To the Reader

As the stock market crashed in America and triggered the Great Depression, and Europe was on the road to World War II, William Gray was worrying about finding a better way to help children learn to read. Gray, one of the nation's leading reading experts, believed children would read more easily if their schoolbooks included illustrations that *showed* a child's world—a colorful world full of fun, suspense and surprise — rather than just *describing* one. When words were used, he knew they would have to ring true.

So beginning in the late 1920s, Gray began to build the world of Dick and Jane, featuring characters created by a reading consultant named Zerna Sharp, for the educational publisher Scott, Foresman and Company. What Gray and Sharp and teams of passionate educators, writers, illustrators and editors produced was the map for the classic illustrated book series that taught eighty-five million children how to read from the 1930s through the 1960s.

Growing Up with Dick and Jane takes us back to the seductive watercolor world where we learned how to read. It's a world where night never comes, knees never scrape, parents never yell and the fun never stops. For schoolchildren who lived through the Depression and World War II, the world of Dick and Jane must have read like a dream. But for baby boomers lucky enough to escape the suffering of their parents and to be born into a postwar paradise, the stories they read in the first months of the first grade felt like their everyday suburban lives.

Growing Up with Dick and Jane steps back in time and reenters the world of mid-century childhood. Remember holding a Dick and Jane primer for the first time? Remember the thrill—the exact moment—when you *knew* you could read? Here it is again, the green grass and the blue skies. And here are Dick and Jane and Sally, Mother and Father and Spot— the happy, happy family. Now, as grown-ups, we can see a bigger picture—how the optimism in these little books, seen alongside the turbulent events of the times, together tell the story of a country defining, pursuing and living the American Dream.

Growing Up with

Dick and Jane

Learning and Living
the American Dream

by CAROLE KISMARIC *and* MARVIN HEIFERMAN
Preface by Bob Keeshan, creator of Captain Kangaroo

A Lookout Book

CollinsPublishersSanFrancisco
A Division of HarperCollinsPublishers

First published 1996
by Collins Publishers San Francisco
1160 Battery Street
San Francisco, California
94111-1213
415-616-4700

Produced by Lookout
1024 Avenue of the Americas
New York, New York 10018

Library of Congress Cataloging-in Publication Data
Kismaric, Carole, 1942-
Growing up with Dick and Jane: learning and living the American dream/
Carole Kismaric, Marvin Heiferman: preface, Captain Kangaroo/Bob Keeshan.
p. cm.
A Lookout Book.
ISBN 0-00-649246-0
1. Readers (Primary)—History and criticism. 2. Children—Conduct of life—Study and teaching—United States—History.
3. Education (Primary)—United States—History—20th century. 4. Reading (Primary)—Social aspects—United States.
5. Textbooks—United States—History and criticism. 6. United States—Civilization—20th century. I. Heiferman, Marvin. II. Title.
PE1119.3.K57 1996
428.6'083–dc20   95-40246

Printed in Hong Kong
10 9 8 7 6 5 4 3 2 1

CONTENTS

BRIEF CONTENTS

Strategic Management, Theory, 12e
Charles W. L. Hill
Melissa A. Schilling
Gareth R. Jones

Vice President, General Manager, Social
    Science & Qualitative Business: Erin
    Joyner

Product Director: Jason Fremder

Senior Product Manager: Scott Person

Content/Media Developer: Tara Singer

Product Assistant: Brian Pierce

Marketing Director: Kristen Hurd

Marketing Manager: Emily Horowitz

Marketing Coordinator:
    Christopher Walz

Senior Content Project Manager:
    Kim Kusnerak

Manufacturing Planner:
    Ron Montgomery

Production Service: MPS Limited

Senior Art Director: Linda May

Cover/Internal Designer: Mike Stratton

Cover Image: mbbirdy/Getty Images

Intellectual Property
    Analyst: Diane Garrity
    Project Manager: Sarah Shainwald

Strategy in Action Sailboat Image:
    © Steve Bly/Getty Images

Part 5 Nautical Compass Image:
    holbox/Shutterstock.com

For product information and technology assistance, contact us at
Cengage Learning Customer & Sales Support, 1-800-354-9706

For permission to use material from this text or product,
submit all requests online at **www.cengage.com/permissions**
Further permissions questions can be emailed to
permissionrequest@cengage.com

Unless otherwise noted all items © Cengage Learning.

Library of Congress Control Number: 2015953360

ISBN: 978-1-305-50233-8

Cengage Learning
20 Channel Center Street
Boston, MA 02210
USA

Cengage Learning is a leading provider of customized learning solutions with employees residing in nearly 40 different countries and sales in more than 125 countries around the world. Find your local representative at **www.cengage.com.**

Cengage Learning products are represented in Canada by Nelson Education, Ltd.

To learn more about Cengage Learning Solutions, visit **www.cengage.com**

Purchase any of our products at your local college store or at our preferred online store **www.cengagebrain.com**

Printed in Canada
Print Number: 01   Print Year: 2016

STRATEGIC MANAGEMENT

12e

THEORY

CHARLES W. L. HILL

University of Washington – Foster School of Business

MELISSA A. SCHILLING

New York University – Stern School of Business

GARETH R. JONES

CENGAGE
Learning·

Australia • Brazil • Mexico • Singapore • United Kingdom • United States

STRATEGIC

12e

MANAGEMENT

THEORY

Contents

The World of Dick and Jane
Bob Keeshan, creator of Captain Kangaroo

I grew up with Dick and Jane, was a contemporary of theirs. You see, I was born, as were Dick and Jane, in the year 1927. Perhaps we even share a birthday.

The world that William Gray and Zerna Sharp created for Dick and Jane was my world. They seemed to suffer little during America's Great Depression. I didn't even *know* there was a depression until I entered my sophisticated teens and became more aware of the world and reality. It wasn't that my father was wealthy; he was not, but we were fortunate to have him well placed in the grocery business, and that insulated our family from much of the hurt that was being endured by others.

I lived in what would now be called suburbia, though we didn't know that at the time. I had nice friends, a nice home, wonderful parents, a couple of dogs but no cats. The ice cream vendor drove by each warm summer evening, bell tinkling, neighborhood children screaming in delight. I sat with many of the other kids on the grassy slopes alongside our homes and played exciting games of imagination. We frightened each other with thrilling ghost stories. Yes, we did believe in ghosts. What would the world be without such tantalizing thoughts?

It was, for me, the world of Dick and Jane, the world that *every* child should inhabit, a world with yellow brick roads, the security of parental love, full stomachs and overflowing hearts filled with warm feelings. Such a world was also filled with the awesome discoveries of childhood, each as tasty as that summer evening's ice cream bar. For most children living in the thirties, Dick and Jane could only be a wonderful dream, a dream of what might be. I was fortunate enough to live the dream.

My world changed in the forties, just as Dick and Jane's did in the fifties and sixties. There were no people quite like Dick and Jane in the Marine Corps, and I was forever transformed. I was "growing up," and World War II accelerated that process. Then along came my children, the baby boomers, and their life was often closer to the ideal. But their world was changing, too, particularly the world of nurturing. The "nurturing place," the family, was being restructured. Mom and Dad sometimes decided they would be better off apart; Mom went to work outside the home, and single-parent families became commonplace.

Highways and jet planes made us a mobile society, and the extended family of grandparents, uncles, aunts and cousins was often miles away when we needed them to help raise the kids. Today's is a very different world from the world of Dick and Jane. Along with the strain placed on the family, much good has come of change. We have become more honest in recognizing that we are not a cookie cutter society. We are far from perfect, but at least we're more realistic and a lot more honest. We are pluralistic, and in that pluralism resides our strength. Most of us have tried to raise our children to understand that American ideal.

By the time *Captain Kangaroo* went on the air in 1955, I had already spent eight years developing programs for children. Television programs such as my first, *Howdy Doody,* were considered by many in the educational community as a threat to good reading habits in children. By 1955, I felt quite to the contrary. I knew that constructive programming could inform children and encourage them to seek more knowledge of a subject that they first learned about on television. The worst fears of educators and reading experts were unfounded. Children read more than ever today. In over nine thousand *Captain Kangaroo* programs we read thousands of books, some of them again and again. We modeled reading habits for children, and today's adults—yesterday's children—often relate how those reading habits became, for them, a lifelong pleasure.

Foster imagination, provide security, feed the mind of the child as well as the body, show your love as well as declaring it, and you will be building self-confidence. Be patient, allow a child to learn from mistakes. "You can do it" should be the most often repeated words of love from parent to child. A child entering kindergarten who has been shown that he or she is capable of accomplishment and high self-esteem is a winner.

Childhood, for every child, should be as close as possible to the ideal world of Dick and Jane. Sometimes the ugliness of our surroundings gets in the way. Never let that ugliness come from you, the parent. With love and security—and an occasional ice cream bar—our children will turn out like Dick and Jane. I'll let you in on a secret. The Dicks and Janes of this world grow into happy human beings. Love!

1. Dreaming the

American Dream

The Declaration of Independence doesn't guarantee that childhood will be a carefree, happy time. In fact, the notion of childhood as a time of innocence, illustrated so convincingly in the Dick and Jane books, was a new idea just beginning to take hold in the 1930s. When the youngest Pilgrims touched down on Plymouth Rock, they had to work hard to survive, helping their mothers and fathers in any way they could. Life was tough in the New World, and it stayed tough. For two hundred years, most Americans eked out their livings on farms, and even the youngest children made a difference hauling water and tools, feeding animals, minding younger siblings, doing chores around the homestead.

In the mid-nineteenth century, when farm families and new immigrants began settling in cities in search of economic opportunity, their working children made another kind of difference, by adding their twenty-five cents a day to the family's pot. And by the century's end, America was experiencing an enormous economic expansion as the industrial revolution created millions of jobs. Many working-class and immigrant children, laboring fourteen-hour days in stifling mills, mines or factories, were valuable assets to bosses, because their nimble little fingers could often outperform those of any adult. Children who didn't have to work were expected to be self-reliant too, even if they spent their day in school instead of at a factory. Discipline was the order of the day. At home, around the dinner table, on the streets, in shops and in churches, children were to be clean and well-behaved, seen but not heard.

Whether children worked in the mines, fields or sweatshops, or folded their hands neatly on their school desks, the very nature of childhood continued to be contested. Philosophers, educators and labor reformers championed the idea of childhood as a sacred time. Child labor laws, protecting children from on-the-job abuse, boosted the notion of youth as a sentimental safe harbor. By the end of the nineteenth century, the majority of states had passed laws making elementary school attendance compulsory.

At the same time, society was starting to pay attention to children in new and different ways. Sigmund Freud was one of the first to argue that children were instinctual creatures, with sexual and psychological needs. Psychologist G. Stanley Hall, who headed the Child Study movement,

During the Depression children saw family shops boarded up or family farms taken over by banks. While fathers traveled to find work or sold apples on street corners and mothers scrimped and saved, crafty youngsters raised money any way they could to contribute to the family or—with a nickel saved—to go to the movies.

1930

Nothing would be too good

endorsed children's needs to express themselves freely, to act and speak like children, to be free of constraining adult morality. By the late nineteenth century, philosopher and educator John Dewey challenged old-fashioned models of education based on rote learning and administered by authoritarian teachers, whose job was to bend a child's will. Dewey's vision respected children as individuals whose intelligence should be stimulated and whose imagination could be encouraged to flourish.

A progressive vision of childhood was taking hold by the early twentieth century. New textbooks, filled with colorful pictures and lively verses, reflected this idealized world of children. Cheaper paper and high-volume printing techniques made it possible for each child to have his or her own reader. Progressive educators began to operate on the premise that each child was an individual who learned differently.

Changes in elementary education paralleled changes in American society. The idea of childhood as a wonderful,

unique stage in life so charmed the culture that childhood became a special time to be cherished and protected. Of course, hard work and good deeds were not forgotten. Children were still expected to behave properly and help out. But there was a sense, at the start of the new century, that childhood was something of a dreamworld.

This dream for children, and the larger American Dream, the firm belief that hard work leads to prosperity, turned into a nightmare when the stock market crashed in 1929. It took two years of further declines in stock prices and in the volume of business for the Great Depression to hit Americans with its full force. In the bust of the thirties, with cash scarce and corporate profits collapsed, salaries were cut. A record high of 25 percent of the work force was unemployed. It felt like a vicious, unending cycle. People lost faith in a government that aided banks and big business but did little to help them. Confidence shaken and marked for life with the guilt of personal failure, adults and children alike bartered, begged and stole to survive, or they went hungry. Feeling betrayed and defeated, men and women put aside their dreams of happy families and a future.

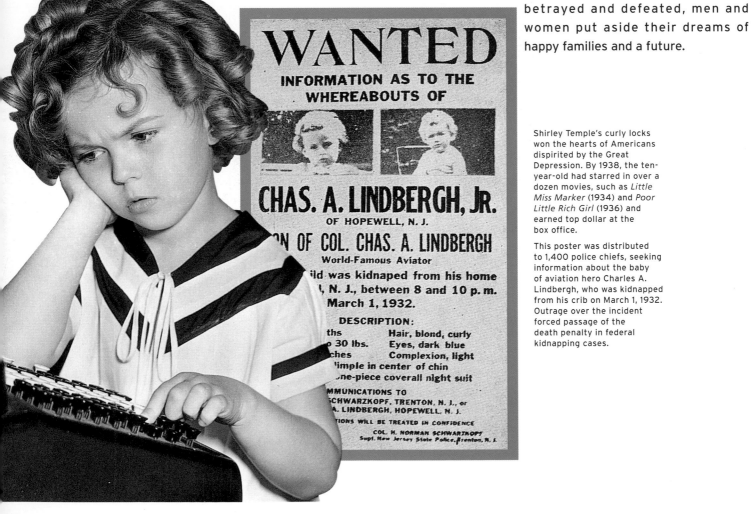

Shirley Temple's curly locks won the hearts of Americans dispirited by the Great Depression. By 1938, the ten-year-old had starred in over a dozen movies, such as *Little Miss Marker* (1934) and *Poor Little Rich Girl* (1936) and earned top dollar at the box office.

This poster was distributed to 1,400 police chiefs, seeking information about the baby of aviation hero Charles A. Lindbergh, who was kidnapped from his crib on March 1, 1932. Outrage over the incident forced passage of the death penalty in federal kidnapping cases.

for children shielded from the Depression and

Maintaining the sanctity of childhood was nearly impossible. Parents couldn't indulge their children or shield them from hardship. Kids needed to help make ends meet. So by selling homegrown produce or scrounging through garbage cans for scraps, from trapping crabs and rabbits, kids brought money home. And whether they lived in the city or on the farm, they were expected to find ways of contributing.

For most middle-class kids, childhood was carefree only when they could escape from everyday life. Radio was free, and after school and every night families tuned in, staring at the dial until their imaginations let them wander along trails with the Lone Ranger, sneak down abandoned silver mines with Jack Armstrong—the all-American boy—or round up arch criminals at the Shadow's side. On Saturday afternoons, kids paid a nickel to enter a world of moody lighting, red carpets and velvet drapes. They stayed all day, watching Movietone newsreels, coming attractions, cliff-hanging serials, cartoons and then a double bill—a western and a musical featuring one of the many child stars of the era.

During the Depression, children became symbols of hope, of better things to come. The Dionne Quintuplets became an international sensation at their birth in 1934, as well-wishers cheered for the survival of five frail baby girls. In their darkest hours, Americans became obsessed with sunny Shirley Temple and her fifty-six curls. She and other glamorized child stars like Mickey Rooney, Judy Garland and Jackie Coogan lightened people's hearts as they sang and danced their way through the Depression. These pint-size movie stars projected all the characteristics of the ideal childhood that educators and reformers had been touting for decades.

As Americans wobbled back to economic stability, Hitler was marching on Poland, and Mussolini was goose-stepping through Rome. When parents pushed children through the turnstiles of New York's 1939 World's Fair, they were in no mood to sacrifice for the people whose lives were being devastated "over there" across the Atlantic. It took the shock of the Japanese bombing of Pearl Harbor to jolt the United States into battle. The war jump-started the American economy, as a massive defense effort created seventeen million new jobs. American men, women and chil-

The B-29 bomber was the ultimate air weapon of WWII. Its use against Japan was a turning point in the Pacific war, and it was used to drop the first atomic bomb on Hiroshima.

During WWII, advertisers, with few consumer goods to sell, focused on getting Americans to support the war. This 1944 Goodyear Tire Company ad shows that home front Americans could help the war effort by investing in U.S. Treasury Bonds.

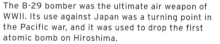

WWII. Postwar affluence would assure kids the

dren vowed to work together to destroy the enemy they all agreed on, the totalitarian evil that threatened democracy and the American way of life.

If the Depression didn't defeat America, neither would fascism, whose threatening voices and faces kids learned to recognize from radio broadcasts, weekly newsreels, movie magazines, advertisements and posters that filled their schoolrooms and community centers. Kids were trained to identify enemy planes, played war games in which they raged against Nazis and the Japanese, collected tin foil from gum and cigarette packs for recycling, gathered milkweed pods for stuffing life preservers, planted Victory gardens to supply their own food, and even turned in their toys as scrap materials.

The terrible war did wonderful things for the American economy. Factories that made lipstick made bullet cases. Assembly lines that produced cars churned out tanks. Money was everywhere. In the first six months of 1942, the government ordered $100 billion in defense equipment. Bank deposits reached record highs as personal savings jumped from $6.3 billion in 1940 to over $37 billion by 1945. Because of war shortages, people on the home front spent their money on the smaller pleasures of life. Movie box office receipts doubled from 1940 to 1945. Sales of cosmetics, self-help paperbacks, and musical instruments skyrocketed. Nightclubs, bars, hotels and resorts were jammed. Kids amused themselves with radio serials, cartoons and comic books. They listened to Kate Smith singing "When the Moon Comes Over the Mountain" and Bing Crosby promising a "White Christmas," and they put their faith in Superman.

With their eyes on victory, Americans' personal lives were in flux. Over thirty million people, a fifth of the population, moved from one part of the country to another, following soldiers and jobs. Doubling up, they lived with relatives in garages and stores and shared homes with strangers, believing that once the war was won, things would get better. Advertising, with few consumer goods to sell, promoted sacrifice as the path to future gain.

And though it brought wealth, the war had real costs: 407,316 Americans were killed, 670,846 came home wounded and 183,000 children were left fatherless. After

1940

Kids played war games and collected newspapers, tin foil and cans for scrap. Once a week, they used their dimes and quarters to buy War Bond Stamps, which they pasted in their books. The book held $18.75 worth of stamps, which could be exchanged for a $25 War Bond, redeemable in ten years.

As oily black smoke from Japanese bombs swirled over Pearl Harbor, the stunning news of the December 7, 1941, sneak attack reached Americans via radio. When President Roosevelt announced that America was at war, everyone was ready to join up; all told, nearly sixteen million Americans served in WWII.

best of everything. Americans were ready to

years of separation, families unraveled. Children had forgotten their fathers; returning servicemen didn't recognize their own children. The divorce rate had doubled. Men who experienced the trauma of war came home shattered, to reenter a world that wouldn't stop for them.

But soon enough, the lure of the future overtook the grim past. Even before the war ended, government and big business had been planning how to turn the booming wartime economy into a prosperous peacetime economy. The money, production lines, new materials and ingenuity that won the war could be directed toward the home front market. Americans were eager for upward mobility and to indulge the pleasures they had deterred during the war.

Americans were ready to move to Easy Street, but first they needed places to live. A returning GI could buy his own dream house on a little plot of land away from the busy cities, where his wife and kids could take a giant step up the ladder of opportunity. With $400 billion in government credit and guaranteed loans, home ownership grew 50 percent from 1940 to 1950. It was in this new suburbia,

a "Babyville" created to cater to children, that childhood finally became the paradise the government and advertisers had promised.

The postwar baby boom supplied America with a new generation of consumers to fulfill the expectations not only of parents, but also of economists who recognized the unprecedented scale of the market. Nothing would be too good for these tots who had been shielded from the impact of both the Depression and the war. Their parents, who ate beans during the Depression and Spam during the war, would soon be grilling steaks in their own backyards. Postwar affluence—and a belief in the permanence of upward mobility—would assure their children the best of everything. More attention, more toys, more security. In their Dick and Jane years, the phenomenal luck of this generation would become clear. Just like Dick and Jane in the stories they would read in first grade, these kids knew they were going to be special.

move to Easy Street, where childhood would

Of the thirteen million homes built in the decade after WWII, eleven million of them were in new suburban developments. The rapid sprawl of suburbia coincided with other major changes: new affluence and social mobility, rising marriage and birth rates, the ethic of family "togetherness."

be the promised paradise.

Dick

Dick is an all-American boy. Master of a little world that stretches from his screen door, across the green lawn, to a white picket fence. It's a world where winter never comes, and the neighbors are nowhere to be seen. It's a world in which troubles from the big world don't trickle down. No Depression. No World War. Surrounded by white space and innocence, Dick (never Richard) is a confident little guy. Dick looks sharp in his shorts and snappy striped polo shirts. When Dick says, "Look, look. Look up. Look up, up, up," everyone else on the page does. He speaks simply, directly, and gets what he wants. Why not?

He's the oldest of three adorable children and the most responsible. He watches out for his younger sisters. He works around the house. Dick waters the lawn, helps set the table and knows how to dial the telephone. He is a little man. Maybe that's why Mother and Father leave Dick alone.

Dick gets top billing in America's best-selling Dick and Jane readers because he is the best a boy can be. A role model for generations of boys, his storybook life is one fun-filled adventure after another, where problems get solved before big tears get shed. Dick is a real boy: always in motion. He climbs trees,

rides a bike, flies a kite, and throughout his forty-year career, plays baseball, basketball and football. And Dick has Spot, the springer spaniel he trains, feeds, walks, plays with and loves.

Dick is organized. He likes routines, because they make his life run smoothly. When his little world spins out of control, it's Dick who stops the runaway red wagon. It's Dick who finds a missing toy, a missing pet, a missing sister. It's Dick, not Father, who keeps order and resolves problems. And it's Dick who makes sure every story ends with a giggle or a smile. That's why we like Dick.

Dick is better than average. He's never, ever afraid, not like other six-year-olds, who sometimes have fears and bad dreams. Dick works and plays well with his sisters and friends and respects his parents and grandparents. He's not boisterous, competitive or mean. He never bullies, never punches, never kicks.

Never cries.

In fact, Dick never gets in trouble.

Little boys once behaved a lot like Dick. They shook hands with adults, never spoke out of turn, and did chores without expecting an allowance. During the Depression, Dick's charmed life was a daydream for boys who sold rags and bottles to bring home extra pennies for food. And during World War II, boys scanned the skies for enemy planes, wondering if they'd ever see their fathers again. Kids had no choice; they had to grow up fast and join America's fight against evil. Even fun had its edge. Games were war games. On Saturday afternoons, war movies

Talking Pictures
Dick and Jane's speech isn't as colorful as the illustrations that capture their true personalities. Dick's repertoire of expressions and gestures reveal his exemplary character traits: his attentiveness (he points things out because his vocabulary is limited); his joie de vivre (Dick often spreads his fingers, palms up, in delight or surprise); and his self-assurance and determination (hands on hips, feet spread) to be a little man.

were preceded by newsreels that showed real people, even children, dying.

It wasn't until after the war that Dick's trouble-free world and the world of real little boys seemed to become a mirror image of each other. If Dick never suffered, neither did the suburban kids of the 1950s, who were the center of their parents' world, lucky to be born into a society exploding with toys, cars, breakfast cereals and multicolored appliances. Boys who read stories about Dick in school were also watching other little boys like Dick star on television shows. Living in a postwar paradise, they grew up believing that they were characters too, living out their lives in front of an adoring audience.

Good Boys, Bad Boys

The 1950s presented a multiple choice of boy wonders, Dick's peers, who either toed the line or broke the rules. Because many of them were entertainers seen week after week on TV, their behavior had to be a little less predictable than Dick's, to keep an audience from changing channels.

Timmy, the adopted orphan caretaker of *Lassie* (1954-74), first played by Tommy Rettig, was too good to be true. Unlike Dick, he was upstaged by his quicker-witted dog. Well-intentioned Beaver Cleaver, played by Jerry Mathers on *Leave It to Beaver* (1957-63), might act selfishly but always knew when he had stepped over the line. A magnet for trouble, cute *Dennis the Menace*, a cartoon character turned TV star, played by Jay North (1959-63), was wild and almost too much for adults to handle.

Timmy Miller

Beaver Cleaver

The Birth of Dick and Jane

Dick and Jane were born in 1927, when Zerna Sharp had an idea that would change how children learned to read. At the turn of the century, American textbooks were full of words. Excerpts from literature or Bible stories preached moralistic values, largely without the help of illustrations. By the 1920s, publisher Scott, Foresman and Company's Elson Readers, edited by reading authority William Gray, had reversed the equation. Big, colorful illustrations told their own stories, and the words with the pictures were simpler and fewer. A reading consultant for Scott Foresman, Sharp believed that children would read even better if they identified with the characters in the illustrations and read words that sounded familiar. She had been listening to kids carefully—how they used a limited vocabulary, spoke with uninhibited energy and repeated words for emphasis.

Sharp pitched her ideas to William Gray, who hired her to develop a family of characters that he could fold into his scientific approach to teaching reading. A revolutionary textbook concept was born. Sharp and a team of editors, consultants, writers, psychologists and illustrators sketched out the main characters and early story lines. After trial and error, they were given names, easy-to-remember four-letter words, Dick and Jane. No last name was necessary, for Dick and Jane were meant to represent Everyboy and Everygirl.

The editorial team that Sharp now supervised went on to create a curriculum of reading books that was interesting from a first-grader's point of view because they reflected a six-year-old's activities and language. The books were more "readable" than earlier textbooks and used attractive illustrations, large legible print and well-written stories full of humor, action, climaxes and suspense. The readers were simple enough for children to experience success reading them, and equally important, teachers would experience success in teaching them. The characters Dick and Jane first appeared in all the stories in the 1930 Elson Basic Reader pre-primer.

Zerna Sharp   William S. Gray

The books were a huge success. Children loved what they saw in Eleanor Campbell's accurately researched, beautifully printed, colorful illustrations. They learned the words that went along with the pictures, using the "whole word" method that taught children to recognize complete words by sight, instead of phonetically sounding words out, letter by letter. Teachers encouraged their pupils to think about the characters' actions and thoughts, and to put themselves in Dick and Jane's place, deepening their connection to the characters and to reading.

The educational techniques and the "look" of the books had been a bold step in educational publishing, and they worked. By the 1950s, 80 percent of the first-graders in the United States who were learning to read were growing up with Dick and Jane.

Dennis the Menace

Jane

Jane is a dream of a girl—pretty, bright and bright-eyed. Stable, responsible, Jane has Ginger Rogers's grace and June Allyson's wholesomeness. She's smart and down-to-earth. Yet for all her charms, Jane is second banana in a famous brother-sister act. She hovers on the outskirts of the action—always there if someone needs her—watching Dick hang confidently from a tree or Sally willfully tear down the street in her little metal pedal car. But Jane is not prissy. She might not skate as well as Dick, or run as fast, but it doesn't stop her from trying.

There's a lot to envy about Jane. Every time she walks onto the page, she's wearing something new. She gardens in a salmon pink dress, she paints in a flowered print dress, she rides a pony wearing a red dress and blue sweater, and she shops in a polka-dot dress. Jane looks like what every little girl dreams about. Her perky dresses never wrinkle or get dirty. She's so neat that even Spot and Puff know enough not to jump on her. Her blond, wavy hair is not too curly, like Shirley Temple's, not too frizzy, like Little Orphan Annie's. Jane's not too fat or too thin. Jane is a lucky girl, with nothing to cry or sulk about. Dick never teases her.

Sugar and Spice

Jane may have been too good to be true. That left the door open in popular culture for girls who didn't have brothers, docile personalities, ordinary pets or perfect manners. None of them had as many outfits, but they still captured the imagination of the American public.

Chunky, dark-haired Nancy (b. 1940) had dark moods and lived in a single-parent home. Her partner in adventure was not a well-behaved brother but Sluggo, a bald, pseudo-tough slum kid. Lucy van Pelt (b. 1950) was the pushy neurotic of the *Peanuts* troupe. She tormented her foil, the meek Charlie Brown, and was often overshadowed by Snoopy, the brilliant beagle. Patty McCormack played Rhoda, an eight-year-old liar, cheat, arsonist and murderer, in the 1956 movie *The Bad Seed*. Her evil behavior terrorized adults as well as good little children, on screen and in the audience.

Nancy

Rhoda Penmark

Lucy van Pelt

Mother and Father, Grandmother and Grandfather give her presents. Baby sister Sally adores her. Jane is cherished.

Jane doesn't make mistakes. She thinks before she speaks. She's thoughtful to her family and friends and is always willing to share what she has, especially her toys. Jane wants people to be happy. Even if she's perfectly capable of going off on her own—and occasionally does—Jane prefers to be one of the group, a part of the family, a link in her circle of friends. That's where she shines and shows how helpful, generous and fair a five-year-old can be.

More like a grown-up than a kid, Jane is a model girl for her time. She is modest, poised, unflappable. Jane watches everyone and everything carefully. She's learning how to set the table, bring in the laundry, go to the store, bake cakes and cookies. Jane thrives as a perfect younger sister, never upstaging Dick. She is a perfect older sister too, watching out for silly Baby Sally. Jane would rather work, helping Mother wash the floor, than run around the backyard. Home is the center of

Reading, the Old Way

efore Dick and Jane books were passed down the aisles in schools across the country in 1930, learning to read was a lot less fun. Even today, the debate continues about how a child learns to read. Reading is complex and requires the ability to pull together motor, perceptual and cognitive processes. As much as schools wanted students to develop reading skills in lockstep, children learn at different rates; they learn to read quickly or slowly, well or poorly, depending on who they are and how they are taught.

Yet America was founded on the concept of an informed and educated citizenry. For democracy to work, access to the printed word was essential. Reading not only gets people through work and everyday life, but facilitates the exchange of opinions, values and information that promotes the survival and evolution of a democratic culture. For a democracy to endure, all citizens, not just an aristocratic few, must be educated and informed to participate. This demanded the radical concept of educating the masses, beginning with reading.

Early American readers taught reading not as a process, but as a way to learn religious, rhetorical, moral and patriotic values. These books combined alphabets with Bible facts and verses. By the nineteenth century, readers were more likely to preach the golden rule and offer moral tales of honesty, obedience, temperance, thrift and patriotism. It wasn't until the early twentieth century that educators began to focus on the learner and not on society's precepts and values. For the first time, children were taught the "how" of reading, instead of the "what."

The 1944 editorial team for Dick and Jane readers

As the content and purpose of reading changed, so did the methods used to teach reading. Two basic techniques have been used since the nineteenth century: phonics, which is the ability to decode the printed word by recognizing letters and knowing the sound those letters stand for, and the whole word method, in which a child is taught to recognize entire words and their meaning at a glance. Educators' preferences used to swing between these two approaches, and it is only in the last few decades that a more holistic approach, which values both sound and words in context, has taken hold. Advocates of "pure" phonics believed that by learning to sound out words, children acquired the underlying skill to read any word they saw by matching it with its spoken equivalent. Whole word advocates maintained that children best learned to read by decoding the word as a whole unit, and understanding its meaning from its context. Current thinking favors the synthesis of sound/symbol relationships and the importance of understanding content in context.

Phonics, popular in the early nineteenth century, was challenged by the whole word method. It's interesting to note that Thomas Gallaudet's 1835 *Mother's Primer*, the first whole word book, included the lines, "Frank had a dog, his name was Spot.... Spot was a good dog." And educator Horace Mann protested in 1838, "eleven-twelfths of all the children in the reading classes did not understand the words they read so glibly," which was probably true, given the rhetoric and abstractness of their readers. He suggested the need for silent reading, with an emphasis on the meaning of words rather than on the sound of the letters.

As America shifted from a rural to an urban society and as waves of immigrants arrived, the mass education of these hordes of learners required a systematic approach to reading. McGuffey Readers, a series of five books graduated in difficulty, were introduced in 1836 and became the most widely used textbooks. Over a period of fifty years, 122 million copies reached classrooms. The readers were used to teach reading aloud, clearly and dramatically according to rules of rhetoric and oratory. These books stressed moral and religious issues such as the importance of family and respect for authority, patriotism and truthfulness. Gradually, other readers introduced restricted vocabulary and less abstract content.

At the turn of the century, inexpensive paper and high-volume printing techniques made it possible to mass produce readers, profusely illustrated with pictures mostly of children and animals. In 1897, Baldwin Readers, the first to use color pictures, became available. It wasn't until the 1930s that school surveys showed what educators suspected—that thousands of children were unable to read effectively. The monotonous memory drills of the nineteenth century had to be replaced with reading activities that freed children from the lockstep of traditional technique.

William S. Gray, an editor of the popular Elson Readers published by Scott Foresman, which featured stories about a family and its home life, conducted many of these early reading studies. In the process, he came up with a model for a new whole word reading system that evolved into Scott Foresman's innovative New Basic Reading Program. It was a system that deeply involved the teacher and would grow to include pre-primers, primers, workbooks, word cards and charts featuring two children named Dick and Jane, who from the 1930s through the 1960s taught millions of children how to read.

Jane's world; it's where she blossoms, where she measures her success and sees her accomplishments add up.

School is important too. Jane would never miss a day of class. She is a perfect student, carrying an armload of books, even if she's too young to read them. Jane is smart in the way little girls were supposed to be smart in the 1950s, when boys could be boys, but girls had to be girls. She is a young lady in training to be a perfect wife and mother. Jane is always calm, self-controlled and free of emotional extremes. No tantrums, no tears, no false moves. Jane is never a problem.

The Jane "Look"

In her forty-year career, Jane wore at least two hundred different ensembles. In story after story, whether Jane is dressed in dainty prints, solids or plaids, she always looks stylish. Jane never slouches, she stands up straight. She's a perfect model for her dresses with Peter Pan collars, jumpers, sweater and skirt sets, and party dresses with crinolines and fitted sashes. Since the illustrators who drew Dick and Jane wanted them to look familiar to readers, the outfits were based on clothing featured in Sears, Roebuck and Montgomery Ward mail order catalogs of the time. The ideal middle-class girl of the 1950s was ladylike and wore dresses everywhere, accessorized with hats, shoes, purses and clean white gloves to create a total "look."

Sears, Roebuck
Summer 1956 catalog

27

Sally

Sally is a force of nature, unpredictable and full of energy. What attracts her, she runs toward. Too young to play by the rules, Sally innocently barges through stories and into situations, spicing up Dick and Jane's life whenever she appears. If a story has a surprise ending, it's usually Sally's silly antics that make the plot spin. Sally is lucky enough to be the baby and gets away with mischief.

Sally walks through puddles in Mother's shoes, while Dick stands by laughing. She powders the noses of pets and toys alike, and everyone thinks she's cute. When she speeds down the street in her toy car, she's on her own, so focused and fearless in her determination to get where she wants, that she's oblivious to whatever might cross her path.

The Boom in Babyville

In the late 1940s, excited mothers and fathers-to-be, millions of them, were buying cribs and carriages and putting up circus wallpaper in nurseries all around the country. Optimistic about the future, these prospective parents were ready to have and cherish their children—seventy-six million American babies born in less than two decades. The baby boomers, as they've been called ever since, came in two tidal waves, the first from 1944 to 1949, the second between 1950 and 1957. *Fortune* magazine, in 1951, pronounced the baby boom "exhilarating.... A civilian market growing by the size of Iowa every year ought to be able to absorb whatever production the military will eventually turn loose." What got turned loose was a flood of postwar consumer goods, and parents across the nation did their share by mass-producing new consumers. The economy and the baby boom lunged forward together, for better and for worse.

When the first wave of babies entered school in the early fifties, the educational system strained and teachers and parents hit the panic button. The generation that was supposed to reap the benefits of America's postwar potential looked like it was going to be cheated out of a world-class education. Seventy-eight thousand makeshift classrooms were set up in vacant stores and churches. Three out of five classes were overcrowded, and forty-five children to a class was common. Students shared everything, including books and desks.

Parents demanded school expansion and new construction. They joined parent-teacher groups in record numbers (PTA membership doubled to eight million by 1952) to agitate for the supplies and reforms they wanted. Bond issues and higher local taxes raised the money for schools to expand. From 1950 to 1970, elementary school enrollment rose by two-thirds. In 1952, 50,000 new classrooms were built, but even that wasn't enough; in 1953, the average daily attendance rose by two million. By 1960, the federal government was spending $18 billion on elementary education, three times the amount spent a decade earlier. There was a staggering teacher shortage. Early in the fifties the country was 72,000 teachers short, and little had improved by 1959, when nearly one-tenth of the nation's 1.3 million teachers were working with substandard credentials.

Regardless of the quality of the educations they received, the baby boomers caused an unprecedented business bonanza. With 11,000 babies being born every day, businesses large and small had to accommodate the huge numbers of children who needed to be fed, clothed, educated and entertained. A *Life* magazine cover story in 1958 called the baby boom and the $33 billion juvenile market a "built-in recession cure." And it was. Each new consumer used up $800 worth of goods and services in the first year of its life: from baby food (1.5 billion cans a year, nationally) and diaper service ($50 million a year), to bronze baby shoes ($5 million a year to one company alone). Every dollar spent seemed like a good investment.

And, of course, there was television, which turned toddlers into a powerful consumer market. TV bypassed parents and appealed directly to kids, who soon learned to recognize brand names before they could read. They learned jingles before "The Star-spangled Banner." It was writer Joyce Maynard who observed, "We are, in the fullest sense, *consumers*, trained to salivate not at a bell, but at the sight of a Kellogg's label or a Dunkin' Donuts box." As they grew up, baby boomers' economic power turned their passing fads and fancies into major businesses. Whatever they did, they were a big and powerful group. Where the baby boomers went, the economy followed.

New supermarkets placed candy on shelves easy for little shoppers to reach.

No matter what she's up to, three-year-old Sally is always learning about the world. Everything that happens to her is new. She's the curious member of the family, free of responsibility and full of imagination. Sally struts, darts and responds to surprises with big theatrical gestures and a tiny vocabulary. Sally makes people pay attention to her, and she makes them laugh. She is so involved in the here and now, she can't think ahead. Sally is a magnet for mishaps. She loses Tim, her teddy bear, again and again. Sally drops her ice cream cone, gets lost on a bus and trapped under a big umbrella. Dick and Jane, who always watch out for her, don't mind, because they're responsible and eager to show Sally what it means to do the right thing. They never lose their patience or get too mad with Sally, because they remember that not so long ago, they were babies too.

Model Children

If Dick and Jane were Zerna Sharp's idea, it was Eleanor Campbell's illustrations that brought them to life. A popular Philadelphia illustrator, Campbell was the artist who defined the characters' looks and personalities and made them so convincing that first-graders counted them as friends. Campbell photographed real-life models—her relatives, friends and even neighborhood pets—who acted out the story lines and sketches Sharp and her editorial team developed. Working from snapshots, she was able to give the action in the stories their movie-like quality, and to capture the spontaneous energy of childhood.

Model for Jane

Models for Dick and Sally

31

Spot

"See Spot run," and he does. Hear Spot speak, "Bow-wow. Bow-wow." Like everyone else, he uses short words, repeated over and over. Dick and Jane and Sally understand Spot because he broadcasts whatever is on his mind. When he is happy to see someone, he smiles. When his ears fold back, he's in hot water, being chased by a chicken or attacked by a flying teddy bear. When Spot rolls his eyes up to the sky, he can't believe what he's gotten himself into.

Spot may be a dog, but he is featured in more stories than Mother and Father combined. That's because Spot wears two hats in Dick and Jane's world. Sure it's his job to make everyone laugh, but he also teaches Dick and Jane how to be responsible children. He can count on them to care for him every

day, to walk, groom and feed him. Spot has fun when he does his jobs too, greeting Father at the front door, shaking hands with Grandfather when he arrives at the farm. If work is fun for Dick and Jane, it's a game for Spot, who rushes to bring in the laundry when it starts to rain.

Sometimes Spot suffers in silence, like the times Dick and Jane dress him up in human clothes or Sally powders him all over with Mother's makeup. Still, Spot maintains his dignity, even when the worst thing happens, when Dick longs for a new puppy. But most of the time, Spot will do anything to be part of the action. He swims, plays hide-and-seek, jumps rope (though not very well), even pulls the kids along on their skates. Good dog.

It is Spot's animal instincts that turn disasters into delight and make for more than a dog's share of happy endings. Time after time, Spot saves the day, finding the toy Sally drops overboard, buries in the sand or loses when she doesn't pay attention. You'd think he was a retriever. Spot first appeared in early Dick and Jane stories as a trim black-and-white terrier, because in the early 1930s, terriers were the most popular breed of dog. Spot turned into a sentimental springer spaniel in 1936, when spaniels became best-selling dogs. But no matter what he looked like, kids loved Spot, because he reminded them of their pets at home and made every story more fun. Smart dog.

Puff

Puff is a soft, purring ball of fur, Jane and Sally's tiny orange kitten. Cute and cuddly, Puff is as frisky as Sally is curious. Pretty Puff, both civilized and brave, unties Mother's apron strings one day and plays fearlessly with barnyard animals the next. Silly Puff gets tangled in a big blue ball of yarn, trapped in a tree and sent on a harrowing swing ride.

It's a good thing Puff has nine lives. In a previous life—c.1930—she was known as Little Mew. With a new name, she became more adventurous. Puff steps in wet paint, chases and breaks balloons and is always knocking something off a table. But she is not bad. Puff never claws the furniture or picks fussily at her food or jumps up on the dining room table. Playing against type, Puff is not aloof. She'd never walk away from an affectionate pat. Puff even gets along with dogs—lucky Spot. Puff's rarely seen alone and seldom disappears to take a nap. Puff is a smarter cat than most and can jump rope a lot better than Spot. By the 1960s she's going for rides on Mother's modern vacuum cleaner and watching other cats on television.

Tim

Tim is the teddy bear, Sally's little sidekick who comforts her even though she treats him carelessly. In Dick and Jane's world, where only a few bad things happen, most of them happen to Tim, the good-natured pal. Tim never complains when Sally drags him wherever she goes, trailing him along the ground, dangling him sideways by an arm or upside down by his leg. In a non-speaking role, Tim can't scream for help when Sally sends him flying down the banister, where he collides with a startled Spot. Tim can't swallow when Sally force-feeds him water at the drinking fountain in the park. He can't budge when he's buried alive at a construction site. Tim can't swim when he slips over the rim of the little blue rowboat and nearly sponges up enough water to sink him forever. Tim may always need help, but it's really Sally who needs Tim. He's her playmate, her confidant, her little brother, her security blanket.

35

Fun with Dick & Jane

Every day is filled with fun in Dick and Jane's world. Every minute, every hour, someone's eyes are sparkling with delight. This is a family that likes to laugh. Everyone, even the  pets, knows the power of a smile, a giggle, a joke. To make reading fun, Dick and Jane's world has been turned into fun. Simple fun, inexpensive fun; you can tell that Mother and Father were children of the Depression. There are very few toys around the house, and all the kids share them: a ball, a wagon, a balsa-wood airplane, a few wooden blocks and some chalk. There are dolls, but none that talk, wet or walk. There's not a battery-operated toy in sight. Only a modest electric train set and a toy telephone. No one complains.

Full of energy like most little kids, Dick and Jane and Sally seldom sit still. They spend most of their time out of the house, out-of-doors, swimming, juggling, kite-flying, racing and throwing balls. In their backyard or on the front sidewalk, they run and jump and swing and slide. They ride bikes and ponies, play on the seesaw and swing from trees. They're pint-size acrobats. They can somersault, stand on their hands and still have energy left to horse around. Dick dangles from trees. Jane jumps rope and skates up a storm. Sally jumps up and down the stairs in the hallway and on the porch and, miraculously, never falls.

Dick and Jane don't count on Mother or Father to amuse them or to organize a game. They make their own fun. They play hide-and-seek, Simon says and blindman's bluff. Dick and Jane are creative. Their imaginations manufacture non-stop entertainment. They ride kitchen broomsticks as if they were frisky horses, turn the laundry basket into a boat and dress up in paper bags to look like scary ghosts.

Spot and Puff have fun too. Spot chases balls and butterflies and frogs, and loves to jump through the air to get his stick. Puff has a great time trying to catch a balloon and even more fun playing with Mother's ball of yarn. The kids have tea parties for the pets, play jokes on them and dress Puff up like a baby and make Spot pretty with Mother's face powder.

Toys Were Us

Fun got to be serious business in the decades following World War II. Toy sales in 1940 totaled only $84 million, but by the end of the 1950s, kids and parents and grandparents were spending $1.25 billion on everything from deluxe boxes of Crayolas to the first glamorous Barbie dolls. The market for toys was huge, but fickle. In December 1954, 40 million people saw Fess Parker as Davy Crockett on TV's *Disneyland*, and frenzied Americans spent more than $100 million on different Davy Crockett items—toothbrushes, snowsuits, coonskin caps, bathing suits, school lunch boxes, guitars and T-shirts—before the market collapsed in July 1955.

Silly Putty (1950) was World War II's gift to kids. This bouncing, stretchy rubber substitute was a pink blob best used to pick up, transfer and distort comic strip pictures. Mr. Potato Head (1952), the first toy advertised on television, was a box full of plastic ears, eyes, lips, mustaches, noses, hats and pipes that turned ordinary potatoes into the wackiest of characters. Chatty Cathy (1960) spoke eleven random phrases when a kid pulled her magic ring. "Tell me a story." "Please comb my hair." "I got hurt." "Where are we going?" "Change my dress," said the doll, who came either as a blue-eyed blonde or brown-eyed brunette.

Food is fun too. The kids devour vanilla ice cream cones whenever they have the chance. Mother and Grandmother bake them delicious layer cakes with white icing, big, round cookies and gingerbread men that the kids gobble up. Sally loves doughnuts, and Spot loves any crumb that falls his way.

Going places is as much fun as staying home. The kids climb the hill near their house and watch the cars on the highway zoom by. They enjoy window shopping with Mother and looking around in toy stores, bookshops and the grocery store. They pile in the car, excited about a trip to the zoo, the Fun Park or Grandmother and Grandfather's farm.

Wherever lighthearted Dick and Jane go, they take fun with them. Who wouldn't want to have them around? Dick and Jane and Sally know that life and everything about it—work, food, chores, school—is meant to be enjoyed. They're the kind of kids who fall asleep with smiles on their faces.

Father

Father is handsome. Father is young. Father is trim. Father is tall. Father has it all. He has a perfect family, a job that gets him home when it's light out and an even temperament that lets him take life one day at a time. Father adores Dick and Jane and Sally. Father loves Mother, the perfect wife and partner. Father, who never says a word about his job, is a breadwinner heading up the ladder of success, ready to do anything he can for his family. His family is his dream come true, and Father is happy.

Father and Mother raise their children together. Father always does his share. When Dick or Jane or Sally needs him, Father doesn't say, "I'm tired. Talk to your Mother." Father never says, "No." Father is fun-loving and energetic. Father is always on the go, fixing broken toys, washing the car, unpacking the new barbecue, building a birdhouse, planting shrubs in the garden. And still, there's energy to spare, to teach Dick to juggle, to jump rope with Jane, to carry Sally and Tim around on his shoulders. Father doesn't play favorites.

Gentle, tolerant, patient, soft-spoken, Father listens, like a modern, model father. No lectures about what the world was like when he was a kid. It is not Father's job to discipline or punish. It is not in his nature to be unfair, to withhold or act

superior because he's older or because he's a man or because he's the husband or the father. No one has to call Father "Sir." He is a realist, not a romantic. Father is one of five citizens in a little democracy where everyone gets to be who he really is.

Every time Father strides up the walk to the front door in his business suit and hat, he steps into the safe world he shares with his family. At home, when Father smiles at everyone, everyone smiles back. That's one more reason for Father to be happy. For Father and the family, the big world and its problems never get through the white picket fence.

World War II
infantry soldiers

Park Forest, Illinois commuters
heading home

Where's Poppa?

Many boys and girls weren't lucky enough to see their fathers as often as Dick and Jane saw theirs. During World War II, 1.24 million fathers left families behind to fight in Europe, Africa and the Pacific; many more had to leave to fight in the Korean War. Separated from them for years at a time, children grew up knowing their fathers through letters, snapshots and stories told around the kitchen table. By the end of the war, many fathers were dead, and other fathers came home wounded or emotionally scarred. The 1944 GI Bill of Rights encouraged close to eight million returning men to go back to school, with the government paying all costs for higher education and on-the-job training programs and a monthly living allowance of up to $120. Their goal? Land a job, climb the corporate ladder, buy homes and cars and braces for the kids and college educations and, years later, retire. If success demanded overtime and three-hour-a-day commutes, at least fathers saw their kids on weekends.

Learning to Read with Dick and Jane

Why are Dick and Jane American icons? What makes us smile when we hear their names? Forty years of first-graders bonded with Dick and Jane, lived in their world and, through their adventures, learned to read. Teachers loved Dick and Jane because they did their job so well, and gave slow and smart kids alike the sequence of skills that turned them into successful readers. School boards chose Dick and Jane books because they were innovative products that got students on an organized learning track and moved them smoothly through the educational process.

Dick and Jane books were an educational breakthrough, the product of a decade of experimentation that fused the talents of educators, reading specialists, classroom teachers, child psychologists, writers and illustrators. The books set new standards in textbook publishing. They were easy to read, designed to be bright and attractive with their big color pictures and bold Century Schoolbook

anticipated what actions would happen next. They learned to interpret simple pictures, learn visual discrimination, recognize simple sentence patterns and practice eye-hand coordination. They also learned how to concentrate and pay attention, and to pick up social skills like working with other children and handling books properly.

William Gray and his associates pioneered the technique of "controlled vocabulary," in which a limited number of new words were introduced and then repeated at least ten times each until new readers learned to recognize them. In the paperbound pre-primers (*Dick and Jane; More Dick and Jane Stories; We Come and Go; We Look and See; We Work and Play; Sally, Dick and Jane; Fun with Our Family* and *Fun Wherever We Are*) and in primers (*Fun with Dick and Jane, New Fun with Dick and Jane* and *Fun with Our Friends*) and in the readers *Our New Friends* and *More Fun with Our Friends*, which were read in the second half of first grade, words printed with the illustrations were the spoken words of the charac-

The 1956 *Before We Read*   *We Work and Play*   *New Fun with Dick and Jane*   *Think-and-Do* workbook

typeface. The stories were short and upbeat, shunning the abstraction, gloom and monotony of earlier readers. Simple sentence structure and limited vocabulary helped kids learn quickly. The whole word or "look-say" method was based on the goal of teaching a student to recognize the form of a word and then to understand its meaning in the context of its use. Teachers also used phonics in every lesson, sounding out letters and letter combinations to reinforce word recognition.

Scott, Foresman and Company's Curriculum Foundation Series was a textbook program that moved students from kindergarten through eighth grade. It was only for the first months of the first grade that Dick and Jane appeared in reading readiness books, pre-primers, a primer, a workbook, on word cards, as cutouts and in oversize Big Books. But they were such unforgettable characters, they made a lasting impression. By the first half of the second grade, however, kids said good-bye to Dick and Jane, who subsequently appeared only in a few stories in readers that introduced a new cast of characters and more difficult stories.

In the 1930s and '40s, reading readiness was a new concept that taught pre-reading skills by getting students to pay attention to the content of pictures. Children looked at the pictures in *Before We Read*—and later, in the 1950s, in *We Read Pictures* and *We Read More Pictures*—and described what characters were saying, then

ters. Children learned to transfer the meaning of a spoken word to its printed form. When children in the 1950s finished reading three pre-primers, they could recognize fifty-eight new words.

When the teacher first passed the primer *Fun with Dick and Jane* down classroom aisles, kids felt that they were finally holding their first "real" book. Clothbound and filled with more words, the stories were longer and presented more complicated ideas than pre-primers. The settings for stories took Dick and Jane out into the world, to the farm, to town, to the zoo and to activities that included a widening circle of friends. Each student was given a *Think-and-Do Book*. These workbooks were filled with visual discrimination and reading exercises that children completed on their own.

The Dick and Jane system was meant to be comprehensive, with enough built-in steps from pre-literacy to literacy to insure that children got all the skills they needed to read. Teacher's Editions made the teacher's job easier. Books were periodically updated. Trained reading specialists traveled around the country to visit teachers and observe how materials were being used and to comment on what worked and what didn't. Every five years, based on specialists' input and requests from state school boards, stories were revised and illustrations updated. The revisions reflected changes in clothing, household furnishings, automobiles and, by the 1960s, the physical and psychological sophistication of children.

43

Mother

Mother is pretty. Mother is graceful. Mother is mellow and Mother is smart. She knows how to do it all: be a good partner to Father, a nurturing Mother to Dick and Jane and Sally and an effortless homemaker, who makes everything look easy. Mother makes the American Dream happen. Mother sews. Mother launders. Mother cooks. Mother sweeps. Mother knits. Mother walks to town to shop. Somehow, every day, Mother must get her work done: washing dishes, cooking

meals, ironing, and washing floors and windows. Mother is happy when the house looks neat and beautiful. Her family doesn't just function, it thrives. That makes Mother happiest of all.

Mother likes to look good and dresses like a lady. She wears hats and gloves and pretty soft day dresses. She has pretty pocketbooks for every occasion. Mother is feminine and sits with ankles crossed and hands clasped. Mother has poise and seems to glide as she walks. No sharp turns, no sudden movements. Even when she jumps rope, Mother has style.

Mother is easy-going. She doesn't hover, doesn't have to check up on Dick or Jane or Sally to see what they're doing, to know that they're OK. Mother trusts Dick and Jane, and trusts them to watch out for Sally. There's no need to lecture or order anyone around. Mother is proud of her efficient, winning team.

Mother's life has no frustrations or setbacks. Just outside the world of Dick and Jane, the new suburban mothers were excited about their new homes and their new

families too. But many whirled like spinning tops from one role to the next—maid, cook, chauffeur, referee, cheerleader, romantic partner and ego booster. Many women had jobs and still got a hot dinner on the table. And many more did not live in the suburbs or enjoy the benefits of the postwar boom.

Dick and Jane's Mother doesn't have an outside-the-home job. She works at home all day and when everything's done sits in her chair, not a hair out of place, reading magazines. Mother is a modern miracle. She teaches quietly, by example. She's cool and doesn't yell and never, never nags or corrects. Mother is selfless, soothing and approving. Mother may be young, but she's wise. Like a Buddha, smiling Mother embraces Dick and Jane and Sally and Father and her world for all it is.

45

Changing Role of Women

If Dick and Jane's mother took pride in her secure and tranquil married life, other women were not so sure. The novelist Pearl S. Buck, in her 1941 book, *Of Men and Women*, described her observations of a prosperous American housewife's day: "She listens to as much as they will tell her, she reads as much as she is inclined, she potters about on the fringes of the world which really goes on without her and comforts herself by having a good hot dinner ready at night anyway. It is not enough." By the end of the fifties, a growing number of women were starting to feel the same way—confused about their traditional roles as wives and mothers and frustrated by their limited options.

In the 1930s, movie audiences applauded and Oscars were awarded to actresses who played tough women making their way in a tough world. The country needed role models who could withstand adversity. With the onset of World War II, millions of women said good-bye to their husbands who went off to war, and took control of their households, often leaving their children with neighbors or family to take over a man's job. The independence some women had longed for was finally theirs. During the war years, more than one-third of the civilian labor force was female, and more than three-quarters of them were married. Between 1941 and 1945, women earned $8 billion and felt the thrill of having, spending and saving their own money. Conventional wisdom might still proclaim that a woman's first allegiance was to home and children. But the truth was that once the war was over, many women didn't want to go home and many simply did not want to give up their financial freedom. Two-thirds of them did not give up working.

It wasn't easy managing a job and a home, or giving back good jobs to returning veterans to take lesser jobs for lesser pay, but the women who stuck it out wouldn't turn back. And society went along with their limited ambitions. As long as women didn't confuse a job with a career, no one could disapprove. Their money made a difference; it helped pay off the new mortgage, was banked for a kid's college tuition or splurged on a vacation.

Suburban women who didn't have jobs may have found themselves with everything they could want, but they were isolated from their mothers, sisters and old friends. Without any on-the-job training, they scoured advice-filled women's magazines on

In the 1930s, the majority of states had laws prohibiting the employment of married women; by 1960, ten million wives were working.

supermarket lines and at home to figure out their changing role in a changing world. How to be an attractive wife, a devoted mother, an optimistic and efficient manager? Magazines like *McCall's*, *Ladies Home Journal*, *Family Circle*, *Woman's Day* and *Redbook* provided road maps to fulfillment, recipes, homemaking tips, ads and editorials that either idolized or chastised women who felt responsible for everything and answerable to everyone. Articles instructed women what to eat, how to dress, how to live and, most importantly, how happiness was to be measured.

The ideal of a fulfilled woman at the helm of a child-centered nuclear family had its heyday for a short time, from the first blush of the postwar boom until the mid-1950s. By 1956, *Life* magazine reported on "Changing Roles in Modern Marriage:" "If there is such a thing as a 'suburban syndrome' it might take this form: the wife, having worked before marriage, or at least having been educated and socially conditioned toward the idea that work... carries prestige," might become depressed about being a mere housewife. Even if she avoids this, "her humiliation still seeks an outlet. This may take various forms: in destructive gossip about other women, in raising hell at the PTA, in becoming a dominating mother."

Despite the decade's glorification of domesticity and togetherness, there was a growing gap between smiling home-all-day wives and the reality of everyday family life. While wives were supposed to take pride in redecorating their houses, volunteering for library work and making home an oasis for a harried husband, these activities couldn't paper over gnawing frustrations and genuine discontent. Tranquilizer and liquor sales were rising, and so were the divorce rates.

Women who were better educated and looking forward to longer lives felt a jolt of recognition when, in 1963, they read Betty Friedan's *The Feminine Mystique*: "It was a strange stirring, a sense of dissatisfaction, a yearning that women suffered in the middle of the twentieth century in the United States. Each suburban wife struggled with it alone. As she made the beds, shopped for groceries, matched slipcover materials, ate peanut butter sandwiches with her children, chauffeured Cub Scouts and Brownies, lay beside her husband at night, she was afraid to ask even of herself the silent question—'Is this all?' "

47

The Family

Dick, Jane and Sally Who? They have no last name, but it doesn't matter. Family matters. A fun-loving, secure family, where everyone plays and nobody yells. A happy family, where the kids are free to be kids and are so good that Mother and Father never say no. A traditional family, with a pretty Mother, a handsome Father, two kind and generous Grandparents, three well-adjusted kids (not too many, not too few), and a menagerie of equally well-adjusted pets. A family where everyone is trusting and shares a sense of humor, the kind of family every child, and every parent, wants.

In the world of Dick and Jane, children get more attention than adults. Self-sufficient Dick and Jane make no great demands. Mother and Father are ready to approve, to

play, to fix things, to amuse. Their job is easy. They don't have to discipline or punish, because none of their children steps out of line. Dick and Jane don't cry, because bad things don't happen to them. Dick and Jane don't tattle, because there's nothing to tattle about. Their family lives in harmony, in a universe all its own. There are no uncles, aunts or cousins. No arguments, no competition, no power plays. No fighting. No secrets.

The nuclear family is a tight-knit, winning team because each member is loved and respected for who he is and what he can do.

This is a family that wants to be together, around the dining room table, playing out in the yard and when they climb in the car to go visiting. No one wants or needs to be alone, because they enjoy each other's company so much. Everyone communicates well. Things don't get fussed over, they get done. Mother and Father watch and listen. It's their job to pay attention to the kids, to care. And it works. Dick and Jane and Sally feel so secure, so wanted, so loved, that parents don't need to say, "Good boy," "Good girl," "You're smart," "You're pretty." "I love you."

As Seen on TV

After reading about Dick and Jane's family during the school day, kids came home and after dinner many sat side by side with their mothers and fathers, watching television. Popular situation comedies, staples of 1950s programming, featured ideal families—understanding fathers who never work and wise and wily mothers who managed happy homes. On these long-running shows, season after season, well-behaved children grew up before America's eyes. These perfect families, watched so loyally, felt like neighbors and were looked up to as role models.

Ozzie and Harriet (1952-66)

Father Knows Best (1954-62)

The Donna Reed Show (1958-66)

Grandparents

Grandmother and Grandfather are the oldest people in Dick and Jane's world. They may not jump rope or crawl under chairs to play follow the leader, but they have as much enthusiasm and energy as Mother and Father. Grandmother and Grandfather live on a farm, far away from Dick and Jane. When they visit Dick and Jane's house to celebrate birthdays, they always bring nice presents and are fun to be with. On the farm, where Grandmother and Grandfather are always busy, they enjoy what they do. They spend their days planting their fields and tending the animals. Grandmother bakes delicious cookies and scrumptious birthday cakes. Grandfather wants Dick and Jane and Sally to learn how farm animals live. He encourages them to try new things, to take risks, to explore. Grandfather cheers the kids on when they race the pony. On every visit to Grandmother and

Grandfather's farm, something exciting happens.

In the 1960s, Dick and Jane's Grandmother and Grandfather looked and felt a lot younger than their peers of a generation earlier. America was getting younger, and Grandmother and Grandfather moved with the flow. They gave up their spectacles, got flattering new hairstyles, started wearing denim clothes and looked a lot younger too. Out on city streets, young people were shouting, "Don't trust anyone over thirty," but Grandmother and Grandfather were still getting the respect they deserved. Even Spot could tell they were special, and as

soon as the car door would open, he'd jump out, stand up, and stick out his paw to shake hands.

Good Morning, Class! Since the nineteenth century, the teaching of children has been considered "women's work." Children went from their mother's care to the care of a female teacher, usually a local woman who trained at a "normal school," as two-year teacher training colleges were then called. Teachers were idealistic but practical women who generally embraced their profession with intensity and dedication. For generations, teaching was one of the very few respectable ways for an unmarried woman to make a living. The stereotypical teacher was a strict disciplinarian who taught by the rules, drilling kids in reading, writing and arithmetic as she paced the aisles and kept up the pace by clapping. After World War II, more men entered the profession, and by 1960 there were an equal number of men teaching, but only at the high school level.

51

On the Farm

A trip to Grandmother and Grandfather's farm is a special treat. The farm is a beautiful place. Dick and Jane's Mother, or maybe it was Father, grew up here. There are big green meadows and taller trees than Dick and Jane have in their backyard. There's a farmhouse, a chicken coop, a red barn and a stable for the horses and ponies. The animals that live on the farm are not pets. Each one has a job to do—horses work, dogs round up animals, cats catch pesky mice.

The farm is where Dick and Jane learn that milk comes from cows, not bottles, that eggs come from hens, not cartons in the market. Grandfather and Grandmother work with their hands and, watching and helping

them, Dick and Jane share in the fun of their accomplishments. It's in the darkness of the barn, discovering a cat with her newborn kittens, that Dick and Jane are reminded by Grandfather about how important families are. On the farm, they learn about self-reliance and see how everyone has to work together, people and animals too.

It's on the farm that Dick and Jane are introduced to farm values and a bigger view of nature. Playing under big old trees; running through grass and not on side-walks; riding on real horses, not on broom-sticks; the farm is far away and very different from Dick and Jane's modern everyday lives.

2. Living the A

merican Dream

By the early 1950s—after nearly twenty years of fine-tuning reading techniques, stories and graphics —Dick and Jane books had hit their stride. Educational theory, content and form were all in sync, a dependable way to teach reading, a system that worked for the market it targeted. The safe, colorful and fun world of Dick and Jane and Sally permeated the lives of millions of children, as the basal series became the most widely used reading program in the history of American education. Children recognized that the seamless world they saw in the books—a place where no need went unanswered, where unhappiness, trouble and fear existed someplace else, far away—would be a great world to live in and a great place to be a child.

The American Dream that promised the postwar generation a storybook world was becoming a reality, put in place bit by bit by businessmen, politicians, the media and millions of enthusiastic new parents. The speed and efficiency that won the war now produced instant homogenized communities, full of tract homes that were promoted as individual little worlds with rooms and closets to fill. People lived next door to people pretty much like themselves, neighbors bound not by friendship or family but by ambition, newly achieved status and shared beliefs and fears. A 1954 *McCall's* magazine picture story endorsed family "togetherness"—working as a team—as one way to claim and enjoy the payoff for two decades of trouble and sacrifice.

Inexperienced suburbanites turned to all sorts of experts for advice. But the expert with the biggest impact was Dr. Benjamin Spock, whose *Common Sense Book of Baby and Child Care* (1946) was the best-selling guide to child-rearing that comforted parents so they could comfort their children. Spock wrote, "You know more than you think you do." Even so, parents placed their trust in Spock's comprehensive index, which walked them, step by step, through tantrums and toilet training.

For the first time in a long time, people had options. Wartime materials, recycled as new products with high-tech names, were put to imaginative uses. Polyethylene, once used as electrical insulation, was molded into Tupperware. The small cathode ray tubes that guided bombers now made television sets cheaper to produce and radios small enough to fit in a pocket. Polystyrene, used for life preservers, was shaped into Styrofoam coffee cups. America, retooled, was back on track.

A multitude of choices encouraged people to create their own postwar life-styles. Early American living room. Traditional bedroom. Modern kitchen. Luxurious, stain-free carpets in every color. Loosely woven Fiberglas drapes that swayed in the breeze. Nubby sectional sofa parts were designed to be rearranged—moved opposite the fireplace, nearer the television set or facing one another to stimulate conversation at cocktail parties.

Technology continually improved on nature. Families could enjoy "fresh" fruit cocktail and frozen Florida orange juice, all year long. TV dinners delivered effortless Thanksgiving feasts of turkey with all the trimmings any day of the week. Cakes rose from foolproof mixes. Fluffy Minute Rice cooked "instantly." Cheese spread. Ketchup flowed. Jell-O was sculpted, and dehydrated onion soup mixes transformed sour cream into party dip. Vitamin-enriched milk and Wonder Bread helped fill a child's daily nutritional needs, and the endless choices of multi-shaped and multi-colored breakfast

cereals made those same children vocal connoisseurs to be reckoned with at the cash register.

There was always one "last" consumer choice to make before life would be perfect. Once the first wave of appliances was bought—frost-free refrigerators, automatic washing machines, electric ranges—housewives moved on to a second tier of steam irons, pressure cookers, Mixmasters, electric blankets and vacuum cleaners with attachments that reached into every corner and crevice. With so many labor-saving devices, women were driven to higher standards of housekeeping perfection and actually spent more time cleaning the house than ever before.

Anyone looking through the picture window could see neighbors wearing the same clothes and doing the same things—planting flowering shrubs, squirting lighter fluid on charcoal briquettes, washing the car, and late at night dragging noisy aluminum garbage cans out to the curb. Men weeded and mowed so their lawns blended into one yard-to-yard green carpet that stretched uninterrupted all the way

1950

How To Plan
THE HOME YOU WANT

The more suburbia sprawled, the more cars became central to an American way of life. Car registration soared from 26 million in 1945 to 40 million in 1950 to 60 million by 1959. When the first baby boomers got their driver's licenses, the number exploded to 88 million.

Packaging was intensely studied in the 1950s by manufacturers and consumers alike. Stodgy labels were updated by industrial designers who aimed to communicate images that would sell as well on the small television screen as from the supermarket shelf.

By 1950, 1.4 million new homes had been built to accommodate first-time home buyers, returning war veterans and their new families. They visited model homes and selected payment options, floor plans and appliances from builders' brochures. From 1950 to 1960, the number of new homeowners rose from 23.6 million to 32.8 million people.

Dwight D. Eisenhower, President from 1952 to 1960, was a plain speaker with an honest face that voters liked. His record as commander of all Allied forces in WWII and his pledge to work for peace during the Korean War won him the 1952 election.

The American Dream had promised

down the street. Entertained and diverted by life's new choices, one choice most people didn't make was to step out of line. Like teams of synchronized swimmers, the smiling American men and women who most benefited from the pursuit of the American Dream also conformed to its ground rules. Husbands went to jobs and came home, like clockwork. Wives cooked and cleaned, then read magazines about how to cook and clean better. Kids lived by the clock too, and went to school, and after school were shuttled to dance classes, scout meetings and Little League games.

Everyone climbed into the car, then out, back and forth on excursions to the outside world. Drive to the station and catch the train to work. Drive to the brightly lit supermarket and survey the alluring packages lined up on metal-edged shelves, or piled deep in finger-numbing freezers. Drive to church. Drive back to the old neighborhood to visit relatives who didn't choose a new life, or didn't have the option. Drive for the fun of driving. To buy an ice cream cone. To go to the beach, a drive-in, an amusement park. Once a year, take a long drive to another state and vacation for a while. Then come home to find that your neighbor had watered the lawn and that everything else was exactly where you'd left it.

At first, suburban life in the 1950s seemed as alluring as a Technicolor movie. The plot was simple: live the American Dream, count on progress without too much pain. New lines of dialogue were written and delivered every day, in newspapers and magazines like *Life* and *Look*. Advertisements, everywhere, stirred desire, defined glamour and accelerated the plot. Buy this! Buy that! Look like him! Be like her! Cash registers rang. Then television changed American life, upping the ante, broadcasting messages morning till night. Hour-long dramas, reinforcing American values, mesmerized the family. Half-hour sitcoms let viewers laugh as they measured the private lives they were living against the small-screen fictional lives they were watching. Some experiences didn't match. But in a suburban culture obsessed with the way things looked, what you couldn't relate to didn't matter.

Then people began to realize that their world was developing cracks. Politicians and increasingly persuasive "media" barraged them about circumstances literally beyond their control. So working even harder together, nuclear families did their best to avoid anything or anyone who might spoil their perfect world—from neighbors of other races, to juvenile delinquents,

Every Saturday and for fifty cents, kids spent the afternoon watching double and triple bill shows, which changed weekly at local movie theaters. Color movies became commonplace in the 1950s, and special techniques like Cinemascope and 3-D tried to lure audiences away from television.

Twenty million Americans watched the Army-McCarthy hearings on television starting in 1950, when Republican Senator Joseph R. McCarthy launched a four-year binge of character assassination. He charged government leaders and cultural figures with a range of offenses, from sympathizing with communists to being committed members of the Communist Party.

the postwar generation a storybook world. Now,

to communists. People shunned, swept under the carpet or repressed any behavior that fell outside the norm, anything "deviant" or weird. The nuclear family was an exaggeration of family harmony, just as domesticity in the 1950s was exaggerated, with its matching stoves, dishwashers, clothes dryers, refrigerators, dish towels and pot holders. The harmony was as much a function of isolationism as it was of togetherness.

A-bombs had won the war. American nuclear power promised to transform the future, but Americans had been nervous since Russia tested its atomic bomb in 1949. At any time, a cold war could turn hot, as people learned when the Korean War broke out in 1950. America's postwar sense of security turned out to be short-lived. People were scared, and the dangers of the time were hard for kids to understand. Why did parents keep watching the scowling face of Senator Joseph McCarthy on TV? Why didn't they like how Elvis Presley sang or the way he danced? Why did soldiers with guns have to walk with black children when they went to school? Why did some kids get polio and others not? Cold war fears seeped through schoolroom windows when alarms rang. Kids crouched in hallways or crawled under desks, covering their heads as they waited for the building to collapse. What would happen if they lived and their parents died? "Duck and cover!" wasn't fun, like a fire drill.

Sexual Behavior in the Human Male and *Sexual Behavior in the Human Female*, Alfred Kinsey's controversial books, exposed the unspoken realities of Americans' sex lives. Sending shock waves through the bedrooms of suburbia, Kinsey's explicit book about women's sex lives caused such an uproar that TV evangelist Billy Graham admonished, "It is impossible to estimate the damage this book will do to the already deteriorating morals of America." American educators were jolted, four years later, when the communists launched Sputnik in 1957. Political leaders and teachers alike feared that the country's "good times" mentality was doing the country in.

In the 1950s, as the cold war raged, the federal government sponsored educational programs to prepare Americans for nuclear war. During monthly air raid drills in schools, children hid under their desks or in designated civil defense areas in hallways and basements at the sound of a screeching one-minute siren and covered their heads until an all-clear signal sounded.

To Americans, Soviet Premier Nikita Khrushchev was a scary and untrustworthy cold war warrior. In 1960, he made headlines when he pounded his shoe on the podium at the United Nations, denying that Russia deprived people of their rights.

bit by bit, it   was becoming a

The tension between the perfect material world the middle class was working so hard to maintain and the uncontrollable forces of history were bound to rub the gloss off America's postwar fantasy. Day after day, while over a third of America's women were working outside their homes, others were depressed and downed record numbers of tranquilizers to keep their lives intact. Men's seeming willingness to trade in conscience for money and a "gray flannel" suit made them feel trapped even if they did spend all weekend trying to be good fathers and husbands. The more people wanted, the more people had to juggle, and the more fragile the "good life" began to feel.

It is not surprising that as traditional beliefs eroded in the late fifties, people tried all kinds of things to keep their own lives under control. More Americans went to church than ever before, to be comforted by a spirituality they hoped would transcend current events and the stress that sometimes kept them awake at night. Science fiction movies about aliens who "passed" as humans and television shows that went forward and backward in time took some of the edge off people's anxieties. It was comforting to think that

the bad world existed outside one's own. Children and adults alike spent more and more of their leisure time re-creating trouble-free worlds that were a hallmark of the 1950s. They played miniature golf and filled in paint-by-number sets. Kids mailed away for ant farms, rearranged miniature furniture in split-level dollhouses, reconfigured electric train sets. Families passed around View-Master slides, and switched from one seamless world to the next on TV.

This theme-park ride of mid-century life, when the American Dream seemed to be within the reach of most middle-class families, felt like it could go on forever. Until the mid-1960s, when long-ignored demands for equal rights and opportunities for minorities would change the political and social fabric of America, the surface of this synthetic suburban world paralleled the candy-colored world of Dick and Jane. These worlds looked alike and each reflected what the majority of American consumers wanted. But America was changing, and no picket fence was tall enough, no driveway long enough, no big city far enough away to insulate the people lucky enough to be living the American Dream from change.

reality, and it felt like it could go on forever.

An Exclusive Gallup Poll
Prepared for the POST:

THE SECRETS OF LONG LIFE

The Saturday Evening

POST

August 15, 1959   15¢

The August 15, 1959, cover of *The Saturday Evening Post* summed up what newlyweds were dreaming about in the 1950s: a house, cars, limitless appliances and power tools, a swimming pool.

At Home

"Ding dong!" the doorbell chimes. The screen door slams. Welcome to Dick and Jane's house, where no room has four walls or any corners. Home is an evocative stage set, with just enough familiar touches to convey a sense of well-being and comfort. There are many doorways for Dick and Jane and Sally to run in and out of, and few rugs to trip on. It's a home with just enough hints of style—patches of homey wallpaper and cheery curtains, a random chair or piece of furniture—to let you know that Mother and Father are solidly middle-class.

Even though we're never exactly sure just what kind of neighborhood Dick and Jane live in, we know

they're lucky, because they don't live in the city. And they don't have to share a house with Grandmother and Grandfather. Dick and Jane have what everybody dreams of—their own rooms in their own house.

Dick and Jane live in a traditional house. Everything in it is supposed to feel familiar and typical. There's a living room that's seldom used, a dining room the family eats in every day, and Mother's busy kitchen. A front hall leads to a staircase to the second floor, where there are at least three bedrooms but maybe only one bathroom. Father has his workshop in the basement. It's not a modern home, like a lot of new houses in the 1950s. There are no kidney-shaped tables, no blond-wood furniture, Corning Ware, Tupperware or harvest gold kitchen appliances. There's not even a record player or a radio. There is no barbecue in the backyard or television in the living room until the 1960s. But it's a comfortable house, bright and airy, where kids can do pretty much what they want. No plastic slipcovers protect the furniture, but well-behaved Dick and Jane know enough to keep their feet off the couch. Sally might not. And Spot and Puff? The opportunity never arises.

Building Blocks

More than one million acres of farmland were plowed under every year during the 1950s to make room for new houses for new families. The American Dream was finally an affordable reality for families who made around $3,000 a year and had never been able to afford a home before. All they had to do was make a $58 down payment and move into their mortgaged house as soon as the painters moved out. Of thirteen million homes built between 1948 and 1958, eleven million were built in the suburbs, which were growing fifteen times faster than any other part of the country. For the first time—using their savings, government loans and mortgages—more Americans owned homes than rented them. It was a new life-style that called for new schools, new churches and new swimming pools.

Nobody built houses faster than William J. Levitt, whose Levittown development in Hempstead, New York, defined suburbia as a place to live, a way of life with its own rules: no fences, no "Negro" families, no laundry hanging on clotheslines. Between 1947 and 1951, Levitt built and immediately sold 17,311 nearly identical Cape Cod and ranch-style homes. It was reported that on one day, he closed on 1,100 homes in five hours. At a price of between $7,770 and $9,500, the profit for each unit averaged $1,000. Using nails and lumber manufactured by Levitt, trained teams of workmen built houses in twenty-seven orderly steps. On a good day, thirty-six houses could be completed.

Built on a concrete slab, each house, with its pitched roof and louvered shutters, sat on a generous 60 X 100-foot plot (2,000 feet more than required by law). The small four-room dwelling had two bedrooms, one bath, a 12 X 16-foot living room and a modern kitchen. Landscaping, including four fruit trees, and all kitchen appliances were included. Some houses even came with a built-in television set and a Bendix washing machine as incentives.

Early Levittown kitchens shared the front of the house with the living room, in an open plan that turned the kitchen into the nerve center of the house. Life was more informal, less traditional. Seventy percent of meals were now eaten in the kitchen. The kitchen was the dining room, the laundry room and the "real" living room, where cooking, socializing and other household chores previously done in

Even when they were closed to the public, Levittown's model homes lured young couples to glimpse a new life-style.

private were now semipublic. The housewife-mother stood center stage in her kitchen, no longer relegated to the background.

Bathrooms were a third of the size they had been in turn-of-the-century houses. Bedrooms were big enough for a bed and a few pieces of furniture. This lack of space reinforced the "togetherness" being lauded in magazines and pushed people out the back door once the weather got warm. The backyard was the biggest room in the house, a place to barbecue, to cool off in the aboveground pool, play badminton and relax on the patio furniture. Fired up with a do-it-yourself mentality, the young men of suburbia mowed lawns, finished basements and repainted furniture. Levitt once joked, "No man who owns his own house and lot can be a communist. He has too much to do."

Parents moved to suburbia for peace and quiet and fresh air for their children. Kids played unsupervised with kids their own age on safe streets and cul-de-sacs. Parents wanted to shield their children from what they considered to be harmful influences, to make sure their children grew up according to their own standards, and not somebody else's. Most of the tensions in suburbia centered around children—how to discipline them, how to achieve quality in their schools, how to promote or ignore the class differences that distinguished one family from another.

Not everyone found suburbia to be a new Eden. Social critics lamented the loss of individualism, worried about the isolation of women and children and the domestication of men. They feared that traditional roles would get distorted, with women turned into overbearing wives and mothers. Men, they cautioned, would appear as overnight guests in their own homes, and children would be spoiled and delinquent. But while critics railed, the most important studies of Levittown showed that while some people were dissatisfied, especially women who missed the families they left behind, Levittowners talked frequently to their relatives on the telephone and visited them often, but did not want to move back to crowded, pressured cities.

The suburb became such a symbol of the American way of life that when Soviet Premier Nikita Khrushchev paid his first visit to America in 1959, President Eisenhower wanted him to visit Levittown to see the American Dream firsthand. Mr. Khrushchev declined.

Backyard Fun

The air is fresh, and the sun always shines. New white picket fences and old, tall, leafy trees mark the edges of Dick and Jane's outdoor domain. In front and back yards, the well-watered grass is very green. It smells good. No weeds, brown spots, bare patches, no dandelions mar the smooth, flat lawn. Everything Dick and Jane see belongs to them in this little utopia, where butterflies float between blossoms, flowers bloom in the garden, and Spot and Puff feel most at home.

Dick and Jane, who spend most of their time outside the house, are lucky that they're left on their own, unsupervised. The backyard is a safe place. No one has to watch them. They play by themselves, and sometimes with friends Susan, Pete and Billy, in their little suburban Arcadia, where it never snows, barely rains and never gets dark. After all, that's why Mother and Father moved here, to the "country," to be a little bit closer to nature. The backyard is Dick and Jane's private landscape, the place to do somersaults, fly a kite or toy plane, take a giant step, test out stilts, swing from strong branches, roll in piles of red and yellow autumn leaves. The fun ends only when Mother stands in the screen door, calling "Diiiiiiick!" "Jaaaaaane!" and it's time to go back inside.

Mother and Father like to be outside as much as they can too. Father mows the lawn and washes the car. Mother hangs up laundry to dry, then takes it down. Everyone works in the garden. Spot digs holes, chases frogs and plays hide-and-seek. When Puff climbs a tree, she can count on being rescued. Tim likes to be out-of-doors too, even if all he does is sit on the back steps, watching everyone else have fun.

Family Values

Big gold stars for Dick and Jane, who behave so well. "Do unto others as you would have others do unto you," says the Golden Rule. And Dick and Jane do. They've learned their lessons well. Where? At home. How? By listening carefully, by trusting and respecting Mother and Father. Why? Dick and Jane are encouraged to say what they mean, and when they speak, people listen. The children are respected for what they think and who they are.

Dick and Jane live in a world where only good exists. They don't hang around with kids who set bad examples. There are no bad influences, no comic books, TV shows or movies. No one in their little world competes or cheats. No one snitches, no one teases and no one ever lies.

Dick and Jane know how to share. They share toys, they share problems, they share fun. Dick and Jane know what it means to be responsible. They take care of Spot and Puff. They take care of their bikes and skates and wagon. They help around the house. Dick and Jane are always polite and well-behaved. They shake hands with their elders, they never talk back or grab things, and they always wait their turn.

But what Dick and Jane and everyone around them knows best is the value of work. "Work. Work. Work," says Sally as she watches a steam shovel in action. "I can work," says Dick as he helps Jane set the table. "I can work," says Jane as she makes a yellow dress for her doll. Mother does housework with a smile on her face. Father, home from work, fixes anything

Lessons to Learn

School is a place where values are passed along. But what values get passed along depends on when, where and how you live. At the peak of Dick and Jane's success, the books—short on vocabulary—were long on traditional American values. Here are some big moral lessons reinforced in these little readers.

Respect your parents

Help your siblings

Families have fun when they work together

Cooperate

Play is valuable

Use your imagination

Don't complain

Be kind to animals

Help others

Be enthusiastic

Take chances

Be considerate

Share what you have

Amuse yourself

Be like your parents

Be curious

Work hard at your job

Mind your manners

Be creative

All people are equal

Be self-assured

Express what you feel

Appreciate nature

Be proud of your accomplishments

Behave in the car and on the bus

Work and play well with others

The older you are, the more you should do

Take school seriously

Cleverness is rewarded

Clean up after yourself

Follow directions and rules

Ask permission when you're in doubt

Watch out for the safety of others

Accept other people's limitations

Be nice to people

Encourage others

Keep your sense of humor

Reading is good

at the drop of a hat. Jane gardens happily. Dick has fun watering the lawn and feeding Spot. Spot works to find Tim, and Sally plays by making believe she's working.

Work is the eighteenth new word in the Dick and Jane vocabulary. Most of the people Dick and Jane meet work, and work happily. The milkman comes to the house as he has for years, cheery and efficient, dropping off milk and cream in glass bottles with paper lids, and picking up the empties. Mother is glad to see the dry cleaner who comes right up to the front door, with arms full of dresses, bedspreads and the curtains Mother can't wash in the new washing machine. People do their jobs well, and Dick and Jane are happy to see them because they make Mother's work just a bit easier.

Who Wants a Toy?

"See the toys," said Sally.

"Horses and cows and pigs!
And a funny red duck!
I want that funny red duck."

"Oh, Sally," said Dick.
"You have a yellow toy duck.
Do you want a red duck, too?"

"Oh, I guess not," said Sally.

74

"See that baby doll," said Jane.
"That doll can talk.
I want it.
I want a doll that talks."

"Oh, Jane," said Dick.
"You have two big dolls.
Do you want a baby doll, too?"

"Oh, I guess not," said Jane.
"I guess I have all the dolls
I want."

75

Two Moral Tales

Impressionable children don't learn values only at home, they pick up information and cues everywhere they go, from the movies to Sunday school. They learn what's important, how to behave and how to tell right from wrong. Traditionally, American reading books have advocated religion and patriotism. The educators who developed plots for Dick and Jane stories understood their power to influence the behavior of millions of children. At a time when values in America were shifting dramatically, and the number of children in classrooms was growing, Dick and Jane became role models whose words

The Dog for Dick

Father said, "Come with me.
I want to get something for Spot."

"Oh, Father," said Dick.
"We want to look at the dogs now."

45

Jane said, "Look at this little dog!
It wants to play with us."

Sally said, "Jump, little dog.
Jump! Jump! Jump!
We like you."

Dick said, "Down, Spot, down.
I want to see the little dogs."

46

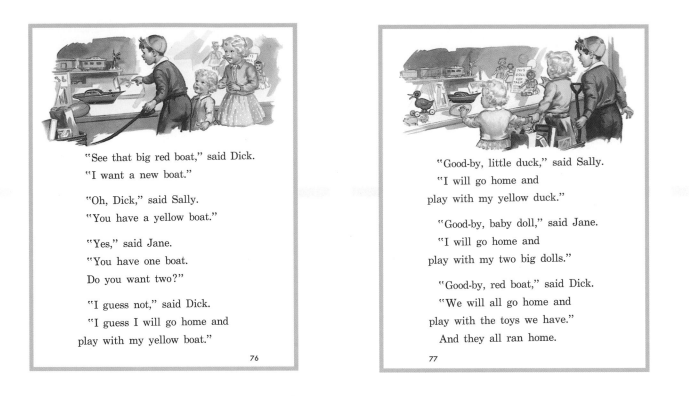

"See that big red boat," said Dick.
"I want a new boat."

"Oh, Dick," said Sally.
"You have a yellow boat."

"Yes," said Jane.
"You have one boat.
Do you want two?"

"I guess not," said Dick.
"I guess I will go home and
play with my yellow boat."

"Good-by, little duck," said Sally.
"I will go home and
play with my yellow duck."

"Good-by, baby doll," said Jane.
"I will go home and
play with my two big dolls."

"Good-by, red boat," said Dick.
"We will all go home and
play with the toys we have."
And they all ran home.

and actions were used to illustrate mainstream values of the time. Family, responsibility, citizenship and the importance of work were foremost. But at a time when children were gaining an upper hand, and adults were fretting over all the choices American culture was throwing their way, kind and considerate Dick and Jane had to come to terms with their own conflicting desires and postwar acquisitiveness. In "Who Wants a Toy?," Dick and Jane and Sally learn to be happy with the toys they already have. In "The Dog for Dick," Dick comes to understand the need for kindness and consideration, even toward animals.

Dick said, "Look here, Father.
This little dog likes us.
And we like it.
Will you get it for us?"

Father said, "You have a dog.
What will you do with Spot?
Do you want Spot to go away?"

Jane said, "Look at Spot!
Spot wants to run away now."

Dick said, "Oh, Spot!
I like that little dog.
But I do not want it.
I want my dog!
I want you!"

Heaven and Health

Parochial schools—a substantial religious educational market—asked Scott Foresman to produce religious editions of their popular textbooks. In 1930 the company obliged, replacing regular Dick and Jane stories with new ones that promoted Catholic values. By the 1950s, Dick and Jane and Sally had been rechristened John and Jean and Judy, named for Catholic saints. Spot, Puff, Mother and Father kept their own names.

In one pre-primer story, "Jesus Is Here," Mother and Father drive the family to church, where Dick and Jane and Sally will pray for Jesus' help. Spot and Puff, who'd like to go to church too, have to stay in the car. In "Blessed Mother Mary and Baby Jesus," Father surprises the family when he brings home a framed picture of the Virgin Mary cuddling the Baby Jesus. The children become excited when he hangs it above a vase of flowers in a place of honor in the living room. In "The Night Baby Jesus Came," John and Father set up a screen and slide projector in the living room and show the story of the Nativity for Jean and an assembled group of her friends. Dick and Jane books were also produced in a Seventh Day Adventist edition.

On another front, Dick and Jane were called into action to teach first-graders about health, personal development and safety. *Good Times with Our Friends* and *Happy Times with Our Friends* appeared in 1948. The Teacher's Edition emphasized that a teacher's first responsibility was to establish the finest physical

Jane said, "Look, look.
It is red.
We can not go now.
Stop, Dick and Sally.
Stop, Spot.
See the cars go.
We do not want to get hurt."

22

The 1941 *Good Times with Our Friends*

environment for her pupils: maintain the classroom at a proper temperature (68°F to 70°F), keep the atmosphere from getting too dry, see that children have properly adjusted chairs and desks, monitor the lighting in the classroom.

Concentrating on health, safety and mental hygiene, stories emphasized: working and playing safely (six-year-olds are accident-prone); the importance of sleep and the willingness to observe a reasonable bedtime hour; an appreciation of milk ("baby food" to most six-year-olds); a willingness to try new foods; proper use of a handkerchief to avoid the spread of germs; as well as good habits in nutrition, dressing, washing and dental care.

The Teacher's Edition reminds teachers that boys and girls should be given "the comforting assurance that they are not alone in their problems or varied emotions, that differences among people are to be prized rather than deplored, that reasonable standards of behavior rather than perfection constitute legitimate goals, that difficult situations usually must be met squarely rather than evaded, and that there are learnable techniques for getting along better with oneself and with others."

These books, like all Dick and Jane books, were not only revised to keep products up-to-date (replacing gauze bandages with band-aids) but also introduced new words to a child's vocabulary: breakfast, wash, milk, hurt, lunch, bump, handkerchief, candy, dinner, clothes, hats, tired, late, clean.

Father said, "Come, come.
Come and find something.
It is for Dick and Jane.
It is for Sally.
Come and find it."

Dick said, "I can find it."
Sally said, "I can find it."

30

The 1941 Cathedral Edition *We Come and Go*

The Power of Positive Thinking

I t's an iffy proposition to expect young boys and girls to do the right thing. Someone has to guide them. Parents start the process off, teaching values and drawing moral boundaries. Schools reinforce broader community values and promote social skills. Religious organizations and community and special interest groups also have their say in molding a child's spiritual and civic behavior.

The sense of suburban well-being filled advertisements, dreams and everyday life in the 1950s, but underneath the surface some leftover fears and some new anxieties were eating away at traditional values. Memories of the insecurity and sacrifice of the Depression and World War II gnawed at the belief in upward spiraling progress. The exaggerated threat of encroaching communism and constant atomic anxieties set off by the cold war undermined the sense of safety and security. A 1954 Supreme Court decision barring segregation in public schools exposed widespread racial bias in America. It triggered fears among white Americans who didn't want to share access to the American Dream, while providing some opportunities for blacks. When the Soviets launched Sputnik in 1957 and beat the Americans into space, fingers pointed at educators, who were criticized for not taking math and the sciences seriously.

Separated by geography from families and traditions, people felt stirrings of alienation. A new value system for suburbia mandated conformity, ambition and a frenzied materialism, taking some of the joy out of upward mobility. Mothers and fathers, faced with moral dilemmas and social uncertainty, clung to the hope that by being part of suburbia, they could keep the threatening outside world at bay.

In 1958, the number of people regularly attending churches and synagogues reached its highest level in American history before decline would set in, two years later. Spiritual leader Norman Vincent Peale's book *The Power of Positive Thinking* was a bestseller throughout the decade. It preached that answers to trouble lay within the individual, in the divine energy stored in the unconscious. According to Peale, all a person needed to do was "picturize" a goal, "prayerize" to learn what God wants, and "actualize" positive energy to leave one's troubles behind. By 1957, Peale was reaching a weekly television audience of thirty million believers.

Children were organized into activities that got them out of the house and expanded their repertoire of social skills while reinforcing traditional values. The scouting movement boomed during the 1950s. Brownie and Girl Scout membership rose from 1.8 million to four million. Girl Scouts hustled so many cookies that commercial bakeries had to fill the orders. Cub Scout enrollment doubled from 766,635 in 1949 to 1.6 million in 1956, and across the nation Boy Scouts gave three-fingered salutes as they repeated the Scout Oath: "On my honor, I will do my best: to do my duty to God and my country, and to obey the Scout Law; to help other people at all times; to keep myself physically strong, mentally awake, and morally straight."

On a scouting trip, a Cub Scout, Brownie and Boy Scout paid their respects to the Liberty Bell.

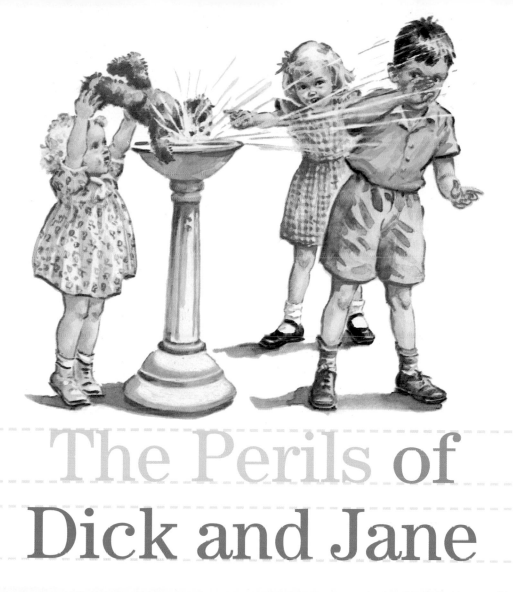

The Perils of
Dick and Jane

Dick and Jane and Sally must have been born under lucky stars. As with all little children, some bad things happen to them. But not too bad. The ball they play with rolls under a car, and only Spot can reach it. Their wagon tips over and Jane tumbles to the ground, but she isn't hurt. Tim falls, over and over again, into a ditch, into the lake, down the stairs, out of the car, but someone always rescues him. When a doll carriage wheel breaks off, Father can repair it. When a dress tears, Mother sits down and mends it.

Wouldn't you know, it's Sally who gets into the most scrapes. She's the baby and makes mistakes because she can't think things through. So because she doesn't pay attention, Sally drops the ice cream from her cone, and lucky Spot and Puff get to lick it up. When Sally offers Tim a drink of water from the fountain in the park, she squirts

everybody, and everybody laughs, "Funny, funny Sally." She'll learn. Mother's face powder looks so pretty, Sally has to try some on—on herself, on Tim, then on Puff and, finally, on Spot, who looks doubtful, but only for a moment.

Animals get in trouble too. Puff breaks a balloon, gets trapped in a yarn ball, is stuck up a tree. Spot knocks over Sally's toy farm—two times—and all the little animals topple to the floor! Spot gets chased by angry hens, has a stand-off with a big French poodle and, in his darkest hour, almost runs away when Dick hurts his feelings. A pet rabbit escapes. Little Quack, visiting from a farm, tries to run away too.

But every bit of trouble, which always comes as a surprise in Dick and Jane's world, has a happy ending. Bad things are turned into good things. Dicey moments get resolved without nasty taunts, little fists flying, mean words or tiny tears.

A Shot in the Arm

Outside the charmed world of storybooks, bad things do happen to good little children. Luckily, most of them are minor mishaps. A child loses a favorite toy or breaks something around the house, falls off a bike, gets stung by a bee. A child complains about a tummy ache and parents cope. Children are more vulnerable and need special care when it comes to scarier illnesses like chicken pox, mumps, whooping cough and measles.

It was in the 1950s, after two decades of escalating and frightening epidemics, that the poliomyelitis virus, which attacks nerve cells that control muscle movement, became every parent's nightmare. In 1952, the worst year on record, 58,000 cases of polio were reported and 1,400 children died. Rumor and fear surrounded the contagious illness. Children were kept away from crowded swimming pools, pulled out of movie theaters, and whisked home from summer camps in the middle of the night. In newspapers and newsreels, images of children doomed to death, paralysis or years in an iron lung haunted the fearful nation. Children were terrified at the sight of flies and mosquitoes thought to carry the virus. Parents dreaded fevers and complaints of sore throats or stiff necks.

In 1951, medical researcher Dr. Jonas Salk began testing a vaccine using dead polio viruses powerful enough to trigger antibodies in people who were inoculated with them. By the spring of 1954, the country mobilized to test the vaccine on 650,000 children in forty-four states. Twenty thousand doctors and public health officials, 40,000 nurses, 64,000 schoolteachers and principals and 200,000 volunteers cooperated in running the trials and in analyzing the results. The success of Salk's vaccine made him a hero, ranked in public opinion polls between Winston Churchill and Mahatma Gandhi.

David Eisenhower (*far right*), grandson of President Dwight Eisenhower, lined up for his polio vaccination.

Easy-to-Read Instructions

During World War II, many women left teaching for higher paying factory jobs and to help the wartime effort. When the war ended, with the baby boom swelling school populations, new teachers were hired, but they often had inadequate training.

That's why Teacher's Editions, which had been part of the Scott Foresman system for many years, became so important to the success of the Dick and Jane reading method. Charged with marching armies of children through the educational system, educators developed instructions for teaching reading that were as reliable as the recipes on cake boxes.

The Teacher's Editions explained what a complicated process reading really was and outlined a clear plan of attack that any teacher could follow. The guides also urged teachers to understand that the needs of each child they taught were different. The 1951 Teacher's Edition to the Dick and Jane pre-primers explained: "Children do not leave their problems behind when they come to school.... Not all homes are happy or filled with warmth and understanding of children. There are noisy, crowded homes surrounded by dirt and squalor.... There are homes where standards of order and cleanliness come first and children second. There are broken homes and unhappy homes where the child feels no sense of belonging....

There are homes in which the air is charged with conflict. When such deprived children lose themselves in stories about Dick, Jane, and Sally, and live for a time with these happy storybook characters, they experience the same release from their problems that the adult does when he loses himself in a good book or a movie.... Family conflicts, the absence of a "real" father or mother, the strain of high standards, or the sense of neglect are forgotten...."

Detailed lesson plans showed teachers the path that moved them through every page of the reading program. For less experienced teachers, scripts suggested the exact words to be repeated if they were to do their jobs successfully. Each lesson was organized around four sections: "Preparing for Reading," "Interpreting the Story," "Extending Skills and Abilities" and "Extending Interests." To teach the pre-primer story "Jump and Play," the teacher begins the class with a discussion of games like hopscotch, leapfrog and jump rope to get youngsters talking about their favorite games. Then, using word cards or writing on the blackboard, the teacher presents the two new words in the story, "you" and "not," and uses them in sentences so children recognize the form of the word and the context in which it can be used. Still "preparing," teachers then ask questions to make certain that the children comprehend the examples.

First-graders, like these Cleveland students, spent 40 percent of their school day learning to read.

In the most important section of the lesson, "Interpreting the Story," here's what the Teacher's Edition advises:

Guided reading: *Open the books to the table of contents and see if the youngsters can find the name of today's story. "It's a jump-rope story," you can hint. "Who can find the name for us?" Later, help everyone find the first page of the story.*

Page 31: *"Who is in this picture? What are Dick and Jane doing? What do you suppose they plan to do?" Talk about why Dick might be waving and what the two children could be saying. Draw attention to the name of the story and ask someone to read it aloud."*

Page 32: *Girls and boys may be surprised to see Mother joining the game. "Do you think this was fun? What makes you think everyone in the story likes it, too?" Notice Sally's excitement and welcome ideas on what she may have said. Ask someone to read aloud Sally's speech before you call attention to the fact that Dick had another idea. Have pupils read the last three lines silently to find out what it was. "What was Dick's idea?" Continue by having the last three lines read aloud. After the entire page has been read as a unit, ask, "Do you suppose Father can jump rope as well as Mother can? What makes you say so?"*

Page 33: *Ask pupils what they think of Father's jumping ability. "Do the children look as if they're enjoying this game?" After the silent reading of the text, ask, "To whom was Sally talking? What did she want Mother to see? What did Sally think of Father? Does Father look funny to you, too?" Following the oral reading, return to the picture again and ask, "Whom else do you see in this picture? Did anyone in the story notice Spot and Puff? What do you think Spot and Puff are doing?"*

Page 34: *Guide the detailed interpretation with such questions as: "What has happened? What do you suppose Jane said? Read the first three lines to yourselves. Who can not jump and play? Is Father the only one who can not jump?" Have the group read the rest of the page to themselves to find out what Dick said.*

After the children reread this story, the section "Extending Skills and Abilities" suggests activities to develop memory and phonetic skills and to reinforce the meaning of the two new words. Finally, in "Extending Interests," the teacher reads aloud two poems about hopping and jumping as children clap and jump along, plays a recording of one more poem, then organizes a jumping contest.

On the Town

Wherever town is, it's not far from home. Sometimes Mother walks there. Sally drives alongside in her metal toy car, and Dick and Jane travel the same route in their red wagon. When they arrive, no one is too tired to shop. Sometimes they take the big bus and look through the windows at the changing scene. There are traffic signs to read and stoplights to pay attention to. Town is a busy, clean, pleasant place, a place to learn grown-up things. There's a main street, lined with cheerful big picture windows piled with things boys and girls like to look at. They learn what it means to shop and that everything has its price. They understand they can't have everything.

Dick, Jane, Sally and Mother go to the grocery store often, where they see pyramids of delicious fruit and bins of healthy vegetables and, in the bakery section, stare at the

pink frosted cupcakes temptingly set out in neat rows. Sally gets to browse for a new book at the bookstore, spinning a book rack around and around. Jane window-shops for a new doll. Everyone gets new outfits for holidays and when it's time to head back to school. Because they behave, the kids get ice cream treats at the soda fountain.

When they leave the main street, there's more to see. There's the service station with lights and gas pumps where Father takes the car to have it checked. There's a zoo filled with elephants, hippos and kangaroos who are fun to look at and even more fun to imitate. But there's no place better than the Fun Park, where there's a merry-go-round that goes up and down and faster and faster and scary rides that make kids squeal with joy. Jane likes the game of ring toss best, because she beats Dick and Father. Atta girl!

Copycats

Dick and Jane books were such successful readers, and baby boomers such a big educational market, that competing textbook publishers came up with copycat versions of the winning Dick and Jane formula. To gain their share of the market, they introduced other brother and sister teams, of which Alice and Jerry (Row, Peterson and Company), Susan and Tom (Ginn and Company), and Ned and Nancy (D.C. Heath and Company) were the most popular. Bill and Susan, Tags and Twinkle, Bill and Linda and Jack and Jane had their followings too.

Alice and Jerry

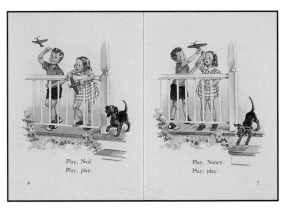

Ned and Nancy

Susan and Tom

Car culture so dramatically changed the American landscape, that a 1965 Highway Beautification Act encouraged communities to plant trees and flowers alongside roads, while the federal government legislated the placement and sizes of roadside signage.

Drive-by Culture

No technological invention has changed the way Americans live as radically as the automobile. From a temperamental plaything, the car became a necessity. The automobile changed the landscape and the way we saw it; it changed how cities were built, and ultimately how we lived.

In 1930, twenty-three million cars were on the road; by 1950 that number had doubled. Eight million cars, the highest number to date, were built in the U.S. in 1955. New car sales totaling $65 billion accounted for 20 percent of America's gross national product. The car was driving the American economy, an optimistic symbol of change and progress. Charles E. Wilson, the former president of General Motors who became President Eisenhower's Secretary of Defense, admitted the obvious: "What was good for our country was good for General Motors, and vice versa."

From 1940 to 1950, the number of highway miles built almost tripled, from 234,000 to 641,000. The practical value of driving on new roads paled in comparison to the other values Americans projected on their cars in the 1950s—to reflect and fantasize about themselves, their status and, most important, their mobility and freedom. Car ownership touched the deepest recesses of the American psyche: You were what you drove. General Motors figured out and targeted markets for each of its products, according to how much consumers would spend and where on the social ladder they saw themselves. Blue-collar workers and young couples just starting out bought Chevys. More confident, successful people who wanted a sportier look chose Pontiacs. Oldsmobiles looked good to white-collar bureaucrats. Buicks were for the local doctor, the lawyer and young professionals on the rise. The Cadillac was the ultimate status symbol for the executive at the top of the ladder.

Americans were ready to trade in newly won stability for mobility, to abandon tradition for a chance to see the "new" world being built. The Sunday drive to the relatives may have been the first on-the-road ritual, but soon people were driving for the fun of it, making up destinations—to the airport to see new jet planes, to neighborhoods where people with more money lived—or just driving around to see what was new. Sundays were no longer for rest, but for shopping in stores that did one-third of their weekly business on that day. Family vacations in the car were another kind of ritual, a quest for education, relaxation and open spaces that quickly became dotted with billboards and roadside attractions meant to lure people off the highways. Architecture and signage, scaled to the motorist's viewpoint, created a roadside environment designed to make an impact at high speed.

The car changed how Americans shopped, as Main Street lost its monopoly, its customers and its luster. Shiny, modern franchises—McDonald's, AAMCO, Holiday Inn, Roto-Rooter, H & R Block, Kentucky Fried Chicken, Dunkin' Donuts, Midas Muffler, Cut & Curl—opened across the country. Each sold an imaginative concept and a predictable product. Advertised locally and nationally, franchises hastened the death of many mom-and-pop businesses, which by comparison seemed slow, shoddy, expensive and old-fashioned. A growing nation on the go wanted speed, efficiency, predictable products and a smiley but impersonal "Hello" and "Thank you," before they jumped back in the car.

Baby boomers were the first generation to be driven before they walked. Cars changed parents' relationships with their teenagers, who, as soon as they were old enough, grabbed for car keys, expressing their independence and looking for entertainment. Cars became couches, where couples found privacy. And by the early 1960s, the car had even become a place to pray when the first drive-in church opened in California; worshipers sat in their "pews from Detroit" and heard sermons broadcast over loudspeakers.

83

In this one-car family, Father drives. Mother sits up front next to Father, and the children and Spot, and sometimes even Puff and Tim, sit in the back. The big four-door sedan is Father's special appliance, and he washes and simonizes it to keep it looking new. Father loves his car. He knows exactly what the motor sounds like. If it doesn't purr like Puff, if it clinks, or clicks, or rattles, off it goes to the service station. Sometimes it just needs gas. Dick and Jane love to go along to watch, to see the numbers spin as the gas tank fills. They like the funny smell of gasoline. And they watch with fascination as attendants—in

bow ties, neat uniforms and smart caps—put on a show. Open the hood. Check the oil. Add water to the radiator. Wash the windshield. Check the tires. Take the money. And when Father starts the car, they wave a friendly good-bye.

On the road, the air feels cool on Dick and Jane's faces. The wind rushes through Sally's curly hair. The car smells like metal, like rubber, like wool. It's fun to sit on the deep car seat, legs dangling above the floor. The car is a beautiful thing, with carpeting, molded plastic locks, stitched upholstery, leather piping, armrests and shiny chrome ashtrays. It's fun to look out the car windows and see trees and buildings and people and other cars go by so fast, to see small things far away get so big, to see big things get so small.

Every time they climb in the family car,

which is almost as big as a room in their house, Dick and Jane and Sally have something to look forward to. A car ride is a treat, not something that happens every day. The car is for drives to special places—not to school or the grocery store—but to the new model houses, to Grandmother and Grandfather's farm, to the lake for a boat ride or a picnic, to the zoo and, once in a while, to the Fun Park.

The family's first car was big and green. Then every five years or so Father got a new one. A sportier car. Then a station wagon. That's how time and progress are measured in Dick and Jane's world, and it's not just the cars that change, but who's in the driver's seat. By 1962, Mother's behind the wheel, and Dick and Jane and Sally can't imagine a day without the fun of a drive.

What You See Is What You Get

Before baby boomers were old enough to read words with Dick and Jane, they were already experts in "reading" pictures. They were growing up in a visual culture where comics, movies, magazines, billboards, store signs, mall order catalogs and, most of all, television showed them—rather than told them—about a world that was vivid, seductive and constantly changing.

Changes in American culture could be measured visually. The exciting ways things could look, the way styles appeared virtually overnight, redefined America as a modern, prosperous, imaginative country. The golden age of consumer culture offered up one new experience, then replaced it with another option. With so many new objects and events swirling around them, people could take pleasure just in looking. Adults and children were excited window-shoppers, surveying new homes and furnishings, clothes and foodstuffs, toys and gadgets before they made their choices. Just seeing so many objects change shape—cars, appliances, hairdos— gave people a sense that the shape of their own lives could change too, and get better and better and better.

After two decades of seeing black-and-white images of a drab, deprived world, the fifties introduced colored cereals, colored appliances and colorful magazine advertisements that promoted optimism and progress to adults and children. Jingle-driven television commercials grabbed kids' attention as they stared at ads for everything, making up their own minds about what was good, what was bad, what was necessary, and what they wanted their own worlds to look like.

Kids already knew what other tiny worlds looked like in pictures. Comic books, popular since the 1930s, taught kids how to "read" stories one frame at a time by studying drawings of characters' gestures, expressions and costumes. They became versatile in decoding comic book graphic shorthand—people "saw" stars when they were punched, light bulbs lit up over characters' heads when they had an idea, something moving across a scene left a trail of black lines.

Adults had their picture books too. Magazines arrived weekly—*Life, Look, The Saturday Evening Post*. Everything was described in picture stories that even kids could figure out: how the president of France spent the day, what a movie star ate for breakfast, what an atom bomb looked like as it exploded. Children could even learn things they weren't supposed to by scrutinizing half-naked bodies in *National Geographic* or the underwear pages of the Sears catalog.

In 1953, a billion comic books were sold at a cost of four times the U.S. library book budget.

Just as interesting as the picture stories were the sophisticated, colorful advertisements that used visual tricks to make chicken pot pies or new convertibles look like they were jumping off the page.

Kids also took their own pictures and using black photo corners glued them into story sequences in family photo albums. Kids were the child stars of home movies, parading back and forth, making faces, always waving, gesturing and mouthing words at the camera. View-Master slide sets supplied 3-D escape routes, and once a week there were the movies, bigger than life.

At the movies was where kids made their strongest, most visceral connection to pictures. Kids used their imaginations to project themselves into the pictures on a screen, to get lost in history or in a science fiction nightmare, to chase the bad guys over a mountain. Sitting in the dark, in the first row or in the back of the balcony, kids added to their repertoire of visual know-how, catching on to how to react to close-ups, long shots, fade-ins and fade-outs and grasping how movies create their own sense of time and reality.

But it was television that finally defined this first visually literate generation as separate from their parents. In the mid-1950s, six-year-olds who were just getting their first Dick and Jane reading readiness book had already watched 5,000 hours of TV programs. By the time they reached sixth grade, they averaged four and a half hours of TV viewing daily, and more than six hours on Sunday. Watching television began to take up one-quarter of a child's life.

Short shows and even shorter commercials trained kids to expect and be ready to switch gears, to jump from an engrossing story to a seductive commercial, to another commercial, to station identification, and then back into the story without missing a narrative beat. Television delivered more information in a day than a teacher could teach in a week. Changing collages of images defined a new reality, linking kids together through the shows they watched and loved.

The visual world was providing its own curriculum. Children learned more of what they needed to know from the pictures they saw—at home, on the street, at the supermarket, in magazines, on television and in movie theaters. This was the first generation to know the world through pictures first—to depend on, and even to value, fast, sophisticated and entertaining pictures more than words.

87

We Look and See

From the 1946 Pre-primer Teacher's Edition

When people remember Dick and Jane, what pops to mind first are the simple words they learned to read. "Look," "See," "Jump," "Oh," "Run." What is less obvious is how great a role the illustrations had in developing skills children had to master before they could read.

William Gray and his cohorts at Scott Foresman were ahead of their time in understanding how important pictures had become in a modern world that was relying more and more on visual information. In a 1946-47 Teacher's Edition, Gray wrote: "Skill in interpreting pictures is becoming increasingly important as a means of securing pleasure and information. Adults today are exposed to 'picture' magazines, cartoons, advertisements, movies, and many types of diagrammatic schemes for the presentation of facts. Children are surrounded with picture books and 'read' the funnies long before they enter school. Regardless of age or situation, the individual who can 'read' pictorial material effectively has access to a vast world of new ideas."

Illustrations in Dick and Jane books worked just as hard as the words printed beneath them. It was the pictures, full of drama and surprise, that really told the stories. As simple as they might seem, they were complex, full of details and information that a child could study and discover: the kind of sneakers Dick wore, how a sprinkler attached to a hose, how Mother bent her knees when she jumped rope. Movie-like, they looked spontaneous and true-to-life because the illustrators worked from photographs.

The teachers encouraged each student to tell a story based upon what he or she had seen in the picture, making certain that the most important incidents were noted. The next step was to introduce a group of pictures that told a story, so students learned to interpret the narrative in a picture sequence. These sequences were called "talking-picture stories."

Students were trained to look carefully at an individual picture, and did exercises in their workbooks identifying the details of what they saw. For instance, a teacher would say, "This picture shows many things happening at one time. Look at it carefully. What do you see?" Teachers encouraged their classes to make inferences about things a picture implied. "What season is it? Is it late spring or summer?" By leading children to notice the clothing worn, the leaves on the tree, the presence of a robin, teachers helped them understand what was implied by a picture, the information that wasn't spelled out but could be figured out. And by studying the differences among objects in a row and figuring out which were alike and which were different, children learned skills they needed to discriminate between one letter form and the next.

In show-and-tell sessions, children brought snapshots or pictures from newspapers and magazines that related to the stories they studied. The pictures were thumbtacked to bulletin boards or arranged in stories in a scrapbook. With so much time spent "reading" the information in pictures, it's not surprising that postwar children were well prepared to navigate a world that, as time passed, was packed with more and more visual information that moved or changed, faster and faster.

Classroom Christmas tree ornament

Love, from Dick and Jane

At the peak of their popularity in the 1950s, Dick and Jane controlled 80 percent of the early reading market. First-graders loved them so much that they sent Dick and Jane thousands of letters a year, most of them asking whether or not the children had a last name. And, as polite, thoughtful children would do, Dick and Jane wrote back. Year after year, teachers and students got Valentines, Christmas cards that could be hung on classroom trees, as well as calendars, pens, pencils and even party napkins.

Party napkin

Valentine's Day card

3. Growing Up wi

At the brink of adulthood, young people in the 1960s looked out over a vista of change, accelerating in every direction. Against a kaleidoscopic backdrop of fun—acid rock, pop art, fast-paced movies, psychedelic posters and outrageous fashions—the media broadcast starker pictures of political and social conflicts, at home and abroad. Teenagers never knew what they were going to see or hear: Laugh-In or another assassination, *Love Story* or *Easy Rider*, Connie Francis or Janis Joplin. It was time to make choices, time to test the limits and, for some, time to rebel.

Raised during a prolonged period of world peace, baby boomers were the most educated, sophisticated and mobile generation the country had turned out. Blessed with a sense of economic security unmatched in history, many were uncomfortable being so comfortable, and were ready to blast off—to be outrageous instead of polite, to reject repression and "let it all hang out."

The cold war had escalated into a deadly political power game. When the young, handsome President John F. Kennedy faced down Nikita Khrushchev over the stockpiling of Soviet missiles in Cuba, tearful baby boomers, watching TV, got their first terrifying whiff of mortality. Nothing, not even security, could be taken for granted. It was obvious, when they read the daily news and looked out their car windows, that while the suburbs might be affluent, cities had become unmanageable, and parts of them unlivable. The gap between privilege and poverty had never been so wide, so clear. A war in Southeast Asia was beginning to cast its dark shadow.

In his Inaugural address, the charismatic Kennedy had challenged American youth to take action: "... ask not what your country can do for you; ask what you can do for your country." Many responded to his idealism by looking around to see where they might make a difference. With no allegiance to the past, and numbers on their side, they would shake up the country.

1960

Student demonstrations, peaceful in the early sixties, became increasingly violent as the decade progressed. In 1964, Berkeley police dragged away protesters who had turned university property into a "People's Park."

The youngest President ever elected, John F. Kennedy projected an image of energy and intellect, family and fun. His moving speeches motivated young Americans to join the Peace Corps and embrace their responsibility as citizens.

By the mid-1960s, high school enrollment had doubled from the previous decade. Twenty million eighteen-to-twenty-four-year-olds were ready to leave home. Some went to college. Some moved south to register black voters. Others went overseas and down the economic ladder, to join the Peace Corps to build schools, health centers and housing for people who could give only their thanks in return.

But in 1963, bullets brought down Kennedy and his vision and shattered the American Dream. Violence slammed shut the gate on the New Frontier, and created a void that some distraught young people had the courage to look into. Everyone was stunned by the country's loss. Some people couldn't move forward and others felt they had nothing left to lose. They rejected the repressive codes of the 1950s, and exposed the hypocrisy of the world they were heirs to. With a precocity and surprising assurance gleaned from the media that had nourished them, they would change the world by triggering a decade of skepticism, rebellion, radical experimentation and instability.

While Dick and Jane were teaching yet another generation of first-graders to "help" and "work" and have "fun," articulate former first-graders were screaming, "Up the establishment," "Tell it like it is" and, above all, "Don't trust anyone over thirty." The rules and values drummed into their heads by parents who had lived through the Depression and a world war did not make any sense in a world where "do your own thing" was replacing family "togetherness" as the rallying cry for a generation. Kennedy had promised a New Frontier, and now Lyndon Johnson was hell-bent on giving all Americans access to his Great Society.

It would not be so simple. Nuclear families were breaking apart. People were tired of telling lies—about who they were, about who they loved, about why they worked so hard, about whether they were happy. There was a bad fit between traditional norms and new social realities. Between a quarter and a third of the people who married in the 1950s were on the road to divorce. The generation

When the single "She Loves You" was released in 1963, Beatlemania hit America. Flower power peaked in 1968, and the Beatles' animated cartoon, *Yellow Submarine*, dazzled audiences with psychedelic animation and clever lyrics.

Under the leadership of Martin Luther King, Jr., southern blacks organized nonviolent marches to register the eleven million blacks who through poll taxes and trumped-up literacy tests had been deprived of their right to vote. The road from Selma to Montgomery, Alabama in 1965 had to be placed under National Guard protection.

It was a time to test the limits. Young people

gap widened when young people refused to turn into Mother or Father. Who needed to listen to parents when there was an edgier counterculture to live in as well as millions of peers who agreed it was time to be different?

When the largest freshman class ever hit college in 1963, their demands for change couldn't be silenced by nervous school administrators. Students held rap sessions, teach-ins, sit-ins, and called strikes to topple values that had stood for generations. Students at Berkeley, many back from civil rights demonstrations in the South, returned with new organizational skills. The Free Speech Movement began when they protested the university's ban on fund-raising and recruiting for political causes on campus. Their action crystallized a national political movement around the New Left.

Middle-class students, sensing that political action would be cleansing, began to identify with the oppressed. They did it out of guilt, for the romance of being involved, as an apprenticeship. Their support would jump from one social cause to another, because they now understood that progress was not automatic. A domino principle was at work. Sparks from the civil rights movement inflamed students who insisted that there was no part of America that couldn't be improved. The women's movement shook up America's psyche, with women demanding equal rights in the kitchen, the bedroom and the boardroom. A sexual revolution was in the works. People either postponed getting married, or didn't bother to marry at all. The birth rate dropped by a third. This was the first generation that made having a child a life-style choice. Gay liberation gave voice to men and women who no longer had to hide who they loved. Consumer rights activists pointed fingers at corporations that built unsafe cars and perfected napalm. The economic growth that everyone had cheered and hoped to share in now was a threat to the whole earth and its fragile environment. And the urban black population, which had doubled since the 1950s, had won its civil rights but now had to battle for fair treatment.

By the mid-1960s, former Dicks and Janes, well-behaved children who had stayed within the lines in their coloring books,

The U.S. started bombing Vietnam in 1965. By 1967, the first major antiwar marches, in New York and Washington, D.C., were covered worldwide by the media, and in the first six months of 1968, 221 demonstrations rocked college campuses. While 58,196 Americans died, hawks and doves debated the morality of America's involvement, until the war ended in 1973.

At Woodstock, the landmark "Aquarian Exposition" held on a dairy farm in upstate New York in the summer of 1969, 400,000 people braved heat, traffic jams, rain and mud for peace, love and sixty hours of rock and blues.

looked out over a vista of change, and with assura

found their fun by acting out. Tie-dyed psychedelic T-shirts were more fun than button-down shirts. Men wore bracelets, women wore more bracelets, and everyone wore love beads. Dogs like Spot wore bandannas. People didn't get dressed, they "dressed up" as sherpas, gypsies, swamis, in costumes of see-through gauze, leather, velvet, showing off their bodies and their individuality. People searched for gurus to help them understand who they were, not what they were supposed to be. Self-expression no longer meant buying a new car every two years, but smoking marijuana and dropping acid. By 1967, "The Summer of Love," these long-haired flower children defined a movement whose social, stylistic and spiritual fallout turned America upside down.

Angrily and visibly, American students opposed the country's involvement in Vietnam and hastened its end. By 1968, the government was spending $30 billion a year on an increasingly unpopular war that many people thought was immoral. Protest turned into resistance. Citizens refused to pay income taxes, burned draft cards and flags and moved to Canada or Sweden to avoid serving in the Army. It was a turning point in American history. Never had a population turned a war's course through widespread civil protest. America's failure to win the war proved that the country's military power could not be used to justify influencing the politics of another country. America's confident sense of itself as the world's democratic role model and policeman—responsibilities assumed after World War II ended—was shattered by the debacle of Vietnam.

The late 1960s were starting to look like the flip side of the 1940s. Fathers had wanted to fight in a just cause; sons were refusing to fight in a "dirty" war. Mothers who had devoted their lives to homemaking couldn't understand why their daughters weren't settling down. Parents who had sacrificed their personal freedom to keep the bonds of nuclear families intact watched their children disdain family values.

At the schoolhouse too, revolution was underway. Students were changing. Elementary kids started school wiser than students before them. They may have cut their teeth watching *Romper Room* and *Ding Dong School* on TV, but

Sixties technologies turned science fiction into reality. Scientists decoded DNA molecules and generated laser light waves, while computers navigated astronauts through their landing on the moon on July 20, 1969.

Oral contraception came into widespread use in America by 1960, reflecting the changes in America's attitudes about sexual freedom. Using "the Pill," American women could choose to protect themselves against unwanted pregnancies for the first time. By the end of the decade, 80 percent of college men and women surveyed said premarital sex was just fine.

nce they changed the world by triggering a decade

they came of age stunned by the evening news, full of war and violence. When student demonstrators at the 1968 Democratic National Convention screamed, "The whole world's watching," as they were beaten by Chicago cops, children were watching too. Kids were wrenched from their storybook lives. Those who lived in one-parent homes took care of themselves when no one else was around. Kids were sophisticated and street-wise, privy to secrets children had been shielded from before—offensive language, sex, racial hatred, and the out-of-control quality of everyday life. The barriers that protected childhood were gone.

Children's experiences in schools were changing too. Kids were being bused out of their own neighborhoods into unfamiliar schools in strange territories. In urban and suburban schools, geographic and racial universes apart, parents and teachers called for books that showed more than a white middle-class suburban world. Forward-thinking elementary school educators, working in university think tanks, were determined to find a way of presenting a more complex world to media-savvy, street-smart kids.

As American institutions were shaken to their core, so was the world of Dick and Jane. From the start, the stories—text, illustration and content—had been adapted and revised taking into account the changing world of the readers. Characters and situations shed their traditional look and were modernized. The easy part was updating illustrations of the clothes, the house and the family car. Mother learned to drive, Father learned to cook, and Dick and Jane and Sally, from time to time, were now less than perfect.

Changing the cast of characters, so that Dick and Jane's world was more diverse, was harder. New people moved into the neighborhood who didn't look anything like Dick and Jane. In 1965, Mike and Pam and Penny and their parents were the first black family on the block and the first to appear in a first-grade basal reading program. Educational publishing was growing up, and so were Dick and Jane.

Across the country, young people in the late 1960s gathered at love-ins to smoke marijuana, renounce capitalism and spread the doctrine of peace and love. Of the 30,000 Flower Children, Love Children and Free People, 70 percent came from middle-class families.

of experimentation.

The New Neighbors

They're here! Mike and the cute little twins, Pam and Penny. Their pretty Mother and handsome Father are here too. It's 1965, and they're the new neighbors who live next door or maybe just down the block. They make great new friends for Dick and Jane and Sally. And like Dick and Jane and Sally's family, they don't have a last name either. Mike and Pam and Penny like to have fun and to work too. And they are happy.

Mike is just like Dick. He's the same height, wears the same kind of clothes and runs around just as much. Mike's a leader too. He is Dick's first real friend, and more than his match at games, bike-riding and making up new things to do. Mike is great at guessing games. He organizes puppet shows, makes chalk drawings on Dick's driveway and puts on a play that makes everyone laugh. Mike's a gentleman too, neat and well-

behaved. Just as Dick and Jane watch out for Sally, Mike watches out for Pam and Penny, even though they are good at taking care of each other.

Pam and Penny are identical twins, exactly alike, adorable with their braided pigtails tied in bows or clipped with colorful barrettes. Sometimes they wear overalls, with matching pink tops with their names, so no one gets them confused. Pam and Penny are as lively and mischievous as Sally and twice as much to handle. They're curious. They climb where they shouldn't. Count on the twins to discover the pink cupcakes before the picnic even starts.

The new kids on the block have the best two-wheeler and tricycles. Mike threads colorful strips of plastic through the wheels and from the ends of the handlebars so they fly in the wind when the kids pedal fast. Mike has big books and Pam and Penny have little books. Mike and the twins read a lot. And they work hard in the yard, helping Father, and in the kitchen, helping Mother. Father drives the car and does a lot of gardening, mowing the lawn and trimming shrubs. Mother cooks and helps outside too. She loves to plant red geraniums.

Mike and Pam and Penny live in a house like Dick and Jane's, except it is made of beautiful stones like the path that leads to their front door. From inside their house, you can see outside through the big picture window. Their living room is as comfortable as Dick and Jane's, but they have landscape paintings on the walls and a couch and chairs you want to sink

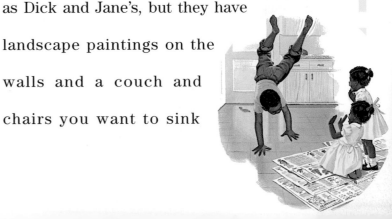

into. Their Mother's shiny kitchen has modern Formica countertops. The new neighbors have style.

Mike and Pam and Penny have Grandparents too. Their Grandmother and Grandfather live in the city in a brownstone apartment house. When the kids visit, they travel by bus, take taxis and go for interesting walks along busy streets. They see all kinds of city things like big construction sites with thick steel girders, a big old red brick school, streets lined with parking meters and filled with cars. Lucky kids. They get to see things that Dick and Jane and Sally only see on television.

Black in a White World

Dick and Jane's world was populated by white people, and white people only, until the 1960s. Designed to sell all across the country, Dick and Jane books reflected what mainstream educators believed America believed in and did not take into account, because no argument was made for, questions of cultural diversity and alternate points of view.

Black children in the South, where the law mandated separation, attended segregated, underfunded elementary schools where, more often than not, they got an inferior education. They spent the day in dilapidated buildings and were taught by untrained teachers, hampered by out-of-date teaching materials and limited supplies. In the 1950s, educator and psychologist Kenneth B. Clark described how segregating black children in schools lowered their motivation and contributed to negative self-images. Clark said that since children weren't encouraged to aspire to success, they saw no point in trying to excel at schoolwork.

It took the ground-breaking 1954 Supreme Court ruling *Brown* v. *Board of Education of Topeka* to shake up the segregated school systems that Americans took for granted. The court ruled unanimously that "separate but equal" was unconstitutional and institutional segregation therefore could not be tolerated. But desegregation went slowly at first in the South, where school boards often chose to shut down rather than face integration, and later in the North, where white flight to the suburbs insured de facto separation of the races in inner city schools.

Mass migrations of blacks out of the South accelerated in the 1950s and 1960s, as people uprooted their lives and moved to northern cities seeking greater opportunities in jobs and education. They moved in just as whites were moving out to suburbia. Between 1950 and 1960, the black urban population doubled, as 70 percent of the nation's blacks settled in the country's largest cities. Instead of life improving for many, it got worse. Unable to find decent jobs, they felt mounting frustration as they faced continued racial bigotry and economic stagnation.

The civil rights movement gained momentum during the 1960s, as blacks raised consciousness and challenged laws, often through nonviolent demonstrations and civil disobedience. They registered voters, sat in at whites-only lunch counters and held strikes to protest unfair treatment of blacks. The movement's efforts culminated when the 1964 Civil Rights Act created sweeping guidelines for the preservation of civil liberties, from voting rights to the withholding of federal funds from schools that practiced discrimination.

By the mid-1960s, popular culture started to make room for black entertainers, who had been influencing American culture since the turn of the century, without getting much credit for it. Market and the power of the pocketbook were the path to acceptance. Motown Records, for example, could top the charts because blacks *and* whites could follow its beat, feel its soul, and buy its records. On TV, black performers like Bill Cosby in *I Spy* (1965) and Diahann Carrol, who starred in *Julia* (1968), were successful because they could fit a white mold and disprove racist typecasting at the same time.

Despite gains, the battle for equality raged on among those urban blacks who faced relentless poverty and day-to-day racism. In the second half of the 1960s, anger and frustration spread, fueled by the murders of civil rights leaders Medgar Evers in 1963, black nationalist Malcolm X in 1965 and the Rev. Martin Luther King, Jr., in 1968. Riots broke out in Cleveland, Detroit, Newark, Oakland and New York. In 1965, as the Watts area in Los Angeles went up in flames, four thousand people were injured and thirty-four killed. And during the first nine months of 1967, there were 164 race-based disorders in 128 American cities. The 1968 Kerner Commission report on urban violence concluded: "Our Nation is moving toward two societies, one black, one white— separate and unequal."

At the 1963 March on Washington, 250,000 people supporting pending civil rights bills heard Martin Luther King, Jr. speak about his hopes for the future: "I have a dream that one day... little black boys and black girls will be able to join hands with little white boys and white girls and walk together as sisters and brothers."

Out of the indifference and pain, blacks reassessed their own identity and celebrated their own power. Black became beautiful. The black power movement grew. By end of the sixties, two-thirds of eligible black voters had been registered and 1,200 black candidates had been elected to political office. Black entrepreneurs began to replace white absentee landlords in local businesses. College students participated in strikes, sit-ins and lockouts, demanding that black studies programs be added to university curricula.

On the elementary school level, these social changes and challenges were felt just as strongly. Empowerment meant that black parents and concerned educators—black and white—would have to redefine what was taught to the youngest of children as they first entered school.

N-O Spells "No"

Dick and Jane were once almost too good to be true. But by the 1960s, like many other Americans, they were changing. Starting in the 1962 editions of Dick and Jane books, the kids looked bigger and older and were more sophisticated. They spent time doing things that were decidedly more cool, like playing basketball and watching TV. Dick and Jane and Sally didn't give up on fun. Their fun was different. They helped Father unpack and set up the new charcoal grill in the backyard. It became their job to feed Spot and Puff. And they used their imaginations in ways they never did before, like when they stared at their shadows and saw Jane as a princess, Dick as a football player and Mike as an Indian chief. And Jane delighted in discovering she had some real power over men, after all. When she trounced Father and Dick in a game of ring toss, she put her hands on her hips, adopting Dick's confident attitude, and laughed at the guys.

The universe that Dick and Jane lived in got bigger. More stylish suburban houses were built, and they filled with new friends. The kids dressed up in plastic space helmets instead of Mother or Father's oversize clothes. The children all knew that the air around them was filled not just with butterflies, but with TV antennas. The sky in suburbia pulsed with television signals. Mother, Dick, Jane and Sally, even Spot and Puff had their favorite TV programs. Fists and voices were raised and an argument broke out when the little kids, Sally or Pam and Penny, blocked the television screen.

What was clear was that Dick and Jane and their crew were more independent and worldly. The kids went off on more far-flung adventures, all on their own. They no longer needed Mother to escort them to the toy store when it was time to buy a birthday present for their friend, little Billy. Dick and Jane shopped on their own, wandering from display to display, looking at shrink-wrapped toys, before they made their decision.

Attitudes changed. Dick and Jane and Sally said words they never would have thought of saying before like, "Help." "Don't." " Can't." "I don't want to." "Get away." "Not now." "No!" They whined a bit and pawned off jobs on each other when they didn't want to do this chore or that. Dick and Jane and Baby Sally had their own priorities. They were full of cute wisecracks when they'd proved themselves right at someone else's expense. And they even pointed fingers and blamed people when they suspected wrongdoing.

And when the fun stopped it was for different reasons than ever before. Father drove his big car over Sally's little toy horse and crushed it in half. He didn't mean to, but Sally was really miserable. To take her mind off her tragedy, to keep her quiet, the whole family piled into the car and drove off to the Fun Park, where they all went off in different directions, seeking their own fun. Sally, too frightened to ride the real white pony (something she liked to do in earlier Dick and Jane books), settled for a spin on the merry-go-round. In the 1950s, when a scoop of ice cream fell off a cone, it was overexcited Spot, jumping up on Sally, who knocked it off. In the 1960s, when ice cream flew, it was because Dick used his pal Tom as a target, dumping his scoop on his friend's head, as a joke.

It was clear that everyone, everything and every place was changing. Even the farm was no longer a safe place. Rabbits now startled ponies who ran away. Plots thickened, and the stories could be almost scary. When Mike disappeared, dogs found his coat in the woods. While everyone was concerned about Mike, something even more dramatic happened. A fire broke out and threatened to burn down the farm. What would happen next?

We Watch and Learn

A lot of the world as seen on TV in the 1960s looked nothing like the innocent world long championed in Dick and Jane readers, where childhood was ideal and the emotional soundtrack played songs of unconditional love. Television, now in 95 percent of American homes, brought a constant stream of information—some of it good, some of it bad, and, many critics would say, a lot of it destructive to children. When kids started watching television it changed childhood, because parents and teachers no longer controlled the information kids had access to. Any child could turn a TV set on anytime and *see* what was happening. Innocence gave way to sophistication, while self-sufficiency gave way to a need for constant excitement. The more television kids watched, the harder it became to feel at home in the world of Dick and Jane.

Learning to read was still a thrill. Instead of just sitting and being read to, kids could read for themselves. It was fun to follow the beginning, middle and surprising end of a simple Dick and Jane adventure. But it was easier and more exciting for children to watch TV. Television told stories by piecing together a convincing collage of rapid shots, which kids learned to "read" without any training. By contrast, Dick and Jane's little world seemed unrealistic and tame.

Skills that made kids media-savvy were not the skills they needed to be good readers. As critics have pointed out, the word c-a-t is a symbol that triggers thoughts about the furry, four-legged animal who likes milk, chases mice, and who purrs like Puff when you pet it. When children read the word "cat," their imaginations take off. When they see a cat on TV, they don't have to do any work—it's the specific cat on the TV screen, no imagination required. Another skill that reading demands and TV dulls is the ability to follow a sequence of ideas. When you read, you concentrate on recognizing sequences of letters and words and sentences and paragraphs, which all add up to an idea. When you watch television, so many things happen so fast, there's just enough time to recognize what you see, watch it move and register what you feel. Words are slow, pictures are fast. Words are ideas, pictures are things. Words make us think, pictures make us feel.

Television alone can't be blamed for drops in reading scores, but the more kids watched TV, the more nervous educators got. Some damned the medium as having a bad effect on kids' educational success. Others embraced television as a new tool for teaching. It was smart and inevitable that a maverick group of educational researchers, advertising personnel and producers would harness television to teach disadvantaged kids pre-reading skills on public television, before commercial television lulled and dulled them. Children's Television Workshop's *Sesame Street* debuted in the summer of 1969. It was an innovative program that wound up appealing to all kids. *Sesame Street*, set in an old neighborhood on an inner city street, used short commercial-length spots to capture viewers' attention. Each show was comprised of thirty to fifty separate segments, some as short as twelve seconds. Shows populated by Jim Henson's puppets, real people and cartoon characters taught numbers and letters at first, then went on to tackle social, ethical, environmental and racial issues. Kids who watched the show shared a little world with characters like Big Bird, a seven-foot-tall canary, Oscar the Grouch, Bert, Ernie and the Cookie Monster, a world that was multiethnic and multiracial.

Educational television took a giant step when *Sesame Street* premiered in 1969. Set on a block of an inner-city street, with a multiracial cast, the program broke with educational tradition by exploiting TV techniques to teach skills to preschoolers.

105

Whatever Happened to Dick and Jane?

Reading theory changes, but the changes come slowly. Once school boards define standards and select the textbooks that will be used, they make a commitment of millions of dollars to a way of teaching and a reading program is firmly set in place. It takes something provocative to rock the establishment, like Rudolf Flesch's book *Why Johnny Can't Read*, which hit the best-seller list in 1955. Flesch claimed that no country had as much trouble teaching reading as America, and blamed the whole word method for making reading English as difficult for kids as Chinese, where every word has its own distinct form. Flesch had a political agenda—the familiar call for a return to America's greatness—and he advocated a return to phonics as a basic step to educational superiority.

From their introduction, Dick and Jane readers were never immune from criticism. Though millions of children were successfully taught to read through Dick and Jane books, some educators complained about the stilted way the characters spoke, about their repetitious language, about their goody-goody behavior. During the 1960s, as American culture was churning, Dick and Jane were challenged on yet another front. Their stories had been based on a family structure that existed in the 1920s—a father, a mother, two or more children. The mother kept house and the father worked.

Pressure groups wanted textbook publishers to show a mother going to work, and a father who did his fair share of housework and child care. Editors were told by teachers and school administrators that the characters had become stereotypes, not right for the time, not representative of the changing demographics of America, its ethnic and racial mix. Special interest groups launched campaigns through local school boards, protesting that society was too complicated for there to be one all-American boy like Dick and one all-American girl like Jane. The books, which had always been adaptable to their milieu, had come to a point where adaptation was really not the answer. Not only Dick and Jane, but the pedagogy that inspired them needed to be rethought, based on the most current information and research about reading.

How to represent multiculturalism in school textbooks had become a core issue, discussed within publishing companies and analyzed in university think tanks. Research groups developed new reading programs for the large segments of population whose lives and experiences were not being represented in elementary readers. One popular concept was "primacy of speech," an idea that led to introducing street language and, inevitably, street values and diversity into first grade reading materials. Federal funds supported university research to develop appropriate reading programs. In cities like Detroit, Chicago and Pittsburgh, multicultural programs were narrowly adopted, and by the end of the decade had helped to alter mainstream educational publishing.

First-graders, in the late 1940s, reading *We Come and Go*

Dick and Jane had been successful because the reading program worked, and they had represented the American Dream understood by the white, middle-class mainstream. But Dick and Jane were now no longer like the majority of kids who were reading about them, not even white middle-class kids. There was no way Dick and Jane could be believable as the characters they were, saying the words they said and living the lives they lived. It was time for Dick and Jane to retire. And they did, quietly. Scott Foresman continued to sell the 1965 editions of the Dick and Jane books through 1970, when they introduced an entirely new reading system. Today's educational reading programs have leapfrogged over the "real/pretend" world of primers and incorporate actual children's book texts. Children learn to read in a variety of ways and settings, in and out of school, with the teacher, and on their own.

Dick and Jane. Gone, but not forgotten. Say their names and watch a former first-grader's eyes light up. Dick and Jane were introduced as new friends, grew to be trusted role models and were then elevated to American icons. What they represent inspires people. Writers, artists and filmmakers celebrate the brother and sister team. Hip advertisements echo their words. Scholars analyze their pivotal role in American education. Museum exhibitions and television shows keep their history alive.

Dick and Jane reached their peak when America, fresh from winning a war, was secure, safe and flourishing in a burst of prosperity and optimism. Dick and Jane stir memories that have lingered for decades because they remind us of our own histories, especially what it was like to grow up when childhood felt like one long summer day.

Producers/Writers: Carole Kismaric and Marvin Heiferman

Design: Spot Design, New York

Project Manager: Alanna Stang

Text Researchers: Susan Jonas and Marilyn Nissenson

Copy Editor: Paula Glatzer

Interns: Carmen Menocal and Amelia Vicini

Acknowledgments

Collins Publishers San Francisco gratefully acknowledges the creative effort and enthusiasm that Carole Kismaric and Marvin Heiferman, of Lookout, brought to this project, and the guidance and cooperation of Scott, Foresman and Company, especially James M. Fitzmaurice, vice president and editor in chief.

Lookout thanks Jenny Barry, vice president and publisher; Maura Carey Damacion, executive editor; Lynne Noone, production director; and Carole Vandermeyde, executive assistant of Collins Publishers San Francisco, who worked with us to capture the spirit of Dick and Jane. Past and present employees at Scott Foresman who were generous in providing us with materials and information about the history of Dick and Jane readers include: James Fitzmaurice; Nancie Mitchell, associate librarian; Judy Besterfeldt, manager, library and information services; Sandra Belton, executive editor, educational technology; Bert Crossland, product manager, reading; Beth Martin, director of advertising; Judy Nyberg, editorial director, elementary language arts; Nick Savastio, creative group manager, advertising; Barbara Schneider, vice president, publishing services; Altienne Hahn, Louise McNutt and Richard Peterson.

Drew Hodges, Adam Levite and Naomi Mizusaki at Spot Design worked with good humor and enthusiasm to give Dick and Jane the design they deserve. Susan Jonas and Marilyn Nissenson provided valuable research on which the writing of this book is based, and George Rosato and Patricia Harrison were especially helpful consultants on education issues. James Keeline, The Prince and the Pauper, San Diego, shared information, materials and insights. David Thompson, WTVP-TV47 Peoria, producer/director of the television documentary *Whatever Happened to Dick and Jane?* and co-curator of a traveling exhibition of Dick and Jane watercolors, has been supportive and generous with sharing his original research. A special thanks to Bob Keeshan and Ruth Manecke. Thanks to Maurice Berger for encouragement and advice.

Other individuals to whom we are grateful for their help and encouragement include: Allison Anderson; Gary Kraut, Alphaville, New York City; Allan Chasanoff; George Darrow, Fun Antiques, New York City; Derek Nelson; David Newell; Nancy Hart, director, Clinton County Historical Society and Historical Museum, Frankfort, Ind.; Maria T. Olmedo; and Kathleen Woith, director of marketing and public affairs, Lakeview Museum of Arts and Sciences, Peoria, Ill. Thanks to Jocelyn Clapp, UPI/Bettmann, Inc.; Michael Shulman, Archive Photos; Christine Argyrakis, FPG International; Roberta Groves, H. Armstrong Roberts and Ron Mandelbaum, Photofest.

Picture Credits

PART THREE STRATEGIES

PART FOUR   IMPLEMENTING STRATEGY

Consistent with our mission to provide students with the most current and up-to-date account of the changes taking place in the world of strategy and management, there have been some significant changes in the 12th edition of *Strategic Management: An Integrated Approach*.

First, our new co-author, Melissa Schilling has taken on a major role in this edition. Melissa is a Professor of Management and Organization at the Leonard Stern School of Business at New York University, where she teaches courses on strategic management, corporate strategy, and technology and innovation management. She has published extensively in top-tier academic journals and is recognized as one of the leading experts on innovation and strategy in high-technology industries. We are very pleased to again have Melissa on the book team. Melissa made substantial contributions to the prior edition, and that continues with this edition. She has revised several chapters and written seven high-caliber case studies. We believe her input has significantly strengthened the book.

Second, a number of chapters have been extensively revised. In the 11th edition, Chapter 5, "Business-Level Strategy," was rewritten from scratch. In addition to the standard material on Porter's generic strategies, this chapter now includes discussion of *value innovation* and *blue ocean strategy* following the work of W. C. Kim and R. Mauborgne. Chapter 6, "Business-Level Strategy and the Industry Environment," was also extensively rewritten and updated to clarify concepts and bring it into the 21st century. For the 12th edition, we significantly revised and updated Chapter 3, building discussion of resources and competitive advantage around Jay Barney's popular VRIO model. We also combined Chapters 12 and 13 into a single chapter on implementing strategy through organization. We think this more streamlined approach greatly strengthens the book and enhances readability, particularly for students.

Third, the examples and cases contained in each chapter have been revised. Every chapter has a new *Opening Case* and a new *Closing Case*. There are also many new *Strategy in Action* features. In addition, there has been significant change in the examples used in the text to illustrate content. In making these changes, our goal has been to make the book relevant for students reading it in the second decade of the 21st century.

To help students learn how to effectively analyze and write a case study, we continue to include a special section on this subject. It has a checklist and an explanation of areas to consider, suggested research tools, and tips on financial analysis. Additionally, the MindTap learning activities include Directed Cases that ask students to complete the steps and offer in-depth explanations to guide them through the process, as well as case-based Branching Activities that place students in the shoes of a manager and require them to move through strategic decisions; students are assessed on the quality of their analysis in making their choices, and the activity concludes with a discussion question for you to implement in class.

Practicing Strategic Management: An Interactive Approach

We have received a lot of positive feedback about the usefulness of the end-of-chapter exercises and assignments in the Practicing Strategic Management sections of our book. They offer a wide range of hands-on and digital learning experiences for students. We are thrilled to announce that we have moved some of these elements into the MindTap digital learning solution to provide a seamless learning experience for students and instructors. We have enhanced these features to give students engaging, multimedia learning experiences that teach them the case analysis framework and provide them multiple opportunities to step into the shoes of a manager and solve real-world strategic challenges. For instructors, MindTap offers a fully customizable, all-in-one learning suite including a digital gradebook, real-time data analytics, and full integration into your LMS. Select from assignments including:

- **Cornerstone to Capstone Diagnostic** assesses students' functional area knowledge and provides feedback and remediation so that students are up to speed and prepared for the strategic management course material.
- **Multimedia Quizzes** assess students' basic comprehension of the reading material to help you gauge their level of engagement and understanding of the content.
- **Directed Cases** engage students by presenting businesses facing strategic challenges, placing concepts in real-world context, and making for great points of discussion. As they complete these activities, students receive instruction and feedback that teaches them the case analysis methodology and helps them build critical thinking and problem-solving skills.
- **Experiential Exercises** are based on the "Practicing Strategic Management" assignments in the end-of-chapter materials in previous editions. They have been updated for the Mind-Tap and challenge students to work in teams using the YouSeeU app in our one-of-a-kind collaborative environment to solve real-world managerial problems and begin to experience firsthand what it's like to work in management.
- **Branching Activities** present challenging problems that cannot be solved with one specific, correct answer. Students are presented with a series of decisions to be made based upon information they are given about a company and are scored according to the quality of their decisions.
- **Case Analysis Projects** are delivered in our online collaborative environment via the You-SeeU app so that students can work together synchronously to complete their comprehensive case analysis projects, papers, and presentations. Offered in conjunction with robust cases written exclusively by Charles Hill and Melissa Schilling, these activities challenge students to think and act like tomorrow's strategic leaders. Upload your case projects and let YouSeeU do the rest.
- **Strategy Sign-On** projects are back by popular demand. They are designed to provide students the opportunity to explore the latest data through digital research activities. Students first research a company that is facing a strategic management problem, and students then follow the company throughout the semester and complete various case analysis assignments.

It is not our intention to suggest that *all* of these exercises should be used for *every* chapter. Strategic management is taught at both undergraduate and graduate levels, and therefore we offer a variety of pedagogically designed activities with numerous challenge levels so that instructors can customize MindTap to best suit their teaching style and the objectives of the course.

We have found that our interactive approach to teaching strategic management appeals to students. It also greatly improves the quality of their learning experience. Our approach is more fully discussed in the *Instructor's Resource Manual*.

Teaching and Learning Aids

Taken together, the teaching and learning features of *Strategic Management* provide a package that is unsurpassed in its coverage and that supports the integrated approach that we have taken throughout the book.

- **Instructor Website.** Access important teaching resources on this companion website. For your convenience, you can download electronic versions of the instructor supplements from the password-protected section of the site, including Instructor's Resource Manual, Comprehensive Case Notes, Cognero Testing, Word Test Bank files, PowerPoint® slides, and Video Segments and Guide. To access these additional course materials and companion resources, please visit www.cengagebrain.com.
- The **Instructor's Resource Manual.** For each chapter, we provide a clearly focused synopsis, a list of teaching objectives, a comprehensive lecture outline, teaching notes for the Ethical Dilemma feature, suggested answers to discussion questions, and comments on the end-of-chapter activities. Each Opening Case, Strategy in Action boxed feature, and Closing Case has a synopsis and a corresponding teaching note to help guide class discussion.
- **Case Teaching Notes.** These include a complete list of case discussion questions, as well as comprehensive teaching notes for each case, which give a complete analysis of case issues.
- **Cognero Test Bank.** A completely online test bank allows the instructor the ability to create comprehensive, true/false, multiple-choice, and essay questions for each chapter in the book. The mix of questions has been adjusted to provide fewer fact-based or simple memorization items and to provide more items that rely on synthesis or application.
- **PowerPoint Presentation Slides.** Each chapter comes complete with a robust PowerPoint presentation to aid with class lectures. These slides can be downloaded from the text website.
- **Cengage Learning Write Experience 3.0.** This new technology is the first in higher education to offer students the opportunity to improve their writing and analytical skills without adding to your workload. Offered through an exclusive agreement with Vantage Learning, creator of the software used for GMAT essay grading, Write Experience evaluates students' answers to a select set of writing assignments for voice, style, format, and originality.
- **Video Segments.** A collection of 13 BBC videos have been included in the MindTap Learning Path. These new videos are short, compelling, and timely illustrations of today's management world. Available on the DVD and Instructor website, and detailed case write-ups including questions and suggested answers appear in the Instructor's Resource Manual and Video Guide.
- **MindTap.** MindTap is the digital learning solution that helps instructors engage students and help them become tomorrow's strategic leaders. All activities are designed to teach students to problem-solve and think like management leaders. Through these activities and real-time course analytics, and an accessible reader, MindTap helps you turn cookie cutter into cutting edge, apathy into engagement, and memorizers into higher-level thinkers.
- **Micromatic Strategic Management Simulation** (for bundles only). The Micromatic Business Simulation Game allows students to decide their company's mission, goals, policies, and strategies. Student teams make their decisions on a quarter-by-quarter basis, determining price, sales and promotion budgets, operations decisions, and financing requirements. Each decision round requires students to make approximately 100 decisions. Students can play in teams or play alone, compete against other players or the computer, or use Micromatic for practice, tournaments, or assessment. You can control any business simulation element

you wish, leaving the rest alone if you desire. Because of the number and type of decisions the student users must make, Micromatic is classified as a medium-to-complex business simulation game. This helps students understand how the functional areas of a business fit together, without being bogged down in needless detail, and provides students with an excellent capstone experience in decision making.

- **Smartsims** (for bundles only). MikesBikes Advanced is a premier strategy simulation providing students with the unique opportunity to evaluate, plan, and implement strategy as they manage their own company while competing online against other students within their course. Students from the management team of a bicycle manufacturing company make all the key functional decisions involving price, marketing, distribution, finance, operations, HR, and R&D. They formulate a comprehensive strategy, starting with their existing product, and then adapt the strategy as they develop new products for emerging markets. Through Smartsims' easy-to-use interface, students are taught the cross-functional disciplines of business and how the development and implementation of strategy involves these disciplines. The competitive nature of MikesBikes encourages involvement and learning in a way that no other teaching methodology can, and your students will have fun in the process!

ACKNOWLEDGMENTS

This book is the product of far more than three authors. We are grateful to our Senior Product Manager, Scott Person; our Content Developer, Tara Singer; our Content Project Manager, Kim Kusnerak; and our Marketing Manager, Emily Horowitz, for their help in developing and promoting the book and for providing us with timely feedback and information from professors and reviewers, which allowed us to shape the book to meet the needs of its intended market. We also want to thank the departments of management at the University of Washington and New York University for providing the setting and atmosphere in which the book could be written, and the students of these universities who react to and provide input for many of our ideas. In addition, the following reviewers of this and earlier editions gave us valuable suggestions for improving the manuscript from its original version to its current form:

Andac Arikan, *Florida Atlantic University*

Ken Armstrong, *Anderson University*

Richard Babcock, *University of San Francisco*

Kunal Banerji, *West Virginia University*

Kevin Banning, *Auburn University- Montgomery*

Glenn Bassett, *University of Bridgeport*

Thomas H. Berliner, *The University of Texas at Dallas*

Bonnie Bollinger, *Ivy Technical Community College*

Richard G. Brandenburg, *University of Vermont*

Steven Braund, *University of Hull*

Philip Bromiley, *University of Minnesota*

Geoffrey Brooks, *Western Oregon State College*

Jill Brown, *Lehigh University*

Amanda Budde, *University of Hawaii*

Lowell Busenitz, *University of Houston*

Sam Cappel, *Southeastern Louisiana University*

Charles J. Capps III, *Sam Houston State University*

Don Caruth, *Texas A&M Commerce*

Gene R. Conaster, *Golden State University*

Steven W. Congden, *University of Hartford*

Catherine M. Daily, *Ohio State University*

Robert DeFillippi, *Suffolk University Sawyer School of Management*

Helen Deresky, *SUNY—Plattsburgh*

Fred J. Dorn, *University of Mississippi*

Gerald E. Evans, *The University of Montana*

John Fahy, *Trinity College, Dublin*

Patricia Feltes, *Southwest Missouri State University*

Bruce Fern, *New York University*

Mark Fiegener, *Oregon State University*

Chuck Foley, *Columbus State Community College*

Isaac Fox, *Washington State University*

Craig Galbraith, *University of North Carolina at Wilmington*

Scott R. Gallagher, *Rutgers University*

Eliezer Geisler, *Northeastern Illinois University*

Gretchen Gemeinhardt, *University of Houston*

Lynn Godkin, *Lamar University*

Sanjay Goel, *University of Minnesota—Duluth*

Robert L. Goldberg, *Northeastern University*

James Grinnell, *Merrimack College*

Russ Hagberg, *Northern Illinois University*

Allen Harmon, *University of Minnesota—Duluth*

Ramon Henson, *Rutgers University*

David Hoopes, *California State University—Dominguez Hills*

Todd Hostager, *University of Wisconsin—Eau Claire*

David Hover, *San Jose State University*

Graham L. Hubbard, *University of Minnesota*

Miriam Huddleston, *Harford Community College*

Tammy G. Hunt, *University of North Carolina at Wilmington*

James Gaius Ibe, *Morris College*

W. Grahm Irwin, *Miami University*

Homer Johnson, *Loyola University—Chicago*

Jonathan L. Johnson, *University of Arkansas Walton College of Business Administration*

Marios Katsioloudes, *St. Joseph's University*

Robert Keating, *University of North Carolina at Wilmington*

Geoffrey King, *California State University—Fullerton*

Rico Lam, *University of Oregon*

Robert J. Litschert, *Virginia Polytechnic Institute and State University*

Franz T. Lohrke, *Louisiana State University*

Paul Mallette, *Colorado State University*

Daniel Marrone, *SUNY Farmingdale*

Lance A. Masters, *California State University—San Bernardino*

Robert N. McGrath, *Embry-Riddle Aeronautical University*

Charles Mercer, *Drury College*

Van Miller, *University of Dayton*

Debi Mishra, *Binghamton University*

Tom Morris, *University of San Diego*

Joanna Mulholland, *West Chester University of Pennsylvania*

James Muraski, *Marquette University*
John Nebeck, *Viterbo University*
Jeryl L. Nelson, *Wayne State College*
Louise Nemanich, *Arizona State University*
Francine Newth, *Providence College*
Don Okhomina, *Fayetteville State University*
Phaedon P. Papadopoulos, *Houston Baptist University*
John Pappalardo, *Keen State College*
Paul R. Reed, *Sam Houston State University*
Rhonda K. Reger, *Arizona State University*
Malika Richards, *Indiana University*
Simon Rodan, *San Jose State*
Stuart Rosenberg, *Dowling College*
Douglas Ross, *Towson University*
Ronald Sanchez, *University of Illinois*
Joseph A. Schenk, *University of Dayton*
Brian Shaffer, *University of Kentucky*
Leonard Sholtis, *Eastern Michigan University*
Pradip K. Shukla, *Chapman University*
Mel Sillmon, *University of Michigan—Dearborn*
Dennis L. Smart, *University of Nebraska at Omaha*
Barbara Spencer, *Clemson University*
Lawrence Steenberg, *University of Evansville*
Kim A. Stewart, *University of Denver*
Ted Takamura, *Warner Pacific College*
Scott Taylor, *Florida Metropolitan University*
Thuhang Tran, *Middle Tennessee University*
Bobby Vaught, *Southwest Missouri State*
Robert P. Vichas, *Florida Atlantic University*
John Vitton, *University of North Dakota*
Edward Ward, *St. Cloud State University*
Kenneth Wendeln, *Indiana University*
Daniel L. White, *Drexel University*
Edgar L. Williams, Jr., *Norfolk State University*
Donald Wilson, *Rochester Institute of Technology*
Jun Zhao, *Governors State University*

Charles W. L. Hill
Melissa A. Schilling
Gareth R. Jones

DEDICATION

To my daughters Elizabeth, Charlotte, and Michelle

— Charles W. L. Hill

For my children, Julia and Conor

— Melissa A. Schilling

For Nicholas and Julia and Morgan and Nia

— Gareth R. Jones

Photomaxx/Shutterstock.com

PART ONE

INTRODUCTION TO STRATEGIC MANAGEMENT

Photomaxx/Shutterstock.com

CHAPTER 1

STRATEGIC LEADERSHIP: MANAGING THE STRATEGY-MAKING PROCESS FOR COMPETITIVE ADVANTAGE

OPENING CASE

The Rise of Lululemon

In 1998, self-described snowboarder and surfer dude Chip Wilson took his first yoga class. The Vancouver native loved the exercises, but hated doing them in the cotton clothing that was standard yoga wear at the time. For Wilson, who had worked in the sportswear business and had a passion for technical athletic fabrics, wearing cotton clothes to do sweaty, stretchy, power yoga exercises seemed inappropriate. Thus the idea for Lululemon was born.

Wilson's vision was to create high-quality, stylishly designed clothing for yoga and related sports activities using the very best technical fabrics. He built a design team, but outsourced manufacturing to low-cost producers in South East Asia. Rather than selling clothing through existing

iStockphoto/Mlenny

2

retailers, Wilson elected to open his own stores. The idea was to staff the stores with employees who were themselves passionate about exercise, and could act as ambassadors for healthy living through yoga and related sports such as running and cycling.

The first store, opened in Vancouver, Canada, in 2000, quickly became a runaway success, and other stores followed. In 2007, the company went public, using the capital raised to accelerate its expansion plans. By late 2014, Lululemon had over 290 stores, mostly in North America, and sales in excess of $1.7 billion. Sales per square foot were estimated to be around $1,800—more than four times that of an average specialty retailer. Lululemon's financial performance was stellar. Between 2007 and 2104, average return on invested capital—an important measure of profitability—was 31%, far outpacing that of other well-known specialty retailers, while earnings per share grew by a staggering 3,183% (see Table 1.1).

How did Lululemon achieve this? It started with a focus on an unmet consumer need: the latent desire among yoga enthusiasts for high-quality, stylish, technical athletic wear. Getting the product offering right was a central part of the company's strategy. An equally important part of the strategy was to stock a limited supply of an item. New colors and seasonal items, for example, get a 3- to 12-week lifecycle, which keeps the product offerings feeling fresh. The goal is to sell gear at full price, and to condition customers to buy it when they see it, rather than wait, because if they do it may soon be "out of stock." The company only allows product returns if the clothes have not been worn and still have the price tags attached. The scarcity strategy has worked. Lululemon never holds sales, and its clothing sells for a premium price. For example, its yoga pants are priced from $78 to $128 a pair, whereas low-priced competitors like Gap Inc.'s Athleta sell yoga pants on their websites for $25 to $50.

To create the right in-store service, Lululemon hires employees who are passionate about fitness. Part of the hiring process involves taking prospective employees to a yoga or spin class. Some 70% of store managers are internal hires; most started on the sales floor and grew up in the culture. Store managers are given funds to repaint their stores, any color, twice a year. The interior design of each store is largely up to its manager. Each store is also given $2,700 a year for employees to contribute to a charity or local event of their own choosing. One store manager in Washington, D.C., used the funds to create, with regional community leaders, a global yoga event in 2010. The result, Salutation Nation, is now an annual event in which over 70 Lululemon stores host a free, all-level yoga practice at the same time.

Employees are trained to eavesdrop on customers, who are called "guests." Clothes-folding tables are placed on the sales floor near the fitting rooms rather than in a back room so that employees can overhear complaints. Nearby, a large chalkboard lets customers write suggestions or complaints that are sent back to headquarters. This feedback is then incorporated into the product design process.

Table 1.1 Lululemon's Financial Performance

	Lululemon	Gap Inc.	Urban Outfitters	Abercrombie & Fitch
Average ROIC 2007–2014	31%	21%	19%	14%
EPS Growth 2007–2014	3183%	295%	274%	15%

Despite the company's focus on providing a quality product, it has not all been clear sailing. In 2010, Wilson caused a stir when he emblazoned the company's tote bags with the phrase "Who is John Galt?" the opening line from Ayn Rand's 1957 novel, *Atlas Shrugged*. *Atlas Shrugged* has become a libertarian bible, and the underlying message that Lululemon supported Rand's brand of unregulated capitalism did not sit well with many of the stores' customers. After negative feedback, the bags were quickly pulled from stores. Wilson himself stepped down from day-to-day involvement in the company in January 2012 and resigned his chairman position in 2014.

In early 2013, Lululemon found itself dealing with another controversy when it decided to recall black yoga pants that were too sheer, and effectively "see through," when stretched due to the lack of "rear-end coverage." In addition to the negative fallout from the product itself, some customers report being mistreated by employees who demanded that customers put the pants on and bend over to determine whether the clothing was see-through enough to warrant a refund. One consequence of this PR disaster was the resignation of then CEO Christine Day. The company is also facing increasing competition from rivals such as Gap's Athleta Urban Outfitters' Without Walls, and Nike Stores. Notwithstanding these challenges, most observers in the media and financial community believe that the company can handle these issues and should be able to continue on its growth trajectory.

Sources: D. Mattoili, "Lululemon's Secret Sauce," *The Wall Street Journal*, March 22, 2012; C. Leahey, "Lululemon CEO: How to Build Trust Inside Your Company," *CNN Money*, March 16, 2012; T. Hsu, "'Pantsgate' to Hurt Lululemon Profit: Customer Told to Bend Over," *latimes.com*, March 21, 2013; C. O'Commor, "Billionaire Founder Chip Wilson Out at Yoga Giant Lululemon," *Forbes*, January 9, 2012; B. Weishaar, "No-moat Lululemon faces increasing competition but is regaining its customer base," *Morningstar*, December 17, 2014.

◤ OVERVIEW

Why do some companies succeed, whereas others fail? Why has Lululemon been able to persistently outperform most other specialty retailers? In the airline industry, how has Southwest Airlines managed to keep increasing its revenues and profits through both good times and bad, whereas rivals such as United Airlines have had to seek bankruptcy protection? What explains the persistent growth and profitability of Nucor Steel, now the largest steelmaker in the United States, during a period when many of its once-larger rivals disappeared into bankruptcy?

In this book, we argue that the strategies that a company's managers pursue have a major impact on the company's performance relative to that of its competitors. A **strategy** is a set of related actions that managers take to increase their company's performance. For most, if not all, companies, achieving superior performance relative to rivals is the ultimate challenge. If a company's strategies result in superior performance, it is said to have a competitive advantage.

Lululemon's strategies produced superior performance from 2007 to 2014; as a result, Lululemon enjoyed a competitive advantage that was translated into stellar financial performance. As described in the Opening Case, Lululemon's strategies included

strategy

A set of related actions that managers take to increase their company's performance.

focusing on a market niche where there was an unmet need for stylish, well-designed, high-quality athletic wear, satisfying that need through excellence in product design, and managing product inventory to limit supply, spur impulse purchases, and keep prices high. Lululemon's founder, Chip Wilson, clearly had a compelling strategic vision, and that vision was well executed.

This book identifies and describes the strategies that managers can pursue to achieve superior performance and provide their companies with a competitive advantage. One of its central aims is to give you a thorough understanding of the analytical techniques and skills necessary to formulate and implement strategies successfully. The first step toward achieving this objective is to describe in more detail what superior performance and competitive advantage mean and to explain the pivotal role that managers play in leading the strategy-making process.

Strategic leadership is about how to most effectively manage a company's strategy-making process to create competitive advantage. The strategy-making process is the process by which managers select and then implement a set of strategies that aim to achieve a competitive advantage. **Strategy formulation** is the task of selecting strategies. **Strategy implementation** is the task of putting strategies into action, which includes designing, delivering, and supporting products; improving the efficiency and effectiveness of operations; and designing a company's organizational structure, control systems, and culture. Lululemon was successful not just because managers formulated a viable strategy, but because that strategy was for the most part very well implemented.

By the end of this chapter, you will understand how strategic leaders can manage the strategy-making process by formulating and implementing strategies that enable a company to achieve a competitive advantage and superior performance. Moreover, you will learn how the strategy-making process can sometimes go wrong, as it did at one point for Lululemon, and what managers can do to make this process more effective.

strategic leadership
Creating competitive advantage through effective management of the strategy-making process.

strategy formulation
Selecting strategies based on analysis of an organization's external and internal environment.

strategy implementation
Putting strategies into action.

◤ STRATEGIC LEADERSHIP, COMPETITIVE ADVANTAGE, AND SUPERIOR PERFORMANCE

Strategic leadership is concerned with managing the strategy-making process to increase the performance of a company, thereby increasing the value of the enterprise to its owners, its shareholders. As shown in Figure 1.1, to increase shareholder value, managers must pursue strategies that increase the profitability of the company and ensure that profits grow (for more details, see the Appendix to this chapter). To do this, a company must be able to outperform its rivals; it must have a competitive advantage.

Superior Performance

Maximizing shareholder value is the ultimate goal of profit-making companies, for two reasons. First, shareholders provide a company with the risk capital that enables managers to buy the resources needed to produce and sell goods and services. **Risk capital** is capital that cannot be recovered if a company fails and goes bankrupt. For

risk capital
Equity capital invested with no guarantee that stockholders will recoup their cash or earn a decent return.

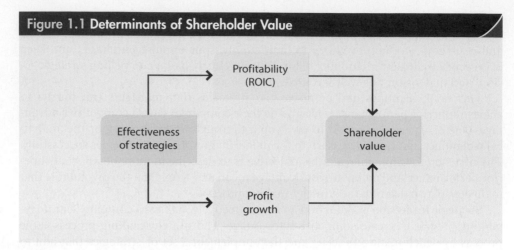

Figure 1.1 Determinants of Shareholder Value

example, when Lululemon went public in 2007, shareholders provided Chip Wilson's company with capital it used to build out its network of stores. Had Lululemon failed to execute, its shareholders would have lost their money—their shares would have been worthless. Thus, shareholders will not provide risk capital unless they believe that managers are committed to pursuing strategies that provide a good return on their capital investment. Second, shareholders are the legal owners of a corporation, and their shares therefore represent a claim on the profits generated by a company. Thus, managers have an obligation to invest those profits in ways that maximize shareholder value.

That being said, as explained later in this book, managers must behave in a legal, ethical, and socially responsible manner while working to maximize shareholder value. Moreover, as we shall see, there is good evidence that the best way to maximize the *long-run* return to shareholders is to focus on customers and employees. Satisfying customer needs, and making sure that employees are fairly treated and work productively, typically translates into better financial performance and superior long-run returns for shareholders. Alternatively, ignoring customer needs, and treating employees unfairly, may boost short-run profits and returns to shareholders, but it will also damage the long-run viability of the enterprise and ultimately depress shareholder value. This is why many successful managers argue that if a company focuses on its customers, and creates incentives for its employees to work productivity, shareholder returns will take care of themselves.

shareholder value
Returns that shareholders earn from purchasing shares in a company.

By **shareholder value**, we mean the returns that shareholders earn from purchasing shares in a company. These returns come from two sources: (a) capital appreciation in the value of a company's shares and (b) dividend payments. For example, during 2014 a share of Microsoft increased in price from $37.35 to $46.73. Each share of Microsoft also paid a dividend of $1.15 to its owners during 2014. Thus, in 2014, shareholders in Microsoft earned a return of 28.2%, 25.1% of which came from capital appreciation in the value of the share and 3.1% of which came in the form of a dividend payout.

profitability
The return a company makes on the capital invested in the enterprise.

One way to measure the **profitability** of a company is by its return on the capital invested in the enterprise.[1] The return on invested capital (ROIC) that a company earns is defined as its net profit over the capital invested in the firm (profit/capital invested). By net profit, we mean net income after tax. By capital, we mean the sum of money invested in the company: that is, stockholders' equity plus debt owed to creditors. So defined, *profitability is the result of how efficiently and effectively managers use the capital at their disposal to produce goods and services that satisfy customer needs.* A company that uses its capital efficiently and effectively makes a positive return on invested capital. Between 2007 and 2014, Lululemon earned an average **return on invested capital** (ROIC) of 31%, far above that of most other specialty retailers, which indicated that its strategies resulted in the very efficient and effective use of its capital.

A company's **profit growth** can be measured by the increase in net profit over time. A company can grow its profits if it sells products in rapidly growing markets, gains market share from rivals, increases sales to existing customers, expands overseas, or diversifies profitably into new lines of business. For example, between 2007 and 2012, Lululemon increased its net profits from $8 million to $280 million by rapidly growing the market for high-end, yoga-inspired clothing. Due to its dramatic profit growth, Lululemon's earnings per share increased from $0.06 to $1.91 over this period, resulting in appreciation in the value of each share in Lululemon.

profit growth
The increase in net profit over time.

Together, profitability and profit growth are the principal drivers of shareholder value (see the Appendix to this chapter for details). *To both boost profitability and grow profits over time, managers must formulate and implement strategies that give their company a competitive advantage over rivals.* This is what Lululemon achieved between 2007 and 2014. As a result, investors who purchased Lululemon shares on July 27, 2007, when it went public, and held on to them until December 31, 2014, saw the value of their shares increase from $14 to $55.79, a capital appreciation of almost 400%. By pursuing strategies that lead to high, sustained profitability and profit growth, Lululemon's managers rewarded shareholders for their decision to invest in the company.

One key challenge managers face is how best to simultaneously generate high profitability and increase profits. Companies that have high profitability but no profit growth will often be less valued by shareholders than companies that have both high profitability and rapid profit growth (see the Appendix for details). At the same time, managers need to be aware that if they grow profits but profitability declines, that too will be less highly valued by shareholders. What shareholders want to see, and what managers must try to deliver through strategic leadership, is *profitable growth*: that is, high profitability and sustainable profit growth. This is not easy, but some of the most successful enterprises of our era have achieved it—companies such as Apple, Google, and Lululemon.

Competitive Advantage and a Company's Business Model

Managers do not make strategic decisions in a competitive vacuum. Their company is competing against other companies for customers. Competition is a rough-and-tumble process in which only the most efficient, effective companies win out. It is a race without end. To maximize long-run shareholder value, managers must formulate and implement strategies that enable their company to outperform rivals—that give it a competitive advantage. A company is said to have a **competitive advantage** over its rivals when its profitability and profit growth are greater than the average of other companies competing for the same set of customers. The higher its profitability and profit growth relative to rivals, the greater its competitive advantage will be. A company has a **sustained competitive advantage** when its strategies enable it to maintain above-average profitability and profit growth for a number of years. This was the case for Lululemon between 2007 and 2014.

competitive advantage
The achieved advantage over rivals when a company's profitability is greater than the average profitability of firms in its industry.

sustained competitive advantage
A company's strategies enable it to maintain above-average profitability for a number of years.

business model
The conception of how strategies should work together as a whole to enable the company to achieve competitive advantage.

The key to understanding competitive advantage is appreciating how the different strategies managers pursue over time can create activities that fit together to make a company unique and able to consistently outperform them. A **business model** is managers' conception of how the set of strategies their company pursues work together as a congruent whole, enabling the company to gain a competitive advantage and achieve superior profitability and profit growth. In essence, a business model is a kind of mental model, or gestalt, of how the various strategies and capital investments a company makes fit together to generate above-average performance. A business model encompasses the totality of how a company will:

- Select its customers.
- Define and differentiate its product offerings.
- Create value for its customers.
- Acquire and keep customers.
- Produce goods or services.
- Increase productivity and lower costs.
- Deliver goods and services to the market.
- Organize activities within the company.
- Configure its resources.
- Achieve and sustain a high level of profitability.
- Grow the business over time.

The business model at discount stores such as Wal-Mart, for example, is based on the idea that costs can be lowered by replacing a full-service retail format for with a self-service format and a wider selection of products sold in a large-footprint store that contains minimal fixtures and fittings. These savings are passed on to consumers in the form of lower prices, which in turn grow revenues and help the company achieve further cost reductions from economies of scale. Over time, this business model has proved superior to the business models adopted by smaller, full-service, "mom-and-pop" stores, and by traditional, high-service department stores such as Sears. The business model—known as the self-service supermarket business model—was first developed by grocery retailers in the 1950s and later refined and improved on by general merchandisers such as Wal-Mart in the 1960s and 1970s. Subsequently, the same basic business model was applied to toys (Toys "R" Us), office supplies (Staples, Office Depot), and home-improvement supplies (Home Depot and Lowes).

Industry Differences in Performance

It is important to recognize that in addition to its business model and associated strategies, a company's performance is also determined by the characteristics of the industry in which it competes. Different industries are characterized by different competitive conditions. In some industries, demand is growing rapidly, and in others it is contracting. Some industries might be beset by excess capacity and persistent price wars, others by strong demand and rising prices. In some, technological change might be revolutionizing competition; others may be characterized by stable technology. In some industries, high profitability among incumbent companies might induce new companies to enter the industry, and these new entrants might subsequently depress prices and profits in the industry. In other industries, new entry might be difficult, and periods of high profitability might persist for a considerable time.

Thus, the different competitive conditions prevailing in different industries may lead to differences in profitability and profit growth. For example, average profitability might be higher in some industries and lower in other industries because competitive conditions vary from industry to industry.

Figure 1.2 shows the average profitability, measured by ROIC, among companies in several different industries between 2002 and 2011. The computer software industry had a favorable competitive environment: demand for software was high and competition was generally not based on price. Just the opposite was the case in the air transport industry, which was extremely price competitive.

Exactly how industries differ is discussed in detail in Chapter 2. For now, it is important to remember that the profitability and profit growth of a company are determined by two main factors: *its relative success in its industry and the overall performance of its industry relative to other industries.*[2]

Performance in Nonprofit Enterprises

A final point concerns the concept of superior performance in the nonprofit sector. By definition, nonprofit enterprises such as government agencies, universities, and charities are not in "business" to make profits. Nevertheless, they are expected to use their resources efficiently and operate effectively, and their managers set goals to measure their performance. The performance goal for a business school might be to

Figure 1.2 Return on Invested Capital (ROIC) in Selected Industries, 2002–2011

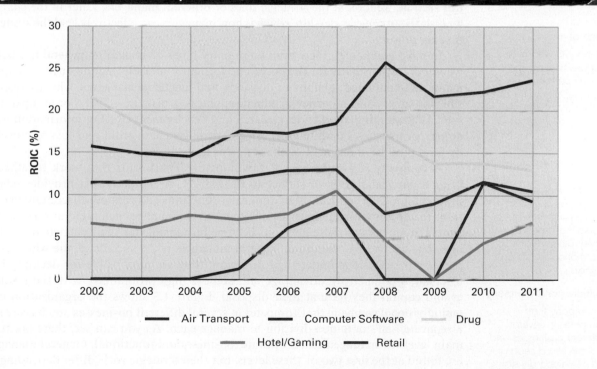

Source: Value Line Investment Survey.

get its programs ranked among the best in the nation. The performance goal for a charity might be to prevent childhood illnesses in poor countries. The performance goal for a government agency might be to improve its services while reducing its need for taxpayer funds. The managers of nonprofits need to map out strategies to attain these goals. They also need to understand that nonprofits compete with each other for scarce resources, just as businesses do. For example, charities compete for scarce donations, and their managers must plan and develop strategies that lead to high performance and demonstrate a track record of meeting performance goals. A successful strategy gives potential donors a compelling message about why they should contribute additional donations. Thus, planning and thinking strategically are as important for managers in the nonprofit sector as they are for managers in profit-seeking firms.

▛ STRATEGIC MANAGERS

Managers are the linchpin in the strategy-making process. Individual managers must take responsibility for formulating strategies to attain a competitive advantage and for putting those strategies into effect through implementation. They must lead the strategy-making process. The strategies that made Lululemon so successful were not chosen by some abstract entity known as "the company"; they were chosen by the company's founder, Chip Wilson, and the managers he hired. Lululemon's success was largely based on how well the company's managers performed their strategic roles. In this section, we look at the strategic roles of different managers. Later in the chapter, we discuss strategic leadership, which is how managers can effectively lead the strategy-making process.

general managers

Managers who bear responsibility for the overall performance of the company or for one of its major self-contained subunits or divisions.

In most companies, there are two primary types of managers: **general managers**, who bear responsibility for the overall performance of the company or for one of its major, self-contained subunits or divisions, and **functional managers**, who are responsible for supervising a particular function; that is, a task, an activity, or an operation such as accounting, marketing, research and development (R&D), information technology, or logistics. Put differently, general managers have profit-and-loss responsibility for a product, a business, or the company as a whole.

functional managers

Managers responsible for supervising a particular function, that is, a task, activity, or operation, such as accounting, marketing, research and development (R&D), information technology, or logistics.

A company is a collection of functions or departments that work together to bring a particular good or service to the market. A company that provides several different goods or services often duplicates functions and creates self-contained divisions (each containing its own set of functions) to manage each good or service. The general managers of these divisions become responsible for their particular product line. The overriding concern of general managers is the success of the whole company or the divisions under their direction; they are responsible for deciding how to create a competitive advantage and achieve high profitability with the resources and capital they have at their disposal. Figure 1.3 shows the organization of a **multidivisional company** that competes in several different businesses and has created a separate, self-contained division to manage each. As you can see, there are three main levels of management: corporate, business, and functional. General managers are found at the first two of these levels, but their strategic roles differ depending on their sphere of responsibility.

multidivisional company

A company that competes in several different businesses and has created a separate, self-contained division to manage each.

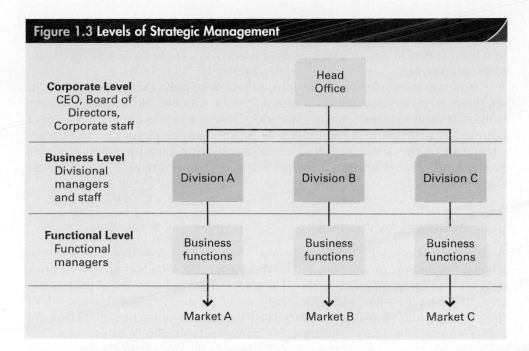

Figure 1.3 Levels of Strategic Management

Corporate Level
CEO, Board of
Directors,
Corporate staff

Head
Office

Business Level
Divisional
managers
and staff

Division A   Division B   Division C

Functional Level
Functional
managers

Business
functions

Business
functions

Business
functions

Market A   Market B   Market C

Corporate-Level Managers

The corporate level of management consists of the chief executive officer (CEO), other senior executives, and corporate staff. These individuals occupy the apex of decision making within the organization. The CEO is the principal general manager. In consultation with other senior executives, the role of corporate-level managers is to oversee the development of strategies for the whole organization. This role includes defining the goals of the organization, determining what businesses it should be in, allocating resources among the different businesses, formulating and implementing strategies that span individual businesses, and providing leadership for the entire organization.

Consider General Electric (GE) as an example. GE is active in a wide range of businesses, including lighting equipment, motor and transportation equipment, turbine generators, construction and engineering services, industrial electronics, medical systems, aerospace, aircraft engines, and financial services. The main strategic responsibilities of its CEO, Jeffrey Immelt, are setting overall strategic goals, allocating resources among the different business areas, deciding whether the firm should divest itself of any of its businesses, and determining whether it should acquire any new ones. In other words, it is up to Immelt to develop strategies that span individual businesses; his concern is with building and managing the corporate portfolio of businesses to maximize corporate profitability.

It is not the CEO's (in this example, Immelt's) specific responsibility to develop strategies for competing in individual business areas such as financial services. The development of such strategies is the responsibility of the general managers in these different businesses, or business-level managers. However, it is Immelt's responsibility to probe the strategic thinking of business-level managers to make sure that they are pursuing robust business models and strategies that will contribute to the maximization of GE's long-run profitability, to coach and motivate those managers, to reward them for attaining or exceeding goals, and to hold them accountable for poor performance.

Corporate-level managers also provide a link between the people who oversee the strategic development of a firm and those who own it (the shareholders). Corporate-level managers, particularly the CEO, can be viewed as the agents of shareholders.[3] It is their responsibility to ensure that the corporate and business strategies that the company pursues are consistent with superior profitability and profit growth. If they are not, then the CEO is likely to be called to account by the shareholders.

Business-Level Managers

business unit

A self-contained division that provides a product or service for a particular market.

A **business unit** is a self-contained division (with its own functions—for example, finance, purchasing, production, and marketing departments) that provides a product or service for a particular market. The principal general manager at the business level, or the business-level manager, is the head of the division. The strategic role of these managers is to translate the general statements of direction and intent from the corporate level into concrete strategies for individual businesses. Whereas corporate-level general managers are concerned with strategies that span individual businesses, business-level general managers are concerned with strategies that are specific to a particular business. At GE, a major corporate goal is to be a market leader in every business in which the corporation competes. The general managers in each division work out for their business the details of a business model that is consistent with this objective.

Functional-Level Managers

Functional-level managers are responsible for the specific business functions or operations (human resources, purchasing, product development, logistics, production, customer service, and so on) found within a company or one of its divisions. Thus, a functional manager's sphere of responsibility is generally confined to one organizational activity, whereas general managers oversee the operation of an entire company or division. Although they are not responsible for the overall performance of the organization, functional managers nevertheless have a major strategic role: to develop functional strategies in their areas that help fulfill the strategic objectives set by business- and corporate-level general managers.

In GE's aerospace business, for instance, production managers are responsible for developing manufacturing strategies consistent with corporate objectives. Moreover, functional managers provide most of the information that makes it possible for business- and corporate-level general managers to formulate realistic and attainable strategies. Indeed, because they are closer to the customer than is the typical general manager, functional managers may generate important ideas that subsequently become major strategies for the company. Thus, it is important for general managers to listen closely to the ideas of their functional managers. An equally great responsibility for managers at the operational level is strategy implementation: the execution of corporate- and business-level plans.

THE STRATEGY-MAKING PROCESS

We can now turn our attention to the process by which managers formulate and implement strategies. Many writers have emphasized that strategy is the outcome of a formal planning process and that top management plays the most important role in this process.[4] Although this view has some basis in reality, it is not the whole story. As we shall see later in the chapter, valuable strategies often emerge from deep within the organization without prior planning. Nevertheless, a consideration of formal, rational planning is a useful starting point for our journey into the world of strategy. Accordingly, we consider what might be described as a typical, formal strategic planning model.

A Model of the Strategic Planning Process

The formal strategic planning process has five main steps:

1. Select the corporate mission and major corporate goals.
2. Analyze the organization's external competitive environment to identify opportunities and threats.
3. Analyze the organization's internal operating environment to identify the organization's strengths and weaknesses.
4. Select strategies that build on the organization's strengths and correct its weaknesses in order to take advantage of external opportunities and counter external threats. These strategies should be consistent with the mission and major goals of the organization. They should be congruent and constitute a viable business model.
5. Implement the strategies.

The task of analyzing the organization's external and internal environments and then selecting appropriate strategies constitutes strategy formulation. In contrast, as noted earlier, strategy implementation involves putting the strategies (or plan) into action. This includes taking actions consistent with the selected strategies of the company at the corporate, business, and functional levels; allocating roles and responsibilities among managers (typically through the design of organizational structure); allocating resources (including capital and money); setting short-term objectives; and designing the organization's control and reward systems. These steps are illustrated in Figure 1.4 (which can also serve as a roadmap for the rest of this book).

Each step in Figure 1.4 constitutes a sequential step in the strategic planning process. At step 1, each round, or cycle, of the planning process begins with a statement of the corporate mission and major corporate goals. The mission statement is followed by the foundation of strategic thinking: external analysis, internal analysis, and strategic choice. The strategy-making process ends with the design of the organizational structure and the culture and control systems necessary to implement the organization's chosen strategy. This chapter discusses how to select a corporate mission and choose major goals. Other aspects of strategic planning are reserved for later chapters, as indicated in Figure 1.4.

Some organizations go through a new cycle of the strategic planning process every year. This does not necessarily mean that managers choose a new strategy each year. In many instances, the result is simply to modify and reaffirm a strategy and structure already in place. The strategic plans generated by the planning process generally

Figure 1.4 Main Components of the Strategic Planning Process

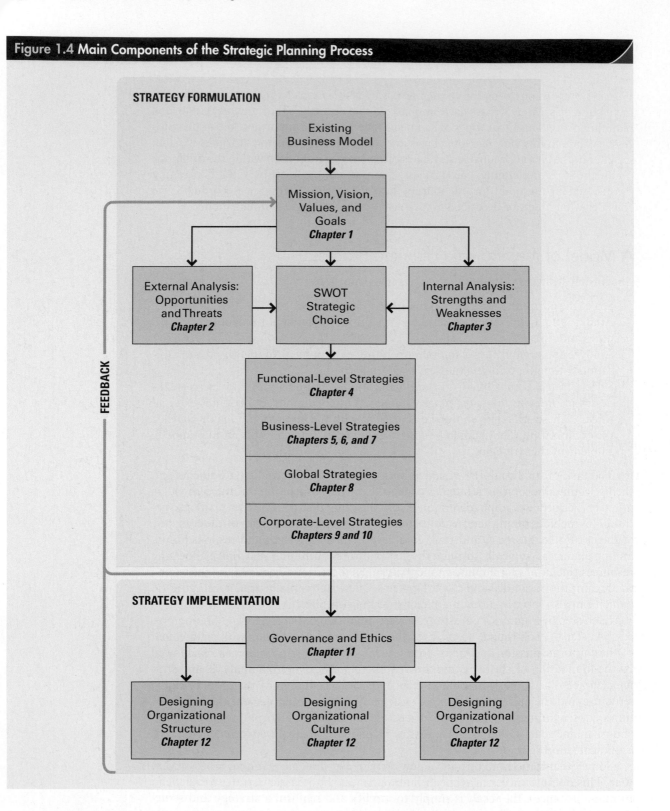

project over a period of 1 to 5 years, and the plan is updated, or rolled forward, every year. The results of the annual strategic planning process should be used as input into the budgetary process for the coming year so that strategic planning shapes resource allocation within the organization.

Mission Statement

The first component of the strategic management process is crafting the organization's mission statement, which provides the framework—or context—within which strategies are formulated. A mission statement has four main components: a statement of the organization's reason for existence—normally referred to as the mission; a statement of some desired future state, usually referred to as the vision; a statement of the key values to which the organization is committed; and a statement of major goals.

The Mission A company's mission describes what the company does. For example, the mission of Google is *to organize the world's information and make it universally accessible and useful.*[5] Google's search engine is the method that is employed to "organize the world's information and make it accessible and useful." In the view of Google's founders, Larry Page and Sergey Brin, information includes not just text on websites, but also images, video, maps, products, news, books, blogs, and much more. You can search through all of these information sources using Google's search engine.

mission
The purpose of the company, or a statement of what the company strives to do.

According to the late Peter Drucker, an important first step in the process of formulating a mission is to come up with a definition of the organization's business. Essentially, the definition answers these questions: "What is our business? What will it be? What should it be?"[6] The responses to these questions guide the formulation of the mission. To answer the question, "What is our business?" a company should define its business in terms of three dimensions: who is being satisfied (what customer groups), what is being satisfied (what customer needs), and how customers' needs are being satisfied (by what skills, knowledge, or distinctive competencies).[7] Figure 1.5 illustrates these dimensions.

This approach stresses the need for a *customer-oriented* rather than a *product-oriented* business definition. A product-oriented business definition focuses on the characteristics of the products sold and the markets served, not on the customer needs the products satisfy. Such an approach obscures the company's true mission, because a product is only the physical manifestation of applying a particular skill to satisfy a particular need for a particular customer group. In practice, that need may be served in many different ways, and a broad, customer-oriented business definition that identifies these ways can safeguard companies from being caught unaware by major shifts in demand.

Google's mission statement is customer oriented. Google's product is search. Its production technology involves the development of complex search algorithms and vast databases that archive information. But Google does not define its self as a search engine company. Rather, it sees itself as organizing information to make it accessible and useful *to customers*.

The need to take a customer-oriented view has often been ignored. History is peppered with the ghosts of once-great corporations that did not define their businesses, or defined them incorrectly, and so ultimately declined. In the 1950s and 1960s, many office equipment companies such as Smith Corona and Underwood defined their businesses as being the production of typewriters. This product-oriented definition ignored the fact that they were really in the business of satisfying customers' needs

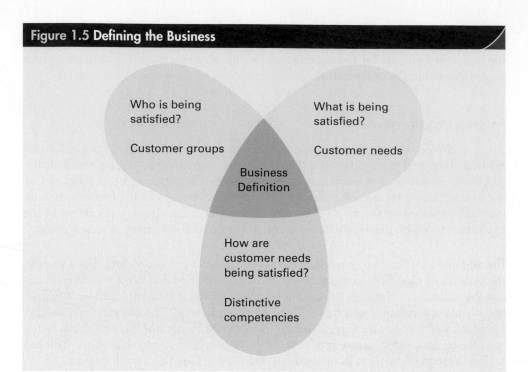

Figure 1.5 Defining the Business

Who is being satisfied?

Customer groups

What is being satisfied?

Customer needs

Business Definition

How are customer needs being satisfied?

Distinctive competencies

for information processing. Unfortunately for those companies, when a new form of technology appeared that better served customer needs for information processing (computers), demand for typewriters plummeted. The last great typewriter company, Smith Corona, went bankrupt in 1996, a victim of the success of computer-based word-processing technology.

In contrast, IBM correctly foresaw what its business would be. In the 1950s, IBM was a leader in the manufacture of typewriters and mechanical tabulating equipment using punchcard technology. However, unlike many of its competitors, IBM defined its business as providing a means for *information processing and storage*, rather than only supplying mechanical tabulating equipment and typewriters.[8] Given this definition, the company's subsequent moves into computers, software systems, office systems, and printers seem logical.

vision

The articulation of a company's desired achievements or future state.

Vision The **vision** of a company defines a desired future state; it articulates, often in bold terms, what the company would like to achieve. In its early days, Microsoft operated with a very powerful vision of a computer on every desk and in every home. To turn this vision into a reality, Microsoft focused on producing computer software that was cheap and useful to business and consumers. In turn, the availability of powerful, inexpensive software such as Windows and Office helped to drive the penetration of personal computers into homes and offices.

values

A statement of how employees should conduct themselves and their business to help achieve the company mission.

Values The **values** of a company state how managers and employees should conduct themselves, how they should do business, and what kind of organization they should build. Insofar as they help drive and shape behavior within a company, values are commonly seen as the bedrock of a company's organizational culture: the set of values, norms, and standards that control how employees work to achieve an organization's mission and goals. An organization's culture is commonly seen as an important source of its competitive advantage.[9] (We discuss the issue of organizational culture in depth in Chapter 12.) For example, Nucor Steel is one of the most productive and profitable steel firms in the world. Its competitive advantage is based, in part, on the extremely high productivity of its workforce, which the company maintains is a direct result of its cultural values, which in turn determine how it treats its employees. These values are as follows:

- "Management is obligated to manage Nucor in such a way that employees will have the opportunity to earn according to their productivity."
- "Employees should be able to feel confident that if they do their jobs properly, they will have a job tomorrow."
- "Employees have the right to be treated fairly and must believe that they will be."
- "Employees must have an avenue of appeal when they believe they are being treated unfairly."[10]

At Nucor, values emphasizing pay for performance, job security, and fair treatment for employees help to create an atmosphere within the company that leads to high employee productivity. In turn, this has helped Nucor achieve one of the lowest cost structures in its industry, and it helps to explain the company's profitability in a very price-competitive business.

In one study of organizational values, researchers identified a set of values associated with high-performing organizations that help companies achieve superior financial performance through their impact on employee behavior.[11] These values included respect for the interests of key organizational stakeholders: individuals or groups that have an interest, claim, or stake in the company, in what it does, and in how well it performs.[12] They include stockholders, bondholders, employees, customers, the communities in which the company does business, and the general public. The study found that deep respect for the interests of customers, employees, suppliers, and shareholders was associated with high performance. The study also noted that the encouragement of leadership and entrepreneurial behavior by mid- and lower-level managers and a willingness to support change efforts within the organization contributed to high performance. The same study identified the attributes of poorly performing companies—as might be expected, these are not articulated in company mission statements: (1) arrogance, particularly in response to ideas from outside the company; (2) lack of respect for key stakeholders; and (3) a history of resisting change efforts and "punishing" mid- and lower-level managers who showed "too much leadership."

MAJOR GOALS

Having stated the mission, vision, and key values, strategic managers can take the next step in the formulation of a mission statement: establishing major goals. A goal is a precise, measurable, desired future state that a company attempts to realize. In this context, the purpose of goals is to specify with precision what must be done if the company is to attain its mission or vision.

Well-constructed goals have four main characteristics:[13]

- They are precise and measurable. Measurable goals give managers a yardstick or standard against which they can judge their performance.
- They address crucial issues. To maintain focus, managers should select a limited number of major goals to assess the performance of the company. The goals that are selected should be crucial or important ones.
- They are challenging but realistic. They give all employees an incentive to look for ways of improving the operations of an organization. If a goal is unrealistic in the challenges it poses, employees may give up; a goal that is too easy may fail to motivate managers and other employees.[14]
- They specify a time period in which the goals should be achieved, when that is appropriate. Time constraints tell employees that success requires a goal to be attained by a given date, not after that date. Deadlines can inject a sense of urgency into goal attainment and act as a motivator. However, not all goals require time constraints.

Well-constructed goals also provide a means by which the performance of managers can be evaluated.

As noted earlier, although most companies operate with a variety of goals, the primary goal of most corporations is to maximize shareholder returns, and doing this requires both high profitability and sustained profit growth. Thus, most companies operate with goals for profitability and profit growth. However, it is important that top managers do not make the mistake of overemphasizing current profitability to the detriment of long-term profitability and profit growth.[15] The overzealous pursuit of current profitability to maximize short-term ROIC can encourage such misguided managerial actions as cutting expenditures judged to be nonessential in the short run—for instance, expenditures for research and development, marketing, and new capital investments. Although cutting current expenditures increases current profitability, the resulting underinvestment, lack of innovation, and diminished marketing can jeopardize long-run profitability and profit growth.

To guard against short-run decision making, managers need to ensure that they adopt goals whose attainment will increase the long-run performance and competitiveness of their enterprise. Long-term goals are related to such issues as product development, customer satisfaction, and efficiency, and they emphasize specific objectives or targets concerning such details as employee and capital productivity, product quality, innovation, customer satisfaction, and customer service.

External Analysis

The second component of the strategic management process is an analysis of the organization's external operating environment. The essential purpose of the external analysis is to identify strategic opportunities and threats within the organization's operating environment that will affect how it pursues its mission. Strategy in Action 1.1 describes how an analysis of opportunities and threats in the external environment led to a strategic shift at Time Inc.

Three interrelated environments should be examined when undertaking an external analysis: the industry environment in which the company operates, the country or national environment, and the wider socioeconomic or macroenvironment. Analyzing

1.1 STRATEGY IN ACTION

Strategic Analysis at Time Inc.

Time Inc., the magazine publishing division of media conglomerate Time Warner, has a venerable history. Its magazine titles include *Time*, *Fortune*, *Sports Illustrated*, and *People*, all long-time leaders in their respective categories. By the mid-2000s, however, Time Inc. was confronted with declining subscription rates.

An external analysis revealed what was happening. The readership of Time's magazines was aging. Increasingly, younger readers were getting what they wanted from the Web. This was both a *threat* for Time Inc., as its Web offerings were not strong, and an *opportunity*, because with the right offerings, Time Inc. could capture this audience. Time also realized that advertising dollars were migrating rapidly to the Web, and if the company was going to maintain its share, its Web offerings had to be every bit as good as its print offerings.

An internal analysis revealed why, despite multiple attempts, Time had failed to capitalize on the opportunities offered by the emergence of the Web. Although Time had tremendous *strengths*, including powerful brands and strong reporting, development of its Web offerings had been hindered by a serious *weakness*— an editorial culture that regarded Web publishing as a backwater. At *People*, for example, the online operation used to be "like a distant moon," according to managing editor Martha Nelson. Managers at Time Inc. had also been worried that Web offerings would cannibalize print offerings and accelerate the decline in the circulation of magazines, with dire financial consequences for the company. As a result of this culture, efforts to move publications onto the Web were underfunded or were stymied entirely by a lack of management attention and commitment.

Martha Nelson showed the way forward for the company. Her *strategy* for overcoming the *weakness* at Time Inc., and better exploiting *opportunities* on the Web, started in 2003 with merging the print and online newsrooms at *People*, removing the distinction between them. Then, she relaunched the magazine's

online site, made major editorial commitments to Web publishing, stated that original content should appear on the Web, and emphasized the importance of driving traffic to the site and earning advertising revenues. Over the next 2 years, page views at People.com increased fivefold.

Ann Moore, then the CEO at Time Inc., formalized this strategy in 2005, mandating that all print offerings should follow the lead of People.com, integrating print and online newsrooms and investing significantly more resources in Web publishing. To drive this initiative home, Time hired several well-known bloggers to write for its online publications. The goal of Moore's strategy was to neutralize the cultural *weakness* that had hindered online efforts in the past and to redirect resources to Web publishing.

In 2006, Time made another strategic move designed to exploit the opportunities associated with the Web. It partnered with the 24-hour news channel CNN to put all of its financial magazines onto a jointly owned site, CNNMoney .com. The site, which offers free access to *Fortune*, *Money*, and *Business 2.0*, quickly took the third spot in online financial websites, behind Yahoo Finance and MSN. This was followed with a redesigned website for *Sports Illustrated* that has rolled out video downloads for iPods and mobile phones.

In 2007, to further its shift to Web-centric publishing, Time Inc. announced another change in strategy: It would sell off 18 magazine titles that, although good performers, did not appear to have much traction on the Web.

Also in 2007, Ann Moore stated that, going forward, Time Inc. would focus its energy, resources, and investments on the company's largest, most profitable brands, those that have demonstrated an ability to draw large audiences in digital form. Since then, the big push has been to develop magazine apps for tablet computers, most notably Apple's iPad and tablets that use the Android operating system.

(continued)

By early 2012, Time Inc. had its entire magazine catalog on every major tablet platform. As of 2014, revenues from digital editions were growing rapidly, while print subscriptions were in a secular decline, which underlined the wisdom of Moore's digitalization strategy.

Sources: A. Van Duyn, "Time Inc. Revamp to Include Sale of 18 Titles," *Financial Times* (September 13, 2006): 24; M. Karnitsching, "Time Inc. Makes New Bid to Be Big Web Player," *The Wall Street Journal* (March 29, 2006): B1; M. Flamm, "Time Tries the Web Again," *Crain's New York Business* (January 16, 2006): 3; T. Carmody, "Time Warner Bringing Digital Magazines, HBO to More Platforms," *Wired* (July 3, 2011); "Time Inc. Q3 2014 Review: Digitalization Underway," Seeking Alpha, November 5, 2014; http://seekingalpha.com/.

the industry environment requires an assessment of the competitive structure of the company's industry, including the competitive position of the company and its major rivals. It also requires analysis of the nature, stage, dynamics, and history of the industry. Because many markets are now global, analyzing the industry environment also means assessing the impact of globalization on competition within an industry. Such an analysis may reveal that a company should move some production facilities to another nation, that it should aggressively expand in emerging markets such as China, or that it should beware of new competition from emerging nations. Analyzing the macroenvironment consists of examining macroeconomic, social, governmental, legal, international, and technological factors that may affect the company and its industry. We look at external analysis in Chapter 2.

Internal Analysis

Internal analysis, the third component of the strategic planning process, focuses on reviewing the resources, capabilities, and competencies of a company in order to identify its strengths and weaknesses. For example, as described in Strategy in Action 1.1, an internal analysis at Time Inc. revealed that although the company had strong, well-known brands such as *Fortune*, *Money*, *Sports Illustrated*, and *People* (a strength), and strong reporting capabilities (another strength), it suffered from a lack of editorial commitment to online publishing (a weakness). We consider internal analysis in Chapter 3.

SWOT Analysis and the Business Model

The next component of strategic thinking requires the generation of a series of strategic alternatives, or choices of future strategies to pursue, given the company's internal strengths and weaknesses and its external opportunities and threats. The comparison of **s**trengths, **w**eaknesses, **o**pportunities, and **t**hreats is normally referred to as a **SWOT analysis**.[16] The central purpose is to identify the strategies to exploit external opportunities, counter threats, build on and protect company strengths, and eradicate weaknesses.

SWOT analysis
The comparison of strengths, weaknesses, opportunities, and threats.

At Time Inc., managers saw the move of readership to the Web as both an *opportunity* that they must exploit and a *threat* to Time's established print magazines. Managers recognized that Time's well-known brands and strong reporting capabilities were *strengths* that would serve it well online, but that an editorial culture that marginalized online publishing was a *weakness* that had to be fixed. The *strategies* that managers at Time Inc. devised included merging the print and online newsrooms to remove distinctions between them; investing significant financial resources in online sites; and entering into a partnership with CNN, which already had a strong online presence.

More generally, the goal of a SWOT analysis is to create, affirm, or fine-tune a company-specific business model that will best align, fit, or match a company's resources and capabilities to the demands of the environment in which it operates. Managers compare and contrast various alternative possible strategies and then identify the set of strategies that will create and sustain a competitive advantage. These strategies can be divided into four main categories:

- *Functional-level strategies*, directed at improving the efficiency and effectiveness of operations within a company, such as manufacturing, marketing, materials management, product development, and customer service. We review functional-level strategies in Chapter 4.
- *Business-level strategies*, which encompass the business's overall competitive theme, the way it positions itself in the marketplace to gain a competitive advantage, and the different positioning strategies that can be used in different industry settings— for example, cost leadership, differentiation, focusing on a particular niche or segment of the industry, or some combination of these. We review business-level strategies in Chapters 5, 6, and 7.
- *Global strategies*, which address how to expand operations outside the home country in order to grow and prosper in a world where competitive advantage is determined at a global level. We review global strategies in Chapter 8.
- *Corporate-level strategies*, which answer the primary questions: What business or businesses should we be in to maximize the long-run profitability and profit growth of the organization, and how should we enter and increase our presence in these businesses to gain a competitive advantage? We review corporate-level strategies in Chapters 9 and 10.

The strategies identified through a SWOT analysis should be congruent with each other. Thus, functional-level strategies should be consistent with, or support, the company's business-level strategies and global strategies. Moreover, as we explain later in this book, corporate-level strategies should support business-level strategies. When combined, the various strategies pursued by a company should constitute a complete, viable business model. In essence, a SWOT analysis is a methodology for choosing between competing business models, and for fine-tuning the business model that managers choose. For example, when Microsoft entered the videogame market with its Xbox offering, it had to settle on the best business model for competing in this market. Microsoft used a SWOT-type analysis to compare alternatives, and settled on a business model referred to as "razor and razor blades," in which the Xbox console is priced at cost to build sales (the "razor"), while profits are generated from royalties on the sale of games for the Xbox (the "blades").

Strategy Implementation

Once managers have chosen a set of congruent strategies to achieve a competitive advantage and increase performance, those strategies have to be implemented. Strategy implementation involves taking actions at the functional, business, and corporate levels to execute a strategic plan. Implementation can include, for example, putting quality improvement programs into place, changing the way a product is designed, positioning the product differently in the marketplace, segmenting the marketing and offering different versions of the product to different consumer groups, implementing price increases or decreases, expanding through mergers and acquisitions, or downsizing the company by closing down or selling off parts of the company. These and other topics are discussed in detail in Chapters 4 through 10.

Strategy implementation also entails designing the best organizational structure and the best culture and control systems to put a chosen strategy into action. In addition, senior managers need to put a governance system in place to make sure that everyone within the organization acts in a manner that is not only consistent with maximizing profitability and profit growth, but also legal and ethical. We look at the topic of governance and ethics in Chapter 11; in Chapter 12 we discuss the organizational structure, culture, and controls required to implement business-level strategies.

The Feedback Loop

The feedback loop in Figure 1.4 indicates that strategic planning is ongoing: it never ends. Once a strategy has been implemented, its execution must be monitored to determine the extent to which strategic goals and objectives are actually being achieved, and to what degree competitive advantage is being created and sustained. This information and knowledge is returned to the corporate level through feedback loops, and becomes the input for the next round of strategy formulation and implementation. Top managers can then decide whether to reaffirm the existing business model and the existing strategies and goals, or suggest changes for the future. For example, if a strategic goal proves too optimistic, a more conservative goal is set. Or, feedback may reveal that the business model is not working, so managers may seek ways to change it. In essence, this is what happened at Time Inc. (see Strategy in Action 1.1).

STRATEGY AS AN EMERGENT PROCESS

The planning model suggests that a company's strategies are the result of a plan, that the strategic planning process is rational and highly structured, and that top management orchestrates the process. Several scholars have criticized the formal planning model for three main reasons: (1) the unpredictability of the real world, (2) the role that lower-level managers can play in the strategic management process, and (3) the fact that many successful strategies are often the result of serendipity, not rational strategizing. These scholars have advocated an alternative view of strategy making.[17]

Strategy Making in an Unpredictable World

Critics of formal planning systems argue that we live in a world in which uncertainty, complexity, and ambiguity dominate, and in which small chance events can have a large and unpredictable impact on outcomes.[18] In such circumstances, they claim, even the most carefully thought-out strategic plans are prone to being rendered useless by rapid and unforeseen change. In an unpredictable world, being able to respond quickly to changing circumstances, and to alter the strategies of the organization accordingly, is paramount. The dramatic rise of Google, for example, with its business model based on revenues earned from advertising links associated with search results (the so-called "pay-per-click" business model), disrupted the business models of companies that made money from more traditional forms of online advertising. Nobody could foresee this development or plan for it, but companies had to respond to it, and rapidly. Companies with a strong online advertising presence, including Yahoo.com and Microsoft's MSN network, rapidly changed their strategies to adapt to the threat Google posed. Specifically, both companies developed their own search engines and copied Google's pay-per-click business model. According to critics of formal systems, such a flexible approach to strategy making is not possible within the framework of a traditional strategic planning process, with its implicit assumption that an organization's strategies only need to be reviewed during the annual strategic planning exercise.

Autonomous Action: Strategy Making by Lower-Level Managers

Another criticism leveled at the rational planning model of strategy is that too much importance is attached to the role of top management, particularly the CEO.[19] An alternative view is that individual managers deep within an organization can—and often do—exert a profound influence over the strategic direction of the firm.[20] Writing with Robert Burgelman of Stanford University, Andy Grove, the former CEO of Intel, noted that many important strategic decisions at Intel were initiated not by top managers but by the autonomous action of lower-level managers deep within Intel who, on their own initiative, formulated new strategies and worked to persuade top-level managers to alter the strategic priorities of the firm.[21] These strategic decisions included the decision to exit an important market (the DRAM memory chip market) and to develop a certain class of microprocessors (RISC-based microprocessors) in direct contrast to the stated strategy of Intel's top managers.

Another example of autonomous action occurred at Starbucks. Anyone who has walked into a Starbucks cannot help but notice that in addition to various coffee beverages and food, the company also sells music CDs. Most Starbucks stores now have racks displaying anywhere between 5 and 20 CDs nearby the cash register. You can also purchase Starbucks music CDs on the company's website, and music published by the company's Hear Music label is available for download via iTunes. The interesting thing about Starbucks' entry into music retailing and publishing is that it was not the result of a formal planning process. The company's journey into music started in the late 1980s, when Tim Jones, then the manager of a Starbucks in Seattle's University Village, started to bring his own mix tapes into the store to play. Soon Jones was getting requests for copies from customers. Jones reported this to Starbucks' CEO, Howard Schultz, and suggested that Starbucks sell music. At first, Schultz was skeptical, but after repeated lobbying efforts by Jones he eventually took up the suggestion. In the late 1990s, Starbucks purchased Hear Music, a small publishing company, so that it could sell and distribute its own music CDs. Today, Starbucks' music business represents a small but healthy part of its overall product portfolio. For some artists, sales through Starbucks can represent an important revenue stream. Although it shifts titles regularly, sales of a CD over, say, 6 weeks, typically accounts for 5 to 10% of the album's overall sales.

Autonomous action may be particularly important in helping established companies deal with the uncertainty created by the arrival of a radical new technology that changes the dominant paradigm in an industry.[22] Top managers usually rise to preeminence by successfully executing the established strategy of the firm. Therefore, they may have an emotional commitment to the status quo and are often unable to see things from a different perspective. In this sense, they can be a conservative force that promotes inertia. Lower-level managers are less likely to have the same commitment to the status quo and have more to gain from promoting new technologies and strategies. They may be the first ones to recognize new strategic opportunities and lobby for strategic change. As described in Strategy in Action 1.2, this seems to have been the case at discount stockbroker Charles Schwab, which had to adjust to the arrival of the Web in the 1990s.

Serendipity and Strategy

Business history is replete with examples of accidental events that helped push companies in new and profitable directions. These examples suggest that many successful strategies are not the result of well-thought-out plans, but of serendipity—stumbling across good outcomes unexpectedly. One such example occurred at 3M during the 1960s. At that time, 3M was producing fluorocarbons for sale as coolant liquid in air-conditioning equipment. One day, a researcher working with fluorocarbons in a 3M lab spilled some of the liquid on her shoes. Later that day when she spilled coffee over her shoes, she watched with interest as the coffee formed into little beads of liquid and then ran off her shoes without leaving a stain. Reflecting on this phenomenon, she realized that a fluorocarbon-based liquid might turn out to be useful for protecting fabrics from liquid stains, and so the idea for Scotchgard was born. Subsequently, Scotchgard became one of 3M's most profitable products and took the company into the fabric protection business, an area within which it had never planned to participate.[23]

Serendipitous discoveries and events can open all sorts of profitable avenues for a company. But some companies have missed profitable opportunities because serendipitous discoveries or events were inconsistent with their prior (planned) conception of their strategy. In one classic example of such myopia, in the 19th century, the telegraph company Western Union turned down an opportunity to purchase the rights to an invention by Alexander Graham Bell. The invention was the telephone, the technology that subsequently made the telegraph obsolete.

Intended and Emergent Strategies

Henry Mintzberg's model of strategy development provides a more encompassing view of strategy. According to this model, illustrated in Figure 1.6, a company's realized strategy is the product of whatever planned strategies are actually put into action (the company's deliberate strategies) and any unplanned, or emergent, strategies. In Mintzberg's view, many planned strategies are not implemented because of unpredicted changes in the environment (they are unrealized). Emergent strategies are the unplanned responses to unforeseen circumstances. They arise from autonomous action by individual managers deep within the organization, from serendipitous discoveries or events, or from an unplanned strategic shift by top-level managers in response to changed circumstances. They are not the product of formal, top-down planning mechanisms.

1.2 STRATEGY IN ACTION

A Strategic Shift at Charles Schwab

In the mid-1990s, Charles Schwab was the most successful discount stockbroker in the world. Over 20 years, it had gained share from full-service brokers like Merrill Lynch by offering deep discounts on the commissions charged for stock trades. Although Schwab had a nationwide network of branches, most customers executed their trades through a telephone system, TeleBroker. Others used online proprietary software, Street Smart, which had to be purchased from Schwab. It was a business model that worked well—then along came E*Trade.

Bill Porter, a physicist and inventor, started the discount brokerage firm E*TRADE in 1994 to take advantage of the opportunity created by the rapid emergence of the World Wide Web. E*TRADE launched the first dedicated website for online trading: E*TRADE had no branches, no brokers, and no telephone system for taking orders, and thus it had a very-low-cost structure. Customers traded stocks over the company's website. Due to its low-cost structure, E*TRADE was able to announce a flat $14.95 commission on stock trades, a figure significantly below Schwab's average commission, which at the time was $65. It was clear from the outset that E*TRADE and other online brokers, such as Ameritrade, which soon followed, offered a direct threat to Schwab. Not only were their cost structures and commission rates considerably lower than Schwab's, but the ease, speed, and flexibility of trading stocks over the Web suddenly made Schwab's Street Smart trading software seem limited and its telephone system antiquated.

Deep within Schwab, William Pearson, a young software specialist who had worked on the development of Street Smart, immediately saw the transformational power of the Web. Pearson believed that Schwab needed to develop its own Web-based software, and quickly. Try as he might, though, Pearson could not get the attention of his supervisor. He tried a number of other executives but found little support. Eventually he approached Anne Hennegar, a former Schwab manager who now worked as a consultant to the company. Hennegar suggested that Pearson meet with Tom Seip, an executive vice president at Schwab who was known for his ability to think outside the box. Hennegar approached Seip on Pearson's behalf, and Seip responded positively, asking her to set up a meeting. Hennegar and Pearson arrived, expecting to meet only Seip, but to their surprise, in walked Charles Schwab, his chief operating officer, David Pottruck, and the vice presidents in charge of strategic planning and electronic brokerage.

As the group watched Pearson's demo, which detailed how a Web-based system would look and work, they became increasingly excited. It was clear to those in the room that a Web-based system using real-time information, personalization, customization, and interactivity all advanced Schwab's commitment to empowering customers. By the end of the meeting, Pearson had received a green light to start work on the project. A year later, Schwab launched its own Web-based offering, eSchwab, which enabled Schwab clients to execute stock trades for a low, flat-rate commission. eSchwab went on to become the core of the company's offering, enabling it to stave off competition from deep discount brokers like E*TRADE.

Sources: J. Kador, *Charles Schwab: How One Company Beat Wall Street and Reinvented the Brokerage Industry* (New York: John Wiley Sons, 2002); E. Schonfeld, "Schwab Puts It All Online," *Fortune* (December 7, 1998): 94–99.

Mintzberg maintains that emergent strategies are often successful and may be more appropriate than intended strategies. In the classic example of this process, Richard Pascale described the entry of Honda Motor Co. into the U.S. motorcycle market.[24] When a number of Honda executives arrived in Los Angeles from Japan in

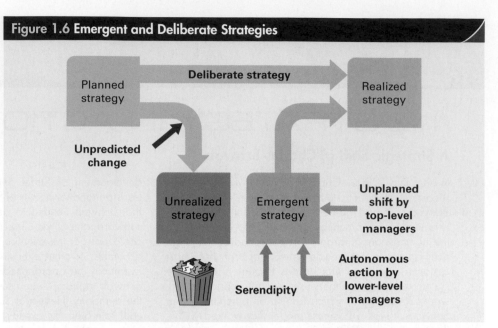

Figure 1.6 Emergent and Deliberate Strategies

Source: Adapted from H. Mintzberg and A. McGugh, *Administrative Science Quarterly* 30:2 (June 1985).

1959 to establish a U.S. operation, their original aim (intended strategy) was to focus on selling 250-cc and 350-cc machines to confirmed motorcycle enthusiasts rather than 50-cc Honda Cubs, which were a big hit in Japan. Their instinct told them that the Honda 50s were not suitable for the U.S. market, where everything was bigger and more luxurious than in Japan.

However, sales of the 250-cc and 350-cc bikes were sluggish, and the bikes themselves were plagued by mechanical failure. It looked as if Honda's strategy was going to fail. At the same time, the Japanese executives who were using the Honda 50s to run errands around Los Angeles were attracting a lot of attention. One day, they got a call from a Sears, Roebuck and Co. buyer who wanted to sell the 50-cc bikes to a broad market of Americans who were not necessarily motorcycle enthusiasts. The Honda executives were hesitant to sell the small bikes for fear of alienating serious bikers, who might then associate Honda with "wimpy" machines. In the end, however, they were pushed into doing so by the failure of the 250-cc and 350-cc models.

Honda had stumbled onto a previously untouched market segment that would prove huge: the average American who had never owned a motorbike. Honda had also found an untried channel of distribution: general retailers rather than specialty motorbike stores. By 1964, nearly one out of every two motorcycles sold in the United States was a Honda.

The conventional explanation for Honda's success is that the company redefined the U.S. motorcycle industry with a brilliantly conceived intended strategy. The fact was that Honda's intended strategy was a near-disaster. The strategy that emerged did so not through planning but through unplanned action in response to unforeseen circumstances. Nevertheless, credit should be given to the Japanese management for recognizing the strength of the emergent strategy and for pursuing it with vigor.

The critical point demonstrated by the Honda example is that successful strategies can often emerge within an organization without prior planning, and in response to unforeseen circumstances. As Mintzberg has noted, strategies can take root wherever people have the capacity to learn and the resources to support that capacity.

In practice, the strategies of most organizations are likely a combination of the intended and the emergent. The message for management is that it needs to recognize the process of emergence and to intervene when appropriate, relinquishing bad emergent strategies and nurturing potentially good ones.[25] To make such decisions, managers must be able to judge the worth of emergent strategies. They must be able to think strategically. Although emergent strategies arise from within the organization without prior planning—that is, without completing the steps illustrated in Figure 1.5 in a sequential fashion—top management must still evaluate emergent strategies. Such evaluation involves comparing each emergent strategy with the organization's goals, external environmental opportunities and threats, and internal strengths and weaknesses. The objective is to assess whether the emergent strategy fits the company's needs and capabilities. In addition, Mintzberg stresses that an organization's capability to produce emergent strategies is a function of the kind of corporate culture that the organization's structure and control systems foster. In other words, the different components of the strategic management process are just as important from the perspective of emergent strategies as they are from the perspective of intended strategies.

◤ STRATEGIC PLANNING IN PRACTICE

Despite criticisms, research suggests that formal planning systems do help managers make better strategic decisions. A study that analyzed the results of 26 previously published studies came to the conclusion that, on average, strategic planning has a positive impact on company performance.[26] Another study of strategic planning in 656 firms found that formal planning methodologies and emergent strategies both form part of a good strategy-formulation process, particularly in an unstable environment.[27] For strategic planning to work, it is important that top-level managers plan not only within the context of the current competitive environment but also within the context of the future competitive environment. To try to forecast what that future will look like, managers can use scenario-planning techniques to project different possible futures. They can also involve operating managers in the planning process and seek to shape the future competitive environment by emphasizing strategic intent.

Scenario Planning

One reason that strategic planning may fail over longer time periods is that strategic managers, in their initial enthusiasm for planning techniques, may forget that the future is entirely unpredictable. Even the best-laid plans can fall apart if unforeseen contingencies occur, and that happens all the time. The recognition that uncertainty makes it difficult to forecast the future accurately led planners at Royal Dutch Shell to pioneer the scenario approach to planning.[28] **Scenario planning** involves formulating plans that are based upon "what-if" scenarios about the future. In the typical scenario-planning exercise, some scenarios are optimistic and some are pessimistic. Teams of

scenario planning
Formulating plans that are based upon "what-if" scenarios about the future.

managers are asked to develop specific strategies to cope with each scenario. A set of indicators is chosen as signposts to track trends and identify the probability that any particular scenario is coming to pass. The idea is to allow managers to understand the dynamic and complex nature of their environment, to think through problems in a strategic fashion, and to generate a range of strategic options that might be pursued under different circumstances.[29] The scenario approach to planning has spread rapidly among large companies. One survey found that over 50% of the *Fortune* 500 companies use some form of scenario-planning methods.[30]

The oil company Royal Dutch Shell has, perhaps, done more than most companies to pioneer the concept of scenario planning, and its experience demonstrates the power of the approach.[31] Shell has been using scenario planning since the 1980s. Today, it uses two primary scenarios to anticipate future demand for oil and refine its strategic planning. The first scenario, called "Dynamics as Usual," sees a gradual shift from carbon fuels (such as oil) to natural gas, and, eventually, to renewable energy. The second scenario, "The Spirit of the Coming Age," looks at the possibility that a technological revolution will lead to a rapid shift to new energy sources.[32] Shell is making investments that will ensure profitability for the company, regardless of which scenario comes to pass, and it is carefully tracking technological and market trends for signs of which scenario will become more likely over time.

The great virtue of the scenario approach to planning is that it pushes managers to think outside the box, to anticipate what they might need to do in different situations. It reminds managers that the world is complex and unpredictable, and to place a premium on flexibility rather than on inflexible plans based on assumptions about the future (which may or may not be correct). As a result of scenario planning, organizations might pursue one dominant strategy related to the scenario that is judged to be most likely, but they make investments that will pay off if other scenarios come to the fore (see Figure 1.7). Thus, the current strategy of Shell is based on the assumption that the world will gradually shift away from carbon-based fuels

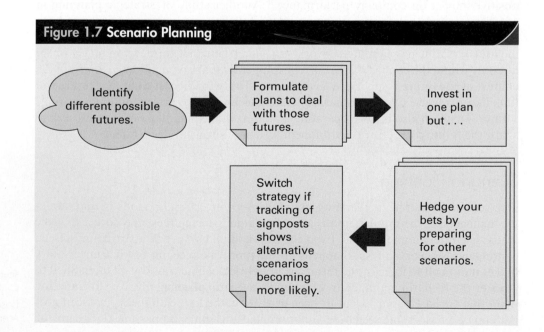

Figure 1.7 Scenario Planning

Identify different possible futures.

Formulate plans to deal with those futures.

Invest in one plan but . . .

Hedge your bets by preparing for other scenarios.

Switch strategy if tracking of signposts shows alternative scenarios becoming more likely.

(its "Dynamics as Usual" scenario), but the company is hedging its bets by investing in new energy technologies and mapping out a strategy should the second scenario come to pass.

Decentralized Planning

Some companies constructing a strategic planning process erroneously treat planning exclusively as a top-management responsibility. This "ivory tower" approach can result in strategic plans formulated in a vacuum by top managers who may be disconnected from current operating realities. Consequently, top managers may formulate suboptimal strategies. For example, when demographic data indicated that houses and families were shrinking, planners at GE's appliance group concluded that smaller appliances were the wave of the future. Because they had little contact with homebuilders and retailers, they did not realize that kitchens and bathrooms were the two rooms that were not shrinking. Nor did they appreciate that two-income families wanted large refrigerators to cut down on trips to the supermarket. GE wasted a lot of time designing small appliances for which there was limited demand.

The ivory tower concept of planning can also lead to tensions between corporate-, business-, and functional-level managers. The experience of GE's appliance group is again illuminating. Many of the corporate managers in the planning group were recruited from consulting firms or top-flight business schools. Many of the functional managers took this pattern of recruitment to mean that the corporate managers did not believe they were smart enough to think through strategic problems. They felt shut out of the decision-making process, which they believed to be unfairly constituted. From this perceived lack of procedural justice sprang an us-versus-them mindset that quickly escalated into hostility. As a result, even when the planners were correct, operating managers would not listen to them. For example, the planners correctly recognized the importance of the globalization of the appliance market and the emerging Japanese threat. However, operating managers, who then saw Sears, Roebuck and Co. as the competition, paid them little heed. Finally, ivory tower planning ignores both the important, strategic role of autonomous action by lower-level managers and the role of serendipity.

Correcting the ivory tower approach to planning requires recognizing that successful strategic planning encompasses managers at all levels of the corporation. Much of the best planning can and should be done by business and functional managers who are closest to the facts; in other words, planning should be decentralized. Corporate-level planners should be facilitators who help business and functional managers do the planning by setting the broad strategic goals of the organization and providing the resources necessary to identify the strategies required to attain those goals.

STRATEGIC DECISION MAKING

Even the best-designed strategic-planning systems will fail to produce the desired results if managers do not effectively use the information at their disposal. Consequently, it is important that strategic managers use that information to understand why they sometimes make poor decisions. One important way to do is to understand how common cognitive biases can result in poor decision making.[33]

Cognitive Biases and Strategic Decision Making

The rationality of decision making is bound by one's cognitive capabilities.[34] Humans are not supercomputers—it is difficult for us to absorb and process large amounts of information effectively. As a result, when we make decisions, we tend to fall back on certain rules of thumb, or heuristics, that help us make sense out of a complex and uncertain world. Sometimes these rules lead to severe, systematic errors in the decision-making process.[35] Systematic errors are those that appear time and time again. They seem to arise from a series of **cognitive biases** in the way we process information and reach decisions. Cognitive biases cause many managers to make poor strategic decisions.

Numerous cognitive biases have been verified repeatedly in laboratory settings, so we can be reasonably sure that these biases exist and that all people are prone to them.[36] The **prior hypothesis bias** refers to the fact that decision makers who have strong prior beliefs about the relationship between two variables tend to make decisions on the basis of these beliefs, even when presented with evidence that their beliefs are incorrect. Moreover, they tend to seek and use information that is consistent with their prior beliefs while ignoring information that contradicts these beliefs. To place this bias in a strategic context, it suggests that a CEO who has a strong prior belief that a certain strategy makes sense might continue to pursue that strategy despite evidence that it is inappropriate or failing.

Another well-known cognitive bias, **escalating commitment**, occurs when decision makers, having already committed significant resources to a project, commit even more resources even if they receive feedback that the project is failing.[37] A more logical response would be to abandon the project and move on (that is, to cut your losses and exit), rather than escalate commitment.

A third bias, **reasoning by analogy**, involves the use of simple analogies to make sense out of complex problems. The problem with this heuristic is that the analogy may not be valid. A fourth bias, **representativeness**, is rooted in the tendency to generalize from a small sample or even a single, vivid anecdote. This bias violates the statistical law of large numbers, which states that it is inappropriate to generalize from a small sample, let alone from a single case. In many respects, the dot-com boom of the late 1990s was based on reasoning by analogy and representativeness. Prospective entrepreneurs saw some early dot-com companies such as Amazon and Yahoo! achieve rapid success, at least as judged by some metrics. Reasoning by analogy from a very small sample, they assumed that any dot-com could achieve similar success. Many investors reached similar conclusions. The result was a massive wave of start-ups that attempted to capitalize on perceived Internet opportunities. The vast majority of these companies subsequently went bankrupt, proving that the analogy was wrong and that the success of the small sample of early entrants was no guarantee that all dot-coms would succeed.

A fifth cognitive bias is referred to as **the illusion of control**, or the tendency to overestimate one's ability to control events. General or top managers seem to be particularly prone to this bias: having risen to the top of an organization, they tend to be overconfident about their ability to succeed. According to Richard Roll, such overconfidence leads to what he has termed the *hubris hypothesis of takeovers*.[38] Roll argues that top managers are typically overconfident about their ability to create value by acquiring another company. Hence, they make poor acquisition decisions, often paying far too much for the companies they acquire. Subsequently, servicing the debt taken on to finance such an acquisition makes it all but impossible to profit from the acquisition.

cognitive biases
Systematic errors in decision making that arise from the way people process information.

prior hypothesis bias
A cognitive bias that occurs when decision makers who have strong prior beliefs tend to make decisions on the basis of these beliefs, even when presented with evidence that their beliefs are wrong.

escalating commitment
A cognitive bias that occurs when decision makers, having already committed significant resources to a project, commit even more resources after receiving feedback that the project is failing.

reasoning by analogy
Use of simple analogies to make sense out of complex problems.

representativeness
A bias rooted in the tendency to generalize from a small sample or even a single ,vivid anecdote.

illusion of control
A cognitive bias rooted in the tendency to overestimate one's ability to control events.

Availability error is yet another common bias. Availability error arises from our predisposition to estimate the probability of an outcome based on how easy the outcome is to imagine. For example, more people seem to fear a plane crash than a car accident, yet statistically one is far more likely to be killed in a car on the way to the airport than in a plane crash. People overweigh the probability of a plane crash because the outcome is easier to imagine, and because plane crashes are more vivid events than car crashes, which affect only small numbers of people at one time. As a result of availability error, managers might allocate resources to a project with an outcome that is easier to imagine, rather than to one that might have the highest return.

availability error
A bias that arises from our predisposition to estimate the probability of an outcome based on how easy the outcome is to imagine.

Techniques for Improving Decision Making

The existence of cognitive biases raises a question: How can critical information affect the decision-making mechanism so that a company's strategic decisions are realistic and based on thorough evaluation? Two techniques known to enhance strategic thinking and counteract cognitive biases are devil's advocacy and dialectic inquiry.[39]

Devil's advocacy requires the generation of a plan and a critical analysis of that plan. One member of the decision-making group acts as the devil's advocate, emphasizing all the reasons that might make the proposal unacceptable. In the process, decision makers become aware of the possible perils of recommended courses of action.

Dialectic inquiry is more complex because it requires the generation of a plan (a thesis) and a counterplan (an antithesis) that reflect plausible but conflicting courses of action.[40] Strategic managers listen to a debate between advocates of the plan and counterplan and then decide which plan will lead to higher performance. The purpose of the debate is to reveal the problems with the definitions, recommended courses of action, and assumptions of both plans. As a result of this exercise, strategic managers are able to form a new and more encompassing conceptualization of the problem, which then becomes the final plan (a synthesis). Dialectic inquiry can promote strategic thinking.

Another technique for countering cognitive biases is the outside view, which has been championed by Nobel Prize winner Daniel Kahneman and his associates.[41] The **outside view** requires planners to identify a reference class of analogous past strategic initiatives, determine whether those initiatives succeeded or failed, and evaluate the project at hand against those prior initiatives. According to Kahneman, this technique is particularly useful for countering biases such as illusion of control (hubris), reasoning by analogy, and representativeness. For example, when considering a potential acquisition, planners should look at the track record of acquisitions made by other enterprises (the reference class), determine if they succeeded or failed, and objectively evaluate the potential acquisition against that reference class. Kahneman argues that such a reality check against a large sample of prior events tends to constrain the inherent optimism of planners and produce more realistic assessments and plans.

devil's advocacy
A technique in which one member of a decision-making team identifies all the considerations that might make a proposal unacceptable.

dialectic inquiry
The generation of a plan (a thesis) and a counterplan (an antithesis) that reflect plausible but conflicting courses of action.

outside view
Identification of past successful or failed strategic initiatives to determine whether those initiatives will work for project at hand.

◤ STRATEGIC LEADERSHIP

One key strategic role of both general and functional managers is to use all their knowledge, energy, and enthusiasm to provide strategic leadership for their subordinates and develop a high-performing organization. Several authors have identified key characteristics of strong strategic leaders that lead to high performance: (1) vision, eloquence, and consistency; (2) articulation of a business model; (3) commitment; (4) being well informed; (5) willingness to delegate and empower; (6) astute use of power; and (7) emotional intelligence.[42]

Vision, Eloquence, and Consistency

One key task of leadership is to give an organization a sense of direction. Strong leaders have a clear, compelling vision of where the organization should go, eloquently communicate this vision to others within the organization in terms that energize people, and consistently articulate their vision until it becomes part of the organization's culture.[43]

In the political arena, John F. Kennedy, Winston Churchill, Martin Luther King, Jr., and Margaret Thatcher are regarded as visionary leaders. Think of the impact of Kennedy's summons, "Ask not what your country can do for you, ask what you can do for your country," of King's "I have a dream" speech, of Churchill's declaration that "we will never surrender", and of Thatcher's statement that "the problem with socialism is that you eventually run out of other peoples' money." Kennedy and Thatcher used their political office to push for governmental actions that were consistent with their visions. Churchill's speech galvanized a nation to defend itself against an aggressor. King pressured the government from outside to make changes within society.

Historic examples of strong business leaders include Microsoft's Bill Gates; Jack Welch, the former CEO of General Electric; and Sam Walton, Wal-Mart's founder. For years, Bill Gates's vision of a world in which there would be a Windows-based personal computer on every desk was a driving force at Microsoft. More recently, that vision has evolved into one of a world in which Windows-based software can be found on any computing device, from PCs and servers to videogame consoles (Xbox), cell phones, and handheld computers. At GE, Jack Welch was responsible for articulating the simple but powerful vision that GE should be first or second in every business in which it competed, or it should exit from that business. Similarly, Wal-Mart founder Sam Walton established and articulated the vision that has been central to Wal-Mart's success: passing on cost savings from suppliers and operating efficiencies to customers in the form of everyday low prices.

Articulation of the Business Model

Another key characteristic of good strategic leaders is their ability to identify and articulate the business model the company will use to attain its vision. A business model is the managers' conception of how the various strategies that the company pursues fit together into a congruent whole. At Dell, for example, Michael Dell identified and articulated the basic business model of the company: the direct sales business model. The various strategies that Dell has pursued over the years have refined this basic model, creating one that is very robust in terms of its efficiency and effectiveness. Although individual strategies can take root in many different places in an organization, and although their identification is not the exclusive preserve of top management, only strategic leaders have the perspective required to make sure that the various strategies fit together into a congruent whole and form a valid and compelling business model. If strategic leaders lack a clear conception of the company's business model (or what it should be), it is likely that the strategies the firm pursues will not fit together, and the result will be lack of focus and poor performance.

Commitment

Strong leaders demonstrate their commitment to their visions and business models by actions and words, and they often lead by example. Consider Nucor's former CEO, Ken Iverson. Nucor is a very efficient steelmaker with perhaps the lowest cost structure in the steel industry. It has achieved 30 years of profitable performance in an industry where most other companies have lost money due to a relentless focus on cost minimization. In his tenure as CEO, Iverson set the example: he answered his own phone, employed only one secretary, drove an old car, flew coach class, and was proud of the fact that his base salary was the lowest of the *Fortune* 500 CEOs (Iverson made most of his money from performance-based pay bonuses). This commitment was a powerful signal to employees that Iverson was serious about doing everything possible to minimize costs. It earned him the respect of Nucor employees and made them more willing to work hard. Although Iverson has retired, his legacy lives on in Nucor's cost-conscious organizational culture or, and like all other great leaders, his impact will last beyond his tenure.

Being Well Informed

Effective strategic leaders develop a network of formal and informal sources who keep them well informed about what is going on within the company. At Starbucks, the first thing that former CEO Jim Donald did every morning was call 5 to 10 stores, talk to the managers and other employees there, and get a sense for how their stores were performing. Donald also stopped at a local Starbucks every morning on the way to work to buy his morning coffee. This allowed him to get to know individual employees very well. Donald found these informal contacts to be a useful source of information about how the company was performing.[44]

Similarly, Herb Kelleher, the founder of Southwest Airlines, was able to gauge the health of his company by dropping in unannounced on aircraft maintenance facilities and helping workers perform their tasks. Herb Kelleher would also often help airline attendants on Southwest flights, distributing refreshments and talking to customers. One frequent flyer on Southwest Airlines reported sitting next to Kelleher three times in 10 years. Each time, Kelleher asked him (and others sitting nearby) how Southwest Airlines was doing in a number of areas, in order to spot trends and inconsistencies.[45]

Using informal and unconventional ways to gather information is wise because formal channels can be captured by special interests within the organization or by gatekeepers—managers who may misrepresent the true state of affairs to the leader. People like Donald and Kelleher who constantly interact with employees at all levels are better able to build informal information networks than leaders who closet themselves and never interact with lower-level employees.

Willingness to Delegate and Empower

High-performance leaders are skilled at delegation. They recognize that unless they learn how to delegate effectively, they can quickly become overloaded with responsibilities. They also recognize that empowering subordinates to make decisions is a good motivational tool and often results in decisions being made by those who must implement them. At the same time, astute leaders recognize that they need to maintain control over certain key decisions. Thus, although they will delegate many important decisions to lower-level employees, they will not delegate those that they judge to be of critical importance to the future success of the organization, such as articulating the company's vision and business model.

The Astute Use of Power

In a now-classic article on leadership, Edward Wrapp noted that effective leaders tend to be very astute in their use of power.[46] He argued that strategic leaders must often play the power game with skill and attempt to build consensus for their ideas rather than use their authority to force ideas through; they must act as members of a coalition or its democratic leaders rather than as dictators. Jeffery Pfeffer articulated a similar vision of the politically astute manager who gets things done in organizations through the intelligent use of power.[47] In Pfeffer's view, power comes from control over resources that are important to the organization: budgets, capital, positions, information, and knowledge. Politically astute managers use these resources to acquire another critical resource: critically placed allies who can help them attain their strategic objectives. Pfeffer stresses that one does not need to be a CEO to assemble power in an organization. Sometimes junior functional managers can build a surprisingly effective power base and use it to influence organizational outcomes.

Emotional Intelligence

Emotional intelligence, a term coined by Daniel Goleman, describes a bundle of psychological attributes that many strong, effective leaders exhibit[48]:

- Self-awareness—the ability to understand one's own moods, emotions, and drives, as well as their effect on others.
- Self-regulation—the ability to control or redirect disruptive impulses or moods; that is, to think before acting.
- Motivation—a passion for work that goes beyond money or status and a propensity to pursue goals with energy and persistence.
- Empathy—the ability to understand the feelings and viewpoints of subordinates and to take those into account when making decisions.
- Social skills—friendliness with a purpose.

According to Goleman, leaders who exhibit a high degree of emotional intelligence tend to be more effective than those who lack these attributes. Their self-awareness and self-regulation help to elicit the trust and confidence of subordinates. In Goleman's view, people respect leaders who, because they are self-aware, recognize their own limitations and, because they are self-regulating, consider decisions carefully. Goleman also argues that self-aware, self-regulating individuals tend to be more self-confident and therefore are better able to cope with ambiguity and are more open to change. A strong motivation exhibited in a passion for work can be infectious, persuading others to join together in pursuit of a common goal or organizational mission. Finally, strong empathy and social skills help leaders earn the loyalty of subordinates. Empathetic, socially adept individuals tend to be skilled at remedying disputes between managers, are better able to find common ground and purpose among diverse constituencies, and are better able to move people in a desired direction compared to leaders who lack these skills. In short, Goleman argues that the psychological makeup of a leader matters.

KEY TERMS

TAKEAWAYS FOR STRATEGIC MANAGERS

1. The major goal of companies is to maximize the returns that shareholders receive from holding shares in the company. To maximize shareholder value, managers must pursue strategies that result in high and sustained profitability and also in profit growth.

2. The profitability of a company can be measured by the return that it makes on the capital invested in the enterprise. The profit growth of a company can be measured by the growth in earnings per share. Profitability and profit growth are determined by the strategies managers adopt.

3. A company has a competitive advantage over its rivals when it is more profitable and has greater profit growth than the average for all firms in its industry. It has a sustained competitive advantage when it is able to maintain above-average performance over a number of years.

4. General managers are responsible for the overall performance of the organization, or for one of its major self-contained divisions. Their overriding strategic concern is for the health of the total organization under their direction.

5. Functional managers are responsible for a particular business function or operation. Although they lack general management responsibilities, they play a very important strategic role.

6. Formal strategic planning models stress that an organization's strategy is the outcome of a rational planning process.

7. The major components of the strategic management process are defining the mission, vision, and major goals of the organization; analyzing the external and internal environments of the organization; choosing a business model and strategies that align an organization's strengths and weaknesses with external environmental opportunities and threats; and adopting organizational structures and control systems to implement the organization's chosen strategies.

8. Strategy can emerge from deep within an organization in the absence of formal plans as lower-level managers respond to unpredicted situations.

9. Strategic planning may fail because executives do not plan for uncertainty and because ivory tower planners lose touch with operating realities.

10. In spite of systematic planning, companies may adopt poor strategies if cognitive biases are allowed to intrude into the decision-making process.

11. Devil's advocacy, dialectic inquiry, and the outside view are techniques for enhancing the effectiveness of strategic decision making.

12. Good leaders of the strategy-making process have a number of key attributes: vision, eloquence, and consistency; ability to craft a business model; commitment; being well informed; willingness to delegate and empower; political astuteness; and emotional intelligence.

DISCUSSION QUESTIONS

1. What do we mean by strategy? How is a business model different from a strategy?
2. What do you think are the sources of sustained superior profitability?
3. What are the strengths of formal strategic planning? What are its weaknesses?
4. Can you think of an example in your own life where cognitive biases resulted in you making a poor decision? How might that mistake have been avoided?

5. Discuss the accuracy of the following statement: Formal strategic planning systems are irrelevant for firms competing in high-technology industries where the pace of change is so rapid that plans are routinely made obsolete by unforeseen events.
6. Pick the current or a past president of the United States and evaluate his performance against the leadership characteristics discussed in the text. On the basis of this comparison, do you think that the president was/is a good strategic leader? Why or why not?

CLOSING CASE

The Evolution of Wal-Mart

Wal-Mart is one of the most extraordinary success stories in business history. Started in 1962 by Sam Walton, Wal-Mart has grown to become the world's largest corporation. In 2014, the discount retailer—whose mantra is "Everyday low prices"—had sales of more than $475 billion, close to 11,000 stores in 27 countries, and more than 2.2 million employees. Some 8% of all retail sales in the United States are made at a Wal-Mart store. Wal-Mart is not only large; it is also very profitable. Between 2005 and 2014, the company's average ROIC was 14.1%–better than its well–managed rivals, Costco and Target, which earned 11.8% and 11%, respectively.

Wal-Mart's persistently superior profitability is based on a number of factors. In 1962, Wal-Mart was one of the first companies to apply the self-service supermarket business model developed by grocery chains to sell general merchandise. Unlike rivals such as K-Mart and Target that focused on urban and suburban locations, Sam Walton's Wal-Mart concentrated on small, southern towns that were ignored by its rivals and which had enough demand to support one large discount store. Walton realized that, in rural America, people would drive an hour to Wal-Mart in a small town rather than

drive 2 to 3 hours to a major city. This meant that a small town with a population of 25,000 actually had a catchment area containing 100,000 people.

Wal-Mart grew quickly by pricing its products lower than those of local retailers, often putting them out of business. By the time its rivals realized that many small towns could support one large discount general merchandise store, Wal-Mart had already pre-empted them and had spread out to small towns across America.

Over time, the company became an innovator in information systems, logistics, and human resource practices. Actions taken in these functional areas resulted in higher productivity and lower costs as compared to rivals, which enabled the company to earn a high ROIC while charging low prices. Wal-Mart led the way among U.S. retailers in developing and implementing sophisticated product-tracking systems using bar-code technology and checkout scanners. This information technology enabled Wal-Mart to track what was selling and adjust its inventory accordingly so that the products found in each store matched local demand. By avoiding over-stocking, Wal-Mart did not have to hold periodic sales to shift unsold inventory. Over time, Wal-Mart linked its information system to a nationwide network of distribution centers in which inventory was shipped from vendors, and then shipped out on a daily basis to stores within a 400-mile radius. The combination of distribution centers and information systems enabled Wal-Mart to reduce the amount of inventory it held in stores, and thus to devote valuable space to selling and to reduce the amount of capital it had tied up in inventory.

With regard to human resources, Sam Walton set the tone. He held a strong belief that employees should be respected and rewarded for helping to improve the profitability of the company. Underpinning this belief, Walton referred to employees as "associates." He established a profit-sharing plan for all employees and, after the company went public in 1970, a program that allowed employees to purchase Wal-Mart stock at a discount to its market value. Wal-Mart was rewarded for this approach by high employee productivity, which translated into lower operating costs and higher profitability.

As Wal-Mart grew, its sheer size and purchasing power enabled it to drive down the prices that it paid suppliers and to pass on those savings to customers in the form of lower prices—which enabled Wal-Mart to gain more market share and hence lower prices even further. To take the sting out of the persistent demands for lower prices, Wal-Mart shared its sales information with suppliers on a daily basis, enabling them to gain efficiencies by configuring their own production schedules for sales at Wal-Mart.

By the 1990s, Wal-Mart was already the largest seller of general merchandise in the United States. To keep growing, it started to diversify into the grocery business, opening 200,000-square-foot supercenter stores that sold groceries and general merchandise under the same roof. Wal-Mart also diversified into the warehouse club business with the establishment of Sam's Club. The company began expanding internationally in 1991 with its entry into Mexico. Today, Wal-Mart generates $175 billion in foreign sales.

For all its success, Wal-Mart is now encountering very real limits to profitable growth. The U.S. market is saturated, and growth overseas has proved more difficult than the company hoped. The company was forced to exit Germany and South Korea after losing money there, and it has faced difficulties in several developed nations. Moreover, rivals Target and Costco have continued to improve their performance, and Costco in particular is now snapping at Wal-Mart's heels.

Sources: "How Big Can It Grow?" *The Economist* (April 17, 2004): 74–78; "Trial by Checkout," *The Economist* (June 26, 2004): 74–76; Wal-Mart 10-K, 2013, www.walmartstores.com; R. Slater, *The Wal-Mart Triumph* (New York: Portfolio Trade Books, 2004); "The Bulldozer from Bentonville Slows; Wal-Mart," *The Economist* (February 17, 2007): 70; K. Perkins, "Wal-Mart still faces challenges, but its scale should allow it to compete amid fierce rivalry," Morningstar, December 2, 2014.

CASE DISCUSSION QUESTIONS

1. What was Sam Walton's original strategic vision for Wal-Mart? How did this enable the company to gain a competitive advantage?

2. How did Wal-Mart continue to strengthen its competitive advantage over time? What does this teach you about the source of a long-term competitive advantage?

3. By the early 1990s, Wal-Mart was encountering limits to growth in the US. How did it overcome these limits to growth? Explain how the expansion moves that Wal-Mart made in the 1990s made economic sense and helped to create value for the company's shareholders.

4. Wal-Mart is once again encountering limits to growth. Why do you think this is the case? What might Wal-Mart do to push back these limits?

5. How much of Wal-Mart's strategy do you think was planned at the outset, and how much evolved over time in response to circumstances? What does this suggest to you about the nature of strategy development?

APPENDIX TO CHAPTER 1: Enterprise Valuation, ROIC, and Growth

The ultimate goal of strategy is to maximize the value of a company to its shareholders (subject to the important constraints that this is done in a legal, ethical, and socially responsible manner). The two main drivers of enterprise valuation are return on invested capital (ROIC) and the growth rate of profits, g.[49]

ROIC is defined as net operating profits less adjusted taxes (NOPLAT) over the invested capital of the enterprise (IC), where IC is the sum of the company's equity and debt (the method for calculating adjusted taxes need not concern us here). That is:

$$ROIC = NOPLAT/IC$$

where:

NOPLAT = revenues − cost of goods sold − operating expenses − depreciation charges − adjusted taxes
IC = value of shareholders' equity + value of debt

The growth rate of profits, g, can be defined as the percentage increase in net operating profits (NOPLAT) over a given time period. More precisely:

$$g = [(NOPLAT_{t+1} - NOPLAT_t)/NOPLAT_t] \times 100$$

Note that if NOPLAT is increasing over time, earnings per share will also increase so long as (a) the number of shares stays constant or (b) the number of shares outstanding increases more slowly than NOPLAT.

The valuation of a company can be calculated using discounted cash flow analysis and applying it to future expected free cash flows (free cash flow in a period is defined as NOPLAT − net investments). It can be shown that the valuation of a company so calculated is related to the company's weighted average cost of capital (WACC), which is the cost of the equity and debt that the firm uses to finance its business, and the company's ROIC. Specifically:

- If ROIC > WACC, the company is earning more than its cost of capital and it is creating value.
- If ROIC = WACC, the company is earning its cost of capital and its valuation will be stable.

- If ROIC < WACC, the company is earning less than its cost of capital and it is therefore destroying value.

A company that earns more than its cost of capital is even more valuable if it can grow its net operating profits less adjusted taxes (NOPLAT) over time. Conversely, a firm that is not earning its cost of capital destroys value if it grows its NOPLAT. This critical relationship between ROIC, g, and value is shown in Table A1.

In Table A1, the figures in the cells of the matrix represent the discounted present values of future free cash flows for a company that has a starting NOPLAT of $100, invested capital of $1,000, a cost of capital of 10%, and a 25-year time horizon after which ROIC = cost of capital.

Table A1 ROIC, Growth, and Valuation

NOPLAT Growth, g	ROIC 7.5%	ROIC 10.0%	ROIC 12.5%	ROIC 15.0%	ROIC 20%
3%	887	1000	1058	1113	1170
6%	708	1000	1117	1295	1442
9%	410	1000	1354	1591	1886

The important points revealed by this exercise are as follows:

1. A company with an already high ROIC can create more value by increasing its profit growth rate rather than pushing for an even higher ROIC. Thus, a company with an ROIC of 15% and a 3% growth rate can create more value by increasing its profit growth rate from 3 to 9% than it can by increasing ROIC to 20%.
2. A company with a low ROIC destroys value if it grows. Thus, if ROIC = 7.5%, a 9% growth rate for 25 years will produce less value than a 3% growth rate. This is because unprofitable growth requires capital investments, the cost of which cannot be covered. Unprofitable growth destroys value.
3. The best of both worlds is high ROIC and high growth.

Very few companies are able to maintain an ROIC > WACC and grow NOPLAT over time, but there are some notable examples, including Dell, Microsoft, and Wal-Mart. Because these companies have generally been able to fund their capital investment needs from internally generated cash flows, they have not had to issue more shares to raise capital. Thus, growth in NOPLAT has translated directly into higher earnings per share for these companies, making their shares more attractive to investors and leading to substantial share-price appreciation. By successfully pursuing strategies that result in a high ROIC and growing NOPLAT, these firms have maximized shareholder value.

NOTES

[1] There are several different ratios for measuring profitability, such as return on invested capital, return on assets, and return on equity. Although these different measures are highly correlated with each other, finance theorists argue that the return on invested capital is the most accurate measure of profitability. See T. Copeland, T. Koller, and J. Murrin, *Valuation: Measuring and Managing the Value of Companies* (New York: Wiley, 1996).

[2] Trying to estimate the relative importance of industry effects and firm strategy on firm profitability has been one of the most important areas of research in the strategy literature during the past decade. See Y. E. Spanos and S. Lioukas, "An Examination of the Causal Logic of Rent Generation," *Strategic Management* 22:10 (October 2001): 907–934; R. P. Rumelt, "How Much Does Industry Matter?" *Strategic Management* 12 (1991): 167–185. See also A. J. Mauri and M. P. Michaels, "Firm and Industry Effects Within Strategic Management: An Empirical Examination," *Strategic Management* 19 (1998): 211–219.

[3] This view is known as "agency theory." See M. C. Jensen and W. H. Meckling, "Theory of the Firm: Managerial Behavior, Agency Costs and Ownership Structure," *Journal of Financial Economics* 3 (1976): 305–360; E. F. Fama, "Agency Problems and the Theory of the Firm," *Journal of Political Economy* 88 (1980): 375–390.

[4] K. R. Andrews, *The Concept of Corporate Strategy* (Homewood, Ill.: Dow Jones Irwin, 1971); H. I. Ansoff, *Corporate Strategy* (New York: McGraw-Hill, 1965); C. W. Hofer and D. Schendel, *Strategy Formulation: Analytical Concepts* (St. Paul, Minn.: West, 1978). See also P. J. Brews and M. R. Hunt, "Learning to Plan and Planning to Learn," *Strategic Management* 20 (1999): 889–913; R. W. Grant, "Planning in a Turbulent Environment," *Strategic Management* 24 (2003): 491–517.

[5] www.google.com/about/company/.

[6] P. F. Drucker, *Management: Tasks, Responsibilities, Practices* (New York: Harper & Row, 1974), pp. 74–94.

[7] D. F. Abell, *Defining the Business: The Starting Point of Strategic Planning* (Englewood Cliffs, N.J.: Prentice-Hall, 1980).

[8] P. A. Kidwell and P. E. Ceruzzi, *Landmarks in Digital Computing* (Washington, D.C.: Smithsonian Institute, 1994).

[9] J. C. Collins and J. I. Porras, "Building Your Company's Vision," *Harvard Business Review* (September–October 1996): 65–77.

[10] www.nucor.com.

[11] See J. P. Kotter and J. L. Heskett, *Corporate Culture and Performance* (New York: Free Press, 1992); Collins and Porras, "Building Your Company's Vision."

[12] E. Freeman, *Strategic Management: A Stakeholder Approach* (Boston: Pitman Press, 1984).

[13] M. D. Richards, *Setting Strategic Goals and Objectives* (St. Paul, Minn.: West, 1986).

[14] E. A. Locke, G. P. Latham, and M. Erez, "The Determinants of Goal Commitment," *Academy of Management Review* 13 (1988): 23–39.

[15] R. E. Hoskisson, M. A. Hitt, and C. W. L. Hill, "Managerial Incentives and Investment in R&D in Large Multiproduct Firms," *Organization Science* 3 (1993): 325–341.

[16] Andrews, *Concept of Corporate Strategy;* Ansoff, *Corporate Strategy;* Hofer and Schendel, *Strategy Formulation.*

[17] For details, see R. A. Burgelman, "Intraorganizational Ecology of Strategy Making and Organizational Adaptation: Theory and Field Research," *Organization Science* 2 (1991): 239–262; H. Mintzberg,

"Patterns in Strategy Formulation," *Management Science* 24 (1978): 934–948; S. L. Hart, "An Integrative Framework for Strategy Making Processes," *Academy of Management Review* 17 (1992): 327–351; G. Hamel, "Strategy as Revolution," *Harvard Business Review* 74 (July–August 1996): 69–83; R. W. Grant, "Planning in a Turbulent Environment," *Strategic Management Journal* 24 (2003): 491–517. See also G. Gavetti, D. Levinthal, and J. W. Rivkin, "Strategy Making in Novel and Complex Worlds: The Power of Analogy," *Strategic Management Journal* 26 (2005): 691–712.

[18]This is the premise of those who advocate that complexity and chaos theory should be applied to strategic management. See S. Brown and K. M. Eisenhardt, "The Art of Continuous Change: Linking Complexity Theory and Time Based Evolution in Relentlessly Shifting Organizations," *Administrative Science Quarterly* 29 (1997): 1–34; R. Stacey and D. Parker, *Chaos, Management and Economics* (London: Institute for Economic Affairs, 1994). See also H. Courtney, J. Kirkland, and P. Viguerie, "Strategy Under Uncertainty," *Harvard Business Review* 75 (November–December 1997): 66–79.

[19]Hart, "Integrative Framework"; Hamel, "Strategy as Revolution."

[20]See Burgelman, "Intraorganizational Ecology," and Mintzberg, "Patterns in Strategy Formulation."

[21]R. A. Burgelman and A. S. Grove, "Strategic Dissonance," *California Management Review* (Winter 1996): 8–28.

[22]C. W. L. Hill and F. T. Rothaermel, "The Performance of Incumbent Firms in the Face of Radical Technological Innovation," *Academy of Management Review* 28 (2003): 257–274.

[23]Personal communication to the author by George Rathmann, former head of 3M's research activities.

[24]Richard T. Pascale, "Perspectives on Strategy: The Real Story Behind Honda's Success," *California Management Review* 26 (1984): 47–72.

[25]This viewpoint is strongly emphasized by Burgelman and Grove, "Strategic Dissonance."

[26]C. C. Miller and L. B. Cardinal, "Strategic Planning and Firm Performance: A Synthesis of More Than Two Decades of Research," *Academy of Management Journal* 37 (1994): 1649–1665. See also P. R. Rogers, A. Miller, and W. Q. Judge, "Using Information Processing Theory to Understand Planning/Performance Relationships in the Context of Strategy," *Strategic Management* 20 (1999): 567–577.

[27]P. J. Brews and M. R. Hunt, "Learning to Plan and Planning to Learn," *Strategic Management Journal* 20 (1999): 889–913.

[28]P. Cornelius, A. Van de Putte, and M. Romani, "Three Decades of Scenario Planning at Shell," *California? Management Review* 48 (2005): 92–110.

[29]H. Courtney, J. Kirkland, and P. Viguerie, "Strategy Under Uncertainty," *Harvard Business Review* 75 (November–December 1997): 66–79.

[30]P. J. H. Schoemaker, "Multiple Scenario Development: Its Conceptual and Behavioral Foundation," *Strategic Management Journal* 14 (1993): 193–213.

[31]P. Schoemaker, P. J. H. van der Heijden, and A. J. M. Cornelius, "Integrating Scenarios into Strategic Planning at Royal Dutch Shell," *Planning Review* 20:3 (1992): 41–47; I. Wylie, "There Is No Alternative to…" *Fast Company* (July 2002): 106–111.

[32]"The Next Big Surprise: Scenario Planning," *The Economist* (October 13, 2001): 71.

[33]See C. R. Schwenk, "Cognitive Simplification Processes in Strategic Decision Making," *Strategic Management* 5 (1984): 111–128; K. M. Eisenhardt and M. Zbaracki, "Strategic Decision Making," *Strategic Management* 13 (Special Issue, 1992): 17–37.

[34]H. Simon, *Administrative Behavior* (New York: McGraw-Hill, 1957).

[35]The original statement of this phenomenon was made by A. Tversky and D. Kahneman, "Judgment Under Uncertainty: Heuristics and Biases," *Science* 185 (1974): 1124–1131. See also D. Lovallo and D. Kahneman, "Delusions of Success: How Optimism Undermines Executives' Decisions," *Harvard Business Review* 81 (July 2003): 56–67; J. S. Hammond, R. L. Keeny, and H. Raiffa, "The Hidden Traps in Decision Making," *Harvard Business Review* 76 (September–October 1998): 25–34.

[36]Schwenk, "Cognitive Simplification Processes," pp. 111–128.

[37]B. M. Staw, "The Escalation of Commitment to a Course of Action," *Academy of Management Review* 6 (1981): 577–587.

[38]R. Roll, "The Hubris Hypotheses of Corporate Takeovers," *Journal of Business* 59 (1986): 197–216.

[39]See R. O. Mason, "A Dialectic Approach to Strategic Planning," *Management Science* 13 (1969): 403–414; R. A. Cosier and J. C. Aplin, "A Critical View of Dialectic Inquiry in Strategic Planning,"

Strategic Management 1 (1980): 343–356; I. I. Mintroff and R. O. Mason, "Structuring III–Structured Policy Issues: Further Explorations in a Methodology for Messy Problems," *Strategic Management* 1 (1980): 331–342.

[40]Mason, "A Dialectic Approach," pp. 403–414.

[41]Lovallo and Kahneman, "Delusions of Success."

[42]For a summary of research on strategic leadership, see D. C. Hambrick, "Putting Top Managers Back into the Picture," *Strategic Management* 10 (Special Issue, 1989): 5–15; D. Goldman, "What Makes a Leader?" *Harvard Business Review* (November–December 1998): 92–105; H. Mintzberg, "Covert Leadership," *Harvard*

Business Review (November–December 1998): 140–148; R. S. Tedlow, "What Titans Can Teach Us," *Harvard Business Review* (December 2001): 70–79.

[43]N. M. Tichy and D. O. Ulrich, "The Leadership Challenge: A Call for the Transformational Leader," *Sloan Management Review* (Fall 1984): 59–68; F. Westley and H. Mintzberg, "Visionary Leadership and Strategic Management," *Strategic Management* 10 (Special Issue, 1989): 17–32.

[44]Comments made by Jim Donald at a presentation to University of Washington MBA students.

[45]B. McConnell and J. Huba. *Creating Customer Evangelists* (Chicago: Dearborn Trade Publishing, 2003).

[46]E. Wrapp, "Good Managers Don't Make Policy Decisions," *Harvard Business Review* (September–October 1967): 91–99.

[47]J. Pfeffer, *Managing with Power* (Boston: Harvard Business School Press, 1992).

[48]D. Goleman, "What Makes a Leader?" *Harvard Business Review* (November–December 1998): 92–105.

[49]C. Y. Baldwin, *Fundamental Enterprise Valuation: Return on Invested Capital*, Harvard Business School Note 9-801-125, July 3, 2004; T. Copeland et al., *Valuation: Measuring and Managing the Value of Companies* (New York: Wiley, 2000).

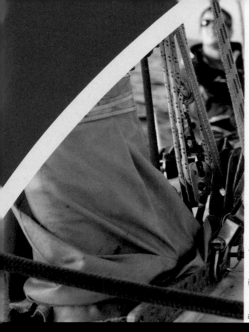

CHAPTER 2

EXTERNAL ANALYSIS: THE IDENTIFICATION OF OPPORTUNITIES AND THREATS

2.1 Review the primary technique used to analyze competition in an industry environment: the Five Forces model

2.2 Explore the concept of strategic groups and illustrate the implications for industry analysis

2.3 Discuss how industries evolve over time, with reference to the industry life-cycle model

2.4 Show how trends in the macroenvironment can shape the nature of competition in an industry

Competition in the U.S. Market for Wireless Telecommunications

Over the last two decades, the wireless telecommunications industry in the United States has been characterized by strong growth as demand for mobile phones—and, since 2007 smartphones—drove industry revenues forward. In 2000, there were 109 million wireless subscribers in the United States. By 2014, the number had risen to almost 360 million, representing a penetration rate of 108% (some people had multiple phones). Moreover, smartphone penetration had risen from 37% of the population in 2010 to 83% by 2014.

As the market has grown, the competitive structure of the industry has become increasingly consolidated. Today four companies dominate the

industry: Verizon with 38% of the market, AT&T with 33%, Sprint with 15%, and T-Mobile also with 15%. Much of the consolidation has been achieved through mergers and acquisitions. In 2004, AT&T bought Cingular for $41 billion; in 2005, Sprint and Nextel closed a $36-billion merger; and in 2009, Verizon bought Alltel for $28.1 billion. Since then regulatory authorities have stymied further merger attempts between large players. In 2011, AT&T tried to purchase T-Mobile, but was blocked by regulators. A 2014 merger proposal between T-Mobile and Sprint was also scuttled by objections from regulators.

The merger wave was driven by a realization among wireless companies that only the largest firms can reap the scale economies necessary to be profitable in this capital-intensive industry. Building out network infrastructure such as cell towers, and constantly upgrading that infrastructure to deliver fast, reliable voice and data service, has consumed over $400 billion in capital spending since 1985; $330 billion of that has been spent since 2000. By 2014, capital expenditures in the industry were running at $35 billion a year. Wireless companies have also spent $53 billion so far to acquire from the government the right to use the wireless spectrum. The government periodically auctions off the spectrum, and competition among wireless providers typically drives up the price. Companies in the industry have also had to spend heavily on marketing to establish their brands, and on building out a nationwide network of retail stores to provide point-of-sale service to their customers.

Until recently, competition in the industry primarily focused on non-price factors such as service coverage and reliability, handset equipment, service packages, and brand. Verizon, for example, emphasized its superior coverage and the high speed of its network; AT&T gained share when it signed a deal in 2007 to be the exclusive supplier of Apple's iPhone for one year; and T-Mobile branded itself as the hip network for young people looking for value. To reduce customer churn and limit price competition, service providers required customers to enter into 2-year contracts with early termination fees in exchange for new equipment (the cost of which was heavily subsidized), or purchase updated service plans.

However, with the market now saturated, and regulators blocking further merger attempts, competition is increasingly based on price. The shift began in early 2013, when T-Mobile broke ranks with the industry and began discarding 2-year contracts and early-termination fees, and eliminating subsidies of several hundred dollars for new phones, instead offering customers the option to pay for new devices in monthly installments. When merger talks broke down between Sprint and T-Mobile in mid-2014, Sprint quickly shifted its strategy and went after market share by offering customers who switch from rivals lower prices and more data. T-Mobile responded with a similar offering of its own, and the price war started to accelerate in the industry. In December 2014, T-Mobile upped the stakes with further price cuts that would save a family of four 50% in their monthly payments compared to a similar plan from Verizon (Verizon continues to subsidize the cost of handsets, T-Mobile does not). Both AT&T and Sprint rolled out their own offers to keep pace with T-Mobile. In signs that the price war is starting to hurt the industry, in December both AT&T and Verizon warned investors that their profits might take a hit going forward due to declining average revenues per customer and high capital expenditures.

Sources: C. Lobello, "Wireless merger madness," *The Week*, April 25, 2013; M. De la Merced and B. Chen, "No merger of Sprint and T-Mobile," *New York Times*, August 6, 2014; "Number of wireless subscribers in the United States," *Statista*, www.statista.com; CTIA Wireless Industry Association Survey Results, 1985-2013, CTIA, archived at www.ctia.org; P. Dave, "Wireless price wars drive down costs for consumers, sales for carriers," *Los Angeles Times*, December 9, 2014.

▛ OVERVIEW

Strategy formulation begins with an analysis of the forces that shape competition within the industry in which a company is based. The goal is to understand the opportunities and threats confronting the firm, and to use this understanding to identify strategies that will enable the company to outperform its rivals. **Opportunities** arise when a company can take advantage of conditions in its industry environment to formulate and implement strategies that enable it to become more profitable. For example, as discussed in the Opening Case, the growth of demand for smartphone data services created an enormous opportunity for wireless companies to grow their revenues during the 2007–2013 time period. **Threats** arise when conditions in the external environment endanger the integrity and profitability of the company's business. The biggest threats confronting wireless service providers today are market saturation and the acceleration of price wars that began in late 2014 (see the Opening Case).

This chapter begins with an analysis of the external industry environment. First, it examines concepts and tools for analyzing the competitive structure of an industry and identifying industry opportunities and threats. Second, it analyzes the competitive implications that arise when groups of companies within an industry pursue similar or different kinds of competitive strategies. Third, it explores the way an industry evolves over time, and the changes present in competitive conditions. Fourth, it looks at the way in which forces in the macroenvironment affect industry structure and influence opportunities and threats. By the end of the chapter, you will understand that, in order to succeed, a company must either fit its strategy to the external environment in which it operates or be able to reshape the environment to its advantage through its chosen strategy.

▛ DEFINING AN INDUSTRY

An **industry** can be defined as a group of companies offering products or services that are close substitutes for each other—that is, products or services that satisfy the same basic customer needs. A company's closest competitors—its rivals—are those that serve the same basic customer needs. For example, carbonated drinks, fruit punches, and bottled water can be viewed as close substitutes for each other because they serve the same basic customer needs for refreshing, cold, nonalcoholic beverages. Thus, we can talk about the soft drink industry, whose major players are Coca-Cola, PepsiCo, and Cadbury Schweppes. Similarly, desktop and laptop computers and tablets satisfy the same basic need that customers have for computer hardware devices on which to run personal productivity software, browse the Internet, send e-mail, play games, music and video, and store, display, or manipulate digital images. Thus, we can talk about the computer hardware device industry, whose participants include Apple, Dell, Hewlett-Packard, Lenovo, Microsoft, and Samsung.

External analysis begins by identifying the industry within which a company competes. To do this, managers must start by looking at the basic customer needs their company is serving—that is, they must take a customer-oriented view of their business rather than a product-oriented view (see Chapter 1). The basic customer needs that are served by a market define an industry's boundaries. It is very important for managers to realize this, for if they define industry boundaries incorrectly, they may be caught

---

opportunities

Elements and conditions in a company's environment that allow it to formulate and implement strategies that enable it to become more profitable.

threats

Elements in the external environment that could endanger the integrity and profitability of the company's business.

industry

A group of companies offering products or services that are close substitutes for each other.

off-guard by the rise of competitors that serve the same basic customer needs but with different product offerings. For example, Coca-Cola long saw itself as part of the soda industry—meaning carbonated soft drinks—whereas it actually was part of the soft drink industry, which includes noncarbonated soft drinks. In the mid-1990s, the rise of customer demand for bottled water and fruit drinks began to cut into the demand for sodas, which caught Coca-Cola by surprise. Coca-Cola moved quickly to respond to these threats, introducing its own brand of water, Dasani, and acquiring several other beverage companies, including Minute Maid and Glaceau (the owner of the Vitamin Water brand). By defining its industry boundaries too narrowly, Coke almost missed the rapid rise of noncarbonated soft drinks within the soft-drinks market.

It is important to realize that industry boundaries may change over time as customer needs evolve, or as emerging new technologies enable companies in unrelated industries to satisfy established customer needs in new ways. We have noted that during the 1990s, as consumers of soft drinks began to develop a taste for bottled water and noncarbonated fruit-based drinks, Coca-Cola found itself in direct competition with the manufacturers of bottled water and fruit-based soft drinks. All were in the same industry.

For another example of how technological change can alter industry boundaries, consider the convergence that has taken place between the computer and telecommunications industries. Historically, the telecommunications equipment industry has been considered an entity distinct from the computer hardware industry. However, as telecommunications equipment moved from analog technology to digital technology, this equipment increasingly resembled computers. The result is that the boundaries between these once distinct industries has been blurred. A smartphone such as Apple's iPhone is nothing more than a small, handheld computer with a wireless connection and telephone capabilities. Thus, Samsung and HTC, which manufacture wireless phones, are now competing directly with traditional computer companies such as Apple and Microsoft.

▼PORTER'S COMPETITIVE FORCES MODEL

Once the boundaries of an industry have been identified, managers face the task of analyzing competitive forces within the industry environment in order to identify opportunities and threats. Michael E. Porter's well-known framework, the Five Forces model, helps managers with this analysis.[1] An extension of his model, shown in Figure 2.1, focuses on *six* forces that shape competition within an industry: (1) the risk of entry by potential competitors, (2) the intensity of rivalry among established companies within an industry, (3) the bargaining power of buyers, (4) the bargaining power of suppliers, (5) the closeness of substitutes to an industry's products, and (6) the power of complement providers (Porter did not recognize this sixth force).

As each of these forces grows stronger, it limits the ability of established companies to raise prices and earn greater profits. Within this framework, a strong competitive force can be regarded as a threat because it depresses profits. A weak competitive force can be viewed as an opportunity because it allows a company to earn greater profits. The strength of the six forces may change over time as industry conditions change. Managers face the task of recognizing how changes in the six forces give rise to new opportunities and threats, and formulating appropriate strategic responses. In addition, it is possible for a company, through its choice of strategy, to alter the strength of one or more of the forces to its advantage. This is discussed in the following chapters.

Figure 2.1 Competitive Forces

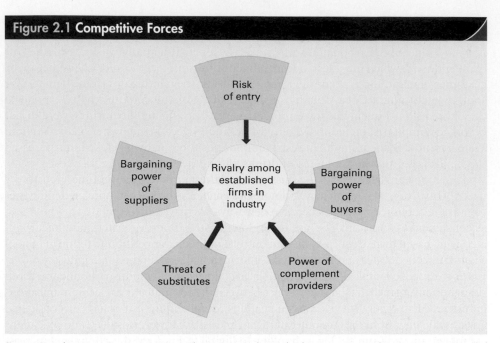

Source: Based on How Competitive Forces Shape Strategy, by Michael E. Porter, Harvard Business Review, March/April 1979.

Risk of Entry by Potential Competitors

potential competitors
Companies that are currently not competing in the industry but have the potential to do so.

Potential competitors are companies that are not currently competing in an industry but have the capability to do so if they choose. For example, in the last decade, cable television companies emerged as potential competitors to traditional phone companies. New digital technologies have allowed cable companies to offer telephone and Internet service over the same cables that transmit television shows.

Established companies already operating in an industry often attempt to discourage potential competitors from entering the industry because their entry makes it more difficult for the established companies to protect their share of the market and generate profits. A high risk of entry by potential competitors represents a threat to the profitability of established companies.

The risk of entry by potential competitors is a function of the height of the barriers to entry; that is, those factors that make it costly for companies to enter an industry. The greater the costs potential competitors must bear to enter an industry, the greater the barriers to entry, and the weaker this competitive force. High entry barriers may keep potential competitors out of an industry even when industry profits are high. Important barriers to entry include economies of scale, brand loyalty, absolute cost advantages, customer switching costs, and government regulation.[2] An important strategy is building barriers to entry (in the case of incumbent firms) or finding ways to circumvent those barriers (in the case of new entrants). We shall discuss this topic in more detail in subsequent chapters.

economies of scale
Reductions in unit costs attributed to large output.

Economies of Scale   **Economies of scale** arise when unit costs fall as a firm expands its output. Sources of scale economies include: (1) cost reductions gained through mass-producing a standardized output; (2) discounts on bulk purchases of raw material inputs and component parts; (3) the advantages gained by spreading fixed production costs over a large production volume; and (4) the cost savings associated with distributing, marketing, and advertising costs over a large volume of output. For example, as discussed in the Opening Case, the economies of scale enjoyed by incumbent firms in the wireless telecommunications industry are large, and this constitutes a significant barrier to new entry into the market. More generally, if the cost advantages from economies of scale are significant, a new company that enters the industry and produces on a small scale suffers a significant cost disadvantage relative to established companies. If the new company decides to enter on a large scale in an attempt to obtain these economies of scale, it must raise the capital required to build large-scale production facilities and bear the high risks associated with such an investment. In addition, an increased supply of products will depress prices and result in vigorous retaliation by established companies, which constitutes a further risk of large-scale entry. For these reasons, the threat of entry is reduced when established companies achieve economies of scale.

Brand Loyalty   **Brand loyalty** exists when consumers have a preference for the products of established companies. A company can create brand loyalty by continuously advertising its brand-name products and company name, patent protection of its products, product innovation achieved through company research and development (R&D) programs, an emphasis on high-quality products, and exceptional after-sales service. Significant brand loyalty makes it difficult for new entrants to take market share away from established companies. Thus, it reduces the threat of entry by potential competitors; they may see the task of breaking down well-established customer preferences as too costly. In the smartphone business, for example, Apple has generated such strong brand loyalty with its iPhone offering and related products that Microsoft is finding it very difficult to attract customers away from Apple and build demand for its Windows phone, introduced in late 2011. Despite its financial might, three years after launching the Windows phone, Microsoft's U.S. market share remained mired at around 3.6%, whereas Apple led the market with a 42% share.[3]

brand loyalty
Preference of consumers for the products of established companies.

Absolute Cost Advantages   Sometimes established companies have an **absolute cost advantage** relative to potential entrants, meaning that entrants cannot expect to match the established companies' lower cost structure. Absolute cost advantages arise from three main sources: (1) superior production operations and processes due to accumulated experience, patents, or trade secrets; (2) control of particular inputs required for production, such as labor, materials, equipment, or management skills, that are limited in supply; and (3) access to cheaper funds because existing companies represent lower risks than new entrants. If established companies have an absolute cost advantage, the threat of entry as a competitive force weakens.

absolute cost advantage
A cost advantage that is enjoyed by incumbents in an industry and that new entrants cannot expect to match.

Customer Switching Costs   **Switching costs** arise when a customer invests time, energy, and money switching from the products offered by one established company to the products offered by a new entrant. When switching costs are high, customers can be locked in to the product offerings of established companies, even if new entrants offer better products.[4] A familiar example of switching costs concerns the costs associated with switching from one computer operating system to another. If a person currently uses Microsoft's Windows operating system and has a library of related software applications and document files, it is expensive for that person to switch to another computer operating system. To effect the change, this person would need to purchase a new set of software applications and convert all existing document

switching costs
Costs that consumers must bear to switch from the products offered by one established company to the products offered by a new entrant.

files to the new system's format. Faced with such an commitment of money and time, most people are unwilling to make the switch unless the competing operating system offers a substantial leap forward in performance. Thus, the higher the switching costs, the higher the barrier to entry for a company attempting to promote a new computer operating system. Similarly, as we saw in the Opening Case, wireless service companies have traditionally created high switching costs by requiring customers to enter into 2-year contracts with early-termination fees whenever they upgrade their equipment.

Government Regulations   Government regulation can constitute a major entry barrier for many industries. For example, until the mid-1990s, U.S. government regulation prohibited providers of long-distance telephone service from competing for local telephone service, and vice versa. Other potential providers of telephone service, including cable television service companies such as Time Warner and Comcast (which could have used their cables to carry telephone traffic as well as TV signals), were prohibited from entering the market altogether. These regulatory barriers to entry significantly reduced the level of competition in both the local and long-distance telephone markets, enabling telephone companies to earn higher profits than they might have otherwise. All this changed in 1996, when the government significantly deregulated the industry. In the months that followed, local, long-distance, and cable TV companies all announced their intention to enter each other's markets, and a host of new players entered the market as well. The competitive forces model predicts that falling entry barriers due to government deregulation will result in significant new entry, an increase in the intensity of industry competition, and lower industry profit rates, and that is what occurred here.

In summary, if established companies have built brand loyalty for their products, have an absolute cost advantage over potential competitors, have significant scale economies, are the beneficiaries of high switching costs, or enjoy regulatory protection, the risk of entry by potential competitors is greatly diminished; it is a weak competitive force. Consequently, established companies can charge higher prices, and industry profits are therefore higher. Evidence from academic research suggests that the height of barriers to entry is one of the most important determinants of profit rates within an industry.[5] Clearly, it is in the interest of established companies to pursue strategies consistent with raising entry barriers to secure these profits. Additionally, potential new entrants must find strategies that allow them to circumvent barriers to entry.

Rivalry Among Established Companies

The second competitive force is the intensity of rivalry among established companies within an industry. Rivalry refers to the competitive struggle between companies within an industry to gain market share. The competitive struggle can be fought using price, product design, advertising and promotional spending, direct-selling efforts, and after-sales service and support. Intense rivalry implies lower prices or more spending on non-price-competitive strategies, or both. Because intense rivalry lowers prices and raises costs, it squeezes profits out of an industry. Thus, intense rivalry among established companies constitutes a strong threat to profitability. Alternatively, if rivalry is less intense, companies may have the opportunity to raise prices or reduce spending on non-price-competitive strategies, leading to higher industry profits. Four factors have a major impact on the intensity of rivalry among established companies within an industry: (1) industry competitive structure, (2) demand conditions, (3) cost conditions, and (4) the height of exit barriers in the industry.

2.1 STRATEGY IN ACTION

Circumventing Entry Barriers into the Soft Drink Industry

Two companies have long dominated the carbonated soft drink industry: Coca-Cola and PepsiCo. By spending large sums of money on advertising and promotion, these two giants have created significant brand loyalty and made it very difficult for new competitors to enter the industry and take away market share. When new competitors have tried to enter, both companies have responded by cutting prices, forcing new entrants to curtail expansion plans.

However, in the early 1990s, the Cott Corporation, then a small Canadian bottling company, worked out a strategy for entering the carbonated soft drink market. Cott's strategy was deceptively simple. The company initially focused on the cola segment of the market. Cott struck a deal with Royal Crown (RC) Cola for exclusive global rights to its cola concentrate. RC Cola was a small player in the U.S. cola market. Its products were recognized as high quality, but RC Cola had never been able to effectively challenge Coke or Pepsi. Next, Cott entered an agreement with a Canadian grocery retailer, Loblaw, to provide the retailer with its own, private-label brand of cola. The Loblaw private-label brand, known as "President's Choice," was priced low, became very successful, and took shares from both Coke and Pepsi.

Emboldened by this success, Cott tried to convince other retailers to carry private-label cola. To retailers, the value proposition was simple because, unlike its major rivals, Cott spent almost nothing on advertising and promotion. This constituted a major source of cost savings, which Cott passed on to retailers in the form of lower prices. Retailers found that they could significantly undercut the price of Coke and Pepsi colas and still make better profit margins on private-label brands than on branded colas.

Despite this compelling value proposition, few retailers were willing to sell private-label colas for fear of alienating Coca-Cola and Pepsi, whose products were a major draw for grocery store traffic. Cott's breakthrough came when it signed a deal with Wal-Mart to supply the retailing giant with a private-label cola, "Sam's Choice" (named after Wal-Mart founder Sam Walton). Wal-Mart proved to be the perfect distribution channel for Cott. The retailer was just beginning to appear in the grocery business, and consumers shopped at Wal-Mart not to buy branded merchandise, but to get low prices. As Wal-Mart's grocery business grew, so did Cott's sales. Cott soon added other flavors to its offerings, such as lemon-lime soda, which would compete with 7-Up and Sprite. Moreover, by the late 1990s, other U.S. grocers pressured by Wal-Mart had also started to introduce private-label sodas and often turned to Cott to supply their needs.

By 2014, Cott's private-label customers included Wal-Mart, Kroger, Costco, and Safeway. Cott had revenues of $2.33 billion and accounted for 60% of all private-label sales of carbonated beverages in the United States, and 6 to 7% of overall sales of carbonated beverages in grocery stores, its core channel. Although Coca-Cola and PepsiCo remain dominant, they have lost incremental market share to Cott and other companies that have followed Cott's strategy.

Sources: A. Kaplan, "Cott Corporation," *Beverage World*, June 15, 2004, p. 32; J. Popp, "2004 Soft Drink Report," *Beverage Industry*, March 2004, pp. 13–18; L. Sparks, "From Coca-Colonization to Copy Catting: The Cott Corporation and Retailers Brand Soft Drinks in the UK and US," *Agribusiness* 13:2 (March 1997), 133–167; E. Cherney, "After Flat Sales, Cott Challenges Pepsi, Coca-Cola," *The Wall Street Journal*, January 8, 2003, pp. B1, B8; "Cott Corporation: Company Profile," *Just Drinks*, August 2006, pp. 19–22; Cott Corp. 2011 Annual Report, www.cott.com.

Industry Competitive Structure   The competitive structure of an industry refers to the number and size distribution of companies within it, something that strategic managers determine at the beginning of an industry analysis. Industry structures vary, and different structures have different implications for the intensity of rivalry. A fragmented industry consists of a large number of small or medium-sized companies, none of which is in a position to determine industry price. A consolidated industry is dominated by a small number of large companies (an oligopoly) or, in extreme cases, by just one company (a monopoly), and such companies often are in a position to determine industry prices. Examples of fragmented industries are agriculture, dry cleaning, health clubs, real estate brokerage, and sun-tanning parlors. Consolidated industries include the aerospace, soft drink, wireless service (see the Opening Case), and small-package express delivery industries. In the small-package express delivery industry, two firms, UPS and FedEx, account for over 85% of industry revenues in the United States.

Low-entry barriers and commodity-type products that are difficult to differentiate characterize many fragmented industries. This combination tends to result in boom-and-bust cycles as industry profits rapidly rise and fall. Low-entry barriers imply that new entrants will flood the market, hoping to profit from the boom that occurs when demand is strong and profits are high. The number of video stores, health clubs, and sun-tanning parlors that exploded onto the market during the 1980s and 1990s exemplifies this situation.

Often, the flood of new entrants into a booming, fragmented industry creates excess capacity, and consequently companies cut prices. The difficulty of differentiating their products from those of competitors can exacerbate this tendency. The result is a price war, which depresses industry profits, forces some companies out of business, and deters potential new entrants. For example, after a decade of expansion and booming profits, many health clubs are now finding that they have to offer large discounts in order to maintain their memberships. In general, the more commodity-like an industry's product, the more vicious the price war will be. The bust phase of this cycle continues until overall industry capacity is brought into line with demand (through bankruptcies), at which point prices may stabilize again.

A fragmented industry structure, then, constitutes a threat rather than an opportunity. Economic boom times in fragmented industries are often relatively short-lived because the ease of new entry can soon result in excess capacity, which in turn leads to intense price competition and the failure of less-efficient enterprises. Because it is often difficult to differentiate products in these industries, minimizing costs is the best strategy for a company that strives to be profitable in a boom and survive any subsequent bust. Alternatively, companies might try to adopt strategies that change the underlying structure of fragmented industries and lead to a consolidated industry structure in which the level of industry profitability is increased. (We shall consider how companies can do this is sider in later chapters.)

In consolidated industries, companies are interdependent because one company's competitive actions (for instance, changes in price or quality) directly affect the market share of its rivals and thus their profitability. One company making a move can force a response from its rivals, and the consequence of such competitive interdependence can be a dangerous competitive spiral. Rivalry increases as companies attempt to undercut each other's prices or offer customers more value, pushing industry profits down in the process. This seems to be happening today in the wireless telecommunications industry (see the Opening Case).

Companies in consolidated industries sometimes seek to reduce this threat by matching the prices set by the dominant company in the industry.[6] However, care must be taken, for explicit, face-to-face, price-fixing agreements are illegal. (Tacit, indirect agreements, arrived at without direct or intentional communication, are legal.) For the most part, though, companies set prices by watching, interpreting, anticipating, and responding to one another's strategies. However, tacit price-leadership agreements often break down under adverse economic conditions, as has occurred in the breakfast cereal industry, profiled in Strategy in Action 2.2.

Industry Demand   The level of industry demand is another determinant of the intensity of rivalry/among established companies. Growing demand from new customers or additional purchases by existing customers tend to moderate competition by providing greater scope for companies to compete for customers. Growing demand tends to reduce rivalry because all companies can sell more without taking market share away from other companies. High industry profits are often the result. This was the case in the U.S. wireless telecommunications industry until recently (see the Opening Case). Conversely, stagnant or declining demand results in increased rivalry as companies fight to maintain market share and revenues (see Strategy in Action 2.2). Demand stagnates when the market is saturated and replacement demand is not enough to offset the lack of first-time buyers. Demand declines when customers exit the marketplace, or when each customer purchases less. When demand is stagnating or declining, a company can grow only by taking market share away from its rivals, as is now occurring in the U.S. wireless telecommunications industry, where aggressive price cuts by T-Mobile and Sprint are designed to grab market share from rivals. Stagnant or declining demand constitutes a threat because for it increases the extent of rivalry between established companies.

Cost Conditions   The cost structure of firms in an industry is a third determinant of rivalry. In industries where fixed costs are high, profitability tends to be highly leveraged to sales volume, and the desire to grow volume can spark intense rivalry. Again, this is the case in the U.S. wireless telecommunications industry (see Opening Case). Fixed costs are costs that must be paid before the firm makes a single sale. For example, before they can offer service, cable TV companies must lay cable in the ground; the cost of doing so is a fixed cost. Similarly, to offer express courier service, a company such as FedEx must first invest in planes, package-sorting facilities, and delivery trucks—all fixed costs that require significant capital investment. In industries where the cost of production is high, firms cannot cover their fixed costs and will not be profitable if sales volume is low. Thus, they have an incentive to cut their prices and/or increase promotional spending to drive up sales volume in order to cover fixed costs. In situations where demand is not rapidly growing and many companies are simultaneously engaged in the same pursuits, the result can be intense rivalry and lower profits. Research suggests that the weakest firms in an industry often initiate such actions precisely because they are struggling to cover their fixed costs.[7]

Exit Barriers   Exit barriers are economic, strategic, and emotional factors that prevent companies from leaving an industry.[8] If exit barriers are high, companies become locked into an unprofitable industry where overall demand is static or declining. The result is often excess productive capacity, leading to even more intense rivalry and price competition as companies cut prices, attempting to obtain the customer orders needed to use their idle capacity and cover their fixed costs.[9] Common exit barriers include:

- Investments in assets such as specific machines, equipment, or operating facilities that are of little or no value in alternative uses, or cannot be later sold. If the company wishes to leave the industry, it must write off the book value of these assets.
- High fixed costs of exit such as severance pay, health benefits, or pensions that must be paid to workers who are being made laid off when a company ceases to operate.

2.2 STRATEGY IN ACTION

Price Wars in the Breakfast Cereal Industry

For decades, the breakfast cereal industry was one of the most profitable in the United States. The industry has a consolidated structure dominated by Kellogg's, General Mills, and Kraft Foods with its Post brand. Strong brand loyalty, coupled with control over the allocation of supermarket shelf space, helped to limit the potential for new entry. Meanwhile, steady demand growth of about 3% per annum kept industry revenues expanding. Kellogg's, which accounted for over 40% of the market share, acted as the price leader in the industry. Every year, Kellogg's increased cereal prices, its rivals followed, and industry profits remained high.

This favorable industry structure began to change in the 1990s, when growth in demand slowed—and then stagnated—as a latte and bagel or muffin replaced cereal as the American morning fare. Then came the rise of powerful discounters such as Wal-Mart (which entered the grocery industry in 1994) that began to aggressively promote their own cereal brands and priced them significantly below the brand-name cereals. As the decade progressed, other grocery chains such as Kroger's started to follow suit, and brand loyalty in the industry began to decline as customers realized that a $2.50 bag of wheat flakes from Wal-Mart tasted about the same as a $3.50 box of cornflakes from Kellogg's. As sales of cheaper, store-brand cereals began to take off, supermarkets, no longer as dependent on brand names to bring traffic into their stores, began to demand lower prices from the branded cereal manufacturers.

For several years, manufacturers of brand-name cereals tried to hold out against these adverse trends, but in the mid-1990s, the dam broke. In 1996, Kraft (then owned by Philip Morris) aggressively cut prices by 20% for its Post brand in an attempt to gain market share. Kellogg's soon followed with a 19% price cut on two-thirds of its brands, and General Mills quickly did the same. The decades of tacit price collusion were officially over.

If breakfast cereal companies were hoping that price cuts would stimulate demand, they were wrong.

Instead, demand remained flat while revenues and margins followed price decreases, and operating margins at Kellogg's dropped from 18% in 1995 to 10.2% in 1996, a trend also experienced by the other brand-name cereal manufacturers.

By 2000, conditions had only worsened. Private-label sales continued to make inroads, gaining over 10% of the market. Moreover, sales of breakfast cereals started to contract at 1% per annum. To cap it off, an aggressive General Mills continued to launch expensive price-and-promotion campaigns in an attempt to take away share from the market leader. Kellogg's saw its market share slip to just over 30% in 2001, behind the 31% now held by General Mills. For the first time since 1906, Kellogg's no longer led the market. Moreover, profits at all three major producers remained weak in the face of continued price discounting.

In mid-2001, General Mills finally blinked and raised prices a modest 2% in response to its own rising costs. Competitors followed, signaling—perhaps—that after a decade of costly price warfare, pricing discipline might once more emerge in the industry. Both Kellogg's and General Mills tried to move further away from price competition by focusing on brand extensions, such as Special K containing berries and new varieties of Cheerios. Efforts with Special K helped Kellogg's recapture market leadership from General Mills, and, more important, the renewed emphasis on non-price competition halted years of damaging price warfare.

After a decade of relative peace, price wars broke out in 2010 once more in this industry. The trigger, yet again, appears to have been falling demand for breakfast cereals due to substitutes such as a quick trip to the local coffee shop. In the third quarter of 2010, prices fell by 3.6% and unit volumes by 3.4%, leading to falling profit rates at Kellogg's. Both General Mills and Kellogg's introduced new products in an attempt to boost demand and raise prices.

Sources: G. Morgenson, "Denial in Battle Creek," *Forbes,* October 7, 1996, p. 44; J. Muller, "Thinking out of the Cereal Box," *Business Week,* January 15, 2001, p. 54; A. Merrill, "General Mills Increases Prices," *Star Tribune,* June 5, 2001, p. 1D; S. Reyes, "Big G, Kellogg's Attempt to Berry Each Other," *Brandweek,* October 7, 2002, p. 8; M. Andrejczak, "Kellogg's Profit Hurt by Cereal Price War," *Market Watch,* November 2, 2010.

- Emotional attachments to an industry, such as when a company's owners or employees are unwilling to exit an industry for sentimental reasons or because of pride.
- Economic dependence because a company relies on a single industry for its entire revenue and all profits.
- The need to maintain an expensive collection of assets at or above a minimum level in order to participate effectively in the industry.
- Bankruptcy regulations, particularly in the United States, where Chapter 11 bankruptcy provisions allow insolvent enterprises to continue operating and to reorganize under this protection. These regulations can keep unprofitable assets in the industry, result in persistent excess capacity, and lengthen the time required to bring industry supply in line with demand.

As an example of exit barriers and effects in practice, consider the small-package express mail and parcel delivery industry. Key players in this industry such as FedEx and UPS rely entirely upon the delivery business for their revenues and profits. They must be able to guarantee their customers that they will deliver packages to all major localities in the United States, and much of their investment is specific to this purpose. To meet this guarantee, they need a nationwide network of air routes and ground routes, an asset that is required in order to participate in the industry. If excess capacity develops in this industry, as it does from time to time, FedEx cannot incrementally reduce or minimize its excess capacity by deciding not to fly to and deliver packages in Miami, for example, because that portion of its network is underused. If it did, it would no longer be able to guarantee to its customers that packages could be delivered to all major locations in the United States, and its customers would switch to another carrier. Thus, the need to maintain a nationwide network is an exit barrier that can result in persistent excess capacity in the air-express industry during periods of weak demand.

The Bargaining Power of Buyers

The third competitive force is the bargaining power of buyers. An industry's buyers may be the individual customers who consume its products (end-users) or the companies that distribute an industry's products to end-users, such as retailers and wholesalers. For example, although soap powder made by Procter & Gamble (P&G) and Unilever is consumed by end-users, the principal buyers of soap powder are supermarket chains and discount stores, which resell the product to end-users. The bargaining power of buyers refers to the ability of buyers to bargain down prices charged by companies in the industry, or to raise the costs of companies in the industry by demanding better product quality and service. By lowering prices and raising costs, powerful buyers can squeeze profits out of an industry. Powerful buyers, therefore, should be viewed as a threat. Alternatively, when buyers are in a weak bargaining position, companies in an industry can raise prices and perhaps reduce their costs by lowering product quality and service, thus increasing the level of industry profits. Buyers are most powerful in the following circumstances:

- When buyers have choice. If the industry is a monopoly, buyers obviously lack choice. If there are two or more companies in the industry, the buyers clearly have choice.
- When the buyers purchase in large quantities, they can use their purchasing power as leverage to bargain for price reductions.

- When the supply industry depends upon buyers for a large percentage of its total orders.
- When switching costs are low and buyers can pit the supplying companies against each other to force down prices.
- When it is economically feasible for buyers to purchase an input from several companies at once, they can pit one company in the industry against another.
- When buyers can threaten to enter the industry and independently produce the product, thus supplying their own needs, they can force down industry prices.

The automobile component supply industry, whose buyers are large manufacturers such as GM, Ford, Honda, and Toyota, is a good example of an industry in which buyers have strong bargaining power, and thus pose a strong competitive threat. Why? The suppliers of auto components are numerous and typically smaller in scale; their buyers, the auto manufacturers, are large in size and few in number. Additionally, to keep component prices down, historically both Ford and GM have used the threat of manufacturing a component themselves rather than buying it from a supplier. The automakers use their powerful position to pit suppliers against one another, forcing down the prices for component parts, and to demand better quality. If a component supplier objects, the automaker can use the threat of switching to another supplier as a bargaining tool.

The Bargaining Power of Suppliers

The fourth competitive force is the bargaining power of suppliers—the organizations that provide inputs into the industry, such as materials, services, and labor (which may be individuals, organizations such as labor unions, or companies that supply contract labor). The bargaining power of suppliers refers to the ability of suppliers to raise input prices, or to raise the costs of the industry in other ways—for example, by providing poor-quality inputs or poor service. Powerful suppliers squeeze profits out of an industry by raising the costs of companies in the industry. Thus, powerful suppliers are a threat. Conversely, if suppliers are weak, companies in the industry have the opportunity to force down input prices and demand higher-quality inputs (such as more productive labor). As with buyers, the ability of suppliers to make demands on a company depends on their power relative to that of the company. Suppliers are most powerful in these situations:

- The product that suppliers sell has few substitutes and is vital to the companies in an industry.
- The profitability of suppliers is not significantly affected by the purchases of companies in a particular industry; in other words, when the industry is not an important customer to the suppliers.
- Companies in an industry would experience significant switching costs if they moved to the product of a different supplier because a particular supplier's products are unique or different. In such cases, the company depends upon a particular supplier and cannot pit suppliers against each other to reduce prices.
- Suppliers can threaten to enter their customers' industry and use their inputs to produce products that would compete directly with those of companies already in the industry.
- Companies in the industry cannot threaten to enter their suppliers' industry and make their own inputs as a tactic for lowering the price of inputs.

An example of an industry in which companies are dependent upon a powerful supplier is the PC industry. Personal computer firms are heavily dependent on Intel, the world's largest supplier of microprocessors for PCs. Intel's microprocessor chips are the industry standard for personal computers. Intel's competitors, such as Advanced Micro Devices (AMD), must develop and supply chips that are compatible with Intel's standard. Although AMD has developed competing chips, Intel still supplies approximately 85% of the chips used in PCs primarily because only Intel has the manufacturing capacity required to serve a large share of the market. It is beyond the financial resources of Intel's competitors to match the scale and efficiency of its manufacturing systems. This means that although PC manufacturers can purchase some microprocessors from Intel's rivals, most notably AMD, they still must turn to Intel for the bulk of their supply. Because Intel is in a powerful bargaining position, it can charge higher prices for its microprocessors than if its competitors were stronger and more numerous (that is, if the microprocessor industry were fragmented).

Substitute Products

The final force in Porter's model is the threat of substitute products: the products of different businesses or industries that can satisfy similar customer needs. For example, companies in the coffee industry compete indirectly with those in the tea and soft drink industries because all three serve customer needs for nonalcoholic, caffeinated drinks. The existence of close substitutes is a strong competitive threat because it limits the price that companies in one industry can charge for their product, which also limits industry profitability. If the price of coffee rises too much relative to that of tea or soft drinks, coffee drinkers may switch to those substitutes.

If an industry's products have few close substitutes (making substitutes a weak competitive force), then companies in the industry have the opportunity to raise prices and earn additional profits. There is no close substitute for microprocessors, which thus gives companies like Intel and AMD the ability to charge higher prices than if there were available substitutes.

Complementors

Andrew Grove, the former CEO of Intel, has argued that Porter's original formulation of competitive forces ignored a sixth force: the power, vigor, and competence of complementors.[10] Complementors are companies that sell products that add value to (complement) the products of companies in an industry because, when used together, the combined products better satisfy customer demands. For example, the complementors to the PC industry are the companies that make software applications. The greater the supply of high-quality software applications running on these machines, the greater the value of PCs to customers, the greater the demand for PCs, and the greater the profitability of the PC industry.

Grove's argument has a strong foundation in economic theory, which has long argued that both substitutes and complements influence demand in an industry.[11] Research has emphasized the importance of complementary products in determining demand and profitability in many high-technology industries such as the computer industry, where Grove made his mark.[12] When complements are an important determinant of demand for an industry's products, industry profits critically depend upon an adequate supply of complementary products. When the number of complementors is increasing and producing attractive complementary products, demand increases and profits in the industry can broaden opportunities for creating value. Conversely, if complementors are weak, and are not producing attractive complementary products, they can become a threat, slowing industry growth and limiting profitability.

It is also possible for complementors to gain so much power that they are able to extract profit from the industry to which they provide complements. Complementors this strong can be a competitive threat. For example, in the videogame industry, the companies that produce the consoles—Nintendo, Microsoft (Xbox), and Sony (PS3)—have historically made the most money in the industry. They have done so by charging game-development companies (the complement providers) a royalty fee for every game sold that runs on their consoles. For example, Nintendo used to charge third-party game developers a 20% royalty fee for every game they sold that was written to run on a Nintendo console. However, two things have changed over the last decade. First, game developers have choices. They can, for example, decide to write for Microsoft Xbox first, and Sony PS3 a year later. Second, some game franchises are now so popular that consumers will purchase whichever platform runs the most recent version of the game. Madden NFL, which is produced by Electronic Arts, has an estimated 5 to 7 million dedicated fans that will purchase each new release. The game is in such demand that Electronic Arts can bargain for lower royalty rates from Microsoft and Sony in return for writing it to run on their gaming platforms. Put differently, Electronic Arts has gained bargaining power over the console producers, and it uses this to extract profit from the console industry in the form of lower royalty rates paid to console manufacturers. The console manufacturers have responded by trying to develop their own powerful franchises that are exclusive to their platforms. Nintendo has been successful here with its long-running Super Mario series, and Microsoft has had a major franchise hit with its Halo series, which is now in its fourth version.

Summary: Why Industry Analysis Matters

The analysis of competition in the industry environment using the competitive forces framework is a powerful tool that helps managers think strategically. It is important to recognize that one competitive force often affects others, and all forces need to be considered when performing industry analysis. For example, if new entry occurs due to low entry barriers, this will increase competition in the industry and drive down prices and profit rates, other things being equal. If buyers are powerful, they may take advantage of the increased choice resulting from new entry to further bargain down prices, increasing the intensity of competition and making it more difficult to make a decent profit in the industry. Thus, it is important to understand how one force might impact upon another.

Industry analysis inevitably leads managers to think systematically about strategic choices. For example, if entry barriers are low, managers might ask themselves, "how can we raise entry barriers into this industry, thereby reducing the threat of new competition?" The answer often involves trying to achieve economies of scale, build brand loyalty, create switching costs, and so on, so that new entrants are at a disadvantage and find it difficult to gain traction in the industry. Or they could ask, "How can we modify the intensity of competition in our industry?" They might do this by emphasizing brand loyalty in an attempt to differentiate their products, or by creating switching costs that reduce buyer power in the industry. As noted in the Opening Case for example, wireless service providers have required their customers to sign a new 2-year contract with early termination fees that may run into hundreds of dollars whenever they upgrade their phone equipment. This action effectively increases the costs of switching to a different wireless provider, thus making it more difficult for new entrants to gain traction in the industry. The increase in switching costs also moderates the intensity of rivalry in the industry by making it less likely that consumers will switch from one provider to another in an attempt to lower the price they pay for their service.

For another example, consider what happened when Coca-Cola looked at its industry environment in the early 2000s. It noticed a disturbing trend—per capita consumption of carbonated beverages had started to decline as people switched to noncarbonated soft drinks. In other words, substitute products were becoming a threat. This realization led to a change in the strategy at Coca-Cola. The company started to develop and offer its own noncarbonated beverages, effectively turning the threat into a strategic opportunity. Similarly, in the 2000s, demand for traditional newspapers began to decline as people increasingly started to consume news content on the Web. In other words, the threat from a substitute product was increasing. Several traditional newspapers responded by rapidly developing their own Web-based content.

In all of these examples, an analysis of industry opportunities and threats led directly to a change in strategy by companies within the industry. This, of course, is the crucial point—analyzing the industry environment in order to identify opportunities and threats leads logically to a discussion of what strategies should be adopted to exploit opportunities and counter threats. We will return to this issue again in Chapters 5, 6, and 7 when we look at the different business-level strategies firms can pursue, and how they can match strategy to the conditions prevailing in their industry environment.

◤ STRATEGIC GROUPS WITHIN INDUSTRIES

Companies in an industry often differ significantly from one another with regard to the way they strategically position their products in the market. Factors such as the distribution channels they use, the market segments they serve, the quality of their products, technological leadership, customer service, pricing policy, advertising policy, and promotions affect product position. As a result of these differences, within most industries, it is possible to observe groups of companies in which each company follows a strategy that is similar to that pursued by other companies in the group, but different from the strategy pursued by companies in other groups. These different groups of companies are known as strategic groups.[13]

For example, in the commercial aerospace industry there has traditionally been two main strategic groups: the manufacturers of regional jets and the manufacturers of large commercial jets (see Figure 2.2). Bombardier and Embraer are the standouts in the regional jet industry, whereas Boeing and Airbus have lone dominated the market for large commercial jets. Regional jets have less than 100 seats and limited range. Large jets have anywhere from 100 to 550 seats, and some models are able to fly across the Pacific Ocean. Large jets are sold to major airlines, and regional jets to small regional carriers. Historically, the companies in the regional jet group have competed against each other, but not against Boeing and Airbus (the converse is also true).

Normally, the basic differences between the strategies that companies in different strategic groups use can be captured by a relatively small number of factors. In the case of commercial aerospace, the differences are primarily in terms of product

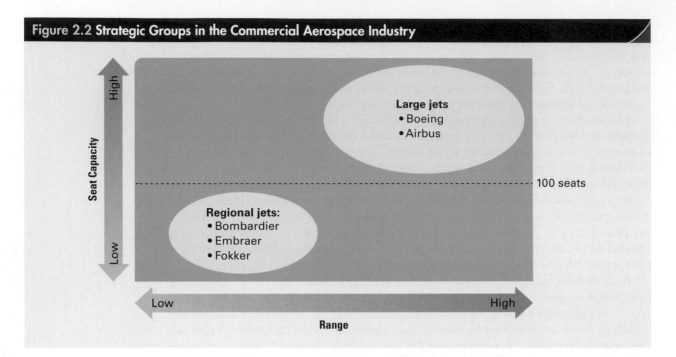

Figure 2.2 Strategic Groups in the Commercial Aerospace Industry

attributes (seat capacity and range), and customer set (large airlines versus smaller regional airlines). For another example, consider the pharmaceutical industry. Here two primary strategic groups stand out.[14] One group, which includes such companies as Merck, Eli Lilly, and Pfizer, is characterized by a business model based on heavy R&D spending and a focus on developing new, proprietary, blockbuster drugs. The companies in this proprietary strategic group are pursuing a high-risk, high-return strategy because basic drug research is difficult and expensive. Bringing a new drug to market can cost up to $800 million in R&D funding and a decade of research and clinical trials. The risks are high because the failure rate in new drug development is very high: only one out of every five drugs entering clinical trials is eventually approved by the U.S. Food and Drug Administration. However, this strategy has potential for a high return because a single successful drug can be patented, giving the innovator a monopoly on the production and sale of the drug for the life of the patent (patents are issued for 20 years). This allows proprietary companies to charge a high price for the drug, earning them millions, if not billions, of dollars over the lifetime of the patent.

The second strategic group might be characterized as the generic-drug strategic group. This group of companies, which includes Forest Labs, Mylan, and Watson Pharmaceuticals, focuses on the manufacture of generic drugs: low-cost copies of drugs that were developed by companies in the proprietary group, which now have expired patents. Low R&D spending, production efficiency, and an emphasis on low prices characterize the business models of companies in this strategic group. They are pursuing a low-risk, low-return strategy. It is low risk because these companies are not investing millions of dollars in R&D, and low return because they cannot charge high prices for their products.

Implications of Strategic Groups

The concept of strategic groups has a number of implications for the identification of opportunities and threats within an industry. First, because all companies in a strategic group are pursuing a similar strategy, customers tend to view the products of such enterprises as direct substitutes for each other. Thus, a company's closest competitors are those in its strategic group, not those in other strategic groups in the industry. The most immediate threat to a company's profitability comes from rivals within its own strategic group. For example, in the retail industry, there is a group of companies that might be characterized as general merchandise discounters. Included in this group are Wal-Mart, K-mart, Target, and Fred Meyer. These companies compete vigorously with each other, rather than with other retailers in different groups, such as Nordstrom or The Gap. K-Mart, for example, was driven into bankruptcy in the early 2000s, not because Nordstrom or The Gap took its business, but because Wal-Mart and Target gained share in the discounting group by virtue of their superior strategic execution of the discounting business model for general merchandise.

A second competitive implication is that different strategic groups can have different relationships to each of the competitive forces; thus, each strategic group may face a different set of opportunities and threats. Each of the following can be a relatively strong or weak competitive force depending on the competitive positioning approach adopted by each strategic group in the industry: the risk of new entry by potential competitors; the degree of rivalry among companies within a group; the bargaining power of buyers; the bargaining power of suppliers; and the competitive force of substitute and complementary products. For example, in the pharmaceutical industry, companies in the proprietary group historically have been in a very powerful position in relation to buyers because their products are patented and there are no substitutes. Also, rivalry based on price competition within this group has been low because competition in the industry depends upon which company is first to patent a new drug ("patent races"), not on drug prices. Thus, companies in this group have been able to charge high prices and earn high profits. In contrast, companies in the generic group have been in a much weaker position because many companies are able to produce different versions of the same generic drug after patents expire. Thus, in this strategic group, products are close substitutes, rivalry has been high, and price competition has led to lower profits than for the companies in the proprietary group.

The Role of Mobility Barriers

It follows from these two issues that some strategic groups are more desirable than others because competitive forces open up greater opportunities and present fewer threats for those groups. Managers, after analyzing their industry, might identify a strategic group where competitive forces are weaker and higher profits can be made. Sensing an opportunity, they might contemplate changing their strategy and move to compete in that strategic group. However, taking advantage of this opportunity may be difficult because of mobility barriers between strategic groups.

Mobility barriers are within-industry factors that inhibit the movement of companies between strategic groups. They include the barriers to entry into a group and the barriers to exit from an existing group. For example, attracted by the promise of higher returns, Forest Labs might want to enter the proprietary strategic group in the pharmaceutical industry, but it might find doing so difficult because it lacks the requisite R&D skills, and building these skills would be an expensive proposition. Over time, companies in different groups develop different cost structures, skills, and competencies that allow them different pricing options and choices. A company contemplating entry into another strategic group must evaluate whether it has the ability to imitate, and outperform, its potential competitors in that strategic group. Managers must determine if it is cost-effective to overcome mobility barriers before deciding whether the move is worthwhile.

At the same time, managers should be aware that companies based in another strategic group within their industry might ultimately become their direct competitors if they can overcome mobility barriers. This now seems to be occurring in the commercial aerospace industry, where two of the regional jet manufacturers, Bombardier and Embraer, have started to move into the large commercial jet business with the development of narrow-bodied aircraft in the 100- to 150-seat range. This implies that Boeing and Airbus will be seeing more competition in the years ahead, and their managers need to prepare for this.

INDUSTRY LIFE-CYCLE ANALYSIS

Changes that take place in an industry over time are an important determinant of the strength of the competitive forces in the industry (and of the nature of opportunities and threats). The similarities and differences between companies in an industry often become more pronounced over time, and its strategic group structure frequently changes. The strength and nature of each competitive force also changes as an industry evolves, particularly the two forces of risk of entry by potential competitors and rivalry among existing firms.[15]

A useful tool for analyzing the effects of industry evolution on competitive forces is the industry life-cycle model. This model identifies five sequential stages in the evolution of an industry that lead to five distinct kinds of industry environment: embryonic, growth, shakeout, mature, and decline (see Figure 2.3). The task managers face is to anticipate how the strength of competitive forces will change as the industry environment evolves, and to formulate strategies that take advantage of opportunities as they arise and that counter emerging threats.

Embryonic Industries

An embryonic industry is one that is just beginning to develop (for example, personal computers and biotechnology in the 1970s, wireless communications in the 1980s, Internet retailing in the 1990s, and nanotechnology today). Growth at this stage is slow because of factors such as buyers' unfamiliarity with the industry's product, high prices due to the inability of companies to leverage significant scale economies, and poorly developed distribution channels. Barriers to entry tend to be based on access to key technological knowhow rather than cost economies or brand loyalty. If the core knowhow required to compete in the industry is complex and difficult to grasp, barriers to entry can be quite high, and established companies will

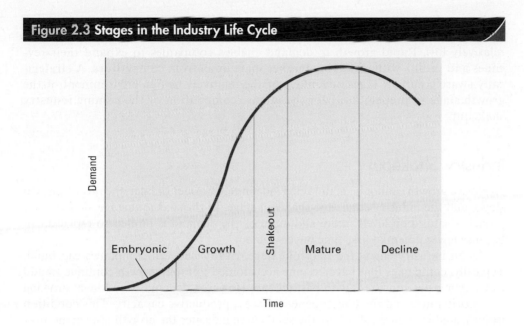

Figure 2.3 Stages in the Industry Life Cycle

be protected from potential competitors. Rivalry in embryonic industries is based not so much on price as on educating customers, opening up distribution channels, and perfecting the design of the product. Such rivalry can be intense, and the company that is the first to solve design problems often has the opportunity to develop a significant market position. An embryonic industry may also be the creation of one company's innovative efforts, as happened with microprocessors (Intel), vacuum cleaners (Hoover), photocopiers (Xerox), small-package express delivery (FedEx), and Internet search engines (Google). In such circumstances, the developing company has a major opportunity to capitalize on the lack of rivalry and build a strong hold on the market.

Growth Industries

Once demand for an industry's product begins to increase, it develops the characteristics of a growth industry. In a growth industry, first-time demand is expanding rapidly as many new customers enter the market. Typically, an industry grows when customers become familiar with the product, prices fall because scale economies have been attained, and distribution channels develop. The U.S. wireless telephone industry remained in the growth stage for most of the 1985–2012 period. In 1990, there were only 5 million cellular subscribers in the nation. In 1997, there were 50 million. By 2014, this figure had increased to about 360 million, or roughly 1.08 accounts per person, implying that the market is now saturated and the industry is mature.

Normally, the importance of control over technological knowledge as a barrier to entry has diminished by the time an industry enters its growth stage. Because few companies have yet to achieve significant scale economies or built brand loyalty, other entry barriers tend to be relatively low early in the growth stage. Thus, the threat from potential competitors is typically highest at this point. Paradoxically, high growth usually means that new entrants can be absorbed into an industry without a marked increase in the intensity of rivalry. Thus, rivalry tends to be relatively low. Rapid growth in demand enables companies to expand their revenues and profits without taking market share away from competitors. A strategically aware company takes advantage of the relatively benign environment of the growth stage to prepare itself for the intense competition of the coming industry shakeout.

Industry Shakeout

Explosive growth cannot be maintained indefinitely. Sooner or later, the rate of growth slows, and the industry enters the shakeout stage. In the shakeout stage, demand approaches saturation levels: more and more of the demand is limited to replacement because fewer potential first-time buyers remain.

As an industry enters the shakeout stage, rivalry between companies can build. Typically, companies that have become accustomed to rapid growth continue to add capacity at rates consistent with past growth. However, demand is no longer growing at historic rates, and the consequence is excess productive capacity. This condition is illustrated in Figure 2.4, where the solid curve indicates the growth in demand over time and the broken curve indicates the growth in productive capacity over time. As you can see, past time t_1, demand growth slows as the industry matures. However, capacity continues to grow until time t_2. The gap between the solid and broken lines signifies excess capacity. In an attempt to use this capacity, companies often cut prices. The result can be a price war that drives inefficient companies into bankruptcy and deters new entry.

Figure 2.4 Growth in Demand and Capacity

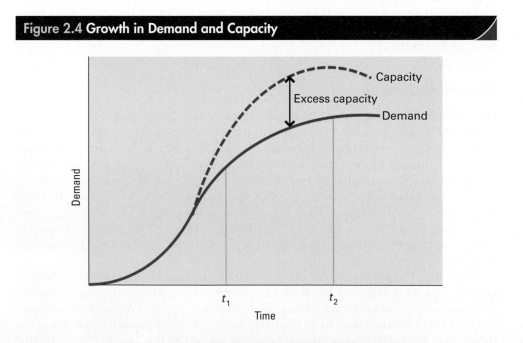

Mature Industries

The shakeout stage ends when the industry enters its mature stage: The market is totally saturated, demand is limited to replacement demand, and growth is low or zero. Typically, the growth that remains comes from population expansion, bringing new customers into the market, or increasing replacement demand.

As an industry enters maturity, barriers to entry increase, and the threat of entry from potential competitors decreases. As growth slows during the shakeout, companies can no longer maintain historic growth rates merely by holding on to their market share. Competition for market share develops, driving down prices and often producing a price war, as has happened in the airline and PC industries. To survive the shakeout, companies begin to focus on minimizing costs and building brand loyalty. The airlines, for example, tried to cut operating costs by hiring nonunion labor, and to build brand loyalty by introducing frequent-flyer programs. Personal computer companies have sought to build brand loyalty by providing excellent after-sales service and working to lower their cost structures. By the time an industry matures, the surviving companies are those that have secured brand loyalty and efficient, low-cost operations. Because both these factors constitute a significant barrier to entry, the threat of entry by potential competitors is often greatly diminished. High entry barriers in mature industries can give companies the opportunity to increase prices and profits, although this does not always occur.

As a result of the shakeout, most industries in the maturity stage consolidate and become oligopolies. Examples include the beer industry, breakfast cereal industry, and wireless service industry. In mature industries, companies tend to recognize their interdependence and try to avoid price wars. Stable demand gives them the opportunity to enter into tacit price-leadership agreements. The net effect is to reduce the threat of intense rivalry among established companies, thereby allowing greater profitability. Nevertheless, the stability of a mature industry is always threatened by further price wars. A general slump in economic activity can depress industry demand. As companies fight to maintain their revenues in the face of declining demand, price-leadership agreements break down, rivalry increases, and prices and profits fall. The periodic price wars that occur in the airline industry appear to follow this pattern.

Declining Industries

Eventually, most industries enter a stage of decline: growth becomes negative for a variety of reasons, including technological substitution (air travel instead of rail travel), social changes (greater health consciousness impacting tobacco sales), demographics (the declining birthrate constricting the market for products for babies and children), and international competition (low-cost, foreign competition pushing the U.S. steel industry into decline). Within a declining industry, the degree of rivalry among established companies usually increases. Depending on the speed of the decline and the height of exit barriers, competitive pressures can become as fierce as in the shakeout stage.[16] The largest problem in a declining industry is that falling demand leads to the emergence of excess capacity. In trying to use this capacity, companies begin to cut prices, thus sparking a price war. The U.S. steel industry experienced these problems during the 1980s and 1990s because steel companies tried to use their excess capacity despite falling demand. The same problem occurred in the airline industry in the 1990–1992 period, in 2001–2005, and again in 2008–2009 as companies cut prices to ensure that they would not be flying with half-empty planes (that is, they would not be operating with substantial excess capacity). Exit barriers play a part in adjusting excess capacity. The higher the exit barriers, the harder it is for companies to reduce capacity, and the greater the threat of severe price competition.

Summary

A third task of industry analysis is to identify the opportunities and threats that are characteristic of different kinds of industry environments in order to develop effective strategies. Managers have to tailor their strategies to changing industry conditions. They must also learn to recognize the crucial points in an industry's development, so they can forecast when the shakeout stage of an industry might begin, or when an industry might be moving into decline. This is also true at the level of strategic groups, for new embryonic groups may emerge because of shifts in customer needs and tastes, or because some groups may grow rapidly due to changes in technology, whereas others will decline as their customers defect.

◤ LIMITATIONS OF MODELS FOR INDUSTRY ANALYSIS

The competitive forces, strategic groups, and life-cycle models provide useful ways of thinking about and analyzing the nature of competition within an industry to identify opportunities and threats. However, each has its limitations, and managers must be aware of these.

Life-Cycle Issues

It is important to remember that the industry life-cycle model is a generalization. In practice, industry life cycles do not always follow the pattern illustrated in Figure 2.3. In some cases, growth is so rapid that the embryonic stage is skipped altogether. In others, industries fail to get past the embryonic stage. Industry growth can be revitalized after long periods of decline through innovation or social change. For example, the health boom brought the bicycle industry back to life after a long period of decline.

The time span of these stages can vary significantly from industry to industry. Some industries can remain mature almost indefinitely if their products are viewed as basic necessities, as is the case for the car industry. Other industries skip the mature stage and go straight into decline, as in the case of the vacuum-tube industry. Transistors replaced vacuum tubes as a major component in electronic products despite that the vacuum tube industry was still in its growth stage. Still other industries may go through several shakeouts before they enter full maturity, as appears to currently be happening in the telecommunications industry.

Innovation and Change

Over any reasonable length of time, in many industries competition can be viewed as a process driven by innovation.[17] Innovation is frequently the major factor in industry evolution and propels a company's movement through the industry life cycle. Innovation is attractive because companies that pioneer new products, processes, or strategies often earn enormous profits. Consider the explosive growth of Toys "R" Us, Dell, and Wal-Mart. In a variety of ways, all of these companies were innovators. Toys "R" Us pioneered a new way of selling toys (through large, discount warehouse-type stores), Dell pioneered an entirely new way of selling personal computers (directly via telephone, and then the Web), and Wal-Mart pioneered the low-price discount superstore concept.

Successful innovation can transform the nature of industry competition. In recent decades, one frequent consequence of innovation has been to lower the fixed costs of production, thereby reducing barriers to entry and allowing new, smaller enterprises to compete with large established organizations. Four decades ago, large, integrated steel companies such as U.S. Steel, LTV, and Bethlehem Steel dominated the steel industry. The industry was an oligopoly, dominated by a small number of large producers, in which tacit price collusion was practiced. Then along came a series of efficient, mini-mill producers such as Nucor and Chaparral Steel, which used a new technology: electric arc furnaces. Over the past 40 years, they have revolutionized the structure of the industry. What was once a consolidated industry is now fragmented and price competitive. U.S. Steel now has only a 12% market share, down from 55% in the mid-1960s. In contrast, the mini-mills as a group now hold over 40% of the market, up from 5% 20 years ago.[18] Thus, the mini-mill innovation has reshaped the nature of competition in the steel industry.[19] A competitive forces model applied to the industry in 1970 would look very different from a competitive forces model applied in 2014.

Michael Porter sees innovation as "unfreezing" and "reshaping" industry structure. He argues that after a period of turbulence triggered by innovation, the structure of an industry once more settles into a fairly stable pattern, and the competitive forces and strategic group concepts can once more be applied.[20] This view of the evolution of industry structure, often referred to as "punctuated equilibrium,"[21] holds that long periods of equilibrium (refreezing), when an industry's structure is stable, are punctuated by periods of rapid change (unfreezing), when industry structure is revolutionized by innovation.

Figure 2.5 depicts punctuated equilibrium for a key dimension of industry structure: competitive structure. From time t_0 to t_1, the competitive structure of the industry is a stable oligopoly, and few companies share the market. At time t_1, a major new innovation is pioneered either by an existing company or a new entrant. The result is a period of turbulence between t_1 and t_2. Afterward, the industry settles into a new state of equilibrium, but now the competitive structure is far more fragmented. Note that the opposite could have happened: the industry could have become more consolidated, although this seems to be less common. In general, innovation seems to lower barriers to entry, allow more companies into the industry, and, as a result, lead to fragmentation rather than consolidation.

During a period of rapid change when industry structure is being revolutionized by innovation, value typically migrates to business models based on new positioning strategies.[22] In the stockbrokerage industry, value migrated from the full-service broker

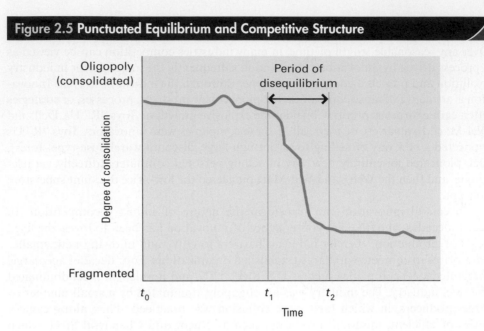

Figure 2.5 Punctuated Equilibrium and Competitive Structure

model to the online trading model. In the steel industry, electric arc technology led to a migration of value away from large, integrated enterprises and toward small mini-mills. In the bookselling industry, value has migrated first away from small boutique "bricks-and-mortar" booksellers toward large bookstore chains like Barnes & Noble, and more recently toward online bookstores such as Amazon.com. Because the competitive forces and strategic group models are static, they cannot adequately capture what occurs during periods of rapid change in the industry environment when value is migrating.

Company Differences

Another criticism of industry models is that they overemphasize the importance of industry structure as a determinant of company performance, and underemphasize the importance of variations or differences among companies within an industry or a strategic group.[23] As we discuss in the next chapter, the profit rates of individual companies within an industry can vary enormously. Research by Richard Rumelt and his associates suggests that industry structure explains only about 10% of the variance in profit rates across companies.[24] This implies that individual company differences account for much of the remainder. Other studies have estimated the explained variance at closer to 20%.[25] Similarly, a numbers of studies have found only weak evidence linking strategic group membership and company profit rates, despite that the strategic group model predicts a strong link.[26] Collectively these studies suggest that a company's individual resources and capabilities may be more important determinants of its profitability than the industry or strategic group of which the company is a member. In other words, there are strong companies in tough industries where average profitability is low (Nucor in the steel industry), and weak companies in industries where average profitability is high.

Although these findings do not invalidate the competitive forces and strategic group models, they do imply that the models are imperfect predictors of enterprise profitability. A company will not be profitable just because it is based in an attractive industry or strategic group. As we will discuss in subsequent chapters, much more is required.

THE MACROENVIRONMENT

Just as the decisions and actions of strategic managers can often change an industry's competitive structure, so too can changing conditions or forces in the wider macroenvironment, that is, the broader economic, global, technological, demographic, social, and political context in which companies and industries are embedded (see Figure 2.6). Changes in the forces within the macroenvironment can have a direct impact on any or all of the forces in Porter's model, thereby altering the relative strength of these forces as well as the attractiveness of an industry.

Figure 2.6 The Role of the Macroenvironment

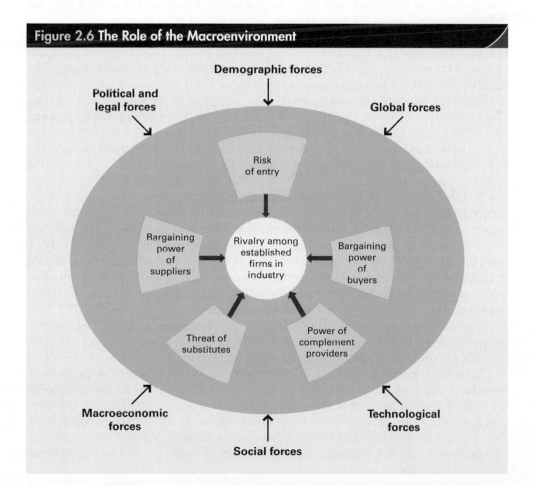

Macroeconomic Forces

Macroeconomic forces affect the general health and well-being of a nation and the regional economy of an organization, which in turn affect companies' and industries' ability to earn an adequate rate of return. The four primary macroeconomic forces are the growth rate of the economy, interest rates, currency exchange rates, and inflation (or deflation) rates. Economic growth, because it leads to an expansion in customer expenditures, tends to ease competitive pressures within an industry. This gives companies the opportunity to expand their operations and earn higher profits. Because economic decline (a recession) leads to a reduction in customer expenditures, it increases competitive pressures. Economic decline frequently causes price wars in mature industries.

Interest rates can determine the demand for a company's products and thus are important whenever customers routinely borrow money to finance their purchase of these products. The most obvious example is the housing market, where mortgage rates directly affect demand. Interest rates also have an impact on the sale of autos, appliances, and capital equipment, to give just a few examples. For companies in such industries, rising interest rates are a threat, and falling rates an opportunity. Interest rates are also important because they influence a company's cost of capital, and therefore its ability to raise funds and invest in new assets. The lower the interest rate, the lower the cost of capital for companies and the more potential investment.

Currency exchange rates define the comparative value of different national currencies. Movement in currency exchange rates has a direct impact on the competitiveness of a company's products in the global marketplace. For example, when the value of the dollar is low compared to the value of other currencies, products made in the United States are relatively inexpensive, and products made overseas are relatively expensive. A low or declining dollar reduces the threat from foreign competitors while creating opportunities for increased sales overseas. The fall in the value of the dollar against several major currencies during 2004–2008 helped to make the U.S. steel industry more competitive, whereas its rise during 2012–2014 made the industry less competitive.

Price inflation can destabilize the economy, producing slower economic growth, higher interest rates, and volatile currency movements. If inflation continues to increase, investment planning becomes hazardous. The key characteristic of inflation is that it makes the future less predictable. In an inflationary environment, it may be impossible to predict with any accuracy the real value of returns that can be earned from a project 5 years later. Such uncertainty makes companies less willing to invest, which in turn depresses economic activity and ultimately pushes the economy into a recession. Thus, high inflation is a threat to companies.

Price deflation also has a destabilizing effect on economic activity. If prices fall, the real price of fixed payments rises. This is damaging for companies and individuals with a high level of debt who must make regular, fixed payments on that debt. In a deflationary environment, the increase in the real value of debt consumes more household and corporate cash flows, leaving less for other purchases and depressing the overall level of economic activity. Although significant deflation has not been seen since the 1930s, in the 1990s it took hold in Japan; in 2008–2009, concerns grew that it might re-emerge in the United States, as the country plunged into a deep recession; and in 2014, economists were increasingly worried about the risk of price deflation in Europe.

Global Forces

The last half-century has seen enormous changes in the world's economic system. We review these changes in some detail in Chapter 8, where we discuss global strategy. For now, the important points to note are that barriers to international trade and investment have tumbled, and more and more countries have enjoyed sustained economic growth. Economic growth in Brazil, China, and India has created large, new markets for companies' goods and services and is giving companies an opportunity to grow their profits faster by entering these nations. Falling barriers to international trade and investment have made it much easier to enter foreign nations. For example, 20 years ago, it was almost impossible for a Western company to set up operations in China. Today, Western and Japanese companies are investing approximately $100 billion annually in China. By the same token, falling barriers to international trade and investment have made it easier for foreign enterprises to enter the domestic markets of many companies (by lowering barriers to entry), thereby increasing the intensity of competition and lowering profitability. Because of these changes, many formerly isolated domestic markets have now become part of a much larger, more competitive global marketplace, creating both threats and opportunities for companies.

Technological Forces

Over the last few decades, the pace of technological change has accelerated.[27] This has unleashed a process that has been called a "perennial gale of creative destruction."[28] Technological change can render established products obsolete overnight and simultaneously create a host of new product possibilities. Thus, technological change is both creative and destructive—both an opportunity and a threat.

Most important, the impacts of technological change can affect the height of barriers to entry and therefore radically reshape industry structure. For example, the Internet lowered barriers to entry into the news industry. Providers of financial news must now compete for advertising dollars and customer attention with new, Internet-based media organizations that developed during the 1990s and 2000s, such as TheStreet .com, The Motley Fool, Yahoo Finance, and most recently, Google News. Advertisers now have more choices due to the resulting increase in rivalry, enabling them to bargain down the prices that they must pay to media companies.

Demographic Forces

Demographic forces result from changes in the characteristics of a population such as age, gender, ethnic origin, race, sexual orientation, and social class. Like the other forces in the general environment, demographic forces present managers with opportunities and threats and can have major implications for organizations. Changes in the age distribution of a population are an example of a demographic force that affects managers and organizations. Currently, most industrialized nations are experiencing the aging of their populations as a consequence of falling birth and death rates and the aging of the Baby-Boom generation. As the population ages, opportunities for organizations that cater to older people are increasing; the home-health-care and recreation industries, for example, are seeing an upswing in demand for their services. As the Bab-Boom generation from the late 1950s to the early 1960s has aged, it has created a host of opportunities and threats. During the 1980s, many Baby Boomers were getting married and creating an upsurge in demand for the customer appliances normally purchased by couples marrying for the first time. Companies such as Whirlpool Corporation and GE capitalized on the resulting upsurge in demand for washing machines, dishwashers, dryers, and the like. In the 1990s, many of these same baby boomers began to save for retirement, creating an inflow of money into mutual fund, and creating a surge in the mutual fund industry. Today many of these same baby boomers are retiring, creating a boom in retirement communities.

Social Forces

Social forces refer to the way in which changing social mores and values affect an industry. Like other macroenvironmental forces, social change creates opportunities and threats. One major social movement of recent decades has been the trend toward greater health consciousness. Its impact has been immense, and companies that recognized the opportunities early have often reaped significant gains. Philip Morris, for example, capitalized on the growing health consciousness trend when it acquired Miller Brewing Company, and then redefined competition in the beer industry with its introduction of low-calorie beer (Miller Lite). Similarly, PepsiCo was able to gain market share from its rival, Coca-Cola, by being the first to introduce diet colas and fruit-based soft drinks. At the same time, the health trend has created a threat for many industries. The tobacco industry, for example, is in decline as a direct result of greater customer awareness of the health implications of smoking.

Political and Legal Forces

Political and legal forces are outcomes of changes in laws and regulations, and significantly affect managers and companies. Political processes shape a society's laws, which constrain the operations of organizations and managers and thus create both opportunities and threats.[29] For example, throughout much of the industrialized world, there has been a strong trend toward deregulation of industries previously controlled by the state, and privatization of organizations once owned by the state. In the United States, deregulation of the airline industry in 1979 allowed 29 new airline companies to enter the industry between 1979 and 1993. The increase in passenger-carrying capacity after deregulation led to excess capacity on many routes, intense competition, and fare wars. To respond to this more competitive task environment, airlines needed to look for ways to reduce operating costs. The development of hub-and-spoke systems, the rise of nonunion airlines, and the introduction of no-frills discount service are all responses to increased competition in the airlines' task environment. Despite these innovations, the airline industry still experiences intense fare wars, which have lowered profits and caused numerous airline-company bankruptcies. The global telecommunications service industry is now experiencing the same kind of turmoil following the deregulation of that industry in the United States and elsewhere.

KEY TERMS

TAKEAWAYS FOR STRATEGIC MANAGERS

1. An industry is a group of companies offering products or services that are close substitutes for each other. Close substitutes are products or services that satisfy the same basic customer needs.

2. The main technique used to analyze competition in the industry environment is the competitive forces model. The forces are: (1) the risk of new entry by potential competitors, (2) the extent of rivalry among established firms, (3) the bargaining power of buyers, (4) the bargaining power of suppliers, (5) the threat of substitute products, and (6) the power of complement providers. The stronger each force is, the more competitive the industry and the lower the rate of return that can be earned.

3. The risk of entry by potential competitors is a function of the height of barriers to entry. The higher the barriers to entry are, the lower the risk of entry and the greater the potential profits in the industry.

4. The extent of rivalry among established companies is a function of an industry's competitive structure, demand conditions, cost conditions, and barriers to exit. Strong demand conditions moderate the competition among established companies and create opportunities for expansion. When demand is weak, intensive competition can develop, particularly in consolidated industries with high exit barriers.

5. Buyers are most powerful when a company depends on them for business, but they are not dependent on the company. In such circumstances, buyers are a threat.

6. Suppliers are most powerful when a company depends on them for business but they are not dependent on the company. In such circumstances, suppliers are a threat.

7. Substitute products are the products of companies serving customer needs similar to the needs served by the industry being analyzed. When substitute products are very similar to one another, companies can charge a lower price without losing customers to the substitutes.

8. The power, vigor, and competence of complementors represent a sixth competitive force. Powerful, vigorous complementors may have a strong positive impact on demand in an industry.

9. Most industries are composed of strategic groups of companies pursuing the same or a similar strategy. Companies in different strategic groups pursue different strategies.

10. The members of a company's strategic group constitute its immediate competitors. Because different strategic groups are characterized by different opportunities and threats, a company may improve its performance by switching strategic groups. The feasibility of doing so is a function of the height of mobility barriers.

11. Industries go through a well-defined life cycle: from an embryonic stage through growth, shakeout, and maturity, and eventually decline. Each stage has different implications for the competitive structure of the industry, and each gives rise to its own opportunities and threats.

12. The competitive forces, strategic group, and industry life-cycles models all have limitations. The competitive forces and strategic group models present a static picture of competition that deemphasizes the role of innovation. Yet innovation can revolutionize industry structure and completely shift the strength of different competitive forces. The competitive forces and strategic group models have been criticized for deemphasizing the importance of individual company

differences. A company will not be profitable just because it is part of an attractive industry or strategic group; much more is required. The industry life-cycle model is a generalization that is not always followed, particularly when innovation revolutionizes an industry.

13. The macroenvironment affects the intensity of rivalry within an industry. Included in the macroenvironment are the macroeconomic environment, the global environment, the technological environment, the demographic and social environment, and the political and legal environment.

DISCUSSION QUESTIONS

1. Under what environmental conditions are price wars most likely to occur in an industry? What are the implications of price wars for a company? How should a company try to deal with the threat of a price war?
2. Discuss the competitive forces model with reference to what you know about the US market for wireless telecommunications services (see the Opening Case). What does the model tell you about the level of competition in this industry?
3. Identify a growth industry, a mature industry, and a declining industry. For each industry,

identify the following: (a) the number and size distribution of companies, (b) the nature of barriers to entry, (c) the height of barriers to entry, and (d) the extent of product differentiation. What do these factors tell you about the nature of competition in each industry? What are the implications for the company in terms of opportunities and threats?
4. Assess the impact of macroenvironmental factors on the likely level of enrollment at your university over the next decade. What are the implications of these factors for the job security and salary level of your professors?

CLOSING CASE

The Market for Large Commercial Aircraft

Two companies, Boeing and Airbus, have long dominated the market for large commercial jet aircraft. Today Boeing planes account for 50% of the world's fleet of commercial jet aircraft, and Airbus planes account for 31%. The reminder of the global market is split between several smaller players, including Embraer of Brazil and Bombardier of Canada, both of which have a 7% share. Embraer and Bombardier, however, have to date focused primarily on the regional jet market, building planes of less than 100 seats. The market for aircraft with more than 100 seats has been totally dominated by Boeing and Airbus.

The overall market is large and growing. In 2014, Boeing delivered 723 aircraft and Airbus delivered 620 aircraft. Demand for new aircraft is driven primarily by demand for air travel, which has grown at 5% per annum compounded since 1980. Looking forward, Boeing predicts that over the next 20 years the world economy will grow at 3.2% per annum, and airline traffic will continue to grow at 5% per annum as more and more people from the world's emerging economies take to the air for business and pleasure trips. Given the anticipated growth in demand, Boeing believes the world's airlines will need 37,000 new aircraft between 2013 and 2033 with a market value of $5.2 trillion dollars in today's prices.

Clearly, the scale of future demand creates an enormous profit opportunity for the two main incumbents, Boeing and Airbus. Given this, many observers wonder if the industry will see new entries. Historically, it has been assumed that the high development cost associated with bringing new commercial jet aircraft to market, and the need to realize substantial economies of scale to cover those costs, has worked as a very effective deterrent to new entries. For example, estimates suggest that it cost Boeing some $18 to $20 billion to develop its latest aircraft, the wide bodied Boeing 787, and that the company will have to sell 1,100 787s to break even, which will take 10 years. Given the costs, risks, and long time horizon here, it has been argued that only Boeing and Airbus can afford to develop new large commercial jet aircraft.

However, in the last few years, three new entrants have appeared. All three are building smaller narrow-bodied jets with a seat capacity between 100 and 190. Boeing's 737 and the Airbus A320 currently dominate the narrow-bodied segment. The Commercial Aircraft Corporation of China (Comac) is building a 170- to 190-seat narrow-bodied jet, scheduled for introduction in 2018. To date, Comac has 430 firm orders for the aircraft, mostly from Chinese domestic airlines. Bombardier is developing a 100- to 150-seat plane that will bring it into direct competition with Boeing and Airbus for the first time. Scheduled for introduction in late 2015, Bombardier has 243 firm orders and another 100 commitments for these aircraft. Embraer too, has developed a 108- to 125-seat plane to compete in the narrow-bodied segment, the E-190/195. It has taken orders for 720 of these aircraft, 640 of which had been delivered by late 2014. The new entry is occurring because all three producers believe that the market for narrow-bodied aircraft is now large enough to support more than Boeing and Airbus. Bombardier and Embraer can leverage the know-how they developed manufacturing regional jets to help them move upmarket. For its part, Comac can count on orders from Chinese airlines and the tacit support of the Chinese government to help it get off the ground.

In response to these competitive threats, Boeing and Airbus are developing new, more fuel-efficient versions of their own narrow-bodied planes, the 737 and A320. Although they hope their new offerings will keep entrants in check, one thing seems clear: with potentially five producers rather than two in the market, it seems likely that competition will become more intense in the narrow-bodied segment of the industry, which could well drive prices and profits down for the big two incumbent producers.

Sources: R. Marowits, "Bombardier's C Series Drought Ends," *The Montreal Gazette*, December 20, 2012; D. Gates, "Boeing Projects Break-Even on 787 Manufacturing in 10 Years," *Seattle Times*, October 26, 2011; Boeing Corporation, "Current Market Outlook 2014–2033," www.boeing.com/commercial/cmo/; D. Cameron, "Boeing delivers record number of jets in 2014," *The Wall Street Journal*, January 6, 2015.

CASE DISCUSSION QUESTIONS

1. Explain why the wide-bodied segment of the large commercial jet aircraft industry can only profitably support two players at present. What are the implications of your answer for barriers to entry into this segment?

2. Are entry barriers into the narrow-bodied segment the same as those into the wide-bodied segment? Explain your answer?

3. Given future projections for demand, how do you think the industry as a whole will do over the next twenty years? How might your forecast differ for the wide-bodied and narrow-bodied segments?

4. If you were a new entrant into the bottom part of the narrow-bodied industry, as are Comac and Bombardier, what would be your long-term development strategy?

5. What can Boeing and Airbus do to deter further entry into this industry, and/or keep new entrants boxed into the bottom end of the market (that is, smaller, narrow-bodied jets)?

NOTES

[1]M. E. Porter, *Competitive Strategy* (New York: Free Press, 1980).

[2]J. E. Bain, *Barriers to New Competition* (Cambridge, Mass.: Harvard University Press, 1956). For a review of the modern literature on barriers to entry, see R. J. Gilbert, "Mobility Barriers and the Value of Incumbency," in R. Schmalensee and R. D. Willig (eds.), *Handbook of Industrial Organization,* vol. 1 (Amsterdam: North-Holland, 1989). See also R. P. McAfee, H. M. Mialon, and M. A. Williams, "What Is a Barrier to Entry?" *American Economic Review* 94 (May 2004): 461–468.

[3]"comScore reports September 2014 U.S. smartphone subscriber market share," comScore, November 6, 2014.

[4]A detailed discussion of switching costs can be found in C. Shapiro and H. R. Varian, *Information Rules: A Strategic Guide to the Network Economy* (Boston: Harvard Business School Press, 1999).

[5]Most information on barriers to entry can be found in the industrial organization economics literature. See especially Bain, *Barriers to New Competition;* M. Mann, "Seller Concentration, Barriers to Entry and Rates of Return in 30 Industries," *Review of Economics and Statistics* 48 (1966): 296–307; W. S. Comanor and T. A. Wilson, "Advertising, Market Structure and Performance," *Review of Economics and Statistics* 49 (1967): 423–440; Gilbert, "Mobility Barriers"; K. Cool, L. H. Roller, and B. Leleux, "The Relative Impact of Actual and Potential Rivalry on Firm Profitability in the Pharmaceutical Industry," *Strategic Management Journal* 20 (1999): 1–14.

[6]For a discussion of tacit agreements, see T. C. Schelling, *The Strategy of Conflict* (Cambridge, Mass.: Harvard University Press, 1960).

[7]M. Busse, "Firm Financial Condition and Airline Price Wars," *Rand Journal of Economics* 33 (2002): 298–318.

[8]For a review, see F. Karakaya, "Market Exit and Barriers to Exit: Theory and Practice," *Psychology and Marketing* 17 (2000): 651–668.

[9]P. Ghemawat, *Commitment: The Dynamics of Strategy* (Boston: Harvard Business School Press, 1991).

[10]A. S. Grove, *Only the Paranoid Survive* (New York: Doubleday, 1996).

[11]In standard microeconomic theory, the concept used for assessing the strength of substitutes and complements is the cross elasticity of demand.

[12]For details and further references, see Charles W. L. Hill, "Establishing a Standard: Competitive Strategy and Technology Standards in Winner Take All Industries," *Academy of Management Executive* 11 (1997): 7–25; Shapiro and Varian, *Information Rules.*

[13]The development of strategic group theory has been a strong theme in the strategy literature. Important contributions include R. E. Caves and M. E. Porter, "From Entry Barriers to Mobility Barriers," *Quarterly Journal of Economics* (May 1977): 241–262; K. R. Harrigan, "An Application of Clustering for Strategic Group Analysis," *Strategic Management Journal* 6 (1985): 55–73; K. J. Hatten and D. E. Schendel, "Heterogeneity Within an Industry: Firm Conduct in the U.S. Brewing Industry, 1952–71," *Journal of Industrial Economics* 26 (1977): 97–113; M. E. Porter, "The Structure Within Industries and Companies' Performance," *Review of Economics and Statistics* 61 (1979): 214–227. See also K. Cool and D. Schendel, "Performance Differences Among Strategic Group Members," *Strategic Management Journal* 9 (1988): 207–233; A. Nair and S. Kotha, "Does Group Membership Matter? Evidence from the Japanese Steel Industry," *Strategic Management Journal* 20 (2001): 221–235; G. McNamara, D. L. Deephouse, and R. A. Luce, "Competitive Positioning Within and Across a Strategic Group Structure," *Strategic Management Journal* 24 (2003): 161–180.

[14]For details on the strategic group structure in the pharmaceutical industry, see K. Cool and I. Dierickx, "Rivalry, Strategic Groups, and Firm Profitability," *Strategic Management Journal* 14 (1993): 47–59.

[15]C. W. Hofer argued that lifecycle considerations may be the most important contingency when formulating business strategy. See Hofer, "Towards a Contingency Theory of Business Strategy," *Academy of Management Journal* 18 (1975): 784–810. For empirical evidence to support this view, see C. R. Anderson and C. P. Zeithaml,

"Stages of the Product Life Cycle, Business Strategy, and Business Performance," *Academy of Management Journal* 27 (1984): 5–24; D. C. Hambrick and D. Lei, "Towards an Empirical Prioritization of Contingency Variables for Business Strategy," *Academy of Management Journal* 28 (1985): 763–788. See also G. Miles, C. C. Snow, and M. P. Sharfman, "Industry Variety and Performance," *Strategic Management Journal* 14 (1993): 163–177; G. K. Deans, F. Kroeger, and S. Zeisel, "The Consolidation Curve," *Harvard Business Review* 80 (December 2002): 2–3.

[16]The characteristics of declining industries have been summarized by K. R. Harrigan, "Strategy Formulation in Declining Industries," *Academy of Management Review* 5 (1980): 599–604. See also J. Anand and H. Singh, "Asset Redeployment, Acquisitions and Corporate Strategy in Declining Industries," *Strategic Management Journal* 18 (1997): 99–118.

[17]This perspective is associated with the Austrian school of economics, which goes back to Schumpeter. For a summary of this school and its implications for strategy, see R. Jacobson, "The Austrian School of Strategy," *Academy of Management Review* 17 (1992): 782–807; C. W. L. Hill and D. Deeds, "The Importance of Industry Structure for the Determination of Industry Profitability: A Neo-Austrian Approach," *Journal of Management Studies* 33 (1996): 429–451.

[18]"A Tricky Business," *Economist,* June 30, 2001, pp. 55–56.

[19]D. F. Barnett and R. W. Crandall, *Up from the Ashes* (Washington, D.C.: Brookings Institution, 1986).

[20]M. E. Porter, *The Competitive Advantage of Nations* (New York: Free Press, 1990).

[21]The term *"punctuated equilibrium"* is borrowed from evolutionary biology. For a detailed explanation of the concept, see M. L. Tushman, W. H. Newman, and E. Romanelli, "Convergence and Upheaval: Managing the Unsteady Pace of Organizational Evolution," *California Management Review* 29:1 (1985): 29–44; C. J. G. Gersick, "Revolutionary Change Theories: A Multilevel Exploration of the Punctuated Equilibrium Paradigm," *Academy of Management Review* 16 (1991): 10–36; R. Adner and D. A. Levinthal, "The Emergence of Emerging Technologies, *"California Management Review* 45 (Fall 2002): 50–65.

[22]A. J. Slywotzky, *Value Migration: How to Think Several Moves Ahead of the Competition* (Boston: Harvard Business School Press, 1996).

[23]Hill and Deeds, "Importance of Industry Structure."

[24]R. P. Rumelt, "How Much Does Industry Matter?" *Strategic Management Journal* 12 (1991): 167–185. See also A. J. Mauri and M. P. Michaels, "Firm and Industry Effects Within Strategic Management: An Empirical Examination," *Strategic Management Journal* 19 (1998): 211–219.

[25]R. Schmalensee, "Inter-Industry Studies of Structure and Performance," in Schmalensee and Willig (eds.), *Handbook of Industrial Organization.* Similar results were found by A. N. McGahan and M. E. Porter, "How Much Does Industry Matter, Really?" *Strategic Management Journal* 18 (1997): 15–30.

[26]For example, see K. Cool and D. Schendel, "Strategic Group Formation and Performance: The Case of the U.S. Pharmaceutical Industry, 1932–1992," *Management Science* (September 1987): 1102–1124.

[27]See M. Gort and J. Klepper, "Time Paths in the Diffusion of Product Innovations," *Economic Journal* (September 1982): 630–653. Looking at the history of 46 products, Gort and Klepper found that the length of time before other companies entered the markets created by a few inventive companies declined from an average of 14.4 years for products introduced before 1930 to 4.9 years for those introduced after 1949.

[28]The phrase was originally coined by J. Schumpeter, *Capitalism, Socialism and Democracy* (London: Macmillan, 1950), p. 68.

[29]For a detailed discussion of the importance of the structure of law as a factor explaining economic change and growth, see D. C. North, *Institutions, Institutional Change, and Economic Performance* (Cambridge: Cambridge University Press, 1990).

THE NATURE OF COMPETITIVE ADVANTAGE

Christopher Halloran/Shutterstock.com

E®

Christopher Halloran/Shutterstock.com

CHAPTER 3

INTERNAL ANALYSIS: RESOURCES AND COMPETITIVE ADVANTAGE

OPENING CASE

Southwest Airlines

Southwest Airlines has long been the standout performer in the U.S. airline industry. It is famous for its fares, which are often some 30% lower than those of its major rivals. These low fares are balanced by an even lower cost structure, which has enabled Southwest to record superior profitability even in its down years. Indeed, Southwest has been profitable for 41 consecutive years, making it the envy of an airline industry that has seen more than 180 bankruptcies since 1978. Even during 2001 to 2005—quite possibly the worst four years in the history of the airline industry—when every other major airline lost money, Southwest made money each year and earned a return on invested capital of 5.8 percent.

Southwest operates differently than many of its competitors. While operators like American Airlines and Delta route passengers through hubs, Southwest Airlines flies point-to-point, often through smaller airports. By operating this way, Southwest has found that it can reduce total travel

© Christopher Parypa / Shutterstock.com

time for its passengers. They are not routed through hubs and spend less time on the ground—something that most passengers value. This boosts demand and keeps planes full. Moreover, because it avoids many hubs, Southwest has experienced fewer long delays, which again helps to reduce total travel time. In 2014, a delayed flight at Southwest was on average 48.79 minutes late leaving the gate, compared to 58.9 minutes at Delta and 60.53 minutes at American Airlines. Southwest's high reliability translates into a solid brand reputation and strong demand, which further helps to fill its planes and consequently, reduce costs.

Furthermore, because Southwest because flies point to point rather than through congested airport hubs, there is no need for dozens of gates and thousands of employees to handle banks of flights that come arrive and depart within a 2-hour window, leaving the hub empty until the next flights arrive a few hours later. The result: Southwest operates with far fewer employees than do airlines that fly through hubs

To further reduce costs and boost reliability, Southwest flies only one type of plane, the Boeing 737. This reduces training costs, maintenance costs, and inventory costs while increasing efficiency in crew and flight scheduling. The operation is nearly ticketless and there is no seat assignment, which reduces costs associated with back-office functions. There are no in-flight meals or movies, and the airline will not transfer baggage to other airlines, reducing the need for baggage handlers. Southwest also has high employee productivity, which means fewer employees per passenger. All of this helps to keep costs low. In 2014, for example, Southwest's cost per available seat miles flown was 13.76 cents, compared to 16.80 cents at Delta and 15.84 cents at American Airlines.

To help maintain high employee productivity, Southwest devotes enormous attention to its staff. On average, the company hires only 3% of candidates interviewed in a year. When hiring, it emphasizes teamwork and a positive attitude. Southwest reasons that skills can be taught, but a positive attitude and a willingness to pitch in cannot. Southwest also creates incentives for its employees to work hard. All employees are covered by a profit-sharing plan, and at least 25% of each employee's share in the plan must to be invested in Southwest Airlines stock. This gives rise to a simple formula: The harder employees work, the more profitable Southwest becomes and the more well off the employees become. The results are clear. At other airlines, one would never see a pilot helping to check passengers onto the plane. At Southwest, pilots and flight attendants have been known to help clean the aircraft and check in passengers at the gate in order to get a plane back into the air as quickly as possible, because no plane makes money when it is sitting on the ground. This flexible, motivated workforce leads to higher productivity and reduces the need for more employees.

Sources: M. Brelis, "Simple Strategy Makes Southwest a Model for Success," *Boston Globe*, November 5, 2000, p. F1; M. Trottman, "At Southwest, New CEO Sits in the Hot Seat," *The Wall Street Journal*, July 19, 2004, p. B1; J. Helyar, "Southwest Finds Trouble in the Air," *Fortune*, August 9, 2004, p. 38; Southwest Airlines 10-K 2013; N. Dihora, "Southwest launched international routes on July 1st," Morningstar, July 24, 2014; Bureau of Transportation Statistics at www.transtats.bts.gov/.

▛OVERVIEW

Why, within a particular industry or market, do some companies outperform others? What is the basis of their sustained competitive advantage? The Opening Case provides some clues. For more than four decades, Southwest Airlines has outperformed its rivals in the U.S. airline industry because it offers a more reliable service that delivers more value to its customers at a lower cost than its rivals. Southwest was an *innovator* with regard to strategy, flying point to point between smaller airports. It was *responsive to the needs of its customers*, pursuing strategies that reduced total travel time and increased the r*eliability* of its service. It has done all of this in a very *efficient* way that has lowered the costs of the business and enabled Southwest to offer lower prices and still make profits when its rivals have been losing money. As you will see in this chapter, responding to customer needs by offering them more *value* through innovative and reliable goods and services, and doing so efficiently, are common themes seen in many enterprises that have established a sustainable competitive advantage over their rivals.

This chapter focuses on internal analysis, which is concerned with identifying the strengths and weaknesses of a company. At Southwest, for example, its point-to-point route structure, its investments in employee productivity, and its utilization of only one type of aircraft can all be seen as strengths. Internal analysis, coupled with an analysis of the company's external environment, gives managers the information they need to choose the strategy that will enable their company to attain a sustained competitive advantage.

As explained in this chapter, internal analysis is a three-step process. First, managers must understand the role of rare, valuable, and hard-to-imitate resources in the establishment of competitive advantage. Second, they must appreciate how such resources lead to superior efficiency, innovation, quality, and customer responsiveness. Third, they must be able to analyze the sources of their company's competitive advantage to identify what drives the profitability of their enterprise, and just as importantly, where opportunities for improvement might lie. In other words, they must be able to identify how the strengths of the enterprise boost its profitability and how its weaknesses result in lower profitability.

After reading this chapter, you will understand the nature of competitive advantage and why managers need to perform internal analysis (just as they must conduct industry analysis) in order to achieve superior performance and profitability.

▛COMPETITIVE ADVANTAGE

A company has a *competitive advantage* over its rivals when its profitability is greater than the average profitability of all companies in its industry. It has a *sustained competitive advantage* when it is able to maintain above-average profitability over a number of years (as Southwest has done in the airline industry). The primary objective of strategy is to achieve a sustained competitive advantage, which in turn results in superior profitability and profit growth. What are the sources of competitive advantage, and what is the link between strategy, competitive advantage, and profitability?

Distinctive Competencies

It has long been argued that competitive advantage is based upon the possession of distinctive competencies. **Distinctive competencies** are firm-specific strengths that allow a company to differentiate its products from those offered by rivals and/or achieve substantially lower costs than its rivals. Apple, for example, has a distinctive competence in design. Customers want to own the beautiful devices that Apple markets. Similarly, it can be argued that Toyota, which historically has been the standout performer in the automobile industry, has distinctive competencies in the development and operation of manufacturing processes. Toyota pioneered an entire range of manufacturing techniques such as just-in-time inventory systems, self-managing teams, and reduced setup times for complex equipment. These competencies, collectively known as the "Toyota lean production system," helped the company attain superior efficiency and product quality as the basis of its competitive advantage in the global automobile industry.[1]

distinctive competencies
Firm-specific strengths that allow a company to differentiate its products and/or achieve substantially lower costs to achieve a competitive advantage.

Resources

Distinctive competencies also can be rooted in one or more of a company's resources.[2] **Resources** refer to the factors of production that a company uses to transform inputs into outputs that it can sell in the marketplace. Resources include basic factors of production such as labor, land, management, physical plant, and equipment.

However, any enterprise is more than just a combination of the basic factors of production. Another important factor of production is **process knowledge** about how to develop, produce, and sell a company's output. Process knowledge can be thought of as the organizational equivalent of human skills. Process knowledge resides in the rules, routines, and procedures of an organization; that is, in the style or manner in which managers make decisions and utilize the company's internal processes to achieve organizational objectives.[3] Process knowledge is accumulated by the organization over time and through experience. Organizations, like people, learn by doing, often through trial and error. Process knowledge is often **socially complex**, which means that it diffused among many different individuals, teams, departments, and functions within the company, no one of which possesses all of the knowledge required to develop, produce, and sell its products. Process knowledge also often has an important **tacit** component, meaning that some of it is not documented or codified, but instead is learned by doing and is transmitted to new employees through the culture of the organization.[4]

The organizational architecture of a company is another very important factor of production. By **organizational architecture** we mean the combination of the organizational structure of a company, its control systems, its incentive systems, its organizational culture, and the human capital strategy of the enterprise, particularly with regard to its hiring and employee development and retention strategies. We will explore the concept of organizational architecture in depth in Chapter 12. For now, it is important to understand that companies with well-designed organizational architecture generally outperform those with poorly designed organizational architecture. Getting the organizational structure, control systems, incentives, culture, and human capital strategy of a company right is extremely important. Differences in the efficacy of organizational architecture are a major reason for performance differentials across companies.

resources
Assets of a company.

process knowledge
Knowledge of the internal rules, routines, and procedures of an organization that managers can leverage to achieve organizational objectives.

socially complex
Something that is characterized by, or is the outcome of, the interaction of multiple individuals.

tacit
A characteristic of knowledge or skills such that they cannot be documented or codified but may be understood through experience or intuition.

organizational architecture
The combination of the organizational structure of a company, its control systems, its incentive systems, its organizational culture, and its human-capital strategy.

intellectual property

Knowledge, research, and information that is owned by an individual or organization.

The codified **intellectual property** that a company has created over time represents another important factor of production. Intellectual property takes many forms, such as engineering blueprints, the molecular structure of a new drug, proprietary software code, and brand logos. Companies establish ownership rights over their intellectual property through patents, copyright, and trademarks. For example, Apple has built a powerful brand based on its reputation for high-quality, elegantly designed computing devices. The Apple logo displayed on its hardware products symbolizes that brand. That logo is Apple's intellectual property. It assures the consumer that this is a genuine Apple product. It is protected from imitation by trademark law.

In sum, a company's resources include not just *basic* factors of production such as land, labor, managers, property, and equipment. They also include more *advanced* factors of production such as process knowledge, organizational architecture, and intellectual property. For example, Coca-Cola has been very successful over a prolonged period in the carbonated beverage business. Coke's factors of production include not just labor, land, management, plants, and equipment, but also the *process knowledge* about how to develop, produce, and sell carbonated beverages. Coke is in fact a very strong marketing company—it really knows how to sell its product. Furthermore, Coke has an *organizational architecture* that enables it to manage its functional process well. Coke also has valuable *intellectual property* such as the recipes for its leading beverages (which Coke keeps secret) and its brand, which is protected from imitation by trademark law.

Similarly, Apple is more than just a combination of land, labor, management, plants, and equipment. Apple has world-class *process knowledge* when it comes to developing, producing, and selling its products. Most notably, Apple probably has the best industrial-design group in the computer business. This design group is ultimately responsible for the format, features, look, and feel of Apple's innovative products, including the iPod, iPhone, iPad, and its striking line of desktop and laptop computers. Apple also has a strong *organizational architecture* that enables it to manage the enterprise productively. In particular, the industrial-design group has a very powerful position within Apple's organizational structure. It initiates and coordinates the core product development processes. This includes ensuring that hardware engineering, software engineering, and manufacturing all work to achieve the product specifications mapped out by the design group. Apple is probably unique among computing-device companies in terms of the power and influence granted to its design group. Furthermore, Apple has created extremely valuable *intellectual property*, including the patents underlying its products and the trademark that protects the logo symbolizing the Apple brand.

basic factors of production

Resources such as land, labor, management, plants, and equipment.

advanced factors of production

Resources such as process knowledge, organizational architecture, and intellectual property that contribute to a company's competitive advantage.

Thus, as in the Coke and Apple examples, the resources (or factors of production) of any enterprise include not just **basic factors of production** but also **advanced factors of production**. The important point to understand is that advanced factors of production are not endowments; they are human creations. Skilled managers can and do create these advanced factors of production, often out of little more than thin air, vision, and drive. Apple founder and CEO Steve Jobs, in combination with his handpicked head of industrial design, Jonny Ive, created the process knowledge that underlies Apple's world-class skills in industrial design, and he built an organizational structure that gave the design group a powerful central role.

To summarize: An expanded list of resources includes labor, land, management, plants, equipment, process knowledge, organizational architecture, and intellectual property. As shown in Figure 3.1, a company is in effect a bundle of resources

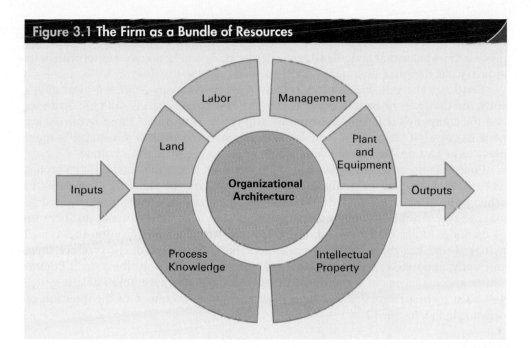

Figure 3.1 The Firm as a Bundle of Resources

(factors of production) that transforms inputs (e.g., raw materials) into outputs (goods or services). The efficiency and effectiveness with which a company performs this transformation process depends critically upon the *quality* of its resources, and most significantly, upon the quality of its advanced factors of production—process knowledge, organizational architecture, and intellectual property. This insight gives rise to other, very important questions. What determines the quality of a company's resources? How do we know if its resources constitute and strength or a weaknesses?

Resource Quality: The VRIO Framework

Jay Barney and Bill Hesterly have developed a framework that represents a useful way for managers to think about the quality of resources.[5] They refer to this framework as the **VRIO framework**, where *V* stands for value, *R* for rarity, *I* for inimitability, and *O* for organization. They encourage managers to ask themselves the following questions when performing an internal analysis:

First, are the company's resources *valuable* in the sense that they enable the enterprise to exploit opportunities and counter threats in the external environment? For example, Apple's product-design skills constitute a valuable resource that has helped the company exploit opportunities to develop new product categories in the computer-device industry with its touch screen iPhone and iPad offerings. At the same time, those skills have also enabled Apple to keep rivals at bay, thereby countering threats. More generally, resources can be judged as valuable if they (a) enable a company to create strong demand for its products, and/or (b) lower the costs of producing those products.

Second, are those resources *rare*? If they are not rare and rivals also have access to them, by definition they cannot be a source of competitive advantage. For a company

VRIO framework

A framework managers use to determine the quality of a company's resources, where *V* is value, *R* is rarity, *I* is inimitability, and *O* is for organization.

to gain a competitive advantage, it must have some resource that is superior to that possessed by its rivals. It cannot be a commodity; it must be uncommon. Thus, the process knowledge that underlies Apple's design skills is rare; no other enterprise in its industry has a similar, high-quality skill set.

Third, are the valuable and rare resources of the company *inimitable*? Put differently, are they easy or hard to copy? If they are easy to copy, rivals will quickly do so, and the company's competitive advantage will erode. However, if those resources are hard to copy—if they are inimitable–the company's competitive advantage is more likely to be sustainable. Apple's design skills appear to be difficult to imitate.

Fourth, is the company *organized* and managed in a way that enables it to exploit its rare, valuable, and inimitable resources and capture the value they produce? In other words, does the firm have the broader *organizational architecture* required to make the most out of its unique strengths? Apple has been successful not just because of its design skills, but because those skills reside within an organization that is well managed and has the capability to take superbly designed products, produce them efficiently, and market and distribute them to customers. Without the correct organization and management systems, even firms with valuable, rare, inimitable resource will be at a competitive disadvantage. As noted above, we return to the question of organizing in Chapter 12.

Resources and Sustained Competitive Advantage

This discussion leads logically to another very important question: Which valuable resources are most likely to result in a long-term, *sustainable* competitive advantage? The quick answer is process knowledge, organizational architecture, and intellectual property. As we shall argue below, these resources or advanced factors of production are more likely to be rare and are in general more difficult for rivals to imitate.

Rare Resource   Consider the issue of rareness or scarcity with regard to basic factors of production. In general, land, labor, management, plants, and equipment are purchased on the open market. Of course, these resources are not homogenous; some employees are more productive than others; some land has more value; some managers have better skills. Over time, however, this becomes evident and the more productive resources will command a higher price for their services. You simply have to pay more for the best land, employees, managers, and equipment. Indeed, in a free market the price of such resources will be bid up to reflect their economic value, and the sellers of those resources, as opposed to the firm, will capture much of that value.

Now consider process knowledge and organizational architecture. These are likely to be heterogeneous. No two companies are exactly the same. Each has its own history, which impacts the way activities are organized and processes managed within the enterprise. The way in which product development is managed at Apple, for example, differs from the way it is managed at Microsoft or Samsung. Marketing at Coca Cola might differ in subtle but important ways from marketing at Pepsi Cola. The human resource function at Nucor Steel might be organized in such a way that it raises employee productivity above the level achieved by U.S. Steel. Each organization has its own culture, its own way of doing certain things. As a result of strategic vision, systematic process-improvement efforts, trial and error, or just blind luck, some companies will develop process knowledge and organizational architecture that is of higher quality than that of their rivals. By definition, such resources will be rare, since they are a *path-dependent* consequence of the history of the company. Moreover, the firm "owns" its process knowledge and organizational architecture. It does not buy these from a provider, so it is in a position to capture the full economic value of these resources.

Intellectual property that is protected by patents, copyright, or trademarks is also by definition rare. You can only patent something that no-one else has patented. A copyright protects the *unique* creation of an individual, or a company, and prevents anyone from copying it. The software code underlying Microsoft Windows, for example, is copyrighted, so no one else can use the same code without express permission from Microsoft. Similarly, a trademark protects the *unique* symbols, names, or logos of a company, preventing them from being copied and in effect making them rare. Rivals cannot use the Apple logo; it is Apple's unique property—thus it is rare.

Barriers to Imitation Now let's consider the issue of inimitability. If a company develops a rare, valuable resource that enables it to create more demand, charge a higher price, and/or lower its costs, how easy will it be for rivals to copy that resource? Put differently, what are the **barriers to imitation**?[6]

barriers to imitation
Factors or characteristics that make it difficult for another individual or company to replicate something.

Consider first intellectual property. The ability of rivals to copy a firm's intellectual property depends foremost upon the efficacy of the intellectual property regime in a nation state. In advanced nations such as the United States or the member states of the European Union, for example, where there is a well-established body of intellectual property law, direct imitation is outlawed and violators are likely to be sued for damages. This legal protection prevents most enterprises from engaging in direct copying of intellectual property. However, in developing nations with no well-established body of intellectual property law, copying may be widespread given the absence of legal sanctions. This used to be the case in China, for example, but it is becoming less common as the Chinese legal system adopts international norms with regard to patents, copyrights, and trademarks.

Even though direct copying is outlawed, it is certainly possible for companies to invent their way around their rivals' intellectual property through reverse engineering, producing a functionally similar piece of technology that works in a slightly different way to produce the same result. This seems to be a particular problem with regard to patented knowledge. Patents accord the inventor 20 years of legal protection from direct imitation, but research suggests that rivals invent their way around 60% of patent innovations within 4 years.[7] On the other hand, trademarks are initially protected from imitation for 10 years but can be renewed every 10 years. Moreover, it is almost impossible for a rival to copy a company's trademark protected logo and brand name without violating the law. This is important, for logos and brand names are powerful symbols. As such trademarks can insulate a company's brand from direct attack by rivals, which builds something of an economic moat around companies with strong brands.

A company's rare and valuable process knowledge can be very hard for rivals to copy; the barriers to imitation are high. There are two main reasons for this. First, process knowledge is often (1) partly tacit, (2) hidden from view within the firm, and (3) socially complex. As such, it is difficult for outsiders to identify with precision the nature of a company's rare and valuable process knowledge. We refer to this problem as **causal ambiguity**.[8] Moreover, the socially complex nature of such knowledge means that hiring individual employees away from a successful firm to gain access to its process knowledge may be futile, because each individual only has direct experience with part of the overall knowledge base.

causal ambiguity
When the way that one thing, A, leads to an outcome (or "causes"), B, is not clearly understood.

Second, even if a rival were able to identify with precision the form of a company's valuable and rare process knowledge, it still has to implement that knowledge within its own organization. This not easy to do; it requires changing the way the imitating company currently operates. Such change can be stymied by organizational inertia. We discuss organizational inertia in more detail in Chapter 12, but for now note that organizational structure, routines, and culture are notoriously hard to change. The reasons include opposition from organizational members whose power and influence will be reduced as a result of the change, and the difficulties associated with changing the culture of an organization, particularly old habits, old ways of doing things, and old ways of perceiving the world. Typically, process change takes a sustained effort over several years, during which time the company that is the target of imitation efforts may have accumulated new knowledge and moved on.

An inability to imitate valuable process knowledge seems to have been a problem in the U.S. automobile industry, where attempts by Ford and GM to imitate Toyota's lean production systems were held back for years, if not decades, by their own internal inertia. These included objections from unions to proposals to change work practices, the legacy of decades of investment in factories configured to mass production rather than lean production, and an organizational culture that resisted change that altered the balance of power and influence within the company.

Organizational architecture that is rare and valuable can also be very hard for rivals to imitate, for many of the same reasons that process knowledge is hard to imitate. Specifically, even if the would-be imitator can identify with precision the features of a successful company's value creating organizational architecture, adopting that architecture might require wholesale organizational change, which is both risky and difficult to do given internal inertia.

Implications   In sum, we have demonstrated how *advanced* factors of production such as intellectual property, process knowledge, and organizational architecture are more likely to be rare, and will be harder to imitate due to high barriers to imitation, than more basic factors of production. Put differently, advanced factors of production are more likely to constitute the unique strengths of an organization. A number of implications flow from this insight.

First, it is clearly important for managers to vigorously protect their intellectual property from imitation both by establishing their intellectual property rights (e.g., by filing for patent, copyright or trademark protection), and by asserting those rights, legally challenging rivals who try to violate them. This said, it is sometimes best not to patent valuable technology but instead keep it as a trade secret, because that can make imitation more difficult. Coca Cola, for example, has never patented the recipe underlying its core Coke brand, because filing a patent would reveal valuable information about the recipe.

Second, given that process knowledge is often an important source of sustainable competitive advantage, managers would be well advised to devote considerable attention to optimizing their processes. They might, for example, invest time and effort in process improvement methodologies such as Six Sigma (which we shall discuss in Chapter 4). Similarly, given the importance of organizational architecture, it is crucial for managers to assure that their company's organization is optimal. Thinking critically and proactively about organizational design becomes a very important task (as we discuss in Chapter 12).

Third, it is important to protect knowledge about superior processes and practices from leaking out. For example, Intel, a very efficient manufacturer of microprocessors, has developed valuable technology to improve its manufacturing processes but has chosen not to patent it. Instead, it treats the underlying knowledge as a trade secret. Intel's reasoning is that if the technology were patented, the patent filing would make available crucial information about the technology, making imitation by rivals more likely.

Fourth, if a company has developed rare and valuable process knowledge in core functional activities of the firm, it would be unwise for the firm to outsource those activities to a third-party producer in pursuit of a perceived short-term cost saving or other transitory benefit. Some observers believed that Boeing made this mistake when it decided to outsource production for horizontal stabilizers for its 737 aircraft to Chinese subcontractors. Horizontal stabilizers are the horizontal winglets on the tail section of an aircraft. Historically, Boeing designed and built these and as a consequence it accumulated rare and valuable design and manufacturing process knowledge. In the late 1990s, Boeing outsourced production of horizontal stabilizers in exchange for the tacit promise for more orders from Chinese airlines. Although this benefitted Boeing in the short run, it gave Chinese manufacturers the chance to develop their own process knowledge, while Boeing stopped accumulating important process knowledge. Today, Chinese aircraft manufacturers are building a competitor to Boeing's 737 aircraft, and Boeing may well have helped them do that through outsource decisions that diminished the company's long-run competitive advantage.

▛ VALUE CREATION AND PROFITABILITY

We have discussed how competitive advantage based upon valuable, rare, inimitable resources that reside within a well-organized, well-managed firm constitute unique strengths that lead to a sustained competitive advantage. In this section, we take a deeper look at how such resources (strengths) translate into superior profitability.

At the most basic level, a company's profitability depends on three factors: (1) the value customers place on the company's products, (2) the price that a company charges for its products, and (3) the costs of creating those products. The value customers place on a product reflects the *utility* they derive from it, or the happiness or satisfaction gained from consuming or owning it. Value must be distinguished from price. Value is something that customers receive from a product. It is a function of the attributes of the product such as its performance, design, quality, and point-of-sale and after-sale service. For example, most customers would place a much higher value on a top-end Lexus from Toyota than on a low-end, basic economy car from Kia, precisely because they perceive Lexus to have better performance and superior design, quality, and service. A company that strengthens the value of its products in the eyes of customers enhances its brand and has more pricing options: It can raise prices to reflect that value, or keep prices lower to induce more customers to purchase its products, thereby expanding unit sales volume.

Regardless of the pricing option a company chooses, that price is typically less than the value placed upon the good or service by the customer. This is because the customer captures some of that value in the form of what economists call a *consumer surplus*.

This occurs because it is normally impossible to segment the market to such a degree that the company can charge each customer a price that reflects that individual's unique assessment of the value of a product—what economists refer to as a customer's *reservation price*. In addition, because the company is competing against rivals for customers, it has to charge a lower price than it could were it a monopoly. For these reasons, the point-of-sale price tends to be less than the value placed on the product by many customers. Nevertheless, remember this basic principle: The more value that consumers derive from a company's goods or services, the more pricing options that company has.

These concepts are illustrated in Figure 3.2. V is the *average* value per unit of a product to a customer; P is the average price per unit that the company decides to charge for that product; and C is the average unit cost of producing that product (including actual production costs and the cost of capital investments in production systems). The company's average profit per unit is equal to $P - C$, and the consumer surplus is equal to $V - P$. In other words, $V - P$ is a measure of the value the consumer captures, and $P - C$ is a measure of the value the company captures. The company makes a profit so long as P is more than C, and its profitability will be greater the lower C is relative to P. Bear in mind that the difference between V and P is in part determined by the intensity of competitive pressure in the marketplace; the lower the competitive pressure's intensity, the higher the price that can be charged relative to V, but the difference between V and P is also determined by the company's pricing choice.[9]

As we shall see, a company may choose to keep prices low relative to volume because lower prices enable the company to sell more products, attain scale economies, and boost its profit margin by lowering C relative to P.

Also, note that the *value created by a company* is measured by the difference between the value or utility a consumer gets from the product (V) and the costs of production (C), that is, $V - C$. A company creates value by converting inputs that cost C into a good or service from which customers derive a value of V. A company can create more value for its customers by lowering C or making the product more attractive through superior design, performance, quality, service, and other factors. When customers assign a greater value to the product (V increases), they are willing to pay a higher price (P increases). This discussion suggests that a company

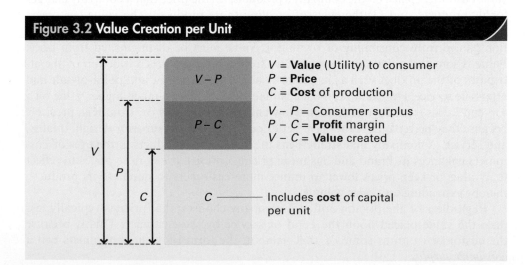

Figure 3.2 Value Creation per Unit

$V - P$

$P - C$

V

P

C

V = **Value** (Utility) to consumer
P = **Price**
C = **Cost** of production

$V - P$ = Consumer surplus
$P - C$ = **Profit** margin
$V - C$ = **Value** created

C ——— Includes **cost** of capital per unit

has a competitive advantage and high profitability when it creates more value for its customers than rivals.[10]

The company's pricing options are captured in Figure 3.3. Suppose a company's current pricing option is the one pictured in the middle column of Figure 3.3. Imagine that the company decides to pursue strategies to increase the utility of its product offering from V to V^* in order to boost its profitability. Increasing value initially raises production costs because the company must spend money in order to increase product performance, quality, service, and other factors. Now there are two different pricing options that the company can pursue. Option 1 is to raise prices to reflect the higher value: the company raises prices more than its costs increase, and profit per unit ($P - C$) increases. Option 2 involves a very different set of choices: The company lowers prices in order to expand unit volume. Generally, customers recognize that they are getting a great bargain because the price is now much lower than the value (the consumer surplus has increased), so they rush out to buy more (demand has increased). As unit volume expands due to increased demand, the company is able to realize scale economies and reduce its average unit costs. Although creating the extra value initially costs more, and although margins are initially compressed by aggressive pricing, ultimately profit margins widen because the average per-unit cost of production falls as volume increases and scale economies are attained.

Managers must understand the dynamic relationships among value, pricing, demand, and costs in order to make decisions that will maximize competitive advantage and profitability. Option 2 in Figure 3.3, for example, may not be a viable strategy if demand did not increase rapidly with lower prices, or if few economies of scale will result by increasing volume. Managers must understand how value creation and pricing decisions affect demand, as well as how unit costs change with increases in volume. In other words, they must clearly comprehend the demand for their company's product and its cost structure at different levels of output if they are to make decisions that maximize profitability.

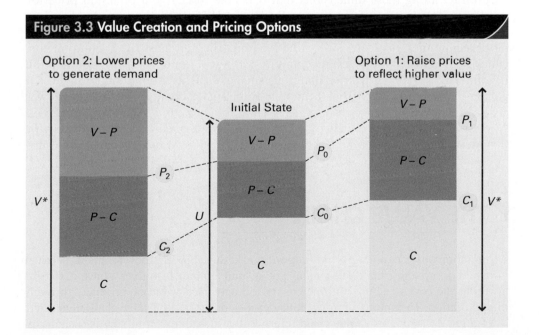

Figure 3.3 Value Creation and Pricing Options

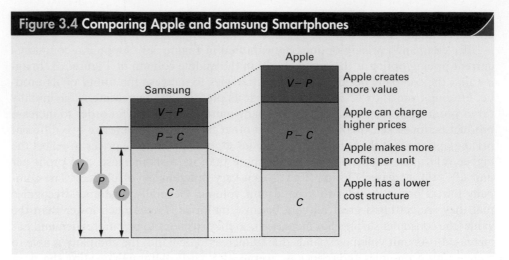

Figure 3.4 Comparing Apple and Samsung Smartphones

The most beneficial position for a company occurs when it can utilize its valuable, rare, inimitable resources and capabilities to deliver a product offering that consumers value more highly than that of rivals (that is, they derive more utility from it), and which can be produced at a lower cost than that of rivals. This is an outcome that many companies strive to achieve. Consider again the example of Apple and its successful iPhone offering. Apple creates value for consumers with the elegance of its design for the iPhone, its intuitive, easy-to-use interface, its onboard applications such as iTunes and iCloud, and the fact that Apple has encouraged a healthy ecosystem of developers to write third-party applications that run on the phone. Apple has been so successful at differentiating its product along these dimensions that it is able to charge a premium price for its iPhone relative to offerings from Samsung, HTC, and the like. At the same time, it sells so many iPhones that the company has been able to achieve enormous economies of scale in production and the purchasing of components, which has driven down the average unit cost of the iPhone. Thus, even though the iPhone makes use of expensive materials such as brushed aluminum casing and a gorilla-glass screen, Apple has been able to charge a higher price *and* has lower costs than its rivals. Hence, although Samsung sold more units than Apple in 2013, Apple was able to capture 75% of all profit in the global smartphone industry for that year. Samsung captured the remaining 25%, with no other smartphone supplier making money.

THE VALUE CHAIN

value chain

The concept that a company consists of a chain of activities that transforms inputs into outputs.

All functions of a company—production, marketing, product development, service, information systems, materials management, and human resources—have a role in lowering the cost structure and increasing the perceived value of products through differentiation. To explore this idea, consider the concept of the value chain illustrated in Figure 3.5.[11] The term **value chain** refers to the idea that a company is a chain of

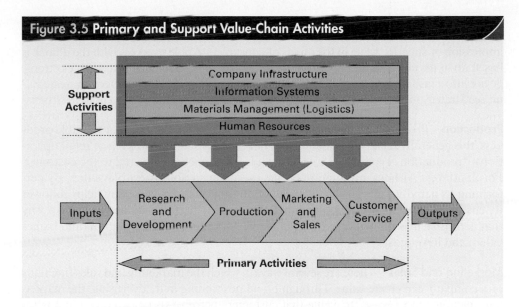

Figure 3.5 Primary and Support Value-Chain Activities

functional activities that transforms inputs into outputs. The transformation process involves both primary activities and support activities. Value is added to the product at each stage in the chain. Valuable, rare, inimitable resources can be found within one or more of a company's value-chain activities.

Primary Activities

Primary activities include the design, creation, and delivery of the product, the product's marketing, and its support and after-sales service. In the value chain illustrated in Figure 3.5, the primary activities are broken down into four functions: research and development, production, marketing and sales, and customer service.

Research and Development   Research and development (R&D) refers to the design of products and production processes. We may think of R&D as being associated with the design of physical products such as an iPhone or a Toyota, and/or production processes in manufacturing enterprises, service companies also undertake R&D. For example, banks compete with each other by developing new financial products and new ways of delivering those products to customers. Online banking and smart debit cards are examples of the fruits of new-product development in the banking industry. Earlier innovations in the banking industry include ATM machines, credit cards, and debit cards.

By creating superior product design, R&D can increase the functionality of products, making them more attractive to customers and thereby adding value. Alternatively, R&D may result in more efficient production processes, thereby lowering production costs. Either way, R&D can lower costs or raise a product's value, thus permitting a company to charge higher prices. At Intel, R&D creates value by developing ever-more powerful microprocessors and pioneering ever-more efficient manufacturing processes (in conjunction with equipment suppliers).

primary activities
activities related to the design, creation, and delivery of the product, its marketing, and its support and after-sales service.

It is important to emphasize that R&D is not just about enhancing the features and functions of a product; it is also about the elegance of product design, which can create an impression of superior value in the minds of consumers. Apple's success with the iPhone is based upon the elegance and appeal of the iPhone design, which has turned an electronic device into a fashion accessory. For another example of how design elegance can create value, see Strategy in Action 3.1, which discusses value creation at the fashion house Burberry.

Production   Production refers to the creation of a good or service. For tangible products, this generally means manufacturing. For services such as banking or retail operations, "production" typically takes place while the service is delivered to the customer. For Southwest Airlines, production occurs every time a Southwest plane flies. By performing its activities efficiently, the production function of a company helps to lower its cost structure. The production function can also perform its activities in a way that is consistent with high product quality, which leads to differentiation (and higher value) and lower costs.

Marketing and Sales   There are several ways in which the marketing and sales functions of a company can create value. Through brand positioning and advertising, the marketing function can increase the value that customers perceive to be contained in a company's product (and thus the utility they attribute to the product). Insofar as these help to create a favorable impression of the company's product in the minds of customers, they increase utility. For example, the French company Perrier persuaded U.S. customers that slightly carbonated, bottled water was worth $2.50 per bottle rather than a price closer to the $1.00 that it cost to collect, bottle, and distribute the water. Perrier's marketing function increased the perception of value that customers ascribed to the product. Similarly, by helping to rebrand the company and its product offering, the marketing department at Burberry helped to create value (see Strategy in Action 3.1). Marketing and sales can also create value by discovering customer needs and communicating them back to the R&D function , which can then design products that better match those needs.

Customer Service   The role of the service function of an enterprise is to provide after-sales service and support. This function can create superior utility by solving customer problems and supporting customers after they have purchased the product. For example, Caterpillar, the U.S.-based manufacturer of heavy earth-moving equipment, can ship spare parts to any location in the world within 24 hours, thereby minimizing the amount of downtime its customers face if their Caterpillar equipment malfunctions. This is an extremely valuable support capability in an industry where downtime is very expensive. The extent of customer support has helped to increase the utility that customers associate with Caterpillar products, and therefore the price that Caterpillar can charge for them.

Support Activities

support activities

Activities of the value chain that provide inputs that allow the primary activities to take place.

The **support activities** of the value chain provide inputs that allow the primary activities to take place. These activities are broken down into four functions: materials management (or logistics), human resources, information systems, and company infrastructure (see Figure 3.5).

Materials Management (Logistics)   The materials-management (or logistics) function controls the transmission of physical materials through the value chain, from

3.1 STRATEGY IN ACTION

Value Creation at Burberry

When Rose Marie Bravo, the highly regarded president of Saks Fifth Avenue, announced in 1997 that she was leaving to become CEO of ailing British fashion house Burberry, people thought she was crazy. Burberry, best known as a designer of raincoats with a trademark tartan lining, had been described as an outdated, stuffy business with a fashion cachet of almost zero. When Bravo stepped down in 2006, she was heralded in Britain and the United States as one of the world's best managers. In her tenure at Burberry, she had engineered a remarkable turnaround, leading a transformation of Burberry into what one commentator called an "achingly hip" high-end fashion brand whose famous tartan bedecks everything from raincoats and bikinis to handbags and luggage in a riot of color from pink to blue to purple. In less than a decade, Burberry had become one of the most valuable luxury fashion brands in the world.

When asked how she achieved the transformation, Bravo explained that there was hidden value in the brand, which was unleashed by constant creativity and innovation. Bravo hired world-class designers to redesign Burberry's tired fashion line and bought in Christopher Bailey, one of the very best, to lead the design team. The marketing department worked closely with advertisers to develop hip ads that would appeal to a younger, well-heeled audience. The ads featured supermodel Kate Moss promoting the line, and Burberry hired a top fashion photographer to shoot Moss in Burberry. Burberry exercised tight control over distribution, pulling its products from stores whose image was not consistent with the Burberry brand, and expanding its own chain of Burberry stores.

Bravo also noted that "creativity doesn't just come from designers ... ideas can come from the sales floor, the marketing department, even from accountants, believe it or not. People at whatever level they are working have a point of view and have something to say that is worth listening to." Bravo emphasized the importance of teamwork: "One of the things I think people overlook is the quality of the team. It isn't one person, and it isn't two people. It is a whole group of people—a team that works cohesively toward a goal—that makes something happen or not." She notes that her job is to build the team and then motivate the team, "keeping them on track, making sure that they are following the vision."

Sources: Quotes from S. Beatty, "Bass Talk: Plotting Plaid's Future," *The Wall Street Journal*, September 9, 2004, p. B1; C. M. Moore and G. Birtwistle, "The Burberry Business Model," *International Journal of Retail and Distribution Management* 32 (2004): 412–422; M. Dickson, "Bravo's Legacy in Transforming Burberry," *Financial Times*, October 6, 2005, p. 22.

procurement through production and into distribution. The efficiency with which this is carried out can significantly lower cost, thereby generating profit. A company that has benefited from very efficient materials management, the Spanish fashion company Zara, is discussed in Strategy in Action 3.2, see Figure 3.4.

Human Resources   There are numerous ways in which the human resource function can help an enterprise create more value. This function ensures that the company has the right combination of skilled people to perform its value creation activities effectively. It is also the job of the human resource function to ensure that people are adequately trained, motivated, and compensated to perform their value creation tasks. If the human resources are functioning well, employee productivity rises (which lowers costs) and customer service

3.2 STRATEGY IN ACTION

Competitive Advantage at Zara

Fashion retailer Zara is one of Spain's fastest-growing and most successful companies, with sales of some $10 billion and a network of 6,500 stores in 88 countries. Zara's competitive advantage centers around one thing: speed. Whereas it takes most fashion houses 6 to 9 months to go from design to delivering merchandise to a store, Zara can complete the entire process in just 5 weeks. This competitive advantage enables Zara to quickly respond to changing fashion trends.

Zara achieves this by breaking many of the rules of operation in the fashion business. Whereas most fashion houses outsource production, Zara has its own factories and keeps approximately half of its production in-house. Zara also has its own designers and its own stores. Its designers, who are in constant contact with the stores, track what is selling on a real-time basis through information systems and talk to store managers weekly to get their impressions of what is "hot." This information supplements data gathered from other sources such as fashion shows.

Drawing on this information, Zara's designers create approximately 40,000 new designs a year, 10,000 of which are selected for production. Zara then purchases basic textiles from global suppliers, but performs capital-intensive production activities in its own factories. These factories use computer-controlled machinery to cut

pieces for garments. Zara does not produce in large volumes to attain economies of scale; instead, it produces in small lots. Labor-intensive activities such as sewing are performed by subcontractors located close to Zara's factories. Zara makes a practice of retaining more production capacity than necessary, so that when a new fashion trend emerges it can quickly respond by designing garments and ramping up production.

Completed garments are delivered to one of Zara's own warehouses, and then shipped to its own stores once a week. Zara deliberately underproduces products, supplying small batches of products in hot demand before quickly shifting to the next fashion trend. Often, its merchandise sells out quickly. The empty shelves in Zara stores create a scarcity value—which helps to generate demand. Customers quickly snap up products they like because they know these styles may soon be out of stock and never produced again.

As a result of this strategy, which is supported by competencies in design, information systems, and logistics management, Zara carries less inventory than its competitors (Zara's inventory equals about 10% of sales, compared to 15% at rival stores such as The Gap and Benetton). This means fewer price reductions to move products that haven't sold, and higher profit margins.

Sources: "Shining Examples," *The Economist: A Survey of Logistics,* June 17, 2006, pp. 4–6; K. Capell et al., "Fashion Conquistador," *Business Week,* September 4, 2006, pp. 38–39; K. Ferdows et al., "Rapid Fire Fulfillment," *Harvard Business Review* 82 (November 2004): 101–107; "Inditex is a leader in the fast fashion industry," *Morningstar,* December 15, 2009; "Pull based centralized manufacturing yields cost efficiencies for Zara," *Morningstar,* June 19, 2014.

improves (which raises value to consumers), thereby enabling the company to create more value. This has certainly been the case at Southwest Airlines, and it helps to explain the persistently low cost structure and high reliability of that company (see the Opening Case).

Information Systems Information systems are, primarily, the digital systems for managing inventory, tracking sales, pricing products, selling products, dealing with customer service inquiries, and so on. Modern information systems, coupled with the communications features of the Internet, have enabled many enterprises to significantly improve the efficiency and effectiveness with which they manage their other value creation activities. World-class information systems are an aspect of Zara's competitive advantage (see Strategy in Action 3.2).

Company Infrastructure   Company infrastructure is the companywide context within which all the other value creation activities take place. This includes organizational structure, control systems, incentive systems, and organizational culture—what we refer to as the organizational architecture of a company. The company infrastructure also includes corporate-level legal, accounting, and finance functions. Because top management can exert considerable influence upon shaping all of these aspects of a company, top management should also be viewed as part of the infrastructure. Indeed, through strong leadership, top management can shape the infrastructure of a company and, through that, the performance of all other value creation activities that take place within it. A good example of this process is given in Strategy in Action 3.1, which looks at how Rose Marie Bravo helped to engineer a turnaround at Burberry.

Value-Chain Analysis: Implications

The concept of the value chain is useful because, when performing an internal analysis, managers can look at the different value-chain activities of the firm, identifying which activities result in the creation of the most value and which are not performing as well as they might be. In other words, value-chain analysis is a useful tool that helps managers identify the company's strengths and weaknesses. Furthermore, it helps managers pinpoint where valuable, rare, and inimitable resources reside within the company.

If managers are to perform a rigorous value-chain analysis, they need to do several things. First, they must analyze how efficiently and effectively each activity is being performed. This should go beyond a qualitative assessment to include an in-depth analysis of quantitative data. For example, the efficiency of the materials-management function might be measured by inventory turnover; the effectiveness of the customer service function might be measured by the speed with which customer complaints are satisfactorily resolved; and ability of the enterprise to deliver reliable products might be measured by customer returns and warranty costs. Managers need to identify those quantitative measures that are important for their business, collect data on them, and assess how well the firm is performing.

Second, as an aid to this process, whenever possible managers should benchmark each activity against a similar activity performed by rivals to see how well the company is doing. **Benchmarking** requires a company to measure how well it is performing against other enterprises using strategically relevant data. An airline, for example, can benchmark its activities against rivals by using publically available data that covers important aspects of airline performance such as departure and arrival delays, revenue per seat mile, and cost per seat mile. Government agencies, industry associations, or third-party providers may collect such data. The Department of Transportation and the Air Transport Industry Association collect a wealth of valuable information on the airline industry. Similarly, the market research company J.D. Power provides important information on product quality and customer satisfaction for companies operating in a number of industries, including automobiles and wireless telecommunications. With regard to Web-based businesses, comScore.com collects a trove of valuable information on web traffic, search-engine performance, advertising conversions, and so on.

Third, in addition to benchmarking performance against rivals, it can be valuable to benchmark performance against best-in-class companies in other industries.

benchmarking
Measuring how well a company is doing by comparing it to another company, or to itself, over time.

For example, Apple is known for excellent customer services in its stores (through the Genius Bar). Comcast has a reputation for poor customer service. Thus, managers at Comcast might want to benchmark their customer service activities against Apple. Although Apple and Comcast are very different organizations, the comparison might yield useful insights that could help Comcast improve its performance.

Fourth, there are a number of process improvement methodologies that managers can and should use to analyze how well value creation activities are performing, and to identify opportunities for improving the efficiency and effectiveness of those activities. One of the most famous process improvement tools, *Six Sigma*, is discussed in more detail in Chapter 4. Finally, whenever there is potential for improvement within a value-chain activity, leaders within the company need to (a) empower managers to take the necessary actions, (b) measure performance improvements over time against goals, (c) reward managers for meeting or exceeding improvement goals, and (d) when goals are not met, analyze why this is so and take corrective action if necessary.

THE BUILDING BLOCKS OF COMPETITIVE ADVANTAGE

Four factors help a company build and sustain competitive advantage: superior efficiency, quality, innovation, and customer responsiveness. We call these factors the building blocks of competitive advantage. Each factor is the *result* of the way the various value-chain activities within an enterprise are performed. By performing value-chain activities to achieve superior efficiency, quality, innovation, and customer responsiveness, a company can (1) differentiate its product offering, and hence offer more value to its customers, and (2) lower its cost structure (see Figure 3.6). Although each factor

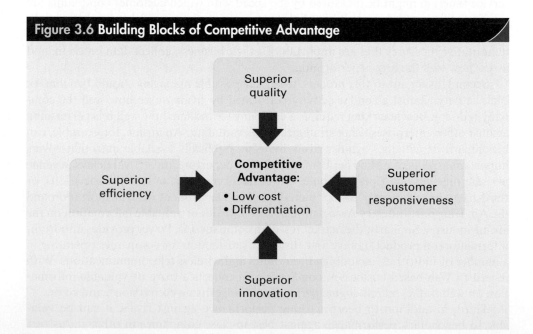

Figure 3.6 Building Blocks of Competitive Advantage

is discussed sequentially below, all are highly interrelated, and the important ways in which these building blocks affect each other should be noted. For example, superior quality can lead to superior efficiency, and innovation can enhance efficiency, quality, and responsiveness to customers.

Efficiency

The simplest measure of efficiency is the quantity of inputs required to produce a given output; that is, efficiency = outputs/inputs. The more efficient a company is, the fewer inputs it requires to produce a particular output, and the lower its costs.

One common measure of efficiency is employee productivity. **Employee productivity** refers to the output produced per employee. For example, if it takes General Motors 30 hours of employee time to assemble a car, and it takes Ford 25 hours, we can say that Ford has higher employee productivity than GM and is more efficient. As long as other factors such as wage rates are equal, we can assume from this information that Ford will have a lower cost structure than GM. Thus, employee productivity helps a company attain a competitive advantage through a lower cost structure.

Another important measure of efficiency is capital productivity. **Capital productivity** refers to the output produced by a dollar of capital invested in the business. Firms that use their capital very efficiently and don't waste it on unproductive assets or activities will have higher capital productivity. For example, a firm that adopts just-in-time inventory systems to reduce both its inventory and its need for warehouse facilities will use less working capital (have less capital tied up in inventory) and less fixed capital (have less capital tied up in warehouses). Consequently, its capital productivity will increase.

employee productivity
The output produced per employee.

capital productivity
The sales produced by a dollar of capital invested in the business.

Quality as Excellence and Reliability

A product can be thought of as a bundle of attributes.[12] The attributes of many physical products include their form, features, performance, durability, reliability, style, and design.[13] A product is said to have *superior quality* when customers perceive that its attributes provide them with higher utility than the attributes of products sold by rivals. For example, a Rolex watch has attributes such as design, styling, performance, and reliability that customers perceive as being superior to the same attributes in many other watches. Thus, we can refer to a Rolex as a high-quality product: Rolex has differentiated its watches by these attributes.

When customers evaluate the quality of a product, they commonly measure it against two kinds of attributes: those related to *quality as excellence* and those related to *quality as reliability*. From a quality-as-excellence perspective, the important attributes are a product's design and styling, its aesthetic appeal, its features and functions, the level of service associated with delivery of the product, and so on. For example, customers can purchase a pair of imitation-leather boots for $20 from Wal-Mart, or they can buy a handmade pair of butter-soft, leather boots from Nordstrom for $500. The boots from Nordstrom will have far superior styling, feel more comfortable, and look much better than those from Wal-Mart. The value consumers get from the Nordstrom boots will in all probability be much greater than the value derived from the Wal-Mart boots, but of course they will have to pay far more for them. That is the point: When excellence is built into a product offering, consumers must pay more to own or consume it.

With regard to quality as reliability, a product can be said to be reliable when it consistently performs the function it was designed for, performs it well, and rarely, if ever, breaks down. As with excellence, reliability increases the value (utility) a consumer derives from a product, and thus affects the price the company can charge for that product and/or the demand for that product.

The position of a product against two dimensions, reliability and other attributes, can be plotted as shown in Figure 3.7. For example, Verizon has the most reliable network in the wireless service industry as measured by factors such as coverage, number of dropped calls, dead zones, and so on. Verizon also has the best ratings when it comes to excellence, as measured by download speeds, customer care, and the like. According to J.D. Power surveys, T-Mobile has the worst position in the industry as measured by reliability and excellence.

The concept of quality applies whether we are talking about Toyota automobiles, clothes designed and sold by Zara, Verizon's wireless service, the customer service department of Citibank, or the ability of airlines to arrive on time. Quality is just as relevant to services as it is to goods.[14]

The impact of high product quality on competitive advantage is twofold.[15] First, providing high-quality products increases the value (utility) those products provide to customers, which gives the company the option of charging a higher price for the products. In the automobile industry, for example, Toyota has historically been able to charge a higher price for its cars because of the higher quality of its products.

Second, greater efficiency and lower unit costs associated with reliable products of high quality impact competitive advantage. When products are reliable, less employee time is wasted making defective products, or providing substandard services, and less time has to be spent fixing mistakes—which means higher employee productivity and lower unit costs. Thus, high product quality not only enables a company to differentiate its product from that of rivals, but, if the product is reliable, it also lowers costs.

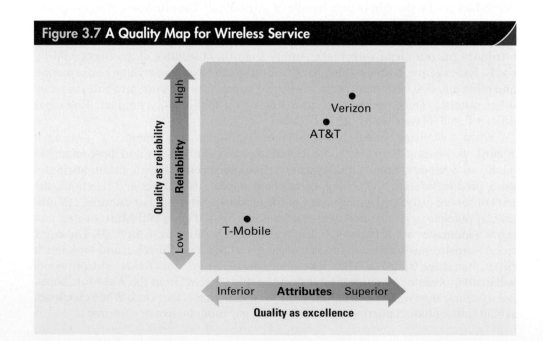

Figure 3.7 A Quality Map for Wireless Service

The importance of reliability in building competitive advantage has increased dramatically over the past 30 years. The emphasis many companies place on reliability is so crucial to achieving high product reliability that it can no longer be viewed as just one way of gaining a competitive advantage. In many industries, it has become an absolute imperative for a company's survival.

Innovation

There are two main types of innovation: product innovation and process innovation. **Product innovation** is the development of products that are new to the world or have superior attributes to existing products. Examples are Intel's invention of the microprocessor in the early 1970s, Cisco's development of the router for routing data over the Internet in the mid-1980s, and Apple's development of the iPod, iPhone, and iPad in the 2000s. **Process innovation** is the development of a new process for producing and delivering products to customers. Examples include Toyota, which developed a range of new techniques collectively known as the "Toyota lean production system" for making automobiles: just-in-time inventory systems, self-managing teams, and reduced setup times for complex equipment.

Product innovation generates value by creating new products, or enhanced versions of existing products, that customers perceive as having more value, thus increasing the company's pricing options. Process innovation often allows a company to create more value by lowering production costs. Toyota's lean production system helped boost employee productivity, thus giving Toyota a cost-based competitive advantage.[16] Similarly, Staples dramatically lowered the cost of selling office supplies by applying the supermarket business model to retail office supplies. Staples passed on some of this cost savings to customers in the form of lower prices, which enabled the company to increase its market share rapidly.

In the long run, innovation of products and processes is perhaps the most important building block of competitive advantage.[17] Competition can be viewed as a process driven by innovations. Although not all innovations succeed, those that do can be a major source of competitive advantage because, by definition, they give a company something unique that its competitors lack (at least until they imitate the innovation). Uniqueness can allow a company to differentiate itself from its rivals and charge a premium price for its product, or, in the case of many process innovations, reduce its unit costs far below those of competitors.

Customer Responsiveness

To achieve superior responsiveness to customers, a company must be able to do a better job than competitors of identifying and satisfying its customers' needs. Customers will then attribute more value to its products, creating a competitive advantage based on differentiation. Improving the quality of a company's product offering is consistent with achieving responsiveness, as is developing new products with features that existing products lack. In other words, achieving superior quality and innovation is integral to achieving superior responsiveness to customers.

Another factor that stands out in any discussion of responsiveness to customers is the need to customize goods and services to the unique demands of individuals or groups. For example, the proliferation of soft drinks and beers can be viewed partly as a response to this trend. An aspect of responsiveness to customers that has drawn increasing attention is **customer response time**: the time that it takes for a good to be

product innovation
Development of products that are new to the world or have superior attributes to existing products.

process innovation
Development of a new process for producing and delivering products to customers.

customer response time
Time that it takes for a good to be delivered or a service to be performed.

delivered or a service to be performed.[18] For a manufacturer of machinery, response time is the time it takes to fill customer orders. For a bank, it is the time it takes to process a loan, or the time that a customer must stand in line to wait for a free teller. For a supermarket, it is the time that customers must stand in checkout lines. For a fashion retailer, it is the time required to take a new product from design inception to placement in a retail store (see Strategy in Action 3.2 for a discussion of how the Spanish fashion retailer Zara minimizes this). Customer survey after customer survey has shown slow response time to be a major source of customer dissatisfaction.[19]

Other sources of enhanced responsiveness to customers are superior design, superior service, and superior after-sales service and support. All of these factors enhance responsiveness to customers and allow a company to differentiate itself from its less responsive competitors. In turn, differentiation enables a company to build brand loyalty and charge a premium price for its products. Consider how much more people are prepared to pay for next-day delivery of Express Mail, compared to delivery in 3 to 4 days. In 2012, a two-page letter sent by overnight Express Mail within the United States cost about $10, compared to $0.48 for regular mail. Thus, the price premium for express delivery (reduced response time) was $9.52, or a premium of 1983% over the regular price.

ANALYZING COMPETITIVE ADVANTAGE AND PROFITABILITY

In order to perform a solid internal analysis and dig into how well different value-chain activities are performed, managers must be able to analyze the financial performance of their company, identifying how its strategies contribute (or not) to profitability. To identify strengths and weaknesses effectively, they must be able to compare, or benchmark, the performance of their company against competitors, as well as against the historic performance of the company itself. This will help them determine whether they are more or less profitable than competitors and whether the performance of the company has been improving or deteriorating through time; whether their company strategies are maximizing the value being created; whether their cost structure is out of alignment compared to competitors; and whether they are using the company resources to the greatest effect.

As we noted in Chapter 1, the key measure of a company's financial performance is its profitability, which captures the return that a company is generating on its investments. Although several different measures of profitability exist, such as return on assets and return on equity, many authorities on the measurement of profitability argue that return on invested capital (ROIC) is the best measure because "it focuses on the true operating performance of the company."[20] (However, return on assets is very similar in formulation to return on invested capital.)

ROIC is defined as net profit over invested capital, or ROIC = net profit/invested capital. Net profit is calculated by subtracting the total costs of operating the company from its total revenues (total revenues – total costs). *Net profit* is what is left over after the government takes its share in taxes. *Invested capital* is the amount that is invested in the operations of a company: property, plants, equipment, inventories, and other assets. Invested capital comes from two main sources: interest-bearing debt and shareholders' equity. *Interest-bearing debt* is money the company borrows from banks and those who purchase its bonds. *Shareholders' equity* is money raised from selling shares to the public, plus earnings that the company has retained in prior years (and that are available to fund current investments). ROIC measures the effectiveness with which a company is using the capital funds that it has available for investment. As such, it is recognized to be an excellent measure of the value a company is creating.[21]

A company's ROIC can be algebraically divided into two major components: return on sales and capital turnover.[22] Specifically:

$$\text{ROIC} = \text{net profits/invested capital}$$
$$= \text{net profits/revenues} \times \text{revenues/invested capital}$$

where net profits/revenues is the return on sales, and revenues/invested capital is capital turnover. Return on sales measures how effectively the company converts revenues into profits. Capital turnover measures how effectively the company employs its invested capital to generate revenues. These two ratios can be further divided into some basic accounting ratios, as shown in Figure 3.8 and defined in Table 3.1.[23]

Figure 3.8 notes that a company's managers can increase ROIC by pursuing strategies that increase the company's return on sales. To increase the company's return on sales, they can pursue strategies that reduce the cost of goods sold (COGS) for a given level of sales revenues (COGS/sales); reduce the level of spending on sales force, marketing, general, and administrative expenses (SG&A) for a given level of sales revenues (SG&A/sales); and reduce R&D spending for a given level of sales revenues (R&D/sales). Alternatively, they can increase return on sales by pursuing strategies that increase sales revenues more than they increase the costs of the business as measured by COGS, SG&A, and R&D expenses. That is, they can increase the return on sales by pursuing strategies that lower costs or increase value through differentiation, and thus allow the company to increase its prices more than its costs.

Figure 3.8 also tells us that a company's managers can boost the profitability of their company by obtaining greater sales revenues from their invested capital, thereby increasing capital turnover. They do this by pursuing strategies that reduce the amount of working capital, such as the amount of capital invested in inventories, needed to generate a given

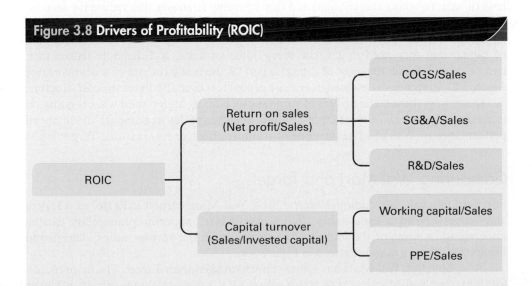

Figure 3.8 Drivers of Profitability (ROIC)

Table 3.1 Definitions of Basic Accounting Terms

Term	Definition	Source
Cost of goods sold (COGS)	Total costs of producing products	Income statement
Sales, general, and administrative expenses (SG&A)	Costs associated with selling products and administering the company	Income statement
Research and development (R&D) expenses	Research and development expenditure	Income statement
Working capital	The amount of money the company has to "work" with in the short term: Current assets – current liabilities	Balance sheet
Property, plant, and equipment (PPE)	The value of investments in the property, plant, and equipment that the company uses to manufacture and sell its products; also known as *fixed capital*	Balance sheet
Return on sales (ROS)	Net profit expressed as a percentage of sales; measures how effectively the company converts revenues into profits	Ratio
Capital turnover	Revenues divided by invested capital; measures how effectively the company uses its capital to generate revenues	Ratio
Return on invested capital (ROIC)	Net profit divided by invested capital	Ratio
Net profit	Total revenues minus total costs before tax	Income statement
Invested capital	Interest-bearing debt plus shareholders' equity	Balance sheet

level of sales (working capital/sales) and then pursuing strategies that reduce the amount of fixed capital that they have to invest in property, plant, and equipment (PPE) to generate a given level of sales (PPE/sales). That is, they pursue strategies that reduce the amount of capital that they need to generate every dollar of sales, and therefore reduce their cost of capital. Recall that cost of capital is part of the cost structure of a company (see Figure 3.2), so strategies designed to increase capital turnover also lower the cost structure.

To see how these basic drivers of profitability help us understand what is going on in a company and identify its strengths and weaknesses, let us compare the financial performance of Wal-Mart against one of its more effective competitors, Target.

Comparing Wal-Mart and Target

For the financial year ending January 2012, Wal-Mart earned a ROIC of 13.61%, and Target earned a respectable 10.01%. Wal-Mart's superior profitability can be understood in terms of the impact of its strategies on the various ratios identified in Figure 3.8. These are summarized in Figure 3.9.

First, note that Wal-Mart has a *lower* return on sales than Target. The main reason for this is that Wal-Mart's cost of goods sold (COGS) as a percentage of sales is higher

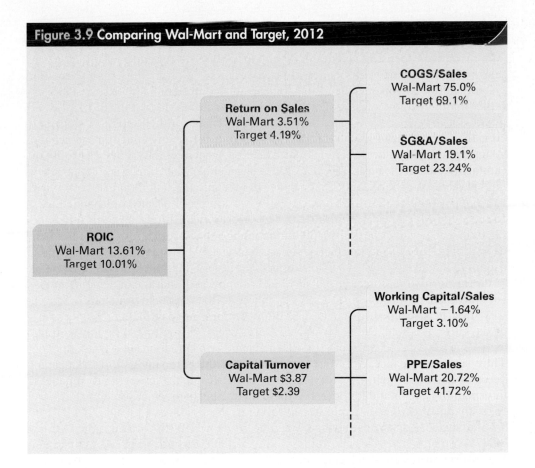

Figure 3.9 Comparing Wal-Mart and Target, 2012

than Target's (75% versus 69.1%). For a retailer, the COGS reflects the price that Wal-Mart pays to its suppliers for merchandise. The lower COGS/sales ratio implies that Wal-Mart does not mark up prices much as Target—its profit margin on each item sold is lower. Consistent with its long-time strategic goal, Wal-Mart passes on the low prices it gets from suppliers to customers. Wal-Mart's higher COGS/sales ratio reflects its strategy of being the lowest-price retailer.

On the other hand, you will notice that Wal-Mart spends less on sales, general, and administrative (SG&A) expenses as a percentage of sales than Target (19.1% versus 22.24%). There are three reasons for this. First, Wal-Mart's early strategy was to focus on small towns that could only support one discounter. In small towns, the company does not have to advertise heavily because it is not competing against other discounters. Second, Wal-Mart has become such a powerful brand that the company does not need to advertise as heavily as its competitors, even when its stores are located close to them in suburban areas. Third, because Wal-Mart sticks to its low-price philosophy, and because the company manages its inventory so well, it does not usually have an overstocking problem. Thus, the company does not need to hold periodic sales—and nor bear the costs of promoting those sales (e.g., sending out advertisements and coupons in local newspapers). Reducing spending on sales promotions reduces Wal-Mart's SG&A/sales ratio.

In addition, Wal-Mart operates with a flat organizational structure that has very few layers of management between the head office and store managers. This reduces administrative expenses (which are a component of SG&A) and hence the SG&A/sales ratio. Wal-Mart can operate with such a flat structure because its information systems allow its top managers to monitor and control individual stores directly, rather than rely upon intervening layers of subordinates to do that for them.

It is when we turn to consider the capital turnover side of the ROIC equation, however, that the financial impact of Wal-Mart's competitive advantage in information systems and logistics becomes apparent. Wal-Mart generates $3.87 for every dollar of capital invested in the business, whereas Target generates $2.39 for every dollar of capital invested. Wal-Mart is much more efficient in its use of capital than Target. Why?

One reason is that Wal-Mart has a lower working capital/sales ratio than Target. In fact, Wal-Mart has a *negative* ratio (–1.64%), whereas Target has a positive ratio (3.10%). The negative working capital ratio implies that Wal-Mart does not need any capital to finance its day-to-day operations—in fact, Wal-Mart is using its *suppliers'* capital to finance its day-to-day operations. This is very unusual, but Wal-Mart is able to do this for two reasons. First, Wal-Mart is so powerful that it can demand and get very favorable payment terms from its suppliers. It does not take ownership of inventory until it is scanned at the checkout, and it does not pay for merchandise until 60 days after it is sold. Second, Wal-Mart turns over its inventory so rapidly—around eight times a year—that it typically sells merchandise *before* it has to pay its suppliers. Thus, suppliers finance Wal-Mart's inventory and the company's short-term capital needs. Wal-Mart's high inventory turnover is the result of strategic investments in information systems and logistics. It is these value-chain activities more than any other that explain Wal-Mart's competitive advantage.

Finally, note that Wal-Mart has a significantly lower PPE/sales ratio than Target: 20.72% versus 41.72%. There are several explanations for this. First, many of Wal-Mart's stores are still located in small towns where land is cheap, whereas most Target stores are located in more expensive, suburban locations. Thus, on average, Wal-Mart spends less on a store than Target—again, strategy has a clear impact on financial performance. Second, because Wal-Mart turns its inventory over so rapidly, it does not need to devote as much space in stores to holding inventory. This means that more floor space can be devoted to selling merchandise. Other things being equal, this will result in a higher PPE/sales ratio. By the same token, efficient inventory management means that it needs less space at a distribution center to support a store, which again reduces total capital spending on property, plant, and equipment. Third, the higher PPE/sales ratio may also reflect the fact that Wal-Mart's brand is so powerful, and its commitment to low pricing so strong, that store traffic is higher than at comparable discounters such as Target. The stores are simply busier and the PPE/sales ratio is higher.

In sum, Wal-Mart's high profitability is a function of its strategy, and the resources and distinctive competencies that its strategic investments have built over the years, particularly in the area of information systems and logistics. As in the Wal-Mart example, the methodology described in this section can be very useful for analyzing why and how well a company is achieving and sustaining a competitive advantage. It highlights a company's strengths and weaknesses, showing where there is room for improvement and where a company is excelling. As such, it can drive strategy formulation. Moreover, the same methodology can be used to analyze the performance of competitors, and gain a greater understanding of their strengths and weakness, which in turn can inform strategy.

KEY TERMS

TAKEAWAYS FOR STRATEGIC MANAGERS

1. Distinctive competencies are the firm-specific strengths of a company. Valuable distinctive competencies enable a company to earn a profit rate that is above the industry average.

2. The distinctive competencies of an organization arise from its resources. Resources include land, labor, management, plants, equipment, process knowledge, intellectual property, and organizational architecture.

3. Resources are likely to result in a competitive advantage when they are valuable, rare, and inimitable, and when the firm is organized to exploit them.

4. Advanced factors of production (resources) such as intellectual property, process knowledge, and organizational architecture are most likely to result in a sustained competitive advantage. Valuable advanced resources are more likely to be rare and inimitable.

5. In order to achieve a competitive advantage, a company needs to pursue strategies that build on its existing resources and formulate strategies that create additional resources (and thus develop new competencies).

6. The amount of value a company creates is measured by the difference between the value (utility) consumers derive from its goods or services and the cost of creating that value.

7. To create more value a company must lower its costs or differentiate its product so that it creates more utility for consumers and can charge a higher price, or do both simultaneously.

8. The four building blocks of competitive advantage are efficiency, quality, innovation, and responsiveness to customers. Superior efficiency enables a company to lower its costs; superior quality allows it to charge a higher price and lower its costs; and superior customer service lets it charge a higher price. Superior innovation can lead to higher prices in the case of product innovations, or lower unit costs in the case of process innovations.

9. In order to perform a solid internal analysis, managers need to be able to analyze the financial performance of their company, identifying how the strategies of the company relate to its profitability as measured by the return on invested capital.

DISCUSSION QUESTIONS

1. What are the primary implications of the material discussed in this chapter for strategy formulation?

2. When is a company's competitive advantage most likely to be sustained over time?

3. It is possible for a company to be the lowest-cost producer in its industry and simultaneously have an output that is the most valued by customers. Discuss this statement.

4. Why is it important to understand the drivers of profitability as measured by the return on invested capital?

5. Which is more important in explaining the success and failure of companies: strategizing to create valuable resources, or luck?

CLOSING CASE

Verizon Wireless

Established in 2000 as a joint venture between Verizon Communications and Britain's Vodafone, over the last 12 years Verizon Wireless has emerged as the largest and consistently most profitable enterprise in the fiercely competitive U.S. wireless service market (see the Chapter 2 Opening Case for details on the industry). Today, the company has almost 136 million subscribers and a 38% market share.

One of the most significant facts about Verizon is that it has the lowest churn rate in the industry. Customer churn refers to the number of subscribers who leave a service within a given time period. Churn is important because it costs between $400 and $600 to acquire a customer (with phone subsidies accounting for a large chunk of that). It can take months just to recoup the fixed costs of a customer acquisition. If churn rates are high, profitability is eaten up by the costs of acquiring customers who do not stay long enough to provide a profit to the service provider.

The risk of churn increased significantly in the United States after November 2003, when the Federal Communications Commission (FCC) allowed wireless subscribers to transfer their phone numbers when they switched to a new service provider. Over the next few years, Verizon Wireless emerged as the clear winner in the battle to limit customer defections. For example, in late 2014, Verizon's churn rate was 1.28% per month, compared to a rate of 1.36% at AT&T, 2.75% at Sprint, and 2.83% at T-Mobile. Verizon's low churn rate has enabled the company to grow its subscriber base faster than its rivals, which allows the company to better achieve economies of scale by spreading the fixed costs of building a wireless network over a larger customer base.

The low customer churn at Verizon is due to a number of factors. First, it has the most extensive network in the United States, blanketing 95% of the nation. This means fewer dropped calls and dead zones as compared to its rivals. For years, Verizon communicated its coverage and quality advantage to customers with its "Test Man" advertisements. In these ads, a Verizon Test Man wearing horn-rimmed glasses and a Verizon uniform wanders around remote spots in the nation asking on his Verizon cell phone, "Can you hear me now?" Verizon claims that the Test Man was actually the personification of a crew of 50 Verizon employees who each drive some 100,000 miles annually in specially outfitted vehicles to test the reliability of Verizon's network.

Second, the company has invested aggressively in high-speed wireless networks, including 3G and now 4G LTE, enabling fast download rates on smartphones. Complementing this, Verizon has a high-speed, fiber-optic backbone for transporting data between cell towers. Verizon has invested some $100 billion in its wireless and fiber-optic network since 2000. For customers, this means a high-quality user experience when accessing data such as streaming video on their smartphones. To drive this advantage home, in 2011, Verizon started offering Apple's market-leading iPhone in addition to the full range of Android smartphones it was already offering (the iPhone was originally exclusive to AT&T).

To further reduce customer churn, Verizon has invested heavily in its customer care function. Its automated software programs analyze the call habits of individual customers. Using that information, Verizon representatives will contact customers and suggest alternative plans that might better suit their needs. For example, Verizon might contact a customer and say, "We see that because of your heavy use of data, an alternative plan might make more sense for you and help reduce your monthly bills."

The goal is to anticipate customer needs and pro-actively satisfy them, rather than have the customer take the initiative and possibly switch to another service provider.

Surveys by J.D. Power have repeatedly confirmed Verizon's advantages. A recent J.D. Power study ranked Verizon best in the industry in terms of overall network performance. The ranking was based on a number of factors, including dropped calls, late text message notifications, Web connection errors, and slow download rates. Another J.D. Power study looked at customer care in three customer contact channels—telephone, walk-in (retail store), and online. Again, Verizon had the best score in the industry, reflecting faster service and greater satisfaction with the efficiency with which costumer service reps resolved problems.

Sources: R. Blackden, "Telecom's Giant Verizon Is Conquering America," *The Telegraph*, January 6, 2013; S. Woolley, "Do You Fear Me Now?" *Forbes*, November 10, 2003, pp. 78–80; A. Z. Cuneo, "Call Verizon Victorious," *Advertising Age*, March 24, 2004, pp. 3–5; M. Alleven, "Wheels of Churn," *Wireless Week*, September 1, 2006; J.D. Power, "2012 U.S. Wireless Customer Care Full-Service Performance Study," July 7, 2012; J.D. Power, "2012 U.S. Wireless Network Quality Performance Study," August 23, 2012; Statista, "Average monthly churn rate for wireless carriers in the United States," January 2015, www.statista.com.

CASE DISCUSSION QUESTIONS

1. What resources underlie Verizon's strong competitive position in the U.S. wireless telecommunications industry?
2. Explain how these resources enable Verizon to improve one or more of the following: efficiency, quality, customer responsiveness, and innovation.
3. Apply the VRIO framework and describe to what extent these resources can be considered valuable, rare, inimitable, and well organized.
4. What must Verizon do to maintain its competitive advantage going forward in the increasingly competitive U.S. wireless telecommunications industry (you might want to reread the Chapter 2 Opening Case)?

NOTES

[1]M. Cusumano, *The Japanese Automobile Industry* (Cambridge, Mass.: Harvard University Press, 1989); S. Spear and H. K. Bowen, "Decoding the DNA of the Toyota Production System," *Harvard Business Review* (September-October 1999): 96–108.

[2]The material in this section relies on the resource-based view of the company. For summaries of this perspective, see J. B. Barney, "Company Resources and Sustained Competitive Advantage," *Journal of Management* 17 (1991): 99–120; J. T. Mahoney and J. R. Pandian, "The Resource-Based View Within the Conversation of Strategic Management," *Strategic Management Journal* 13 (1992): 63–380.

[3]R. Amit and P. J. H. Schoemaker, "Strategic Assets and Organizational Rent," *Strategic Management Journal* 14 (1993): 33–46; M. A. Peteraf, "The Cornerstones of Competitive Advantage: A Resource-Based View," *Strategic Management Journal* 14 (1993): 179–191; B. Wernerfelt, "A Resource-Based View of the Company," *Strategic Management Journal* 15 (1994): 171–180; K. M. Eisenhardt and J. A. Martin, "Dynamic Capabilities: What Are They?" *Strategic Management Journal* 21 (2000): 1105–1121.

[4]For a discussion of organizational capabilities, see R. R. Nelson and S. Winter, *An Evolutionary Theory of Economic Change* (Cambridge, Mass.: Belknap Press, 1982).

[5]J. B. Barney and W. S. Hesterly, *Strategic Management and Competitive Advantage* (Boston: Pearson, 2005).

[6]The concept of barriers to imitation is grounded in the resource-based view of the company. For details, see R. Reed and R. J. DeFillippi, "Causal Ambiguity, Barriers to Imitation, and Sustainable Competitive Advantage," *Academy of Management Review* 15 (1990): 88–102.

[7]E. Mansfield, "How Economists See R&D," *Harvard Business Review* (November-December 1981): 98–106.

[8]R. Reed and R. J. DeFillippi, "Causal Ambiguity, Barriers to Imitation, and Sustainable Competitive Advantage," *Academy of Management Review* 15 (1990): 88–102.

[9]However, $P = V$ only in the special case when the company has a perfect monopoly and can charge each customer a unique price that reflects the utility of the product to that customer (i.e., where perfect price discrimination is possible). More generally, except in the limiting case of perfect price discrimination, even a monopolist will see most customers capture some of the value of a product in the form of a consumer surplus.

[10]This point is central to the work of Michael Porter. See M. E. Porter, *Competitive Advantage* (New York: Free Press, 1985). See also P. Ghemawat, *Commitment: The Dynamic of Strategy* (New York: Free Press, 1991), Chapter 4.

[11]Porter, *Competitive Advantage.*

[12]This approach goes back to the pioneering work by K. Lancaster, *Consumer Demand: A New Approach* (New York: Columbia University Press, 1971).

[13]D. Garvin, "Competing on the Eight Dimensions of Quality," *Harvard Business Review* (November-December 1987): 101–119; P. Kotler, *Marketing Management* (Millennium Ed.) (Upper Saddle River, N.J.: Prentice-Hall, 2000).

[14]C. K. Prahalad and M. S. Krishnan, "The New Meaning of Quality in the Information Age," *Harvard Business Review* (September-October 1999): 109–118.

[15]See D. Garvin, "What Does Product Quality Really Mean?" *Sloan Management Review* 26 (Fall 1984): 25–44; P. B. Crosby, *Quality Is Free* (New York: Mentor, 1980); A. Gabor, *The Man Who Discovered Quality* (New York: Times Books, 1990).

[16]M. Cusumano, *The Japanese Automobile Industry* (Cambridge, Mass.: Harvard University Press, 1989); S. Spear and H. K. Bowen, "Decoding the DNA of the Toyota Production System," *Harvard Business Review* (September-October 1999): 96–108.

[17]W. C. Kim and R. Mauborgne, "Value Innovation: The Strategic Logic of High Growth," *Harvard Business Review* (January–February 1997): 102–115.

[18]G. Stalk and T. M. Hout, *Competing Against Time* (New York: Free Press, 1990).

[19]Ibid.

[20]T. Copeland, T. Koller, and J. Murrin, *Valuation: Measuring and Managing the Value of Companies* (New York: Wiley, 1996). See also S. F. Jablonsky and N. P. Barsky, *The Manager's Guide to Financial Statement Analysis* (New York: Wiley, 2001).

[21]Copeland, Koller, and Murrin, *Valuation.*

[22]This is done as follows. Signifying net profit by =, invested capital by K, and revenues by R, then ROIC = $=/K$. If we multiply through by revenues, R, this becomes $R = (K) = (= = R)/(K = R)$, which can be rearranged as $=/R = R/K$, where $=/R$ is the return on sales and R/K is capital turnover.

[23]Figure 3.8 is a simplification that ignores other important items that enter the calculation, such as depreciation/sales (a determinant of ROS) and other assets/sales (a determinant of capital turnover).

CHAPTER 4

COMPETITIVE ADVANTAGE THROUGH FUNCTIONAL-LEVEL STRATEGIES

Christapher Halloran/Shutterstock.com

Trouble at McDonald's

For most of its history McDonald's has been an extraordinarily successful enterprise. It began in 1955, when the legendary Ray Kroc decided to franchise the McDonald brothers' fast-food concept. Since its inception, McDonald's has grown into the largest restaurant chain in the world, with almost 32,000 stores in 120 countries.

For decades, McDonald's success was grounded in a simple formula: give consumers value for money, good quick service, and consistent quality in a clean environment, and they will return time and time again. To deliver value for money and consistent quality, McDonalds standardized the process of order taking, making food, and providing service. Standardized processes raised employee productivity while ensuring that customers had the same experience in all branches of the restaurant. McDonald's also developed close ties with wholesalers and food producers, managing its supply chain to reduce costs. As it became

4.1 Explain how an enterprise can use functional-level strategies to increase its efficiency

4.2 Explain how an enterprise can use functional-level strategies to increase its quality

4.3 Explain how an enterprise can use functional-level strategies to increase its innovation

4.4 Explain how an enterprise can use functional-level strategies to increase its customer responsiveness

Najlah Feamny/Corbis

109

larger, buying power enabled McDonald's to realize economies of scale in purchasing and pass on cost savings to customers in the form of low-priced meals, which drove increased demand. There was also the ubiquity of McDonald's; their restaurants could be found everywhere. This accessibility, coupled with the consistent experience and low prices, built brand loyalty.

The formula worked well until the early 2000s. By then, McDonald's was under attack for contributing to obesity. Its low-priced, high-fat foods were dangerous, claimed critics. By 2002, sales were stagnating and profits were falling. It seemed that McDonald's had lost its edge. The company responded with a number of steps. It scrapped its supersize menu and added healthier options such as salads and apple slices. Executives mined data to discover that people were eating more chicken and less beef. So McDonald's added grilled chicken sandwiches, chicken wraps, Southern-style chicken sandwiches, and most recently, chicken for breakfast to their menu. Chicken sales doubled at McDonald's between 2002 and 2008, and the company now buys more chicken than beef.

McDonald's also shifted its emphasis on beverages. For decades, drinks were an afterthought, but executives couldn't help but note the rapid growth of Starbucks. In 2006, McDonald's decided to offer better coffee, including lattes. McDonald's improved the quality of its coffee by purchasing high-quality beans, using better equipment, and filtering its water. The company did not lose sight of the need to keep costs low and service quick, however, and continues to add coffee-making machines that produce lattes and cappuccinos in 45 seconds, at the push of a button. Starbucks it is not, but for many people a latte from the McDonald's drive-through window is comparable. Today, the latte machines have been installed in almost half of the stores in the United States.

All of these strategies seemed to work. Revenues, net profits and profitability all improved between 2002 and 2013. By 2014, however, McDonald's was once more running into headwinds. Same-store sales declined in 2014, impacting profitability. Among the problems that analysts identified at McDonald's was an inability to attract customers in the 19- to 30-year-old age group. Rivals offering healthier alternatives, such as Chipotle Mexican Grill, and "better burger" chains that appeal to this demographic, such as Smashburger, are gaining ground at the expense of McDonald's. A recent *Consumer Reports* survey ranked McDonald's burgers the worst among its peers. Another problem is that the quality of customer service at McDonald's seems to have slipped. Many customers say that employees at McDonalds are rude and unprofessional. One reason why McDonald's employees might be feeling stressed out is that the menu has grown quite large in recent years, and many restaurants are not longer staffed given the diversity of the menu. Management at McDonalds has promised to fix these problems, but how they will do this remains to be seen.

Sources: Jonathan Beer, "5 Reasons McDonald's Has Indigestion," *CBS Money Watch*, August 12, 2014; A. Martin, "McDonald's, the Happiest Meal is Hot Profits," *New York Times*, January 11, 2009; M. Vella, "A New Look for McDonald's," *Business Week Online*, December 4, 2008; M. Warner, "Salads or No, Cheap Burgers Revive McDonald's," *New York Times*, April 19, 2006.

OVERVIEW

In Chapter 3, we saw how valuable, rare, inimitable resources that are well organized within an enterprise form the foundation of competitive advantage. These resources reside in the value creation activities (functions) of a company. In this chapter, we take a close look at how a firm can use functional-level strategies to build valuable resources that enable it to attain superior efficiency, quality, innovation, and customer responsiveness (see Figure 4.1). **Functional-level strategies** are actions that managers take to improve the efficiency and effectiveness of one or more of value creation activities (see Figure 3.5 in the previous chapter).

The Opening Case illustrates some of these relationships. Historically, McDonald's has been a standout performer in the fast-food industry. McDonald's was a fast-food *innovator*, developing many of the practices that have become standard in the industry. It was *responsive to customer needs* for inexpensive fast food, good, quick service, and a clean environment. By standardizing the process of making fast food and working closely with its suppliers, McDonald's improved its *efficiency*, thereby lowering costs and prices, while offering a product of *reliable quality* that was the same no matter where it was purchased.

However, by the early 2000s, the company's distinctive competence in providing inexpensive fast food of reliable quality was under attack. Eating habits were changing. McDonald's responded to shifting customer needs by changing its menu, and for a few years this seemed to work. By 2014, however, same-store sales and profits were once more declining. This time, the problem was not only McDonald's menu but also a perception that the quality of customer service had declined. To fix these problems, McDonald's will have to take many actions at the functional level to enhance the perceived quality of its product offering, reconfigure the menu, and improve in-store customer service, all while keeping costs under control through efficient operations.

functional-level strategies
Actions that managers take to improve the efficiency and effectiveness of one or more value creation activities.

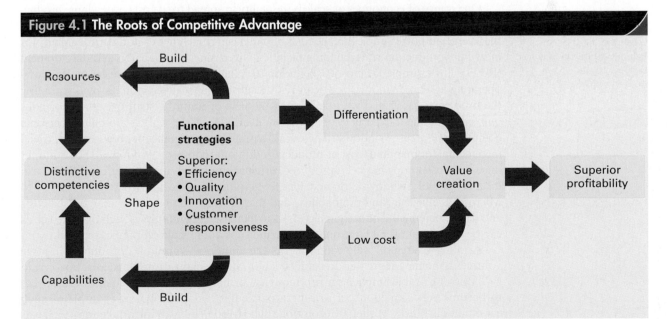

Figure 4.1 The Roots of Competitive Advantage

McDonald's, in other words, needs to adjust many of its functional strategies. The content in this chapter is germane to the problems McDonald's is facing today, for much of it is devoted to looking at the basic strategies that can be adopted at the functional level to improve efficiency, quality, innovation, and customer responsiveness of the enterprise. By the end of this chapter, you will understand how functional-level strategies can be used to build a sustainable competitive advantage.

◤ACHIEVING SUPERIOR EFFICIENCY

A company is a device for transforming inputs (labor, land, capital, management, and technological knowhow) into outputs (the goods and services produced). The simplest measure of efficiency is the quantity of inputs that it takes to produce a given output; that is, efficiency = outputs/inputs. The more efficient a company, the fewer the inputs required to produce a given output, and therefore the lower its cost structure. Put another way, an efficient company has higher productivity and therefore lower costs than its rivals. Here we review the steps that companies can take at the functional level to increase efficiency and lower cost structure.

Efficiency and Economies of Scale

economies of scale

Reductions in unit costs attributed to larger output.

Economies of scale are unit cost reductions associated with large-scale output. You will recall from the Chapter 3 that it is very important for managers to understand how the cost structure of their enterprise varies with output, because this understanding should help to drive strategy. For example, if unit costs fall significantly as output is expanded—that is, if there are significant economies of scale—a company may benefit by keeping prices down and increasing volume.

fixed costs

Costs that must be incurred to produce a product regardless of level of output.

One source of economies of scale is the ability to spread fixed costs over a large production volume. **Fixed costs** are costs that must be incurred to produce a product regardless of the level of output; examples are the costs of purchasing machinery, setting up machinery for individual production runs, building facilities, advertising, and research and development (R&D). For example, Microsoft spent approximately $5 billion to develop its Windows operating system, Windows 8. It can realize substantial scale economies by distributing the fixed costs associated with developing the new operating system over the enormous unit sales volume it expects for this system (over 90% of the world's 1.6 billion personal computers (PCs) use Windows). These scale economies are significant because of the trivial incremental (or marginal) cost of producing additional copies of Windows 8. For example, once the master copy has been produced, original equipment manufacturers (OEMs) can install copies of Windows 8 on new PCs for zero marginal cost to Microsoft. The key to Microsoft's efficiency and profitability (and that of other companies with high fixed costs and trivial incremental or marginal costs) is to increase sales rapidly enough that fixed costs can be spread out over a large unit volume and substantial scale economies realized.

Another source of scale economies is the ability of companies producing in large volumes to achieve a greater division of labor and specialization. Specialization is said to have a favorable impact on productivity, primarily because it enables employees to become very skilled at performing a particular task. The classic example of such economies is Ford's Model T automobile. The Model T Ford, introduced in 1923, was the world's first mass-produced car. Until 1923, Ford had made cars using an expensive, hand-built, craft production method. Introducing mass-production techniques allowed the company to achieve greater division of labor (it split assembly into small, repeatable tasks) and specialization, which boosted employee productivity. Ford was also able to distribute the fixed costs of developing a car and setting up production machinery over a large volume of output. As a result of these economies, the cost of manufacturing a car at Ford fell from $3,000 to less than $900 (in 1958 dollars).

The concept of scale economies is depicted in Figure 4.2, which illustrates that, as a company increases its output, unit costs decrease. This process comes to an end at an output of Q1, where all scale economies are exhausted. Indeed, at outputs of greater than Q1, the company may encounter **diseconomies of scale**, which are the unit cost increases associated with a large scale of output. Diseconomies of scale occur primarily because of the increased bureaucracy associated with large-scale enterprises and the managerial inefficiencies that can result.[1] Larger enterprises have a tendency to develop extensive managerial hierarchies in which dysfunctional political behavior is commonplace. Information about operating matters can accidentally and/or deliberately be distorted by the number of managerial layers through which the information must travel to reach top decision makers. The result is poor decision making. Therefore, past a specific point—such as Q1 in Figure 4.2—inefficiencies that result from such developments outweigh any additional gains from economies of scale. As output expands, unit costs begin to rise.

diseconomies of scale
Unit cost increases associated with a large scale of output.

Managers must know the extent of economies of scale, and where diseconomies of scale begin to occur. At Nucor Steel, for example, the realization that diseconomies of scale exist has led to the company's decision to build plants that employ only 300 individuals or less. The belief is that it is more efficient to build two plants, each employing 300 people, than one plant employing 600 people. Although the larger plant may theoretically make it possible to reap greater scale economies, Nucor's management believes that larger plants would suffer from the diseconomies of scale associated with large organizational units.

Figure 4.2 Economies and Diseconomies of Scale

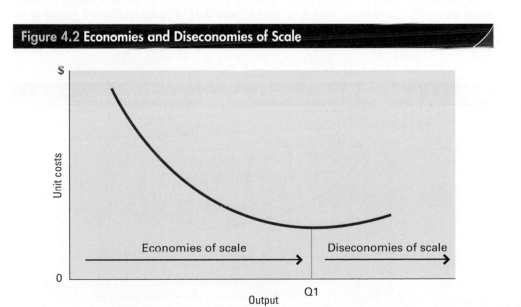

Efficiency and Learning Effects

learning effects

Cost savings that come from learning by doing.

Learning effects are cost savings that result from "learning by doing." Labor, for example, learns by repetition how to best carry out a task. Therefore, labor productivity increases over time, and unit costs decrease as individuals learn the most efficient way to perform a particular task. Equally important, management in a new manufacturing facility typically learns over time how best to run the new operation. Hence, production costs decline because of increasing labor productivity and management efficiency. Put differently, over time, management and labor accumulate valuable process knowledge that leads to higher productivity. Japanese companies such as Toyota are noted for making the accumulation of process knowledge central to their operating philosophy.

Learning effects tend to be more significant when a technologically complex task is repeated because there is more to learn. Thus, learning effects will be more significant in an assembly process that has 1,000 complex steps than in a process with 100 simple steps. Although learning effects are normally associated with the manufacturing process, there is substantial evidence that they are just as important in service industries. One famous study of learning in the health-care industry discovered that more-experienced medical providers posted significantly lower mortality rates for a number of common surgical procedures, suggesting that learning effects are at work in surgery.[2] The authors of this study used the evidence to argue in favor of establishing regional referral centers for the provision of highly specialized medical care. These centers would perform many specific surgical procedures (such as heart surgery), replacing local facilities with lower volumes and presumably higher mortality rates. Another recent study found strong evidence of learning effects in a financial institution. This study looked at a newly established document-processing unit with 100 staff members and found that, over time, documents were processed much more rapidly as the staff learned the process. Overall, the study concluded that unit costs decreased every time the cumulative number of documents processed doubled.[3] Strategy in Action 4.1 looks at the determinants of differences in learning effects across a sample of hospitals performing cardiac surgery.

In terms of the unit cost curve of a company, economies of scale imply a movement along the curve (say, from A to B in Figure 4.3). The realization of learning effects implies a downward shift of the entire curve (B to C in Figure 4.3) as both labor and management become more efficient over time at performing their tasks at every

Figure 4.3 The Impact of Learning and Scale Economies on Unit Costs

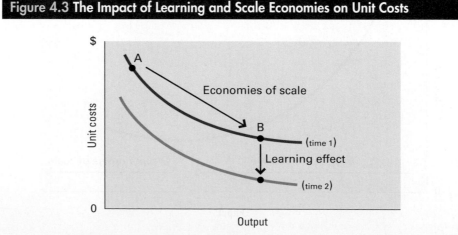

4.1 STRATEGY IN ACTION

Learning Effects in Cardiac Surgery

Researchers at the Harvard Business School carried out a study to estimate the importance of learning effects in the case of a new technology for minimally invasive heart surgery that was approved by federal regulators. The researchers looked at 16 hospitals and obtained data on operations for 660 patients who underwent surgery using the new technology. They examined how the time required to undertake the procedure varied with cumulative experience. Across the 16 hospitals, they found that average time decreased from 280 minutes for the first procedure with the new technology to 220 minutes once a hospital had performed 50 procedures (note that not all hospitals performed 50 procedures, and the estimates represent an extrapolation based on the data).

Next, the study observed differences across hospitals; here they found evidence of very large differences in learning effects. One hospital, in particular, stood out. This hospital, which they called "Hospital M," reduced its net procedure time from 500 minutes on case 1 to 132 minutes by case 50. Hospital M's 88-minute procedure time advantage over the average hospital at case 50 meant a cost savings of approximately $2,250 per case, which allowed surgeons at the hospital to complete one more revenue-generating procedure per day.

The researchers inquired into factors that made Hospital M superior. They noted that all hospitals had similar, state-of-the-art operating rooms, all used the same devices, approved by the Food and Drug Administration

(FDA), all surgeons who adopted the new technology completed the same training courses, and all surgeons came from highly respected training hospitals. Follow-up interviews, however, suggested that Hospital M differed in how it implemented the new procedure. The adopting surgeon handpicked the team that would perform the surgery. Members of the team had significant prior experience working together, which was a key criterion for member selection, and the team trained together to perform the surgery with the new technology. Before undertaking the surgery, the entire team met with the operating room nurses and anesthesiologists to discuss it. In addition, the adopting surgeon mandated that no changes would be made to either the team or the procedure in the early stages of using the technology. The initial team completed 15 procedures before members were added or substituted, and completed 20 cases before the procedure was modified. The adopting surgeon also insisted that the team meet prior to each of the first 10 cases, and after the first 20 cases, to debrief.

The picture that emerges is a core team selected and managed to maximize gains from learning Unlike other hospitals where team members and procedures were less consistent, and where there was not the same attention to briefing, debriefing, and learning, surgeons at Hospital M learned much faster and ultimately achieved higher productivity than their peers in other institutions. Clearly, differences in the implementation of the new procedure were very significant.

Source: G. P. Pisano, R. M. J. Bohmer, and A. C. Edmondson, "Organizational Differences in Rates of Learning: Evidence from the Adoption of Minimally Invasive Cardiac Surgery," Management Science 47 (2001): 752–768.

level of output. In accounting terms, learning effects in a production setting reduce the cost of goods sold as a percentage of revenues, enabling the company to earn a higher return on sales and return on invested capital.

No matter how complex the task, learning effects typically diminish in importance after a period of time. Indeed, it has been suggested that they are most important during the start-up period of a new process and become trivial after 2 or 3 years.[4] When a company's production system changes—as a result of the use of new information technology, for example—the learning process must begin again.

Efficiency and the Experience Curve

experience curve

The systematic lowering of the cost structure and consequent unit cost reductions that have been observed to occur over the life of a product.

The **experience curve** refers to the systematic lowering of the cost structure, and consequent unit cost reductions, that have been observed to occur over the life of a product.[5] According to the experience-curve concept, per-unit production costs for a product typically decline by some characteristic amount each time accumulated output of the product is doubled (accumulated output is the total output of a product since its introduction). This relationship was first observed in the aircraft industry, where it was found that each time the accumulated output of airframes doubled, unit costs declined to 80% of their previous level.[6] As such, the fourth airframe typically cost only 80% of the second airframe to produce, the eighth airframe only 80% of the fourth, the sixteenth only 80% of the eighth, and so on. The outcome of this process is a relationship between unit manufacturing costs and accumulated output similar to the illustration in Figure 4.3. Economies of scale and learning effects underlie the experience-curve phenomenon. Put simply, as a company increases the accumulated volume of its output over time, it is able to realize both economies of scale (as volume increases) and learning effects. Consequently, unit costs and cost structure fall with increases in accumulated output.

The strategic significance of the experience curve is clear: Increasing a company's product volume and market share will lower its cost structure relative to its rivals. In Figure 4.4, Company B has a cost advantage over Company A because of its lower cost structure, and because it is farther down the experience curve. This concept is very important in industries that mass-produce a standardized output—for example, the manufacture of semiconductor chips. A company that wishes to become more efficient and lower its cost structure must try to move down the experience curve as quickly as possible. This means constructing manufacturing facilities that are scaled for efficiency even before the company has generated demand for its product, and aggressively pursuing cost reductions from learning effects. It might also need to adopt an aggressive marketing strategy, cutting prices drastically and stressing heavy sales promotions and extensive advertising in order to build up demand and accumulated volume as quickly as possible. A company is likely to have a significant cost advantage

Figure 4.4 The Experience Curve

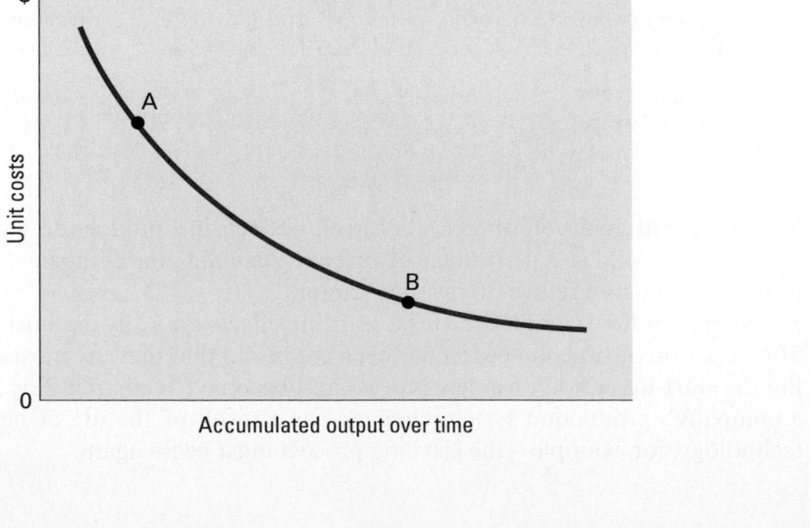

over its competitors because of its superior efficiency once it is down the experience curve. It has been argued that Intel uses such tactics to ride down the experience curve and gain a competitive advantage over its rivals in the microprocessor market.[7]

It is worth emphasizing that this concept is just as important outside of manufacturing. For example, as it invests in its distribution network, online retailer Amazon is trying to both realize economies of scale (spreading the fixed costs of its distribution centers over a large sales volume) and improve the efficiency of its inventory-management and order-fulfillment processes at distribution centers (a learning effect). Together these two sources of cost savings should enable Amazon to ride down the experience curve ahead of its rivals, thereby gaining a low-cost position that enables it to make greater profits at lower prices than its rivals.

Managers should not become complacent about efficiency-based cost advantages derived from experience effects. First, because neither learning effects nor economies of scale are sustained forever, the experience curve will bottom out at some point; it must do so by definition. When this occurs, further unit-cost reductions from learning effects and economies of scale will be difficult to attain. Over time, other companies can lower their cost structures and match the cost leader. Once this happens, many low-cost companies can achieve cost parity with each other. In such circumstances, a sustainable competitive advantage must rely on strategic factors other than the minimization of production costs by using existing technologies— factors such as better responsiveness to customers, product quality, or innovation.

Second, cost advantages gained from experience effects can be rendered obsolete by the development of new technologies. For example, the large, "big box" bookstores Borders and Barnes & Noble may have had cost advantages that were derived from economies of scale and learning. However, those advantages diminished when Amazon, utilizing Web technology, launched its online bookstore in 1994. By selling online, Amazon was able to offer a larger selection at a lower cost than established rivals with physical storefronts. When Amazon introduced its Kindle digital reader in 2007 and started to sell eBooks, it changed the basis of competition once more, effectively nullifying the experience-based advantage enjoyed by Borders and Barnes & Noble. By 2012, Borders was bankrupt and Barnes & Noble was in financial trouble and closing stores. Amazon, in the meantime, has gone from strength to strength.

Efficiency, Flexible Production Systems, and Mass Customization

Central to the concept of economies of scale is the idea that a lower cost structure, attained through the mass production of a standardized output, is the best way to achieve high efficiency. There is an implicit tradeoff in this idea between unit costs and product variety. Wide product variety shipped from a single factory implies shorter production runs, which implies an inability to realize economies of scale and thus higher costs. That is, greater product variety makes it difficult for a company to increase its production efficiency and reduce its unit costs. According to this logic, the way to increase efficiency and achieve a lower cost structure is to limit product variety and produce a standardized product in large volumes (see Figure 4.5a).

This view of production efficiency has been challenged by the rise of flexible production technologies. The term **flexible production technology** covers a range of

flexible production technology

A range of technologies designed to reduce setup times for complex equipment, increase the use of machinery through better scheduling, and improve quality control at all stages of the manufacturing process.

Figure 4.5 Tradeoff Between Costs and Product Variety

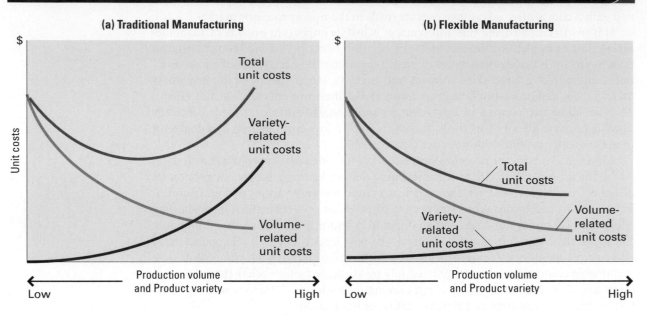

technologies designed to reduce setup times for complex equipment, increase the use of individual machines through better scheduling, and improve quality control at all stages of the manufacturing process.[8] Flexible production technologies allow the company to produce a wider variety of end products at a unit cost that at one time could be achieved only through the mass production of a standardized output (see Figure 4.5b). Research suggests that the adoption of flexible production technologies may increase efficiency and lower unit costs relative to what can be achieved by the mass production of a standardized output, while at the same time enabling the company to customize its product offering to a much greater extent than was once thought possible. The term **mass customization** has been coined to describe a company's ability to use flexible manufacturing technology to reconcile two goals that were once thought to be incompatible: low cost and differentiation through product customization.[9]

Dell Computer pursues a mass-customization strategy when it allows its customers to build their own machines online. Dell keeps costs and prices under control by allowing customers to make choices within a limited menu of options (different amounts of memory, hard-drive capacity, video card, microprocessor, and so on). The result is to create more value for customers than is possible for rivals that sell a limited range of PC models through retail outlets. Similarly, Mars offers a service, My M&Ms, that enables customers to design "personalized" M&Ms online. Customers can pick different colors and have messages or pictures printed on their M&Ms. Another example of mass customization is the Internet radio service Pandora, which is discussed in Strategy in Action 4.2.

The effects of installing flexible production technology on a company's cost structure can be dramatic. Over the last decade, the Ford Motor Company has been introducing such technologies in its automotive plants around the world. These technologies

mass customization

The use of flexible manufacturing technology to reconcile two goals that were once thought to be incompatible: low cost and differentiation through product customization.

4.2 STRATEGY IN ACTION

Pandora: Mass Customizing Internet Radio

Pandora Media streams music to PCs and mobile devices. Customers start by typing in the kind of music that they want to listen to. With a database of over 100,000 artists, there is a good chance that Pandora has something for you, however particular your tastes. Customers can then rate the music that Pandora plays for them (thumbs up or down). Pandora takes this feedback and refines the music it streams to a customer. The company also uses sophisticated predictive statistical analysis (what do other customers who also like this song listen to?) and product analysis (what Pandora calls its Music Genome, which analyzes songs and identifies similar songs) to further customize the experience for the individual listener. The Music Genome has the added benefit of introducing listeners to new songs they might like based on an analysis of their listening habits. The result is a radio station attuned to each individual's unique listening preferences. This is mass customization at its most pure.

Launched in 2000, by late 2014 Pandora's annualized revenue run rate was 920 million. There were 250 million registered users and 77 million active users, giving Pandora a 78% share of the online radio market in the United States. Pandora's revenue comes primarily from advertising, although premium subscribers can pay $36 a year and get commercial-free music.

Despite its rapid growth—a testament to the value of mass customization—Pandora does have its problems. Pandora pays more than half of its revenue in royalties to music publishers. By comparison, satellite-radio company Sirius-XM pays out only 7.5% of its revenue in the form of royalties, and cable companies that stream music pay only 15%. The different royalty rates are due to somewhat arcane regulations under which three judges who serve on the Copyright Royalty Board, an arm of the Library of Congress, set royalty fees for radio broadcasters. This method of setting royalty rates has worked against Pandora, although the company is lobbying hard to have the law changed. Pandora is also facing growing competition from Spotify and Rdio, two customizable music-streaming services that have sold equity stakes to recording labels in exchange for access to their music libraries. There are also reports that Apple will soon be offering its own customizable music-streaming service. Whatever happens to Pandora in the long run, however, it would seem that the mass customization of Internet radio is here to stay.

Sources: A. Fixmer, "Pandora Is Boxed in by High Royalty Fees," Bloomberg Businessweek, December 24, 2012; E. Smith and J. Letzing, "At Pandora Each Sales Drives up Losses," *The Wall Street Journal*, December 6, 2012; E. Savitz, "Pandora Swoons on Weak Outlook," Forbes.com, December 5, 2012; G. Peoples, "Pandora Revenue up 40 percent, Listening Growth Softens," Billboardbiz, October 23, 2014.

---

have enabled Ford to produce multiple models from the same line and to switch production from one model to another much more quickly than in the past. Ford removed $2 billion out of its cost structure between 2006 and 2010 through flexible manufacturing, and is striving to remove more.[10]

Marketing and Efficiency

marketing strategy

The position that a company takes with regard to pricing, promotion, advertising, product design, and distribution.

The marketing strategy that a company adopts can have a major impact on its efficiency and cost structure. **Marketing strategy** refers to the position that a company takes with regard to market segmentation, pricing, promotion, advertising, product design, and distribution. Some of the steps leading to greater efficiency are fairly obvious. For example, moving down the experience curve to achieve a lower cost structure can be facilitated by aggressive pricing, promotion, and advertising—all of which are tasks of the marketing function. Other aspects of marketing strategy have a less obvious—but no less important—impact on efficiency. One important aspect is the relationship of customer defection rates, cost structure, and unit costs.[11]

customer defection

The percentage of a company's customers who defect every year to competitors.

Customer defection (or "churn rate") is the percentage of a company's customers who defect every year to competitors. Defection rates are determined by customer loyalty, which in turn is a function of the ability of a company to satisfy its customers. Because acquiring a new customer often entails one-time fixed costs, there is a direct relationship between defection rates and costs. For example, when a wireless service company signs up a new subscriber, it has to bear the administrative cost of opening a new account and the cost of a subsidy that it pays to the manufacturer of the handset the new subscriber chooses. There are also the costs of advertising and promotions designed to attract new subscribers. The longer a company retains a customer, the greater the volume of customer-generated unit sales that can be set against these fixed costs, and the lower the average unit cost of each sale. Thus, lowering customer defection rates allows a company to achieve a lower cost structure.

One consequence of the defection–cost relationship illustrated in Figure 4.6. Because of the relatively high fixed costs of acquiring new customers, serving customers who stay with the company only for a short time before switching to competitors often leads to a loss on the investment made to acquire those customers. The longer a customer stays with the company, the more the fixed costs of acquiring that customer can be distributed over repeat purchases, boosting the profit per customer. Thus, there is a positive relationship between the length of time that a customer stays with a company and profit per customer.

Figure 4.6 The Relationship Between Customer Loyalty and Profit per Customer

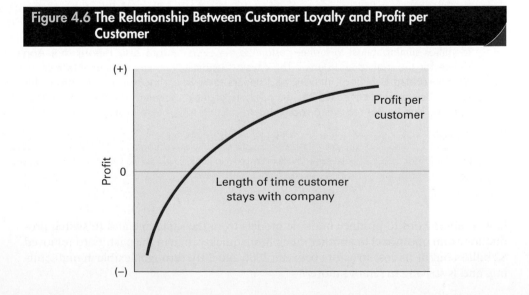

A company that can reduce customer defection rates can make a much better return on its investment in acquiring customers, and thereby boost its profitability.

For example, consider the credit card business.[12] Most credit card companies spend an average of $50 per customer for recruitment and new account setup. These costs accrue from the advertising required to attract new customers, the credit checks required for each customer, and the mechanics of setting up an account and issuing a card. These one-time fixed costs can be recouped only if a customer stays with the company for at least 2 years. Moreover, when customers stay a second year, they tend to increase their use of the credit card, which raises the volume of revenues generated by each customer over time. As a result, although the credit card business loses $50 per customer in year 1, it makes a profit of $44 in year 3 and $55 in year 6.

Another economic benefit of long-time customer loyalty is the free advertising that customers provide for a company. Loyal customers can dramatically increase the volume of business through referrals. A striking example is Britain's largest retailer, the clothing and food company Marks & Spencer, whose success is built on a well-earned reputation for providing its customers with high-quality goods at reasonable prices. The company has generated such customer loyalty that it does not need to advertise in Britain—a major source of cost savings.

The key message, then, is that reducing customer defection rates and building customer loyalty can be major sources of a lower cost structure. One study has estimated that a 5% reduction in customer defection rates leads to the following increases in profits per customer over average customer life: 75% in the credit card business, 50% in the insurance brokerage industry, 45% in the industrial laundry business, and 35% in the computer software industry.[13]

A central component of developing a strategy to reduce defection rates is to identify customers who have defected, find out why they defected, and act on that information so that other customers do not defect for similar reasons in the future. To take these measures, the marketing function must have information systems capable of tracking customer defections.

◤ MATERIALS MANAGEMENT, JUST-IN-TIME SYSTEMS, AND EFFICIENCY

The contribution of materials management (logistics) to boosting the efficiency of a company can be just as dramatic as the contribution of production and marketing. Materials management encompasses the activities necessary to get inputs and components to a production facility (including the costs of purchasing inputs), through the production process, and out through a distribution system to the end-user.[14] Because there are so many sources of cost in this process, the potential for reducing costs through more efficient materials-management strategies is enormous. For a typical manufacturing company, materials and transportation costs account for 50 to 70% of its revenues, so even a small reduction in these costs can have a substantial impact on profitability. According to one estimate, for a company with revenues of $1 million, a return on invested capital (ROIC) of 5% and materials-management costs that amount to 50% of sales revenues (including purchasing costs), increasing total profits by $15,000 would require either a 30% increase in sales revenues or a 3% reduction in

just-in-time (JIT) inventory system

System of economizing on inventory holding costs by scheduling components to arrive just in time to enter the production process or only as stock is depleted.

materials costs.[15] In a typical competitive market, reducing materials costs by 3% is usually much easier than increasing sales revenues by 30%.

Improving the efficiency of the materials-management function typically requires the adoption of a **just-in-time (JIT) inventory system**, which is designed to economize on inventory holding costs by scheduling components to arrive at a manufacturing plant just in time to enter the production process, or to have goods arrive at a retail store only when stock is almost depleted. The major cost saving comes from increasing inventory turnover, which reduces both inventory holding costs, such as warehousing and storage costs, and the company's need for working capital. For example, through efficient logistics, Wal-Mart can replenish the stock in its stores at least twice a week; many stores receive daily deliveries if they are needed. The typical competitor replenishes its stock every 2 weeks, so it must carry a much higher inventory, which requires more working capital per dollar of sales. Compared to its competitors, Wal-Mart can maintain the same service levels with a lower investment in inventory—a major source of its lower cost structure. Thus, faster inventory turnover has helped Wal-Mart achieve an efficiency-based competitive advantage in the retailing industry.[16]

More generally, in terms of the profitability model developed in Chapter 3, JIT inventory systems reduce the need for working capital (because there is less inventory to finance) and the need for fixed capital to finance storage space (because there is less to store), which reduces capital needs, increases capital turnover, and, by extension, boosts ROIC.

The drawback of JIT systems is that they leave a company without a buffer stock of inventory. Although buffer stocks are expensive to store, they can help a company prepare for shortages on inputs brought about by disruption among suppliers (for instance, a labor dispute at a key supplier), and can help a company respond quickly to increases in demand. However, there are ways around these limitations. For example, to reduce the risks linked to dependence on just one supplier for an important input, a company might decide to source inputs from multiple suppliers.

supply chain management

The task of managing the flow of inputs and components from suppliers into the company's production processes to minimize inventory holding and maximize inventory turnover.

Recently, the efficient management of materials and inventory has been recast in terms of **supply chain management**: the task of managing the flow of inputs and components from suppliers into the company's production processes to minimize inventory holding and maximize inventory turnover. Dell, whose goal is to streamline its supply chain to such an extent that it 'replaces inventory with information,' is exemplary in terms of supply chain management.

Research and Development Strategy and Efficiency

The role of superior research and development (R&D) in helping a company achieve a greater efficiency and a lower cost structure is twofold. First, the R&D function can boost efficiency by designing products that are easy to manufacture. By cutting down on the number of parts that make up a product, R&D can dramatically decrease the required assembly time, which results in higher employee productivity, lower costs, and higher profitability. For example, after Texas Instruments redesigned an infrared sighting mechanism that it supplies to the Pentagon, it found that it had reduced the number of parts from 47 to 12, the number of assembly steps from 56 to 13, the time spent fabricating metal from 757 minutes per unit to 219 minutes per unit, and unit assembly time from 129 minutes to 20 minutes. The result was a substantial decline in production costs. Design for manufacturing requires close coordination between the production and R&D functions of the company. Cross-functional teams that contain production and R&D personnel who work jointly can best achieve this.

Pioneering process innovations is the second way in which the R&D function can help a company achieve a lower cost structure. A process innovation is a new, unique way that production processes can operate more efficiently. Process innovations are often a major source of competitive advantage. Toyota's competitive advantage is based partly on the company's invention of new, flexible manufacturing processes that dramatically reduce setup times. This process innovation enabled Toyota to obtain efficiency gains associated with flexible manufacturing systems years ahead of its competitors.

Human Resource Strategy and Efficiency

Employee productivity is a key determinant of an enterprise's efficiency, cost structure, and profitability.[17] Productive manufacturing employees can lower the cost of goods sold as a percentage of revenues; a productive sales force can increase sales revenues for a given level of expenses; and productive employees in the company's R&D function can boost the percentage of revenues generated from new products for a given level of R&D expenses. Thus, productive employees lower the costs of generating revenues, increase the return on sales, and, by extension, boost the company's ROIC. The challenge for a company's human resource function is to devise ways to increase employee productivity. Among its choices are using certain hiring strategies, training employees, organizing the workforce into self-managing teams, and linking pay to performance.

Hiring Strategy

Many companies that are well known for their productive employees devote considerable attention to hiring. Southwest Airlines hires people who have a positive attitude and who work well in teams because it believes that people who have a positive attitude will work hard and interact well with customers, therefore helping to create customer loyalty. Nucor hires people who are self-reliant and goal-oriented because its employees, who work in self-managing teams, require these skills to perform well. As these examples suggest, it is important to be sure that the hiring strategy of the company is consistent with its internal organization, culture, and strategic priorities. A company's hires should have attributes that match its strategic objectives.

Employee Training

Employees are a major input into the production process. Those who are highly skilled can perform tasks faster and more accurately, and are more likely to learn the complex tasks associated with many modern production methods than individuals with lesser skills. Training upgrades employee skill levels, bringing the company productivity-related efficiency gains from learning and experimentation.[18]

Self-Managing Teams   The use of **self-managing teams**, whose members coordinate their own activities and make their own hiring, training, work, and reward decisions, has been spreading rapidly. The typical team comprises 5 to 15 employees who produce an entire product or undertake an entire task. Team members learn all team tasks and rotate from job to job. Because a more flexible workforce is one result, team members can fill in for absent coworkers and take over managerial duties such as scheduling work and vacation, ordering materials, and hiring new members. The greater

self-managing teams
Teams where members coordinate their own activities and make their own hiring, training, work, and reward decisions.

responsibility delegated to team members, and the empowerment that it implies, are seen as motivators. (*Empowerment* is the process of giving lower-level employees decision-making power.) People often respond well to being given greater autonomy and responsibility. Performance bonuses linked to team production and quality targets work as an additional motivator.

The effect of introducing self-managing teams is reportedly an increase in productivity of 30% or more and a substantial increase in product quality. Further cost savings arise from eliminating supervisors and creating a flatter organizational hierarchy, which lowers the cost structure of the company. In manufacturing companies, perhaps the most potent way to lower the cost structure is to combine self-managing teams with flexible manufacturing cells. For example, after the introduction of flexible manufacturing technology and work practices based on self-managing teams, a General Electric (GE) plant in Salisbury, North Carolina, increased productivity by 250% compared with GE plants that produced the same products 4 years earlier.[19]

Still, teams are no panacea. In manufacturing companies, self-managing teams may fail to live up to their potential unless they are integrated with flexible manufacturing technology. Also, many management responsibilities are placed upon team members, and helping team members cope with these responsibilities often requires substantial training—a fact that many companies often forget in their rush to drive down costs. Haste can result in teams that don't work out as well as planned.[20]

Pay for Performance

It is hardly surprising that linking pay to performance can help increase employee productivity, but the issue is not quite as simple as just introducing incentive pay systems. It is also important to define what kind of job performance is to be rewarded and how. Some of the most efficient companies in the world, mindful that cooperation among employees is necessary to realize productivity gains, link pay to group or team (rather than individual) performance. Nucor Steel divides its workforce into teams of about 30, with bonus pay, which can amount to 30% of base pay, linked to the ability of the team to meet productivity and quality goals. This link creates a strong incentive for individuals to cooperate in pursuit of team goals; that is, it facilitates teamwork.

Information Systems and Efficiency

With the rapid spread of computers and devices, the explosive growth of the Internet and corporate intranets (internal corporate computer networks based on Internet standards), and the spread of high-bandwidth fiber-optics and digital wireless technology, the information systems function has moved to center stage in the quest for operating efficiencies and a lower cost structure.[21] The impact of information systems on productivity is wide ranging and potentially affects all other activities of a company. For example, Cisco Systems was able to realize significant cost savings by moving its ordering and customer service functions online. The company found it could operate with just 300 service agents handling all of its customer accounts, compared to the 900 it would need if sales were not handled online. The difference represented an annual savings of $20 million a year. Moreover, without automated customer service functions, Cisco calculated that it would need at least 1,000 additional service engineers, at a cost of close to $75 million.[22]

Like Cisco, many companies are using Web-based information systems to reduce the costs of coordination between the company and its customers and the company and its suppliers. By using Web-based programs to automate customer and supplier interactions, they can substantially reduce the staff required to manage these interfaces, thereby reducing costs. This trend extends beyond high-tech companies. Banks and financial-service companies are finding that they can substantially reduce costs by moving customer accounts and support functions online. Such a move reduces the need for customer service representatives, bank tellers, stockbrokers, insurance agents, and others. For example, it costs an average of about $1.07 to execute a transaction at a bank, such as shifting money from one account to another; executing the same transaction over the Internet costs $0.01.[23]

Similarly, the concept behind Internet-based retailers such as Amazon.com is that replacing physical stores and their supporting personnel with an online, virtual store and automated ordering and checkout processes allows a company to eliminate significant costs from the retailing system. Cost savings can also be realized by using Web-based information systems to automate many internal company activities, from managing expense reimbursements to benefits planning and hiring processes, thereby reducing the need for internal support personnel.

Infrastructure and Efficiency

A company's infrastructure—including its organizational structure, culture, style of strategic leadership, and control system—determines the context within which all other value creation activities take place. It follows that improving infrastructure can help a company increase efficiency and lower its cost structure. Above all, an appropriate infrastructure can help foster a companywide commitment to efficiency and promote cooperation among different functions in pursuit of efficiency goals. These issues are addressed at length in Chapter 12.

For now, it is important to note that strategic leadership is especially important in building a companywide commitment to efficiency. The leadership task is to articulate a vision that recognizes the need for all functions of a company to focus on improving efficiency. It is not enough to improve the efficiency of production, or of marketing, or of R&D in a piecemeal fashion. Achieving superior efficiency requires a companywide commitment to this goal that must be articulated by general and functional managers. A further leadership task is to facilitate the cross-functional cooperation needed to achieve superior efficiency. For example, designing products that are easy to manufacture requires that production and R&D personnel communicate; integrating JIT systems with production scheduling requires close communication between materials management and production; and designing self-managing teams to perform production tasks requires close cooperation between human resources and production.

Summary

Table 4.1 summarizes the primary roles of various functions in achieving superior efficiency. Keep in mind that achieving superior efficiency is not something that can be tackled on a function-by-function basis. It requires organizationwide commitment and the ability to ensure close cooperation among functions. Top management, by exercising leadership and influencing the infrastructure, plays a significant role in this process.

Table 4.1 Primary Roles of Value Creation Functions in Achieving Superior Efficiency

Value Creation Function	Primary Roles
Infrastructure (leadership)	1. Provide companywide commitment to efficiency. 2. Facilitate cooperation among functions.
Production	1. Where appropriate, pursue economies of scale and learning economics. 2. Implement flexible manufacturing systems.
Marketing	1. Where appropriate, adopt aggressive marketing to ride down the experience curve. 2. Limit customer defection rates by building brand loyalty.
Materials management	1. Implement JIT systems. 2. Implement supply chain coordination.
R&D	1. Design products for ease of manufacture. 2. Seek process innovations.
Information systems	1. Use information systems to automate processes. 2. Use information systems to reduce costs of coordination.
Human resources	1. Institute training programs to build skills. 2. Implement self-managing teams. 3. Implement pay for performance.

ACHIEVING SUPERIOR QUALITY

In Chapter 3, we noted that quality can be thought of in terms of two dimensions: *quality as reliability* and *quality as excellence*. High-quality products are reliable, do well the job for which they were designed, and are perceived by consumers to have superior attributes. We also noted that superior quality provides a company with two advantages. First, a strong reputation for quality allows a company to differentiate its products from those offered by rivals, thereby creating more value in the eyes of customers and giving the company the option of charging a premium price for its products. Second, eliminating defects or errors from the production process reduces waste, increases efficiency, lowers the cost structure of the company, and increases its profitability. For example, reducing the number of defects in a company's manufacturing process will lower the cost of goods sold as a percentage of revenues, thereby raising the company's return on sales and ROIC. In this section, we look in more depth at what managers can do to enhance the reliability and other attributes of the company's product offering.

Attaining Superior Reliability

The principal tool that most managers now use to increase the reliability of their product offering is the Six Sigma quality improvement methodology. Six Sigma is a direct descendant of the **total quality management** (TQM) philosophy that was widely adopted, first by Japanese companies and then by American companies, during the 1980s and early 1990s.[24] The TQM concept was developed by a number of American management consultants, including W. Edwards Deming, Joseph Juran, and A. V. Feigenbaum.[25]

total quality management Increasing product reliability so that it consistently performs as it was designed to and rarely breaks down.

Originally, these consultants won few converts in the United States. However, managers in Japan embraced their ideas enthusiastically, and even named their premier annual prize for manufacturing excellence after Deming. Underlying TQM, according to Deming, are five factors:

1. Improved quality means that costs decrease because of less rework, fewer mistakes, fewer delays, and better use of time and materials.
2. As a result, productivity improves.
3. Better quality leads to higher market share and allows the company to raise prices.
4. Higher prices increase the company's profitability and allow it to stay in business.
5. Thus, the company creates more jobs.[26]

Deming identified a number of steps that should be part of any quality improvement program:

1. Management should embrace the philosophy that mistakes, defects, and poor-quality materials are not acceptable and should be eliminated.
2. Quality of supervision should be improved by allowing more time for supervisors to work with employees, and training employees in appropriate skills for the job.
3. Management should create an environment in which employees will not fear reporting problems or recommending improvements.
4. Work standards should not only be defined as numbers or quotas, but should also include some notion of quality to promote the production of defect-free output.
5. Management is responsible for training employees in new skills to keep pace with changes in the workplace.
6. Achieving better quality requires the commitment of everyone in the company.

Western businesses were blind to the importance of the TQM concept until Japan rose to the top rank of economic powers in the 1980s. Since that time, quality improvement programs have spread rapidly throughout Western industry. Strategy in Action 4.3 describes one of the most successful implementations of a quality improvement process, General Electric's Six Sigma program.

Implementing Reliability Improvement Methodologies

Among companies that have successfully adopted quality improvement methodologies, certain imperatives stand out. These are discussed in the following sections in the order in which they are usually tackled in companies implementing quality improvement programs. However, it is essential to understand that improvement in product reliability is a cross-functional process. Its implementation requires close cooperation among all functions in the pursuit of the common goal of improving quality; it is a process that works across functions. The roles played by the different functions in implementing reliability improvement methodologies are summarized in Table 4.2.

4.3 STRATEGY IN ACTION

General Electric's Six Sigma Quality Improvement Process

Six Sigma, a quality and efficiency program adopted by many major corporations, including Motorola, General Electric, and AlliedSignal, aims to reduce defects, boost productivity, eliminate waste, and cut costs throughout a company. "Sigma" refers to the Greek letter that statisticians use to represent a standard deviation from a mean: the higher the number of sigmas, the smaller the number of errors. At Six Sigma, a production process would be 99.99966% accurate, creating just 3.4 defects per million units. Although it is almost impossible for a company to achieve such precision, several companies strive toward that goal.

General Electric (GE) is perhaps the most well-known adopter of the Six Sigma program. Under the direction of long-serving CEO Jack Welch, GE spent nearly $1 billion to convert all of its divisions to the Six Sigma method.

One of the first products designed using Six Sigma processes was a $1.25-million diagnostic computer tomography (CT) scanner, the LightSpeed VCT, which produces rapid, three-dimensional images of the human body. The new scanner captured multiple images simultaneously, requiring only 20 seconds to do full-body scans that once took 3 minutes—important because patients must remain perfectly still during the scan. GE spent $50 million to run 250 separate Six Sigma analyses designed to improve the reliability and lower the manufacturing cost of the new scanner. Its efforts were rewarded when LightSpeed VCT's first customers soon noticed that it ran without downtime between patients—a testament to its reliability.

Achieving that reliability took immense work. GE's engineers deconstructed the scanner into its basic components and tried to improve the reliability of each component through a detailed step-by-step analysis. For example, the most important components of CT scanners are vacuum tubes that focus x-ray waves. The tubes that GE used in previous scanners, which cost $60,000 each, suffered from low reliability. Hospitals and clinics wanted the tubes to operate for 12 hours a day for at least 6 months, but typically they lasted only half that long. Moreover, GE was scrapping some $20 million in tubes each year because they failed preshipping performance tests, and disturbing numbers of faulty tubes were slipping past inspection, only to prove dysfunctional upon arrival.

To try to solve the reliability problem, the Six Sigma team took the tubes apart. They knew that one problem was a petroleum-based oil used in the tubes to prevent short circuits by isolating the anode (which has a positive charge) from the negatively charged cathode. The oil often deteriorated after a few months, leading to short circuits, but the team did not know why. Using statistical "what-if" scenarios on all parts of the tube, the researchers discovered that the lead-based paint on the inside of the tube was contaminating the oil. Acting on this information, the team developed a paint that would preserve the tube and protect the oil.

By pursuing this and other improvements, the Six Sigma team was able to extend the average life of a vacuum tube in the CT scanner from 3 months to over 1 year. Although the improvements increased the cost of the tube from $60,000 to $85,000, the increased cost was outweighed by the reduction in replacement costs, making it an attractive proposition for customers.

Source: C. H. Deutsch, "Six-Sigma Enlightenment," *New York Times*, December 7, 1998, p. 1; J. J. Barshay, "The Six-Sigma Story," *Star Tribune*, June 14, 1999, p. 1; D. D. Bak, "Rethinking Industrial Drives," Electrical/Electronics Technology, November 30, 1998, p. 58. G. Eckes, *The Six-Sigma Revolution* (New York: Wiley, 2000); General Electric, "What Is Six Sigma?," http://www.ge.com/en/company/companyinfo/quality/whatis.htm.

Table 4.2 Roles Played by Different Functions in Implementing Reliability Improvement Methodologies

Infrastructure (leadership)	1. Provide leadership and commitment to quality.
	2. Find ways to measure quality.
	3. Set goals and create incentives.
	4. Solicit input from employees.
	5. Encourage cooperation among functions.
Production	1. Shorten production runs.
	2. Trace defects back to the source.
Marketing	1. Focus on the customer.
	2. Provide customer feedback on quality.
Materials management	1. Rationalize suppliers.
	2. Help suppliers implement quality improvement methodologies.
	3. Trace defects back to suppliers.
R&D	1. Design products that are easy to manufacture.
Information systems	1. Use information systems to monitor defect rates.
Human resources	1. Institute quality improvement training programs.
	2. Identify and train black belts.
	3. Organize employees into quality teams

First, it is important that senior managers agree to a quality improvement program and communicate its importance to the organization. Second, if a quality improvement program is to be successful, individuals must be identified to lead the program. Under the Six Sigma methodology, exceptional employees are identified and put through a "black belt" training course on the Six Sigma methodology. The black belts are taken out of their normal job roles, and assigned to work solely on Six Sigma projects for the next 2 years. In effect, the black belts become internal consultants *and* project leaders. Because they are dedicated to Six Sigma programs, the black belts are not distracted from the task at hand by day-to-day operating responsibilities. To make a black belt assignment attractive, many companies now endorse the program as an advancement in a career path. Successful black belts might not return to their prior job after 2 years, but could instead be promoted and given more responsibility.

Third, quality improvement methodologies preach the need to identify defects that arise from processes, trace them to their source, find out what caused the defects, and make corrections so that they do not recur. Production and materials management are primarily responsible for this task. To uncover defects, quality improvement methodologies rely upon the use of statistical procedures to pinpoint variations in the quality of goods or services. Once variations have been identified, they must be traced to their respective sources and eliminated.

One technique that helps greatly in tracing defects to the source is reducing lot sizes for manufactured products. With short production runs, defects show up immediately. Consequently, they can quickly be sourced, and the problem can be rectified. Reducing lot sizes also means that defective products will not be produced in large lots, thus decreasing waste. Flexible manufacturing techniques can be used to reduce lot sizes without raising costs. JIT inventory systems also play a part. Under a JIT system, defective parts enter the manufacturing process immediately; they are not warehoused for several months before use. Hence, defective inputs can be quickly spotted. The problem can then be traced to the supply source and corrected before more defective parts are produced. Under a more traditional system, the practice of warehousing parts for months before they are used may mean that suppliers deliver large quantities of parts with defects before they are detected in the production process.

Fourth, another key to any quality improvement program is to create a metric that can be used to measure quality. In manufacturing companies, quality can be measured by criteria such as defects per million parts. In service companies, suitable metrics can be devised with a little creativity. For example, one of the metrics Florida Power & Light uses to measure quality is meter-reading errors per month.

Fifth, once a metric has been devised, the next step is to set a challenging quality goal and create incentives for reaching it. Under Six Sigma programs, the goal is 3.4 defects per million units. One way of creating incentives to attain such a goal is to link rewards such as bonus pay and promotional opportunities to the goal.

Sixth, shop floor employees can be a major source of ideas for improving product quality, so these employees must participate and be incorporated into a quality improvement program.

Seventh, a major source of poor-quality finished goods is poor-quality component parts. To decrease product defects, a company must work with its suppliers to improve the quality of the parts they supply.

Eighth, the more assembly steps a product requires, the more opportunities there are for mistakes. Thus, designing products with fewer parts is often a major component of any quality improvement program.

Finally, implementing quality improvement methodologies requires organizationwide commitment and substantial cooperation among functions. R&D must cooperate with production to design products that are easy to manufacture; marketing must cooperate with production and R&D so that customer problems identified by marketing can be acted on; and human resource management must cooperate with all the other functions of the company in order to devise suitable quality-training programs.

Improving Quality as Excellence

As we stated in Chapter 3, a product is comprised of different attributes. Reliability is just one attribute, albeit an important one. Products can also be *differentiated* by attributes that collectively define product excellence. These attributes include the form, features, performance, durability, and styling of a product. In addition, a company can create quality as excellence by emphasizing attributes of the service associated with the

Table 4.3 Attributes Associated with a Product Offering

Product Attributes	Service Attributes	Associated Personnel Attributes
Form	Ordering ease	Competence
Features	Delivery	Courtesy
Performance	Installation	Credibility
Durability	Customer training	Reliability
Reliability	Customer consulting	Responsiveness
Style	Maintenance and repair	Communication

product. Dell Inc., for example, differentiates itself on ease of ordering (via the Web), prompt delivery, easy installation, and the ready availability of customer support and maintenance services. Differentiation can also be based on the attributes of the people in the company with whom customers interact when making a purchase, such as competence, courtesy, credibility, responsiveness, and communication. Singapore Airlines enjoys an excellent reputation for quality service, largely because passengers perceive their flight attendants as competent, courteous, and responsive to their needs. Thus, we can talk about the product attributes, service attributes, and personnel attributes associated with a company's product offering (see Table 4.3).

To be regarded as being high in the excellence dimension, a company's product offering must be seen as superior to that of rivals. Achieving a perception of high quality on any of these attributes requires specific actions by managers. First, it is important for managers to collect marketing intelligence indicating which attributes are most important to customers. For example, consumers of personal computers (PCs) may place a low weight on durability because they expect their PCs to be made obsolete by technological advances within 3 years, but they may place a high weight on features and performance. Similarly, ease of ordering and timely delivery may be very important attributes for customers of online booksellers (as indeed they are for customers of Amazon.com), whereas customer training and consulting may be very important attributes for customers who purchase complex, business-to-business software to manage their relationships with suppliers.

Second, once the company has identified the attributes that are important to customers, it needs to design its products (and the associated services) in such a way that those attributes are embodied in the product. It also needs to train personnel in the company so that the appropriate attributes are emphasized during design creation. This requires close coordination between marketing and product development (the topic of the next section) and the involvement of the human resource management function in employee selection and training.

Third, the company must decide which significant attributes to promote and how best to position them in the minds of consumers; that is, how to tailor the marketing message so that it creates a consistent image in the minds of customers.[27] At this point, it is important to recognize that although a product might be differentiated on the basis of six attributes, covering all of those attributes in the company's communications may lead to an unfocused message. Many marketing experts advocate promoting only one or two central attributes. For example, Volvo consistently emphasizes the safety and durability of its vehicles in all marketing messages, creating the perception in the minds of consumers (backed by product design) that Volvos are safe and durable. Volvos are also very reliable and have high performance, but the company does not emphasize these attributes in its marketing messages. In contrast, Porsche emphasizes performance and styling in all of its marketing messages; thus, a Porsche is positioned differently in the minds of consumers than Volvo. Both are regarded as high-quality products because both have superior attributes, but each company differentiates its models from the average car by promoting distinctive attributes.

Finally, it must be recognized that competition is not stationary, but instead continually produces improvement in product attributes, and often the development of new-product attributes. This is obvious in fast-moving high-tech industries where product features that were considered leading edge just a few years ago are now obsolete—but the same process is also at work in more stable industries. For example, the rapid diffusion of microwave ovens during the 1980s required food companies to build new attributes into their frozen-food products: they had to maintain their texture and consistency while being cooked in the microwave; a product could not be considered high quality unless it could do that. This speaks to the importance of a strong R&D function within the company that can work with marketing and manufacturing to continually upgrade the quality of the attributes that are designed into the company's product offerings. Exactly how to achieve this is covered in the next section.

◤ ACHIEVING SUPERIOR INNOVATION

In many ways, innovation is the most important source of competitive advantage. This is because innovation can result in new products that better satisfy customer needs, can improve the quality (attributes) of existing products, or can reduce the costs of making products that customers want. The ability to develop innovative new products or processes gives a company a major competitive advantage that allows it to: (1) differentiate its products and charge a premium price, and/or (2) lower its cost structure below that of its rivals. Competitors, however, attempt to imitate successful innovations and often succeed. Therefore, maintaining a competitive advantage requires a continuing commitment to innovation.

Successful new-product launches are major drivers of superior profitability. Robert Cooper reviewed more than 200 new-product introductions and found that of those classified as successes, some 50% achieve a return on investment in excess of 33%, half have a payback period of 2 years or less, and half achieve a market share in excess of 35%.[28] Many companies have established a track record for successful innovation. Among them are Apple, whose successes include the iPod, iPhone, and iPad; Pfizer, a drug company that during the 1990s and early 2000s produced eight new blockbuster drugs; 3M, which has applied its core competency in tapes and adhesives to developing a wide range of new products; and Intel, which has consistently managed to lead in the development of innovative microprocessors to run PCs.

The High Failure Rate of Innovation

Although promoting innovation can be a source of competitive advantage, the failure rate of innovative products is high. Research evidence suggests that only 10 to 20% of major R&D projects give rise to commercial products.[29] Well-publicized product failures include Apple's Newton, an early, handheld computer that flopped in the marketplace; Sony's Betamax format in the videocassette recorder segment; Sega's Dreamcast videogame console; and Windows Mobile, an early smartphone operating system created by Microsoft that was made obsolete in the eyes of consumers by the arrival of Apple's iPhone. Although many reasons have been advanced to explain why so many new products fail to generate an economic return, five explanations for failure repeatedly appear.[30]

First, many new products fail because the demand for innovation is inherently uncertain. It is impossible to know prior to market introduction whether the new product has tapped an unmet customer need, and if there is sufficient market demand to justify manufacturing the product. Although good market research can reduce the uncertainty about likely future demand for a new technology, that uncertainty cannot be fully eradicated; a certain failure rate is to be expected.

Second, new products often fail because the technology is poorly commercialized. This occurs when there is definite customer demand for a new product, but the product is not well adapted to customer needs because of factors such as poor design and poor quality. For instance, the failure of Microsoft to establish an enduring, dominant position in the market for smartphones, despite the fact that phones using the Windows Mobile operating system were introduced in 2003—4 years before Apple's iPhone hit the market—can be traced to its poor design. Windows Mobile phones had a physical keyboard, and a small, cluttered screen that was difficult to navigate, which made the product unattractive to many consumers. In contrast, the iPhone's large touchscreen and associated keyboard appealed to many consumers, who rushed out to buy it in droves.

Third, new products may fail because of poor positioning strategy. **Positioning strategy** is the specific set of options a company adopts for a product based upon four main dimensions of marketing: price, distribution, promotion and advertising, and product features. Apart from poor design, another reason for the failure of Windows Mobile phones was poor positioning strategy. They were targeted at business users, whereas Apple developed a mass market by targeting the iPhone at retail consumers.

positioning strategy
The specific set of options a company adopts for a product based upon four main dimensions of marketing: price, distribution, promotion and advertising, and product features.

Fourth, many new-product introductions fail because companies make the mistake of marketing a technology for which there is not enough demand. A company can become blinded by the wizardry of a new technology and fail to determine whether there is sufficient customer demand for it. A classic example is the Segway two-wheeled personal transporter. Despite the fact that its gyroscopic controls were highly sophisticated, and that the product introduction was accompanied by massive media hype, sales fell well below expectations when it transpired that most consumers had no need for such a conveyance.

Finally, companies fail when products are slowly marketed. The more time that elapses between initial development and final marketing—the slower the "cycle time"—the more likely it is that a competitor will beat the company to market and gain a first-mover advantage.[31] In the car industry, General Motors long suffered from being a slow innovator. Its typical product development cycle used to be about 5 years, compared with 2 to 3 years at Honda, Toyota, and Mazda, and 3 to 4 years at Ford. Because GM's offerings were based on 5-year-old technology and design concepts, they are already out of date when they reached the market.

Reducing Innovation Failures

One of the most important things that managers can do to reduce the high failure rate associated with innovation is to make sure that there is tight integration between R&D, production, and marketing.[32] Tight, cross-functional integration can help a company ensure that:

1. Product development projects are driven by customer needs.
2. New products are designed for ease of manufacture.
3. Development costs are not allowed to spiral out of control.
4. The time it takes to develop a product and bring it to market is minimized.
5. Close integration between R&D and marketing is achieved to ensure that product development projects are driven by the needs of customers.

A company's customers can be a primary source of new-product ideas. The identification of customer needs, particularly unmet needs, can set the context within which successful product innovation takes place. As the point of contact with customers, the marketing function can provide valuable information. Moreover, integrating R&D and marketing is crucial if a new product is to be properly commercialized—otherwise, a company runs the risk of developing products for which there is little or no demand.

Integration between R&D and production can help a company ensure that products are designed with manufacturing requirements in mind. Design for manufacturing lowers manufacturing costs and leaves less room for error; thus it can lower costs and increase product quality. Integrating R&D and production can help lower development costs and speed products to market. If a new product is not designed with manufacturing capabilities in mind, it may prove too difficult to build with existing manufacturing technology. In that case, the product will need to be redesigned, and both overall development costs and time to market may increase significantly. Making design changes during product planning can increase overall development costs by 50% and add 25% to the time it takes to bring the product to market.[33]

One of the best ways to achieve cross-functional integration is to establish cross-functional product development teams composed of representatives from R&D, marketing, and production. The objective of a team should be to oversee a product development project from initial concept development to market introduction. Specific attributes appear to be important in order for a product development team to function effectively and meet all its development milestones.[34]

First, a project manager who has high status within the organization and the power and authority required to secure the financial and human resources that the team needs to succeed should lead the team and be dedicated primarily, if not entirely, to the project. The leader should believe in the project (be a champion for the project) and be skilled at integrating the perspectives of different functions and helping personnel from different functions work together for a common goal. The leader should also act as an advocate of the team to senior management.

Second, the team should be composed of at least one member from each key function or position. Individual team members should have a number of attributes, including an ability to contribute functional expertise, high standing within their function, a willingness to share responsibility for team results, and an ability to put functional advocacy aside. It is generally preferable if core team members are 100% dedicated to the project for its duration. This ensures that their focus is on the project, not on their ongoing, individual work.

Third, team members work in proximity to one another to create a sense of camaraderie and facilitate communication. Fourth, the team should have a clear plan and clear goals, particularly with regard to critical development milestones and development budgets. The team should have incentives to attain those goals; for example, bonuses paid when major development milestones are attained. Fifth, each team needs to develop its own processes for communication, as well as conflict resolution. For example, one product development team at Quantum Corporation, a California-based manufacturer of disk drives for PCs, mandated that all major decisions would be made and conflicts resolved during meetings that were held every Monday afternoon. This simple rule helped the team meet its development goals.[35]

Finally, there is substantial evidence that developing competencies in innovation requires managers to proactively learn from their experience with product development, and to incorporate the lessons from past successes and failures into future new-product development processes.[36] This is easier said than done. To learn, managers need to undertake an objective assessment after a product development project has been completed, identifying key success factors and the root causes of failures, and allocating resources to repairing failures. Leaders also must admit their own failures if they are to encourage other team members to responsibly identify what they did wrong.

The primary role that the various functions play in achieving superior innovation is summarized in Table 4.4. The table makes two matters clear. First, top management must bear primary responsibility for overseeing the entire development process. This entails both managing the development process and facilitating cooperation among the functions. Second, the effectiveness of R&D in developing new products and processes depends upon its ability to cooperate with marketing and production.

Table 4.4 Functional Roles for Achieving Superior Innovation

Value Creation Function	Primary Roles
Infrastructure (leadership)	1. Manage overall project (i.e., manage the development function).
	2. Facilitate cross-functional cooperation.
Production	1. Cooperate with R&D on designing products that are easy to manufacture.
	2. Work with R&D to develop process innovations.
Marketing	1. Provide market information to R&D.
	2. Work with R&D to develop new products.
Materials management	No primary responsibility.
R&D	1. Develop new products and processes.
	2. Cooperate with other functions, particularly marketing and manufacturing, in the development process.
Information systems	1. Use information systems to coordinate cross-functional, cross-company product development.
Human resources	1. Hire talented scientists and engineers.

ACHIEVING SUPERIOR CUSTOMER RESPONSIVENESS

To achieve superior customer responsiveness, a company must give customers what they want, when they want it, and at a price they are willing to pay—and not compromise the company's long-term profitability in the process. Customer responsiveness is an important differentiating attribute that can help build brand loyalty. Strong product differentiation and brand loyalty give a company more pricing options; it can charge a premium price for its products, or keep prices low to sell more goods and services to customers. Whether prices are at a premium or kept low, the company that is most responsive to customers' needs will gain the competitive advantage.

Achieving superior responsiveness to customers means giving customers value for their money, and steps taken to improve the efficiency of a company's production process and the quality of its products should be consistent with this aim. In addition, giving customers what they want may require the development of new products with new features. In other words, achieving superior efficiency, quality, and innovation are all part of achieving superior responsiveness to customers. There are two other prerequisites for attaining this goal. First, a company must develop a competency in listening to its customers, focusing on its customers, and investigating and identifying their needs. Second, it must constantly seek better ways to satisfy those needs.

Focusing on the Customer

A company cannot respond to its customers' needs unless it knows what those needs are. Thus, the first step to building superior customer responsiveness is to motivate the entire company to focus on the customer. The means to this end are demonstrating leadership, shaping employee attitudes, and using mechanisms for making sure that customer needs are well known within the company.

Demonstrating Leadership

Customer focus must emanate from the top of the organization on down. A commitment to superior responsiveness to customers brings attitudinal changes throughout a company that can only be built through strong leadership. A mission statement that puts customers first is one way to send a clear message to employees about the desired focus. Another avenue is top management's own actions. For example, Tom Monaghan, the founder of Domino's Pizza, stayed close to the customer by eating Domino's pizza regularly, visiting as many stores as possible every week, running some deliveries himself, and insisting that top managers do the same.[37]

Shaping Employee Attitudes

Leadership alone is not enough to attain superior customer responsiveness. All employees must see the customer as the focus of their activity and be trained to concentrate on the customer—whether their function is marketing, manufacturing, R&D, or accounting. The objective should be to put employees in customers' shoes, a perspective that enables them to become better able to identify ways to improve the quality of a customer's experience with the company.

To reinforce this mindset, incentive systems should reward employees for satisfying customers. For example, senior managers at the Four Seasons hotel chain, who pride themselves on customer focus, tell the story of Roy Dyment, a doorman in Toronto who neglected to load a departing guest's briefcase into his taxi. The doorman called the guest, a lawyer, in Washington, D.C., and found that he desperately needed the briefcase for a morning meeting. Dyment hopped on a plane to Washington and returned it—without first securing approval from his boss. Far from punishing Dyment for not checking with management before going to Washington, the Four Seasons responded by naming Dyment Employee of the Year.[38] This sent a powerful message to Four Seasons employees, stressing the importance of satisfying customer needs.

Knowing Customer Needs

"Know thy customer" is one of the keys to achieving superior responsiveness to customers. Knowing the customer not only requires that employees think like customers; it also demands that they listen to what customers have to say. This involves communicating customers' opinions by soliciting feedback from customers on the company's goods and services, and by building information systems that disseminate the feedback to the relevant people.

For an example, consider clothing retailer Lands' End. Through its catalog, the Internet, and customer-service telephone operators, Lands' End actively solicits comments about the quality of its clothing and the kind of merchandise customers want Lands' End to supply. Indeed, it was customer insistence that initially prompted the company to move into the clothing segment. Lands' End formerly supplied equipment for sailboats through mail-order catalogs. However, it received so many requests from customers to include outdoor clothing in its offering that it responded by expanding the catalog to fill this need. Soon, clothing became its main business, and Lands' End ceased selling sailboat equipment. Today, the company continues to pay close attention to customer requests. Every month, data on customer requests and comments is reported to managers. This feedback helps the company fine-tune the merchandise it sells; new lines of merchandise are frequently introduced in response to customer requests.

Satisfying Customer Needs

Once customer focus is integral to the organization, the next requirement is to satisfy those customer needs that have been identified. As already noted, efficiency, quality, and innovation are crucial competencies that help a company satisfy customer needs. Beyond that, companies can provide a higher level of satisfaction if they differentiate their products by (1) customizing them, where possible, to the requirements of individual customers, and (2) reducing the time it takes to respond to or satisfy customer needs.

Customization

Customization involves varying the features of a good or service to tailor it to the unique needs or tastes of a group of customers, or—in the extreme case—individual customers. Although extensive customization can raise costs, the development of flexible manufacturing technologies has made it possible to customize products to a greater extent than was feasible 10 to 15 years ago, without experiencing a prohibitive rise in cost structure (particularly when flexible manufacturing technologies are linked with Web-based information systems). For example, online retailers such as Amazon. com have used Web-based technologies to develop a homepage customized for each individual user. When a customer accesses Amazon.com, he or she is offered a list of recommended books and music to purchase based on an analysis of prior buying history—a powerful competency that gives Amazon.com a competitive advantage.

The trend toward customization has fragmented many markets, particularly customer markets, into ever-smaller niches. An example of this fragmentation occurred in Japan in the early 1980s when Honda dominated the motorcycle market there. Second-place Yamaha was determined to surpass Honda's lead. It announced the opening of a new factory that, when operating at full capacity, would make Yamaha the world's largest manufacturer of motorcycles. Honda responded by proliferating its product line and increasing its rate of new-product introduction. At the start of what became known as the "Motorcycle Wars," Honda had 60 motorcycles in its product line. Over the next 18 months thereafter, it rapidly increased its range to 113 models, customizing them to ever-smaller niches. Because of its competency in flexible manufacturing, Honda accomplished this without bearing a prohibitive cost penalty. The flood of Honda's customized models pushed Yamaha out of much of the market, effectively stalling its bid to overtake Honda.[39]

Response Time

To gain a competitive advantage, a company must often respond to customer demands very quickly, whether the transaction is a furniture manufacturer's completion of an order , a bank's processing of a loan application, an automobile manufacturer's delivery of a spare part, or the wait in a supermarket checkout line. We live in a fast-paced society where time is a valuable commodity. Companies that can satisfy customer demands for rapid response build brand loyalty, differentiate their products, and can charge higher prices for products.

Increased speed often lets a company opt for premium pricing, as the mail delivery industry illustrates. The air-express niche of the mail delivery industry is based on the notion that customers are often willing to pay substantially more for overnight express mail than for regular mail. Another exemplar of the value of rapid response is Caterpillar, the manufacturer of heavy-earthmoving equipment, which can deliver a spare part to any location in the world within 24 hours. Downtime for heavy-construction equipment is very costly, so Caterpillar's ability to respond quickly in the event of equipment malfunction is of prime importance to its customers. As a result, many customers have remained loyal to Caterpillar despite the aggressive, low-price competition from Komatsu of Japan.

In general, reducing response time requires: (1) a marketing function that can quickly communicate customer requests to production, (2) production and materials-management functions that can quickly adjust production schedules in response to unanticipated customer demands, and (3) information systems that can help production and marketing in this process.

Table 4.5 summarizes the steps different functions must take if a company is to achieve superior responsiveness to customers. Although marketing plays a critical role in helping a company attain this goal (primarily because it represents the point of contact with the customer), Table 4.5 shows that the other functions also have major roles. Achieving superior responsiveness to customers requires top management to lead in building a customer orientation within the company.

Table 4.5 Primary Roles of Different Functions in Achieving Superior Customer Responsiveness

Value Creation Function	Primary Roles
Infrastructure (leadership)	• Through leadership by example, build a companywide commitment to responsiveness to customers
Production	• Achieve customization through implementation of flexible manufacturing • Achieve rapid response through flexible manufacturing
Marketing	• Know the customer • Communicate customer feedback to appropriate functions
Materials management	• Develop logistics systems capable of responding quickly to unanticipated customer demands (JIT)
R&D	• Bring customers into the product development process
Information systems	• Use Web-based information systems to increase responsiveness to customers
Human resources	• Develop training programs that get employees to think like customers

KEY TERMS

functional-level
  strategies   111
economies of scale   112
fixed costs   112
diseconomies of scale   113
learning effects   114

experience curve   116
flexible production
  technology   117
mass customization   118
marketing strategy   120
customer defection   120

just-in-time (JIT) inventory
  system   122
supply chain
  management   122
self-managing
  teams   123

total quality
  management   127
positioning strategy   133

TAKEAWAYS FOR STRATEGIC MANAGERS

1. A company can increase efficiency through a number of steps: exploiting economies of scale and learning effects; adopting flexible manufacturing technologies; reducing customer defection rates; implementing just-in-time systems; getting the R&D function to design products that are easy to manufacture; upgrading the skills of employees through training; introducing self-managing teams; linking pay to performance; building a companywide commitment to efficiency through

strong leadership; and designing structures that facilitate cooperation among different functions in pursuit of efficiency goals.

2. Superior quality can help a company lower its costs, differentiate its product, and charge a premium price.

3. Achieving superior quality demands an organizationwide commitment to quality and a clear focus on the customer. It also requires metrics to measure quality goals and incentives that

emphasize quality; input from employees regarding ways in which quality can be improved; a methodology for tracing defects to their source and correcting the problems that produce them; a rationalization of the company's supply base; cooperation with approved suppliers to implement total quality management programs; products that are designed for ease of manufacturing; and substantial cooperation among functions.

4. The failure rate of new-product introductions is high because of factors such as uncertainty, poor commercialization, poor positioning strategy, slow cycle time, and technological shortsightedness.

5. To achieve superior innovation, a company must build skills in basic and applied research; design good processes for managing development projects; and achieve close integration between the different functions of the company, primarily through the adoption of cross-functional product development teams and partly parallel development processes.

6. Achieving superior customer responsiveness often requires that the company achieve superior efficiency, quality, and innovation.

7. Furthermore, to achieve superior customer responsiveness, a company must also give customers what they want, when they want it. It must ensure a strong customer focus, which can be attained by emphasizing customer focus through leadership; training employees to think like customers; bringing customers into the company through superior market research; customizing products to the unique needs of individual customers or customer groups; and responding quickly to customer demands.

DISCUSSION QUESTIONS

1. How are the four building blocks of competitive advantage related to each other?

2. What role can top management play in helping a company achieve superior efficiency, quality, innovation, and responsiveness to customers?

3. Over time, will the adoption of Six Sigma quality improvement processes give a company a competitive advantage, or will it be required only to achieve parity with competitors?

4. What is the relationship between innovation and competitive advantage?

CLOSING CASE

Amazon.Com

When Jeff Bezos founded Amazon.com in 1995, the online retailer focused just on selling books. Music and videos were soon added to the mix. Today, you can purchase a wide range of media and general-merchandise products from Amazon, which is now the world's largest online retailer, with over $85 billion in annual sales. According to Bezos, Amazon's success is based on three core factors: a relentless focus on delivering value to customers, operating efficiencies, and a willingness to innovate.

Amazon offers customers a much wider selection of merchandise than they can find in a physical store, and does so at a low price. Online shopping and purchasing is made easy with a user-friendly interface, product recommendations, customer wish lists, and a one-click purchasing option for repeat customers. The percentage of traffic that Amazon gets from search engines such as Google has been falling for several years, whereas other online retailers are becoming more dependent on third-party search engines. This indicates that Amazon is increasingly becoming the starting point for online purchases. As a result, its active customer base is now approaching 250 million.

To deliver products to customers quickly and accurately, Amazon has been investing heavily in a network of distribution centers. In the United States alone there are now over 40 such centers. Sophisticated software analyzes customer purchasing patterns and informs the company what to order, where to store it in the distribution network, what to charge for it, and when to mark it down to shift it. The goal is to reduce inventory-holding costs while always having product in stock. The increasingly dense network of distribution centers enables Amazon to reduce the time it takes to deliver products to consumers and to cut down on delivery costs. As Amazon grows it can support a denser distribution network, which it turn enables it to fulfill customer orders more rapidly and at a lower cost, thereby solidifying its competitive advantage over smaller rivals.

To make its distribution centers even more efficient, Amazon is embracing automation. Until recently, most picking and packing of products at Amazon distribution centers was done by hand, with employees walking as much as 20 miles per shift to pick merchandise off shelves and bring it to packing stations. Although walking 20 miles a day may be good for the physical health of employees, it represents much wasted time and hurts productivity. In 2012, Amazon purchased Kiva, a leading manufacturer of robots that service warehouses. Post the acquisition, Kiva announced that, for the next 2 to 3 years, it would take no external orders and instead focus on automating Amazon's distribution centers. Kiva robots pick products from shelves and deliver them to packing stations. This reduces the staff needed per distribution center by 30 to 40%, and boosts productivity accordingly.

On the innovation front, Amazon has been a leader in pushing the digitalization of media. Its invention of the Kindle digital reader, and the ability of customers to use that reader either on a dedicated Kindle device or on a general-purpose device such as an iPad, turbocharged the digital distribution of books—a market segment where Amazon is the clear leader. Digitalization of books is disrupting the established book-retailing industry and strengthening Amazon's advantage in this segment. To store digital media, from books to films and music, and to enable rapid customer download, Amazon has built huge server farms. Its early investment in "cloud-based" infrastructure has turned Amazon into a leader in this field. It is now leveraging its expertise and infrastructure to build another business, Amazon Web Services (AWS), which will host websites, data, and associated software for other companies. In 2014, this new business generated over $2.5 billion in revenues, making Amazon one of the early leaders in the emerging field of cloud computing. Jeff Bezos is on record as stating that he believes AWS will ultimately match Amazon's online retail business in sales volume.

Sources: "Amazon to Add 18 New Distribution Centers," *Supply Chain Digest,* August 7, 2012; A. Lashinsky, "Jeff Bezos: The Ultimate Disrupter," *Fortune,* December 3, 2012, pp. 34–41; S. Banker, "The New Amazon Distribution Model," *Logistics Viewpoints,* August 6, 2012; G. A. Fowler, "Holiday Hiring Call: People Vs Robots," *The Wall Street Journal,* December 10, 2010, p. B1.

CASE DISCUSSION QUESTIONS

1. What functional-level strategies has Amazon pursued to boost its efficiency?
2. What functional-level strategies has Amazon pursued to boost its customer responsiveness?
3. What does product quality mean for Amazon? What functional-level strategies has Amazon pursued to boost its product quality?
4. How has innovation helped Amazon improve its efficiency, customer responsiveness, and product quality?
5. Do you think that Amazon has any rare and valuable resources? In what value creation activities are these resources located?
6. How sustainable is Amazon's competitive position in the online retail business?

NOTES

[1] G. J. Miller, *Managerial Dilemmas: The Political Economy of Hierarchy* (Cambridge: Cambridge University Press, 1992).

[2] H. Luft, J. Bunker, and A. Enthoven, "Should Operations Be Regionalized?" *New England Journal of Medicine* 301 (1979): 1364–1369.

[3] S. Chambers and R. Johnston, "Experience Curves in Services," *International Journal of Operations and Production Management* 20 (2000): 842–860.

[4] G. Hall and S. Howell, "The Experience Curve from an Economist's Perspective," *Strategic Management Journal* 6 (1985): 197–212; M. Lieberman, "The Learning Curve and Pricing in the Chemical Processing Industries," *RAND Journal of Economics* 15 (1984): 213–228; R. A. Thornton and P. Thompson, "Learning from Experience and Learning from Others," *American Economic Review* 91 (2001): 1350–1369.

[5] Boston Consulting Group, *Perspectives on Experience* (Boston: Boston Consulting Group, 1972); Hall and Howell, "The Experience Curve," pp. 197–212; W. B. Hirschmann, "Profit from the Learning Curve," *Harvard Business Review* (January–February 1964): 125–139.

[6] A. A. Alchian, "Reliability of Progress Curves in Airframe Production," *Econometrica* 31 (1963): 679–693.

[7] M. Borrus, L. A. Tyson, and J. Zysman, "Creating Advantage: How Government Policies Create Trade in the Semi-Conductor Industry," in P. R. Krugman (ed.), *Strategic Trade Policy and the New International Economics* (Cambridge, Mass.: MIT Press, 1986); S. Ghoshal and C. A. Bartlett, "Matsushita Electrical Industrial (MEI) in 1987," Harvard Business School Case #388-144 (1988).

[8] See P. Nemetz and L. Fry, "Flexible Manufacturing Organizations: Implications for Strategy Formulation," *Academy of Management Review* 13 (1988): 627–638; N. Greenwood, *Implementing Flexible Manufacturing Systems* (New York: Halstead Press, 1986); J. P. Womack, D. T. Jones, and D. Roos, *The Machine That Changed the World* (New York: Rawson Associates, 1990); R. Parthasarthy and S. P. Seith, "The Impact of Flexible Automation on Business Strategy and Organizational Structure," *Academy of Management Review* 17 (1992): 86–111.

[9] B. J. Pine, *Mass Customization: The New Frontier in Business Competition* (Boston: Harvard Business School Press, 1993); S. Kotha, "Mass Customization: Implementing the Emerging Paradigm for Competitive Advantage," *Strategic Management Journal* 16 (1995): 21–42; J. H. Gilmore and B. J. Pine II, "The Four Faces of Mass Customization," *Harvard Business Review* (January–February 1997): 91–101.

[10] P. Waurzyniak, "Ford's Flexible Push," *Manufacturing Engineering*, September 1, 2003: 47–50.

[11] F. F. Reichheld and W. E. Sasser, "Zero Defections: Quality Comes to Service," *Harvard Business Review* (September–October 1990): 105–111.

[12] Ibid.

[13] The example comes from Reichheld and Sasser.

[14] R. Narasimhan and J. R. Carter, "Organization, Communication and Coordination of International Sourcing," *International Marketing Review* 7 (1990): 6–20.

[15] H. F. Busch, "Integrated Materials Management," *IJDP & MM* 18 (1990): 28–39.

[16] G. Stalk and T. M. Hout, *Competing Against Time* (New York: Free Press, 1990).

[17] See P. Bamberger and I. Meshoulam, *Human Resource Strategy: Formulation, Implementation, and Impact* (Thousand Oaks, Calif.: Sage, 2000); P. M. Wright and S. Snell, "Towards a Unifying Framework for Exploring Fit and Flexibility in Human Resource Management," *Academy of Management Review* 23 (October 1998): 756–772.

[18] A. Sorge and M. Warner, "Manpower Training, Manufacturing Organization, and Work Place Relations in Great Britain and West Germany," *British Journal of Industrial Relations* 18 (1980): 318–333; R. Jaikumar, "Postindustrial Manufacturing," *Harvard Business Review,* November–December 1986, pp. 72–83.

[19] J. Hoerr, "The Payoff from Teamwork," *Business Week,* July 10, 1989, pp. 56–62.

[20] "The Trouble with Teams," *The Economist,* January 14, 1995, p. 61.

[21] T. C. Powell and A. Dent Micallef, "Information Technology as Competitive Advantage: The Role of Human, Business, and Technology Resource," *Strategic Management Journal* 18 (1997):

375–405; B. Gates, *Business @ the Speed of Thought* (New York: Warner Books, 1999).

[22]"Cisco@speed," *The Economist,* June 26, 1999, p. 12; S Tully, "How Cisco Mastered the Net," *Fortune,* August 17, 1997, pp. 207 210; C. Kano, "The Real King of the Internet," *Fortune,* September 7, 1998, pp. 82–93

[23]Gates, *Business @ the Speed of Thought.*

[24]See the articles published in the special issue of the *Academy of Management Review on Total Quality Management* 19:3 (1994). The following article provides a good overview of many of the issues involved from an academic perspective: J. W. Dean and D. E. Bowen, "Management Theory and Total Quality," *Academy of Management Review* 19 (1994): 392–418. See also T. C. Powell, "Total Quality Management as Competitive Advantage," *Strategic Management Journal* 16 (1995): 15–37.

[25]For general background information, see "How to Build Quality," *The Economist,* September 23, 1989, pp. 91–92; A. Gabor, *The Man Who Discovered Quality* (New York: Penguin, 1990); P. B. Crosby, *Quality Is Free* (New York: Mentor, 1980).

[26]W. E. Deming, "Improvement of Quality and Productivity Through Action by Management," *National Productivity Review* 1 (Winter 1981–1982): 12–22.

[27]A. Ries and J. Trout, *Positioning: The Battle for Your Mind* (New York: Warner Books, 1982).

[28]R. G. Cooper, *Product Leadership* (Reading, Mass.: Perseus Books, 1999).

[29]See Cooper, *Product Leadership*; A. L. Page "PDMA's New Product Development Practices Survey: Performance and Best Practices," presentation at PDMA 15th Annual International Conference, Boston, MA, October 16, 1991; E. Mansfield, "How Economists See R&D," *Harvard Business Review* (November–December 1981): 98–106.

[30]S. L. Brown and K. M. Eisenhardt, "Product Development: Past Research, Present Findings, and Future Directions," *Academy of Management Review* 20 (1995): 343–378; M. B. Lieberman and D. B. Montgomery, "First Mover Advantages," *Strategic Management Journal* 9 (Special Issue, Summer 1988): 41–58; D. J. Teece, "Profiting from Technological Innovation: Implications for Integration, Collaboration, Licensing and Public Policy," *Research Policy* 15 (1987): 285–305; G. J. Tellis and P. N. Golder, "First to Market, First to Fail?" *Sloan Management Review,* Winter 1996, pp. 65 75; G. A. Stevens and J. Burley, "Piloting the Rocket of Radical Innovation," *Research Technology Management* 46 (2003): 16–26.

[31]G. Stalk and T. M. Hout, *Competing Against Time* (New York: Free Press, 1990).

[32]K. B. Clark and S. C. Wheelwright, *Managing New Product and Process Development* (New York: Free Press, 1993); M. A. Schilling and C. W. L. Hill, "Managing the New Product Development Process," *Academy of Management Executive* 12:3 (August 1998): 67–81.

[33]O. Port, "Moving Past the Assembly Line," *Business Week* (Special Issue, "Reinventing America," 1992). 177–180.

[34]K. B. Clark and T. Fujimoto, "The Power of Product Integrity," *Harvard Business Review* (November–December 1990): 107–118; Clark and Wheelwright, *Managing New Product and Process Development*; Brown and Eisenhardt, "Product Development"; Stalk and Hout, *Competing Against Time.*

[35]C. Christensen, "Quantum Corporation –Business and Product Teams," *Harvard Business School Case,* #9-692-023.

[36]H. Petroski, *Success Through Failure: The Paradox of Design* (Princeton, NJ: Princeton University Press, 2006). See also A. C. Edmondson, "Learning from Mistakes Is Easier Said Than Done," *Journal of Applied Behavioral Science* 40 (2004): 66–91.

[37]S. Caminiti, "A Mail Order Romance: Lands' End Courts Unseen Customers," *Fortune,* March 13, 1989, pp. 43–44.

[38]Sellers, "Getting Customers to Love You."

[39]Stalk and Hout, *Competing Against Time.*

3

STRATEGIES

sergign/Shutterstock.com

CHAPTER 5

BUSINESS-LEVEL STRATEGY

5.1 Explain the difference between low-cost and differentiation strategies

5.2 Articulate how the attainment of a differentiated or low-cost position can give a company a competitive advantage

5.3 Explain how a company executes its business-level strategy through function-level strategies and organizational arrangements

5.4 Describe what is meant by the term "value innovation"

5.5 Discuss the concept of blue ocean strategy, and explain how innovation in business-level strategy can change the competitive game in an industry, giving the innovator a sustained competitive advantage

OPENING CASE

Virgin America

Virgin America is consistently rated as one of the top U.S. airlines. The 7-year-old airline serves 20 destinations out of its main hub in San Francisco. Virgin America is known for its leather seats, cocktail lounge-style lighting, onboard Wi-Fi, in-seat power outlets for electronics devices, full-service meals, and that most scarce of all assets in coach class, legroom! The airline has earned a host of awards since its launch in 2007, including being named the "Best U.S. Airline" in the *Condé Nast* Traveler Readers' Choice Awards every year from 2008-2014; and "Best Domestic Airline" in the *Travel + Leisure* World's Best Awards, both for the past 7 years. Furthermore, *Consumer* Reports named Virgin America the "Best U.S. Airline" in 2013 and 2014. Industry statistics support these accolades. In 2014, Virgin was #1 in on-time arrivals in the United States, with 83.5% of aircraft arriving on time. Virgin America

Bob Riha Jr/Getty Images

also had the lowest level of denied boarding's (0.07 per 1,000 passengers), and mishandled baggage (0.87 per 1,000 passengers), and the fewest customer complaints (1.50 per 1,000 passengers).

Virgin America is an offshoot of the Virgin Group, the enterprise started by British billionaire Richard Branson. Branson got his start in the music business with Virgin Records stores (established in 1971) and the Virgin Record record label (established in 1973). In 1984, he leveraged the Virgin brand to enter an entirely new industry, airlines, with Virgin Atlantic. Virgin Atlantic became a major competitor to British Airways on a number of long-haul routes out of London, winning market share through superior customer service, innovative touches for premium travelers, and competitive pricing. Branson has also licensed the right to use the Virgin brand name across a wide array of businesses, including Virgin Media (a major U.K. cable operator), Virgin Money (a U.K. financial services company), and Virgin Mobile (a wireless brand that exists in many countries). This strategy has made Virgin one of the most recognizable brands in the world. Interestingly, Branson makes money from royalty payments irrespective of whether companies licensing the Virgin brand are profitable or not. Branson himself describes the Virgin brand as representing, "innovation, quality, and a sense of fun."

For all of its accolades and the power of the Virgin brand, Virgin America has had a hard time making money. One problem is that, as a small airline, Virgin only has a few flights a day on many routes and is unable to offer consumers the choice of multiple departure times, something that many travelers value. For example, on the popular route for tech workers between San Francisco and Austin, Texas, United offers six flights a day and Jet Blue offers two, compared with just one for Virgin America.

Another serious problem is that providing all of the extra frills necessary to deliver a high-quality experience costs money. In its first 5 years of operation, Virgin America accumulated $440 million in losses before registering a small profit of $67 million on revenues of $1.4 billion in 2013. In 2014, Virgin America went public and managed to post a respectable $150 million in net profits on revenues of close to $1.5 billion. The company was helped by an improving economy, strong demand, and lower jet fuel costs.

The key competitive issue the company faces is that it is a niche player in a much larger industry where low-cost carriers such as Southwest Airlines and Jet Blue are putting constant pressure on prices and crowding out routes with multiple flights daily. Virgin America does charge prices that are 10-20% above those of its no-frills rivals, but it cannot raise prices too far without losing customers and flying with empty seats, which is a recipe for failure in an industry where margins are slim. On the route between New York's Kennedy Airport and Los Angeles during late 2012, for example, Virgin passengers were paying an average of $305 a ticket compared to an industry average of $263. Virgin's passenger-load factor on that route was 96% of the industry average during the same period. Virgin CEO David Cush, however, is adamant that the airline "… won't get into a fare war. Our product is good; we've got good loyalty. People will be willing to pay $20 or $30 more." Is he correct? Only time will tell. History, however, is not on Virgin's side. Since airline deregulation in 1978, all but a handful of the roughly 250 new airlines have failed.

Sources: M. Richtel, "At Virgin America, a fine line between pizazz and profit," *New York Times*, September 7, 2013; B. Tuttle, "Why an airline that travelers love is failing," *Time*, October 25, 2012; T. Huddleston, "Virgin America goes public," *Fortune*, November 13, 2014; A. Levine-Weinberg, "How Richard Branson built a $5-billion fortune from scratch," *Motley Fool*, October 19, 2014, www.fool.com.

◤ OVERVIEW

business-level strategy
A business's overall competitive theme; the way it positions itself in the marketplace to gain a competitive advantage, and the different positioning strategies that it can use in different industry settings.

In this chapter we look at the formulation of **business-level strategy**. As you may recall from Chapter 1, business-level strategy refers to the overarching competitive theme of a company in a given market. At its most basic, business-level strategy is about *whom* a company decides to serve (which customer segments), what customer *needs* and *desires* the company is trying to satisfy, and *how* the company decides to satisfy those needs and desires.[1] If this sounds familiar, it is because we have already discussed this in Chapter 1 when we considered how companies construct a mission statement.

The airline Virgin America provides us with an illustration of how this works (see the Opening Case). Virgin America is targeting mid- to upper-income travelers, many of them in the technology industry, who are willing to pay 10–20% extra for a more pleasant flying experience. Virgin attempts to satisfy the desires of this customer segment through excellent customer service and a range of inflight offerings that includes leather seats, more legroom, and full-service meals. As proven by the many awards that it has won, Virgin America has certainly *differentiated* itself from rival carriers. However, like many enterprises that pursue a differentiation strategy, Virgin America also has to deal with an incrementally higher cost structure than its rivals. This is particularly problematic in the airline industry, where low-cost carriers such as Southwest and Jet Blue have conditioned customers to shop for the lowest price. Unless Virgin America can fill its aircraft at higher price points, the strategy may not lead to higher profitability and a sustained competitive advantage.

In this chapter, we will look at how managers decide what business-level strategy to pursue, and how they go about executing that strategy in order to attain a sustainable competitive advantage. We start by looking at the two basic ways that companies compete in a marketplace—by *lowering costs* and by *differentiating* their goods or services from those offered by rivals so that they create more value. Next, we consider the issue of *customer choice* and *market segmentation*, and discuss the decisions that managers must make when it comes to their company's segmentation strategy. Then, synthesizing this, we discuss the various business-level strategies that an enterprise can adopt, and what must be done to successfully implement those strategies. The chapter closes with a discussion of how managers can think about formulating an innovative, business-level strategy that gives their company a unique and defendable position in the marketplace.

◤ LOW COST AND DIFFERENTIATION

Strategy is about the search for competitive advantage. As we saw in Chapter 3, at the most fundamental level, a company has a competitive advantage if it can lower costs relative to rivals and/or if it can differentiate its product offering from those of rivals, thereby creating more value. We will look at lowering costs first, and then at differentiation.[2]

Lowering Costs

Imagine that all enterprises in an industry offer products that are very similar in all respects except for price, and that each company is small relative to total market demand, so that they are unable to influence the prevailing price. This is the situation that exists in commodity markets such as those for oil, wheat, aluminum, and steel. In the global oil market, for example, prices are set by the interaction of supply and demand. Even the world's largest private oil producer, Exxon Mobile, only produces around 3.5% of world output and cannot influence the prevailing price.

In commodity markets, competitive advantage goes to the company that has the lowest costs. Low costs enable a company to make a profit at price points where its rivals are losing money. Low costs can also allow a company to undercut rivals on price, gain market share, and maintain or even increase profitability. Being the low-cost player in an industry can be a very advantageous position.

Although lowering costs below those of rivals is a particularly powerful strategy in a pure commodity industry, it can also have great utility in other settings. General merchandise retailing, for example, is not a classic commodity business. Nevertheless, Wal-Mart has built a very strong competitive position in the U.S. market by being the low-cost player. Because its costs are so low, Wal-Mart can cut prices, grow its market share, and still make profits at price points where its competitors lose money. The same is true in the airline industry, where Southwest Airlines has established a low-cost position. Southwest's operating efficiencies have enabled it to make money in an industry that has been hit by repeated bouts of price warfare, and where many of its rivals have been forced into bankruptcy.

Differentiation

Now let's look at the differentiation side of the equation. Differentiation involves distinguishing your company from its rivals by offering something that they find hard to match. As we saw in the Opening Case, Virgin America has differentiated itself from its rivals through excellence in customer service and offering inflight amenities that its rivals do not. A company can differentiate itself from rivals in many ways A product can be differentiated by superior reliability (it breaks down less often, or not at all), better design, superior functions and features, better point-of-sale service, better after-sales service and support, better branding, and so on. A Rolex watch is differentiated from a Timex watch by superior design, materials, and reliability; a Toyota car is differentiated from a General Motors car by superior reliability (historically, new Toyota models have had fewer defects than new GM models); Apple differentiates its iPhone from rival offerings through superior product design, ease of use, excellent customer service at its Apple stores, and easy synchronization with other Apple products, such as its computers, tablets, iTunes, and iCloud.

Differentiation gives a company two advantages. First, it can allow the company to charge a premium price for its good or service, should it chose to do so. Second, it can help the company grow overall demand and capture market share from its rivals. In the case of the iPhone, Apple has reaped both of these benefits through its successful differentiation strategy. Apple charges more for its iPhone than people pay for rival smartphone offerings, and the differential appeal of Apple products has led to strong demand growth.

It is important to note that differentiation often (but not always) raises the cost structure of the firm. It costs Virgin America more to create a comfortable, full-service, inflight experience. It is often the case that companies pursuing a differentiation strategy have a higher cost structure than companies pursuing a low-cost strategy. On the other hand, somewhat counter intuitively, there are situations where successful differentiation, because it increases primary demand so much, can actually lower costs. Apple's iPhone is a case in point. Apple uses very expensive materials in the iPhone—Gorilla Glass for the screen and brushed aluminum for the case. It could have used cheap plastic, but then the product would not have looked as good and would have scratched easily. Although these decisions about materials originally raised the unit cost of the iPhone, the fact is that Apple has sold so many iPhones that it now enjoys economies of scale in purchasing and can effectively bargain down the price it pays for expensive materials. The result for Apple—successful differentiation of the iPhone—not only helped the company charge a premium price, it has also gown demand to the point where it can lower costs through the attainment of scale economies, thereby widening profit margins. This is why Apple captured 89% of all profits in the global smartphone business in the second half of 2014.

The Apple example points to an essential truth: Successful differentiation gives managers options. One option is to raise the price to reflect the differentiated nature of the product offering and cover any incremental increase in costs (see Figure 5.1). Many firms pursue this option, which can by itself enhance profitability as long as prices increase more than costs. For example, Four Seasons hotels are very luxurious. It certainly costs a lot to provide that luxury, but Four Seasons also charges very high prices for its rooms, and the firm is profitable as a result.

However, the Apple example also suggests that increased profitability and profit growth can come from the increased demand associated with successful differentiation, which enables the firm to use its assets more efficiently and thereby realize *lower costs* from scale economies. This leads to another option: The successful differentiator can hold prices constant, or only increase them slightly, sell more, and boost profitability through the attainment of scale economies (see Figure 5.1).[3]

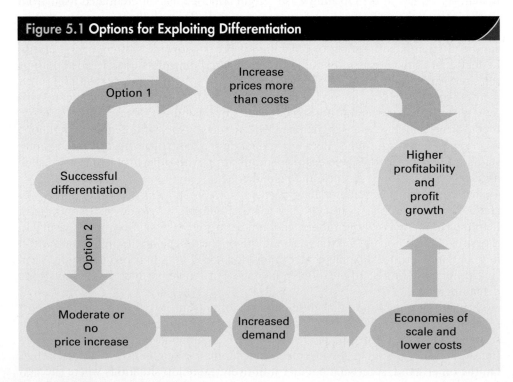

Figure 5.1 Options for Exploiting Differentiation

Source: Charles W.L. Hill © Copyright 2013.

For another example, consider Starbucks. The company has successfully differentiated its product offering from that of rivals such as Tully's by the excellent quality of its
coffee-based drinks; by the quick, efficient, friendly service that its baristas offer customers; by the comfortable atmosphere created by the design of its stores; and by its strong
brand image. This differentiation increases traffic volume in each Starbucks store, thereby increasing the productivity of employees (they are always busy) and the productivity
of the capital invested in the store. Thus, each store realizes scale economies from greater
volume, which lowers the average unit costs at each store. Spread across the 12,000 stores
that Starbucks operates, this represents potentially huge cost savings that translate into
higher profitability. Add this to the enhanced demand that comes from successful differentiation—which in the case of Starbucks not only enables the firm to sell more from
each store, but also to open more stores—and profit growth will also accelerate.

The Differentiation–Low Cost Tradeoff

The thrust of our discussion so far is that a low-cost position and a differentiated position are two very different ways of gaining a competitive advantage. The enterprise striving for the lowest costs does everything it can to be productive and drive down its cost
structure, whereas the enterprise striving for differentiation necessarily has to bear higher costs to achieve that differentiation. Put simply, one cannot be both Wal-Mart and
Nordstrom, Virgin America and Southwest, Porsche and Kia, Rolex and Timex. Managers
must choose between these two basic ways of attaining a competitive advantage.

However, presenting the choice between differentiation and low costs in these terms
is something of a simplification. As we have already noted, the successful differentiator might be able to subsequently reduce costs if differentiation leads to significant
demand growth and the attainment of scale economies. But in actuality, the relationship between low cost and differentiation is subtler than this. In reality, strategy is not
so much about making discrete choices as it is about achieving the right balance is
between differentiation and low costs.

To understand these issues, see Figure 5.2. The convex curve in Figure 5.2 illustrates
what is known as an *efficiency frontier* (also known in economics as a production possibility frontier).[4] The efficiency frontier shows all of the different positions that a company can adopt with regard to differentiation and low cost, *assuming* that its internal
functions and organizational arrangements are configured efficiently to support a particular position (note that the horizontal axis in Figure 5.2 is reverse scaled—moving
along the axis to the right implies lower costs). The efficiency frontier has a convex
shape because of diminishing returns. Diminishing returns imply that when an enterprise already has significant differentiation built into its product offering, increasing
differentiation by a relatively small amount requires significant additional costs. The
converse also holds: A company that already has a low-cost structure must relinquish
much differentiation in its product offering to achieve additional cost reductions.

The efficiency frontier shown in Figure 5.2 is for the U.S. retail apparel business
(Wal-Mart sells more than apparel, but that need not concern us here). As you can see,
the high-end retailer Nordstrom and the low-cost retailer Wal-Mart are both shown to
be on the frontier, implying that both organizations have configured their internal functions and organizations efficiently. However, they have adopted very different positions;
Nordstrom has high differentiation and high costs, whereas Wal-Mart has low costs and
low differentiation. These are not the only viable positions in the industry, however. The

Figure 5.2 The Differentiation–Low Cost Tradeoff

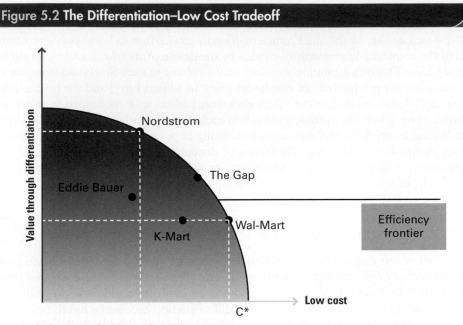

Gap, too, is on the frontier. The Gap offers higher-quality apparel merchandise than Wal-Mart, sold in a more appealing environment, but its offering is nowhere near as differentiated as that of Nordstrom; it is positioned between Wal-Mart and Nordstrom. This mid-level position, offering moderate differentiation at a higher cost than Wal-Mart, makes perfect sense because there are enough consumers demanding this option. They don't want to look as if they purchased their clothes at Wal-Mart; they want fashionable, casual clothes that are more affordable than those available at Nordstrom.

The essential point is that *there are often multiple positions on the differentiation–low-cost continuum that are viable in the sense that they have enough demand to support an offering.* The task for managers is to identify a position in the industry that is viable and then configure the functions and organizational arrangements of the enterprise so that they are run as efficiently and effectively as possible, and enable the firm to reach the frontier. Not all companies are able to do this. Only those that can get to the frontier have a competitive advantage. Getting to the frontier requires excellence in strategy implementation. As has been suggested already in this chapter, business-level strategy is implemented through function and organization. Therefore, *to successfully implement a business-level strategy and reach the efficiency frontier, a company must pursue the right functional-level strategies and be appropriately organized; business-level strategy, functional-level strategy, and organizational arrangement must all be in alignment.*

It should be noted that not all positions on an industry's efficiency frontier are equally attractive. For some positions, there may not be sufficient demand to support a product offering. For other positions, there may be too many competitors going after the same basic position—the competitive space might be too crowded—and the resulting competition might drive prices below acceptable levels.

In Figure 5.2, K-Mart is inside the frontier. K-Mart is trying to position itself in the same basic space as Wal-Mart, but its internal operations are not efficient (the company was operating under bankruptcy protection in the early 2000s, although it is now out of bankruptcy). Also shown in Figure 5.2 is Seattle-based clothing retailer Eddie Bauer, which is owned by Spiegel. Like K-Mart, Eddie Bauer is not an efficiently run operation relative to its rivals. Its parent company has operated under bankruptcy protection three times in the last 20 years.

Value Innovation: Greater Differentiation at a Lower Cost

The efficiency frontier is not static; it is continually being pushed outward by the efforts of managers to improve their firm's performance through innovation. For example, in the mid-1990s, Dell pushed out the efficiency frontier in the personal computer (PC) industry (see Figure 5.3). Dell pioneered the online sale of PCs allowing customers to build their own machines and effectively creating value through customization. In other words, the strategy of selling online allowed Dell to *differentiate* itself from rivals that sold PCs through retail outlets. At the same time, Dell used order information submitted over the Web to efficiently coordinate and manage the global supply chain, driving down production costs in the process. The net result was that Dell was able to offer more value (through superior *differentiation*) at a *lower cost* than its rivals. Through its process innovations, it redefined the frontier of what was possible in the industry.

We use the term **value innovation** to describe what happens when innovation pushes out the efficiency frontier in an industry, allowing for greater value to be offered through superior differentiation at a lower cost than was previously thought possible.[5] When

value innovation
When innovations push out the efficiency frontier in an industry, allowing for greater value to be offered through superior differentiation at a lower cost than was previously thought possible.

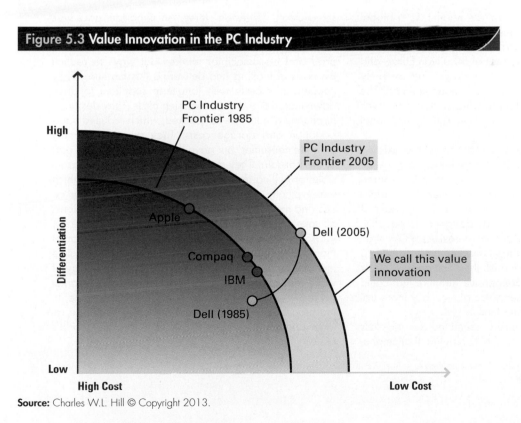

Figure 5.3 Value Innovation in the PC Industry

Source: Charles W.L. Hill © Copyright 2013.

a company pioneers process innovations that lead to value innovation, it effectively changes the game in an industry and may be able to outperform its rivals for a long period of time. This is what happened to Dell. After harnessing the power of the Internet to sell PCs online and coordinate the global supply chain, Dell outperformed its rivals in the industry for over a decade while they scrambled to catch up with the industry leader.

Toyota is another company that benefitted from value innovation. As we have discussed in Chapters 3 and 4, Toyota pioneered lean production systems that improved the quality of automobiles, while simultaneously lowering costs. Toyota *redefined what was possible in the automobile industry*, effectively pushing out the efficiency frontier and enabling the company to better differentiate its product offering at a cost level that its rivals couldn't match. The result was a competitive advantage that persisted for over two decades. For another example of value innovation, see Strategy in Action 5.1,which describes how IKEA redefined competition in the furniture business.

5.1 STRATEGY IN ACTION

IKEA: Value Innovation in Furniture Retailing

IKEA, the privately held furniture retailer, is a global colossus. The world's largest furniture retailer, in 2014 IKEA had 361 stores around the globe, 164,000 employees, revenues in excess of 30 billion Euros, and 861 million customer visits to its stores. The company started out with a single store in Sweden in 1958. The vision of the company's founder, Ingvar Kamprad, was to "democratize furniture," making stylish, functional furniture available at a low cost.

Kamprad's vision was a reaction to the existing market for furniture. Furniture was either seen as an expensive heirloom, which typically had to be ordered from the manufacturer after the consumer had made a purchase decision in a retail store, and might take 3 months to deliver, or was poorly designed, low-quality, cheap furniture sold in discount stores. As IKEAs strategy evolved, its core target market became young professionals looking to furnish their first apartments or homes with stylish but inexpensive furniture that could be disposed off when they were able to buy more traditional, heirloom-style furniture.

Over the years, Kamprad assembled a world-class team that designed stylish, quality furniture that empha-

sized clean, "Swedish" lines. An important goal was to make IKEA offerings 30% cheaper than comparable items produced by rivals. To drive down costs, Kamprad and his associates worked out ways to reduce the costs of making and delivering this furniture. They cooperated closely with long-term suppliers to drive down material and manufacturing costs. They designed furniture that could be flat packed, which reduced transportation and storage costs. They pushed assembly onto the consumer, but gave them lower prices as part of the bargain. They even made the consumer responsible for pulling inventory out of the warehouse, which was typically placed between the product-display areas and the cash registers. As a result of these actions, all taken at the functional level within the company, IKEA was able to offer more value to its target market than rivals, and to do so at a lower cost. Through astute market segmentation and a well-thought-out strategy of value innovation, IKEA redefined the furniture market not just in Sweden but in countries around the globe, in the process becoming the world's largest furniture retailer and making Ingvar Kamprad one of the world's richest men.

Source: C.W.L. Hill, "IKEA in 2013: Furniture Retailer to the World," in C.W.L Hill, G.R. Jones, and M. Shilling, *Strategic Management*, 11ᵗʰ edition (Boston: Cengage, 2015).

WHO ARE OUR CUSTOMERS? MARKET SEGMENTATION

As noted in the introduction to this chapter, business-level strategy begins with deciding *who* the company is going to serve, what *needs* or *desires* it is trying to satisfy, and *how* it is going to satisfy those needs and desires. Answering these questions is not straightforward, because customers in a market are not homogenous. They often differ in fundamental ways. Some are wealthy, some are not; some are old, some are young; some are women, some are men; some are influenced by popular culture, some never watch TV; some live in cities, some in the suburbs; some care deeply about status symbols, others do not; some place a high value on luxury, others value for money; some exercise every day, others have never seen the inside of a gym; some speak English most of the time, while for others Spanish is their first language; and so on.

One fundamental decision that every company faces is whether to recognize such differences in customers, and if so, how to tailor its approach depending on which customer segment or segments it decides to serve. The first step toward answering these questions is to segment the market according to differences in customer demographics, needs, and desires.

Market segmentation refers to the process of subdividing a market into clearly identifiable groups of customers with similar needs, desires, and demand characteristics. Customers within these segments are relatively homogenous, whereas they differ in important ways from customers in other segments of the market. For example, Nike segments the athletic shoe market according to sport and gender because it believes that people participating in different sports expect different things from an athletic shoe (a shoe designed for running is not suitable for playing basketball), and that men and women desire different shoe styling and construction (most men don't want to wear pink shoes). Similarly, in the market for colas, Coca-Cola segments the market by needs—regular Coke for the average consumer, and diet cola for consumers concerned about their weight. The diet cola segment is further subdivided by gender, with Diet Coke targeted at women, and Coke Zero targeted at men.

market segmentation
The way a company decides to group customers, based on important differences in their needs, in order to gain a competitive advantage.

Three Approaches to Market Segmentation

Companies adopt one of three basic approaches to market segmentation. The first is to *not* tailor different offerings to different segments and instead produce and sell a standardized product that is targeted at the average customer in that market. This was the approach adopted by Coca-Cola until the early 1980s, before the introduction of Diet Coke and flavored cola drinks such as Cherry Cola. In those days, Coke was *the* drink for everyone. Coke was differentiated from the offerings of rivals, and particularly Pepsi Cola, by lifestyle advertising that positioned Coke as the iconic American drink, the "real thing." Some network broadcast news programs adopt this approach today. The coverage offered by ABC News, for example, is tailored toward the average American viewer. The giant retailer Wal-Mart targets the average customer in the market, although, unlike Coca-Cola, Wal-Mart's goal is to drive down costs so that it can charge everyday low prices, give its customers value for money, and still make a profit.

A second approach is to recognize differences between segments and create different product offerings for each segment. Coca-Cola has adopted this approach since the 1980s. In 1982, it introduced Diet Coke, targeting that drink at the weight and health conscious. In 2007, it introduced Coke Zero, also a diet cola, but this time targeted at men. Coca Cola did this because company research found that men tended to associate Diet Coke with women. Since 2007, Diet Coke has been repositioned as more of a women's diet drink. Similarly, in the automobile industry, Toyota has brands that address the entire market—Scion for budget-constrained, young, entry-level buyers, Toyota for the middle market, and Lexus for the luxury end of the market. In each of these segments Toyota tries to differentiate itself from rivals in the segment by the excellent reliability and high quality of its offerings.

A third approach is to target only a limited number of market segments, or just one, and to become the very best at serving that particular segment. In the automobile market, Porsche focuses exclusively on the very top end of the market, targeting wealthy, middle-aged, male consumers who have a passion for the speed, power, and engineering excellence associated with its range of sports cars. Porsche is clearly pursuing a differentiation strategy with regard to this segment, although it emphasizes a different type of differentiation than Toyota. Alternatively, Kia of South Korea has positioned itself as low-cost player in the industry, selling vehicles that are aimed at value-conscious buyers in the middle- and lower-income brackets. In the network broadcasting news business, Fox News and MSNBC have also adopted a focused approach. Fox tailors its content toward viewers on the right of the political spectrum, whereas MSNBC is differentiated toward viewers on the left.

When managers decide to ignore different segments and produce a standardized product for the average consumer, we say they are pursuing a **standardization strategy**. When they decide to serve many segments, or even the entire market, producing different offerings for different segments, we say they are pursuing a **segmentation strategy**. When they decide to serve a limited number of segments, or just one segment, we say they are pursuing a **focus strategy**. Today, Wal-Mart is pursuing a standardization strategy, Toyota a segmentation strategy, and Nordstrom a focus strategy.

Market Segmentation, Costs and Revenues

It is important to understand that these different approaches to market segmentation have different implications for costs and revenues. Consider first the comparison between a standardization strategy and a segmentation strategy.

A standardization strategy, which is typically associated with lower costs than a segmentation strategy, involves the company producing one, basic offering and trying to attain economies of scale by achieving high-volume sales. Wal-Mart pursues a standardization strategy and achieves enormous economies of scale in purchasing, driving down its cost of goods sold.

In contrast, a segmentation strategy requires that the company customize its product offering to different segments, producing multiple offerings, one for each segment. Customization can drive up costs for two reasons; first, the company may sell less of each offering, making it harder to achieve economies of scale; second, products targeted at segments at the higher-income end of the market may require more functions and features, which can raise the costs of production and delivery.

standardization strategy
When a company decides to ignore different segments and produces a standardized product for the average consumer.

segmentation strategy
When a company decides to serve many segments, or even the entire market, producing different offerings for different segments.

focus strategy
When a company decides to serve a limited number of segments, or just one segment.

On the other hand, it is important not to lose sight of the fact that advances in production technology, and particularly lean production techniques, have allowed for *mass customization*—that is, the production of more product variety without a large cost penalty (see Chapter 4 for details). In addition, by designing products that share common components, some manufacturing companies achieve substantial economies of scale in component production while still producing a variety of end products aimed at different segments. This is an approach adopted by large automobile companies, which try to utilize common components and platforms across a wide range of models. To the extent that mass customization and component sharing is possible, the cost penalty borne by a company pursuing a segmentation strategy may be limited.

Although a standardization strategy may have lower costs than a segmentation strategy, a segmentation strategy has one big advantage: It allows the company to capture incremental revenues by customizing its offerings to the needs of different groups of consumers and thus selling more in total. A company pursuing a standardization strategy where a product is aimed at the average consumer may lose sales from customers who desire more functions and features and are prepared to pay more for them. Similarly, it may lose sales from customers who cannot afford to purchase the average product but might enter the market if a more basic offering was available.

This reality was first recognized in the automobile industry back in the 1920s. The early leader in the automobile industry was Ford with its Model T offering. Henry Ford famously said that consumers could have it in "any color as long as it's black." Ford was in essence pursuing a standardization strategy. However, in the 1920s, Ford rapidly lost market share to General Motors, a company that pursued a segmentation strategy and offered a range of products aimed at different customer groups.

For a focus strategy, the impact on costs and revenues is subtler. Companies that focus on the higher-income or higher-value end of the market will tend to have a higher cost structure for two reasons. First, they have to add features and functions to their products that appeal to higher-income consumers, and this raises costs. For example, luxury retailer Nordstrom locates its stores in areas where real estate is expensive; its stores have costly fittings and fixtures and a wide-open store plan with lots of room to browse; and the merchandise is expensive and does not turn over as fast as the basic clothes and shoes sold at stores like Wal-Mart. Second, the relatively limited nature of demand associated with serving a given segment of the market may make it hard to attain economies of scale. Offsetting this, however, is the fact that the customization and exclusivity associated with a strategy of focusing on the high-income end of the market may enable a firm to charge significantly higher prices than enterprises pursuing standardization and segmentation strategies.

For companies focusing on the lower-income end of the market, or a segment that desires value for money, a different calculus comes into play. First, such companies tend to produce a more basic offering that is relatively inexpensive to produce and deliver. This may help them to drive down their cost structures. The retailer Costco, for example, focuses on consumers who seek value for money and are less concerned about brand than they are about price. Costco sells a limited range of merchandise in large, warehouse-like stores. A Costco store has about 3,750 stock-keeping units (SKUs), compared to 142,000 SKUs at the average Wal-Mart superstore. Products are stored on pallets stacked on utilitarian metal shelves. Costco offers consumers the opportunity to purchase basic goods such as breakfast cereal, dog food, and paper towels in bulk purchases and at lower prices than found elsewhere. It turns over

generic business-level strategy

A strategy that gives a company a specific form of competitive position and advantage vis-à-vis its rivals, resulting in above-average profitability.

broad low-cost strategy

When a company lowers costs so that it can lower prices and still make a profit.

broad differentiation strategy

When a company differentiates its product in some way, such as by recognizing different segments or offering different products to each segment.

focus low-cost strategy

When a company targets a certain segment or niche and tries to be the low-cost player in that niche.

focus differentiation strategy

When a company targets a certain segment or niche and customizes its offering to the needs of that particular segment through the addition of features and functions.

inventory rapidly, typically selling it before it has to pay its suppliers and thereby reducing its working capital needs. Thus, by tailoring its business to the needs of a segment, Costco is able to undercut the cost structure and pricing of a retail gain such as Wal-Mart, even though it lacks Wal-Mart's enormous economies of scale in purchasing. The drawback, of course, is that Costco offers much less choice than you will find at a Wal-Mart superstore; so, for customers looking for one-stop shopping at a low price, Wal-Mart is likely to be the store of choice.

BUSINESS-LEVEL STRATEGY CHOICES

We now have enough information to identify the basic, business-level strategy choices that companies make. These basic choices are sometimes called **generic business-level strategy**. The various choices are illustrated in Figure 5.4.

Companies that pursue a standardized or segmentation strategy both target a broad market. However, those pursuing a segmentation strategy recognize different segments and tailor their offering accordingly, whereas those pursuing a standardization strategy focus on serving the average consumer. Companies that target the broad market can either concentrate on lowering their costs so that they can lower prices and still make a profit, in which case they are pursuing a **broad low-cost strategy**, or they can try to differentiate their product in some way, in which case they are pursuing a **broad differentiation strategy**. Companies that decide to recognize different segments and offer different product to each one are by default pursuing a broad differentiation strategy. It is possible, however, to pursue a differentiation strategy while not recognizing different segments, as Coca-Cola did prior to the 1980s. Today, Wal-Mart pursues a broad low-cost strategy, whereas Toyota and Coca-Cola pursue a broad differentiation strategy.

Companies that target a few segments, or more typically, just one, are pursuing a focus or niche strategy. These companies can either try to be the low-cost player in that niche, as Costco has done, in which case we say they pursuing a **focus low-cost strategy**, or they can try to customize their offering to the needs of that particular segment through the addition of features and functions, as Virgin America has done, in which case we say they are pursuing a **focus differentiation strategy**.

Figure 5.4 Generic Business-Level Strategies

It is important to understand that there is often no one best way to compete in an industry. Different strategies may be equally viable. Wal-Mart, Costco, and Nordstrom are all in the retail industry, all three compete in different ways, and all three have done very well financially. The important thing is that managers are confident in their business-level strategy, have clear logic for pursuing that strategy, have an offering that matches their strategy, and have aligned functional activities and organizational arrangements with that strategy in order to execute it well.

Michael Porter, the originator of the concept of generic business-level strategies, has argued that companies must make a clear choice between the different options outlined in Figure 5.4.[6] If they don't, Porter argues, they may become "stuck in the middle" and experience relatively poor performance. Central to Porter's thesis is the assertion that it is not possible to be both a differentiated company and a low-cost enterprise. According to Porter, differentiation by its very nature raises costs and makes it impossible to attain the low-cost position in an industry. By the same token, to achieve a low-cost position companies necessarily must limit spending on product differentiation.

There is certainly considerable value in this perspective. As we have noted, one company cannot be both Nordstrom and Wal-Mart, Timex and Rolex, Porsche and Kia, or Southwest and Virgin America. Low cost and differentiation are very different ways of competing—they require different functional strategies and different organizational arrangements. Trying to do both at the same time may not work. On the other hand, there are important caveats to this argument.

First—as we have already seen in this chapter when we discussed value innovation through improvements in process and product—a company can push out the efficiency frontier in its industry, redefining what is possible, and deliver more differentiation at a lower cost than its rivals. In such circumstances, a company might find itself in the fortunate position of being both the differentiated player in its industry and having a low-cost position. Ultimately its rivals might catch up, in which case it may well have to make a choice between emphasizing low cost and differentiation, but as we have seen from the case histories of Dell and Toyota, value innovators can gain a competitive advantage that lasts for years, if not decades (another example of value innovation is given in Strategy in Action 5.2, which recounts the history of Microsoft Office).

Second, it is important for the differentiated company to recognize that it cannot waver in its focus on efficiency. Similarly, the low-cost company cannot ignore product differentiation. The task facing a company pursuing a differentiation strategy is to be as efficient as possible given its choice of strategy. The differentiated company should not cut costs so deeply that it harms its capability to differentiate its offering from that of rivals. At the same time, it cannot let costs get out of control. Nordstrom, for example, is very efficient given its choice of strategic position. It is not a low-cost company by any means, but given its choice of how to compete it operates as efficiently as possible. Similarly, the low-cost company cannot totally ignore key differentiators in its industry. Wal-Mart does not provide the high level of customer service found at Nordstrom, but Wal-Mart cannot simply ignore customer service. Even though Wal-Mart has a self-service business model, employees are on hand to help customers with questions if needed. The task for low-cost companies such as Wal-Mart is to be "good enough" with regard to key differentiators. For another example of how this plays out, see Strategy in Action 5.2, which examines the competition between Google and Microsoft in the market for office-productivity software.

5.2 STRATEGY IN ACTION

Microsoft Office Versus Google Apps

Microsoft has long been the dominant player in the market for office productivity software with its Office suite of programs, which includes a word processor, spreadsheet, presentation software, and an e-mail client. Microsoft's rise to dominance in this market was the result of an important innovation—in 1989, Microsoft was the first company to bundle word processing, spreadsheet, and presentation programs together into a single offering that was interoperable. At the time, the market leader in word-processing software was Word Perfect; in spreadsheet software it was Lotus; and in presentation software it was Harvard Graphics. Microsoft was number 2 in each of these markets. However, by offering a bundle and pricing it below the price of each program purchased on its own, Microsoft grabbed share from its competitors, none of which had a full suite of offerings. In effect, Microsoft Office offered consumers more value (interoperability), at a lower price, than could be had from rivals.

As demand for Office expanded, Microsoft was able to spread the fixed costs of product development over a much larger volume than its rivals, and unit costs fell, giving Microsoft the double advantage of a differentiated product offering and a low-cost position. The results included the creation of a monopoly position in office- productivity software and two decades of extraordinary high returns for Microsoft in this market.

The landscape shifted in 2006, when Google introduced Google Apps, an online suite of office productivity software that was aimed squarely at Microsoft's profitable Office franchise. Unlike Office at the time, Google Apps was an online service. The basic programs reside on the cloud, and documents are saved on the cloud. At first, Google lacked a full suite of programs, and traction was slow, but since 2010 adoption of Google Apps has accelerated. Today, Google Apps offers the same basic programs as Office—a word processer, spreadsheet, presentation software, and an e-mail client—but far fewer features. Google's approach is not to match Office on features, but to *be good enough* for the majority of users. This helps to reduce development costs. Google also distributes Google Apps exclusively over the Internet, which is a very-low-cost distribution model, whereas Office still has a significant presence in the physical retail channel, raising costs.

In other words, Google is pursuing a low-cost strategy with regard to Google Apps. Consistent with this, Google Apps is priced significantly below Office. Google charges $50 a year for each person using its product. In contrast, Microsoft Office costs $400 per computer for business users (although significant discounts are often negotiated). Initially, Google Apps was targeted at small businesses and start-ups, but more recently, Google seems to be gaining traction in the enterprise space, which is Microsoft's core market for Office. In 2012, Google scored an impressive string of wins, including licenses with the Swiss drug company Hoffman La Roche, where over 80,000 employees use the package, and with the U.S. Interior Department, where 90,000 use it. In total, Google Apps earned approximately $1 billion in revenue in 2012. Estimates suggest that the company has more than 30 million paying subscribers. This still makes it a small offering relative to Microsoft Office, which is installed on over 1 billion computers worldwide. Microsoft Office, which generated $24 billion in revenue in 2012, remains Microsoft's most profitable business. However, Microsoft cannot ignore Google Apps.

Indeed, Microsoft is not standing still. In 2012, Microsoft rolled out its own cloud-based Office offering, Office 365. Office 365 starts at a list price of $72 a year per person, and it can cost as much as $240 per user annually in versions that offer many more features and software-development capabilities. According to a Microsoft spokesperson, demand for Office 365 is strong. Microsoft argues that Google cannot match the quality of the enterprise experience that Microsoft can provide in in areas like privacy, security, and data handling. Microsoft's message is clear—it still believes that Office is the superior product offering, differentiated by features, functions, privacy, data handing, and security. Whether Office 365 will keep Google Apps in check, however, remains to be seen.

Sources: Author interviews at Microsoft and Google; Q. Hardy, "Google Apps Moving onto Microsoft's Business Turf," *New York Times*, December 26, 2012; A. R. Hickey, "Google Apps: A $1-Billion Business?," *CRN*, February 3, 2012, www.crn.com.

BUSINESS-LEVEL STRATEGY, INDUSTRY, AND COMPETITIVE ADVANTAGE

Properly executed, a well-chosen, well-crafted business-level strategy can give a company a competitive advantage over actual and potential rivals. More precisely, it can put the company in an advantageous position relative to each of the competitive forces that we discussed in Chapter 2—specifically, the threat of entrants, the power of buyers and suppliers, the threat posed by substitute goods or services, and the intensity of rivalry between companies in the industry.

Consider first the low-cost company; by definition, the low-cost enterprise can make profits at price points that its rivals cannot profitably match. This makes it very hard for rivals to enter its market. In other words, the low-cost company can build an entry barrier into its market; it can, in effect, erect an economic moat around its business that thwarts higher-cost rivals. Amazon has done this in the online retail business. Through economies of scale and other operating efficiencies, Amazon has attained a very-low-cost structure that effectively constitutes a high entry barrier into this business. Rivals with less volume and fewer economies of scale than Amazon cannot match it on price without losing money—not a very appealing proposition.

A low-cost position and the ability to charge low prices and still make profits also protect a company against substitute goods or services. Low costs can help a company absorb cost increases that may be passed on downstream by powerful suppliers. Low costs can also enable the company to respond to demands for deep price discounts from powerful buyers and still make money. The low-cost company is often best positioned to survive price rivalry in its industry. Indeed, a low-cost company may deliberately initiate a price war in order to grow volume and drive its weaker rivals out of the industry. Dell did this during its glory days in the early 2000s, when it repeatedly cut prices for PCs to drive up sales volume and force marginal competitors out of the business. This strategy enabled Dell to become the largest computer company in the world by the mid-2000s.

Now let us consider the differentiated company. The successful differentiator is also protected against each of the competitive forces we discussed in Chapter 2. The brand loyalty associated with differentiation can constitute an important entry barrier, protecting the company's market from potential competitors. The brand loyalty enjoyed by Apple in the smartphone business has set a very high hurdle for any new entrant to match, and effectively acts as a deterrent to entry. Because the successful differentiator sells on non-price factors such as design or customer service, it is also less exposed to pricing pressure from powerful buyers. Indeed, the opposite may be the case—the successful differentiator may be able to implement price increases without encountering much, if any, resistance from buyers. The differentiated company can also fairly easily absorb price increases from powerful suppliers and pass them on downstream in the form of higher prices for its offerings, without suffering much, if any, loss in market share. The brand loyalty enjoyed by the differentiated company also protects it from substitute goods and service.

The differentiated company is protected from intense price rivalry within its industry by its brand loyalty, and by the fact that non-price factors are important to its customer set. At the same time, the differentiated company often does have to invest significant effort and resources in non-price rivalry, such as brand building through marketing campaigns or expensive product development efforts, but to the extent that it is successful, it can reap the benefits of these investments in the form of stable or higher prices.

This being said, it is important to note that focused companies often have an advantage over their broad market rivals in the segment or niche in which they compete in. For example, although Wal-Mart and Costco are both low-cost companies, Costco has a cost advantage over Wal-Mart in the segment that it serves. This primarily is due to the fact that Costco carries far fewer SKUs, and those it does are sold in bulk. However, if Costco tried to match Wal-Mart and serve the broader market, the need to carry a wider product selection (Wal-Mart has over 140,000 SKUs) means that its cost advantage would be lost.

The same can be true for a differentiated company. By focusing on a niche, and customizing the offering to that segment, a differentiated company can often outsell differentiated rivals that target a broader market. Thus, Porsche can outsell broad market companies like Toyota or General Motors in the high-end sports car niche of the market, in part because the company does not sell outside of its core niche. Porsche creates an image of exclusivity that appeals to its customer base. Were Porsche to start moving down market, it would lose this exclusive appeal and become just another broad market differentiator.

IMPLEMENTING BUSINESS-LEVEL STRATEGY

As we have already suggested in this chapter, for a company's business-level strategy to translate into a competitive advantage, it must be well implemented. This means that actions taken at the functional level should support the business-level strategy, as should the organizational arrangements of the enterprise. There must, in other words, be *alignment* or *fit* between business-level strategy, functional strategy, and organization (see Figure 5.5). We have discussed functional strategy in Chapter 4; detailed discussion of organizational arrangements is postponed until Chapter 12. Notwithstanding, we will make some basic observations about the functional strategies and

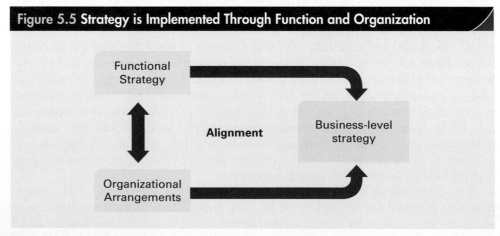

Figure 5.5 Strategy is Implemented Through Function and Organization

Source: Charles W.L. Hill © Copyright 2013.

organizational arrangements required to implement the business-level strategies of low cost and differentiation.

Lowering Costs Through Functional Strategy and Organization

Companies achieve a low-cost position primarily by pursuing functional-level strategies that result in *superior efficiency* and *superior product reliability*, which we discussed in detail in Chapter 4 when we looked at functional-level strategy and the building blocks of competitive advantage. As you will recall from Chapter 4, the following are clearly important:

- Achieving economies of scale and learning effects.
- Adopting lean production and flexible manufacturing technologies.
- Implementing quality improvement methodologies to ensure that the goods or services the company produces are reliable, so that time, materials, and effort are not wasted producing and delivering poor-quality products that have to be scrapped, reworked, or reproduced from scratch
- Streamlining processes to take out unnecessary steps
- Using information systems to automate business process
- Implementing just-in-time inventory control systems
- Designing products that can be produced and delivered at as low a cost as possible
- Taking steps to increase customer retention and reduce customer churn

In addition, to lower costs the firm must be *organized* in such a way that the structure, control systems, incentive systems, and culture of the company all emphasize and reward employee behaviors and actions that are consistent with, or lead to, higher productivity and greater efficiency. As will be explained in detail in Chapter 12, the kinds of organizational arrangements that are favored in such circumstances include a flat organizational structure with very few levels in the management hierarchy, clear lines of accountability and control, measurement and control systems that focus on productivity and cost containment, incentive systems that encourage employees to work in as productive a manner as possible and empower them to suggest and pursue initiatives that are consistent with productivity improvements, and a frugal culture that emphasizes the need to control costs. Companies that operate with these organizational arrangements include Amazon and Wal-Mart.

Differentiation Through Functional-Level Strategy and Organization

As with low costs, to successfully differentiate itself a company must pursue the right actions at the functional level and organize itself appropriately. Pursuing functional-level strategies that enable the company to achieve *superior quality* in terms of both reliability and excellence are important, as is an emphasis upon *innovation* in the product offering, and high levels of *customer responsiveness*. You will recall from Chapters 3 and 4 that superior quality, innovation, and customer responsiveness are three of the four building blocks of competitive advantage, the other being *efficiency*. Remember, too, that the differentiated firm cannot ignore efficiency; by virtue of its strategic choice, the differentiated company is likely to have a higher cost structure than the low-cost player in its industry. Specific functional-level strategies designed to improve differentiation include:

- Customization of the product offering and marketing mix to different market segments
- Designing product offerings that have high perceived quality in terms of their functions, features, and performance, in addition to being reliable
- A well-developed customer-care function for quickly handling and responding to customer inquiries and problems
- Marketing efforts focused on brand building and perceived differentiation from rivals
- Hiring and employee development strategies designed to ensure that employees act in a manner that is consistent with the image that the company is trying to project to the world

As demonstrated in the opening case, Virgin America's successful differentiation is due to its excellent customer service, which is an element of customer responsiveness. Similarly, Apple has an excellent customer care function, as demonstrated by its in-store "Genius Bars," where well-trained employees are available to help customers with inquiries and problems, and provide tutorials to help them get the best value out of their purchases. Apple has also been very successful at building a brand that differentiates it from rivals such as Microsoft (for example, the long-running TV advertisements featuring "Mac," a very hip guy, and "PC," a short, overweight man in a shabby gray suit).

As regards organization, creating the right structure, controls, incentives, and culture can all help a company differentiate itself. In a differentiated enterprise, one key issue is to make sure that marketing, product design, customer service, and customer care functions all play a key role. Again consider Apple; following the return of Steve Jobs to the company in 1997, he reorganized to give the industrial design group the lead on all new product development efforts. Under this arrangement, industrial design, headed by Johnny Ive, reported directly to Jobs, and engineering reported to industrial design for purposes of product development. This meant that designers rather than engineers specified the look and feel of a new product, and engineers then had to design according to the parameters imposed by the design group. This is in contrast to almost all other companies in the computer and smartphone business, where engineering typically takes the lead on product development. Jobs felt that this organizational arrangement was necessary to ensure that Apple produced beautiful products that not only worked well, but also looked and felt elegant. Because Apple under Jobs was differentiating by design, design was given a pivotal position in the organization.[7]

Making sure that control systems, incentive systems, and culture are aligned with the strategic thrust is also extremely important for differentiated companies. We will return to and expand upon these themes in Chapter 12.

◤ COMPETING DIFFERENTLY: BLUE OCEAN STRATEGY

We have already suggested in this chapter that sometimes companies can fundamentally shift the game in their industry by figuring out ways to offer more value through differentiation at a lower cost than their rivals. We referred to this as *value innovation*, a term first coined by Chan Kim and Renee Mauborgne.[8] Kim and Mauborgne developed their ideas further in the bestselling book *Blue Ocean Strategy*.[9] Their basic proposition is that many successful companies have built their competitive advantage by redefining their product offering through value innovation and, in essence, creating a new market space. They describe the process of thinking through value innovation as searching for the blue ocean—which they characterize as a wide-open market space where a company can chart its own course.

One of their examples of a company that found its blue ocean is Southwest Airlines. From its conception, Southwest competed differently than other companies in the U.S. airline industry. Most important, Southwest saw its main competitors not as other airlines but as people who would typically drive or take a bus to travel. For Southwest, the focus was to reduce travel time for its customer set and do so in a way that was cheap, reliable, and convenient, so that they would prefer to fly rather than drive.

The first route that Southwest operated was between Houston and Dallas. To reduce total travel time, it decided to fly into the small, downtown airports in both cities, Hobby in Houston and Love Field in Dallas, rather than the large, intercontinental airports located an hour's drive outside of both cities. The goal was to reduce total travel time by eliminating the need to drive to reach a major airport outside the city before even beginning one's journey. Southwest put as many flights a day on the route as possible to make it convenient, and did everything possible to drive down operating costs so that it could charge low prices and still make a profit.

As the company grew and opened more routes, it followed the same basic strategy. Southwest always flew point to point, never routing passengers through hubs. Changing planes in a hub adds to total travel time and can hurt reliability, measured by on-time departures and arrivals, if connections are slow arriving or departing a hub due to adverse events such as bad weather delaying traffic somewhere in an airline's network. Southwest also dispensed with inflight meals, only offers coach-class seating, does not have lounges in airports for business-class passengers, and has standardized on one type of aircraft, the Boeing 737, which helps to raise reliability. The net result is that Southwest delivers more value *to its customer set* and does so at a lower cost than its rivals, enabling it to price lower than them and still make a profit. Southwest is a value innovator.

Kim and Mauborgne use the concept of a *strategy canvas* to map out how value innovators differ from their rivals. The strategy canvas for Southwest shown in Figure 5.6, shows that Southwest charges a low price and does not provide meals or lounges in airports, business-class seating, or connections through hubs (it flies point to point), but does provide friendly, quick, convenient, reliable low-cost service, *which is exactly what its customer set values*.

The whole point of the Southwest example, and other business case histories Kim and Mauborgne review, is to illustrate how many successful enterprises compete differently than their less successful rivals: They carve out a unique market space for themselves through value innovation. When thinking about how a company might redefine its market and craft a new business-level strategy, Kim and Mauborgne suggest that managers ask themselves the following questions:

1. **Eliminate**: Which factors that rivals take for granted in our industry can be eliminated, thereby reducing costs?
2. **Reduce**: Which factors should be reduced well below the standard in our industry, thereby lowering costs?
3. **Raise**: Which factors should be raised above the standard in our industry, thereby increasing value?
4. **Create**: What factors can we create that rivals do not offer, thereby increasing value?

Southwest *eliminated* lounges, business seating, and meals in flight; it *reduced* inflight refreshment to be well below industry standards; but by flying point to point it

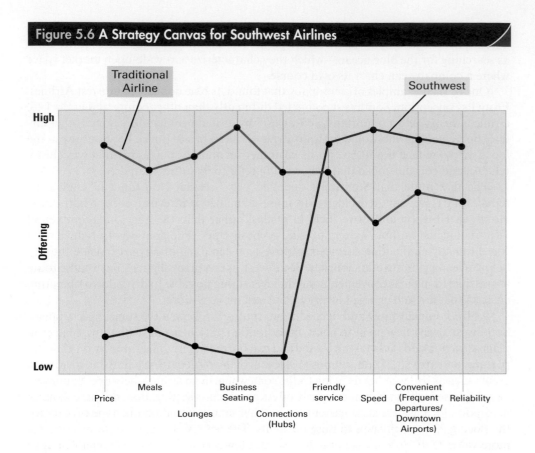

Figure 5.6 A Strategy Canvas for Southwest Airlines

raised speed (reducing travel time), convenience, and reliability. Southwest also *created* more value by flying between smaller, downtown airports whenever possible, something that other airlines did not typically do.

This is a useful framework, and it directs managerial attention to the need to think differently than rivals in order to create an offering and strategic position that are unique. If such efforts are successful, they can help a company build a sustainable advantage.

One great advantage of successful value innovation is that it can catch rivals off guard and make it difficult for them to catch up. For example, when Dell Computer started to sell direct to customers via the Internet, it was very difficult for rivals to respond because they had already invested in a different way of doing business—selling though a physical retail channel. Dell's rivals could not easily adopt the Dell model without alienating their channel, which would have resulted in lost sales. The prior strategic investment of Dell's rivals in distribution channels—which, at the time they were made, seemed reasonable—became a source of inertia that limited their ability to rapidly respond to Dell's innovations. The same holds true in the airline industry, where the prior strategic investments of traditional airlines have made it very difficult for them to respond to the threat posed by Southwest.

In sum, value innovation, because it shifts the basis of competition, can result in a sustained competitive advantage for the innovating company due to the relative inertia of rivals and their inability to respond in a timely manner without breaking prior strategic commitments.

KEY TERMS

business-level
strategy 148
value innovation 153
market segmentation 155
standardization
strategy 156

segmentation
strategy 156
focus strategy 156
generic business-level
strategy 158

broad low-cost
strategy 158
broad differentiation
strategy 158

focus low-cost
strategy 158
focus differentiation
strategy 158

TAKEAWAYS FOR STRATEGIC MANAGERS

1. Business-level strategy refers to the overarching competitive theme of a company in a given market.
2. At the most basic level, a company has a competitive advantage if it can lower costs relative to rivals and/or differentiate its product offering from those of rivals.
3. A low-cost position enables a company to make money at price points where its rivals are losing money.
4. A differentiated company can charge a higher price for its offering, and/or it can use superior value to generate growth in demand.
5. There are often multiple positions along the differentiation–low cost continuum that are viable in a market.
6. Value innovation occurs when a company develops new products, processes, or strategies that enable it to offer more value through differentiation at a lower cost than its rivals.
7. Formulating business-level strategy starts with deciding *who* the company is going to serve, what *needs* or *desires* it is trying to satisfy, and *how* it is going to satisfy those needs and desires.
8. Market segmentation is the process of subdividing a market into clearly identifiable groups of customers that have similar needs, desires, and demand characteristics.
9. A company's approach to market segmentation is an important aspect of its business-level strategy.
10. There are four generic business-level strategies: broad low cost, broad differentiation, focus low cost, and focus differentiation.
11. Business-level strategy is executed through actions taken at the functional level and through organizational arrangements.
12. Many successful companies have built their competitive advantage by redefining their product offering through value innovation and creating a new market space. The process of thinking through value innovation has been described as searching for a "blue ocean"—a wide-open market space where a company can chart its own course.

DISCUSSION QUESTIONS

1. What are the main differences between a low-cost strategy and a differentiation strategy?
2. Why is market segmentation such an important step in the process of formulating a business-level strategy?
3. How can a business-level strategy of (a) low cost and (b) differentiation offer some protection against competitive forces in a company's industry?
4. What is required to transform a business-level strategy from a concept to a reality?
5. What is meant by the term *value innovation*? Can you identify a company not discussed in the text that has established a strong competitive position through value innovation?

CLOSING CASE

Nordstrom is one of American's most successful fashion retailers. John Nordstrom, a Swedish immigrant, established the company in 1901 with a single shoe store in Seattle. From the very start, Nordstrom's approach to business was to provide exceptional customer service, selection, quality, and value. This approach remains Nordstrom's hallmark today.

The modern Nordstrom is a fashion specialty chain with 240 stores in 31 states. Nordstrom generated almost $12.5 billion in sales in 2014 and makes consistently higher-than-average returns on invested capital. Its return on invested capital (ROIC) has consistently been in the mid teens to low 20s, and was 16.3% in 2014–strong performance for a retailer.

Nordstrom is a niche company. It focuses on a relatively affluent customer base that is looking for affordable luxury. The stores, located in upscale areas, have expensive fittings and fixtures that convey an impression of luxury. The stores invite browsing. Touches such as live music played on a grand piano help create an appealing atmosphere. The merchandise is fashionable and of high quality. What truly differentiates Nordstrom from many of its rivals, however, is its legendary excellence in customer service.

Nordstrom's salespeople are typically well groomed and dressed, polite and helpful, and known for their attention to detail. They are selected for their ability to interact with customers in a positive way. During the interview process for new employees, one of the most important questions asked of candidates is their definition of good customer service. Thank-you cards, home deliveries, personal appointments, and access to personal shoppers are the norm at Nordstrom. There is a no-questions-asked returns policy, with no receipt required. Nordstrom's philosophy is that the customer is always right. The company's salespeople are well compensated, with good benefits and commissions on sales that range from 6.75% to 10% depending on the department. Top salespeople at Nordstrom have the ability to earn over $100,000 a year, mostly in commissions.

The customer service ethos is central to the culture and organization of Nordstrom. The organization chart is an inverted pyramid, with salespeople on the top and the CEO at the bottom. According to CEO Blake Nordstrom, this is because "I work for them. My job is to make them as successful as possible." Management constantly shares anecdotes emphasizing the primacy of customer service at Nordstrom in order to reinforce the culture. One story relates that when a customer in Fairbanks, Alaska, wanted to return two tires (which Nordstrom does not sell), bought some time ago from another store once on the same site, a sales clerk looked up their price and gave him his money back!

Despite its emphasis on quality and luxury, Nordstrom has not neglected operating efficiency. Sales per square foot are $400 despite the large, open-plan nature of the stores, and inventory turns exceed 5 times per year, up from 3.5 times a decade ago. These are good figures for a high-end department store. Management constantly seeks ways to improve efficiency and customer service; recently, it put mobile checkout devices into the hands of 5,000 salespeople, eliminating the need for customers to wait in a checkout line.

Sources: A. Martinez, "Tale of Lost Diamond Adds Glitter to Nordstrom's Customer Service," *Seattle Times*, May 11, 2011 (www.seattletimes.com); C. Conte, "Nordstrom Built on Customer Service," *Jacksonville Business Journal*, September 7, 2012 (www.bizjournals.com/Jacksonville); W. S. Goffe, "How Working as a Stock Girl at Nordstrom Prepared Me for Being a Lawyer," *Forbes*, December 3, 2012; and P. Swinand, "Nordstrom Inc," Morningstar, February 22, 2013, www. Morningstar.com.

CASE DISCUSSION QUESTIONS

1. What is Nordstrom's segmentation strategy? Who does it serve?
2. With regard to its core segment, what does Nordstrom offer its customers?
3. Using the Porter model, which generic business-level strategy is Nordstrom pursuing?
4. What actions taken at the functional level have enabled Nordstrom to successfully implement its strategy?

5. What is the source of Nordstrom's long-term, sustainable competitive advantage? What valuable and rare resources does Nordstrom have that its rivals find difficult to imitate?
6. Is Nordstrom organized for success?

NOTES

[1] D. F. Abell, *Defining the Business: The Starting Point of Strategic Planning* (Englewood Cliffs, NJ: Prentice-Hall, 1980).

[2] M. E. Porter, *Competitive Advantage* (New York: Free Press, 1985); M. E. Porter, *Competitive Strategy* (New York, Free Press, 1980).

[3] C. W. L. Hill, "Differentiation Versus Low Cost or Differentiation and Low Cost: A Contingency Framework," *Academy of Management Review* 13 (1988): 401–412.

[4] M. E. Porter, "What Is Strategy?" *Harvard Business Review,* Onpoint Enhanced Edition Article, February 1, 2000.

[5] W.C. Kim and R. Mauborgne, "Value Innovation: The Strategic Logic of High Growth," *Harvard Business Review* (January–February 1997).

[6] Porter, *Competitive Advantage* and *Competitive Strategy*.

[7] The story was related to author Charles Hill by an executive at Apple.

[8] Kim and Mauborgne, "Value Innovation: The Strategic Logic of High Growth."

[9] W.C. Kim and R. Mauborgne, *Blue Ocean Strategy* (Boston, Mass: Harvard Business School Press, 2005).

sergign/Shutterstock.com

CHAPTER 6

BUSINESS-LEVEL STRATEGY AND THE INDUSTRY ENVIRONMENT

LEARNING OBJECTIVES

6.1 Identify the strategies managers can develop to increase profitability in fragmented industries

6.2 Discuss the special problems that exist in embryonic and growth industries and how companies can develop strategies to effectively compete

6.3 Understand competitive dynamics in mature industries and discuss the strategies managers can develop to increase profitability even when competition is intense

6.4 Outline the different strategies that companies in declining industries can use to support their business models and profitability

OPENING CASE

Can Best Buy Survive the Rise of E-commerce?

Best Buy Co., Inc. is the world's largest retailer of consumer electronics, computers, mobile phones, and related products. In the United States it operates under the brands of Best Buy, Magnolia Audio Video, Pacific Sales, and Geek Squad. In Canada it owns the chain of stores Future Shop, and in China it operates the Five Star stores. In 2014, Best Buy was one of the top twenty retail brands in America.

The rise of e-commerce had been hard on consumer electronics stores. Many notable rivals such as Circuit City and CompUSA did not survive the pressure online shopping put on prices and margins, and liquidated their stores. In early 2015, even long-time electronics industry veteran Radio Shack announced it too would file bankruptcy and close its doors. Best Buy was the sole surviving multinational electronics retail chain.

©Vdovichenko Denis/Shutterstock.com

170

Globally, the consumer electronics market was maturing. The industry had experienced modest growth in the last few years—a compound annual growth rate of 0.8% from 2009-2013—and revenues of $253.9 billion in 2013. Most of that growth, however, was occurring in emerging markets. In the United States, consumer electronics spending was flat. Making things tougher for Best Buy was the fact that a growing percentage of consumer electronics spending was occurring online (over 20% in 2012) (see Figure 6.1). The online sales channel was a difficult one in which to compete. There was intense pressure on prices, almost no customer loyalty, and big, general purpose competitors such as Amazon, Target, and Wal-Mart (see Figure 6.2), along with large computer manufactures that sold in direct-to-customer channels.

Figure 6.1 U.S. Consumer Electronics Sales, Online versus Bricks and Mortar, 1999-2012

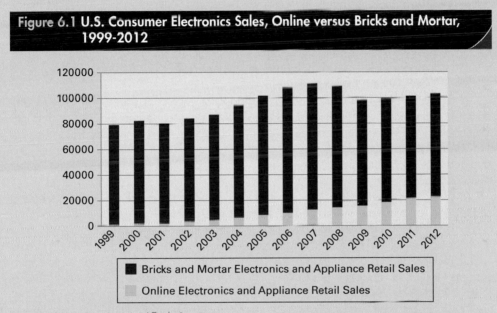

■ Bricks and Mortar Electronics and Appliance Retail Sales

□ Online Electronics and Appliance Retail Sales

Sources: Census Bureau, Annual Trade Survey

Figure 6.2 Major Consumer Electronics Retailers, 2013 sales (in $billions)

Best Buy	30.48
HP	29.07
Dell	24.93
Wal-Mart	22.27
Apple Stores	14.9
CDW Corp.	10.84
Staples	7.47
Target	7.4
Gamestop	7.19

Source: www.Hoovers.com

Though Best Buy had been working hard to build its web presence, online sales still only accounted for 8% of its U.S. revenues. Best Buy was thus still primarily a bricks-and-mortar retail chain that depended heavily on new product introductions in categories in which people wanted to physically compare products. When a new smartphone was introduced, for example, people often wanted to test it before committing to a purchase. Unfortunately for Best Buy, however, in many product categories people were increasingly relying on online reviews to make their purchase decisions; they could browse among various vendors to find the best price. This led to extreme price competition that made it difficult for retailers with a strong physical presence to compete, because that physical presence typically resulted in a high cost structure.

To combat online heavyweights like Amazon, Wal-Mart, and Target (and the growing threat from office-supply stores like Staples and Office Depot), Best Buy implemented a price-matching policy: If customers found a better price online, Best Buy would match it. This put intense pressure on margins, so the company engaged in several cost-cutting measures, including shuttering many stores and cutting 40,000 jobs between 2010 and 2014. It also implemented a program whereby online purchases would be shipped directly from local stores, which helped to match Amazon's speedy delivery times while simultaneously reducing inventory costs.

At the same time, Best Buy worked hard to differentiate its stores from the general purpose competitors. Best Buy salespeople underwent extensive training to ensure that they could provide knowledgeable assistance to customers, and its Geek Squad service provided advanced technical support and home installation services. Best Buy also avoided paying commissions to individual salespeople in order to prevent the use of aggressive sales tactics.

To attract shoppers, Best Buy created programs that would make their stores a destination for consumers to experience electronics products in ways that were more complex or immersive. For example, in 2014, it created "Connected Home" sections in 400 stores, where customers could experience ways of automating their homes with products like programmable lights and thermostats, and home surveillance systems that would enable them to keep an eye on the family pet. Customers found it difficult to shop for such products online; it was a product category that was still not well understood, and customers were often confused about the different components or features they might want to use. As described by Josh Will, senior vice president and general merchandise manager for cellphones, connected home products, and mobile stores, "We want to show them what's possible. That's very difficult to do in a digital-only environment."

To survive, Best Buy would have to be both lean and differentiated. By 2015, it looked like its efforts might pay off. Though the company had suffered losses in 2012 and 2013, it posted profits of $532 million for 2014, resulting in a razor-thin 1.25% profit margin. Though the company had taken a beating with the rise of online commerce, many analysts were betting that it would weather the storm, become a tougher competitor, and remain the winner in an increasingly difficult industry.

Sources: L. Gensler, "Best Buy Battered after Soft Sales Forecast, But Optimists Still Abound," *Forbes*, January 15, 2015, p. 4; J. Wieczner, "Which Fortune 500 Stocks Will Lift Off?," *Fortune*, June 16, 2014, pp. 90–92; Marketline; Hoovers.

OVERVIEW

In Chapter 2 we learned that industries go through a life cycle. Some industries are young and dynamic, with rapidly growing demand. Others are mature and relatively stable, whereas still other industries, like the bricks-and-mortar consumer electronics retailers described in the Opening Case, are in decline.

In this chapter we look at the different strategies that companies can pursue to strengthen their competitive position in each of these different stages of the industry life cycle. We will see that each stage in the evolution of its industry raises interesting challenges for a business. Managers must adopt the appropriate strategies to deal with these challenges.

For example, as illustrated in the Opening Case, many retailers that counted on having a physical presence in the form of local stores are now under intense pricing pressure from online retailers. Some, like Wal-Mart, Target, and Best Buy, have responded by investing heavily in an online presence. Others, like Circuit City, Border's bookstores, and Tower Records, succumbed to competitive pressure and disappeared. However, paradoxically, there is often still good money to be made in a declining industry if managers can figure out the right strategy. A niche strategy of focusing on market segments where demand remains strong is a classic way of making money in a declining industry. There are still many categories of products that customers want to experience in person before purchasing, for example, and Best Buy is hoping it can remain the leader in its declining industry by providing an exceptional experience to these customers.

Before we look at the different stages of an industry life cycle, we first consider strategy in a fragmented industry. We do this because fragmented industries can offer unique opportunities for enterprises to pursue strategies that result in the consolidation of those industries, often creating significant wealth for the consolidating enterprise and its owners.

STRATEGY IN A FRAGMENTED INDUSTRY

A **fragmented industry** is composed of a large number of small- and medium-sized companies. Examples of fragmented industries include the dry-cleaning, hair salon, restaurant, health club, massage, and legal services industries. There are several reasons that an industry may consist of many small companies rather than a few large ones.[1]

fragmented industry
An industry composed of a large number of small- and medium-sized companies.

Reasons for Fragmentation

There are three reasons for fragmentation. First, a lack of scale economies may mean that there are few, if any, cost advantages to large size. There are no obvious scale economies in landscaping and massage services, for example, which helps explain why these industries remain highly fragmented. In some industries customer needs are so specialized that only a small amount of a product is required; hence, there is no scope for a large, mass-production operation to satisfy the market. Custom-made jewelry and catering are examples of this. In some industries there may even be diseconomies of scale. In the restaurant business, for example, customers often prefer the unique food and style of a popular, local restaurant, rather than the standardized offerings of a national chain. This diseconomy of scale places a limit on the ability of large restaurant chains to dominate the market.

Second, brand loyalty in the industry may primarily be local. It may be difficult to build a brand through differentiation that transcends a particular location or region. Many homebuyers, for example, prefer dealing with local real estate agents, whom they perceive as having better local knowledge than national chains. Similarly, there are no large chains in the massage services industry because differentiation and brand loyalty are primarily driven by differences in the skill sets of individual massage therapists.

Third, the lack of scale economies and national brand loyalty implies low entry barriers. When this is the case, a steady stream of new entrants may keep the industry fragmented. The massage services industry exemplifies this situation. Due to the absence of scale requirements, the costs of opening a massage services business can be shouldered by a single entrepreneur. The same is true of landscaping services, which helps to keep that industry fragmented.

In industries that have these characteristics, focus strategies tend to work best. Companies may specialize by customer group, customer need, or geographic region. Many small, specialty companies may operate in local or regional markets. All kinds of specialized or custom-made products fall into this category, as do all small, service operations that cater to personalized customer needs.

Consolidating a Fragmented Industry Through Value Innovation

Business history is full of examples of entrepreneurial organizations that have pursued strategies to create meaningful scale economies and national brands where none previously existed. In the process they have consolidated industries that were once fragmented, reaping enormous gains for themselves and their shareholders in the process.

For example, until the 1980s, the office-supply business was a highly fragmented industry composed of many small, "mom-and-pop" enterprises that served local markets. The typical office-supply enterprise in those days had a limited selection of products, low inventory turnover, limited operating hours, and a focus on providing personal service to local businesses. Customer service included having a small sales force, which visited businesses and took orders, along with several trucks that delivered merchandise to larger customers. Then along came Staples, started by executives who had cut their teeth in the grocery business; they opened a big-box store with a wide product selection, long operating hours, and a self-service business model. They implemented computer information systems to track product sales and make sure that inventory was replenished just before it was out of stock, which drove up inventory turnover. True, Staples did not initially offer the same level of personal service that established office-supply enterprises did, but the managers of Staples made a bet that small-business customers were more interested in value from a wide product selection, long opening hours, and low prices—and they were right! Put differently, the managers at Staples had a different view of what was important to their customer set than did the established enterprises. Today, Staples, Office Depot, and Office Max dominate the office-supply industry, and most of their small rivals have gone out of businesses.

You may recognize in the Staples story a theme that we discussed in the Chapter 5: Staples is a *value innovator*.[2] The company's founders figured out a way to offer more value to their customer set, and to do so at a lower cost. Nor have they been alone in doing so. In the retail sector, for example, Wal-Mart and Target did a similar thing in general merchandise, Lowes and Home Depot pulled off the same trick in building materials and home improvement, and Barnes and Noble did this in book retailing. In the restaurant sector, MacDonald's, Taco Bell, Kentucky Fried Chicken, and, more recently, Starbucks have all followed a similar course. In each case, these enterprises succeeded in consolidating once-fragmented industries.

The lesson is clear: Fragmented industries are wide-open market spaces—blue oceans—just waiting for entrepreneurs to transform them through the pursuit of value innovation. A key to understanding this process is to recognize that in each case, the value innovator defines value differently than do the established companies, and finds a way to offer that value that lowers costs through the creation of scale economies. In fast food, for example, McDonald's offers reliable, quick, convenient fast food, and does so at a low cost. The low cost has two sources—first, the standardization of processes within each store, which boosts labor productivity, and second, the attainment of scale economics on the input side due to McDonald's considerable purchasing power (which grew over time as the McDonald's chain grew). McDonald's was a value innovator in its day, and through its choice of strategy it helped to drive consolidation in the fast-food segment of the restaurant industry.

Chaining and Franchising

In many fragmented industries that have been consolidated through value innovation, the transforming company often starts with a single location, or just a few locations. This was true for Best Buy, which started as a single store (called Sound of Music) in Saint Paul, Minnesota, and Starbucks, which had just three stores in Seattle, Washington, when Howard Shultz took over and started to transform the business. The key is to get the strategy right at the first few locations, and then expand as rapidly as possible to build a national brand and realize scale economies before rivals move into the market. If this is done right, the value innovator can build formidable barriers to new entry by establishing strong brand loyalty and enjoying the scale economics that come from large size (often, these scale economies are associated with purchasing power).

There are two strategies that enterprises use to *replicate* their offering once they get it right. One is chaining and the other is franchising.[3]

Chaining involves opening additional locations that adhere to one, basic formula, *and that the company owns*. Thus, Staples pursued a chaining strategy when it quickly opened additional stores after perfecting its formula at its first location in Boston. Today, Staples has over 2,000 stores worldwide. Starbuck, too, has pursued a chaining strategy, offering the same basic formula in every store that it opens. Its store count now exceeds 21,000 in 63 countries. Best Buy, Wal-Mart, Barnes & Noble, and Home Depot have also all pursued a chaining strategy.

By expanding through chaining, a value innovator can quickly build a national brand. This may be of significant value in a mobile society, such as the United States, where people move and travel frequently, and when in a new town or city they look for familiar offerings. At the same time, by rapidly opening locations, and by knitting those locations together through good information systems, the value innovator can

chaining

A strategy designed to obtain the advantages of cost leadership by establishing a network of linked merchandising outlets interconnected by information technology that functions as one large company.

realize many of the cost advantages that come from large size. Wal-Mart, for example, uses a hub-and-spoke distribution system that is monitored real-time through a satellite-based information system that enables it to tightly control the flow of inventory through its stores. This tight control allows it to customize inventory for particular regions based on sales patterns and maximize inventory turnover (a major source of cost savings). In addition, as Wal-Mart grew, it was able to exercise more and more bargaining power over suppliers, driving down the price for the goods that it then resold in its stores.

franchising
A strategy in which the franchisor grants to its franchisees the right to use the franchisor's name, reputation, and business model in return for a franchise fee and often a percentage of the profits.

Franchising is similar in many respects to chaining, except that in the case of franchising the founding company—the franchisor—licenses the right to open and operate a new location to another enterprise—franchisee—in return for a fee. Typically, franchisees must adhere to some strict rules that require them to adopt the same basic business model and operate in a certain way. Thus, a McDonald's franchisee has to have the same basic look, feel, offerings, pricing, and business processes as other restaurants in the system, and has to report standardized financial information to McDonald's on a regular basis.

There are advantages to using a franchising strategy. First, normally the franchisee puts up some or all of the capital to establish his or her operation. This helps to finance the growth of the system and can result in more rapid expansion. Second, because franchisees are the owners of their operations, and because they often put up capital, they have a strong incentive to make sure that their operations are run as efficiently and effectively as possible, which is good for the franchisor.

Third, because the franchisees are entrepreneurs who own their own businesses, they have an incentive to improve the efficiency and effectiveness of their operations by developing new offerings and/or processes. Typically, the franchisor will give them some latitude to do this, as long as they do not deviate too much from the basic business model. Ideas developed in this way may then be transferred to other locations, improving the performance of the entire system. For example, McDonald's has recently been changing the design and menu of its restaurants in the United States based on ideas first pioneered by a franchisee in France.

The drawbacks of a franchising strategy are threefold. First, it may allow less control than can be achieved through a chaining strategy, because, by definition, a franchising strategy delegates some authority to the franchisee. Howard Shultz of Starbucks, for example, decided to expand primarily via a chaining strategy rather than a franchising strategy because he felt that franchising would not give Starbucks the necessary control over customer service in each store. Second, in a franchising system the franchisee captures some of the economic profit from a successful operation, whereas in a chaining strategy it all flows to the company. Third, because franchisees are small relative to the founding enterprise, they may face a higher cost of capital, which raises system costs and lowers profitability. Given these various pros and cons, the choice between chaining and franchising depends on managers evaluating which strategy is best given the circumstances facing the founding enterprise.

Horizontal Mergers

Another way of consolidating a fragmented industry is to merge with or acquire competitors, combining them into a single, larger enterprise that is able to realize scale economies and build a compelling national brand. For example, in the aerospace and defense contracting business there are many small, niche producers that build the components installed into large products such as Boeing jets or military aircraft. Esterline, a company based in Bellevue, Washington, has been pursuing horizontal mergers and acquisitions, trying to consolidate this tier of suppliers. Esterline started off as a small supplier. Over the last decade it has acquired another 30 or so niche companies, building a larger enterprise that now has sales of almost $2 billion. Esterline's belief is that, as a larger enterprise offering a full portfolio of defense and avionic products, it can gain an edge over smaller rivals when selling to companies like Boeing and Lockheed, while its larger size enables it to realize scale economies and lowers its cost of capital.

It is worth noting that although mergers and acquisitions can help a company consolidate a fragmented industry, the road to success when pursuing this strategy is littered with failures. Some companies pay too much for the companies they acquire. Others find out after the acquisition that they have bought a "lemon" that is nowhere as efficient as they thought prior to the acquisition. Still others discover that the gains envisaged for an acquisition are difficult to realize due to a clash between the culture of the acquiring and acquired enterprises. We will consider the benefits, costs, and risks associated with a strategy of horizontal mergers and acquisitions in Chapters 9 and 10 when we look at corporate-level strategy.

STRATEGIES IN EMBRYONIC AND GROWTH INDUSTRIES

As Chapter 2 discusses, an embryonic industry is one that is just beginning to develop, and a growth industry is one in which first-time demand is rapidly expanding as many new customers enter the market. Choosing the strategies needed to succeed in such industries poses special challenges because new groups of customers with different needs enter the market. Managers must be aware of the way competitive forces in embryonic and growth industries change over time because they frequently need to develop new competencies and refine their business strategy in order to effectively compete in the future.

Most embryonic industries emerge when a technological innovation creates a new product opportunity. For example, in 1975, the personal computer (PC) industry was born after Intel developed the microprocessor technology that allowed companies to build the world's first PCs; this spawned the growth of the PC software industry that took off after Microsoft developed an operating system for IBM.[4]

Customer demand for the products of an embryonic industry is initially limited for a variety of reasons, including: (1) the limited performance and poor quality of the first products; (2) customer unfamiliarity with what the new product can do for them; (3) poorly developed distribution channels to get the product to customers; (4) a lack of complementary products that might increase the value of the product for customers; and (5) high production costs because of small volumes of production.

Customer demand for the first cars, for example, was limited by their poor performance (they were no faster than a horse, far noisier, and frequently broke down), a lack of important complementary products (such as a network of paved roads and gas stations), and high production costs that made these cars an expensive luxury (before Ford invented the assembly line, cars were built by hand in a craft-based production setting). Similarly, demand for electric cars is currently limited because many customers are unfamiliar with the technology and its implications for service and resale value. Customers also worry about whether there are charging stations along routes they will drive, or worry that charging will take too long. Because of such concerns, early demand for the products of embryonic industries typically comes from a small set of technologically savvy customers willing and able to tolerate, and even enjoy, the imperfections in their new purchase. Early adopters of electric cars, for example, tend to have higher-than-average incomes and are highly motivated to buy a car that is environmentally friendly.

mass market
One in which large numbers of customers enter the market.

An industry moves from the embryonic stage to the growth stage when a mass market starts to develop for its product. A **mass market** is one in which large numbers of customers enter the market. Mass markets emerge when three things happen: (1) ongoing technological progress makes a product easier to use, and increases its value for the average customer; (2) complementary products are developed that also increase its value; and (3) companies in the industry work to find ways to reduce the costs of producing the new products so they can lower their prices and stimulate high demand.[5] For example, the mass market for cars emerged and the demand for cars surged when: (1) technological progress increased the performance of cars; (2) a network of paved roads and gas stations was established; and (3) Henry Ford began to mass-produce cars using an assembly-line process, dramatically reducing production costs and enabling him to decrease prices and build consumer demand. Similarly, the mass market for PCs emerged when technological advances made computers easier to use, a supply of complementary software (such as spreadsheet and word-processing programs) was developed, and companies in the industry (such as Dell) began to use mass production to build PCs at low cost.

The Changing Nature of Market Demand

Managers who understand how the demand for a product is affected by the changing needs of customers can focus on developing new strategies that will protect and strengthen their competitive position, such as building competencies to lower production costs or speed product development. In most product markets, the changing needs of customers lead to the S-shaped growth curve in Figure 6.3.[6] This illustrates how different groups of customers with different needs enter the market over time. The curve is S-shaped because adoption is initially slow when an unfamiliar technology is introduced to the market. Adoption accelerates as the technology becomes better understood and utilized by the mass market, and eventually the market is saturated. The rate of new adoptions then declines as demand is increasingly limited to replacement demand.[7] For instance, electronic calculators were adopted upon their introduction by a relatively small pool of scientists and engineers. This group had previously used slide rules. Then, the calculator began to penetrate the larger markets of accountants and commercial users, followed by the still-larger market that included students and the general public. After these markets had become saturated, fewer opportunities remained for new adoptions. This curve has major implications for a company's differentiation, cost, and pricing decisions.

The first group of customers to enter the market is referred to as *innovators*. Innovators are "technocrats" or "gadget geeks"; people who are delighted to be the first to purchase and experiment with a product based on a new technology—even if it is imperfect and expensive. Frequently, innovators have technical talents and interests,

Figure 6.3 Market Development and Customer Groups

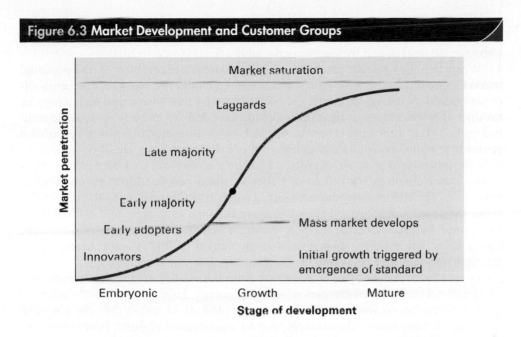

which drive them to "own" and develop new technology. They tend to be less risk averse than other customer groups, and often have greater resources to spare. Though they are not always well integrated into social networks, they are influential in new-product adoption because they are the first to bring a new idea into the social system. In the PC market, the first customers were software engineers and computer hobbyists who wanted to write computer code at home.[8]

Early adopters are the second group of customers to enter the market; they understand that the technology may have important future applications and are willing to experiment with it to see if they can pioneer new uses for the technology. They are comfortable with technical information, and will adopt products that seem appealing even if none of their peers have purchased those products. Early adopters often envision how the technology may be used in the future, and they try to be the first to profit from its use. Jeff Bezos, the founder of Amazon.com, was an early adopter of Web technology. In 1994, before anyone else, he saw that the Web could be used in innovative ways to sell books.

Innovators and early adopters alike enter the market while the industry is in its embryonic stage. The next group of customers, the *early majority*, forms the leading wave or edge of the mass market. Their entry into the market signifies the beginning of the growth stage. Customers in the early majority are practical and generally understand the value of new technology. They weigh the benefits of adopting new products against the costs, and wait to enter the market until they are confident they will benefit. When the early majority decides to enter the market, a large number of new buyers may be expected. This occurred in the PC market after IBM's introduced the PC in 1981. For the early majority, IBM's entry into the market signaled that the benefits of adopting the new PC technology would be worth the cost to purchase, and the time spent to learn how to use, a PC. The growth of the PC market was further strengthened by the development of applications that added value to the PC and transformed it from a hobby into a business-productivity tool. The same process unfolded in the smartphone market after Apple introduced its iPhone in 2007. The early majority entered the market at that point because these customers saw the value that a smartphone could deliver, and they were comfortable adopting new technology.

When the mass market reaches a critical mass, with about 30% of the potential market penetrated, the next group of customers enters the market. This group is characterized as the *late majority*, the customers who purchase a new technology or product only when many of their peers already have done so and it is obvious the technology has great utility and is here to stay. A typical late majority customer group is a somewhat "older" and more conservative set of customers. They are often unfamiliar with the advantages of new technology. The late majority can be a bit nervous about buying new technology but will do so if they see many people adopting it and finding value in it. The late majority did not start to enter the PC market until the mid-1990s, when they saw people around them engaging in email exchanges and browsing the Web, and it became clear that these technologies were here to stay. In the smartphone business, the late majority started to enter the market in 2012, when it became clear that smartphones were becoming the dominant mobile-phone technology.

Laggards, the last group of customers to enter the market, are inherently conservative and unappreciative of the uses of new technology. Laggards frequently refuse to adopt new products even when the benefits are obvious, or unless they are forced to do so by circumstances—for example, due to work-related reasons. People who use typewriters rather than computers to write letters and books are laggards. Given the fast rate of adoption of smartphones in the United States, it will not be long before the only people not in the smartphone market are laggards. These consumers will either continue to use basic wireless phones, or may reject a wireless phone altogether, relying instead on increasingly outdated, traditional, landline phones.

In Figure 6.4, the bell-shaped curve represents the total market, and the divisions in the curve show the average percentage of buyers who fall into each of these customer groups. Note that early adopters are a very small percentage of the market; hence, the

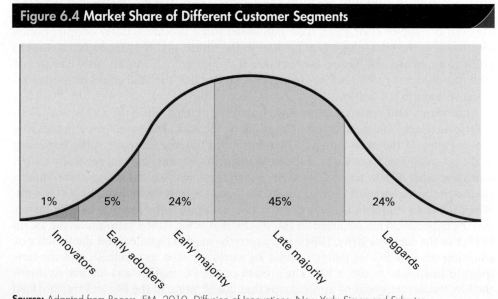

Figure 6.4 Market Share of Different Customer Segments

1%   5%   24%   45%   24%

Innovators   Early adopters   Early majority   Late majority   Laggards

Source: Adapted from Rogers, EM. 2010. Diffusion of Innovations. New York: Simon and Schuster.

figure illustrates a vital competitive dynamic—the highest market demand and industry profits arise when the early and late majority groups enter the market. Additionally, research has found that although early pioneering companies succeed in attracting innovators and early adopters, many of these companies often *fail* to attract a significant share of early and late majority customers, and ultimately go out of business.[9]

Strategic Implications: Crossing the Chasm

Why are pioneering companies often unable to create a business model that allows them to be successful over time and remain as market leaders? *Innovators and early adopters have very different customer needs from the early majority*. In an influential book, Geoffrey Moore argues that because of the differences in customer needs between these groups, the business-level strategies required for companies to succeed in the emerging mass market are quite different from those required to succeed in the embryonic market.[10] Pioneering companies that do not change the strategies they use to pursue their business model will therefore lose their competitive advantage to those companies that implement new strategies aimed at best serving the needs of the early and late majority. New strategies are often required to strengthen a company's business model as a market develops over time for the following reasons:

- Innovators and early adopters are technologically sophisticated customers willing to tolerate the limitations of the product. The early majority, however, values ease of use and reliability. Companies competing in an embryonic market typically pay more attention to increasing the performance of a product than to its ease of use and reliability. Those competing in a mass market need to make sure that the product is reliable and easy to use. Thus, the product development strategies required for success vary as a market develops over time.
- Innovators and early adopters are typically reached through specialized distribution channels, and products are often sold by word of mouth. They are active consumers of technical information. Reaching the early majority requires mass-market distribution channels and mass-media advertising campaigns that require a different set of marketing and sales strategies.
- Because innovators and the early majority are relatively few in number and are not particularly price sensitive, companies serving them typically pursue a focus model, produce small quantities of a product, and price high. To serve the rapidly growing mass market, large-scale mass production may be critical to ensure that a high-quality product can be reliably produced at a low price point.

In sum, the business models and strategies required to compete in an embryonic market populated by early adopters and innovators are very different from those required to compete in a high-growth, mass market populated by the early majority. As a consequence, the transition between the embryonic market and the mass market is not a smooth, seamless one. Rather, it represents a *competitive chasm* or gulf that companies must cross. According to Moore, many companies do not or cannot develop the right business model; they fall into the chasm and go out of business. Thus, although embryonic markets are typically populated by numerous small companies, once the mass market begins to develop, the number of companies sharply decreases.[11] For a detailed example of how this unfolds, see Strategy in Action 6.1, which explains how Microsoft and Research in Motion fell into the chasm in the smartphone market, whereas Apple leaped across it with its iPhone, a product designed for the early majority.

6.1 STRATEGY IN ACTION

Crossing the Chasm in the Smartphone Market

The first smartphones appeared in the early 2000s. Early market leaders included Research in Motion (RIM), with its Blackberry line of smartphones, and Microsoft, whose Windows Mobile operating system powered a number of early smartphone offerings made by companies such as Motorola. These phones were sold to business users and marketed as business productivity tools. They had small screens and a physical keyboard crammed onto a relatively small device. Although they had the ability to send and receive e-mails, browse the Web, and so on, there was no independent applications market, and consequently the utility of the phones was very limited. Nor were they always easy to use. System administrators were often required to set up basic features such as corporate e-mail access. They were certainly not consumer-friendly devices. The customers at this time were primarily innovators and early adopters.

The market changed dramatically after the introduction of the Apple iPhone in 2007 (see Figure 6.5). First, this phone was aimed not at power business users, but at a broader consumer market. Second, the phone was easy to use, with a large, touch-activated screen and a virtual keyboard that vanished when not in use. Third, the phone was stylishly designed, with an elegance that appealed to many consumers. Fourth, Apple made it very easy for independent developers to write applications that could run on the phone, and they set up an App store that made it easy for developers to market their apps. Very quickly, new applications started to appear that added value to the phone. These included mapping applications, news feeds, stock information, and a wide array of games, several of which soon became big hits. Clearly, the iPhone was a device squarely aimed not at business users but at consumers. The ease of use and utility of the iPhone quickly drew the early majority into the market, and sales surged. Meanwhile, sales of Blackberry devices and Windows Mobile phones started to spiral downward.

Both Microsoft and Blackberry were ultimately forced to abandon their existing phone platforms and

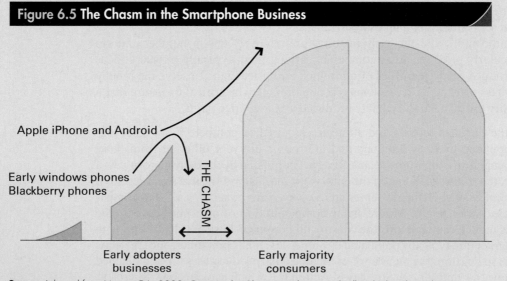

Figure 6.5 The Chasm in the Smartphone Business

Apple iPhone and Android

Early windows phones
Blackberry phones

THE CHASM

Early adopters
businesses

Early majority
consumers

Source: Adapted from Moore, GA. 2009. Crossing the Chasm: Marketing and selling high tech products to mainstream customers. New York: Harper Collins.

strategies, and reorient themselves. Both developed touch-activated screens similar to those on the iPhone, launched app stores, and targeted consumers. However, it may have been too late for them. By early 2015, both former market leaders had market shares in the single digits, whereas Apple's iPhone and Google's Android (which imitated many of the design and technical features of the iPhone) dominated the market.

Sources: Anonymous, "iPhone tops 1 Millionth Sale," *Information Today* 24 (9), 2007, p. 27; Anonymous, "The Battle for the Smartphone's Soul," *The Economist*, November 22, 2008, pp. 76–77; L. Dignan, "Android, Apple iOS Flip Consumer, Corporate Market Share," *Between the Lines*, February 13, 2013; IDC, Smartphone OS Market Share, Q1, 2015, www.idc.com.

The implication is clear: To cross the chasm successfully, managers must correctly identify the needs of the first wave of early majority users—the leading edge of the mass market. Then they must adjust their business models by developing new strategies to redesign products and create distribution channels and marketing campaigns to satisfy the needs of the early majority. They must have a suitable product available at a reasonable price to sell to the early majority when they begin to enter the market in large numbers. At the same time, industry pioneers must abandon outdated, focused business models directed at the needs of innovators and early adopters. Focusing on an outdated model leads managers to ignore the needs of the early majority—and the need to develop the strategies necessary to pursue a differentiation or cost-leadership business model in order to remain a dominant industry competitor.

Strategic Implications of Differences in Market Growth Rates

Managers must understand a final, important issue in embryonic and growth industries: Different markets develop at different rates. The speed at which a market develops can be measured by its growth rate, that is, the rate at which customers in that market purchase the industry's product. A number of factors explain the variation in market growth rates for different products, and thus the speed with which a particular market develops. It is important for managers to understand the source of these differences because their choice of strategy can accelerate or retard the rate at which a market grows.[12]

The first factor that accelerates customer demand is a new product's *relative advantage*; that is, the degree to which a new product is perceived as being better at satisfying customer needs than the product it supersedes. For example, the early growth in demand for cell phones was partly driven by their economic benefits. Studies showed that because business customers could always be reached by cell phone, they made better use of their time—for example, by not showing up at a meeting that had been cancelled at the last minute—and saved 2 hours per week in time that would otherwise have been wasted. For busy executives—the early adopters—the productivity benefits of owning a cell phone outweighed the costs. Cell phones also rapidly diffused for social reasons, in particular, because they conferred glamour or prestige upon their users (something that also drives demand for today's most advanced smartphones).

A second factor of considerable importance is *complexity*. Products that are viewed by consumers as being complex and difficult to master will diffuse more slowly than products that are easy to master. The early PCs diffused quite slowly because many people saw the archaic command lines needed operate a PC as being very complex and intimidating. PCs did not become a mass-market device until graphical user interfaces with onscreen icons became widespread, enabling users to open programs and perform functions by pointing and clicking with a mouse. In contrast, the first cell phones were simple to use and quickly adopted.

Another factor driving growth in demand is *compatibility*, the degree to which a new product is perceived as being consistent with the current needs or existing values of potential adopters. Demand for cell phones grew rapidly because their operation was compatible with the prior experience of potential adopters who used traditional, landline phones. A fourth factor is *trialability*, the degree to which potential customers can experiment with a new product during a hands-on trial basis. Many people first used cell phones by borrowing them from colleagues to make calls, and their positive experiences helped accelerate growth rates. In contrast, early PCs were more difficult to experiment with because they were rare and expensive, and because some training was needed in how to use them. These complications led to slower growth rates for PCs. A final factor is *observability*, the degree to which the results of using and enjoying a new product can be seen and appreciated by other people. Originally, the iPhone and Android phones diffused rapidly because it became obvious that their owners were putting them to many different uses.

Thus, managers must devise strategies that educate customers about the value of their new products if they are to grow demand over time. In addition, they need to design their products to overcome barriers to adoption by making them less complex and intimidating, and easy to use, and by showcasing their relative advantage over prior technology. This is exactly what Apple did with the iPhone, which helps explain the rapid diffusion of smartphones after Apple introduced its first iPhone in 2007.

When a market is rapidly growing, and the popularity of a new product increases or spreads in a way that is analogous to a *viral model of infection*, a related strategic issue arises. Lead adopters (the first customers who buy a product) in a market become "infected" or enthused with the product, as exemplified by iPhone users. Subsequently, lead adopters infect others by telling them about the advantages of products. After observing its benefits, these people also adopt and use the product. Companies promoting new products can take advantage of viral diffusion by identifying and aggressively courting opinion leaders in a particular market—the customers whose views command respect. For example, when the manufacturers of new, high-tech medical equipment such as magnetic resonance imaging (MRI) scanners market a new product, they try to get well-known doctors at major research and teaching hospitals to use the product first. Companies may give these opinion leaders (the doctors) free machines for research purposes, and work closely with the doctors to further develop the technology. Once these opinion leaders commit to the product and give it their stamp of approval, doctors at other hospitals often follow.

In sum, understanding competitive dynamics in embryonic and growth industries is an important strategic issue. The ways in which different kinds of customer groups emerge and the ways in which customer needs change are important determinants of the strategies that need to be pursued to make a business model successful over time. Similarly, understanding the factors that affect a market's growth rate allows managers to tailor their business model to a changing industry environment. (Competition in high-tech industries is discussed further in the Chapter 7.)

STRATEGY IN MATURE INDUSTRIES

A mature industry is commonly dominated by a small number of large companies. Although a mature industry may also contain many medium-sized companies and a host of small, specialized companies, the large companies often determine the nature of competition in the industry because they can influence the six competitive forces. Indeed, these large companies hold their leading positions because they have developed the most successful business models and strategies in an industry.

By the end of the shakeout stage, companies have learned how important it is to analyze each other's business model and strategies. They also know that if they change their strategies, their actions are likely to stimulate a competitive response from industry rivals. For example, a differentiator that starts to lower its prices because it has adopted a more cost-efficient technology not only threatens other differentiators, but may also threaten cost leaders that see their competitive advantage being eroded. Hence, by the mature stage of the life cycle, companies have learned the meaning of competitive interdependence.

As a result, in mature industries, business-level strategy revolves around understanding how established companies *collectively* attempt to moderate the intensity of industry competition in order to preserve both company and industry profitability. Interdependent companies can protect their competitive advantage and profitability by adopting strategies and tactics, first, to deter entry into an industry, and second, to reduce the level of rivalry within an industry.

Strategies to Deter Entry

In mature industries, successful enterprises have normally gained substantial economies of scale and established strong brand loyalty. As we saw in Chapter 2, the economies of scale and brand loyalty enjoyed by incumbents in an industry constitute strong barriers to entry. However, there may be cases in which scale and brand, although significant, are not sufficient to deter entry. In such circumstances there are other strategies that companies can pursue to make new entry less likely. These strategies include product proliferation, limit pricing, technology upgrading, and strategic commitments.[13]

Product Proliferation   One way in which companies try to enter a mature industry is by looking for market segments or niches that are poorly served by incumbent enterprises. This strategy involves entering these segments, gaining experience, scale, and brand in that segment, and then progressively moving upmarket. This is how Japanese automobile companies first entered the U.S. market in the late 1970s and early 1980s. They targeted segments at the bottom end of the market for small, inexpensive, fuel-efficient cars. These segments were not well served by large American manufacturers such as Ford and GM. Once companies like Toyota and Honda had gained a strong position in these segments, they started to move upmarket with larger offerings and ultimately entered the pickup truck and SUV markets, which historically had been the most profitable segments of the automobile industry for American companies.

A **product proliferation strategy** involves incumbent companies attempting to forestall entry by making sure that *every* niche or segment in the marketplace is well served. Had U.S. automobile companies pursued product proliferation in the 1970s and early

product proliferation strategy

The strategy of "filling the niches" or catering to the needs of customers in all market segments to deter entry by competitors.

1980s, and produced a line of smaller, fuel-efficient cars, it may have been more difficult for Japanese automobile companies to enter the U.S. market. Another example concerns breakfast cereal companies, which are famous for pursuing a product proliferation strategy. Typically they produce many different types of cereal, so that they can cater to all likely consumer needs. The net result is that the three big breakfast cereal companies—General Mills, Post, and Kellogg—have been able to occupy all of the valuable real estate in the industry—shelf space in supermarkets—filling it with a multiplicity of offerings and leaving very little room for new entrants. Moreover, when new entry does occur—as happened when smaller companies selling granola and organic cereals entered the market —the big three have moved rapidly to offer their own versions of these products, effectively foreclosing entry. A product proliferation strategy can thus effectively deter entry because it gives new entrants very little opportunity to find an unoccupied niche in an industry.

limit price strategy
Charging a price that is lower than that required to maximize profits in the short run to signal to new entrants that the incumbent has a low-cost structure that the entrant likely cannot match.

Limit Price   A limit price strategy may be used to deter entry when incumbent companies in an industry enjoy economies of scale, but the resulting cost advantages are *not* enough to keep potential rivals out of the industry. A **limit price strategy** involves charging a price that is lower than that required to maximize profits in the short run to signal to a potential entrant that the incumbent could price the new entrant out of the market, thereby deterring entry. Though limit pricing may not be sustainable in the long run for the incumbent, new entrants often do not have full information about the incumbent's costs and thus do not know how long the incumbent can keep prices low.

For illustration, consider Figure 6.6, which shows that incumbent companies have a unit cost structure that is lower than that of potential entrants. However, if incumbents charge the price that the market will bear (Figure 6.6a), this will be above the unit cost structure of new entrants (Figure 6.6b), allowing them to enter and still make a profit under the pricing umbrella set by incumbents. In this situation, the best option for incumbents might be to charge a price that is still above their own cost structure but just below the cost structure of any potential new entrants (Figure 6.6c). Now there is no incentive for companies to attempt to enter the market, because at the lower limit price they cannot make a profit. Thus, because it deters entry, the limit price

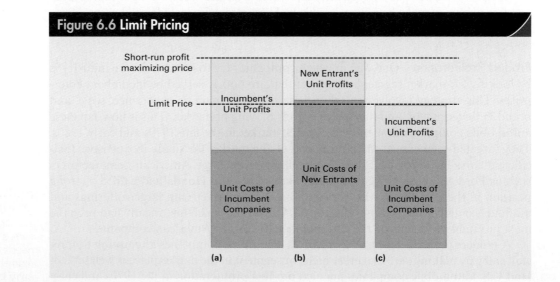

Figure 6.6 Limit Pricing

might be thought of as the long-run, profit-maximizing price. For example, in the U.S. cable industry, incumbents such as Time Warner and Comcast often have near-monopolies over the regions they serve. However, when companies attempt to enter their markets, the incumbents often engage in limit pricing to deter entry. Research by Robert Seamans showed that when new entrants came from outside industries—and thus were unlikely to have full information on the incumbent's costs (e.g., telecom companies such as Verizon FIOS)—incumbent cable companies often used limit pricing to deter their entry. On the other hand, when new entrants were city-owned and thus less sensitive to profit margins, incumbents would use large investments in technology upgrading (discussed below) that city-owned operators had difficulty matching.[14]

Technology Upgrading   If an incumbent is limited in its pricing strategies or faces potential entrants that may be willing to match its pricing, it can deter entry through investments in **technology upgrading** that the new entrant has difficulty matching. For example, though municipal cable TV entrants may be relatively insensitive to profit margins (as described above), they may have difficulty matching investments that a large incumbent can make in state-of-the-art technologies. Thus, when incumbent cable companies were threatened by potential, city-owned entrants, they invested in upgrading their cable infrastructure to provide the two-way communication needed to provide Internet service, thereby slowing municipal entry.[15]

Strategic Commitments   Incumbent companies can deter entry by engaging in strategic commitments that send a signal to potential new entrants that entry will be difficult. **Strategic commitments** are investments that signal an incumbent's long-term commitment to a market, or a segment of that market.[16] As an entry-deterring strategy, strategic commitments involve raising the perceived costs of entering a market, thereby reducing the likelihood of entry. To the extent that such actions are successful, strategic commitments can protect an industry and lead to greater long-run profits for those already in the industry.

One example of strategic commitment occurs when incumbent companies invest in excess productive capacity. The idea is to signal to potential entrants that if they do enter, the incumbents have the ability to expand output and drive down prices, making the market less profitable for new entrants. It has been argued, for example, that chemical companies may overinvest in productive capacity as a way of signaling their commitment to a particular market, and indicating that new entrants will find it difficult to compete.[17]

Other strategic commitments that might act as an entry deterrent include making significant investments in basic research, product development, or advertising beyond those necessary to maintain a company's competitive advantage over its existing rivals.[18] In all cases, for such actions to deter entry, potential rivals must be aware of what incumbents are doing, and the investments must be sufficient to deter entry.

Incumbents might also be able to deter entry if they have a history of responding aggressively to new entry through price cutting, accelerating product development efforts, increasing advertising expenditures, or some combination of these. For example, in the 1990s, when a competitor announced a new software product Microsoft would often attempt to make entry difficult by quickly announcing that it had a similar software product under development that would work well with Windows (the implication being that consumers should wait for the Microsoft product). The term "vaporware" was often used to describe such aggressive product preannouncements. Many observers believe that the practice did succeed on occasion in forestalling entry.[19]

technology upgrading
Incumbent companies deterring entry by investing in costly technology upgrades that potential entrants have trouble matching.

strategic commitments
Investments that signal an incumbent's long-term commitment to a market or a segment of that market.

A history of such actions sends a strong signal to potential rivals that market entry will not be easy and that the incumbents will respond vigorously to any encroachment on their turf. When established companies succeed in signaling this position to potential rivals through past actions, we say that they have established a *credible commitment* to respond to new entry.

One thing to note is that, when making strategic commitments, a company must be careful not to fall afoul of antitrust law. For example, it is illegal to engage in predatory pricing, or pricing a good or service below the cost of production with the express intent of driving a rival out of business and monopolizing a market. In the late 1990s, Microsoft violated antitrust laws when it informed PC manufacturers that they had to display Internet Explorer on the PC desktop if they wanted to license the company's Windows operating system. Because Windows was the only viable operating system for PCs at the time, this was basically viewed as strong-arming PC makers. The intent was to give Internet Explorer an edge over rival browsers, particularly one produced by Netscape. The U.S. Justice Department ruled that Microsoft's actions were predatory. Microsoft was forced to pay fines and change its practices.

Strategies to Manage Rivalry

Beyond seeking to deter entry, companies may wish to develop strategies to manage their competitive interdependence and decrease price rivalry. Unrestricted competition over prices reduces both company and industry profitability. Companies use several strategies to manage industry rivalry. The most important are price signaling, price leadership, non-price competition, and capacity control.

Price Signaling   A company's ability to choose the price option that leads to superior performance is a function of several factors, including the strength of demand for a product and the intensity of competition between rivals. Price signaling is a method whereby companies attempt to control rivalry among competitors to allow the *industry* to choose the most favorable pricing option. **Price signaling** is the process by which companies increase or decrease product prices to convey their intentions to other companies and influence the way other companies price their products. Companies use price signaling to improve industry profitability.

Companies may use price signaling to communicate that they will vigorously respond to hostile competitive moves that threaten them. For example, they may signal that if one company starts to aggressively cut prices, they will respond in kind. A *tit-for-tat strategy* is a well-known price signaling maneuver in which a company exactly mimics its rivals: If its rivals cut prices, the company follows; if they raise prices, the company follows. By consistently pursuing this strategy over time, a company sends a clear signal to its rivals that it will mirror any pricing moves they make; sooner or later, rivals learn that the company will always pursue a tit-for-tat strategy. Because rivals know that it will match any price reductions– and thus reduce profits–price cutting becomes less common in the industry. Moreover, a tit-for-tat strategy also signals to rivals that price increases will be imitated, growing the probability that rivals will initiate price increases to raise profits. Thus, a tit-for-tat strategy can be a useful way of shaping pricing behavior in an industry.[20]

The airline industry is a good example of the power of price signaling when prices typically rise and fall depending upon the current state of customer demand. If one carrier signals the intention to lower prices, a price war frequently ensues as carriers

price signaling
The process by which companies increase or decrease product prices to convey their intentions to other companies and influence the price of an industry's products.

copy one another's signals. If one carrier feels demand is strong, it tests the waters by signaling an intention to increase prices, and price signaling becomes a strategy to obtain uniform price increases. Nonrefundable tickets or charges for a second bag, another strategy adopted to allow airlines to charge higher prices, also originated as a market signal by one company that was quickly copied by all other companies in the industry (it is estimated that extra bag charges have so far allowed airlines to raise over $1 billion in revenues). Carriers have recognized that they can stabilize their revenues and earn interest on customers' money if they collectively act to force customers to assume the risk of buying airline tickets in advance. In essence, price signaling allows companies to exchange information that enables them to understand each other's competitive product or market strategy and make coordinated, price-competitive moves.

Price Leadership   When one company assumes the responsibility for setting the pricing option that maximizes industry profitability, that company assumes the position of price leader—a second tactic used to reduce price rivalry between companies in a mature industry. Explicit price leadership, when companies jointly set prices, is illegal under antitrust laws; therefore, the process of **price leadership** is often very subtle. In the car industry, for example, prices are set by imitation. The price set by the weakest company—that is, the company with the highest cost structure—is often used as the basis for competitors' pricing. Thus, in the past, U.S. carmakers set their prices and Japanese carmakers then set their prices in response to the U.S. prices. The Japanese are happy to do this because they have lower costs than U.S. carmakers and still make higher profits without having to compete on price. Pricing is determined by market segment. The prices of different auto models in a particular range indicate the customer segments that the companies are targeting, and the price range the companies believe each segment can tolerate. Each manufacturer prices a model in the segment with reference to the prices charged by its competitors, not with reference to competitors' costs. Price leadership also allows differentiators to charge a premium price.

Although price leadership can stabilize industry relationships by preventing head-to-head competition and raising the level of profitability within an industry, it has its dangers. It allows companies with high cost structures to survive without needing to implement strategies to become more efficient, although in the long term such behavior makes them vulnerable to new entrants that have lower costs because they have developed low-cost production techniques. This happened in the U.S. car industry. After decades of tacit price fixing, and GM as the price leader, U.S. carmakers were threatened by growing, low-cost, overseas competition. In 2009, the U.S. government bailed out Chrysler and GM, loaning them billions of dollars while forcing them to enter and then emerge from, bankruptcy. This dramatically lowered the cost structures of these companies and has made them more competitive today. (This also applies to Ford, which obtained similar benefits while managing to avoid bankruptcy.)

Non-price Competition   A third very important aspect of product and market strategy in mature industries is the use of **non-price competition** to manage rivalry within an industry. The use of strategies to try to prevent costly price cutting and price wars does not preclude competition by product differentiation. In many industries, product differentiation strategies are the principal tools companies use to deter potential entrants and manage rivalry.

Product differentiation allows industry rivals to compete for market share by offering products with different or superior features, such as smaller, more powerful,

price leadership
When one company assumes the responsibility for determining the pricing strategy that maximizes industry profitability.

non-price competition
The use of product differentiation strategies to deter potential entrants and manage rivalry within an industry.

or more sophisticated computer chips, as AMD, Intel, and NVIDIA compete to offer, or by applying different marketing techniques, as Procter & Gamble, Colgate, and Unilever do. In Figure 6.7, product and market segment dimensions are used to identify four non-price competitive strategies based on product differentiation: market penetration, product development, market development, and product proliferation. (Note that this model applies to new market *segments*, *not* new markets.)

Market Penetration   When a company concentrates on expanding market share in its existing product markets, it is engaging in a strategy of *market penetration* . Market penetration involves heavy advertising to promote and build product differentiation. For example, Intel has actively pursued penetration with its aggressive marketing campaign of "Intel Inside." In a mature industry, advertising aims to influence customers' brand choice and create a brand-name reputation for the company and its products. In this way, a company can increase its market share by attracting its rival's customers. Because brand-name products often command premium prices, building market share in this situation is very profitable.

In some mature industries—for example, soap and detergent, disposable diapers, and brewing—a market-penetration strategy becomes a long-term strategy. In these industries, all companies engage in intensive advertising and battle for market share. Each company fears that if it does not advertise it will lose market share to rivals who do. Consequently, in the soap and detergent industry, Procter & Gamble spends more than 20% of sales revenues on advertising, with the aim of maintaining, and perhaps building, market share. These huge advertising outlays constitute a barrier to entry for prospective competitors.

product development

The creation of new or improved products to replace existing products.

Product Development   **Product development** is the creation of new or improved products to replace existing ones. The wet-shaving industry depends on product replacement to create successive waves of customer demand, which then create new sources of revenue for companies in the industry. Gillette, for example, periodically unveils a new, improved razor such as its vibrating razor (which competes with Schick's four-bladed razor) to try to boost its market share. Similarly, in the car industry, each major car company replaces its models every 3 to 5 years to encourage customers to trade in old models and purchase new ones.

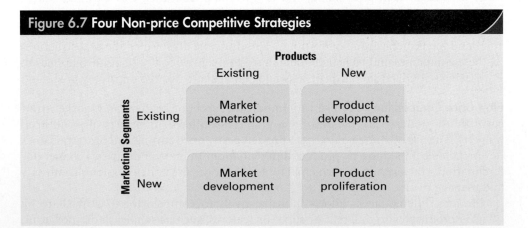

Figure 6.7 Four Non-price Competitive Strategies

	Products	
	Existing	New
Marketing Segments Existing	Market penetration	Product development
New	Market development	Product proliferation

Product development is crucial for maintaining product differentiation and building market share. For instance, the laundry detergent Tide has gone through more than 50 changes in formulation during the past 40 years to improve its performance. The product is always advertised as Tide, but it is a different product each year. Refining and improving products is a crucial strategy companies use to fine-tune and improve their business models in a mature industry, but this kind of competition can be as vicious as a price war because it is very expensive and can dramatically increase a company's cost structure. This occurred in the computer-chip industry, where intense competition to make the fastest or most powerful chip and become the market leader has dramatically increased the cost structure of Intel, AMD, and NVIDIA, and sharply reduced their profitability.

Market Development   **Market development** seeks new market segments for a company's products. A company pursuing this strategy wants to capitalize on the brand name it has developed in one market segment by locating new market segments in which to compete— just as Mattel and Nike do by entering many different segments of the toy and shoe markets, respectively. In this way, a company can leverage the product differentiation advantages of its brand name. Japanese auto manufacturers provide an interesting example of the use of market development. When each manufacturer entered the market, it offered a car model aimed at the economy segment of the auto market, such as the Toyota Corolla and the Honda Accord. Then, these companies upgraded each model over time to target a more expensive market segment. The Honda Accord is a leading contender in the mid-sized car segment, and the Toyota Corolla fills the small-car segment. By redefining their product offerings, Japanese manufacturers have profitably developed their market segments and successfully attacked their U.S. rivals, wresting market share from them. Although the Japanese once competed primarily as cost leaders, market development has allowed them to become differentiators as well. In fact, as we noted in the previous chapter, Toyota has used market development to become a broad differentiator. Over time, it has used market development to create a vehicle for almost every segment of the car market, a tactic discussed in Strategy in Action 6.2.

market development
When a company searches for new market segments for its existing products in order to increase sales.

Product Proliferation   We have already seen how product proliferation can deter entry into an industry. The same strategy can be used to manage rivalry within an industry. As noted earlier, product proliferation generally means that large companies in an industry have a product in each market segment (or niche). If a new niche develops, such as SUVs, designer sunglasses, or shoe-selling websites, the leader gets a first-mover advantage—but soon thereafter, all the other companies catch up. Once again, competition is stabilized, and rivalry within the industry is reduced. Product proliferation thus allows the development of stable industry competition based on product differentiation, not price—that is, non-price competition based on the development of new products. The competitive battle is over a product's perceived uniqueness, quality, features, and performance, not its price. Nike, for example, was founded as a running shoe company, and early in its history it shunned markets for gear for sports such as golf, soccer, basketball, tennis, and skateboarding. However, when its sales declined Nike realized that using marketing to increase sales in a particular market segment (market penetration) could only grow sales and profits so much. The company thus directed its existing design and marketing competencies to the crafting of new lines of shoes for those market segments and others.

6.2 STRATEGY IN ACTION

Toyota Uses Market Development to Become the Global Leader

The car industry has always been one of the most competitive in the world because of the huge revenues and profits at stake. Given the difficult economic conditions in the late-2000s, it is hardly surprising that rivalry has increased as global carmakers struggle to develop new models that better satisfy the needs of particular groups of buyers. One company at the competitive forefront is Toyota.

Toyota produced its first car 40 years ago—an ugly, boxy vehicle that was, however, cheap. As the quality of its car became apparent, sales increased. Toyota, which was then a focused cost leader, reinvested its profits into improving the styling of its vehicles, and into efforts to continually reduce production costs. Over time, Toyota has taken advantage of its low-cost structure to make an ever-increasing range of reasonably priced vehicles tailored to different segments of the car market. The company's ability to begin with the initial design stage and move to the production stage in 2 to 3 years allowed it to make new models available more rapidly than its competitors, and to capitalize on the development of new market segments.

Toyota has been a leader in positioning its entire range of vehicles to take advantage of new, emerging market segments. In the SUV segment, for example, its first offering was the expensive Toyota Land Cruiser, even then priced at over $35,000. Realizing the need for SUVs in lower price ranges, it next introduced the 4Runner, priced at $20,000 and designed for the average SUV customer; the RAV4, a small SUV in the low $20,000 range, followed; then came the Sequoia, a bigger, more powerful version of the 4Runner in the upper $20,000 range. Finally, drawing on technology from its Lexus division, it introduced the luxury Highlander SUV in the low $30,000 range. Today, it sells six SUV models, each offering a particular combination of price, size, performance, styling, and luxury to appeal to a particular customer group within the SUV segment of the car market. In a similar way, Toyota positions its sedans to appeal to the needs of different sets of customers. For example, the Camry is targeted at the middle of the market to customers who can afford to pay about $25,000 and want a balance of luxury, performance, safety, and reliability.

Toyota's broad-differentiation business model is geared toward making a range of vehicles that optimizes the amount of value it can create for different groups of customers. At the same time, the number of models it makes is constrained by the need to keep costs under strict control so that its pricing options that will generate maximum revenues and profits. Competition in every car market segment is now intense, so all carmakers must balance the advantages of showcasing more cars to attract customers against the increasing costs that result when their line of models expands to suit different customers' needs.

Capacity Control   Although non-price competition helps mature industries avoid the cutthroat price cutting that reduces company and industry levels of profitability, price competition does periodically occur when excess capacity exists in an industry. Excess capacity arises when companies collectively produce too much output; to dispose of it, they cut prices. When one company cuts prices, others quickly do the same because they fear that the price cutter will be able to sell its entire inventory and leave them with unwanted goods. The result is a developing price war.

Excess capacity may be caused by a shortfall in demand, as when a recession lowers the demand for cars and causes automakers to offer customers price incentives to purchase new cars. In this situation, companies can do nothing but wait for better times. By and large, however, excess capacity results from companies within an industry simultaneously responding to favorable conditions; they all invest in new plants to take advantage of the predicted upsurge in demand. Paradoxically, each individual company's effort to outperform the others means that, collectively, companies create industry overcapacity, which hurts all companies. Although demand is rising, the consequence of each company's decision to increase capacity is a surge in industry capacity, which drives down prices. To prevent the accumulation of costly excess capacity, companies must devise strategies that enable them to control—or at least benefit from   capacity-expansion programs. Before we examine these strategies, however, we need to consider in greater detail the factors that cause excess capacity.[21]

Factors Causing Excess Capacity   Excess capacity often derives from technological developments. New, low-cost technology sometimes can create an issue because all companies invest in it simultaneously to prevent being left behind. Excess capacity occurs as the new technology produces more efficiently than the old. In addition, new technology is often introduced in large increments, which generates overcapacity. For instance, an airline that needs more seats on a route must add another plane, thereby adding hundreds of seats even if only 50 are needed. To take another example, a new chemical process may efficiently operate at the rate of only 1,000 gallons per day, whereas the previous process was efficient at 500 gallons per day. If all companies within an industry change technologies, industry capacity may double, and enormous problems can ensue.

Competitive factors within an industry can cause overcapacity. Entry into an industry is one such factor. The economic recession of 2008-2009 caused global overcapacity and the price of steel plunged; with global recovery the price has increased. Sometimes the age of a company's physical assets is the source of the problem. For example, in the hotel industry, given the rapidity with which the quality of hotel room furnishings decline, customers are always attracted to new hotels. When new hotel chains are built alongside the old chains, excess capacity can result. Often, companies are simply making simultaneous competitive moves based on industry trends—but these moves lead to head-to-head competition. Most fast-food chains, for instance, establish new outlets whenever demographic data show population increases. However, companies seem to forget that all other chains use the same data—they do not anticipate their rivals' actions. Thus, a certain locality that has few fast-food outlets may suddenly have several new outlets being built at the same time. Whether all the outlets survive depends upon the growth rate of customer demand, but often the least popular outlets close.

Choosing a Capacity-Control Strategy   Given the various ways in which capacity can expand, companies clearly need to find means of controlling it. Companies that are always plagued by price cutting and price wars will be unable to recoup their investments in generic strategies. Low profitability caused by overcapacity forces not only the weakest companies but also sometimes major players to exit the industry. In general, companies have two strategic choices: (1) each company must try to preempt its rivals and seize the initiative, or (2) the companies must collectively find indirect means of coordinating with each other so that they are all aware of the mutual effects of their actions.

To *preempt* rivals, a company must forecast a large increase in demand in the product market and then move rapidly to establish large-scale operations that will be able to satisfy the predicted demand. By achieving a first-mover advantage, the company may deter other firms from entering the market because the preemptor will usually be able to move down the experience curve, reduce its costs, and therefore reduce its prices as well—and threaten a price war if necessary.

This strategy, however, is extremely risky, for it involves investing resources before the extent and profitability of the future market are clear. A preemptive strategy is also risky if it does not deter competitors that decide to enter the market. If competitors can develop a stronger generic strategy, or have more resources (think of Google and Microsoft), they can make the preemptor suffer. Thus, for the strategy to succeed, the preemptor must generally be a credible company with enough resources to withstand a possible advertising/price war.

To *coordinate* with rivals as a capacity-control strategy, caution must be exercised because collusion on the timing of new production capacity investments is illegal under antitrust law. However, tacit coordination is practiced in many industries as companies attempt to understand and forecast one another's competitive moves. Generally, companies use market signaling to secure coordination. They make announcements about their future investment decisions in trade journals and newspapers. In addition, they share information about their production levels and their forecasts of demand within an industry to bring supply and demand into equilibrium. Thus, a coordination strategy reduces the risks associated with investment in the industry. This is very common in the chemical refining and oil businesses, where new capacity investments frequently cost hundreds of millions of dollars.

◤ STRATEGIES IN DECLINING INDUSTRIES

Sooner or later, many industries enter into a decline stage in which the size of the total market begins to shrink. Examples are the railroad industry, the tobacco industry, the steel industry, and the newspaper business (see the Closing Case). Industries decline for many reasons, including technological change, social trends, and demographic shifts. The railroad and steel industries began to decline when technological changes brought viable substitutes for their products. The advent of the internal combustion engine drove the railroad industry into decline, and the steel industry fell into decline with the rise of plastics and composite materials. Similarly, as noted in the Closing Case, the newspaper industry is in decline because of the rise of news sites on the Web. As for the tobacco industry, changing social attitudes and warnings about the health effects of smoking have caused the decline.

The Severity of Decline

Competition tends to intensify in a declining industry, and profit rates tend to fall. The intensity of competition in a declining industry depends on four critical factors, which are depicted in Figure 6.8. First, the intensity of competition is greater in industries in which decline is rapid, as opposed to industries such as tobacco in which decline is slow and gradual.

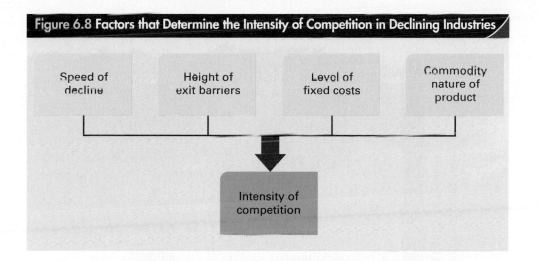

Figure 6.8 Factors that Determine the Intensity of Competition in Declining Industries

Second, the intensity of competition is greater in declining industries in which exit barriers are high. Recall from Chapter 2 that high exit barriers keep companies locked into an industry, even when demand is falling. The result is excess productive capacity and hence an increased probability of fierce price competition.

Third, and related to the previous point, the intensity of competition is greater in declining industries in which fixed costs are high (as in the steel industry). The reason is that the need to cover fixed costs such as the costs of maintaining productive capacity can drive companies to try to use excess capacity by slashing prices, which can trigger a price war.

Finally, the intensity of competition is greater in declining industries in which the product is perceived as a commodity (as it is in the steel industry) in contrast to industries in which differentiation gives rise to significant brand loyalty, as was true (until very recently) of the declining tobacco industry.

Not all segments of an industry typically decline at the same rate. In some segments, demand may remain reasonably strong despite decline elsewhere. The steel industry illustrates this situation. Although bulk steel product, such as sheet steel have suffered a general decline, demand has actually risen for specialty steels such as those used in high-speed machine tools. Vacuum tubes provide another example. Although demand for the tubes collapsed when transistors replaced them as a key component in many electronics products, vacuum tubes still had limited applications in radar equipment for years afterward. Consequently, demand in this one segment remained strong despite the general decline in demand for vacuum tubes. The point is that there may be pockets of demand in an industry in which demand is declining more slowly than in the industry as a whole—or where demand is not declining at all. Price competition may be far less intense among companies serving pockets of demand than within the industry as a whole.

Choosing a Strategy

There are four main strategies that companies can adopt to deal with decline: (1) a **leadership strategy**, by which a company seeks to become the dominant player in a declining industry; (2) a **niche strategy**, which focuses on pockets of demand that are declining more slowly than the industry as a whole; (3) a **harvest strategy**, which

leadership strategy
When a company develops strategies to become the dominant player in a declining industry.

niche strategy
When a company focuses on pockets of demand that are declining more slowly than the industry as a whole to maintain profitability.

harvest strategy
When a company reduces to a minimum the assets it employs in a business to reduce its cost structure and extract ("milk") maximum profits from its investment.

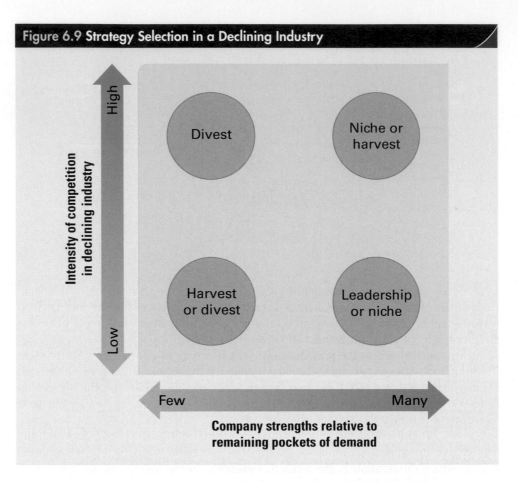

Figure 6.9 Strategy Selection in a Declining Industry

Divest

Niche or harvest

Harvest or divest

Leadership or niche

Intensity of competition in declining industry

High

Low

Few

Many

Company strengths relative to remaining pockets of demand

divestment strategy

When a company exits an industry by selling its business assets to another company.

optimizes cash flow; and (4) a **divestment strategy**, by which a company sells the business to others.[22] Figure 6.9 provides a simple framework for guiding strategic choice. Note that the intensity of competition in the declining industry is measured on the vertical axis, and a company's strengths relative to remaining pockets of demand are measured on the horizontal axis.

Leadership Strategy A leadership strategy aims at growing in a declining industry by picking up the market share of companies that are leaving the industry. A leadership strategy makes most sense when (1) the company has distinctive strengths that allow it to capture market share in a declining industry, and (2) the speed of decline and the intensity of competition in the declining industry are moderate. Philip Morris used this strategy in the tobacco industry. While other cigarette companies were responding to slumping demand by cutting costs or exiting the market, Philip Morris increased its advertising, and subsequently its market share, in the declining industry. It earned enormous profits in the process.

The tactical steps companies might use to achieve a leadership position include using aggressive pricing and marketing to build market share, acquiring established competitors to consolidate the industry, and raising the stakes for other competitors, for example by making new investments in productive capacity. Such competitive tactics signal to rivals that the company is willing and able to stay and compete in the declining industry. These signals may persuade other companies to exit the industry, which would further enhance the competitive position of the industry leader.

Niche Strategy   A niche strategy focuses on pockets of demand in the industry in which demand is stable or declining less rapidly than the industry as a whole. This strategy makes sense when the company has unique strengths relative to those niches in which demand remains relatively strong. Consider Naval, a company that manufactures whaling harpoons (and small guns to fire them) and makes adequate profits. This might be considered rather odd because the world community has outlawed whaling. However, Naval survived the terminal decline of the harpoon industry by focusing on the one group of people who are still allowed to hunt whales, although in very limited numbers: North American Inuit, who are permitted to hunt bowhead whales provided that they do so only for food and not for commercial purposes. Naval is the sole supplier of small harpoon whaling guns to Inuit communities, and its monopoly position allows the company to earn a healthy return in this small market.

Harvest Strategy   As noted earlier, a harvest strategy is the best choice when a company wishes to exit a declining industry and optimize cash flow in the process. This strategy makes the most sense when the company foresees a steep decline and intense future competition, or when it lacks strengths relative to remaining pockets of demand in the industry. A harvest strategy requires the company to halt all new investments in capital equipment, advertising, research and development (R&D), and so forth. The inevitable result is that the company will lose market share, but because it is no longer investing in the business, initially its positive cash flow will increase. Essentially, the company is accepting cash flow in exchange for market share. Ultimately, cash flow will start to decline, and when that occurs, it makes sense for the company to liquidate the business. Although this strategy can be very appealing in theory, it can be somewhat difficult to put into practice. Employee morale in a declining business may suffer. Furthermore, if customers realize what the company is doing, they may rapidly defect, and market share may decline much faster than the company expects. Research by Professors Daniel Elfenbein and Anne Marie Knott found that U.S. banks often delayed exiting the market well past the time when it would have been rational to do so based on their profits. Elfenbein and Knott argue that banks appear to exit late in part because of rational demand uncertainty, and in part because of irrational optimism or escalating commitment that results in management overweighting positive signals that profits might rebound.[23]

Divestment Strategy   A divestment strategy rests on the idea that a company can recover most of its investment in an underperforming business by selling it early, before the industry has entered into a steep decline. This strategy is appropriate when the company has few strengths relative to whatever pockets of demand are likely to remain in the industry, and when the competition in the declining industry is likely to be intense. The best option may be to sell to a company that is pursuing a leadership strategy in the industry. The drawback of the divestment strategy is that its success depends upon the ability of the company to spot industry decline before it becomes detrimental, and to sell while the company's assets are still valued by others.

KEY TERMS

TAKEAWAYS FOR STRATEGIC MANAGERS

1. In fragmented industries composed of many small- and medium-sized companies, the principal forms of competitive strategy are chaining, franchising, and horizontal merger.

2. In embryonic and growth industries, strategy is partly determined by market demand. Innovators and early adopters have different needs than the early and the late majority, and a company must have the right strategies in place to cross the chasm and survive. Similarly, managers must understand the factors that affect a market's growth rate so that they can tailor their business model to a changing industry environment.

3. Mature industries are composed of a few large companies whose actions are so highly interdependent that the success of one company's strategy depends upon the responses of its rivals.

4. The principal strategies used by companies in mature industries to deter entry are product proliferation, price cutting, and maintaining excess capacity.

5. The principal strategies used by companies in mature industries to manage rivalry are price signaling, price leadership, non-price competition, and capacity control.

6. In declining industries, in which market demand has leveled off or is decreasing, companies must tailor their price and non-price strategies to the new competitive environment. Companies also need to manage industry capacity to prevent the emergence of capacity-expansion problems.

7. There are four main strategies a company can pursue when demand is falling: leadership, niche, harvest, and divestment. The strategic choice is determined by the severity of industry decline and the company's strengths relative to the remaining pockets of demand.

DISCUSSION QUESTIONS

1. Why are industries fragmented? What are the primary ways in which companies can turn a fragmented industry into a consolidated industry?

2. What are the key problems in maintaining a competitive advantage in embryonic and growth industry environments? What are the dangers associated with being the leader in an industry?

3. What investment strategies should be made by: (a) differentiators in a strong competitive position, and (b) differentiators in a weak competitive position, while managing a company's growth through the life cycle?

4. Discuss how companies can use: (a) product differentiation, and (b) capacity control to manage rivalry and increase an industry's profitability.

5. What strategies might these enterprises use to strengthen their business models (a) a small pizza place operating in a crowded college market, and (b) a detergent manufacturer seeking to unveil new products in an established market?

CLOSING CASE

How to Make Money in Newspaper Advertising

The U.S. newspaper business is a declining industry. Since 1990, newspaper circulation been steadily falling, with the drop accelerating in recent years. According to the Newspaper Association of America, in 1990, 62.3 million newspapers were sold every day. By 2011, this figure had dropped to 44.4 million. The fall in advertising revenue has been even steeper, with revenues peaking in 2000 at $48.7 billion, and falling to just $20.7 billion in 2013. Reasons for the decline in circulation and advertising revenue are not hard to find; digitalization has disrupted the industry; news consumption has moved to the Web, and advertising has followed suit. The online classified advertising website Craigslist has been particularly damaging to newspapers. Advertisers can post ads on Craigslist for free (in most cases) that are easy to search and update in real time, unlike a newspaper. According to research by professors Robert Seamans and Feng Zhu, Craigslist alone was responsible for over $5 billion in lost revenues in the newspaper industry between 2000-2007.

Declining demand for printed newspapers has left established players in the industry reeling and searching for responses. Gannett Co., which publishes *USA Today* and a host of local newspapers, has seen its revenues slip to $4.3 billion in 2014, down from $6.77 billion in 2008. The venerable *New York Times* has seen revenues fall from $2.9 billion to $1.6 billion over the same period. The industry has responded in multiple ways, but implementing a response has proven to be anything but easy, as a change to one side of a newspaper's business model requires changes to its other side. Newspapers traditionally relied so heavily on advertising that they subsidized the consumer news side. According to research by Professor Seamans and Zhu, without classified advertising revenue to subsidize subscriptions, many newspapers decided to increase their subscription prices, by 5 to 10%. This led, however, to falling numbers of subscribers. In addition, some newspapers have rapidly expanded Web-based news properties at the risk of cannibalizing their offline print customers. As of 2014, almost 30% of total newspaper circulation in the United States was online, and for the fifteen largest newspapers, over 45% of their total circulation was online. Of the country's 1,380 daily newspapers, 450 had adopted digital pay plans that offered a combination of online and print subscription. The *New York Times*, for example, had a range of subscription options that included everything from online only, to select days of print in addition to online, to print only. Many newspapers increased the price of single copies, and this, combined with the digital paywall movement of charging for online content, appeared to stabilize circulation revenues and helped reduce the industry's historic dependence on advertising revenues.

Against this background, one local newspaper company is swimming against the tide, and making money at it. Community Impact Newspaper produces 13 hyperlocal editions that are delivered free each month to 855,000 homes in the Austin, Houston, and Dallas areas. The paper is the brainchild of John Garrett, who used to work as an advertising director for the *Austin Business Journal*. In 2005, Garrett noticed that the large-circulation local newspapers in Texas did not cover news that was relevant to smaller neighborhoods—such as the construction of a local toll road, or the impact of a new corporate campus for Exxon Mobil. Nor could news about these projects be gleaned from the Web. Yet Garrett believed that local people were still hungry for news about local projects and events that

(continued)

might impact them. So he launched the inaugural issue of his paper in September 2005, and financing it with $40,000 borrowed from low-interest credit cards.

Today, the paper has a staff of 30 journalists, about 35% of the total workforce. The reporting is pretty straight stuff. There is no investigative reporting, although *Impact* will run in-depth stories on controversial local issues, being careful not to take sides. "That would just lose us business," says Garrett. About half of each edition is devoted to local advertisements, and this is where *Impact* makes money. For their part, the advertisers seem happy with the paper. "We've tried everything, from Google Ads to Groupon, but this is the most effective," says Richard Hunter, who spends a few hundred dollars each month to advertise his Houston restaurant, Catfish Station. Another advertiser, Rob Sides, who owns a toy store, Toy Time, places 80% of his advertising dollars with *Impact*'s local edition in order to reach 90,000 homes in the area.

An analysis by *Forbes* estimated that each 40-page issue of *Impact* brings in about $2.50 in ad revenue per printed copy. About 50 cents of that goes to mailing and distribution costs, 80 cents to payroll, and another 80 cents to printing and overhead, leaving roughly 40 cents per copy for Garrett and his wife, who own the entire company. If this analysis is right, *Impact* is making very good money for its owners in an industry where most players are struggling just to survive.

Sources: C. Helman, "Breaking: A Local Newspaper Chain That's Actually Making Good Money," *Forbes*, January 21, 2013, www.forbes.com; News Paper Association of America, "Trends and Numbers," www.naa.org/Trends-and-Numbers/Research .aspx; J. Agnese, "Publishing and Advertising," S&P netAdvantage, April 12, 2012, http://eresources.library.nd.edu/ databases /netadvantage; R. Edmonds, E. Guskin, A. Mitchell, and M. Jurkowitz, 2013; *Newspapers by the Numbers. The State of the News Media 2014*, annual report on American journalism, Pew Research Center, New York; Yahoo Finance, finance.yahoo. com; R. Seamans and F. Zhu, "Responses to Entry in Multi-Sided Markets: The Impact of Craigslist on Local Newspapers," *Management Science*, 60 (2), 2014, pp. 476-493; R. Seamans and F. Zhu, "Repositioning and Cost Cutting: The Impact of Competition on Newspaper Strategies," NYU Stern Working Paper, 2014.

CASE DISCUSSION QUESTIONS

1. What advantages do traditional print newspapers have for entering the online news business? What disadvantages do they have?
2. What do you think determines whether people will use print, online, or both sources for their news?
3. When a print newspaper initiates an online version of its newspaper, what are the possible outcomes for its current display advertisers? Are they likely to prefer one channel over the other to reach their customers, or are they likely to select both? If both, are they likely to expect a discount for a bundle of print and online advertising? How do these outcomes affect the newspaper's bargaining power?
4. How do you think the cost structure of online advertising compares to the cost structure of print advertising?
5. Which print newspapers do you think will fare the best as online news continues to expand? Why?

NOTES

1. M. E. Porter, *Competitive Strategy: Techniques for Analyzing Industries and Competitors* (New York: Free Press, 1980), pp. 191–200.

2. W. C. Kim and R. Mauborgne, "Value Innovation: The Strategic Logic of High Growth," *Harvard Business Review* (January–February 1997): pp. 103–112.

3. S. A. Shane, "Hybrid Organizational Arrangements and Their Implications for Firm Growth and Survival: A Study of New Franchisors," *Academy of Management Journal* 1 (1996): 216–234.

4. Microsoft is often accused of not being an innovator, but the fact is that Bill Gates and Paul Allen wrote the first commercial software program for the first commercially available personal computer. Microsoft was the first mover in its industry. See P. Freiberger and M. Swaine, *Fire in the Valley* (New York: McGraw-Hill, 2000).

5. J. M. Utterback, *Mastering the Dynamics of Innovation* (Boston: Harvard Business School Press, 1994).

6. E. M. Rogers, *Diffusion of Innovations,* 5th ed. Free Press, 2003. Ibid.

7. R. Brown "Managing the 'S' Curves of Innovation, *"Journal of Consumer Marketing* 9 (1992): 61–72; P. A. Geroski. "Models of Technology Diffusion," *Research Policy* 29 (2000): 603–25.

8. Freiberger and Swaine, *Fire in the Valley.*

9. Utterback, *Mastering the Dynamics of Innovation.*

10. G. A. Moore, *Crossing the Chasm* (New York: HarperCollins, 1991).

11. Utterback, *Mastering the Dynamics of Innovation.*

12. E. Rogers, *Diffusion of Innovations* (New York: Free Press, 1995).

13. R. J. Gilbert, "Mobility Barriers and the Value of Incumbency," in R. Schmalensee and R. D. Willig (eds.), *Handbook of Industrial Organization* (Elsevier Science Publishers, 1989).

14. R. Seamans, "Threat of Entry, Asymmetric Information, and Pricing," *Strategic Management Journal* 34 (2013): 426–44.

15. R. Seamans. "Fighting City Hall: Entry Deterrence and Technology Upgrades in Cable TV Markets," *Management Science* 58 (2012): 461–75.

16. P. Ghemawat, *Commitment: The Dynamic of Strategy* (Harvard Business School Press, 1991).

17. M. B. Lieberman, "Excess Capacity as a Barrier to Entry: An Empirical Appraisal," *Journal of Industrial Economics* 35 (1987): 607–27

18. R. Lukach, P. M. Kort, and J. Plasmans, "Optimal R&D Investment Strategies Under the Threat of New Technology Entry," *International Journal of Industrial Organization* 25 (February 2007): 103–19.

19. W. B. Arthur, "Increasing Returns and the New World of Business," *Harvard Business Review* (July 1996): 100–109

20. R. Axelrod, *The Evolution of Cooperation* (New York: Basic Books, 1984).

21. The next section draws heavily on Marvin B. Lieberman, "Strategies for Capacity Expansion," *Sloan Management Review* 8 (1987): 19–27; Porter, *Competitive Strategy*, 324–38.

22. K. R. Harrigan, "Strategy Formulation in Declining Industries," *Academy of Management Review* 5 (1980): 599–604.

23. D. W. Elfenbein and A. W. Knott. "Time to Exit: Rational, Behavioral, and Organizational Delays," *Strategic Management Journal* (June 2014): 957–75.

sergign/Shutterstock.com

CHAPTER 7

STRATEGY AND TECHNOLOGY

OPENING CASE

Blu-ray versus HD-DVD and Streaming: Standards Battles in Video

In 2003, Sony officially launched its Blu-ray disc, an optical disc data-storage format that could offer high-definition video, with hopes of replacing the DVD format. Sony's technology had the backing of a consortium that included Philips, Panasonic, Pioneer, Sharp, Samsung, Hitachi, and others. Toshiba, on the other hand, was not eager to let Sony dominate the market with its Blu-ray technology; Sony and Philips had controlled the original standard for compact discs (CDs), and every producer of CDs, CD players, and CD recorders, had been required to pay licensing fees to Sony and Philips–an extremely lucrative arrangement for the partners. Toshiba thus formed a consortium, the DVD Forum, which developed a competing high-definition DVD standard, HD-DVD, making it the "official" successor to the DVD format.

Both new formats were intended to deliver a theaterlike experience at home, with brilliantly clear video and surround-sound audio, on high-end LCD and plasma televisions. The formats, however, would be incompatible. Consumers, retailers, and movie producers all groaned at the prospect of a format war similar to the battle that had taken place between Sony's Betamax and JVC's VHS video standard three decades earlier. That war had left many bloodied—consumers who bought

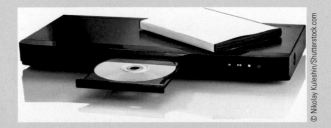
© Nikolay Kuleshin/Shutterstock.com

Betamax players, for example, found that very few movies were ultimately made available in the format, and retailers got stuck with unwanted inventory in Betamax players and movies. The threat of another format war caused many retailers and consumers to delay their purchases of the next-generation players while they waited to see if the market would pick a winner. Fearing a lengthy, costly battle, consumer electronics producers began working on players that would be compatible with both standards, even though that would significantly increase their cost.

Initially, the HD-DVD standard had a head start. Blu-ray players were considered to be too expensive and buggy, and there were few movie titles available in the standard. Toshiba, on the other hand, already had the cooperation of several major Hollywood studios for its format, including Time Warner's Warner Brothers, Viacom's Paramount Pictures and Dreamworks Animation, and NBC Universal's Universal Pictures. Sony had only its own Sony Pictures Entertainment, Disney, News Corporation's 20th Century Fox, and Lions Gate Entertainment.

Both companies also used videogame consoles to promote their standards. Sony incorporated the Blu-ray format into its PlayStation 3, dramatically raising the cost of the devices. Though it sold the consoles at a very low price relative to cost, the consoles were still significantly more expensive than traditional videogame consoles, causing PlayStation 3 to sell only about half as many total units as PlayStation2 had sold (85.23 million versus 157.68 million, respectively). Sony was willing, however, to concede some ground in the PlayStation battle to win the Blu-ray war. Toshiba's HD-DVD was offered as an optional, add-on drive for Microsoft's Xbox 360.

However, on the eve of the Consumer Electronics Show in Las Vegas in early January 2008, Warner Brothers announced that it would no longer support the HD DVD standard. This set off a chain reaction among content providers and retailers. By late February, New Line Cinema, Universal Studios, and Paramount announced that they would be releasing movies on the Blu-ray format, and Best Buy, Wal-Mart, Circuit City, Future Shop, Blockbuster, and Netflix all announced that they would exclusively stock Blu-ray DVDs. The blow was unexpected—and devastating—for Toshiba. On February 19, 2008, Toshiba's CEO, Atsutoshi Nishida, conceded defeat by publicly announcing that Toshiba would no longer produce HD-DVD players, recorders, or components. By late 2009, Toshiba had released its own Blu-ray disc player.

Sony's Blu-ray victory, however, was not the landslide that it expected. On September 12, 2008, a consortium of tech heavyweights (including Intel and Hewlett Packard) announced that they would collaborate with Hollywood to create standards that would make downloading movies fast and easy. If consumers were able to download high-quality movies off the Internet, it would become increasingly difficult to persuade them to spend $300 or more on a Blu-ray player. Carmi Levi, senior vice president at consulting firm AR Communications, predicted that "Blu-ray is probably going to be the last physical [product] where you walk into a store, get a movie in a box, and bring it home."

By 2012, about one-third of US households had a device that could play a Blu-ray movie (including PlayStation 3); at the same point in the DVD format's life, over half of U.S. households had a device for playing DVDs. Video streaming revenues had reached $5.7 billion in the United States by 2014 and were expected to reach $14 billion by 2018. Physical DVD and Blu-ray sales, on the other hand, were expected to drop from $12.2 billion in 2013 to $8.7 billion by 2018. Though the availability of Blu-ray format streamed content was increasing, many people preferred to stream content in standard (versus high definition) format because it was faster, reducing the buffering time necessary for watching content. In fact, one study found that nearly one-quarter of U.S. households did not have adequate bandwidth to stream high-definition content, and another study found that even in households that could stream high-definition content, many viewers still chose standard definition viewing. On May 1, 2014, Sony issued a warning to investors that it expected to take a hit on earnings because Blu-ray sales were contracting faster than it had expected.

Sources: Anonymous, "Battle of the Blue Lasers," *The Economist*, December 2, 2004, p. 16; B. Schlender, "The Trouble with Sony," *Fortune*, February 22, 2007, p. 46; C. Edwards, "R.I.P., HD DVD," *BusinessWeek Online*, February 20, 2008; K. Hall, "DVD Format Wars: Toshiba Surrenders," *BusinessWeek Online*, February 20, 2008; C. Edwards, "Blu-ray: Playing for a Limited Engagement?," *BusinessWeek Online*, September 18, 2008; M. Snider, "Blu-ray Caught in Shift to Streaming," *USA Today*, August 23, 2012, www.USAToday.com; Yahoo Finance; R. McCormick, "Video Streaming Services Could Make More Money than the U.S. Box Office by 2017," *The Verge*, June 4, 2014, www.theverge.com; M. Willens, "Home Entertainment 2014: US DVD Sales and Rentals Crater, DVD Subscriptions Soar," *International Business Times*, March 10, 2015; vgchartz.com, March 10, 2015; J. Rietveld and J. Lampel, "Nintendo: Fighting the Video Game Console Wars," in *The Strategy Process* (H. Mintzberg, Ed.) (5th ed.). FT Press, 2014.

◤ OVERVIEW

The high-stakes battle that Sony faced in video formats is typical of the nature of competition in high-technology industries (see the Opening Case). In industries where standards and compatibility are important strategic levers, a technology that gains an initial advantage can sometimes rise to achieve a nearly insurmountable position. Such industries can thus become "winner-take-all" markets. Being successful in such industries can require very different strategies than those used in more traditional industries. Firms may aggressively subsidize adoption of their preferred technology (including sometimes giving away products for free) in order to win the standards battle.

In this chapter, we will take a close look at the nature of competition and strategy in high-technology industries. Technology refers to the body of scientific knowledge used in the production of goods or services. High-technology (high-tech) industries are those in which the underlying scientific knowledge that companies in the industry use is rapidly advancing, and, by implication, so are the attributes of the products and services that result from its application. The computer industry is often thought of as the quintessential example of a high-technology industry. Other industries often considered high-tech are telecommunications, where new technologies based on wireless and the Internet have proliferated in recent years; consumer electronics, where the digital technology underlying products from high-definition DVD players to video-game terminals and digital cameras is advancing rapidly; pharmaceuticals, where new technologies based on cell biology, recombinant DNA, and genomics are revolutionizing the process of drug discovery; power generation, where new technologies based on fuel cells and cogeneration may change the economics of the industry; and aerospace, where the combination of new composite materials, electronics, and more efficient jet engines is giving birth to a new era of superefficient commercial jet aircraft such as Boeing's 787.

This chapter focuses on high-technology industries for a number of reasons. First, technology is accounting for an ever-larger share of economic activity. Estimates suggest that in the last decade, nearly 25% of growth in domestic product was accounted for by information technology industries.[1] This figure actually underestimates the true impact of technology on the economy, because it ignores the other high-technology areas we just mentioned. Moreover, as technology advances, many low-technology industries are becoming more high-tech. For example, the development of biotechnology and genetic engineering transformed the production of seed corn, long considered a low-tech business, into a high-technology business. Retailing was once considered a low-tech business, but the shift to online retailing, led by companies like Amazon.com, has changed this. In addition, high-tech products are making their way into a wide range of businesses; today, most automobiles contain more computing power than the multimillion-dollar mainframe computers used in the *Apollo* space program, and the competitive advantage of physical stores such as Wal-Mart is based on their use of information technology. The circle of high-technology industries is both large and expanding, and technology is revolutionizing aspects of the product or production system even in industries not typically considered high-tech.

Although high-tech industries may produce very different products, when developing a business model and strategies that will lead to a competitive advantage and superior profitability and profit growth, they often face a similar situation. For example, "winner-take-all" format wars are common in many high-tech industries such as the consumer electronics and computer industries. In mobile payments, for example, it is possible that a new payment system will emerge that could displace Visa, MasterCard, and American Express as the dominant firms for managing payment transactions worldwide. This could result in a tremendous windfall for the firm(s) controlling the new standard (and a tremendous loss for Visa, MasterCard, and American Express). Firms are thus carefully forging alliances and backing standards they believe will best position them to capture the billions of dollars in transactions fees that are at stake (see the Closing Case). This chapter examines the competitive features found in many high-tech industries and the kinds of strategies that companies must adopt to build business models that will allow them to achieve superior profitability and profit growth.

◤ TECHNICAL STANDARDS AND FORMAT WARS

Especially in high-tech industries, ownership of **technical standards**—a set of technical specifications that producers adhere to when making the product, or a component of it—can be an important source of competitive advantage.[2] Indeed, in many cases product differentiation is based on a technical standard. Often, only one standard will dominate a market, so many battles in high-tech industries involve companies that compete to set the standard. For example, for the last three decades, Microsoft has controlled the market as the dominant operating system for personal computers (PCs), sometimes exceeding a 90% market share. Notably, however, Microsoft held very small shares of the tablet (roughly 4.8%) and smartphone (roughly 3.6%) operating system markets in 2014, suggesting the possibility of turbulent times ahead for the firm (see Strategy in Action 7.1).

Battles to set and control technical standards in a market are referred to as **format wars**—essentially, battles to control the source of differentiation, and thus the value

technical standards
A set of technical specifications that producers adhere to when making a product or component.

format wars
Battles to control the source of differentiation, and thus the value that such differentiation can create for the customer.

7.1 STRATEGY IN ACTION

"Segment Zero"—A Serious Threat to Microsoft?

From 1980 to 2013, Microsoft's Windows was entrenched as the dominant PC operating system, giving it enormous influence over many aspects of the computer hardware and software industries. Although competing operating systems had been introduced during that time (e.g., Unix, Geoworks, NeXTSTEP, Linux, and the Mac OS), Microsoft's share of the PC operating system market held stable at roughly 85% throughout most of that period. By 2015, however, Microsoft's position in the computing industry was under greater threat than it had ever been. A high-stakes race for dominance over the next generation of computing was well under way, and Microsoft was not in the front pack.

"Segment Zero"

As Andy Grove, former CEO of Intel, noted in 1998, in many industries—including microprocessors, software, motorcycles, and electric vehicles—technologies improve faster than customer demands of those technologies increase. Firms often add features such as speed and power to products more quickly than customers' capacity to absorb them. Why would firms provide higher performance than that required by the bulk of their customers? The answer appears to lie in the market segmentation and pricing objectives of a technology's providers. As competition in an industry drives prices and margins lower, firms often try to shift sales into progressively higher tiers of the market. In these tiers, high-performance and feature-rich products can command higher margins. Although customers may also expect to have better-performing products over time, their ability to fully utilize such performance improvements is slowed by the need to learn how to use new features and adapt their work and lifestyles accordingly. Thus, both the trajectory of technology improvement and the trajectory of customer demands are upward sloping, but the trajectory for technology improvement is steeper.

In Figure 7.1 the technology trajectory begins at a point where it provides performance close to that demanded by the mass market, but over time it increases faster than the expectations of the mass market as the firm targets the high-end market. As the price of the technology rises, the mass market may feel it is overpaying for technological features it does not value. In Figure 7.1 the low-end market is not being served; it either pays far more for technology that it does not need, or it goes without. It is this market that Andy Grove, former CEO of Intel, refers to as segment zero.

For Intel, segment zero was the market for low-end personal computers (those less than $1,000). Although segment zero may seem unattractive in terms of margins, if it is neglected, it can become the breeding ground for companies that provide lower-end versions of the technology. As Grove notes, "The overlooked, underserved, and seemingly unprofitable end of the market can provide fertile ground for massive competitive change."

As the firms serving low-end markets with simpler technologies ride up their own trajectories (which are also steeper than the slope of the trajectories of customer expectations), they can eventually reach a performance level that meets the demands of the mass market while offering a much lower price than the premium technology (see Figure 7.2). At this point, firms offering premium technology may suddenly find they are losing the bulk of their sales revenue to industry contenders that do not look so low-end anymore. For example, by 1998, the combination of rising microprocessor power and decreasing prices enabled PCs priced under $1,000 to capture 20% of the market.

The Threat to Microsoft

So where was the segment zero that could threaten Microsoft? Look in your pocket. In 2015, Apple's iPhone operating system (iOS) and Google's Android collectively controlled over 95% of the worldwide market for smartphones. Estimates put Microsoft's share

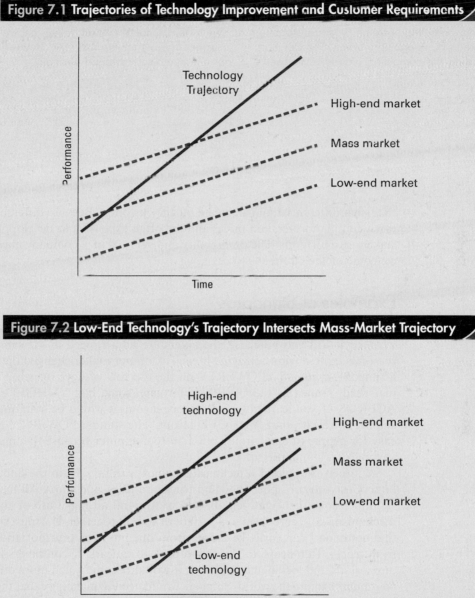

Figure 7.1 Trajectories of Technology Improvement and Customer Requirements

Technology
Trajectory

High-end market

Mass market

Low-end market

Performance

Time

Figure 7.2 Low-End Technology's Trajectory Intersects Mass-Market Trajectory

High-end
technology

High-end market

Mass market

Low-end market

Performance

Low-end
technology

Time

at 3.6%. The iOS and Android interfaces offered a double whammy of beautiful aesthetics and remarkable ease of use. The applications business model used for the phones was also extremely attractive to both developers and customers, and quickly resulted in enormous libraries of applications that ranged from ridiculous to indispensable.

From a traditional economics perspective, the phone operating system market should not be that attractive to Microsoft—people do not spend as much on the applications, and the carriers have too much bargaining power, among other reasons. However, those smartphone operating systems soon became tablet operating systems, and tablets were rapidly

(*continued*)

becoming fully functional computers. Suddenly, all of the mindshare that Apple and Google had achieved in smartphone operating systems was transforming into mindshare in PC operating systems. Despite years of masterminding the computing industry, Microsoft's dominant position was at risk of evaporating. The outcome is still uncertain—in 2015, Microsoft had an impressive arsenal of capital, talent, and relationships in its armory, but for the first time, it was fighting the battle from a disadvantaged position.

Sources: Adapted from M. A. Schilling, "'Segment Zero': A Serious Threat to Microsoft?" Conceptual Note, New York University, 2013; A. S. Grove, "Managing Segment Zero," *Leader to Leader* 11 (1999); L. Dignan, "Android, Apple iOS Flip Consumer, Corporate Market Share," *Between the Lines,* February 13, 2013; J. Edwards, "The iPhone 6 Had Better Be Amazing and cheap, Because Apple Is Losing the War to Android," *Business Insider,* May 31, 2014; M. Hachman, "Android, iOS Gobble Up Even More Global Smartphone Share," *PC World,* August 14, 2014.

that such differentiation can create for the customer. Because differentiated products often command premium prices and are often expensive to develop, the competitive stakes are enormous. The profitability and survival of a company may depend on the outcome of the battle.

Examples of Standards

A familiar example of a standard is the layout of a computer keyboard. No matter what keyboard you purchase, the letters are all arranged in the same pattern.[3] The reason is quite obvious. Imagine if each computer maker changed the ways keys were arranged—if some had QWERTY on the top row of keys (which is indeed the format used, known as the QWERTY format), some had YUHGFD, and some had ACFRDS. If you learned to type on one layout, it would be irritating and time consuming to relearn on a YUHGFD layout. The standard QWERTY format makes it easy for people to move from computer to computer because the input medium, the keyboard, is standardized.

Another example of a technical standard can be seen in the dimensions of containers used to transport goods on trucks, railcars, and ships. All have the same basic dimensions of height, length, and width, and all make use of the same locking mechanisms to secure them to a surface or to bolt together. Having a standard ensures that containers can easily be moved from one mode of transportation to another—from trucks, to railcars, to ships, and back to railcars. If containers lacked standard dimensions and locking mechanisms, it would become much more difficult to deliver containers around the world. Shippers would need to make sure that they had the right kind of container to go on the ships, trucks, and railcars scheduled to carry a particular container around the world—a very complicated process.

Consider, finally, PCs. Most share a common set of features: an Intel or Intel-compatible microprocessor, random access memory (RAM), a Microsoft operating system, an internal hard drive, a DVD drive, a keyboard, a monitor, a mouse, a modem, and so on. We call this set of features the dominant design for personal computers. **Dominant design** refers to a common set of features or design characteristics. Embedded in this design are several technical standards (see Figure 7.3). For example, there is the Wintel technical standard based on an Intel microprocessor and a Microsoft operating system. Microsoft and Intel "own" that standard, which is central to the PC.

dominant design

Common set of features or design characteristics.

Figure 7.3 Technical Standards for Personal Computers

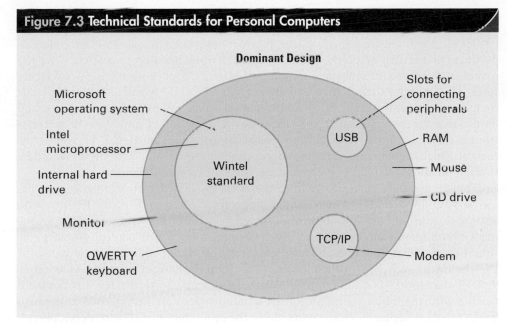

Developers of software applications, component parts, and peripherals such as printers adhere to this standard when developing their products because this guarantees that they will work well with a PC based on the Wintel standard. Another technical standard for connecting peripherals to the PC is the universal serial bus (or USB), established by an industry-standards-setting board. No one owns it; the standard is in the public domain. A third technical standard is for communication between a PC and the Internet via a modem. Known as TCP/IP, this standard was also set by an industry association and is in the public domain. Thus, as with many other products, the PC is actually based on several technical standards. It is also important to note that when a company owns a standard, as Microsoft and Intel do with the Wintel standard, it may be a source of competitive advantage and high profitability.

Benefits of Standards

Standards emerge because there are economic benefits associated with them. First, a technical standard helps to guarantee compatibility between products and their complements. For example, containers are used with railcars, trucks, and ships, and PCs are used with software applications. Compatibility has the tangible economic benefit of reducing the costs associated with making sure that products work well with each other.

Second, a standard can help reduce confusion in the minds of consumers. As noted in the opening case, when Blu-ray was launched it was competing against HD-DVD to be the dominant video standard. Players based on the different standards were incompatible; a disc designed to run on a Blu-ray player would not run on a HD-DVD player, and vice versa. The companies feared that selling these incompatible versions of the same technology would produce confusion in the minds of consumers, who would not know which version to purchase and might decide to wait and see which technology would dominate the marketplace. With lack of demand, both technologies might fail to gain traction in the marketplace and be unsuccessful. After Toshiba conceded the defeat of the HD-DVD standard, Blu-ray sales grew rapidly.

Third, a standard can help reduce production costs. Once a standard emerges, products that are based on the standard design can be mass produced, enabling the manufacturers to realize substantial economies of scale while lowering their cost structures. The fact that there is a central standard for PCs (the Wintel standard) means that the component parts for a PC can be mass produced. A manufacturer of internal hard drives, for example, can mass produce drives for Wintel PCs and thus realize substantial scale economies. If there were several competing and incompatible standards, each of which required a unique hard drive, production runs for hard drives would be shorter, unit costs would be higher, and the cost of PCs would increase.

Fourth, standards can help reduce the risks associated with supplying complementary products, and thus increase the supply for those complements. For instance, writing software applications to run on PCs is a risky proposition, requiring the investment of considerable sums of money for developing the software before a single unit is sold. Imagine what would occur if there were ten different operating systems in use for PCs, each with only 10% of the market, rather than the current situation, where over 90% of the world's PCs adhere to the Wintel standard. Software developers would need to write ten different versions of the same software application, each for a much smaller market segment. This would change the economics of software development, increase its risks, and reduce potential profitability. Moreover, because of their higher cost structure and fewer economies of scale, the price of software programs would increase.

Thus, although many people complain about the consequences of Microsoft's near-monopoly of PC operating systems, that dominance does have at least one good effect: It substantially reduces the risks facing the makers of complementary products and the costs of those products. In fact, standards lead to both low-cost and differentiation advantages for individual companies and can help raise the level of industry profitability.

Establishment of Standards

Standards emerge in an industry in three primary ways. First, when the benefits of establishing a standard are recognized, companies in an industry might lobby the government to mandate an industry standard. In the United States, for example, the Federal Communications Commission (FCC), after detailed discussions with broadcasters and consumer electronics companies, mandated a single technical standard for digital television broadcasts (DTV) and required analog television broadcasts to be terminated in 2009. The FCC took this step because it believed that without government action to set the standard, the DTV rollout would be very slow. Given a standard set by the government, consumer electronics companies have greater confidence that a market will emerge, and this should encourage them to develop DTV products.

Second, technical standards are often set by cooperation among businesses, without government help, and often through the medium of an industry association, as the example of the DVD forum illustrates. Companies cooperate in this way when they decide that competition to create a standard might be harmful because of the uncertainty that it would create in the minds of consumers or the risk it would pose to manufacturers and distributors.

Government- or association-set standards fall into the **public domain**, meaning that any company can freely incorporate the knowledge and technology upon which the standard is based into its products. For example, no one owns the QWERTY format, and therefore no company can profit from it directly. Similarly, the language that underlies the presentation of text and graphics on the Web, hypertext markup language (HTML), is in the public domain; it is free for all to use. The same is true for TCP/IP, the communications standard used for transmitting data on the Internet.

Often, however, the industry standard is selected competitively by the purchasing patterns of customers in the marketplace—that is, by market demand. In this case, the strategy and business model a company has developed for promoting its technological standard are of critical importance because ownership of an industry standard that is protected from imitation by patents and copyrights is a valuable asset—a source of sustained competitive advantage and superior profitability. Microsoft and Intel, for example, both owe their competitive advantage to their ownership of a specific technological standard or format. As noted earlier, format wars occur when two or more companies compete to get their designs adopted as the industry standard. Format wars are common in high-tech industries where standards are important. The Wintel standard became the dominant standard for PCs only after Microsoft and Intel won format wars against Apple's proprietary system, and later against IBM's OS/2 operating system. There is an ongoing format war within the smartphone business, as Apple, Google, Research in Motion, and Microsoft all battle to get their respective operating systems and phones adopted as the industry standard, as described in Strategy in Action 7.1.

public domain
Government- or association-set standards of knowledge or technology that any company can freely incorporate into its product.

Network Effects, Positive Feedback, and Lockout

There has been a growing realization that when standards are set by competition between companies promoting different formats, network effects are a primary determinant of how standards are established.[4] **Network effects** arise in industries where the size of the "network" of complementary products is a primary determinant of demand for an industry's product. For example, the demand for automobiles early in the 20th century was an increasing function of the network of paved roads and gas stations. Similarly, the demand for early telephones was an increasing function of the multitude of numbers that could be called; that is, of the size of the telephone network (the telephone network being the complementary product). When the first telephone service was introduced in New York City, only 100 numbers could be dialed. The network was very small because of the limited number of wires and telephone switches, which made the telephone a relatively useless piece of equipment. But, as an increasing number of people acquired telephones and the network of wires and switches expanded, the telephone connection gained value. This led to an upsurge in demand for telephone lines, which further increased the value of owning a telephone, setting up a positive feedback loop.

network effects
The network of complementary products as a primary determinant of the demand for an industry's product.

To understand why network effects are important in the establishment of standards, consider the classic example of a format war: the battle between Sony and Matsushita to establish their respective technologies for videocassette recorders (VCRs) as the standard in the marketplace. Sony was first to market with its Betamax technology, followed by JVC with its VHS technology. Both companies sold VCR recorder-players, and movie studios issued films prerecorded on VCR tapes for rental to consumers. Initially, all tapes were issued in Betamax format to play on Sony's machine. Sony did not license its Betamax technology, preferring to make all player-recorders itself. Because Japan's Ministry of International Trade and Industry (MITI) appeared poised to select Sony's Betamax as a standard for Japan, JVC decided to liberally license its format and turned to Matsushita (now Panasonic) for support. Matsushita was the largest Japanese electronics manufacturer at that time. JVC and Matushita realized that to make the VHS format players valuable to consumers, they would need to encourage movie studios to issue movies for rental in VHS format. The only way to do that, they reasoned, was to increase the installed base of VHS players as rapidly as possible. They believed that the greater the installed base of VHS players, the greater the incentive for movie studios to issue films in VHS format for rental. As more prerecorded VHS tapes were made available for rental, VHS players became more valuable to consumers and demand for them increased (see Figure 7.4). JVC and Matsushita wanted to exploit a positive feedback loop.

JVC and Matsushita chose a licensing strategy under which any consumer electronics company was allowed to manufacture VHS-format players under license. This strategy worked. A large number of companies signed on to manufacture VHS players, and soon far more VHS players were available for purchase in stores than Betamax players. As sales of VHS players grew, movie studios issued more films for rental in VHS format, and this stoked demand. Before long, it was clear to anyone who entered a video rental store that there were more VHS tapes available for rent than Betamax tapes. This served to reinforce the positive feedback loop, and ultimately Sony's Betamax technology was shut out of the market. The pivotal difference between the two companies was strategy: JVC and Matsushita chose a licensing strategy; Sony did not. As a result, JVC's VHS technology became the de facto standard for VCRs.

The general principle that underlies this example is that when two or more companies compete to get technology adopted as an industry standard, and when network effects and positive feedback loops are important, *the company whose strategy best exploits positive feedback loops wins the format war*. This is a very important strategic principle in many high-technology industries, particularly computer hardware, software, telecommunications, and consumer electronics. Microsoft is where it is today because it exploited a positive feedback loop. Dolby presents us with another example of a company

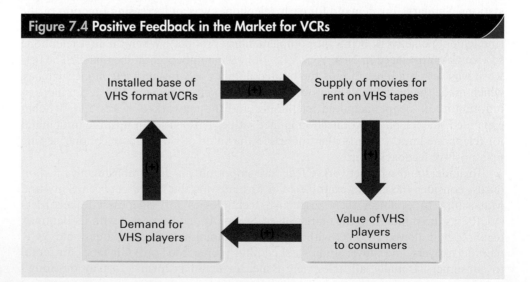

Figure 7.4 Positive Feedback in the Market for VCRs

that exploited a positive feedback loop. When Ray Dolby invented a technology for reducing the background hiss in professional tape recording, he adopted a licensing model that charged a very modest fee. He knew his technology was valuable, but he also understood that charging a high fee would encourage manufacturers to develop their own noise-reduction technology. He also decided to license the technology for use on prerecorded tapes for free, collecting licensing fees on the players only. This set up a powerful, positive feedback loop: Growing sales of prerecorded tapes encoded with Dolby technology created a demand for tape players that contained Dolby technology, and as the installed base of tape players with Dolby technology grew, the proportion of prerecorded tapes that were encoded with Dolby technology surged—further boosting demand for players incorporating Dolby technology. By the mid-1970s, virtually all prerecorded tapes were encoded with Dolby noise-reduction technology.

As the market settles on a standard, an important implication of the positive feedback process occurs: Companies promoting alternative standards can be locked out of the market when consumers are unwilling to bear the switching costs required to abandon the established standard and adopt the new standard. In this context, consumers must bear the costs of switching from a product based on one technological standard to a product based on another technological standard.

For illustration, imagine that a company developed an operating system for personal computers that was both faster and more stable than the current standard in the marketplace, Microsoft Windows. This company would be able to gain significant market share from Microsoft only with great difficulty. Consumers choose PCs not for their operating system but for the applications that run on the operating system. A new operating system would initially have a very small installed base, so few developers would be willing to take the risks involved in writing word-processing programs, spreadsheets, games, and other applications for that operating system. Because there would be very few applications available, consumers who did make the switch would have to bear the switching costs associated with giving up some of their applications, which they might be unwilling to do. Moreover, even if applications were available for the new operating system, consumers would have to bear the costs of purchasing those applications—another source of switching costs. In addition, they would have to bear the costs associated with learning to use the new operating system, yet another source of switching costs. Thus, many consumers would be unwilling to switch even if the new operating system performed better than Windows, and the company promoting the new operating system would be locked out of the market.

However, consumers will bear switching costs if the benefits of adopting the new technology outweigh the costs of switching. For example, in the late 1980s and early 1990s, millions of people switched from analog record players to digital CD players despite the fact that switching costs were significant: Consumers had to purchase the new player technology, and many people purchased CD versions of favorite musical recordings that they already owned. Nevertheless, people made the switch because, for many, the perceived benefit—the incredibly better sound quality associated with CDs—outweighed the costs of switching.

As this switching process continued, a positive feedback loop developed. The installed base of CD players grew, leading to an increase in the number of musical recordings issued on CD as opposed to, or in addition to, vinyl records. The installed base of CD players got so big that mainstream music companies began to issue recordings only in CD format. Once this occurred, even those who did not want to switch to the new technology were required to do so if they wished to purchase new music recordings. The industry standard had shifted: new technology had locked in as the standard, and the old technology was locked out.

Extrapolating from this example, it can be argued that despite its dominance, the Wintel standard for PCs could one day be superseded if a competitor finds a way of providing sufficient benefits that enough consumers are willing to bear the switching costs associated with moving to a new operating system. Indeed, there are signs that Apple and Google are chipping away at the dominance of the Wintel standard, primarily by using elegant design and ease of use as tools to get people to bear the costs of switching from Wintel computers..

STRATEGIES FOR WINNING A FORMAT WAR

From the perspective of a company pioneering a new technological standard in a marketplace where network effects and positive feedback loops operate, the key question becomes: "What strategy should we pursue to establish our format as the dominant one?"

The various strategies that companies should adopt in order to win format wars are centered upon *finding ways to make network effects work in their favor and against their competitors*. Winning a format war requires a company to build the installed base for its standard as rapidly as possible, thereby leveraging the positive feedback loop, inducing consumers to bear switching costs and ultimately locking the market to its technology. It requires the company to jump-start and then accelerate demand for its technological standard or format such that it becomes established as quickly as possible as the industry standard, thereby locking out competing formats. A number of key strategies and tactics can be adopted to try to achieve this.[5]

Ensure a Supply of Complements

It is important for a company to make sure that there is an adequate supply of complements for its product. For example, no one will purchase the Sony PlayStation 4 unless there is an adequate supply of games to run on that machine. Companies typically take two steps to ensure an adequate supply of complements.

First, they may diversify into the production of complements and seed the market with sufficient supply to help jump-start demand for their format. Before Sony produced the original PlayStation in the early 1990s, for example, it established its own in-house unit to produce videogames for the console. When it launched PlayStation, Sony also simultaneously released 16 games to run on the it, giving consumers a reason to purchase the format. Tesla is similarly constructing its own network of supercharging stations at which customers can charge its electric vehicles for free.

Second, companies may create incentives or make it easy for independent companies to produce complements. Sony also licensed the right to produce games to a number of independent game developers, charged the developers a lower royalty rate than they had to pay to competitors such as Nintendo and Sega, and provided them with software tools that made it easier for them to develop games (Apple is now doing the same thing with its smartphones). Thus, the launch of the Sony PlayStation was accompanied by the simultaneous launch of approximately 30 games, which quickly helped to stimulate demand for the machine.

Leverage Killer Applications

Killer applications are applications or uses of a new technology or product that are so compelling that they persuade customers to adopt the new format or technology in droves, thereby "killing" demand for competing formats. Killer applications often help to jump-start demand for the new standard. For example, the killer applications that induced consumers to sign up for online services such as AOL in the 1990s were e-mail, chat rooms, and Web browsers.

Ideally, the company promoting a technological standard will also want to develop its own killer applications—that is, develop the appropriate complementary products. However, it may also be able to leverage applications that others develop. For example, the early sales of the IBM PC following its 1981 introduction were primarily driven by IBM's decision to license two important software programs for the PC: VisiCalc (a spreadsheet program) and EasyWriter (a word-processing program), both developed by independent companies. IBM saw that they were driving rapid adoption of rival personal computers, such as the Apple II, so it quickly licensed software, produced versions that would run on the IBM PC, and sold these programs as complements to the IBM PC, a very successful strategy. In video games, console producers such as Microsoft, Nintendo, and Sony often award endorsements to exceptional games developed by third-party developers. For example, PlayStation designates the best games for each console generation with the award "Platinum: The Best of PlayStation." Nintendo similarly has a "Nintendo Selects" endorsement, and Microsoft has a "Microsoft Xbox 360 Classics" endorsement. These endorsements signal potential customers about the quality of the game and help to generate "buzz" about the game and the console. Endorsing a complement in this way can help to turn the complement into a blockbuster, which in turn fuels more sales of the platform.[6]

killer applications Applications or uses of a new technology or product that are so compelling that customers adopt them in droves, killing competing formats.

Aggressive Pricing and Marketing

A common tactic used to jump-start demand is to adopt a **razor and blade strategy**: pricing the product (razor) low in order to stimulate demand and increase the installed base, and then trying to make high profits on the sale of complements (razor blades), which are priced relatively high. This strategy owes its name to Gillette, the company that pioneered this strategy to sell its razors and blades. Many other companies have followed this strategy—for example, Hewlett-Packard typically sells its printers at cost but makes significant profits on the subsequent sales of replacement cartridges. In this case, the printer is the "razor" and is priced low to stimulate demand and induce consumers to switch from their existing printer, while the cartridges are the "blades," which are priced high to make profits. The inkjet printer represents a proprietary technological format because only HP cartridges can be used with HP printers; cartridges designed for competing inkjet printers such as those sold by Canon will not work in HP printers. A similar strategy is used in the videogame industry: manufacturers price videogame consoles at cost to induce consumers to adopt their technology, while they make profits on royalties from the sales of games that run on the system.

Aggressive marketing is also a key factor in jump-starting demand to get an early lead in an installed base. Substantial upfront marketing and point-of-sales promotion techniques are often used to try to attract potential early adopters who will bear the switching costs associated with adopting the format. If these efforts are successful, they can be the start of a positive feedback loop. Again, the Sony PlayStation provides a good example. Sony co-linked the introduction of the PlayStation with nationwide

razor and blade strategy Pricing the product low in order to stimulate demand, and pricing complements high.

television advertising aimed at its primary demographic (18- to 34-year-olds) and in-store displays that allowed potential buyers to play games on the machine before making a purchase.

Cooperate with Competitors

Companies have been close to simultaneously introducing competing and incompatible technological standards a number of times. A good example is the compact disc. Initially four companies—Sony, Philips, JVC, and Telefunken—were developing CD players using different variations of the underlying laser technology. If this situation had persisted, they might have introduced incompatible technologies into the marketplace; a CD made for a Philips CD player would not play on a Sony CD player. Understanding that the nearly simultaneous introduction of such incompatible technologies can create significant confusion among consumers, and often lead them to delay their purchases, Sony and Philips decided to join forces and cooperate on developing the technology. Sony contributed its error-correction technology, and Philips contributed its laser technology. The result of this cooperation was that momentum among other players in the industry shifted toward the Sony–Philips alliances; JVC and Telefunken were left with little support. Most important, recording labels announced that they would support the Sony–Philips format but not the Telefunken or JVC format.

Telefunken and JVC subsequently abandoned their efforts to develop CD technology. The cooperation between Sony and Philips was important because it reduced confusion in the industry and allowed a single format to rise to the fore, which accelerated adoption of the technology. The cooperation was a win-win situation for both Philips and Sony, which eliminated competitors and enabled them to share in the success of the format.

License the Format

Licensing the format to other enterprises so that they too can produce products based on the format is another strategy often adopted. The company that pioneered the format gains from the licensing fees that return to it, as well as from the enlarged supply of the product, which can stimulate demand and help accelerate market adoption. This was the strategy that JVC and Matsushita adopted with the VHS format for the VCR. As discussed previously, in addition to producing VCRs at Matsushita's factory in Osaka, JVC licensed a number of other companies produce VHS format players, and so VHS players became widely available. (Sony decided not to license its competing Betamax format and produced all Betamax format players itself.)

The correct strategy to pursue in a particular scenario requires that the company consider all of these different strategies and tactics and pursue those that seem most appropriate given the competitive circumstances prevailing in the industry and the likely strategy of rivals. Although there is no single best combination of strategies and tactics, the company must keep the goal of rapidly increasing the installed base of products based on its standard at the forefront of its endeavors. By helping to jump-start demand for its format, a company can induce consumers to bear the switching costs associated with adopting its technology and leverage any positive feedback process that might exist. It is also important not to pursue strategies that have the opposite effect. For example, pricing high to capture profits from early adopters, who tend not to be as price sensitive as later adopters, can have the unfortunate effect of slowing demand growth and allowing a more aggressive competitor to pick up share and establish its format as the industry standard.

COSTS IN HIGH-TECHNOLOGY INDUSTRIES

In many high-tech industries, the fixed costs of developing the product are very high, but the costs of producing one extra unit of the product are very low. This is most obvious in the case of software. For example, it reportedly cost Microsoft $5 billion to develop Windows Vista, but the cost of producing one more copy of Windows Vista is virtually zero. Once the Windows Vista program was complete, Microsoft duplicated its master disks and sent the copies to PC manufacturers, such as Dell Computer, which then installed a copy of Windows Vista onto every PC sold. Microsoft's cost was, effectively, zero, and yet the company receives a significant licensing fee for each copy of Windows Vista installed on a PC.[7] For Microsoft, the marginal cost of making one more copy of Windows Vista is close to zero, although the fixed costs of developing the product were around $5 billion.

Many other high-technology products have similar cost economics: very high fixed costs and very low marginal costs. Most software products share these features, although if the software is sold through stores, the costs of packaging and distribution will raise the marginal costs, and if it is sold by a sales force direct to end-users, this too will raise the marginal costs. Many consumer electronics products have the same basic economics. The fixed costs of developing a DVD player or a videogame console can be very expensive, but the costs of producing an incremental unit are very low. Similarly, the fixed costs of developing a new drug can are typically estimated to be at least $1.6 billion (and potentially much more if one factors in the cost of all the failed drug development efforts),[8] but the marginal cost of producing each additional pill is at most a few cents.

Comparative Cost Economics

To grasp why this cost structure is strategically important, a company must understand that, in many industries, marginal costs rise as a company tries to expand output (economists call this the *law of diminishing returns*). To produce more of a good, a company must hire more labor and invest in more plant and machinery. At the margin, the additional resources used are not as productive, so this leads to increasing marginal costs. However, the law of diminishing returns often does not apply in many high-tech settings such as the production of software or sending data through a digital telecommunications network.

Consider two companies, α and β (see Figure 7.5). Company α is a conventional producer and faces diminishing returns, so as it tries to expand output, its marginal costs rise. Company β is a high-tech producer, and its marginal costs do not rise at all as output is increased. Note that in Figure 7.5, company β's marginal cost curve is drawn as a straight line near to the horizontal axis, implying that marginal costs are close to zero and do not vary with output, whereas company α's marginal costs rise as output is expanded, illustrating diminishing returns. Company β's flat, low

Figure 7.5 Cost Structures in High-Technology Industries

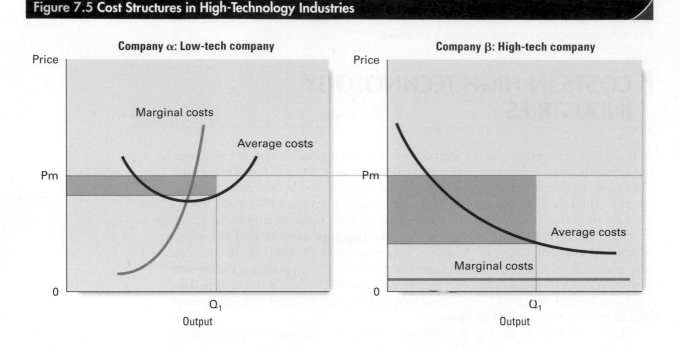

marginal cost curve means that its average cost curve will continuously fall over all ranges of output as it spreads its fixed costs out over greater volume. In contrast, the rising marginal costs encountered by company α mean that its average cost curve is the U-shaped curve familiar from basic economics texts. For simplicity, assume that both companies sell their product at the same price, Pm, and both sell exactly the same quantity of output, $0 - Q_1$. Figure 7.5 shows that, at an output of Q_1, company β has much lower average costs than company α and as a consequence is making far more profit (profit is the shaded area in Figure 7.5).

Strategic Significance

If a company can shift from a cost structure where it encounters increasing marginal costs to one where fixed costs may be high but marginal costs are much lower, its profitability may increase. In the consumer electronics industry, such a shift has been playing out for two decades. Musical recordings were once based on analog technology where marginal costs rose as output expanded due to diminishing returns (as in the case of company α in Figure 7.5). In the 1980s and 1990s, digital systems such as CD players replaced analog systems. Digital systems are software based, and this implies much lower marginal costs of producing one more copy of a recording. As a result, music companies were able to lower prices, expand demand, and see their profitability increase (their production system has more in common with company β in Figure 7.5).

This process, however, was still unfolding. The latest technology for copying musical recordings is based on distribution over the Internet (e.g., by downloading songs onto a smartphone). Here, the marginal costs of making one more copy of a recording are lower still. In fact, they are close to zero, and do not increase with output. The only problem is that the low costs of copying and distributing music recordings can lead to widespread illegal fire sharing, which ultimately leads to a very large decline in overall revenues in recorded music. According to the International Federation of the Phonographic Industry, worldwide revenues for CDs, vinyl, cassettes, and digital downloads dropped from $36.9 billion in 2000 to $15.9 billion in 2010. We discuss copyright issues in more detail shortly when we consider intellectual property rights. The same shift is now beginning to affect other industries. Some companies are building their strategies around trying to exploit and profit from this shift. For an example, Strategy in Action 7.2 looks at SonoSite.

7.2 STRATEGY IN ACTION

Lowering the Cost of Ultrasound Equipment Through Digitalization

The ultrasound unit has been an important piece of diagnostic equipment in hospitals for some time. Ultrasound units use the physics of sound to produce images of soft tissues in the human body. Ultrasounds can produce detailed, three-dimensional, color images of organs and, by using contrast agents, track the flow of fluids through them. A cardiologist, for example, can use an ultrasound in combination with contrast agents injected into the bloodstream to track the flow of blood through a beating heart. In addition to the visual diagnosis, ultrasound also produces an array of quantitative diagnostic information of great value to physicians.

Modern ultrasound units are sophisticated instruments that cost about $250,000 to $300,000 each for a top-line model. They are bulky instruments, weighing approximately 300 pounds, wheeled around hospitals on carts.

A few years ago, a group of researchers at ATL, one of the leading ultrasound companies, proposed an idea for reducing the size and cost of a basic machine. They theorized that it might be possible to replace up to 80% of the solid circuits in an ultrasound unit with software, and in the process significantly shrink the size and reduce the weight of machines, thereby producing portable ultrasound units. Moreover, by digitalizing much of the ultrasound (replacing hardware with software), they could considerably decrease the marginal costs of making additional units, and would thus be able to make a better profit at much lower price points.

The researchers reasoned that a portable, inexpensive ultrasound unit would find market opportunities in totally new niches. For example, a smaller ultrasound unit could be placed in an ambulance or carried into battle by an army medic, or purchased by family physicians for use in their offices. Although they realized that it would be some time, perhaps decades, before such a unit could attain the image quality and diagnostic sophistication of top-of-the-line machines, they saw the opportunity in terms of creating market niches that previously could not be served by ultrasound companies because of the high costs and bulk of the product.

The researchers later became part of a project team within ATL, and thereafter became an entirely new company, SonoSite. In late-1999, SonoSite introduced its first portable product, which weighed just 6 pounds and cost about $25,000. SonoSite targeted niches that full-sized ultrasound products could not reach: ambulatory care and foreign markets that could not afford the more expensive equipment. In 2010, the company sold over $275 million of product. In 2011, Fujifilm Holdings bought SonoSite for $995 million to expand its range of medical imaging products and help it overtake the dominant portable ultrasound equipment producer, General Electric.

Source: Interviews by C. W. L. Hill.

When a high-tech company faces high fixed costs and low marginal costs, its strategy should emphasize the low-cost structure option: deliberately drive down prices in order to increase volume. Figure 7.5 shows that the high-tech company's average costs fall rapidly as output expands. This implies that prices can be reduced to stimulate demand, and as long as prices fall less rapidly than average costs, per-unit profit margins will expand as prices fall. This is a consequence of low marginal costs that do not rise with output. This strategy of pricing low to drive volume and reap wider profit margins is central to the business model of some very successful high-tech companies, including Microsoft.

CAPTURING FIRST-MOVER ADVANTAGES

first mover

A firm that pioneers a particular product category or feature by being first to offer it to market.

In high-technology industries, companies often compete by striving to be the first to develop revolutionary new products, that is, to be a **first mover**. By definition, the first mover that creates a revolutionary product is in a monopoly position. If the new product satisfies unmet consumer needs and demand is high, the first mover can capture significant revenues and profits. Such revenues and profits signal to potential rivals that imitating the first mover makes money. Figure 7.6 implies that in the absence of strong barriers to imitation, imitators will rush into the market created by the first mover, competing away the first mover's monopoly profits and leaving all participants in the market with a much lower level of returns.

Despite imitation, some first movers have the ability to capitalize on and reap substantial first-mover advantages—the advantages of pioneering new technologies and products that lead to an enduring competitive advantage. Intel introduced the world's first microprocessor in 1971; today, it still dominates the microprocessor segment of the semiconductor industry. Xerox introduced the world's first photocopier and for a long time enjoyed a leading position in the industry. Cisco introduced the first Internet

Figure 7.6 The Impact of Imitation on Profits of a First Mover

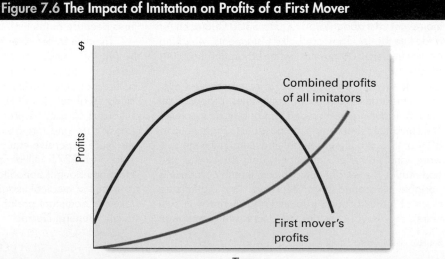

protocol network router in 1986, and still leads the market for that equipment today. Microsoft introduced the world's first software application for a personal computer in 1979, Microsoft BASIC, and it remains a dominant force in PC software.

Some first movers can reap substantial advantages from their pioneering activities that lead to an enduring competitive advantage. They can, in other words, limit or slow the rate of imitation.

But there are plenty of counterexamples suggesting that first-mover advantages might not be easy to capture and, in fact, that there might be **first-mover disadvantages**— the competitive disadvantages associated with being first. For example, Apple was the first company to introduce a handheld computer, the Apple Newton, but the product failed; a second mover, Palm, succeeded where Apple had failed (although Apple has recently had major success as a first mover with the first true tablet computer, the iPad). In the market for commercial jet aircraft, DeHavilland was first to market with the Comet, but it was the second mover, Boeing, with its 707 jetliner, that went on to dominate the market.

Clearly, being a first mover does not by itself guarantee success. As we shall see, the difference between innovating companies that capture first-mover advantages and those that fall victim to first-mover disadvantages in part incites the strategy that the first mover pursues. Before considering the strategy issue, however, we need to take a closer look at the nature of first-mover advantages and disadvantages.[9]

first-mover disadvantages
Competitive disadvantages associated with being first to market.

First-Mover Advantages

There are five primary sources of first-mover advantages.[10] First, the first mover has an opportunity to exploit network effects and positive feedback loops, locking consumers into its technology. In the VCR industry, Sony could have exploited network effects by licensing its technology, but instead the company ceded its first-mover advantage to the second mover, Matsushita.

Second, the first mover may be able to establish significant brand loyalty, which is expensive for later entrants to break down. Indeed, if the company is successful in this endeavor, its name may become closely associated with the entire class of products, including those produced by rivals. People still talk of "Xeroxing" when making a photocopy, or "FedExing" when they will be sending a package by overnight mail.

Third, the first mover may be able to increase sales volume ahead of rivals and thus reap cost advantages associated with the realization of scale economies and learning effects (see Chapter 4). Once the first mover has these cost advantages, it can respond to new entrants by cutting prices in order to retain its market share and still earn significant profits.

Fourth, the first mover may be able to create switching costs for its customers that subsequently make it difficult for rivals to enter the market and take customers away from the first mover. Wireless service providers, for example, will give new customers a "free" wireless phone, but customers must sign a contract agreeing to pay for the phone if they terminate the service contract within a specified time period such as 1 or 2 years. Because the real cost of a wireless phone may run from $100 to $200, this represents a significant switching cost that later entrants must overcome.

Finally, the first mover may be able to accumulate valuable knowledge related to customer needs, distribution channels, product technology, process technology, and so on. Knowledge so accumulated can give it an advantage that later entrants might find difficult or expensive to match. Sharp, for example, was the first mover in the commercial manufacture of active matrix liquid crystal displays used in laptop computers.

The process for manufacturing these displays is very difficult, with a high rejection rate for flawed displays. Sharp has accumulated such an advantage with regard to production processes that it has been very difficult for later entrants to match it on product quality, and therefore on costs.

First-Mover Disadvantages

Balanced against these first-mover advantages are a number of disadvantages.[11] First, the first mover has to bear significant pioneering costs that later entrants do not. The first mover must pioneer the technology, develop distribution channels, and educate customers about the nature of the product. This can be expensive and time consuming. Later entrants, by way of contrast, might be able to free-ride on the first mover's investments in pioneering the market and customer education. That is, they do not have to bear the pioneering costs of the first mover. Generic drug makers, for example, spend very little on R&D compared to the costs borne by the developer of an original drug because they can replicate the finished chemical or biological product (that is,, they do not have to explore many alternative paths to a solution), and they can bypass most of the clinical testing process.[12]

Related to this, first movers are more prone to make mistakes because there are so many uncertainties in a new market. Later entrants may learn from the mistakes made by first movers, improve on the product or the way in which it is sold, and come to market with a superior offering that captures significant market share from the first mover. For example, one reason that the Apple Newton failed was that the software in the handheld computer failed to recognize human handwriting. The second mover in this market, Palm, learned from Apple's error. When it introduced the PalmPilot, it used software that recognized letters written in a particular way, graffiti style, and then persuaded customers to learn this method of inputting data into the handheld computer.

Third, first movers run the risk of building the wrong resources and capabilities because they focus on a customer set that is not characteristic of the mass market. This is the "crossing the chasm" problem that we discussed in the previous chapter. You will recall that the customers in the early market—those we categorized as innovators and early adopters—have different characteristics from the first wave of the mass market, the early majority. The first mover runs the risk of directing its resources and capabilities to the needs of innovators and early adopters, and not being able to switch when the early majority enters the market. As a result, first movers run a greater risk of plunging into the chasm that separates the early market from the mass market.

Finally, the first mover may invest in inferior or obsolete technology. This can happen when its product innovation is based on underlying technology that is rapidly advancing. Basing its product on an early version of a technology may lock a company into a resource that rapidly becomes obsolete. In contrast, later entrants may be able to leapfrog the first mover and introduce products that are based on later versions of the underlying technology. This happened in France during the 1980s when, at the urging of the government, France Telecom introduced the world's first consumer on-line service, Minitel. France Telecom distributed free terminals to consumers , which connected to the phone line and could be used to browse phone directories. Other simple services were soon added, and before long the French could shop, bank, make travel arrangements, and check weather and news "online"—years before the Web was invented. The problem was that by the standards of the Web, Minitel was very crude and inflexible, and France Telecom, as the first mover, suffered. The French were very slow to adopt personal computers and the Internet primarily because Minitel had such a presence. As late as 1998, only one-fifth of French households had a computer, compared with two-fifths in the United States, and only 2% of households were connected to the Internet, compared to over 30% in the United States. As the result of a government decision, France Telecom, and the entire nation of France, was slow to adopt a revolutionary new online medium—the Web —because they were the first to invest in a more primitive version of the technology.[13]

Strategies for Exploiting First-Mover Advantages

First movers must strategize and determine how to exploit their lead and capitalize on first-mover advantages to build a sustainable, long-term competitive advantage while simultaneously reducing the risks associated with first-mover disadvantages. There are three basic strategies available: (1) develop and market the innovation; (2) develop and market the innovation jointly with other companies through a strategic alliance or joint venture; and (3) license the innovation to others and allow them to develop the market.

The optimal choice of strategy depends on the answers to three questions:

1. Does the innovating company have the complementary assets to exploit its innovation and capture first-mover advantages?
2. How difficult is it for imitators to copy the company's innovation? In other words, what is the height of barriers to imitation?
3. Are there capable competitors that could rapidly imitate the innovation?

Complementary Assets   Complementary assets are required to exploit a new innovation and gain a competitive advantage.[14] Among the most important complementary assets are competitive manufacturing facilities capable of handling rapid growth in customer demand while maintaining high product quality. State-of-the-art manufacturing facilities enable the first mover to quickly move down the experience curve without encountering production bottlenecks or problems with the quality of the product. The inability to satisfy demand because of these problems, however, creates the opportunity for imitators to enter the marketplace. For example, in 1998, Immunex was the first company to introduce a revolutionary biological treatment for rheumatoid arthritis. Sales for this product, Enbrel, very rapidly increased, reaching $750 million in 2001. However, Immunex had not invested in sufficient manufacturing capacity. In mid-2000, it announced that it lacked the capacity to satisfy demand and that bringing additional capacity on line would take at least 2 years. This manufacturing bottleneck gave the second mover in the market, Johnson & Johnson, the opportunity to rapidly expand demand for its product, which by early 2002 was outselling Enbrel. Immunex's first-mover advantage had been partly eroded because it lacked an important complementary asset, the manufacturing capability required to satisfy demand.

Complementary assets also include marketing knowhow, an adequate sales force, access to distribution systems, and an after-sales service and support network. All of these assets can help an innovator build brand loyalty and more rapidly achieve market penetration.[15] In turn, the resulting increases in volume facilitate more rapid movement down the experience curve and the attainment of a sustainable, cost-based advantage due to scale economies and learning effects. EMI, the first mover in the market for computerized tomography (CT) scanners, ultimately lost out to established medical equipment companies such as GE Medical Systems because it lacked the marketing knowhow, sales force, and distribution systems required to effectively compete in the world's largest market for medical equipment, the United States.

Developing complementary assets can be very expensive, and companies often need large infusions of capital for this purpose. That is why first movers often lose out to late movers that are large, successful companies in other industries with the resources to quickly develop a presence in the new industry. Microsoft and 3M exemplify companies that have moved quickly to capitalize on the opportunities when other companies open up new product markets, such as compact discs or floppy disks. For example, although Netscape pioneered the market for Internet browsers with the Netscape Navigator, Microsoft's Internet Explorer ultimately dominated that market.

Height of Barriers to Imitation   Recall from Chapter 3 that barriers to imitation are factors that prevent rivals from imitating a company's distinctive competencies and innovations. Although any innovation can be copied, the higher the barriers are, the longer it takes for rivals to imitate the innovation, and the more time the first mover has to build an enduring competitive advantage.

Barriers to imitation give an innovator time to establish a competitive advantage and build more enduring barriers to entry in the newly created market. Patents, for example, are among the most widely used barriers to imitation. By protecting its photocopier technology with a thicket of patents, Xerox was able to delay any significant imitation of its product for 17 years. However, patents are often easy to "invent around." For example, one study found that this happened to 60% of patented innovations within 4 years.[16] If patent protection is weak, a company might try to slow imitation by developing new products and processes in secret. The most famous example of this approach is Coca-Cola, which has kept the formula for Coke a secret for generations. But Coca-Cola's success in this regard is an exception. A study of 100 companies has estimated that rivals learn about a company's decision to develop a major new product or process and its related proprietary information within 12 to 18 months of the original development decision.[17]

Capable Competitors   Capable competitors are companies that can move quickly to imitate the pioneering company. Competitors' capability to imitate a pioneer's innovation depends primarily on two factors: (1) R&D skills; and (2) access to complementary assets. In general, the greater the number of capable competitors with access to the R&D skills and complementary assets needed to imitate an innovation, the more rapid imitation is likely to be.

In this context, R&D skills refer to the ability of rivals to reverse-engineer an innovation to find out how it works and quickly develop a comparable product. As an example, consider the CT scanner. GE bought one of the first CT scanners produced by EMI, and its technical experts reverse-engineered the machine. Despite the product's technological complexity, GE developed its own version, which allowed it to quickly imitate EMI and replace it as the major supplier of CT scanners.

Complementary assets—the access that rivals have to marketing, sales knowhow, and manufacturing capabilities—are key determinants of the rate of imitation. If would-be imitators lack critical complementary assets, not only will they have to imitate the innovation, but they may also need to imitate the innovator's complementary assets. This is expensive, as AT&T discovered when it tried to enter the PC business in 1984. AT&T lacked the marketing assets (sales force and distribution systems) necessary to support personal computer products. The lack of these assets and the time it takes to build the assets partly explains why: Four years after it entered the market, AT&T had lost $2.5 billion and still had not emerged as a viable contender. It subsequently exited this business.

Three Innovation Strategies The way in which these three factors—complementary assets, height of barriers to imitation, and the capability of competitors—influence the choice of innovation strategy is summarized in Table 7.1. The competitive strategy of developing and marketing the innovation alone makes most sense when: (1) the innovator has the complementary assets necessary to develop the innovation, (2) the barriers to imitating a new innovation are high, and (3) the number of capable competitors is limited. Complementary assets allow rapid development and promotion of the innovation. High barriers to imitation give the innovator time to establish a competitive advantage and build enduring barriers to entry through brand loyalty or experience-based cost advantages. The fewer capable competitors there are, the less likely it is that any one of them will succeed in circumventing barriers to imitation and quickly imitating the innovation.

The competitive strategy of developing and marketing the innovation jointly with other companies through a strategic alliance or joint venture makes most sense when: (1) the innovator lacks complementary assets, (2) barriers to imitation are high, and (3) there are several capable competitors. In such circumstances, it makes sense to enter into an alliance with a company that already has the complementary assets—in other words, with a capable competitor. Theoretically, such an alliance should prove to be mutually beneficial, and each partner can share in high profits that neither could earn on its own. Moreover, such a strategy has the benefit of co-opting a potential rival. For example, had EMI teamed with a capable competitor to develop the market for CT scanners, such as GE Medical Systems, instead of going it alone, the company might have been able to build a more enduring competitive advantage and also co-opt a powerful rival into its camp.

The third strategy, licensing, makes most sense when: (1) the innovating company lacks the complementary assets, (2) barriers to imitation are low, and (3) there are many capable competitors. The combination of low barriers to imitation and many capable competitors makes rapid imitation almost certain. The innovator's lack of

Table 7.1 Strategies for Profiting from Innovation

Strategy	Does the Innovator Have the Required Complementary Assets?	Likely Height of Barriers to Imitation	Number of Capable Competitors
Going it alone	Yes	High	Very few
Entering into an alliance	No	High	Moderate number
Licensing the innovation	No	Low	Many

complementary assets further suggests that an imitator will soon capture the innovator's competitive advantage. Given these factors, because rapid diffusion of the innovator's technology through imitation is inevitable, the innovator can at least share in some benefits of this diffusion by licensing out its technology.[18] Moreover, by setting a relatively modest licensing fee, the innovator may be able to reduce the incentive that potential rivals have to develop their own competing, and possibly superior, technology. As described previously, Dolby adopted this strategy to get its technology established as the standard for noise reduction in the music and film businesses.

◤TECHNOLOGICAL PARADIGM SHIFTS

technological paradigm shift

Shifts in new technologies that revolutionize the structure of the industry, dramatically alter the nature of competition, and require companies to adopt new strategies in order to survive.

Technological paradigm shifts occur when new technologies revolutionize the structure of the industry, dramatically alter the nature of competition, and require companies to adopt new strategies in order to survive. A good example of a paradigm shift is the evolution of photography from chemical to digital printing processes. For over half a century, the large, incumbent enterprises in the photographic industry such as Kodak and Fujifilm have generated most of their revenues from selling and processing film using traditional silver halide technology. The rise of digital photography has been a huge disruptive threat to their business models. Digital cameras do not use film, the mainstay of Kodak's and Fuji's business. In addition, these cameras are more like specialized computers than conventional cameras, and are therefore based on scientific knowledge in which Kodak and Fuji have little expertise. Although both Kodak and Fuji have heavily invested in the development of digital cameras, they are facing intense competition from companies such as Sony, Canon, and Hewlett-Packard, which have developed their own digital cameras; from software developers such as Adobe and Microsoft, which make software for manipulating digital images; and from printer companies such as Hewlett-Packard and Canon, which make printers that consumers use to print high-quality pictures from home. As digital substitution gathers speed in the photography industry, it is not clear that the traditional incumbents will survive this shift; the new competitors might rise to dominance in the new market.

Kodak and Fuji are hardly the first large incumbents to be felled by a technological paradigm shift in their industry. In the early 1980s, the computer industry was revolutionized by the arrival of personal computer technology, which gave rise to client–server networks that replaced traditional mainframe and minicomputers for many business uses. Many incumbent companies in the mainframe era, such as Wang, Control Data, and DEC, ultimately did not survive, and even IBM went through a decade of wrenching changes and large losses before it reinvented itself as a provider of e-business solutions. Instead, new entrants such as Microsoft, Intel, Dell, and Compaq rose to dominate this new computer industry.

Today, many believe that the advent of cloud computing is ushering in a paradigm shift in the computer industry. Microsoft, the dominant incumbent in the PC software business, is very vulnerable to this shift. If the center of computing does move to the cloud, with most data and applications stored there, and if all one needs to access data and run applications is a Web browser, then the value of a PC operating system such as Windows is significantly reduced. Microsoft understands this as well as anyone, which is why the company is pushing aggressively into the cloud computing market with Windows Azure.

Examples such as these raise four questions:

1. When do paradigm shifts occur, and how do they unfold?
2. Why do so many incumbents go into decline following a paradigm shift?
3. What strategies can incumbents adopt to increase the probability that they will survive a paradigm shift and emerge on the other side of the market abyss created by the arrival of new technology as a profitable enterprise?
4. What strategies can new entrants into a market adopt to profit from a paradigm shift?

We shall answer each of these questions in the remainder of this chapter.

Paradigm Shifts and the Decline of Established Companies

Paradigm shifts appear to be more likely to occur in an industry when one, or both, of the following conditions are in place.[19] First, the established technology in the industry is mature, and is approaching or at its "natural limit." Second, a new "disruptive technology" has entered the marketplace and is taking root in niches that are poorly served by incumbent companies using established technology.

Natural Limits to Technology   Richard Foster has formalized the relationship between the performance of a technology and time in terms of what he calls the technology S-curve (see Figure 7.7).[20] This curve shows the relationship over time of cumulative investments in R&D and the performance (or functionality) of a given technology. Early in its evolution, R&D investments in a new technology tend to yield rapid improvements in performance as basic engineering problems are solved. After a time, diminishing returns to cumulative R&D begin to set in, the rate of improvement in performance slows, and the technology starts to approach its natural limit, where further advances are not possible. For example, one can argue that there was more improvement in the first 50 years of the commercial aerospace business following the pioneering flight by the Wright Brothers than there has been in the second 50 years. Indeed, the venerable Boeing 747 is based on a 1960's design. In commercial aerospace, therefore, we are now in the region of diminishing returns and may be approaching the natural limit to improvements in the technology of commercial aerospace.

Figure 7.7 The Technology S-Curve

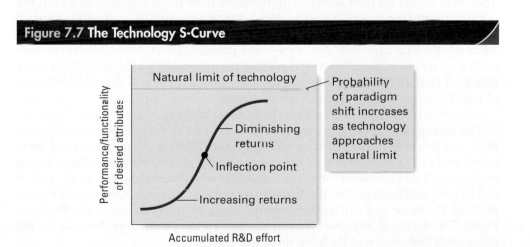

Similarly, it can be argued that we are approaching the natural limit to technology in the performance of silicon-based semiconductor chips. Over the past two decades, the performance of semiconductor chips has been increased dramatically; companies can now manufacture a larger amount of transistors in a single, small silicon chip. This process has helped to increase the power of computers, lower their cost, and shrink their size. But we are starting to approach limits to the ability to shrink the width of lines on a chip and therefore pack ever more transistors onto a single chip. The limit is imposed by the natural laws of physics. Light waves are used to etch lines onto a chip, and one cannot etch a line that is smaller than the wavelength of light being used. Semiconductor companies are already using light beams with very small wavelengths, such as extreme ultraviolet, to etch lines onto a chip, but there are limits to how far this technology can be pushed, and many believe that we will reach those limits within the decade. Does this mean that our ability to make smaller, faster, cheaper computers is coming to an end? Probably not. It is more likely that we will find another technology to replace silicon-based computing and enable us to continue building smaller, faster, cheaper computers. In fact, several exotic competing technologies are already being developed that may replace silicon-based computing. These include self-organizing molecular computers, three-dimensional microprocessor technology, quantum computing technology, and using DNA to perform computations.[21]

What does all of this have to do with paradigm shifts? According to Foster, when a technology approaches its natural limit, research attention turns to possible alternative technologies, and sooner or later one of those alternatives might be commercialized and replace the established technology. That is, the probability that a paradigm shift will occur increases. Thus, sometime in the next decade or two, another paradigm shift might shake up the foundations of the computer industry as exotic computing technology replaces silicon-based computing. If history is any guide, if and when this happens, many incumbents in today's computer industry will go into decline, and new enterprises will rise to dominance.

Foster pushes this point a little further, noting that, initially, the contenders for the replacement technology are not as effective as the established technology in producing the attributes and features that consumers demand in a product. For example, in the early years of the 20th century, automobiles were just beginning to be produced. They were valued for their ability to move people from place to place, but so was the horse and cart (the established technology). When automobiles originally appeared, the horse and cart was still quite a bit better than the automobile (see Figure 7.8). After all, the first cars were slow, noisy, and prone to break down. Moreover, they needed a network of paved roads and gas stations to be really useful, and that network didn't yet exist. For most applications, the horse and cart was still the preferred mode of transportation—in part because it was cheaper.

However, this comparison ignored the fact that in the early 20th century, automobile technology was at the very start of its S-curve and about to experience dramatic improvements in performance as major engineering problems were solved (and those paved roads and gas stations were built). In contrast, after 3,000 years of continuous improvement and refinement, the horse and cart was almost definitely at the end of its technological S-curve. The result was that the rapidly improving automobile soon replaced the horse and cart as the preferred mode of transportation. At time T_1 in Figure 7.8, the horse and cart was still superior to the automobile. By time T_2, the automobile had surpassed the horse and cart.

Figure 7.8 Established and Successor Technologies

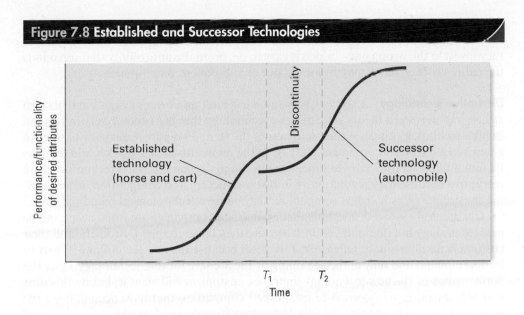

Foster notes that because successor technology is initially less efficient than established technology, established companies and their customers often make the mistake of dismissing it, only to be surprised by its rapid performance improvement. Many people are betting that this is the process unfolding in the electric vehicle industry. Although electric vehicles still have technical disadvantages to internal combustion vehicles (e.g., limited range, time spent recharging), and cost significantly more than comparable internal combustion vehicles, it is possible that dramatic improvements in battery technology could simultaneously address technical disadvantages while reducing the costs of the vehicles.

A final point is that often there is not a single potential successor technology but a swarm of potential successor technologies, only one of which might ultimately rise to the fore (see Figure 7.9). When this is the case, established companies are put at a

Figure 7.9 Swarm of Successor Technologies

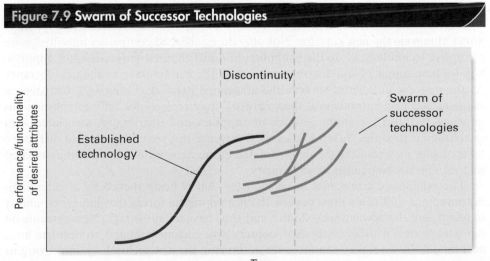

disadvantage. Even if they recognize that a paradigm shift is imminent, companies may not have the resources to invest in all the potential replacement technologies. If they invest in the wrong one—which is easy to do, given the uncertainty that surrounds the entire process—they may be locked out of subsequent development.

Disruptive Technology   Clayton Christensen has built on Foster's insights and his own research to develop a theory of disruptive technology that has become very influential in high-technology circles.[22] Christensen uses the term *disruptive technology* to refer to a new technology that originates away from the mainstream of a market and then, as its functionality improves over time, invades the main market. Such technologies are disruptive because they revolutionize industry structure and competition, often causing the decline of established companies. They cause a technological paradigm shift.

Christensen's greatest insight is that established companies are often aware of the new technology but do not invest in it because they listen to their customers, and their customers do not want it. Of course, this arises because the new technology is early in its development and only at the beginning of the S-curve for that technology. Once the performance of the new technology improves, customers will want it, but by this time it is new entrants, as opposed to established companies, that have accumulated the required knowledge to bring the new technology into the mass market.

In addition to listening too closely to their customers, Christensen also identifies a number of other factors that make it very difficult for established companies to adopt a new disruptive technology. He notes that many established companies decline to invest in new disruptive technologies because initially they serve such small market niches that it seems unlikely there would be an impact on the company's revenues and profits. As the new technology starts to improve in functionality and invade the main market, their investment can often be hindered by the difficult implementation of a new business model required to exploit the new technology.

Both of these points can be illustrated by reference to one more example: the rise of online discount stockbrokers during the 1990s such as Ameritrade and E*TRADE, which made use of a new technology—the Internet—to allow individual investors to trade stocks for a very low commission fee, whereas full-service stockbrokers such as Merrill Lynch, which required that orders be placed through a stockbroker who earned a commission for performing the transaction, did not.

Christensen also notes that a new network of suppliers and distributors typically grows alongside the new entrants. Not only do established companies initially ignore disruptive technology, so do their suppliers and distributors. This creates an opportunity for new suppliers and distributors to enter the market to serve the new entrants. As the new entrants grow, so does the associated network. Ultimately, Christensen suggests, the new entrants and their network may replace not only established enterprises, but also the entire network of suppliers and distributors associated with established companies. Taken to its logical extreme, this view suggests that disruptive technologies may result in the demise of the entire network of enterprises associated with established companies in an industry.

The established companies in an industry that is being rocked by a technological paradigm shift often must cope with internal inertia forces that limit their ability to adapt, but the new entrants do not and thus have an advantage. New entrants do not have to deal with an established, conservative customer set and an obsolete business model. Instead, they can focus on optimizing the new technology, improving its performance, and riding the wave of disruptive technology into new market segments until they invade the main market and challenge the established companies. By then, they may be well equipped to surpass the established companies.

Strategic Implications for Established Companies

Although Christensen has uncovered an important tendency, it is by no means written in stone that all established companies are doomed to fail when faced with disruptive technologies, as we have seen with IBM and Merrill Lynch. Established companies must meet the challenges created by the emergence of disruptive technologies.[23]

First, having access to the knowledge about how disruptive technologies can revolutionize markets is a valuable strategic asset. Many of the established companies that Christensen examined failed because they took a myopic view of the new technology and asked their customers the wrong question. Instead of asking: "Are you interested in this new technology?" they should have recognized that the new technology was likely to improve rapidly over time and instead have asked: "Would you be interested in this new technology if it improves its functionality over time?" If established enterprises had done this, they may have made very different strategic decisions.

Second, it is clearly important for established enterprises to invest in newly emerging technologies that may ultimately become disruptive technologies. Companies have to hedge their bets about new technology. As we have noted, at any time, there may be a swarm of emerging technologies, any one of which might ultimately become a disruptive technology. Large, established companies that are generating significant cash flows can, and often should, establish and fund central R&D operations to invest in and develop such technologies. In addition, they may wish to acquire emerging companies that are pioneering potentially disruptive technologies, or enter into alliances with others to jointly develop the technology. The strategy of acquiring companies that are developing potentially disruptive technology is one that Cisco Systems, a dominant provider of Internet network equipment, is famous for pursuing. At the heart of this strategy must be recognition on behalf of the incumbent enterprise that it is better for the company to develop disruptive technology, and then cannibalize its established sales base, than to have the sales base taken away by new entrants.

However, Christensen makes a very important point: Even when established companies undertake R&D investments in potentially disruptive technologies, they often fail to commercialize those technologies because of internal forces that suppress change. For example, managers who are currently generating the most cash in one part of the business may claim that they need the greatest R&D investment to maintain their market position, and may lobby top management to delay investment in a new technology. This can be a powerful argument when, early in the S-curve, the long-term prospects of a new technology are very unclear. The consequence, however, may be that the company fails to build competence in the new technology, and suffers accordingly.

In addition, Christensen argues that the commercialization of new disruptive technology often requires a radically different value chain with a completely different cost structure—a new business model. For example, it may require a different manufacturing system, a different distribution system, and different pricing options, and may involve very different gross margins and operating margins. Christensen argues that it is almost impossible for two distinct business models to coexist within the same organization. When companies try to implement both models, the already established model will almost inevitably suffocate the model associated with the disruptive technology.

The solution to this problem is to create an autonomous operating division devoted solely to the new technology. For example, during the early 1980s, HP built a very successful laserjet printer business. Then inkjet technology was invented. Some employees at HP believed that inkjet printers would cannibalize sales of laserjet printers, and consequently argued that HP should not produce inkjet printers. Fortunately for HP, senior management saw inkjet technology for what it was: a potential disruptive technology. Instead of choosing to not invest in inkjet technology, HP allocated significant R&D funds toward its commercialization. Furthermore, when the technology was ready for market introduction, HP established an autonomous inkjet division at a different geographical location, including manufacturing, marketing, and distribution departments. HP senior managers accepted that the inkjet division might take sales away from the laserjet division and decided that it was better for an HP division to cannibalize the sales of another HP division, than allow those sales to be cannibalized by another company. Happily for HP, inkjets cannibalize sales of laserjets only on the margin, and both laserjet and inkjet printers have profitable market niches. This felicitous outcome, however, does not detract from the message of this example: If a company is developing a potentially disruptive technology, the chances for success will be enhanced if it is placed in a stand-alone product division and given its own mandate.

Strategic Implications for New Entrants

Christensen's work also holds implications for new entrants. The new entrants, or attackers, have several advantages over established enterprises. Pressures to continue the existing, out-of-date business model do not hamstring new entrants, which do not need to worry about product cannibalization issues. They need not worry about their established customer base or about relationships with established suppliers and distributors. Instead, they can focus all their energies on the opportunities offered by the new disruptive technology, move along the S-curve of technology improvement, and rapidly grow with the market for that technology. This does not mean that the new entrants do not have problems to solve. They may be constrained by a lack of capital or must manage the organizational problems associated with rapid growth; most important, they may need to find a way to take their technology from a small, out-of-the-way niche into the mass market.

Perhaps one of the most important issues facing new entrants is choosing whether to partner with an established company or go it alone in an attempt to develop and profit from a new disruptive technology. Although a new entrant may enjoy all the advantages of the attacker, it may lack the resources required to fully exploit them. In such a case, the company might want to consider forming a strategic alliance with a larger, established company to gain access to those resources. The main issues here are the same as those discussed earlier when examining the three strategies that a company can pursue to capture first-mover advantages: go it alone, enter into a strategic alliance, or license its technology.

KEY TERMS

TAKEAWAYS FOR STRATEGIC MANAGERS

1. Technical standards are important in many high-tech industries. They guarantee compatibility, reduce confusion in the minds of customers, allow for mass production and lower costs, and reduce the risks associated with supplying complementary products.
2. Network effects and positive feedback loops often determine which standard will dominate a market.
3. Owning a standard can be a source of sustained competitive advantage.
4. Establishing a proprietary standard as the industry standard may require the company to win a format war against a competing and incompatible standard. Strategies for doing this include producing complementary products, leveraging killer applications, using aggressive pricing and marketing, licensing the technology, and cooperating with competitors.
5. Many high-tech products are characterized by high fixed costs of development but very low or zero marginal costs of producing one extra unit of output. These cost economics create a presumption in favor of strategies that emphasize aggressive pricing to increase volume and drive down average total costs.
6. It is very important for a first mover to develop a strategy to capitalize on first-mover advantages. A company can choose from three strategies: develop and market the technology itself, do so jointly with another company, or license the technology to existing companies. The choice depends on the complementary assets required to capture a first-mover advantage, the height of barriers to imitation, and the capability of competitors.
7. Technological paradigm shifts occur when new technologies emerge that revolutionize the structure of the industry, dramatically alter the nature of competition, and require companies to adopt new strategies in order to succeed.
8. Technological paradigm shifts are more likely to occur when progress in improving the established technology is slowing because of diminishing returns and when a new disruptive technology is taking root in a market niche.
9. Established companies can deal with paradigm shifts by investing in technology or setting up a stand-alone division to exploit technology.

DISCUSSION QUESTIONS

1. What is different about high-tech industries? Were all industries once high-tech?
2. Why are standards so important in high-tech industries? What are the competitive implications of this?
3. You work for a small company that has the leading position in an embryonic market. Your boss believes that the company's future is ensured because it has a 60% share of the market, the lowest cost structure in the industry, and the most reliable and highest-valued product. Write a memo to your boss outlining why the assumptions posed might be incorrect.
4. You are working for a small company that has developed an operating system for PCs that is faster and more stable than Microsoft's

Windows operating system. What strategies might your company pursue to unseat Windows and establish its own operating system as the dominant technical standard in the industry?

5. You are a manager for a major record label. Last year, music sales declined by 10%, primarily because of illegal file sharing. Your boss has asked you to develop a strategy for reducing illegal file sharing. What would you suggest that the company do?

6. Reread the Strategy in Action 7.1, on Microsoft's "segment zero" threat. Do you think one operating system for smartphones or tablets will become dominant? If so, which one and why?

CLOSING CASE

A Battle Emerging in Mobile Payments

By 2014, there were 6.6 billion mobile phone subscriptions in the world, and of those, 2.3 billion had active mobile broadband subscriptions that would enable users to access the mobile web. Mobile payment systems offered the potential of enabling all of these users to perform financial transactions on their phones, similar to how they would perform those transactions using personal computers. However, in 2015, there was no dominant mobile payment system, and a battle among competing mobile payment mechanisms and standards was unfolding.

In the United States, several large players, including Apple, Samsung, and a joint venture called Softcard between Google, AT&T, T-Mobile, and Verizon Wireless, had developed systems based on near field communication (NFC) chips in smartphones. NFC chips enable communication between a mobile device and a point-of-sale system just by having the devices in close proximity. The systems being developed by Apple, Samsung, and Softcard transferred the customer's information wirelessly, and then used merchant banks and credit card systems such as Visa or MasterCard to complete the transaction. These systems were thus very much like existing ways of using credit cards, but enabled completion of the purchase without contact.

Other competitors such as Square (with Square Wallet) and PayPal did not require a smartphone with an NFC chip, but instead used a downloadable application and the Web to transmit a customer's information. Square had gained early fame by offering small, free, credit card readers that could be plugged into the audio jack of a smartphone. These readers enabled vendors that would normally only take cash (for example, street vendors and babysitters) to accept major credit cards. Square processed $30 billion in payments in 2013, making the company one of the fastest-growing tech start-ups in Silicon Valley. Square takes about 2.75 to 3% from each transaction it processes, but must split that with credit card companies and other financial institutions. In terms of installed base, however, PayPal had the clear advantage, with over 161 million active registered accounts. With PayPal, customers could complete purchases simply by entering their phone numbers and a pin number, or use a PayPal-issued magnetic stripe cards linked to their PayPal accounts. Users could opt to link their PayPal accounts to their credit cards, or directly to their bank accounts. PayPal also owned a service, Venmo, that enabled peer-to-peer exchanges with a Facebook-like interface that was growing in popularity as a way to exchange money without carrying cash. Venmo charged a 3% fee if the transaction used a major credit card, but was free if the consumer used it with a major bank card and debit card.

As noted above, some of the systems being developed did not require involvement of the major credit card companies, which potentially meant that billions of dollars in transaction fees might be avoided, or captured by a new player. PayPal, and its peer-to-peer system Venmo, for instance, did not require credit cards. A group of large merchants that included Wal-Mart, Old Navy, Best Buy, 7-Eleven, and more had also developed their own payment system –"Current-C"—a downloadable application for a smartphone that enabled purchases to be deducted directly from the customer's bank accounts. This would enable merchants to avoid the 2-4% charges that they paid on credit card transactions, amounting to billions of dollars in savings for the participating merchants.

For consumers, the key dimensions that influenced adoption were convenience (would the customer have to type in a code at the point of purchase? was it easily accessible on a device the individual already owned?), risk of fraud (was the individual's identity and financial information at risk?)n and ubiquity (could the system be used everywhere? did it enable peer-to-peer transactions?). For merchants, fraud was also a big concern, especially in situations where the transaction was not guaranteed by a third party, and cost (what were the fixed costs and transaction fees of using the system?) Apple Pay had a significant convenience advantage in that a customer could pay via their fingerprint. Current-C, by contrast, had a serious convenience disadvantage because consumers would have to open the application on their phone and get a QR code to be scanned at the checkout aisle. Both Apple Pay and Current-C also experienced fraud problems, with multiple reports of hacked accounts emerging by early 2015.

In the United States, almost half of all consumers had used their smartphones to make a payment at a merchant location by early 2015. Mobile payments accounted for $52 billion in transactions in 2014 and were expected to be $67 billion in 2015.

In other parts of the world, intriguing alternatives for mobile banking were gaining traction even faster. In India and Africa, for example, there are enormous populations of "unbanked" or "underbanked" people (individuals who do not have bank accounts or make limited use of banking services). In these regions, the proportion of people with mobile phones vastly exceeds the proportion of those with credit cards. In Africa, for example, less than 3% of the population was estimated to have a credit card, whereas 69% of the population was estimated to have mobile phones. Notably, the maximum fixed-line phone penetration ever achieved in Africa was 1.6%—reached in 2009–demonstrating the power of mobile technology to "leapfrog" land-based technology in the developing world. The opportunity, then, of giving such people access to fast and inexpensive funds transfer is enormous.

The leading system in India is the Inter-bank Mobile Payment Service developed by National Payments Corporation of India (NPCI). NPCI leveraged its ATM network (connecting more than 65

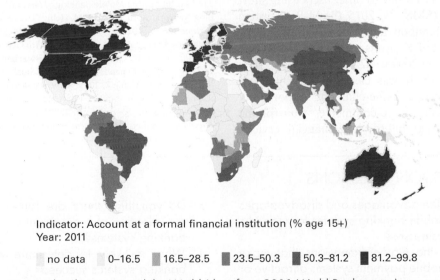

Indicator: Account at a formal financial institution (% age 15+)
Year: 2011

no data   0–16.5   16.5–28.5   23.5–50.3   50.3–81.2   81.2–99.8

Financial Inclusion around the World (data from 2011 World Bank survey)

(continued)

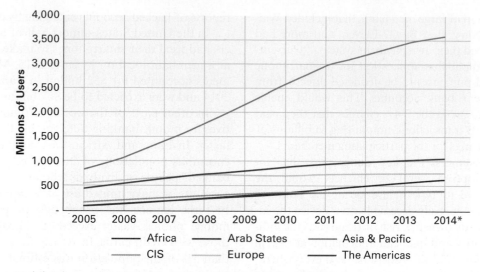

Mobile phone penetration around the world, 2005 - 2014

Sources: United Nations Telecommunications, ICT Report 2014

large banks in India) to create a person-to-person mobile banking system that works on mobile phones. The system uses a unique identifier for each individual who links directly to a bank account. In parts of Africa, where the proportion of people who are unbanked is even larger, a system called M-Pesa ("M" for mobile and "pesa," which is Kiswahili for money) enables any individual with a passport or national ID card to deposit money into his or her phone account and transfer money to other users using short message service (SMS). By 2015, the M-Pesa system had roughly12.2 million active users. The system enabled the percent of Kenyans with access to banking to rise from 41% in 2009 to 67% in 2014.

By early 2015, it was clear that mobile payments represented a game-changing opportunity that could accelerate e-commerce, smartphone adoption, and the global reach of financial services.

However, lack of compatibility between many of the mobile payment systems, and uncertainty over what type of mobile payment system will become dominant, still pose significant obstacles to consumer and merchant adoption.

Sources: J. Kent, "Dominant Mobile Payment Approaches and Leading Mobile Payment Solution Providers: A Review," *Journal of Payments Strategy & Systems* 6 (4), 2012, pp. 315–324; V. Govindarajan and M. Balakrishnan, "Developing Countries Are Revolutionizing Mobile Banking," *Harvard Business Review*, Blog Network, April 30, 2012; M. Helft, "The Death of Cash," *Fortune* 166 (2), 2012, www.fortune.com; D. Pogue, "How Mobile Payments Are Failing and Credit Cards Are Getting Better," *Scientific American*, January 20, 2015, www.scientificamerican.com; M. Isaac, "Square Expands Its Reach into Small-business Services." *New York Times*, March 8, 2015, www.nytimes.com; C. McKay and R. Mazer, "10 Myths about M-PESA: 2014 Update," *Consultative Group to Assist the Poor*, October 1, 2014; *United Nations Telecommunications Development Sector*, ICT Report, 2014.

CASE DISCUSSION QUESTIONS

1. What are the advantages and disadvantages of using mobile banking systems for individuals and businesses?
2. What are the major dimensions that make different mobile payment systems attractive or unattractive to a) consumers, b) merchants, c) banks, and d) credit card companies?

3. Do you think there are forces encouraging the adoption of a dominant design in mobile banking systems?
4. What is likely to determine which mobile banking systems succeed?

NOTES

[1]Data from Bureau of Economic Analysis, 2013, www.bea.gov.

[2]J. M. Utterback, *Mastering the Dynamics of Innovation* (Boston: Harvard Business School Press, 1994); C. Shapiro and H. R. Varian, *Information Rules: A Strategic Guide to the Network Economy* (Boston: Harvard Business School Press, 1999); M. A. Schilling, "Technology Success and Failure in Winner-take-all Markets: Testing a Model of Technological Lock Out," *Academy of Management Journal* 45 (2002): 387–398.

[3]The layout is not universal, although it is widespread. The French, for example, use a different layout.

[4]For details, see C. W. L. Hill, "Establishing a Standard: Competitive Strategy and Technology Standards in Winner Take All Industries," *Academy of Management Executive* 11 (1997): 7–25; Shapiro and Varian, *Information Rules;* B. Arthur, "Increasing Returns and the New World of Business," *Harvard Business Review,* July–August 1996, pp. 100–109; G. Gowrisankaran and J. Stavins, "Network Externalities and Technology Adoption: Lessons from Electronic Payments," *Rand Journal of Economics* 35 (2004): 260–277; V. Shankar and B. L. Bayus, "Network Effects and Competition: An Empirical Analysis of the Home Video Game Industry," *Strategic Management Journal* 24 (2003): 375–394; R. Casadesus-Masanell and P. Ghemawat, "Dynamic Mixed Duopoly: A Model Motivated by Linux vs Windows," *Management Science* 52 (2006): 1072–1085.

[5]See Shapiro and Varian, *Information Rules;* Hill, "Establishing a Standard"; M. A. Schilling, "Technological Lockout: An Integrative Model of the Economic and Strategic Factors Driving Technology Success and Failure," *Academy of Management Review* 23 (2) (1998): 267–285.

[6]J. Reitveld, C. Bellavitus, & M. A. Schilling, "Relaunch and Reload: Platform Governance and the Creation and Capture of Value in Ecosystems," New York University Working Paper, 2015.

[7]Microsoft does not disclose the per-unit licensing fee that it receives from original equipment manufacturers, although media reports speculate that it is around $50 a copy.

[8]M. Herper, "The Truly Staggering Costs of Inventing New Drugs," *Forbes,* February 10, 2012; Pharmaceutical Industry 2008, *Standard & Poor's Industry Surveys;* J. A. DiMasi and H. G. Grabowski, "R&D Costs and Returns to New Drug Development: A Review of the Evidence," in P. M. Danzon and S. Nicholson (ed.), *The Oxford Handbook of the Economics of the Biopharmaceutical Industry* (Oxford, UK: Oxford University Press, 2012), chapter 2, pp. 21–46; Innovation.org, 2007; *Drug Discovery and Development: Understanding the R&D Process* (Washington, DC: PhRMA, February), www.phrma.org (accessed August 1, 2015).

[9]Much of this section is based on C. W. L. Hill, M. Heeley, and J. Sakson, "Strategies for Profiting from Innovation," in *Advances in Global High Technology Management* (3rd ed.). (Greenwich, CT: JAI Press, 1993), pp. 79–95.

[10]M. Lieberman and D. Montgomery, "First Mover Advantages," *Strategic Management Journal* 9 (Special Issue, Summer 1988): 41–58

[11]W. Boulding and M. Christen, "Sustainable Pioneering Advantage? Profit Implications of Market Entry Order?" *Marketing Science* 22 (2003): 371–386; C. Markides and P. Geroski, "Teaching Elephants to Dance and Other Silly Ideas," *Business Strategy Review* 13 (2003): 49–61.

[12]M. A. Schilling, Towards dynamic efficiency: Innovation and its implications for antitrust. *Antitrust Bulletin,* forthcoming.

[13]J. Borzo, "Aging Gracefully," *Wall Street Journal,* October 15, 2001, p. R22.

[14]The importance of complementary assets was first noted by D. J. Teece. See D. J. Teece, "Profiting from Technological Innovation," in D. J. Teece (ed.), *The Competitive Challenge* (New York: Harper & Row, 1986), pp. 26–54

[15]M. J. Chen and D. C. Hambrick, "Speed, Stealth, and Selective Attack: How Small Firms Differ from Large Firms in Competitive Behavior," *Academy of Management Journal* 38 (1995): 453–482.

[16]E. Mansfield, M. Schwartz, and S. Wagner, "Imitation Costs and Patents: An Empirical Study," *Economic Journal* 91 (1981): 907–918.

[17]E. Mansfield, "How Rapidly Does New Industrial Technology Leak Out?" *Journal of Industrial Economics* 34 (1985): 217–223.

[18]This argument has been made in the game theory literature. See

R. Caves, H. Cookell, and P. J. Killing, "The Imperfect Market for Technology Licenses," *Oxford Bulletin of Economics and Statistics* 45 (1983): 249–267; N. T. Gallini, "Deterrence by Market Sharing: A Strategic Incentive for Licensing," *American Economic Review* 74 (1984): 931–941; C. Shapiro, "Patent Licensing and R&D Rivalry," *American Economic Review* 75 (1985): 25–30.

[19]M. Christensen, *The Innovator's Dilemma* (Boston: Harvard Business School Press, 1997); R. N. Foster, *Innovation: The Attacker's Advantage* (New York: Summit Books, 1986).

[20]Foster, *Innovation*.

[21]Ray Kurzweil, *The Age of the Spiritual Machines* (New York: Penguin Books, 1999).

[22]See Christensen, *The Innovator's Dilemma;* C. M. Christensen and M. Overdorf, "Meeting the Challenge of Disruptive Change," *Harvard Business Review* (March–April 2000): 66–77.

[23]C. W. L. Hill and F. T. Rothaermel, "The Performance of Incumbent Firms in the Face of Radical Technological Innovation," *Academy of Management Review* 28 (2003): 257–274; F. T. Rothaermel and Charles W. L. Hill, "Technological Discontinuities and Complementary Assets: A Longitudinal Study of Industry and Firm Performance," *Organization Science* 16 (1) (2005): 52–70.

CHAPTER 8

STRATEGY IN THE GLOBAL ENVIRONMENT

OPENING CASE

The Globalization of Starbucks

Thirty years ago, Starbucks was a single store in Seattle's Pike Place Market selling premium-roasted coffee. Today, it is a global roaster and retailer of coffee with more than 20,000 stores, 40% of which are in 50 countries outside of the United States. Starbucks set out on its current course in the 1980s, when the company's director of marketing, Howard Schultz, came back from a trip to Italy enchanted with the Italian coffeehouse experience. Schultz, who later became CEO, persuaded the company's owners to experiment with the coffeehouse format, and the Starbucks experience was born. The strategy was to sell the company's own, premium-roasted coffee and freshly brewed, espresso-style coffee beverages, along with a variety of pastries, coffee

8.1 Understand the process of globalization and how it impacts a company's strategy

8.2 Discuss the motives for expanding internationally

8.3 Review the different strategies that companies use to compete in the global marketplace

8.4 Explain the pros and cons of different modes for entering foreign markets

Nic Cleave Photography/Alamy

accessories, teas, and other products, in a tastefully designed coffeehouse setting. From the outset, the company focused on selling "a third-place experience" (in other words, spending significant time at a place that is neither work nor home), rather than just the coffee. The formula led to spectacular success in the United States, where, within a decade, Starbucks went from obscurity to one of the best-known brands in the country. Thanks to Starbucks, coffee stores became places for relaxation, chatting with friends, reading the newspaper, holding business meetings, or (more recently) browsing the web.

In 1995, with 700 stores across the United States, Starbucks began exploring foreign opportunities. The first target market was Japan. The company established a joint venture with a local retailer, Sazaby Inc. Each company held a 50% stake in the venture, Starbucks Coffee of Japan. Starbucks initially invested $10 million in this venture, its first foreign direct investment. The Starbucks format was then licensed to the venture, which was charged with growing Starbucks' presence in Japan.

To make sure the Japanese operations replicated the "Starbucks experience" in North America, Starbucks transferred some employees to oversee the Japanese operation. The licensing agreement required all Japanese store managers and employees to attend training classes similar to those given to U.S. employees. The agreement also required that stores adhere to the design parameters established in the United States. In 2001, the company introduced a stock option plan for all Japanese employees, making it the first company in Japan to do so. Skeptics doubted that Starbucks would be able to replicate its North American success overseas but, by 2014, Starbucks' had 1,034 stores and a profitable business in Japan.

After Japan, the company embarked on an aggressive foreign investment program. In 1998, it purchased Seattle Coffee, a British coffee chain with 60 retail stores, for $84 million. An American couple, originally from Seattle, had started Seattle Coffee with the intention of establishing a Starbucks-like chain in Britain. By 2014, there were 530 stores in the United Kingdom. In the late 1990s, Starbucks opened stores in Taiwan, China, Singapore, Thailand, New Zealand, South Korea, and Malaysia. In Asia, Starbucks' most common strategy was to license its format to a local operator in return for initial licensing fees and royalties on store revenues. As in Japan, Starbucks insisted on an intensive employee-training program and strict specifications regarding the format and layout of the store. By 2002, Starbucks was pursuing an aggressive expansion in mainland Europe, primarily through joint ventures with local companies. Its largest footprints are in Switzerland, France, and Germany.

To succeed in some countries, Starbucks has found that it has to adjust its basic formula to accommodate local differences. France, for example, has a well-established café culture. The French find Starbuck's lattes too bland, and the espresso too burnt, so Starbucks has had to change the recipe for its drinks to match French tastes. Since French consumers like to sit and chat while they drink their coffee, Starbucks has had to add more seating per store than is common elsewhere.

As it has grown its global footprint, Starbucks has also embraced ethical sourcing policies and environmental responsibility. Now one of the world's largest buyers of coffee, in 2000 Starbuck's started to purchase Fair Trade Certified coffee. The goal was to empower small-scale farmers organized in cooperatives to invest in their farms and communities, to protect the environment, and to develop the business skills necessary to compete in the global marketplace. In short, Starbucks was trying to use its influence to not only change the way people consumed coffee around the world, but also to change the way coffee was produced in a manner that benefited the farmers and the environment. By 2010, some 75% of the coffee Starbucks purchased was Fair Trade Certified, and the company has a goal of increasing that to 100% by 2015.

Sources: Starbucks 10K, various years; C. McLean, "Starbucks Set to Invade Coffee-Loving Continent," *Seattle Times*, October 4, 2000, p. E1; J. Ordonez, "Starbucks to Start Major Expansion in Overseas Market," *The Wall Street Journal*, October 27, 2000, p. B10; S. Homes and D. Bennett, "Planet Starbucks," *BusinessWeek*, September 9, 2002, pp. 99–110; "Starbucks Outlines International Growth Strategy," *Business Wire*, October 14, 2004; A. Yeh, "Starbucks Aims for New Tier in China," *Financial Times*, February 14, 2006, p. 17; C. Matlack, "Will Global Growth Help Starbucks?" *Business Week*, July 2, 2008; Liz Alderman, "In Europe, Starbucks Adjusts to a Café Culture," *New York Times*, March 30, 2012.

◤OVERVIEW

One of the striking developments of the last 30 years has been the globalization of markets. As a result of declining barriers to cross-border trade and investment, along with the rapid economic development of countries like Brazil, Russia, India, and China, segmented national markets have increasingly merged into much larger global markets. In this chapter, we discuss the implications of this phase shift in the global competitive environment for strategic management.

The chapter begins with a discussion of ongoing changes in the global competitive environment. Next, it discusses the various ways in which global expansion can increase a company's profitability and profit growth. We then discuss the advantages and disadvantages of the different strategies companies can pursue to gain a competitive advantage in the global marketplace. This is followed by a discussion of two related strategic issues: (1) how managers decide which foreign markets to enter, when to enter them, and on what scale; and (2) what kind of vehicle or method a company should use to expand globally and enter a foreign country.

The global expansion of Starbucks, profiled in the Opening Case, gives a preview of some issues explored in this chapter. Starbucks expanded overseas to boost its profit growth by leveraging its product offering to markets that typically lacked indigenous competitors. Today, over 40% of Starbucks stores are outside of its core North American market. *Leveraging product offering* to achieve greater growth is a common motive for global expansion. For the most part, Starbucks' strategy has been to use the same basic formula that worked in the United States. We call this a *global standardization* strategy. However, in certain countries, such as France, where there already was a strong coffee/café culture, Starbucks has had to adapt its format to capture local demand. We call this a *localization* strategy. Starbucks has often favored a *joint venture* strategy for entering foreign markets, teaming up with a local company in order to learn about the unique characteristics of each national market from its venture partners, thereby increasing its chances of successful entry. As we shall see, the choice of entry strategy is an important consideration for any firm expanding globally.

We shall discuss the issues touched on in the Starbucks' case, along with many others, and by the time you have completed the chapter, you will have a good understanding of the various strategic issues that companies face when they decide to expand their operations abroad to achieve superior profitability and/or profit growth.

▛ GLOBAL AND NATIONAL ENVIRONMENTS

Fifty years ago, most national markets were isolated from one another by significant barriers to international trade and investment. In those days, managers could focus on analyzing only those national markets in which their company competed. They did not need to pay much attention to entry by global competitors, for there were few and entry was difficult. Nor did they need to pay much attention to entering foreign markets, because that was often prohibitively expensive. All of this has now changed. Barriers to international trade and investment have tumbled, huge global markets for goods and services have been created, and companies from different nations are entering each other's home markets on an unprecedented scale, increasing the intensity of competition. Rivalry can no longer be understood merely in terms of what happens within the boundaries of a nation; managers now need to consider how globalization is impacting the environment in which their company competes and what strategies their company should adopt to exploit the unfolding opportunities and counter competitive threats. In this section, we look at the changes ushered in by falling barriers to international trade and investment, and we discuss a model for analyzing the competitive situation in different nations.

The Globalization of Production and Markets

The past half-century has seen a dramatic lowering of barriers to international trade and investment. For example, the average tariff rate on manufactured goods traded between advanced nations has fallen from around 40% to under 4%. For some goods, such as information technology, tariff rates have approached zero. Similarly, in nation after nation, regulations prohibiting foreign companies from entering domestic markets and establishing production facilities, or acquiring domestic companies, have been removed. As a result of these developments, there has been a surge in both the volume of international trade and the value of foreign direct investment. The volume of world merchandise trade has been growing faster than the world economy since the 1950s. Between 1970 and 2012, the volume of world merchandise trade increased 32 times, compared to a 9-fold increase in the size of the world economy.[1] As for foreign direct investment, between 1992 and 2013, the total flow of foreign direct investment from all countries increased over 500%, while world trade by value grew by some 150% and world output by around 40%.[2] These trends have led to the globalization of production and the globalization of markets.[3]

The globalization of production has been increasing as companies take advantage of lower barriers to international trade and investment to disperse important parts of their production processes around the globe. Doing so enables them to exploit national differences in the cost and quality of factors of production such as labor, energy, land, and capital, which allows companies to lower their cost structures and boost profits. For example, foreign companies build nearly 65% by value of Boeing's 787 commercial jet aircraft. Three Japanese companies build 35% of the 787, and another 20% is allocated to companies located in Italy, Singapore, and the United Kingdom.[4] Part of Boeing's rationale for outsourcing so much production to foreign suppliers is that these suppliers are the best in the world at performing their particular activity. Therefore, the result of having foreign suppliers build specific parts is a better final product and higher profitability for Boeing.

As for the globalization of markets, it has been argued that the world's economic system is moving from one in which national markets are distinct entities, isolated from each other by trade barriers and barriers of distance, time, and culture, toward a system in which national markets are merging into one huge, global marketplace. Increasingly, customers around the world demand and use the same basic product offerings. Consequently, in many industries, it is no longer meaningful to talk about the German market, the U.S. market, or the Chinese market; there is only the global market. The global acceptance of Coca-Cola, Citigroup credit cards, Starbucks, McDonald's hamburgers, Samsung and Apple smartphones, IKEA furniture, and Microsoft's Windows operating system are examples of this trend.[5]

The trend toward the globalization of production and markets has several important implications for competition within an industry. First, industry boundaries do not stop at national borders. Because many industries are becoming global in scope, competitors and potential future competitors exist not only in a company's home market but also in international markets. Managers who analyze only their home market can be caught unprepared by the entry of efficient foreign competitors. The globalization of markets and production implies that companies around the globe are finding their home markets under attack from foreign competitors. For example, in Japan, American financial institutions such as J.P. Morgan have been making inroads against Japanese financial service institutions. In the United States, South Korea's Samsung has been battling Apple for a share of the smartphone market. In the European Union, the once-dominant Dutch company Philips has seen its market share in the customer electronics industry taken by Japan's Panasonic and Sony, and Samsung of South Korea.

Second, the shift from national to global markets has intensified competitive rivalry in many industries. National markets that once were consolidated oligopolies, dominated by three or four companies and subjected to relatively little foreign competition, have been transformed into segments of fragmented global industries in which many companies battle each other for market share in many countries. This rivalry has threatened to drive down profitability and made it more critical for companies to maximize their efficiency, quality, customer responsiveness, and innovative ability. The painful restructuring and downsizing that has been occurring at companies such as the once dominant and now bankrupt photographic company Kodak is as much a response to the increased intensity of global competition as it is to any other factor. However, not all global industries are fragmented. Many remain consolidated oligopolies, except that now they are consolidated, global (rather than national) oligopolies. In the videogame industry, for example, three companies are battling for global dominance: Microsoft from the United States, and Nintendo and Sony from Japan. In the market for smartphones, Apple is in a global battle with Samsung from South Korea and Xiaomi from China.

Finally, although globalization has increased both the threat of entry and the intensity of rivalry within many formerly protected national markets, it has also created enormous opportunities for companies based in those markets. The steady decline in barriers to crossborder trade and investment has opened up many once-protected national markets to companies based outside these nations. Thus, for example, Western European, Japanese, and U.S. companies have accelerated their investment in the nations of Eastern Europe, Latin America, and Southeast Asia as they try to take advantage of growth opportunities in those areas.

National Competitive Advantage

Despite the globalization of production and markets, many of the most successful companies in certain industries are still clustered in a small number of countries. For example, many of the world's most successful biotechnology and computer companies are based in the United States, and many of the most successful consumer electronics companies are based in Japan, Taiwan, South Korea, and China. Germany is the base for many successful chemical and engineering companies. These facts suggest that the nation-state within which a company is based may have an important bearing on the competitive position of that company in the global marketplace.

In a study of national competitive advantage, Michael Porter identified four attributes of a national or country-specific environment that have an important impact on the global competitiveness of companies located within that nation:[6]

- *Factor endowments*: A nation's position in factors of production such as skilled labor or the infrastructure necessary to compete in a given industry
- *Local demand conditions*: The nature of home demand for the industry's product or service
- *Related and supporting industries*: The presence or absence in a nation of supplier industries and related industries that are internationally competitive
- *Firm strategy, structure, and rivalry*: The conditions in the nation governing how companies are created, organized, and managed, and the nature of domestic rivalry

Porter speaks of these four attributes as constituting the "diamond," arguing that companies from a given nation are most likely to succeed in industries or strategic groups in which the four attributes are favorable (see Figure 8.1). He also argues that

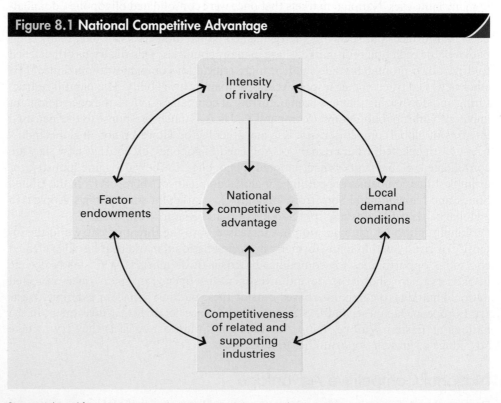

Figure 8.1 National Competitive Advantage

Source: Adapted from M. E. Porter, "The Competitive Advantage of Nations," *Harvard Business Review*, March–April 1990, p. 77.

the diamond's attributes form a mutually reinforcing system in which the effect of one attribute is dependent on the state of others.

Factor Endowments Factor endowments—the cost and quality of factors of production—are a prime determinant of the competitive advantage that certain countries might have in certain industries. Factors of production include basic factors such as land, labor, capital, and raw materials, and advanced factors such as technological knowhow, managerial sophistication, and physical infrastructure (roads, railways, and ports). The competitive advantage that the United States enjoys in biotechnology might be explained by the presence of certain advanced factors of production—for example, technological knowhow—in combination with some basic factors, which might be a pool of relatively low-cost venture capital that can be used to fund risky start-ups in industries such as biotechnology.

Local Demand Conditions Home demand plays an important role in providing the impetus for "upgrading" competitive advantage. Companies are typically most sensitive to the needs of their closest customers. Thus, the characteristics of home demand are particularly important in shaping the attributes of domestically made products and creating pressures for innovation and quality. A nation's companies gain competitive advantage if their domestic customers are sophisticated and demanding, and pressure local companies to meet high standards of product quality and produce innovative products. Japan's sophisticated and knowledgeable buyers of cameras helped stimulate the Japanese camera industry to improve product quality and introduce innovative models. A similar example can be found in the cell phone equipment industry, where sophisticated, demanding local customers in Scandinavia helped push Nokia of Finland and Ericsson of Sweden to invest in cellular phone technology long before demand for cellular phones increased in other developed nations. As a result, Nokia and Ericsson, together with Motorola, became significant players in the global cellular telephone equipment industry.

Competitiveness of Related and Supporting Industries The third broad attribute of national advantage in an industry is the presence of internationally competitive suppliers or related industries. The benefits of investments in advanced factors of production by related and supporting industries can spill over into an industry, thereby helping it achieve a strong competitive position internationally. Swedish strength in fabricated steel products such as ball bearings and cutting tools has drawn on strengths in Sweden's specialty-steel industry. Switzerland's success in pharmaceuticals is closely related to its previous international success in the technologically related dye industry. One consequence of this process is that successful industries within a country tend to be grouped into clusters of related industries. Indeed, this is one of the most pervasive findings of Porter's study. One such cluster is the German textile and apparel sector, which includes high-quality cotton, wool, synthetic fibers, sewing machine needles, and a wide range of textile machinery.

Intensity of Rivalry The fourth broad attribute of national competitive advantage in Porter's model is the intensity of rivalry of firms within a nation. Porter makes two important points. First, different nations are characterized by different management ideologies, which either help them or do not help them to build national competitive advantage. For example, Porter noted the predominance of engineers in top management at German and Japanese firms. He attributed this to these firms' emphasis on improving manufacturing processes and product design. In contrast, Porter noted a predominance of people with finance backgrounds leading many U.S. firms. He linked this to U.S. firms' lack of attention to improving manufacturing processes and product design. He argued that the dominance of finance led to an overemphasis on maximizing short-term financial returns. According to Porter, one consequence of these different management ideologies was a relative loss of U.S. competitiveness in those engineering-based industries where manufacturing processes and product design issues are all-important (such as the automobile industry).

Porter's second point is that there is a strong association between vigorous domestic rivalry and the creation and persistence of competitive advantage in an industry. Rivalry compels companies to look for ways to improve efficiency, which makes them better international competitors. Domestic rivalry creates pressures to innovate, improve quality, reduce costs, and invest in upgrading advanced factors. All this helps to create world-class competitors.

Using the Framework The framework just described can help managers identify where their most significant global competitors are likely to originate. For example, there is a cluster of computer service and software companies in Bangalore, India, that includes two of the fastest-growing information technology companies in the world, Infosys and Wipro. These companies have emerged as aggressive competitors in the global market. Both companies have recently opened up offices in the European Union and United States so they can better compete against Western rivals such as IBM and Hewlett Packard, and both are gaining share in the global marketplace.

The framework can also be used to help managers decide where they might want to locate certain productive activities. Seeking to take advantage of U.S. expertise in biotechnology, many foreign companies have set up research facilities in San Diego, Boston, and Seattle, where U.S. biotechnology companies tend to cluster. Similarly, in an attempt to take advantage of Japanese success in consumer electronics, many U.S. electronics companies have set up research and production facilities in Japan, often in conjunction with Japanese partners.

Finally, the framework can help a company assess how tough it might be to enter certain national markets. If a nation has a competitive advantage in certain industries, it might be challenging for foreigners to enter those industries. For example, the highly competitive retailing industry in the United States has proved to be a very difficult industry for foreign companies to enter. Successful foreign retailers such as Britain's Tesco and Sweden's IKEA have found it tough going into the United States because the U.S. retailing industry is the most competitive in the world.

GLOBAL EXPANSION, PROFITABILITY, AND PROFIT GROWTH

Expanding globally allows firms to increase their profitability and rate of profit growth in ways not available to purely domestic enterprises.[7] Firms that operate internationally are able to:

1. Expand the market for their domestic product offerings by selling those products in international markets.

2. Realize location economies by dispersing individual value creation activities to those locations around the globe where they can be performed most efficiently and effectively.

3. Realize greater cost economies from experience effects by serving an expanded global market from a central location, thereby reducing the costs of value creation.

4. Earn a greater return by leveraging any valuable skills developed in foreign operations and transferring them to other entities within the firm's global network of operations.

As we will see, however, a firm's ability to increase its profitability and profit growth by pursuing these strategies is constrained by the need to customize its product offering, marketing strategy, and business strategy to differing national or regional conditions— that is, by the imperative of localization.

Expanding the Market: Leveraging Products

A company can increase its growth rate by taking goods or services developed at home and selling them internationally; almost all multinationals started out doing this. Procter & Gamble (P&G), for example, developed most of its bestselling products at home and then sold them around the world. Similarly, from its earliest days, Microsoft has focused on selling its software around the world. Automobile companies such as Ford, Volkswagen, and Toyota also grew by developing products at home and then selling them in international markets. The returns from such a strategy are likely to be greater if indigenous competitors in the nations a company enters lack comparable products. Thus, Toyota has grown its profits by entering the large automobile markets of North America and Europe and offering products differentiated from those offered by local rivals (Ford and GM) by superior quality and reliability.

The success of many **multinational companies** that expand in this manner is based not just on the goods or services that they sell in foreign nations, but also upon the distinctive competencies (i.e., unique resources) that underlie the production and marketing of those goods or services. Thus, Toyota's success is based on its distinctive competency in manufacturing automobiles. International expansion can be seen as a way for Toyota to generate greater returns from this competency. Similarly, P&G's global success was based on more than its portfolio of consumer products; it was also based on the company's competencies in mass-marketing consumer goods. P&G grew rapidly in international markets between 1950 and 1990 because it was one of the most skilled mass-marketing enterprises in the world and could "out-market" indigenous competitors in the nations it entered. Global expansion was, therefore, a way of generating higher returns from its valuable, rare, and inimitable resources in marketing.

multinational company
A company that does business in two or more national markets.

The same can be said of companies engaged in the service sectors of an economy, such as financial institutions, retailers, restaurant chains, and hotels. Expanding the market for their services often means replicating their business model in foreign nations (albeit with some changes to account for local differences, which we will discuss in more detail shortly). Starbucks, for example, has expanded globally by taking the basic business model it developed in the United States and using that as a blueprint for establishing international operations.

Realizing Cost Economies from Global Volume

In addition to growing profits more rapidly, a company can realize cost savings from economies of scale, thereby boosting profitability, by expanding its sales volume through international expansion. Such scale economies come from several sources. First, by spreading the fixed costs associated with developing a product and setting up production facilities over its global sales volume, a company can lower its average unit cost. Thus, Microsoft can garner significant scale economies by spreading the $5- to $10- billion cost of developing Windows 8 over global demand.

Second, by serving a global market, a company can potentially utilize its production facilities more intensively, which leads to higher productivity, lower costs, and greater profitability. For example, if Intel sold microprocessors only in the United States, it might only be able to keep its factories open for 1 shift, 5 days a week. But by serving a global market from the same factories, it might be able to utilize those assets for two shifts, 7 days a week. In other words, the capital invested in those factories is used more intensively if Intel sells to a global—as opposed to a national—market, which translates into higher capital productivity and a higher return on invested capital.

Third, as global sales increase the size of the enterprise, its bargaining power with suppliers increases, which may allow it to bargain down the cost of key inputs and boost profitability that way. For example, Wal-Mart has been able to use its enormous sales volume as a lever to bargain down the price it pays to suppliers for merchandise sold through its stores.

In addition to the cost savings that come from economies of scale, companies that sell to a global rather than a local marketplace may be able to realize further cost savings from learning effects. We first discussed learning effects in Chapter 4, where we noted that employee productivity increases with cumulative increases in output over time. (For example, it costs considerably less to build the 100th aircraft from a Boeing assembly line than the 10th because employees learn how to perform their tasks more efficiently over time.) Selling to a global market may enable a company to increase its sales volume more rapidly, and thus the cumulative output from its plants, which in turn should result in accelerated learning, higher employee productivity, and a cost advantage over competitors that are growing more slowly because they lack international markets.

Realizing Location Economies

location economies

The economic benefits that arise from performing a value creation activity in an optimal location.

Earlier in this chapter, we discussed how countries differ from each other along a number of dimensions, including differences in the cost and quality of factors of production. These differences imply that some locations are more suited than others for producing certain goods and services.[8] **Location economies** are the economic benefits that arise from performing a value creation activity in the optimal location for that activity, wherever in the world that might be (transportation costs and trade barriers permitting). Thus, if the best designers for a product live in France, a firm should base its design operations in France. If the most productive labor force for assembly operations is in Mexico, assembly operations should be based in Mexico. If the best marketers are in the United States, the marketing strategy should be formulated in the United States—and so on. Apple, for example, designs the iPhone and develops the associated software in California, but undertakes final assembly in China precisely because the company believes that these are the best locations in the world for carrying out these different value creation activities.

Locating a value creation activity in the optimal location for that activity can have one of two effects: (1) it can lower the costs of value creation, helping the company achieve a low-cost position; or (2) it can enable a company to differentiate its product offering, which gives it the option of charging a premium price or keeping prices low and using differentiation as a means of increasing sales volume. Thus, efforts to realize location economies are consistent with the business-level strategies of low cost and differentiation.

In theory, a company that realizes location economies by dispersing each of its value creation activities to the optimal location for that activity should have a competitive advantage over a company that bases all of its value creation activities at a single location. It should be able to better differentiate its product offering and lower its cost structure more than its single-location competitor. In a world where competitive pressures are increasing, such a strategy may well become an imperative for survival.

Introducing transportation costs and trade barriers can complicate the process of realizing location economies. New Zealand might have a comparative advantage for low-cost car assembly operations, but high transportation costs make it an uneconomical location from which to serve global markets. Factoring transportation costs and trade barriers into the cost equation helps explain why some U.S. companies have shifted production from Asia to Mexico. Mexico has three distinct advantages over many Asian countries as a location for value creation activities: low labor costs; Mexico's proximity to the large U.S. market, which reduces transportation costs; and the North American Free Trade Agreement (NAFTA), which has removed many trade barriers between Mexico, the United States, and Canada, increasing Mexico's appeal as a production site for the North American market. Thus, although the relative costs of value creation are important, transportation costs and trade barriers also must be considered in location decisions.

Leveraging the Competencies of Global Subsidiaries

You will recall from Chapter 3 that competitive advantage is based upon valuable, rare, and inimitable resources, in particular process knowledge, intellectual property, and organizational architecture. Initially, many multinational companies develop the valuable resources and competencies that underpin their competitive advantage in their home nation and then expand internationally, primarily by selling products and services based on those competencies. However, for more mature multinational enterprises that have already established a network of subsidiary operations in foreign markets, the development of valuable resources and competencies can just as well occur in foreign subsidiaries.[9] Competencies can be created anywhere within a multinational's global network of operations, wherever people have the opportunity and incentive to try new ways of doing things. The creation of resources and competencies such as unique process knowledge that helps to lower the costs of production, or to enhance perceived value and support higher product pricing, is not the monopoly of the corporate center.

Leveraging the valuable resources created within subsidiaries and applying them to other operations within the firm's global network may create value. For example, McDonald's is increasingly finding that its foreign franchisees are a source of valuable new ideas. Faced with slow growth in France, its local franchisees have begun to experiment with the menu, as well as the layout and theme of restaurants. Gone are the ubiquitous Golden Arches; gone too are many of the utilitarian chairs and tables and other plastic features of the fast-food giant. Many McDonald's restaurants in

France now have hardwood floors, exposed brick walls, and even armchairs. Half of the outlets in France have been upgraded to a level that would make them unrecognizable to an American. The menu, too, has been changed to include premier sandwiches, such as chicken on focaccia bread, priced some 30% higher than the average hamburger. In France, this strategy seems to be working. Following these changes, increases in same-store sales rose from 1% annually to 3.4%. Impressed with the impact, McDonald's executives are now considering adopting similar changes at other restaurants in markets where same-store sales growth is sluggish, including the United States.[10]

For the managers of a multinational enterprise, this phenomenon creates important new challenges. First, managers must have the humility to recognize that valuable resources such as unique process knowledge or intellectual property can arise anywhere within the firm's global network, not just at the corporate center. Second, they must establish an incentive system that encourages local employees to acquire and build new resources and competencies. This is not as easy as it sounds. Creating new competencies involves a degree of risk. Not all new skills add value. For every valuable idea created by a McDonald's subsidiary in a foreign country, there may be several failures. The management of the multinational must install incentives that encourage employees to take necessary risks, reward them for successes, and not sanction them for taking risks that did not pan out. Third, managers must have a process for identifying when valuable new resources and competencies have been created in a subsidiary. Finally, they need to act as facilitators, helping to transfer valuable resources and competencies within the firm.

COST PRESSURES AND PRESSURES FOR LOCAL RESPONSIVENESS

Companies that compete in the global marketplace typically face two types of competitive pressures: *pressures for cost reductions and pressures to be locally responsive* (see Figure 8.2).[11] These competitive pressures place conflicting demands on a company. Responding to pressures for cost reductions requires that a company attempt to minimize its unit costs. To attain this goal, it may have to base its productive activities at the most favorable low-cost location, wherever in the world that might be. It may also need to offer a standardized product to the global marketplace in order to realize the cost savings that come from economies of scale and learning effects. On the other hand, responding to pressures to be locally responsive requires that a company differentiate its product offering and marketing strategy from country to country in an effort to accommodate the diverse demands arising from national differences in consumer tastes and preferences, business practices, distribution channels, competitive conditions, and government policies. Because differentiation across countries can involve significant duplication and a lack of product standardization, it may raise costs.

Whereas some companies, such as Company A in Figure 8.2, face high pressures for cost reductions and low pressures for local responsiveness, and others, such as Company B, face low pressures for cost reductions and high pressures for local responsiveness, many companies are in the position of Company C. They face high

Figure 8.2 Pressures for Cost Reductions and Local Responsiveness

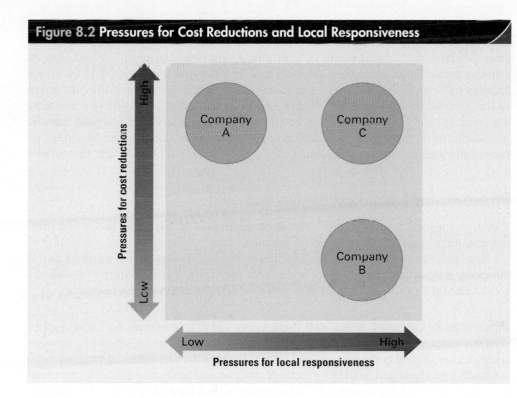

pressures for both cost reductions and local responsiveness. Dealing with these conflicting and contradictory pressures is a difficult strategic challenge, primarily because local responsiveness tends to raise costs.

Pressures for Cost Reductions

In competitive global markets, international businesses often face pressures for cost reductions. To respond to these pressures, a firm must try to lower the costs of value creation. A manufacturer, for example, might mass-produce a standardized product at an optimal site to realize economies of scale and location economies. Alternatively, it might outsource certain functions to low-cost foreign suppliers in an attempt to reduce costs. Thus, many computer companies have outsourced their telephone-based customer service functions to India, where qualified technicians who speak English can be hired for a lower wage rate than in the United States. In the same vein, Wal-Mart pushes its suppliers (which are manufacturers) to also lower their prices. In fact, the pressure that Wal-Mart has placed on its suppliers to reduce prices has been cited as a major cause of the trend among North American manufacturers to shift production to China.[12] A service business such as a bank might move back-office functions such as information processing to developing nations where wage rates are lower.

Cost-reduction pressures can be particularly intense in industries producing commodity-type products where meaningful differentiation on non-price factors is difficult, and price is the main competitive weapon. This tends to be the case for products that serve universal needs. Universal needs exist when the tastes and preferences of consumers in different nations are similar, if not identical, such as for bulk chemicals, petroleum, steel, sugar, and similar products. Pressures for cost reductions also exist for many industrial and consumer products—for example, hand-held calculators, semiconductor chips, personal computers, and liquid crystal display screens. Pressures for cost reductions are also intense in industries where major competitors are based in low-cost locations, where there is persistent excess capacity, and where consumers are powerful and face low switching costs. Many commentators have argued that the liberalization of the world trade and investment environment in recent decades, by facilitating greater international competition, has generally increased cost pressures.[13]

Pressures for Local Responsiveness

Pressures for local responsiveness arise from differences in consumer tastes and preferences, infrastructure and traditional practices, distribution channels, and host government demands. Responding to pressures to be locally responsive requires that a company differentiate its products and marketing strategy from country to country to accommodate these factors, all of which tend to raise a company's cost structure.

Differences in Customer Tastes and Preferences   Strong pressures for local responsiveness emerge when customer tastes and preferences differ significantly between countries, as they may for historic or cultural reasons. In such cases, a multinational company's products and marketing message must be customized to appeal to the tastes and preferences of local customers. The company is then typically pressured to delegate its production and marketing responsibilities and functions to overseas subsidiaries.

For example, the automobile industry in the 1980s and early 1990s moved toward the creation of "world cars." The idea was that global companies such as General Motors, Ford, and Toyota would be able to sell the same basic vehicle globally, sourcing it from centralized production locations. If successful, the strategy would have enabled automobile companies to reap significant gains from global-scale economies. However, this strategy frequently ran aground upon the hard rocks of consumer reality. Consumers in different automobile markets have historically had different tastes and preferences, and these require different types of vehicles. North American consumers show a strong demand for pickup trucks. This is particularly true in the South and West, where many families have a pickup truck as a second or third vehicle. But in European countries, pickup trucks are seen purely as utility vehicles and are purchased primarily by firms rather than individuals. As a consequence, the product mix and marketing message need to be tailored to take into account the different nature of demand in North America and Europe.

Some commentators have argued that customer demands for local customization are on the decline worldwide.[14] According to this argument, modern communications and transport technologies have created the conditions for a convergence of the tastes and preferences of customers from different nations. The result is the emergence of enormous global markets for standardized consumer products. The worldwide acceptance of McDonald's hamburgers, Coca-Cola, GAP clothes, the Apple iPhone, and Sony television sets, all of which are sold globally as standardized products, is often cited as evidence of the increasing homogeneity of the global marketplace.

However, this argument may not hold in many consumer goods markets. Significant differences in consumer tastes and preferences still exist across nations and cultures.

Managers in international businesses do not yet have the luxury of being able to ignore these differences, and they may not for a long time to come. For an example of a company that has discovered the importance of pressures for local responsiveness, see Strategy in Action 8.1 on MTV Networks.

Differences in Infrastructure and Traditional Practices   Pressures for local responsiveness also arise from differences in infrastructure or traditional practices among countries, creating a need to customize products accordingly. To meet this need, companies may have to delegate manufacturing and production functions to foreign subsidiaries. For example, in North America, consumer electrical systems are based on 110 volts, whereas in some European countries 240-volt systems are standard. Thus, domestic electrical appliances must be customized to take this difference in infrastructure into

8.1 STRATEGY IN ACTION

Local Responsiveness at MTV Networks

MTV Networks has become a symbol of globalization. Established in 1981, the U.S.-based TV network has been expanding outside of its North American base since 1987, when it launched MTV Europe. MTV Networks figures that, every second of every day, over 2 million people are watching MTV around the world, the majority outside the United States. Despite its international success, MTV's global expansion got off to a weak start. In the 1980s, when its main programming fare was music videos, it piped a single feed across Europe almost entirely composed of American programming with English-speaking veejays. Naively, the network's U.S. managers thought Europeans would flock to the American programming. But although viewers in Europe shared a common interest in a handful of global superstars, their tastes turned out to be surprisingly local. After losing share to local competitors that focused more on local tastes, MTV changed it strategy in the 1990s. It broke its service into "feeds" aimed at national or regional markets. Although MTV Networks

exercises creative control over these different feeds, and although all the channels have the same familiar, frenetic look and feel of MTV in the United States, a significant share of the programming and content is now local.

Today, an increasing share of programming is local in conception. Although many programming ideas still originate in the United States, with staples such as "The Real World" having equivalents in different countries, an increasing share of programming is local in conception. In Italy, "MTV Kitchen" combines cooking with a music countdown. "Erotica" airs in Brazil and features a panel of youngsters discussing sex. The Indian channel produces twenty-one homegrown shows hosted by local veejays who speak "Hinglish," a city-bred version of Hindi and English. Many feeds still feature music videos by locally popular performers. This localization push reaped big benefits for MTV, allowing the network to capture viewers back from local imitators.

Sources: M. Gunther, "MTV's Passage to India," *Fortune*, August 9, 2004, pp. 117–122; B. Pulley and A. Tanzer, "Sumner's Gemstone," *Forbes*, February 21, 2000, pp. 107–11; K. Huffman, "Youth TV's Old Hand Prepares for the Digital Challenge," *Financial Times*, February 18, 2000, p. 8; presentation by Sumner M. Redstone, chairman and CEO, Viacom Inc., delivered to the Salomon Smith Barney 11th Annual Global Entertainment Media, Telecommunications Conference, Scottsdale, AZ, January 8, 2001, www.viacom.com; Viacom 10K Statement, 2005.

account. Traditional social practices also often vary across nations. In Britain, people drive on the left-hand side of the road, creating a demand for right-hand-drive cars, whereas in France and the rest of Europe, people drive on the right-hand side of the road (and therefore want left-hand-drive cars).

Although many differences in infrastructure are rooted in history, some are quite recent. In the wireless telecommunications industry, different technical standards are found in different parts of the world. A technical standard known as GSM is common in Europe, and an alternative standard, CDMA, is more common in the United States and parts of Asia. The significance of these different standards is that equipment designed for GSM will not work on a CDMA network, and vice versa. Thus, companies that manufacture wireless handsets and infrastructure such as switches need to customize their product offerings according to the technical standard prevailing in a given country.

Differences in Distribution Channels   A company's marketing strategies may have to be responsive to differences in distribution channels among countries, which may necessitate delegating marketing functions to national subsidiaries. In the pharmaceutical industry, for example, the British and Japanese distribution system is radically different from the U.S. system. British and Japanese doctors will not accept or respond favorably to a U.S.-style, high-pressure sales force. Thus, pharmaceutical companies must adopt different marketing practices in Britain and Japan compared with the United States—soft sell versus hard sell.

Similarly, Poland, Brazil, and Russia all have similar per capita income on the basis of purchasing-power parity, but there are big differences in distribution systems across the three countries. In Brazil, supermarkets account for 36% of food retailing; in Poland, for 18%; and in Russia, for less than 1%.[15] These differences in channels require that companies adapt their own distribution and sales strategies.

Host Government Demands   Finally, economic and political demands imposed by host-country governments may require local responsiveness. For example, pharmaceutical companies are subject to local clinical testing, registration procedures, and pricing restrictions, all of which make it necessary that the manufacturing and marketing of a drug meet local requirements. Moreover, because governments and government agencies control a significant portion of the health-care budget in most countries, they are in a powerful position to demand a high level of local responsiveness. More generally, threats of protectionism, economic nationalism, and local content rules (which require that a certain percentage of a product be manufactured locally) can dictate that international businesses manufacture locally.

The Rise of Regionalism   Typically, we think of pressures for local responsive as deriving from *national* differences in tastes and preferences, infrastructure, and the like. While this is still often the case, there is also a tendency toward the convergence of tastes, preferences, infrastructure, distribution channels, and host-government demands within a broader *region* that is composed of two or more nations.[16] We sometimes see this when there are strong pressures for convergence due to, for example, a shared history and culture, or the establishment of a trading block where there are deliberate attempts to harmonize trade policies, infrastructure, regulations, and the like.

The most obvious example of a region is the European Union (EU), and particularly the eurozone countries within that trade block, where institutional forces are pushing toward convergence. The creation of a single EU market, with a single currency, common business regulations, standard infrastructure, and so on, cannot help but result in the reduction of certain national differences between countries within the EU, and the creation of one regional rather than several national markets. Indeed, at the economic level at least, that is the explicit intent of the EU.

Another example of regional convergence is North America, which includes the United States, Canada, and to some extent in some product markets, Mexico. Canada and the United States share history, language, and much of their culture, and both are members of NAFTA. Mexico is clearly different in many regards, but its proximity to the United States, along with its membership in NAFTA, implies that for some product markets (e.g., automobiles) it might be reasonable to consider it part of a relatively homogenous regional market. In the Latin America region, shared Spanish history, cultural heritage, and language (with the exception of Brazil, which was colonized by the Portuguese) mean that national differences are somewhat moderated. One can argue that Greater China, which includes the city-states of Honk Kong and Singapore, along with Taiwan, is a coherent region, as is much of the Middle East, where a strong Arab culture and shared history may limit national differences. Similarly, Russia and some former states of the Soviet Union such as Belarus and the Ukraine might be considered part of a larger regional market, at least for some products.

Taking a regional perspective is important because it may suggest that localization at the regional rather than the national level is the appropriate strategic response. For example, rather than produce cars for each national market within Europe or North America, it makes far more sense for car manufacturers to build cars for the European or North American regions. The ability to standardize a product offering within a region allows for the attainment of greater scale economies, and hence lower costs, than if each nation required its own offering. At the same time, one should be careful about not pushing this perspective too far. There are still deep, profound, cultural differences between the United Kingdom, France, Germany, and Italy—all members of the EU—which may require some degree of local customization at the national level. Managers must thus make a judgment call about the appropriate level of aggregation given (1) the product market they are looking at, and (2) the nature of national differences and trends for regional convergence. What might make sense for automobiles might not be appropriate for packaged food products.

◤ CHOOSING A GLOBAL STRATEGY

Pressures for local responsiveness imply that it may not be possible for a firm to realize the full benefits from economies of scale and location economies. It may not be possible to serve the global marketplace from a single, low-cost location, producing a globally standardized product, and marketing it worldwide to achieve economies of scale. In practice, the need to customize the product offering to local conditions may work against the implementation of such a strategy. For example, automobile firms have found that Japanese, American, and European consumers demand different kinds of cars, and this necessitates producing products that are customized for local markets. In response, firms such as Honda, Ford, and Toyota are pursuing a strategy of establishing top-to-bottom design and production facilities in each of these regions so that they can better serve local demands. Although such customization brings benefits, it also limits the ability of a firm to realize significant scale economies and location economies.

In addition, pressures for local responsiveness imply that it may not be possible to leverage skills and products associated with a firm's distinctive competencies wholesale from one nation to another. Concessions often have to be made to local conditions. Despite being depicted as "poster child" for the proliferation of standardized, global products, even McDonald's has found that it has to customize its product offerings (its menu) in order to account for national differences in tastes and preferences.

Given the need to balance the cost and differentiation (value) sides of a company's business model, how do differences in the strength of pressures for cost reductions versus those for local responsiveness affect the choice of a company's strategy? Companies typically choose among four main strategic postures when competing internationally: a global standardization strategy, a localization strategy, a transnational strategy, and an international strategy.[17] The appropriateness of each strategy varies with the extent of pressures for cost reductions and local responsiveness. Figure 8.3 illustrates the conditions under which each of these strategies is most appropriate.

Global Standardization Strategy

global standardization strategy

A business model based on pursuing a low-cost strategy on a global scale.

Companies that pursue a **global standardization strategy** focus on increasing profitability by reaping the cost reductions that come from economies of scale and location economies; that is, they pursue a low-cost strategy on a global scale. The production, marketing, and R&D activities of companies pursuing a global strategy are

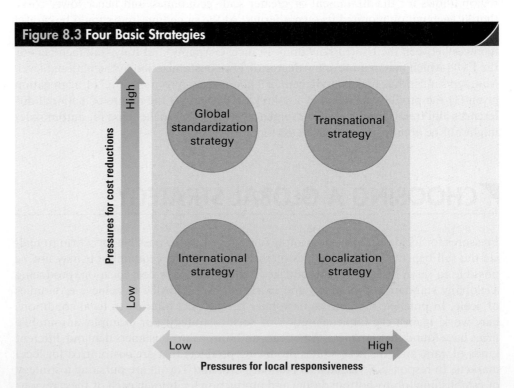

Figure 8.3 Four Basic Strategies

concentrated in a few favorable locations. These companies try not to customize their product offerings and marketing strategy to local conditions because customization, which involves shorter production runs and the duplication of functions, can raise costs. Instead, they prefer to market a standardized product worldwide so that they can reap the maximum benefits from economies of scale. They also tend to use their cost advantage to support aggressive pricing in world markets.

This strategy makes most sense when there are strong pressures for cost reductions and demand for local responsiveness is minimal. Increasingly, these conditions prevail in many industrial-goods industries, whose products often serve universal needs. In the semiconductor industry, for example, global standards have emerged, creating enormous demands for standardized, global products. Accordingly, companies such as Intel, Texas Instruments, and Motorola all pursue a global strategy.

These conditions are not always found in consumer goods markets, where demands for local responsiveness remain high. However, even some consumer goods companies are moving toward a global standardization strategy in an attempt to drive down their costs.

Localization Strategy

A **localization strategy** focuses on increasing profitability by customizing the company's goods or services so that they provide a favorable match to tastes and preferences in different national or regional markets. Localization is most appropriate when there are substantial differences across nations or regions with regard to consumer tastes and preferences, and where cost pressures are not too intense. By customizing the product offering to local demands, the company increases the value of that product in the local market. On the downside, because it involves some duplication of functions and smaller production runs, customization limits the ability of the company to capture the cost reductions associated with mass-producing a standardized product for global consumption. The strategy may make sense, however, if the added value associated with local customization supports higher pricing, which would enable the company to recoup its higher costs, or if it leads to substantially greater local demand, enabling the company to reduce costs through the attainment of scale economies in the local market.

MTV is a good example of a company that has had to pursue a localization strategy. If MTV localized its programming to match the demands of viewers in different nations, it would have lost market share to local competitors, its advertising revenues would have fallen, and its profitability would have declined. Thus, even though it raised costs, localization became a strategic imperative at MTV.

At the same time, it is important to realize that companies like MTV still have to closely monitor costs. Companies pursuing a localization strategy still need to be efficient and, whenever possible, capture scale economies from their global reach. As noted earlier, many automobile companies have found that they have to customize some of their product offerings to local market demands—for example, by producing large pickup trucks for U.S. consumers and small, fuel-efficient cars for European and Japanese consumers. At the same time, these companies try to achieve scale economies from their global volume by using common vehicle platforms and components across many different models and by manufacturing those platforms and components at efficiently scaled factories that are optimally located. By designing their products in this way, these companies have localized their product offerings and simultaneously capture some scale economies.

localization strategy
A strategy focused on increasing profitability by customizing a company's goods or services so that they provide a favorable match to tastes and preferences in different national markets.

Transnational Strategy

We have argued that a global standardization strategy makes most sense when cost pressures are intense and demands for local responsiveness limited. Conversely, a localization strategy makes most sense when demands for local responsiveness are high but cost pressures are moderate or low. What happens, however, when the company simultaneously faces both strong cost pressures and strong pressures for local responsiveness? How can managers balance out such competing and inconsistent demands? According to some researchers, pursuing a transnational strategy is the answer.

Two of these researchers, Christopher Bartlett and Sumantra Ghoshal, argue that, in today's global environment, competitive conditions are so intense that, to survive, companies must do all they can to respond to pressures for both cost reductions and local responsiveness. They must try to realize location economies and economies of scale from global volume, transfer distinctive competencies and skills within the company, and simultaneously pay attention to pressures for local responsiveness.[18]

Moreover, Bartlett and Ghoshal note that, in the modern, multinational enterprise, valuable competencies and resources do not reside just in the home country but can develop in any of the company's worldwide operations. Thus, they maintain that the flow of skills and product offerings should not be all one way, from home company to foreign subsidiary. Rather, the flow should also be from foreign subsidiary to home country, and from foreign subsidiary to foreign subsidiary. Transnational companies, in other words, must focus on leveraging subsidiary skills.

In essence, companies that pursue a **transnational strategy** are trying to develop a strategy that simultaneously achieves low costs, differentiates the product offering across geographic markets, and fosters a flow of resources such as process knowledge between different subsidiaries in the company's global network of operations. As attractive as this may sound, the strategy is not easy to pursue because it places conflicting demands on the company. Differentiating the product to respond to local demands in different geographic markets raises costs, which runs counter to the goal of reducing costs. Companies such as 3M and ABB (a Swiss-based, multinational engineering conglomerate) have tried to implement a transnational strategy and found it difficult.

Indeed, how best to implement a transnational strategy is one of the most complex questions that large, global companies grapple with today. It may be that few, if any, companies have perfected this strategic posture. But some clues to the right approach can be derived from a number of companies. Consider, for example, the case of Caterpillar. The need to compete with low-cost competitors such as Komatsu of Japan forced Caterpillar to look for greater cost economies. However, variations in construction practices and government regulations across countries meant that Caterpillar also had to be responsive to local demands. Therefore, it confronted significant pressures for cost reductions and for local responsiveness.

To deal with cost pressures, Caterpillar redesigned its products to use many identical components and invested in a few large-scale, component-manufacturing facilities, sited at favorable locations, to fill global demand and realize scale economies. At the same time, the company augments the centralized manufacturing of components with assembly plants in each of its major global markets. At these plants, Caterpillar adds local product features, tailoring the finished product to local needs. Thus, Caterpillar

transnational strategy
A business model that simultaneously achieves low costs, differentiates the product offering across geographic markets, and fosters a flow of skills between different subsidiaries in the company's global network of operations.

realizes many of the benefits of global manufacturing while reacting to pressures for local responsiveness by differentiating its product among national markets.[19] Caterpillar started to pursue this strategy in the 1980s. By the 2000s, it had succeeded in doubling output per employee, significantly reducing its overall cost structure in the process. Meanwhile, Komatsu and Hitachi, which are still wedded to a Japan-centric global strategy, have seen their cost advantages evaporate and have been steadily losing market share to Caterpillar.

However, building an organization capable of supporting a transnational strategy is a complex, challenging task. Indeed, some would say it is too complex because the strategy implementation problems of creating a viable organizational structure and set of control systems to manage this strategy are immense. We return to this issue in Chapter 12.

International Strategy

Sometimes it is possible to identify multinational companies that find themselves in the fortunate position of being confronted with low cost pressures and low pressures for local responsiveness. Typically these enterprises sell a product that serves universal needs, but because they do not face significant competitors, they are not confronted with pressures to reduce their cost structure. Xerox found itself in this position in the 1960s, after its invention and commercialization of the photocopier. Strong patents protected the technology comprising the photocopier, so for several years Xerox did not face competitors—it had a monopoly. Because the product was highly valued in most developed nations, Xerox was able to sell the same basic product all over the world and charge a relatively high price for it. At the same time, because it did not face direct competitors, the company did not have to deal with strong pressures to minimize its costs.

Historically, companies like Xerox have followed a similar pattern as they developed their international operations. They tend to centralize product development functions such as R&D at home. However, companies also tend to establish manufacturing and marketing functions in each major country or geographic region in which they do business. Although they may undertake some local customization of product offering and marketing strategy, this tends to be rather limited in scope. Ultimately, in most international companies, the head office retains tight control over marketing and product strategy.

Other companies that have pursued this strategy include P&G, which had historically always developed innovative new products in Cincinnati and thereafter transferred them wholesale to local markets. Microsoft has followed a similar strategy. The bulk of Microsoft's product development work takes place in Redmond, Washington, where the company is headquartered. Although some localization work is undertaken elsewhere, it is limited to producing foreign-language versions of popular Microsoft programs such as Office.

Changes in Strategy over Time

The Achilles heel of the international strategy is that, over time, competitors inevitably emerge, and if managers do not take proactive steps to reduce their cost structure, their company may be rapidly outflanked by efficient, global competitors. This is exactly what happened to Xerox. Japanese companies such as Canon ultimately invented their way around Xerox's patents, produced their own photocopying equipment in very efficient manufacturing plants, priced the machines below Xerox's products, and rapidly took global market share from Xerox. Xerox's demise was not due to the emergence of competitors, for ultimately that was bound to occur, but rather to its failure to proactively reduce its cost structure in advance of the emergence of competitors. The message here is that an international strategy may not be viable in the long term, and to survive, companies that are able to pursue it need to shift toward a global standardization strategy, or perhaps a transnational strategy, ahead of competitors (see Figure 8.4).

The same can be said about a localization strategy. Localization may give a company a competitive edge, but if it is simultaneously facing aggressive competitors, the company will also need to reduce its cost structure—and the only way to do that may be to adopt a transnational strategy. Thus, as competition intensifies, international and localization strategies tend to become less viable, and managers need to orientate their companies toward either a global standardization strategy or a transnational strategy. Strategy in Action 8.2 describes how this process occurred at Coca-Cola.

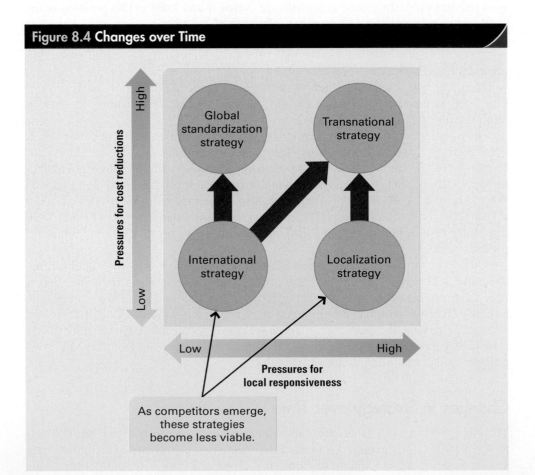

Figure 8.4 Changes over Time

8.2 STRATEGY IN ACTION

The Evolving Strategy of Coca-Cola

Coca-Cola, the Iconic American soda maker, has long been among the most international of enterprises. The company made its first move outside the United States in 1902, when it entered Cuba. By 1929, Coke was marketed in 76 countries. In World War II, Coke struck a deal to supply the U.S. military with Coca-Cola wherever soldiers might be stationed. During this era, the company built 63 bottling plants around the world. Its global push continued after the war, fueled in part by the belief that the U.S. market would eventually reach maturity and by the perception that huge growth opportunities awaited overseas. By 2012, Coca Cola was operating in more than 200 countries, and over 80% of Coke's case volume was in international markets.

Up until the early 1980s, Coke's strategy could best be characterized as one of considerable localization. Local operations were granted a high degree of independence to oversee operations as managers saw fit. This changed in the 1980s and 1990s, under the leadership of Roberto Goizueta, a talented Cuban immigrant who became the CEO of Coke in 1981. Goizueta placed renewed emphasis on Coke's flagship brands, which were extended with the introduction of Diet Coke, Cherry Coke, and similar flavors. His prime belief was that the main difference between the United States and international markets was the lower level of penetration overseas, where consumption per capita of colas was only 10 to 15% of the U.S. figure. Goizueta pushed Coke to become a global company, centralizing many management and marketing activities at the corporate headquarters in Atlanta, focusing on core brands, and taking equity stakes in foreign bottlers so that the company could exert more strategic control over them. This one-size-fits-all strategy was built around standardization and the realization of economies of scale by, for example, using the same advertising message worldwide.

Goizueta's global strategy was adopted by his successor, Douglas Ivester, but by the late 1990s, the drive toward a one-size-fits-all strategy was running out of steam, as smaller, more nimble local competitors that were marketing local beverages began to halt the Coke growth engine. When Coke began failing to hit its financial targets for the first time in a generation, Ivester resigned in 2000 and was replaced by Douglas Daft. Daft instituted a 180-degree shift in strategy. His belief was that Coke needed to put more power back in the hands of local country managers. He thought that strategy, product development, and marketing should be tailored to local needs. He laid off 6,000 employees, many of them in Atlanta, and granted country managers much greater autonomy. Moreover, in a striking move for a marketing company, he announced that the company would stop using global advertisements and placed advertising budgets and control over creative content back in the hands of country managers.

Ivester's move was, in part, influenced by the experience of Coke in Japan, the company's second most profitable market, where the bestselling Coca-Cola product is not a carbonated beverage but a canned, cold coffee drink, Georgia Coffee, which is sold from vending machines. The Japanese experience seemed to signal that products should be customized to local tastes and preferences, and that Coke would do well to decentralize more decision-making authority to local managers.

However, the shift toward localization didn't produce the growth that had been expected and, by 2002, the trend was moving back toward more central coordination, with Atlanta exercising *oversight* over marketing and product development in different nations outside the United States. But this time, it was not the one-size-fits-all ethos of the Goizueta era. Under the leadership of Neville Isdell, who became CEO in March 2004, senior managers at corporate headquarters now reviewed and helped to guide local marketing and product development. However, Isdell adopted the belief that strategy (including pricing, product offerings, and marketing message) should vary from market to market to match local conditions. Isdell's position, in other words, represented a midpoint

(continued)

between the strategy of Goizueta and the strategy of Daft. Moreover, Isdell has stressed the importance of leveraging good ideas across nations–such as Georgia Coffee, for example. Having seen the success of this beverage in Japan, in 2007, Coke entered into a strategic alliance with Illycaffè, one of Italy's premier coffee makers, to build a global franchise for canned or bottled cold coffee beverages. Similarly, in 2003, the Coke subsidiary in China developed a low-cost, noncarbonated, orange-based drink that has rapidly become one of the bestselling drinks in that nation. Sensing the potential of the drink, Coke rolled it out in other Asian countries such as Thailand, where it has been a huge hit.

Sources: "Orange Gold," *The Economist*, March 3, 2007, p. 68; P. Bettis, "Coke Aims to Give Pepsi a Routing in Cold Coffee War," *Financial Times*, October 17, 2007, p. 16; P. Ghemawat, *Redefining Global Strategy* (Boston, Mass: Harvard Business School Press, 2007); D. Foust, "Queen of Pop," *Business Week*, August 7, 2006, pp. 44–47; W. J. Holstein, "How Coca-Cola Manages 90 Emerging Markets," *Strategy+Business*, November 7, 2011, www.strategy-business.com/article/00093?pg=0.

THE CHOICE OF ENTRY MODE

Any firm contemplating entering a different national market must determine the best mode or vehicle for such entry. There are five primary choices of entry mode: exporting, licensing, franchising, entering into a joint venture with a host-country company, and setting up a wholly owned subsidiary in the host country. Each mode has advantages and disadvantages, and managers must weigh these carefully when deciding which mode to use.[20]

Exporting

Most manufacturing companies begin their global expansion as exporters and only later switch to one of the other modes for serving a foreign market. Exporting has two distinct advantages: It avoids the costs of establishing manufacturing operations in the host country, which are often substantial, and it may be consistent with scale economies and location economies. By manufacturing the product in a centralized location and then exporting it to other national markets, a company may be able to realize substantial scale economies from its global sales volume. That is how Sony came to dominate the global television market, how many Japanese auto companies originally made inroads into the U.S. auto market, and how Samsung gained share in the market for computer memory chips.

There are a number of drawbacks to exporting. First, exporting from the company's home base may not be appropriate if there are lower-cost locations for manufacturing the product abroad (that is, if the company can achieve location economies by moving production elsewhere). Thus, particularly in the case of a company pursuing a global standardization or transnational strategy, it may pay to manufacture in a location where conditions are most favorable from a value creation perspective and then export from that location to the rest of the globe. This is not so much an argument against exporting as it is an argument against exporting from the company's home country. For example, many U.S. electronics companies have moved some manufacturing to Asia because low-cost but highly skilled labor is available there. They export from Asia to the rest of the globe, including the United States (as Apple does with the iPhone).

Another drawback is that high transport costs can make exporting uneconomical, particularly in the case of bulk products. One way of alleviating this problem is to manufacture bulk products on a regional basis, thereby realizing some economies from large-scale production while limiting transport costs. Many multinational chemical companies manufacture their products on a regional basis, serving several countries in a region from one facility.

Tariff barriers, too, can make exporting uneconomical, and a government's threat to impose tariff barriers can make the strategy very risky. Indeed, the implicit threat from the U.S. Congress to impose tariffs on Japanese cars imported into the United States led directly to the decision by many Japanese auto companies to set up manufacturing plants in the United States.

Finally, a common practice among companies that are just beginning to export also poses risks. A company may delegate marketing activities in each country in which it does business to a local agent, but there is no guarantee that the agent will act in the company's best interest. Often, foreign agents also carry the products of competing companies and thus have divided loyalties. Consequently, agents may not perform as well as the company would if it managed marketing itself. One way to solve this problem is to set up a wholly owned subsidiary in the host country to handle local marketing. In this way, the company can reap the cost advantages that arise from manufacturing the product in a single location and exercise tight control over marketing strategy in the host country.

Licensing

International licensing is an arrangement whereby a foreign licensee purchases the rights to produce a company's product in the licensee's country for a negotiated fee (normally, royalty payments on the number of units sold). The licensee then provides most of the capital necessary to open the overseas operation.[21] The advantage of licensing is that the company does not have to bear the development costs and risks associated with opening up a foreign market. Licensing therefore can be a very attractive option for companies that lack the capital to develop operations overseas. It can also be an attractive option for companies that are unwilling to commit substantial financial resources to an unfamiliar or politically volatile foreign market where political risks are particularly high.

Licensing has three serious drawbacks, however. First, it does not give a company the tight control over manufacturing, marketing, and strategic functions in foreign countries that it needs to have in order to realize scale economies and location economies—as companies pursuing both global standardization and transnational strategies try to do. Typically, each licensee sets up its manufacturing operations. Hence, the company stands little chance of realizing scale economies and location economies by manufacturing its product in a centralized location. When these economies are likely to be important, licensing may not be the best way of expanding overseas.

Second, competing in a global marketplace may make it necessary for a company to coordinate strategic moves across countries so that the profits earned in one country can be used to support competitive attacks in another. Licensing, by its very nature, severely limits a company's ability to coordinate strategy in this way. A licensee is unlikely to let a multinational company take its profits (beyond those due in the form of royalty payments) and use them to support an entirely different licensee operating in another country.

Third, there is risk associated with licensing technological knowhow to foreign companies. For many multinational companies, technological knowhow forms the basis of their competitive advantage, and they want to maintain control over how this competitive advantage is put to use. By licensing its technology, a company can quickly lose control over it. RCA, for instance, once licensed its color television technology to a number of Japanese companies. The Japanese companies quickly assimilated RCA's technology and then used it to enter the U.S. market, where they soon gained a larger share of the U.S. market than the RCA brand holds.

There are ways of reducing this risk. One way is by entering into a cross-licensing agreement with a foreign firm. Under a cross-licensing agreement, a firm might license some valuable, intangible property to a foreign partner and, in addition to a royalty payment, also request that the foreign partner license some of its valuable knowhow to the firm. Such agreements are reckoned to reduce the risks associated with licensing technological knowhow, as the licensee realizes that if it violates the spirit of a licensing contract (by using the knowledge obtained to compete directly with the licensor), the licensor can do the same to it. Put differently, cross-licensing agreements enable firms to hold each other hostage, thereby reducing the probability that they will behave opportunistically toward each other.[22] Such cross-licensing agreements are increasingly common in high-technology industries. For example, the U.S. biotechnology firm Amgen licensed one of its key drugs, Neupogen, to Kirin, the Japanese pharmaceutical company. The license gives Kirin the right to sell Neupogen in Japan. In return, Amgen receives a royalty payment, and through a licensing agreement it gains the right to sell certain Kirin products in the United States.

Franchising

In many respects, franchising is similar to licensing, although franchising tends to involve longer-term commitments than licensing. Franchising is basically a specialized form of licensing in which the franchiser not only sells intangible property to the franchisee (normally a trademark), but also insists that the franchisee abide by strict rules governing how it does business. The franchiser will often assist the franchisee run the business on an ongoing basis. As with licensing, the franchiser typically receives a royalty payment, which amounts to a percentage of the franchisee revenues.

Whereas licensing is a strategy pursued primarily by manufacturing companies, franchising, which resembles it in some respects, is a strategy employed chiefly by service companies. McDonald's provides a good example of a firm that has grown by using a franchising strategy. McDonald's has set down strict rules as to how franchisees should operate a restaurant. These rules extend to controlling the menu, cooking methods, staffing policies, and restaurant design and location. McDonald's also organizes the supply chain for its franchisees and provides management training and financial assistance.[23]

The advantages of franchising are similar to those of licensing. Specifically, the franchiser does not need to bear the development costs and risks associated with opening up a foreign market on its own, for the franchisee typically assumes those costs and risks. Thus, using a franchising strategy, a service company can build up a global presence quickly and at a low cost.

The disadvantages of franchising are less pronounced than in licensing. Because service companies often use franchising, there is no reason to consider the need for coordination of manufacturing to achieve experience curve and location economies. But franchising may inhibit the firm's ability to take profits out of one country to support competitive attacks in another. A more significant disadvantage of franchising is quality control. The foundation of franchising arrangements is that the firm's brand name conveys a message to consumers about the quality of the firm's product. Thus, a business traveler checking in at a Four Seasons hotel in Hong Kong can reasonably expect the same quality of room, food, and service that would be received in New York, Hawaii, or Ontario, Canada. The Four Seasons name is assumed to guarantee consistent product quality. This presents a problem in that foreign franchisees may not be as concerned about quality as they are supposed to be, and the result of poor quality can cascade beyond lost sales in a particular foreign market to a decline in the firm's worldwide reputation. For example, if a business traveler has a bad experience at the Four Seasons in Hong Kong, he or she may never go to another Four Seasons hotel, and may urge colleagues to avoid the chain as well. The geographical distance of the firm from its foreign franchisees can make poor quality difficult to detect. In addition, the numbers of franchisees—in the case of McDonald's, tens of thousands—can make quality control difficult.

To reduce these problems, a company can set up a subsidiary in each country or region in which it is expanding. The subsidiary, which might be wholly owned by the company or a joint venture with a foreign company, then assumes the rights and obligations to establish franchisees throughout that particular country or region. The combination of proximity and the limited number of independent franchisees that need to be monitored reduces the quality control problem. Because the subsidiary is at least partly owned by the company, it can place its own managers in the subsidiary to ensure the level of quality monitoring it demands. This organizational arrangement has proved very popular in practice; it has been used by McDonald's, KFC, and Hilton Worldwide to expand international operations, to name just three examples.

Joint Ventures

Establishing a joint venture with a foreign company has long been a favored mode for entering a new market. The most typical form of joint venture is a 50/50 joint venture, in which each party takes a 50% ownership stake and a team of managers from both parent companies shares operating control. Some companies seek joint ventures wherein they become the majority shareholder (for example, a 51 to 49% ownership split), which permits tighter control by the dominant partner.[24]

Joint ventures have several advantages. First, a company may feel that it can benefit from a local partner's knowledge of a host country's competitive conditions, culture, language, political systems, and business systems. Second, when the development costs and risks of opening up a foreign market are high, a company might gain by sharing these costs and risks with a local partner. Third, in some countries, political considerations make joint ventures the only feasible entry mode. For example, historically, many U.S. companies found it much easier to obtain permission to set up operations in Japan if they joined with a Japanese partner than if they tried to enter on their own.

Despite the advantages, there are major disadvantages with joint ventures. First, as with licensing, a firm that enters into a joint venture risks yielding control of its technology to its partner. Thus, a proposed joint venture in 2002 between Boeing and Mitsubishi Heavy Industries to build Boeing's new, wide-body jet (the 787) raised fears that Boeing might unwittingly give its commercial airline technology to the Japanese. However, joint-venture agreements can be constructed to minimize this risk. One option is to hold majority ownership in the venture. This allows the dominant partner to exercise great control over its technology—but it can be difficult to find a foreign partner who is willing to settle for minority ownership. Another option is to "wall off" from a partner technology that is central to the core competence of the firm while sharing other technology.

A second disadvantage is that a joint venture does not give a firm the tight control over subsidiaries that it might need to realize experience-curve or location economies. Nor does it give a firm the control over a foreign subsidiary it might need for engaging in coordinated, global attacks against its rivals. Consider the entry of Texas Instruments (TI) into the Japanese semiconductor market. When TI established semiconductor facilities in Japan, it did so for the dual purpose of checking Japanese manufacturers' market share and limiting the cash they had available for invading TI's global market. In other words, TI was engaging in global strategic coordination. To implement this strategy, TI's subsidiary in Japan had to be prepared to take instructions from corporate headquarters regarding competitive strategy. The strategy also required the Japanese subsidiary to run at a loss if necessary. Few, if any, potential joint-venture partners would have been willing to accept such conditions, as it would have necessitated a willingness to accept a negative return on investment. Indeed, many joint ventures establish a degree of autonomy that would make such direct control over strategic decisions all but impossible to establish.[25] Thus, to implement this strategy, TI set up a wholly owned subsidiary in Japan.

Wholly Owned Subsidiaries

A wholly owned subsidiary is one in which the parent company owns 100% of the subsidiary's stock. To establish a wholly owned subsidiary in a foreign market, a company can either set up a completely new operation in that country or acquire an established host-country company to promote its products in the host market.

Setting up a wholly owned subsidiary offers three advantages. First, when a company's competitive advantage is based on its control of a technological competency, a wholly owned subsidiary will normally be the preferred entry mode because it reduces the company's risk of losing this control. Consequently, many high-tech companies prefer wholly owned subsidiaries to joint ventures or licensing arrangements. Wholly owned subsidiaries tend to be the favored entry mode in the semiconductor, computer, electronics, and pharmaceutical industries.

Second, a wholly owned subsidiary gives a company the kind of tight control over operations in different countries that it needs if it is going to engage in global strategic coordination—taking profits from one country to support competitive attacks in another.

Third, a wholly owned subsidiary may be the best choice if a company wants to realize location economies and the scale economies that flow from producing a standardized output from a single or limited number of manufacturing plants. When pressures on costs are intense, it may pay a company to configure its value chain in such a way that value added at each stage is maximized. Thus, a national subsidiary may specialize in manufacturing only part of the product line, or certain components of the end product, exchanging parts and products with other subsidiaries in the company's global system. Establishing such a global production system requires a high degree of control over the operations of national affiliates. Different national operations must be prepared to accept centrally determined decisions as to how they should produce, how much they should produce, and how their output should be priced for transfer between operations. A wholly owned subsidiary would have to comply with these mandates, whereas licensees or joint-venture partners would most likely shun such a subservient role.

On the other hand, establishing a wholly owned subsidiary is generally the most costly method of serving a foreign market. The parent company must bear all the costs and risks of setting up overseas operations—in contrast to joint ventures, where the costs and risks are shared, or licensing, where the licensee bears most of the costs and risks. But the risks of learning to do business in a new culture diminish if a company acquires an established host-country enterprise. Acquisitions, however, raise a whole set of additional problems, such as trying to marry divergent corporate cultures, and these may more than offset the benefits. (The problems associated with acquisitions are discussed in Chapter 10.)

Choosing an Entry Strategy

The advantages and disadvantages of the various entry modes are summarized in Table 8.1. Inevitably, there are tradeoffs in choosing one entry mode over another. For example, when considering entry into an unfamiliar country with a track record of nationalizing foreign-owned enterprises, a company might favor a joint venture with a local enterprise. Its rationale might be that the local partner will help it establish operations in an unfamiliar environment and speak out against nationalization should the possibility arise. But if the company's distinctive competency is based on proprietary technology, entering into a joint venture might mean risking loss of control over that technology to the joint venture partner, which would make this strategy unattractive. Despite such hazards, some generalizations can be offered about the optimal choice of entry mode.

Distinctive Competencies and Entry Mode When companies expand internationally to earn greater returns from their differentiated product offerings, entering markets where indigenous competitors lack comparable products, the companies are pursuing an international strategy. The optimal entry mode for such companies depends to some degree upon the nature of their distinctive competency. In particular, we need to distinguish between companies with a distinctive competency in technological knowhow and those with a distinctive competency in management knowhow.

If a company's competitive advantage—its distinctive competency—derives from its control of proprietary technological knowhow (i.e., intellectual property), licensing and joint-venture arrangements should be avoided if possible to minimize the risk of losing control of that technology. Thus, if a high-tech company is considering setting up operations in a foreign country in order to profit from a distinctive competency in technological knowhow, it should probably do so through a wholly owned subsidiary.

However, this should not be viewed as a hard-and-fast rule. For instance, a licensing or joint-venture arrangement might be structured in such a way as to reduce the

Table 8.1 The Advantages and Disadvantages of Different Entry Modes

Entry Mode	Advantages	Disadvantages
Exporting	• Ability to realize location- and scale-based economies	• High transport costs • Trade barriers • Problems with local marketing agents
Licensing	• Low development costs and risks	• Inability to realize location- and scale-based economies • Inability to engage in global strategic coordination • Lack of control over technology
Franchising	• Low development costs and risks	• Inability to engage in global strategic coordination • Lack of control over quality
Joint Ventures	• Access to local partner's knowledge • Shared development costs and risks • Political dependency	• Inability to engage in global strategic coordination • Inability to realize location- and scale-based economies • Lack of control over technology
Wholly Owned Subsidiaries	• Protection of technology • Ability to engage in global strategic coordination • Ability to realize location- and scale-based economies	• High costs and risks

risks that licensees or joint-venture partners will expropriate a company's technological knowhow. (We consider this kind of arrangement in more detail later in the chapter when we discuss the issue of structuring strategic alliances.) Or consider a situation where a company believes its technological advantage will be short lived and expects rapid imitation of its core technology by competitors. In this situation, the company might want to license its technology as quickly as possible to foreign companies in order to gain global acceptance of its technology before imitation occurs.[26] Such a strategy has some advantages. By licensing its technology to competitors, the company may deter them from developing their own, possibly superior, technology. It also may be able to establish its technology as the dominant design in the industry, ensuring a steady stream of royalty payments. Such situations aside, however, the attractions of licensing are probably outweighed by the risks of losing control of technology, and therefore licensing should be avoided.

The competitive advantage of many service companies such as McDonald's or Hilton Worldwide is based on management knowhow (i.e., process knowledge). For such companies, the risk of losing control of their management skills to franchisees or joint-venture partners is not that great. The reason is that the valuable asset of such companies is their brand name, and brand names are generally well protected by intellectual property laws pertaining to trademarks. Given this fact, many issues that arise in the case of technological knowhow do not arise in the case of management knowhow. As a result, many service companies favor a combination of franchising and subsidiaries to control franchisees within a particular country or region. The subsidiary may be wholly owned or a joint venture. In most cases, however, service companies have found that entering into a joint venture with a local partner in order to set up a controlling subsidiary in a country or region works best because a joint venture is often politically more acceptable and brings a degree of local knowledge to the subsidiary.

Pressures for Cost Reduction and Entry Mode   The greater the pressures for cost reductions, the more likely that a company will want to pursue some combination of exporting and wholly owned subsidiaries. By manufacturing in the locations where factor conditions are optimal and then exporting to the rest of the world, a company may be able to realize substantial location economies and substantial scale economies. The company might then want to export the finished product to marketing subsidiaries based in various countries. Typically, these subsidiaries would be wholly owned and have the responsibility for overseeing distribution in a particular country. Setting up wholly owned marketing subsidiaries is preferable to a joint-venture arrangement or using a foreign marketing agent because it gives the company the tight control over marketing that might be required to coordinate a globally dispersed value chain. In addition, tight control over a local operation enables the company to use the profits generated in one market to improve its competitive position in another market. Hence companies pursuing global or transnational strategies prefer to establish wholly owned subsidiaries.

◤ GLOBAL STRATEGIC ALLIANCES

Global strategic alliances are cooperative agreements between companies from different countries that are actual or potential competitors. Strategic alliances range from formal joint ventures in which two or more companies have an equity stake, to short-term contractual agreements in which two companies may agree to cooperate on a particular problem (such as developing a new product).

global strategic alliances Cooperative agreements between companies from different countries that are actual or potential competitors.

Advantages of Strategic Alliances

Companies enter into strategic alliances with competitors to achieve a number of strategic objectives.[27] First, strategic alliances may facilitate entry into a foreign market. For example, many firms feel that if they are to successfully enter the Chinese market, they need a local partner who understands business conditions and has good connections. Thus, Warner Brothers entered into a joint venture with two Chinese partners to produce and distribute films in China. As a foreign film company, Warner found that if it wanted to produce films on its own for the Chinese market, it had to go through a complex approval process for every film. It also had to farm out distribution to a local company, which made doing business in China very difficult. Due to the participation of Chinese firms, however, the joint-venture films will require a streamlined approval process, and the venture will be able to distribute any films it produces. Moreover, the joint venture will be able to produce films for Chinese TV, something that foreign firms are not allowed to do.[28]

Second, strategic alliances allow firms to share the fixed costs (and associated risks) of developing new products or processes. An alliance between Boeing and a number of Japanese companies to build Boeing's latest commercial jetliner, the 787, was motivated by Boeing's desire to share the estimated $8-billion investment required to develop the aircraft.

Third, an alliance is a way to bring together complementary skills and assets that neither company could easily develop on its own.[29] In 2011, for example, Microsoft and Nokia established an alliance aimed at developing and marketing smartphones that used Microsoft's Windows 8 operating system. Microsoft contributed its software engineering skills, particularly with regard to the development of a version of its Windows operating system for smartphones, and Nokia contributed its design, engineering, and marketing knowhow. The first phones resulting from this collaboration reached the market in late 2012 (Microsoft subsequently purchased Nokia's mobile phone business in 2013.)

Fourth, it can make sense to form an alliance that will help firms establish technological standards for the industry that will benefit them. This was also a goal of the alliance between Microsoft and Nokia. The idea is to try to establish Windows 8 as the de facto operating system for smartphones in the face of strong competition from Apple, with its iPhone, and Google, whose Android operating system was the most widely used smartphone operating system in the world in 2012.

Disadvantages of Strategic Alliances

The advantages we have discussed can be very significant. Despite this, some commentators have criticized strategic alliances on the grounds that they give competitors a low-cost route to new technology and markets.[30] For example, a few years ago, some commentators argued that many strategic alliances between U.S. and Japanese firms were part of an implicit Japanese strategy to keep high-paying, high-value-added jobs in Japan while gaining the project engineering and production process skills that underlie the competitive success of many U.S. companies.[31] They argued that Japanese success in the machine tool and semiconductor industries was built on U.S. technology acquired through strategic alliances. And they argued that U.S. managers were aiding the Japanese by entering alliances that channel new inventions to Japan and provide a U.S. sales and distribution network for the resulting products. Although such deals may generate short-term profits, the argument goes, in the long term, the result is to "hollow out" U.S. firms, leaving them with no competitive advantage in the global marketplace.

These critics have a point; alliances have risks. Unless a firm is careful, it can give away more than it receives. But there are so many examples of apparently successful alliances between firms—including alliances between U.S. and Japanese firms—that this position appears extreme. It is difficult to see how the Boeing–Mitsubishi alliance for the 787, or the long-term Fuji–Xerox alliance, fit the critics' thesis. In these cases, both partners seem to have gained from the alliance. Why do some alliances benefit both firms while others benefit one firm and hurt the other? The next section provides an answer to this question.

Making Strategic Alliances Work

The failure rate for international strategic alliances is quite high. For example, one study of 49 international strategic alliances found that two-thirds run into serious managerial and financial troubles within 2 years of their formation, and that although many of these problems are ultimately solved, 33% are rated as failures by the parties involved.[32] The success of an alliance seems to be a function of three main factors: partner selection, alliance structure, and the manner in which the alliance is managed.

Partner Selection   One key to making a strategic alliance work is selecting the right partner. A good partner has three principal characteristics. First, a good partner helps the company achieve strategic goals such as achieving market access, sharing the costs and risks of new-product development, or gaining access to critical core competencies. In other words, the partner must have capabilities that the company lacks and that it values. Second, a good partner shares the firm's vision for the purpose of the alliance. If two companies approach an alliance with radically different agendas, the chances are great that the relationship will not be harmonious and the partnership will end.

Third, a good partner is unlikely to try to exploit the alliance for its own ends—that is, to expropriate the company's technological knowhow while giving away little in return. In this respect, firms with reputations for fair play probably make the best partners. For example, IBM is involved in so many strategic alliances that it would not pay for the company to trample over its individual alliance partners.[33] This would tarnish IBM's reputation of being a good ally and would make it more difficult for it to attract alliance partners. Because IBM attaches great importance to its alliances, it is unlikely to engage in the kind of opportunistic behavior that critics highlight. Similarly, their reputations make it less likely (but by no means impossible) that such Japanese firms as Sony, Toshiba, and Fuji, which have histories of alliances with non-Japanese firms, would exploit an alliance partner.

To select a partner with these three characteristics, a company needs to conduct comprehensive research on potential alliance candidates. To increase the probability of selecting a good partner, the company should collect as much pertinent, publicly available information about potential allies as possible; collect data from informed third parties, including companies that have had alliances with the potential partners, investment bankers who have had dealings with them, and former employees; and get to know potential partners as well as possible before committing to an alliance. This last step should include face-to-face meetings between senior managers (and perhaps middle-level managers) to ensure that the chemistry is right.

Alliance Structure   Having selected a partner, the alliance should be structured so that the company's risk of giving too much away to the partner is reduced to an acceptable level. First, alliances can be designed to make it difficult (if not impossible) to transfer technology not meant to be transferred. Specifically, the design, development, manufacture, and service of a product manufactured by an alliance can be structured to "wall off" sensitive technologies to prevent their leakage to the other participant. In the alliance between General Electric and Snecma to build commercial aircraft engines, for example, GE reduced the risk of "excess transfer" by walling off certain steps of the production process. The modularization effectively cut off the transfer of what GE regarded as key competitive technology while permitting Snecma access to final assembly. Similarly, in the alliance between Boeing and the Japanese to build the 787, Boeing walled off research, design, and marketing functions considered central to its competitive position, while allowing the Japanese to share in production technology. Boeing also walled off new technologies not required for 787 production.[34]

opportunism
Seeking one's own self-interest, often through the use of guile.

Second, contractual safeguards can be written into an alliance agreement to guard against the risk of **opportunism** by a partner. For example, TRW has three strategic alliances with large Japanese auto component suppliers to produce seat belts, engine valves, and steering gears for sale to Japanese-owned auto assembly plants in the United States. TRW has clauses in each of its alliance contracts that bar the Japanese firms from competing with TRW to supply U.S.-owned auto companies with component parts. By doing this, TRW protects itself against the possibility that the Japanese companies are entering into the alliances merely as a means of gaining access to the North American market to compete with TRW in its home market.

Third, both parties in an alliance can agree in advance to exchange skills and technologies that the other covets, thereby ensuring a chance for equitable gain. Cross-licensing agreements are one way to achieve this goal.

Fourth, the risk of opportunism by an alliance partner can be reduced if the firm extracts a significant, credible commitment from its partner in advance. The long-term alliance between Xerox and Fuji to build photocopiers for the Asian market perhaps best illustrates this. Rather than enter into an informal agreement or a licensing arrangement (which Fujifilm initially preferred), Xerox insisted that Fuji invest in a 50/50 joint venture to serve Japan and East Asia. This venture constituted such a significant investment in people, equipment, and facilities that Fujifilm was committed from the outset to making the alliance work in order to earn a return on its investment. By agreeing to the joint venture, Fuji essentially made a credible commitment to the alliance. In turn, Xerox felt secure in transferring its photocopier technology to Fuji.

Managing the Alliance   Once a partner has been selected and an appropriate alliance structure agreed upon, the task facing the company is to maximize benefits from the alliance. One important ingredient of success appears to be sensitivity to cultural differences. Many differences in management style are attributable to cultural differences, and managers need to make allowances for these when dealing with their partners. Beyond this, maximizing benefits from an alliance seems to involve building trust between partners and learning from partners.[35]

Managing an alliance successfully requires building interpersonal relationships between the firms' managers, or what is sometimes referred to as *relational capital*.[36] This is one lesson that can be drawn from the strategic alliance between Ford and Mazda. Ford and Mazda set up a framework of meetings within which their managers not only discuss matters pertaining to the alliance, but also have time to get to know one another. The belief is that the resulting friendships help build trust and facilitate harmonious relations between the two firms. Personal relationships also foster an informal management network between the firms. This network can then be used to help solve problems arising in more formal contexts (such as in joint committee meetings between personnel from the two firms).

Academics have argued that a major determinant of how much knowledge a company acquires from an alliance is its ability to learn from its alliance partner.[37]

For example, in a study of 15 strategic alliances between major multinationals, Gary Hamel, Yves Doz, and C. K. Prahalad focused on a number of alliances between Japanese companies and Western (European or American) partners.[38] In every case in which a Japanese company emerged from an alliance stronger than its Western partner, the Japanese company had made a greater effort to learn. Few Western companies studied seemed to want to learn from their Japanese partners. They tended to regard the alliance purely as a cost-sharing or risk-sharing arrangement, rather than an opportunity to learn how a potential competitor does business.

For an example of an alliance in which there was a clear learning asymmetry, consider the agreement between General Motors and Toyota Motor Corp. to build the Chevrolet Nova. This alliance was structured as a formal joint venture, New United Motor Manufacturing, in which both parties had a 50% equity stake. The venture owned an auto plant in Fremont, California. According to one of the Japanese managers, Toyota achieved most of its objectives from the alliance: "We learned about U.S. supply and transportation. And we got the confidence to manage U.S. workers." All that knowledge was then quickly transferred to Georgetown, Kentucky, where Toyota opened a plant of its own. By contrast, although General Motors (GM) got a new product, the Chevrolet Nova, some GM managers complained that their new knowledge was never put to good use inside GM. They say that they should have been kept together as a team to educate GM's engineers and workers about the Japanese system. Instead, they were dispersed to different GM subsidiaries.

When entering an alliance, a company must take measures to ensure that it learns from its alliance partner and then puts that knowledge to good use within its own organization. One suggested approach is to educate all operating employees about the partner's strengths and weaknesses and make clear to them how acquiring particular skills will bolster their company's competitive position. For such learning to be of value, the knowledge acquired from an alliance must be diffused throughout the organization—which did not happen at GM. To spread knowledge, the managers involved in an alliance should be used as a resource to educate others within the company about the skills of the alliance partner.

KEY TERMS

multinational company 247
location economies 248
global standardization strategy 256
localization strategy 257
transnational strategy 258
global strategic alliances 269
opportunism 272

TAKEAWAYS FOR STRATEGIC MANAGERS

1. For some companies, international expansion represents a way of earning greater returns by transferring the skills and product offerings derived from their distinctive competencies to markets where indigenous competitors lack those skills. As barriers to international trade

have fallen, industries have expanded beyond national boundaries and industry competition, and opportunities have increased.

2. Because of national differences, it pays for a company to base each value creation activity it performs at the location where factor conditions are most conducive to the performance of that activity. This strategy is known as focusing on the attainment of location economies.

3. By building sales volume more rapidly, international expansion can help a company gain a cost advantage through the realization of scale economies and learning effects.

4. The best strategy for a company to pursue depends on the pressures it must cope with: pressures for cost reductions or for local responsiveness. Pressures for cost reductions are greatest in industries producing commodity-type products, where price is the main competitive weapon. Pressures for local responsiveness arise from differences in consumer tastes and preferences, as well as from national infrastructure and traditional practices, distribution channels, and host government demands.

5. Companies pursuing an international strategy transfer the skills and products derived from distinctive competencies to foreign markets, while undertaking some limited local customization.

6. Companies pursuing a localization strategy customize their product offerings, marketing strategies, and business strategies to national conditions.

7. Companies pursuing a global standardization strategy focus on reaping the cost reductions that come from scale economies and location economies.

8. Many industries are now so competitive that companies must adopt a transnational strategy. This involves a simultaneous focus upon reducing costs, transferring skills and products, and being locally responsive. Implementing such a strategy may prove difficult.

9. There are five different ways of entering a foreign market: exporting, licensing, franchising, entering into a joint venture, and setting up a wholly owned subsidiary. The optimal choice among entry modes depends on the company's strategy.

10. Strategic alliances are cooperative agreements between actual or potential competitors. The advantages of alliances are that they facilitate entry into foreign markets, enable partners to share the fixed costs and risks associated with new products and processes, facilitate the transfer of complementary skills between companies, and help companies establish technical standards.

11. The drawbacks of a strategic alliance are that the company risks giving away technological knowhow and market access to its alliance partner, while getting very little in return.

12. The disadvantages associated with alliances can be reduced if the company selects partners carefully, paying close attention to reputation, and structures the alliance in order to avoid unintended transfers of knowhow.

DISCUSSION QUESTIONS

1. Plot the position of the following companies on Figure 8.3: Microsoft, Google, Coca-Cola, Dow Chemicals, Pfizer, and McDonald's. In each case, justify your answer.

2. Are the following global standardization industries, or industries where localization is more important: bulk chemicals, pharmaceuticals, branded food products, moviemaking, television manufacture, personal computers, airline travel, fashion retailing?

3. Discuss how the need for control over foreign operations varies with the strategy and distinctive competencies of a company. What are the implications of this relationship for the choice of entry mode?

4. Licensing proprietary technology to foreign competitors is the best way to give up a company's competitive advantage. Discuss.

5. What kind of companies stand to gain the most from entering into strategic alliances with potential competitors? Why?

CLOSING CASE

Ford's Global Strategy

When Ford CEO Alan Mulally arrived at the company in 2006, after a long career at Boeing, he was shocked to learn that the company produced one Ford Focus for Europe, and a totally different one for the United- States. "Can you imagine having one Boeing 737 for Europe and one 737 for the United States?," he said at the time. Due to this product strategy, Ford was unable to buy common parts for the vehicles, could not share development costs, and couldn't use its European Focus plants to make cars for the United States, or vice versa. In a business where economies of scale are important, the result was high costs. Nor were these problems limited to the Ford Focus—the strategy of designing and building different cars for different regions was the standard approach at Ford.

Ford's long-standing strategy of regional models was based upon the assumption that consumers in different regions had different tastes and preferences, which required considerable local customization. Americans, it was argued, loved their trucks and SUVs, whereas Europeans preferred smaller, fuel-efficient cars. Notwithstanding such differences, Mulally still could not understand why small car models like the Focus or the Escape SUV, which were sold in different regions, were not built on the same platform and did not share common parts. In truth, the strategy probably had to do with the autonomy of different regions within Ford's organization, a fact that was deeply embedded in Ford's history as one of the oldest multinational corporations.

When the global financial crisis rocked the world's automobile industry in 2008-2009, and precipitated the steepest drop in sales since the Great Depression, Mulally decided that Ford had to change its traditional practices in order to get its costs under control. Moreover, he felt that there was no way that Ford would be able to compete effectively in the large, developing markets of China and India unless Ford leveraged its global scale to produce low-cost cars. The result was Mulally's "One Ford" strategy, which aims to create a handful of car platforms that Ford can use everywhere in the world.

Under this strategy, new models—such as the 2013 Fiesta, Focus, and Escape—share a common design, are built on a common platform, use the same parts, and will be built in identical factories around the world. Ultimately, Ford hopes to have only five platforms to deliver sales of more than 6 million vehicles by 2016. In 2006, Ford had 15 platforms that accounted for sales of 6.6 million vehicles. By pursuing this strategy, Ford can share the costs of design and tooling, and it can attain much greater scale economies in the production of component parts. Ford has stated that it will take about one-third out of the $1-billion cost of developing a new car model and should significantly reduce its $50-billion annual budget for component parts. Moreover, because the different factories producing these cars are identical in all respects, useful knowledge acquired through experience in one factory can quickly be transferred to other factories, resulting in systemwide cost savings.

Ford hopes this strategy will bring down costs sufficiently to enable it to improve profit margins in developed markets and achieve good margins at lower price points in hypercompetitive developing nations such as China, now the world's largest car market, where Ford currently trails global rivals such as General Motors and Volkswagen. Indeed, the strategy is central to Mulally's goal for growing Ford's sales from $5.5 million in 2010 to $8 million by 2015.

(continued)

Sources: M. Ramsey, "Ford SUV Marks New World Car Strategy," *The Wall Street Journal*, November 16, 2011; B. Vlasic, "Ford Strategy Will Call for Stepping up Expansion, Especially in Asia," *New York Times*, June 7, 2011; "Global Manufacturing Strategy Gives Ford Competitive Advantage," Ford Motor Company, http://media.ford .com/article_display.cfm?article_id=13633.

CASE DISCUSSION QUESTIONS

1. Why do you think that Ford historically made different cars in different regions? What are the advantages of Ford's historic strategy? What are the drawbacks?
2. What global developments forced Ford to rethink its historic strategy?
3. How will the "One Ford" strategy benefit Ford? What does this strategy mean for Ford's ability to compete in established markets like the United States and Europe, and emerging markets like China?
4. Using the framework outlined in this chapter and summarized in Figure 8.3, how would you describe Ford's global strategy?

NOTES

[1] World Trade Organization (WTO), *International Trade Statistics 2013* (Geneva: WHO, 2013).

[2] Ibid.; United Nations, *World Investment Report, 2013* (New York and Geneva: United Nations, 2013).

[3] P. Dicken, *Global Shift* (New York: Guilford Press, 1992).

[4] D. Pritchard, "Are Federal Tax Laws and State Subsidies for Boeing 7E7 Selling America Short?" *Aviation Week,* April 12, 2004, pp. 74–75.

[5] T. Levitt, "The Globalization of Markets," *Harvard Business Review,* May–June 1983, pp. 92–102.

[6] M. E. Porter, *The Competitive Advantage of Nations* (New York: Free Press, 1990). See also R. Grant, "Porter's Competitive Advantage of Nations: An Assessment," *Strategic Management Journal* 7 (1991): 535–548.

[7] Empirical evidence does seem to indicate that, on average, international expansion is linked to greater firm profitability. For recent examples, see M. A. Hitt, R. E. Hoskisson, and H. Kim, "International Diversification, Effects on Innovation and Firm Performance," *Academy of Management Journal* 40 (4) (1997): 767–98; S. Tallman and J. Li, "Effects of International Diversity and Product Diversity on the Performance of Multinational Firms," *Academy of Management Journal* 39 (1) (1996): 179–196.

[8] Porter, *Competitive Advantage of Nations.*

[9] See J. Birkinshaw and N. Hood, "Multinational Subsidiary Evolution: Capability and Charter Change in Foreign Owned Subsidiary Companies," *Academy of Management Review* 23 (October 1998): 773–795; A. K. Gupta and V. J. Govindarajan, "Knowledge Flows Within Multinational Corporations," *Strategic Management Journal* 21 (2000): 473–496; V. J. Govindarajan and A. K. Gupta, *The Quest for Global Dominance* (San Francisco: Jossey-Bass, 2001); T. S. Frost, J. M. Birkinshaw, and P. C. Ensign, "Centers of Excellence in Multinational Corporations," *Strategic Management Journal* 23 (2002): 997–1018; U. Andersson, M. Forsgren, and U. Holm, "The Strategic Impact of External Networks," *Strategic Management Journal* 23 (2002): 979–996.

[10] S. Leung, "Armchairs, TVs and Espresso: Is It McDonald's?," *The Wall Street Journal,* August 30, 2002, pp. A1, A6.

[11] C. K. Prahalad and Yves L. Doz, *The Multinational Mission: Balancing Local Demands and*

Global Vision (New York: Free Press, 1987). See also J. Birkinshaw, A. Morrison, and J. Hulland, "Structural and Competitive Determinants of a Global Integration Strategy," *Strategic Management Journal* 16 (1995): 637–655.

[12]J. E. Garten, "Walmart Gives Globalization a Bad Name," *Business Week*, March 8, 2004, p. 24.

[13]Prahalad and Doz, *Multinational Mission*. Prahalad and Doz actually talk about local responsiveness rather than local customization.

[14]Levitt, "Globalization of Markets."

[15]W.W. Lewis. *The Power of Productivity* (Chicago, University of Chicago Press, 2004).

[16]For an extended discussion, see G.S. Yip and G. Tomas M. Hult, *Total Global Strategy* (Boston: Pearson, 2012); A. M. Rugman and A. Verbeke, "A perspective on regional and global strategies of multinational enterprises," *Journal of International Business Studies* 35 (1) (2004): 3–18.

[17]Bartlett and Ghoshal, *Managing Across Borders*.

[18]Ibid.

[19]T. Hout, M. E. Porter, and E. Rudden, "How Global Companies Win Out," *Harvard Business Review* (September–October 1982), pp. 98–108.

[20]This section draws on numerous studies, including C. W. L. Hill, P. Hwang, and W. C. Kim, "An Eclectic Theory of the Choice of International Entry Mode," *Strategic Management Journal* 11 (1990): 117–28; C. W. L. Hill and W. C. Kim, "Searching for a Dynamic Theory of the Multinational Enterprise: A Transaction Cost Model," *Strategic Management Journal* 9 (Special Issue on Strategy Content, 1988): 93–104; E. Anderson and H. Gatignon, "Modes of Foreign Entry: A Transaction Cost Analysis and Propositions," *Journal of International Business Studies* 17 (1986): 1–26; F. R. Root, *Entry Strategies for International Markets* (Lexington, MA: D. C. Heath, 1980); A. Madhok, "Cost, Value and Foreign Market Entry: The Transaction and the Firm," *Strategic Management Journal* 18 (1997): 39–61; K. D. Brouthers and L. B. Brouthers, "Acquisition or Greenfield Start-Up?" *Strategic Management Journal* 21 (1) (2000): 89–97; X. Martin and R. Salmon, "Knowledge Transfer Capacity and Its Implications for the Theory of the Multinational Enterprise," *Journal of International Business Studies,* July 2003, p. 356; A. Verbeke, "The Evolutionary View of the MNE and the Future of Internalization Theory," *Journal of International Business Studies,* November 2003, pp. 498–515.

[21]F. J. Contractor, "The Role of Licensing in International Strategy," *Columbia Journal of World Business,* Winter 1982, pp. 73–83.

[22]Andrew E. Serwer, "McDonald's Conquers the World," *Fortune,* October 17, 1994, pp. 103–116.

[23]For an excellent review of the basic theoretical literature of joint ventures, see B. Kogut, "Joint Ventures: Theoretical and Empirical Perspectives," *Strategic Management Journal* 9 (1988): 319–32. More recent studies include T. Chi, "Option to Acquire or Divest a Joint Venture," *Strategic Management Journal* 21 (6), 2000: 665–688; H. Merchant and D. Schendel, "How Do International Joint Ventures Create Shareholder Value?" *Strategic Management Journal* 21 (7) (2000): 723–737; H. K. Steensma and M A. Lyles, "Explaining IJV Survival in a Transitional Economy Through Social Exchange and Knowledge Based Perspectives," *Strategic Management Journal* 21 (8), 2000: 831–851; J. F. Hennart and M. Zeng, "Cross Cultural Differences and Joint Venture Longevity," *Journal of International Business Studies,* December 2002, pp. 699–717.

[24]J. A. Robins, S. Tallman, and K. Fladmoe-Lindquist, "Autonomy and Dependence of International Cooperative Ventures," *Strategic Management Journal,* October 2002, pp. 881–902.

[25]C. W. L. Hill, "Strategies for Exploiting Technological Innovations," *Organization Science* 3 (1992): 428–441.

[26]See K. Ohmae, "The Global Logic of Strategic Alliances," *Harvard Business Review*, March–April 1989, pp. 143–154; G. Hamel, Y. L. Doz, and C. K. Prahalad, "Collaborate with Your Competitors and Win!" *Harvard Business Review,* January–February 1989, pp. 133–139; W. Burgers, C. W. L. Hill, and W. C. Kim, "Alliances in the Global Auto Industry," *Strategic Management Journal* 14 (1993): 419–432; P. Kale, H. Singh, and H. Perlmutter, "Learning and Protection of Proprietary Assets in Strategic Alliances: Building Relational Capital," *Strategic Management Journal* 21 (2000): 217–237.

[27]L. T. Chang, "China Eases Foreign Film Rules," *The Wall Street Journal,* October 15, 2004, p. B2.

[28]B. L. Simonin, "Transfer of Marketing Knowhow in International Strategic Alliances," *Journal of International Business Studies,*

Vol 30 issue 3 1999, pp. 463–91; J. W. Spencer, "Firms' Knowledge Sharing Strategies in the Global Innovation System," *Strategic Management Journal* 24 (2003): 217–233.

[29]Kale et al., "Learning and Protection of Proprietary Assets."

[30]R. B. Reich and E. D. Mankin, "Joint Ventures with Japan Give Away Our Future," *Harvard Business Review,* March–April 1986, pp. 78–90.

[31]J. Bleeke and D. Ernst, "The Way to Win in Cross-Border Alliances," *Harvard Business Review,* November–December 1991, pp. 127–135.

[32]E. Booker and C. Krol, "IBM Finds Strength in Alliances," *B to B,* February 10, 2003, pp. 3, 27.

[33]W. Roehl and J. F. Truitt, "Stormy Open Marriages Are Better," *Columbia Journal of World Business,* Summer 1987, pp. 87–95.

[34]See T. Khanna, R. Gulati, and N. Nohria, "The Dynamics of Learning Alliances: Competition, Cooperation, and Relative Scope," *Strategic Management Journal* 19 (1998): 193–210; Kale et al., "Learning and Protection of Proprietary Assets."

[35]Kale et al., "Learning and Protection of Proprietary Assets."

[36]Hamel et al., "Collaborate with Competitors"; Khanna et al., "The Dynamics of Learning Alliances"; E. W. K. Tang, "Acquiring Knowledge by Foreign Partners from International Joint Ventures in a Transition Economy: Learning by Doing and Learning Myopia," *Strategic Management Journal* 23 (2002): 835–854.

[37]Hamel et al., "Collaborate with Competitors."

[38]B. Wysocki, "Cross Border Alliances Become Favorite Way to Crack New Markets," *The Wall Street Journal,* March 4, 1990, p. A1.

CHAPTER 9

CORPORATE-LEVEL STRATEGY: HORIZONTAL INTEGRATION, VERTICAL INTEGRATION, AND STRATEGIC OUTSOURCING

sergign/Shutterstock.com

OPENING CASE

The Proposed Merger of Comcast and Time Warner Cable

In February 2014, Comcast and Time Warner announced their intention to merge—a deal worth about $45 billion. The merger would form the largest cable TV and Internet provider in the United States and enable the company to control 27 of the top 30 markets in the United States, and three-fourths of the overall cable market. The merger first had to be approved, however, by the Department of Justice (to assess antitrust concerns) and the Federal Communications Commission (FCC, which evaluates media deals to assess their influence on the public interest).

Drew Angerer/Getty Images

9.1 Discuss how corporate-level strategy can be used to strengthen a company's business model and business-level strategies

9.2 Define horizontal integration and discuss the primary advantages and disadvantages associated with this corporate-level strategy

9.3 Explain the difference between a company's internal value chain and the industry value chain

9.4 Describe why, and under what conditions, cooperative relationships such as strategic alliances and outsourcing may become a substitute for vertical integration

Comcast and Time-Warner argued that the deal would not significantly influence competition in the cable industry because the companies operated in nonoverlapping geographic markets, so customers would not be losing an option for getting cable service. They also argued that the merger would enable the companies to make investments that would provide customers with faster broadband, greater network reliability and security, better in-home Wi-Fi, and greater Video on Demand choices. As argued by David Cohen, Comcast's executive vice president, in front of a Senate panel: "I can make you and the members of this committee one absolute commitment, which is that there is nothing in this transaction that will cause anybody's cable bills to go up."

Opponents of the merger, however, argued that the size and scale of the merged company (particularly given that Comcast had recently acquired NBC Universal) would make the company dangerously powerful. Whereas the merger might not change the cable options available for end consumers, it definitely would change the options available for content providers such as Disney or Viacom, or on-demand programming providers such as Netflix, Cinema Now, Hulu, and others. The merged company's overwhelming bargaining power over suppliers could also create cost advantages other TV or Internet providers might be unable to match, thereby enabling it to squeeze competitors out of the market. For example, satellite operator Dish Network argued that the combined company would be able to use its size to force providers of content to lower their prices, and that companies such as Dish Network would be at a competitive disadvantage. Dish also argued that the merged company might undermine video services such as Netflix or Cinema Now by altering streaming speeds either at the "last mile" of the Internet (where it is delivered into people's homes) or at interconnection points between Internet providers. In support of this, Netflix noted that Comcast had already required the Netflix to pay "terminating access fees" to ensure that customers did not get a downgraded signal. If the cable companies downgraded the signal for on-demand providers, customers would abandon services like Netflix and turn to on-demand options the cable operators themselves were providing. Senator Al Franken pointed out that when Comcast had acquired NBC Universal in 2010, it had defended that vertical integration move by referring to Time Warner as a fierce competitor. "Comcast can't have it both ways," Franken argued. "It can't say that the existence of competition among distributors, including Time Warner Cable, was a reason to approve the NBC deal in 2010 and then turn around a few years later and say the absence of competition with Time Warner Cable is reason to approve this deal."

For Brian Roberts, CEO and chairman of Comcast, the merger would be yet another milestone in the megadeal acquisition spree he had used to grow the company into a $68-billion media behemoth. The deal was a more nuanced proposition for Robert Marcus, who had been CEO at Time Warner Cable for less than 2 months when the deal was announced: he would get a $79.9-million severance payoff to walk away. The investment bankers advising the deal also stood to rake in $140 million in fees. After a year of reviewing the proposed merger, the FCC announced it needed more time and would delay its decision until at least August 2015. Many industry observers, however, still thought the deal was likely to be approved.

Sources: V. Luckerson, "Dish Network Slams Potential Comcast-Time Warner Merger," www.Time.com, July 10, 2014; A. Fitzpatrick, "Time Warner Cable Outage Raises Questions about Comcast Merger," www.Time.com, August 28, 2014; A. Rogers, "Comcast Urges Congress to Back Time Warner Cable Merger," www.Time.com, April 11, 2014; D. Pomerant, "Netflix Calls on the FCC to Deny the Time Warner Comcast Merger," www.Forbes.com, August 26, 2014, p.1; A. Timms, "Deals of the Year 2014: Comcast Faces Screen Test," *Institutional Investor*, December 2014.

◤ OVERVIEW

The overriding goal of managers is to maximize the value of a company for its shareholders. The Opening Case about the proposed merger between Comcast and Time Warner illustrates how companies might horizontally integrate to achieve greater economies of scale or bargaining power over suppliers and customers. This is likely to benefit Comcast and Time Warner's shareholders, although the net effect on consumer welfare is in question.

In general, corporate-level strategy involves choices strategic managers must make: (1) deciding in which businesses and industries a company should compete; (2) selecting which value creation activities it should perform in those businesses; and (3) determining how it should enter, consolidate, or exit businesses or industries to maximize long-term profitability. When formulating corporate-level strategy, managers must adopt a long-term perspective and consider how changes taking place in an industry and in its products, technology, customers, and competitors will affect their company's current business model and its future strategies. They then decide how to implement specific corporate-level strategies that redefine their company's business model to allow it to increase its competitive advantage in a changing industry environment by taking advantage of opportunities and countering threats. Thus, the principal goal of corporate-level strategy is to enable a company to sustain or promote its competitive advantage and profitability in its present business—*and in any new businesses or industries that it chooses to enter*.

This chapter is the first of two that describe the role of corporate-level strategy in repositioning and redefining a company's business model. We discuss three corporate-level strategies—horizontal integration, vertical integration, and strategic outsourcing—that are primarily directed toward improving a company's competitive advantage and profitability in its current business or industry. Diversification, which entails entry into new kinds of businesses or industries, is examined in the next chapter, along with guidelines for choosing the most profitable way to enter new businesses or industries, or to exit others. By the end of this chapter and the next, you will understand how the different levels of strategy contribute to the creation of a successful, profitable business or multibusiness model. You will also be able to distinguish between the types of corporate strategies managers use to maximize long-term company profitability.

◤ CORPORATE-LEVEL STRATEGY AND THE MULTIBUSINESS MODEL

The choice of corporate-level strategies is the final part of the strategy-formulation process. Corporate level strategies drive a company's business model over time and determine which types of business- and functional-level strategies managers will choose to maximize long-term profitability. The relationship between business-level strategy and functional-level strategy was discussed in Chapter 5. Strategic managers develop a business model and strategies that use their company's distinctive competencies to strive for a cost-leadership position and/or to differentiate its products. Chapter 8 described how global strategy is an extension of these basic principles.

In this chapter and the next, we repeatedly emphasize that, to increase profitability, a corporate-level strategy should enable a company or one or more of its business divisions or units *to perform value-chain functional activities (1) at a lower cost and/or (2) in a way that results in increased differentiation*. Only when it selects the appropriate corporate-level strategies can a company choose the pricing option (lowest, average, or premium price) that will allow it to maximize profitability. In addition, corporate-level strategy will increase profitability if it helps a company reduce industry rivalry by reducing the threat of damaging price competition. In sum, a company's corporate-level strategies should be chosen to promote the success of its business-level strategies, which allows it to achieve a sustainable competitive advantage, leading to higher profitability.

Many companies choose to expand their business activities beyond one market or industry and enter others. When a company decides to expand into new industries, it must construct its business model at two levels. First, it must develop a business model and strategies for each business unit or division in every industry in which it competes. Second, it must develop a higher-level *multibusiness model* that justifies its entry into different businesses and industries. This multibusiness model should explain how and why entering a new industry will allow the company to use its existing functional competencies and business strategies to increase its overall profitability. This model should also explain any other ways in which a company's involvement in more than one business or industry can increase its profitability. IBM, for example, might argue that its entry into online computer consulting, data storage, and cloud computing enables it to offer its customers a lineup of computer services that allows it to better compete with HP, Oracle, and Amazon.com. Apple might argue that its entry into digital music and entertainment has given it a commanding lead over rivals such as Sony, Google, and Microsoft.

This chapter first focuses on the advantages of staying inside one industry by pursuing horizontal integration. It then looks at why companies use vertical integration and expand into new industries. In the next chapter, we examine two principal corporate strategies companies use to enter new industries to increase their profitability—related and unrelated diversification—and several other strategies companies use to enter and compete in new industries.

◤ HORIZONTAL INTEGRATION: SINGLE-INDUSTRY CORPORATE STRATEGY

Managers use corporate-level strategy to identify industries in which their company should compete in order to maximize its long-term profitability. For many companies, profitable growth and expansion often entail finding ways to successfully compete within a single market or industry over time. In other words, a company confines its value creation activities to just one business or industry. Examples of such single-business companies include McDonald's, with its focus on the global fast-food business, and Wal-Mart, with its focus on global discount retailing.

Staying within one industry allows a company to focus all of its managerial, financial, technological, and functional resources and capabilities on competing successfully in one area. This is important in fast-growing, changing industries in which demands on a company's resources and capabilities are likely to be substantial, but where the long-term profits from establishing a competitive advantage are also likely to be substantial.

A second advantage of staying within a single industry is that a company "sticks to the knitting," meaning that it stays focused on what it knows and does best. A company does not make the mistake of entering new industries in which its existing resources and capabilities create little value and/or where a whole new set of competitive industry forces—new competitors, suppliers, and customers—present unanticipated threats. Coca-Cola, like many other companies, has committed this strategic error in the past. Coca-Cola once decided to expand into the movie business and acquired Columbia Pictures; it also acquired a large California winemaker. It soon found it lacked the competencies to successfully compete in these new industries and had not foreseen the strong competitive forces that existed in these industries from movie companies such as Paramount and winemakers such as Gallo. Coca-Cola concluded that entry into these new industries had reduced rather than created value and lowered its profitability; it divested or sold off these new businesses at a significant loss.

Even when a company stays in one industry, sustaining a successful business model over time can be difficult because of changing conditions in the environment, such as advances in technology that allow new competitors into the market, or because of changing customer needs. Two decades ago, the strategic issue facing telecommunications providers was how to shape their landline phone services to best meet customer needs in local and long-distance telephone service. However, when wireless telephone service emerged and quickly gained in popularity, landline providers like Verizon and AT&T had to quickly change their business models, lower the price of landline service, merge with wireless companies, and offer broadband services to ensure their survival.

Even within one industry, it is very easy for strategic managers to fail to see the "forest" (changing nature of the industry that results in new product/market opportunities) for the "trees" (focusing only on how to position current products). A focus on corporate-level strategy can help managers anticipate future trends and then change their business models to position their companies to compete successfully in a changing environment. Strategic managers must not become so committed to improving their company's *existing* product or service lines that they fail to recognize *new* product or service opportunities and threats. Apple has been so successful because it recognized the increasing number of product opportunities offered by digital entertainment. The task for corporate-level managers is to analyze how emerging technologies will impact their business models, how and why these technologies might change customer needs and customer groups in the future, and what kinds of new distinctive competencies will be needed to respond to these changes.

One corporate-level strategy that has been widely used to help managers strengthen their company's business model is horizontal integration, a strategy illustrated in the Opening Case. **Horizontal integration** is the process of acquiring or merging with industry competitors to achieve the competitive advantages that arise from a large size and scope of operations. An **acquisition** occurs when one company uses capital resources such as stock, debt, or cash, to purchase another company. A **merger** is an agreement between equals to pool their operations and create a new entity.

Mergers and acquisitions are common in most industries. In the aerospace industry, Boeing merged with McDonnell Douglas to create the world's largest aerospace company; in the pharmaceutical industry, Pfizer acquired Warner-Lambert to become the largest pharmaceutical firm; and global airlines are increasingly merging their

horizontal integration
The process of acquiring or merging with industry competitors to achieve the competitive advantages that arise from a large size and scope of operations.

acquisition
When a company uses its capital resources to purchase another company.

merger
An agreement between two companies to pool their resources and operations and join together to better compete in a business or industry.

operations in order to rationalize the number of flights offered between destinations and increase their market power. The pace of mergers and acquisitions has been rising as companies try to gain a competitive advantage over their rivals. This is because horizontal integration often significantly improves the competitive advantage and profitability of companies whose managers choose to stay within one industry and focus on managing its competitive position to keep the company at the value creation frontier.

Benefits of Horizontal Integration

In pursuing horizontal integration, managers invest their company's capital resources to purchase the assets of industry competitors to increase the profitability of its single-business model. Profitability increases when horizontal integration (1) lowers the cost structure, (2) increases product differentiation, (3) leverages a competitive advantage more broadly, (4) reduces rivalry within the industry, and (5) increases bargaining power over suppliers and buyers.

Lower Cost Structure   Horizontal integration can lower a company's cost structure because it creates increasing *economies of scale*. Suppose five major competitors exist, each of which operates a manufacturing plant in some region of the United States, but none of the plants operate at full capacity. If one competitor buys another and closes that plant, it can operate its own plant at full capacity and reduce its manufacturing costs. Achieving economies of scale is very important in industries that have a high-fixed-cost structure. In such industries, large-scale production allows companies to spread their fixed costs over a large volume, and in this way drive down average unit costs. In the telecommunications industry, for example, the fixed costs of building advanced 4G and LTE broadband networks that offer tremendous increases in speed are enormous, and to make such an investment profitable, a large volume of customers is required. Thus, AT&T and Verizon purchased other telecommunications companies to acquire their customers, increase their customer base, increase utilization rates, and reduce the cost of servicing each customer. In 2011, AT&T planned to acquire T-Mobile, but abandoned the deal in response to antitrust concerns raised by the U.S. Department of Justice and the FCC. Similar considerations were involved in the hundreds of acquisitions that have taken place in the pharmaceutical industry in the last decade because of the need to realize scale economies in research and development (R&D) and sales and marketing. The fixed costs of building a nationwide pharmaceutical sales force are enormous, and pharmaceutical companies such as Pfizer and Merck must possess a wide portfolio of drugs to sell to effectively make use of their sales forces.

A company can also lower its cost structure when horizontal integration allows it to *reduce the duplication of resources* between two companies, such as by eliminating the need for two sets of corporate head offices, two separate sales teams, and so forth. Notably, however, these cost savings are often overestimated. If two companies are operating a function such as a call center, for example, and both are above the minimum efficient scale for operating such a center, there may be few economies from consolidating operations: If each center was already optimally utilized, the consolidated call center could require just as many service people, computers, phone lines, and real estate as the two call centers previously required. Similarly, one justification made for banks consolidating during the late 1990s was that they could save by consolidating their information technology (IT) resources. Ultimately, however, most merged banks realized that their potential savings were meager at best, and the costs of attempting to harmonize their information systems were high; thus, most of them continued to run the separate legacy systems they had prior to merging.

Increased Product Differentiation   Horizontal integration may also increase profitability when it increases product differentiation; for example, by increasing the flow of innovative products that a company's sales force can sell to customers at premium prices. Desperate for new drugs to fill its pipeline, for example, Eli Lilly paid $6.5 billion to ImClone Systems to acquire its new, cancer-preventing drugs in order to outbid rival Bristol-Myers Squibb. Google, anxious to provide its users with online coupons, offered to pay $6 billion for Groupon to fill this niche in its online advertising business in order to increase its differentiation advantage—and reduce industry rivalry. Similarly, in the opening case, Comcast argued to the FCC that a merger with Time Warner Cable would enable the companies to offer faster, more reliable, more secure internet service to their customers.

Horizontal integration may also increase differentiation when it allows a company to combine the product lines of merged companies so that it can offer customers a wider range of products that can be bundled together. **Product bundling** involves offering customers the opportunity to purchase a range of products at a single, combined price. This increases the value of a company's product line because customers often obtain a price discount when purchasing a set of products at one time, and customers become used to dealing with only one company and its representatives. A company may obtain a competitive advantage from increased product differentiation.

Another way to increase product differentiation is through **cross-selling**, which is when a company takes advantage of or leverages its established relationship with customers by way of acquiring additional product lines or categories that it can sell to them. In this way, a company increases differentiation because it can provide a "total solution" and satisfy all of a customer's specific needs. Cross-selling and becoming a total-solution provider is an important rationale for horizontal integration in the computer sector, where IT companies attempt to increase the value of their offerings by satisfying all of the hardware and service needs of corporate customers. Providing a total solution saves customers' time and money because they do not have to work with several suppliers, and a single sales team can ensure that all the components of a customer's IT seamlessly work together. When horizontal integration increases the differentiated appeal and value of the company's products, the total solution provider gains market share.

Leveraging a Competitive Advantage More Broadly   For firms that have resources or capabilities that could be valuably deployed across multiple market segments or geographies, horizontal integration may offer opportunities to become more profitable. In the retail industry, for example, Wal-Mart's enormous bargaining power with suppliers and its exceptional efficiency in inventory logistics enabled it to have a competitive advantage in other discount retail store formats, such as its chain of Sam's Clubs (an even-lower-priced warehouse segment). It also expanded the range of products it offers customers when it entered the supermarket business and established a nationwide chain of Wal-Mart supercenters that sell groceries as well as all the clothing, toys, and electronics sold in regular Wal-Mart stores. It has also replicated its business model globally, although not always with as much success as it has had in the United States because many of its efficiencies in logistics (such as its hub-and-spoke distribution system and inventory tracked by satellite) employ fixed assets that are geographically limited (see the Strategy in Action 9.1 for more on this).

product bundling
Offering customers the opportunity to purchase a range of products at a single, combined price; this increases the value of a company's product line because customers often obtain a price discount when purchasing a set of products at one time, and customers become used to dealing with only one company and its representatives.

cross-selling
When a company takes advantage of or leverages its established relationship with customers by way of acquiring additional product lines or categories that it can sell to them. In this way, a company increases differentiation because it can provide a "total solution" and satisfy all of a customer's specific needs.

9.1 STRATEGY IN ACTION

Wal-Mart's Expansion into Other Retail Formats

In 2014, Wal-Mart was the largest firm in the world, with sales of $485.7 billion, more than 11,000 stores worldwide, and employing 2.2 million people. However, as the U.S. discount retail market was mature (where Wal-Mart earned 70% of its revenues), it looked for other opportunities to apply its exceptional retailing power and expertise. In the United States it had expanded into supercenters that sold groceries in addition to general merchandise and even-lower-priced warehouse store formats (Sam's Club), both of which were doing well. These stores could directly leverage Wal-Mart's bargaining power over suppliers (for many producers of general merchandise, Wal-Mart accounted for more than 70% of their sales, giving it unrivaled power to negotiate prices and delivery terms), and benefitted from its exceptionally efficient system for transporting, managing, and tracking inventory. Wal-Mart had invested relatively early in advanced information technology: it adopted radio frequency identification (RFID) tagging well ahead of its competitors, and satellites tracked inventory in real time. Wal-Mart knew where each item of inventory was at all times and when it had sold, enabling it to simultaneously minimize its inventory holding costs while optimizing the inventory mix in each store. As a result, it had higher sales per square foot and inventory turnover than either Target or Kmart. It handled inventory through a massive, hub-and-spoke distribution system that included more than 140 distribution centers that each served approximately 150 stores within a 150-mile radius. As supercenters and Sam's Clubs were also approaching saturation, however, growth had become harder and harder to sustain. Wal-Mart began to pursue other types of expansion opportunities. It expanded into smaller-format neighborhood stores, international stores (many of which were existing chains that were acquired), and was considering getting into organic foods and trendy fashions. While expansion into contiguous geographic regions (e.g., Canada and Mexico) had gone well, its success at overseas expansions was spottier. Wal-Mart's forays into Germany and South Korea, for example, resulted in large losses, and it ultimately exited the markets. Wal-Mart's entry into Japan was also not as successful as hoped, resulting in many years of losses and never gaining a large share of the market. The challenge was that many of these markets already had tough competitors by the time Wal-Mart entered—they weren't the sleepy, underserved markets that had initially helped it grow in the United States. Furthermore, Wal-Mart's IT and logistics advantages could not easily be leveraged into overseas markets—they would require massive, upfront investments to replicate, and it would be hard to break even on those investments without achieving massive scale in those markets. This rasied important questions such as: "Which of Wal-Mart's advantages could be leveraged overseas and to which markets?" "Was Wal-Mart better off trying to diversify its product offerings within North America?" "Should it perhaps reconsider its growth objectives altogether?"

Source: www.walmart.com.

Reduced Industry Rivalry   Horizontal integration can help to reduce industry rivalry in two ways. First, acquiring or merging with a competitor helps to *eliminate excess capacity* in an industry, which, as we discuss in Chapter 6, often triggers price wars. By taking excess capacity out of an industry, horizontal integration creates a more benign environment in which prices might stabilize—or even increase.

Second, by reducing the number of competitors in an industry, horizontal integration often makes it easier to implement *tacit price coordination* between rivals; that is, coordination reached without communication. (Explicit communication to fix prices is illegal in most countries.) In general, the larger the number of competitors in an industry, the more difficult it is to establish informal pricing agreements—such as price leadership by the dominant company—which increases the possibility that a price war will erupt. By increasing industry concentration and creating an oligopoly, horizontal integration can make it easier to establish tacit coordination among rivals.

Both of these motives seem to have been behind Oracle's many software acquisitions. There was significant excess capacity in the corporate software industry, and major competitors were offering customers discounted prices that had led to a price war and falling profit margins. Oracle hoped to eliminate excess industry capacity, which would reduce price competition.

Increased Bargaining Power   Finally, horizontal integration allows some companies to obtain bargaining power over suppliers or buyers and increase profitability at their expense. By consolidating the industry through horizontal integration, a company becomes a much larger buyer of suppliers' products and uses this as leverage to bargain down the price it pays for its inputs, thereby lowering its cost structure. Wal-Mart, for example, is well known for pursuing this strategy, and it may also have been a major motivation for the proposed merger of Comcast and Time Warner described in the Opening Case. Consolidation among competitors also gives companies more bargaining power over customers: By gaining control over a greater percentage of an industry's product or output, a company can increase its power to raise prices and profits because customers have less choice of suppliers and are more dependent on the company for their products. When a company has greater ability to raise prices to buyers or bargain down the price paid for inputs, it has obtained increased market power.

Problems with Horizontal Integration

Although horizontal integration can strengthen a company's business model in several ways, there are problems, limitations, and dangers associated with pursuing this corporate-level strategy. Implementing a horizontal integration strategy is no easy task for managers. As we discuss in Chapter 10, there are several reasons why mergers and acquisitions may fail to result in higher profitability: problems associated with merging very different company cultures; high management turnover in the acquired company when the acquisition is a hostile one; and a tendency of managers to overestimate the potential benefits from a merger or acquisition and underestimate the problems involved in merging their operations.

When a company uses horizontal integration to become a dominant industry competitor in the United States, it may come into conflict with the Federal Trade Commission (FTC) or the Department of Justice (DOJ), two government agencies that help to enforce antitrust laws. Antitrust authorities are concerned about the potential for abuse of market power; more competition is generally better for consumers than less competition. Antitrust authorities are likely to intervene when a few companies within one industry try to make acquisitions that will allow them to raise consumer prices above the level that would exist in a more competitive situation, and thus abuse their market power. The FTC and DOJ try to prevent dominant companies from using their market power to crush potential competitors, for example, by cutting prices when a new competitor enters the industry and forcing the competitor out of business, then raising prices after the threatening company has been eliminated.

Because of these concerns, any merger or acquisition the FTC perceives as creating too much consolidation, and the *potential* for future abuse of market power, may, for antitrust reasons, be blocked. The proposed merger between the two dominant satellite radio companies Sirius and XM was blocked for months until it became clear that customers had many other options to obtain high-quality radio programming—for example, through their computers and cell phones—so substantial competition would still exist in the industry. Similarly, as discussed in the Opening Case, in 2015 the FTC was still in the process of reviewing the Comcast/Time Warner merger to evaluate whether it would harm the public interest.

▚ VERTICAL INTEGRATION: ENTERING NEW INDUSTRIES TO STRENGTHEN THE "CORE" BUSINESS MODEL

Many companies that use horizontal integration to strengthen their business model and improve their competitive position also use the corporate-level strategy of vertical integration for the same purpose. When pursuing vertical integration, however, a company is entering new industries to support the business model of its "core" industry, that is, the industry which is the primary source of its competitive advantage and profitability. At this point, therefore, a company must formulate a multibusiness model that explains how entry into a new industry using vertical integration will enhance its long-term profitability. The model that justifies the pursuit of vertical integration is based on a company entering industries that *add value* to its core products because this increases product differentiation and/or lowers its cost structure, thus increasing its profitability.

vertical integration

When a company expands its operations either backward into an industry that produces inputs for the company's products (backward vertical integration) or forward into an industry that uses, distributes, or sells the company's products (forward vertical integration).

A company pursuing a strategy of **vertical integration** expands its operations either backward into an industry that produces inputs for the company's products (*backward vertical integration*) or forward into an industry that uses, distributes, or sells the company's products (*forward vertical integration*). To enter an industry, it may establish its own operations and build the value chain needed to compete effectively, or it may acquire a company that is already in the industry. A steel company that supplies its iron ore needs from company-owned iron ore mines illustrates backward integration. A maker of personal computers (PCs) that sells its laptops through company-owned retail outlets illustrates forward integration. For example, Apple entered the retail industry in 2001 when it decided to establish a chain of Apple stores to sell, promote, and service its products. IBM is a highly vertically integrated company; it integrated backward into the chip and memory disk industry to produce the components that work inside its mainframes and servers, and integrated forward into the computer software and consulting services industries.

Figure 9.1 illustrates four *main* stages in a typical raw-materials-to-customer value-added chain. For a company based in the final assembly stage, backward integration means moving into component parts manufacturing and raw materials production.

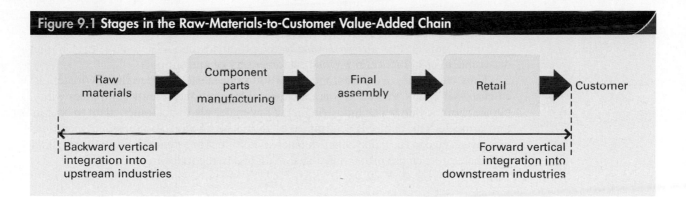

Figure 9.1 Stages in the Raw-Materials-to-Customer Value-Added Chain

Forward integration means moving into distribution and sales (retail). At each stage in the chain *value is added* to the product, transforming it in such a way that it is worth more to the company at the next stage in the chain and, ultimately, to the customer. It is important to note that each stage of the value-added chain involves a separate industry, or industries, in which many different companies compete. Moreover, within each industry, each company has a value chain composed of the value creation activities we discussed in Chapter 3: R&D, production, marketing, customer service, and so on. In other words, we can think of a value chain that runs *across* industries, and embedded within that are the value chains of companies *within* each industry.

As an example of the value-added concept, consider how companies in each industry involved in the production of a PC contribute to the final product (Figure 9.2). The first stage in the chain includes raw-materials companies that make specialty ceramics, chemicals, and metal, such as Kyocera of Japan, which manufactures the ceramic substrate for semiconductors. Companies at the first stage in the chain sell their products to the makers of PC component products such as Intel and AMD, which transform the ceramics, chemicals, and metals they purchase into PC components such as microprocessors, disk drives, and memory chips. In the process, companies *add value* to the raw materials they purchase. At the third stage, the manufactured components are sold to PC makers such as Apple, Dell, and HP, and these companies decide which components to purchase and assemble to *add value* to the finished PCs (that they make or outsource to a contract manufacturer). At stage four, the finished PCs are then either

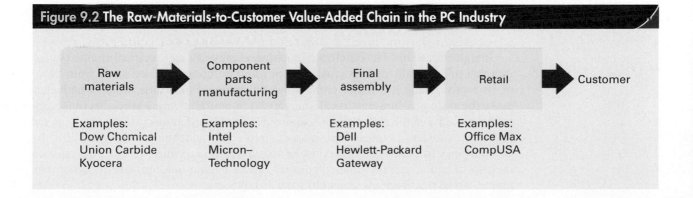

Figure 9.2 The Raw-Materials-to-Customer Value-Added Chain in the PC Industry

sold directly to the final customer over the Internet, or sold to retailers such as Best Buy and Staples, which distribute and sell them to the final customer. Companies that distribute and sell PCs also *add value* to the product because they make the product accessible to customers and provide customer service and support.

Thus, companies in different industries add value at each stage in the raw-materials-to-customer chain. Viewed in this way, vertical integration presents companies with a choice about within which industries in the raw-materials-to-customer chain to operate and compete. This choice is determined by the degree to which establishing operations at a given stage in the value chain will increase product differentiation or lower costs—and therefore increase profitability—as we discuss in the following section.

Increasing Profitability Through Vertical Integration

As noted earlier, a company pursues vertical integration to strengthen the business model of its original or core business and to improve its competitive position.[1] Vertical integration increases product differentiation, lowers costs, or reduces industry competition when it (1) facilitates investments in efficiency-enhancing, specialized assets, (2) protects product quality, and (3) results in improved scheduling.

Facilitating Investments in Specialized Assets   A specialized asset is one that is designed to perform a specific task and the value of which is significantly reduced in its next-best use.[2] The asset may be a piece of equipment that has a firm-specific use or the knowhow or skills that a company or employees have acquired through training and experience. Companies invest in specialized assets because these assets allow them to lower their cost structure or to better differentiate their products, which facilitates premium pricing. A company might invest in specialized equipment to lower manufacturing costs, as Toyota does, for example, or it might invest in an advanced technology that allows it to develop better-quality products than its rivals, as Apple does. Thus, specialized assets can help a company achieve a competitive advantage at the business level.

Just as a company invests in specialized assets in its own industry to build competitive advantage, it is often necessary that suppliers invest in specialized assets to produce the inputs that a specific company needs. By investing in these assets, a supplier can make higher-quality inputs that provide its customers with a differentiation advantage, or inputs at a lower cost so it can charge its customers a lower price to keep their business. However, it is often difficult to persuade companies in adjacent stages of the value chain to invest in specialized assets. Often, to realize the benefits associated with such investments, a company must vertically integrate and enter into adjacent industries and invest its own resources. Why does this happen?

Imagine that Ford has developed a unique, energy-saving, electrical engine system that will dramatically increase fuel efficiency and differentiate Ford's cars from those of its rivals, giving it a major competitive advantage. Ford must decide whether to make the system in-house (vertical integration) or contract with a specialist outsourcing manufacturer to make the new engine system. Manufacturing these new systems requires a substantial investment in specialized equipment that can be used only for this purpose. In other words, because of its unique design, the equipment cannot be used to manufacture any other type of electrical engine for Ford or any other carmaker. Thus, this is an investment in specialized assets.

Consider this situation from the perspective of the outside supplier deciding whether or not to make this investment. The supplier might reason that once it has made the investment, it will become dependent on Ford for business because *Ford is the only possible customer for the electrical engine made by this specialized equipment*. The supplier realizes that this puts Ford in a strong bargaining position, and that Ford might use its buying power to demand lower prices for the engines. Given the risks involved, the supplier declines to make the investment in specialized equipment.

Now consider Ford's position. Ford might reason that if it outsources production of these systems to an outside supplier, it might become too dependent on that supplier for a vital input. Because specialized equipment is required to produce the engine systems, Ford cannot switch its order to other suppliers. Ford realizes that this increases the bargaining power of the supplier, which might demand higher prices.

The situation of *mutual dependence* that would be created by the investment in specialized assets makes Ford hesitant to allow outside suppliers to make the product and makes suppliers hesitant to undertake such a risky investment. The problem is a lack of trust—neither Ford nor the supplier can trust the other to operate fairly in this situation. The lack of trust arises from the risk of **holdup**—that is, being taken advantage of by a trading partner *after* the investment in specialized assets has been made.[3] Because of this risk, Ford reasons that the only cost-effective way to get the new engine systems is for it to invest in specialized assets and manufacture the engine in-house.

To generalize from this example, if achieving a competitive advantage requires one company to make investments in specialized assets so it can trade with another, *the risk of holdup* may serve as a deterrent, and the investment may not take place. Consequently, the potential for higher profitability from specialization will be lost. To prevent such loss, companies vertically integrate into adjacent stages in the value chain. Historically, the problems surrounding specific assets have driven automobile companies to vertically integrate backward into the production of component parts, steel companies to vertically integrate backward into the production of iron, computer companies to vertically integrate backward into chip production, and aluminum companies to vertically integrate backward into bauxite mining. Often such firms practice **tapered integration**, whereby the firm makes some input and buys some input. Purchasing part or most of its needs for a given input from suppliers enables the firm to tap the advantages of the market (e.g., choosing from suppliers that are competing to improve quality or lower the cost of the product). At the same time, meeting some of its needs for input through internal production improves the firm's bargaining power by reducing the likelihood of holdup by its supplier. A firm that is engaged in production of an input is also better able to evaluate the cost and quality of external suppliers of that input.[4]

Enhancing Product Quality   By entering industries at other stages of the value-added chain, a company can often enhance the quality of the products in its core business and strengthen its differentiation advantage. For example, the ability to control the reliability and performance of complex components such as engine and transmission systems may increase a company's competitive advantage in the luxury-sedan market and enable it to charge a premium price. Conditions in the banana industry also illustrate the importance of vertical integration in maintaining product quality. Historically, a problem facing food companies that import bananas has been the variable quality of delivered bananas, which often arrive on the shelves of U.S. supermarkets too ripe or not ripe enough. To correct this problem, major U.S. food companies such as Del Monte have integrated backward and now own banana plantations, putting them in control of the

holdup

When a company is taken advantage of by another company it does business with after it has made an investment in expensive specialized assets to better meet the needs of the other company.

tapered integration

When a firm uses a mix of vertical integration and market transactions for a given input. For example, a firm might operate limited semiconductor manufacturing while also buying semiconductor chips on the market. Doing so helps to prevent supplier holdup (because the firm can credibly commit to not buying from external suppliers) and increases its ability to judge the quality and cost of purchased supplies.

banana supply. As a result, they can distribute and sell bananas of a standard quality at the optimal time to better satisfy customers. Knowing they can rely on the quality of these brands, customers are also willing to pay more for them. Thus, by vertically integrating backward into plantation ownership, banana companies have built customer confidence, which has, in turn, enabled them to charge a premium price for their product.

The same considerations can promote forward vertical integration. Ownership of retail outlets may be necessary if the required standards of after-sales service for complex products are to be maintained. For example, in the 1920s, Kodak owned the retail outlets that distributed its photographic equipment because the company felt that few existing retail outlets had the skills necessary to sell and service its complex equipment. By the 1930s, new retailers had emerged that could provide satisfactory distribution and service for Kodak products, so it left the retail industry.

McDonald's has also used vertical integration to protect product quality and increase efficiency. In the 1990s, McDonald's faced a problem: After decades of rapid growth, the fast-food market was beginning to show signs of market saturation. McDonald's responded to the slowdown by rapidly expanding abroad. In 1980, 28% of the chain's new restaurant openings were abroad; in 1990, it was 60%, and by 2000, 70%. In 2014, McDonalds had 14,350 restaurants in the United States, and 21,908 restaurants in 110 countries outside the United States.[5] Replication of its value creation skills was the key to successful global expansion and spurred the growth of McDonald's in the countries and regions in which it operates. McDonald's U.S. success was built on a formula of close relations with suppliers, nationwide marketing might, and tight control over store-level operating procedures.

The biggest problem McDonald's has faced is replicating its U.S. supply chain in other countries; its domestic suppliers are fiercely loyal to the company because their fortunes are closely linked to its success. McDonald's maintains very rigorous specifications for all the raw ingredients it uses—the key to its consistency and quality control. Outside of the United States, however, McDonald's has found suppliers far less willing to make the investments required to meet its specifications. In Great Britain, for example, McDonald's had problems getting local bakeries to produce the hamburger bun. After experiencing quality problems with two local bakeries, McDonald's had to vertically integrate backward and build its own bakeries to supply its British stores. When McDonald's decided to operate in Russia, it found that local suppliers lacked the capability to produce ingredients of the quality it demanded. It was then forced to vertically integrate through the local food industry on an epic scale, importing potato seeds and bull semen and indirectly managing dairy farms, cattle ranches, and vegetable plots. It also needed to construct the world's largest food-processing plant at a huge cost. In South America, McDonald's purchased huge ranches in Argentina upon which it could raise its own cattle. In short, vertical integration has allowed McDonald's to protect product quality and reduce its global cost structure.[6]

Improved Scheduling Sometimes important strategic advantages can be obtained when vertical integration makes it quicker, easier, and more cost-effective to plan, coordinate, and schedule the transfer of a product such as raw materials or component parts between adjacent stages of the value-added chain.[7] Such advantages can be crucial when a company wants to realize the benefits of just-in-time (JIT) inventory systems. For example, in the 1920s, Ford profited from the tight coordination and scheduling that backward vertical integration made possible. Ford integrated backward into steel foundries, iron ore shipping, and iron ore production—it owned mines in

Upper Michigan. Deliveries at Ford were coordinated to such an extent that iron ore unloaded at Ford's steel foundries on the Great Lakes was turned into engine blocks within 24 hours, which lowered Ford's cost structure.

Problems with Vertical Integration

Vertical integration can often be used to strengthen a company's business model and increase profitability. However, the opposite can occur when vertical integration results in (1) an increasing cost structure, (2) disadvantages that arise when technology is changing fast, and (3) disadvantages that arise when demand is unpredictable. Sometimes these disadvantages are so great that vertical integration, rather than increasing profitability, may actually reduce it—in which case a company engages in **vertical disintegration** and exits industries adjacent to its core industry in the industry value chain. For example, Ford, which was highly vertically integrated, sold all its companies involved in mining iron ore and making steel when more efficient and specialized steel producers emerged that were able to supply lower-priced steel.

vertical disintegration
When a company decides to exit industries, either forward or backward in the industry value chain, to its core industry to increase profitability.

Increasing Cost Structure   Although vertical integration is often undertaken to lower a company's cost structure, it can raise costs if, over time, a company makes mistakes such as continuing to purchase inputs from company-owned suppliers when low-cost independent suppliers that can supply the same inputs exist. For decades, for example, GM's company-owned suppliers made more than 60% of the component parts for its vehicles; this figure was far higher than that for any other major carmaker, which is why GM became such a high-cost carmaker. In the 2000s, it vertically disintegrated by selling off many of its largest component operations, such as Delhi, its electrical components supplier. Thus, vertical integration can be a major disadvantage when company-owned suppliers develop a higher cost structure than those of independent suppliers. Why would a company-owned supplier develop such a high cost structure?

In this example, company-owned or in-house suppliers know that they can always sell their components to the car-making divisions of their company—they have a "captive customer." Because company-owned suppliers do not have to compete with independent, outside suppliers for orders, they have much less *incentive* to look for new ways to reduce operating costs or increase component quality. Indeed, in-house suppliers simply pass on cost increases to the car-making divisions in the form of higher **transfer prices**, the prices one division of a company charges other divisions for its products. Unlike independent suppliers, which constantly need to increase their efficiency to protect their competitive advantage, in-house suppliers face no such competition and the resulting rising cost structure reduces a company's profitability.

transfer pricing
The price that one division of a company charges another division for its products, which are the inputs the other division requires to manufacture its own products.

The term *bureaucratic costs* refers to the costs of solving the transaction difficulties that arise from managerial inefficiencies and the need to manage the handoffs or exchanges between business units to promote increased differentiation, or to lower a company's cost structure. Bureaucratic costs become a significant component of a company's cost structure because considerable managerial time and effort must be spent to reduce or eliminate managerial inefficiencies such as those that result when company-owned suppliers lose their incentive to increase efficiency or innovation.

Technological Change   When technology is changing fast, vertical integration may lock a company into an old, inefficient technology and prevent it from changing to a new one that would strengthen its business model.[8] Consider Sony, which had integrated backward to become the leading manufacturer of now-outdated cathode ray tubes (CRTs) used in TVs and computer monitors. Because Sony was locked into the outdated CRT technology, it was slow to recognize that the future was in liquid crystal display (LCD) flatscreens and it did not exit the CRT business. Sony's resistance to change in technology forced it to enter into a strategic alliance with Samsung to supply the LCD screens that are used in its BRAVIA TVs. As a result, Sony lost its competitive advantage and experienced a major loss in TV market share. Thus, vertical integration can pose a serious disadvantage when it prevents a company from adopting new technology, or changing its suppliers or distribution systems to match the requirements of changing technology.

Demand Unpredictability Suppose the demand for a company's core product, such as cars or washing machines, is predictable, and the company knows how many units it needs to make each month or year. Under these conditions, vertical integration allows a company to schedule and coordinate efficiently the flow of products along the industry value-added chain, which may result in major cost savings. However, suppose the demand for cars or washing machines wildly fluctuates and is unpredictable. If demand for cars suddenly plummets, the carmaker may find itself burdened with warehouses full of component parts it no longer needs, which is a major drain on profitability—something that has hurt major carmakers during the recent recession. Thus, vertical integration can be risky when demand is unpredictable because it is hard to manage the volume or flow of products along the value-added chain.

For example, a PC maker might vertically integrate backward to acquire a supplier of memory chips so that it can make exactly the number of chips it needs each month. However, if demand for PCs falls because of the popularity of mobile computing devices, the PC maker finds itself locked into a business that is now inefficient because it is not producing at full capacity, and therefore its cost structure starts to rise. In general, high-speed environmental change (e.g., technological change, changing customer demands, and major shifts in institutional norms or competitive dynamics) provides a disincentive for integration, as the firm's asset investments are at greater risk of rapid obsolescence.[9] It is clear that strategic managers must carefully assess the advantages and disadvantages of expanding the boundaries of their company by entering adjacent industries, either backward (upstream) or forward (downstream), in the industry value-added chain. Moreover, although the decision to enter a new industry to make crucial component parts may have been profitable in the past, it may make no economic sense today because so many low-cost, global, component parts suppliers exist that compete for the company's business. The risks and returns on investing in vertical integration must be continually evaluated, and companies should be as willing to vertically disintegrate as to vertically integrate in order to strengthen their core business model.

ALTERNATIVES TO VERTICAL INTEGRATION: COOPERATIVE RELATIONSHIPS

Is it possible to obtain the differentiation and cost-savings advantages associated with vertical integration without having to bear the problems and costs associated with this strategy? In other words, is there another corporate-level strategy that managers can use to obtain the advantages of vertical integration while allowing other companies to perform upstream and downstream activities? Today, companies have found that they can realize many of the benefits associated with vertical integration by entering into *long-term cooperative relationships* with companies in industries along the value-added chain, also known as **quasi integration**. Such moves could include, for example, sharing the expenses of investment in production assets or inventory, or making long-term supply or purchase guarantees. Apple's decision to invest in production equipment for its suppliers is a prime example (in the Closing Case).

Short-Term Contracts and Competitive Bidding

Many companies use short-term contracts that last for a year or less to establish the price and conditions under which they will purchase raw materials or components from suppliers or sell their final products to distributors or retailers. A classic example is the carmaker that uses a *competitive bidding strategy*, in which independent component suppliers compete to be chosen to supply a particular component, such as brakes, made to agreed-upon specifications, at the lowest price. For example, GM typically solicits bids from global suppliers to produce a particular component and awards a 1-year contract to the supplier that submits the lowest bid. At the end of the year, the contract is once again put out for competitive bid, and once again the lowest-cost supplier is most likely to win the bid.

The advantage of this strategy for GM is that suppliers are forced to compete over price, which drives down the cost of its components. However, GM has no long-term commitment to outside suppliers—and it drives a hard bargain. For this reason, suppliers are unwilling to make the expensive, long-term investments in specialized assets that are required to produce higher-quality or better-designed component parts over time. In addition, suppliers will be reluctant to agree upon the tight scheduling that makes it possible to use a JIT inventory system because this may help GM lower its costs but will increase a supplier's costs and reduce its profitability.

As a result, short-term contracting does not result in the specialized investments that are required to realize differentiation and cost advantages *because it signals a company's lack of long-term commitment to its suppliers*. Of course, this is not a problem when there is minimal need for cooperation, and specialized assets are not required to improve scheduling, enhance product quality, or reduce costs. In this case, competitive bidding may be optimal. However, when there is a need for cooperation—something that is becoming increasingly significant today—the use of short-term contracts and competitive bidding can be a serious drawback.

Strategic Alliances and Long-Term Contracting

Unlike short-term contracts, **strategic alliances** between buyers and suppliers are long term, cooperative relationships; both companies agree to make specialized investments and work jointly to find ways to lower costs or increase product quality so that they both gain from their relationship. A strategic alliance becomes a *substitute* for vertical integration because it creates a relatively stable, long-term partnership that allows both companies to obtain the same kinds of benefits that result from vertical integration. However, it also avoids the problems (bureaucratic costs) that arise from managerial inefficiencies that result when a company owns its own suppliers, such as

quasi integration
The use of long-term relationships, or investment in some activities normally performed by suppliers or buyers, in place of full ownership of operations that are backward or forward in the supply chain.

strategic alliances
Long-term agreements between two or more companies to jointly develop new products or processes that benefit all companies that are a part of the agreement.

those that arise because of a lack of incentives, or when a company becomes locked into an old technology even when technology is rapidly changing.

Consider the cooperative relationships that often were established decades ago, which many Japanese carmakers have with their component suppliers (the *keiretsu* system). Japanese carmakers and suppliers cooperate to find ways to maximize the value added they can obtain from being a part of adjacent stages of the value chain. For example, they do this by jointly implementing JIT inventory systems, or sharing future component-parts designs to improve quality and lower assembly costs. As part of this process, suppliers make substantial investments in specialized assets to better serve the needs of a particular carmaker, and the cost savings that result are shared. Thus, Japanese carmakers have been able to capture many of the benefits of vertical integration without having to enter the component industry.

Similarly, component suppliers also benefit because their business and profitability grow as the companies they supply grow, and they can invest their profits in investing in ever more specialized assets.[10] An interesting example of this is the computer chip outsourcing giant Taiwan Semiconductor Manufacturing Company (TSMC), which makes chips for many companies such as NVIDIA, Acer, and AMD. The cost of investing in the machinery necessary to build a state-of-the-art chip factory can exceed $10 billion. TSMC is able to make this huge (risky) investment because it has developed cooperative, long-term relationships with its computer-chip partners. All parties recognize that they will benefit from this outsourcing arrangement, which does not preclude some hard bargaining between TSMC and the chip companies, because all parties want to maximize their profits and reduce their risks.

Building Long-Term Cooperative Relationships

How does a company create a long-term strategic alliance with another company when the fear of holdup exists, and the possibility of being cheated arises if one company makes a specialized investment with another company? How do companies such as GM or Nissan manage to develop such profitable, enduring relationships with their suppliers?

There are several strategies companies can adopt to promote the success of a long-term, cooperative relationship and lessen the chance that one company will renege on its agreement and cheat the other. One strategy is for the company that makes the specialized investment to demand a *hostage* from its partner. Another is to establish a *credible commitment* from both companies that will result in a trusting, long-term relationship.[11]

hostage taking

A means of exchanging valuable resources to guarantee that each partner to an agreement will keep its side of the bargain.

Hostage Taking   **Hostage taking** is essentially a means of guaranteeing that each partner will keep its side of the bargain. The cooperative relationship between Boeing and Northrop Grumman illustrates this type of situation. Northrop is a major subcontractor for Boeing's commercial airline division, providing many components for its aircraft. To serve Boeing's special needs, Northrop has had to make substantial investments in specialized assets, and, in theory, because of this investment Northrop has become dependent on Boeing—which can threaten to change orders to other suppliers as a way of driving down Northrop's prices. In practice, Boeing is highly unlikely to change suppliers because it is, in turn, a major supplier to Northrop's defense division and provides many parts for its Stealth aircraft; it also has made major investments in specialized assets to serve Northrop's needs. Thus, the companies are *mutually dependent*; each company holds a hostage—the specialized investment the other has made. Thus, Boeing is unlikely to renege on any pricing agreements with Northrop because it knows that Northrop would respond the same way

Credible Commitments   A **credible commitment** is a believable promise or pledge to support the development of a long-term relationship between companies. Consider the way GE and IBM developed such a commitment. GE is a major supplier of advanced semiconductor chips to IBM, and many of the chips are customized to IBM's requirements. To meet IBM's specific needs, GE has had to make substantial investments in specialized assets that have little other value. As a consequence, GE is dependent on IBM and faces a risk that IBM will take advantage of this dependence to demand lower prices. In theory, IBM could back up its demand by threatening to switch its business to another supplier. However, GE reduced this risk by having IBM enter into a contractual agreement that committed IBM to purchase chips from GE for a 10-year period. In addition, IBM agreed to share the costs of the specialized assets needed to develop the customized chips, thereby reducing the risks associated with GE's investment. Thus, by publicly committing itself to a long-term contract and putting money into the chip development process, IBM made a *credible commitment* that it would continue to purchase chips from GE. When a company violates a credible commitment with its partners, the results can be dramatic, as discussed in Strategy in Action 9.2.

Maintaining Market Discipline   Just as a company pursuing vertical integration faces the problem that its company-owned suppliers might become inefficient, a company that forms a strategic alliance with an independent component supplier runs the risk that its alliance partner might become inefficient over time, resulting in higher component costs or lower quality. This also happens because the outside supplier knows it does not need to compete with other suppliers for the company's business. Consequently, a company seeking to form a mutually beneficial, long-term strategic alliance needs to possess some kind of power that it can use to discipline its partner should the need arise.

A company holds two strong cards over its supplier partner. First, all contracts, including long-term contracts, are periodically renegotiated, usually every 3 to 5 years, so the supplier knows that if it fails to live up to its commitments, its partner may refuse to renew the contract. Second, many companies that form long-term relationships with suppliers use a **parallel sourcing policy**—that is, they enter into long-term contracts with at least *two* suppliers for the *same* component (this is Toyota's policy, for example).[12] This arrangement protects a company against a supplier that adopts an uncooperative attitude because the supplier knows that if it fails to comply with the agreement, the company can switch *all* its business to its other supplier partner. When both the company and its suppliers recognize that the parallel sourcing policy allows a supplier to be replaced at short notice, most suppliers behave because the policy brings market discipline into their relationship.

The growing importance of JIT inventory systems as a way to reduce costs and enhance quality and differentiation is increasing the pressure on companies to form strategic alliances in a wide range of industries. The number of strategic alliances formed each year, especially global strategic alliances, is increasing, and the popularity of vertical integration is falling because so many low-cost global suppliers exist in countries such as Malaysia, Korea, and China.

credible commitment
A believable promise or pledge to support the development of a long-term relationship between companies.

parallel sourcing policy
A policy in which a company enters into long-term contracts with at least two suppliers for the same component to prevent any incidents of opportunism.

9.2 STRATEGY IN ACTION

eBay's Changing Commitment to Its Sellers

Since its founding in 1995, eBay has cultivated good relationships with the millions of sellers that advertise their goods for sale on its website. Over time, however, to increase its revenues and profits, eBay has steadily increased the fees it charges sellers to list their products on its sites, to insert photographs, to use its PayPal on-line payment service, and for other additional services. Although this has caused grumbling among sellers because it reduces their profit margins, eBay increasingly engages in extensive advertising to attract millions more buyers to its website, so sellers can receive better prices and increase their total profits. As a result, they remained largely satisfied with eBay's fee structure.

These policies changed when a new CEO, John Donohue, took the place of eBay's long-time CEO, Meg Whitman, who had built the company into a dot. com giant. By 2008, eBay's profits had not increased rapidly enough to keep its investors happy, and its stock price plunged. To increase performance, one of Donohue's first moves was to announce a major over-haul of eBay's fee structure and feedback policy. The new fee structure would reduce upfront seller listing costs but increase back-end commissions on completed sales and payments. For smaller sellers that already had thin profit margins, these fee hikes were painful. In addition, in the future, eBay announced it would block sellers from leaving negative feedback about buyers—feedback such as buyers didn't pay for the goods they purchased, or buyers took too long to pay for goods. The feedback system that eBay had originally devel-oped had been a major source of its success; it allowed buyers to be certain they were dealing with reputable sellers, and vice versa. All sellers and buyers have feedback scores that provide them with a reputation as good—or bad—individuals with whom to do business, and these scores helped reduce the risks involved in online transactions. Donohue claimed this change was implemented in order to improve the buyer's experi-ence because many buyers had complained that if they left negative feedback on a seller, the seller would in turn leave negative feedback for the buyer.

Together, however, throughout 2009, these chang-es resulted in conflict between eBay and its millions of sellers, who perceived they were being harmed by these changes. Their bad feelings resulted in a revolt. Blogs and forums all over the Internet were filled with messages claiming that eBay had abandoned its small-er sellers, and was pushing them out of business in favor of high-volume "powersellers" who contributed more to eBay's profits. Donohue and eBay received millions of hostile e-mails, and sellers threatened they would do business elsewhere, such as on Amazon. com and Yahoo!, two companies that were both trying to break into eBay's market. Sellers also organized a 1-week boycott of eBay during which they would list no items with the company to express their dismay and hostility! Many sellers did shut down their eBay online storefronts and moved to Amazon.com, which claimed in 2011 that its network of sites had overtaken eBay in monthly unique viewers or "hits" for the first time. The bottom line was that the level of commitment between eBay and its sellers had fallen dramatically; the bitter feelings produced by the changes eBay had made were likely to result in increasing problems that would hurt its future performance.

Realizing that his changes had backfired, Donohue reversed course and eliminated several of eBay's fee increases and revamped its feedback system; sellers and buyers can now respond to one another's com-ments in a fairer way. These changes did improve hostility and smooth over the bad feelings between sellers and eBay, but the old "community relationship" it had enjoyed with sellers in its early years largely disappeared. As this example suggests, finding ways to maintain cooperative relationships—such as by test-ing the waters in advance and asking sellers for their reactions to fee and feedback changes—could have avoided many of the problems that arose.

Source: www.ebay.com.

STRATEGIC OUTSOURCING

Vertical integration and strategic alliances are alternative ways of managing the value chain *across industries* to strengthen a company's core business model. However, just as low-cost suppliers of component parts exist, so today many *specialized companies* exist that can perform one of a company's *own value-chain activities* in a way that contributes to a company's differentiation advantage or that lowers its cost structure. For example, as noted in the Closing Case, Apple found that using Foxconn factories in China to assemble its iPhones enabled it to not only benefit by lower costs, but to also much more rapidly incorporate design changes and scale up production.

Strategic outsourcing is the decision to allow one or more of a company's value-chain activities or functions to be performed by independent specialist companies that focus all their skills and knowledge on just one kind of function, such as the manufacturing function, or on just one kind of activity that a function performs. For example, many companies outsource the management of their pension systems while keeping other human resource management (HRM) activities within the company. When a company chooses to outsource a value-chain activity, it is choosing to focus on a *fewer* number of value creation activities to strengthen its business model.

strategic outsourcing
The decision to allow one or more of a company's value-chain activities to be performed by independent, specialist companies that focus all their skills and knowledge on just one kind of activity to increase performance.

There has been a clear move among many companies to outsource activities that managers regard as being "noncore" or "nonstrategic," meaning they are not a source of a company's distinctive competencies and competitive advantage.[13] The vast majority of companies outsource manufacturing or some other value-chain activity to domestic or overseas companies today; some estimates are that over 60% of all global product manufacturing is outsourced to manufacturing specialists because of pressures to reduce costs. Some well-known companies that outsource include Nike, which does not make its athletic shoes; Gap Inc., which does not make its jeans and clothing; and Microsoft, which does not make its Xbox consoles. These products are made under contract at low-cost, global locations by contract manufacturers that specialize in low-cost assembly.

Although manufacturing is the most common form of strategic outsourcing, as we noted earlier, many other kinds of noncore activities are also outsourced. Microsoft has long outsourced its entire customer technical support operation to an independent company, as does Dell. Both companies have extensive customer support operations in India staffed by skilled operatives who are paid a fraction of what their U.S. counterparts earn. British Petroleum outsourced almost all of its human resource function to Exult, a San Antonio company, in a 5-year deal worth $600 million; a few years later, Exult won a 10-year, $1.1 billion contract to handle HRM activities for Bank of America's 150,000 employees. Similarly, American Express outsourced its entire IT function to IBM in a 7-year deal worth $4 billion. In 2006, IBM announced it was outsourcing its purchasing function to an Indian company to save $2 billion a year, and it has steadily increased its use of outsourcing ever since. For example, in 2009, IBM announced it would lay off 5,000 IT employees in the United States and move their jobs to India.[14]

Companies engage in strategic outsourcing to strengthen their business models and increase their profitability. The process of strategic outsourcing typically begins with strategic managers identifying the value-chain activities that form the basis of a company's competitive advantage; these are obviously kept within the company to protect them from competitors. Managers then systematically review noncore functions to assess whether independent companies that specialize in those activities can perform them more effectively and efficiently. Because these companies specialize in

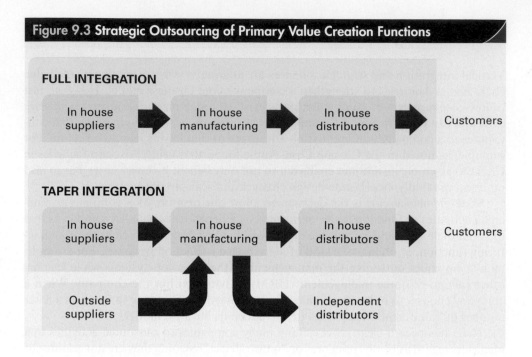

Figure 9.3 Strategic Outsourcing of Primary Value Creation Functions

FULL INTEGRATION

In house suppliers → In house manufacturing → In house distributors → Customers

TAPER INTEGRATION

In house suppliers → In house manufacturing → In house distributors → Customers

Outside suppliers → Independent distributors

particular activities, they can perform them in ways that lower costs or improve differentiation. If managers determine that there are differentiation or cost advantages, these activities are outsourced to those specialists.

This is illustrated in Figure 9.3, which shows the primary value-chain activities and boundaries of a company before and after it has pursued strategic outsourcing. In this example, the company decided to outsource its production and customer service functions to specialist companies, leaving only R&D and marketing and sales within the company. Once outsourcing has been executed, the relationships between the company and its specialists are then often structured as long-term contractual relationships, with rich information sharing between the company and the specialist organization to which it has contracted the activity. The term **virtual corporation** has been coined to describe companies that have pursued extensive strategic outsourcing.[15]

Benefits of Outsourcing

Strategic outsourcing has several advantages. It can help a company (1) lower its cost structure, (2) increase product differentiation,[16] and (3) focus on the distinctive competencies that are vital to its long-term competitive advantage and profitability.

Lower Cost Structure   Outsourcing will reduce costs when the price that must be paid to a specialist company to perform a particular value-chain activity is less than what it would cost the company to perform that activity in-house. Specialists are often able to perform an activity at a lower cost than the company because they are able to realize scale economies or other efficiencies not available to the company. For example, performing HRM activities such as managing benefit and pay systems requires a significant investment in sophisticated HRM IT; purchasing these IT systems represents

virtual corporation
When companies pursued extensive strategic outsourcing to the extent that they only perform the central value creation functions that lead to competitive advantage.

a considerable fixed cost for one company. But, by aggregating the HRM IT needs of many individual companies, companies that specialize in HRM such as Exult and Paychex can obtain huge economics of scale in IT that any single company could not hope to achieve. Some of these cost savings are then passed to the client companies in the form of lower prices, which reduces their cost structure. A similar dynamic is at work in the contract manufacturing business. Manufacturing specialists like Foxconn, Flextronics, and Jabil Circuit make large capital investments to build efficient-scale manufacturing facilities, but then are able to spread those capital costs over a huge volume of output and drive down unit costs so that they can make a specific product—an Apple iPod or Motorola XOOM, for example—at a lower cost than the company.

Specialists are also likely to obtain the cost savings associated with learning effects much more rapidly than a company that performs an activity just for itself (see Chapter 4 for a review of learning effects). For example, because a company like Flextronics is manufacturing similar products for several different companies, it is able to build up *cumulative* volume more rapidly, and it learns how to manage and operate the manufacturing process more efficiently than any of its clients could. This drives down the specialists' cost structure and also allows them to charge client companies a lower price for a product than if they made that product in-house.

Specialists are also often able to perform activities at lower costs than a specific company because of lower wage rates in those locations. For example, many workers at the Foxconn factory that assembles iPhones in China earn less than $17 a day; moving production of iPhones to the United States would, according to estimates, raise the cost of an iPhone by $65.[17] Similarly, Nike outsources the manufacture of its running shoes to companies based in China because of much lower wage rates. Even though wages have doubled in China since 2010, a Chinese-based specialist can assemble shoes (a very labor-intensive activity) at a much lower cost than could be done in the United States. Although Nike could establish its own operations in China to manufacture running shoes, it would require a major capital investment and limit its ability to switch production to an even lower-cost location later—for example, Vietnam; many companies are moving to Vietnam because wage rates are lower there. So, for Nike and most other consumer goods companies, outsourcing manufacturing activities lowers costs and gives companies the flexibility to switch to a more favorable location if labor costs change is the most efficient way to handle production.

Enhanced Differentiation   A company may also be able to differentiate its final products better by outsourcing certain noncore activities to specialists. For this to occur, the *quality* of the activity performed by specialists must be greater than if that same activity was performed by the company. On the reliability dimension of quality, for example, a specialist may be able to achieve a lower error rate in performing an activity precisely because it focuses solely on that activity and has developed a strong, distinctive competency in it. Again, this is one advantage claimed for contract manufacturers. Companies like Flextronics have adopted Six Sigma methodologies (see Chapter 4) and driven down the defect rate associated with manufacturing a product. This means they can provide more reliable products to their clients and differentiate their products on the basis of their superior quality.

A company can also improve product differentiation by outsourcing to specialists when they stand out on the excellence dimension of quality. For example, the excellence of Dell's U.S. customer service is a differentiating factor, and Dell outsources its PC repair and maintenance function to specialist companies. A customer who has a problem with a product purchased from Dell can get excellent help over the phone, and if there is a defective part in the computer, a maintenance person will be dispatched to replace the part within a few days. The excellence of this service differentiates Dell and helps to guarantee repeat purchases, which is why HP has worked hard to match Dell's level of service quality. In a similar way, carmakers often outsource specific vehicle component design activities such as microchips or headlight, to specialists that have earned a reputation for design excellence in this particular activity.

Focus on the Core Business   A final advantage of strategic outsourcing is that it allows managers to focus their energies and their company's resources on performing the core activities that have the most potential to create value and competitive advantage. In other words, companies can enhance their core competencies and are able to push out the value frontier and create more value for their customers. For example, Cisco Systems remains the dominant competitor in the Internet router industry because it has focused on building its competencies in product design, marketing and sales, and supply-chain management. Companies that focus on the core activities essential for competitive advantage in their industry are better able to drive down the costs of performing those activities and thus better differentiate their final products.

Risks of Outsourcing

Although outsourcing noncore activities has many benefits, there are also risks associated with it, risks such as holdup and the possible loss of important information when an activity is outsourced. Managers must assess these risks before they decide to outsource a particular activity, although, as we discuss the following section, these risks can be reduced when the appropriate steps are taken.

Holdup   In the context of outsourcing, holdup refers to the risk that a company will become too dependent upon the specialist provider of an outsourced activity and that the specialist will use this fact to raise prices beyond some previously agreed-upon rate. As with strategic alliances, the risk of holdup can be reduced by outsourcing to several suppliers and pursuing a parallel sourcing policy, as Toyota and Cisco do. Moreover, when an activity can be performed well by any one of several different providers, the threat that a contract will not be renewed in the future is normally sufficient to keep the chosen provider from exercising bargaining power over the company. For example, although IBM enters into long-term contracts to provide IT services to a wide range of companies, it would be unadvisable for those companies to attempt to raise prices after the contract has been signed because it knows full well that such an action would reduce its chance of getting the contract renewed in the future. Moreover, because IBM has many strong competitors in the IT services business, such as Accenture, Capgemini, and HP, it has a very strong incentive to deliver significant value to its clients.

Increased Competition   As firms employ contract manufacturers for production, they help to build an industrywide resource that lowers barriers to entry in that industry. In industries that have efficient, high-quality contract manufacturers, large firms may find that their size no longer affords them protection against competitive pressure; their high investments in fixed assets can become a constraint rather than a source of advantage.[18] Furthermore, firms that use contract manufacturing pay, in essence, for the contract manufacturer to progress down its own learning curve. Over time, the contract manufacturer's capabilities improve, putting it at a greater manufacturing advantage over the firm. Contract manufacturers in many industries increase the scope of their activities over time, adding a wider range of services (e.g., component purchasing, redesign-for-manufacturability, testing, packaging, and after-sales service) and may eventually produce their own end products in competition with their customers. Contracts to manufacture goods for U.S. and European electronics manufacturers, for example, helped to build the electronics manufacturing giants that exist today in Japan and Korea.

Loss of Information and Forfeited Learning Opportunities   A company that is not careful can lose important competitive information when it outsources an activity. For example, many computer hardware and software companies have outsourced their customer technical support function to specialists. Although this makes good sense from a cost and differentiation perspective, it may also mean that a critical point of contact with the customer, and a source of important feedback, is lost. Customer complaints can be useful information and valuable inputs into future product design, but if those complaints are not clearly communicated to the company by the specialists performing the technical support activity, the company can lose the information. Similarly, a firm that manufactures its own products also gains knowledge about how to improve their design in order to lower the costs of manufacturing or produce more reliable products. Thus, a firm that forfeits the development of manufacturing knowledge could unintentionally forfeit opportunities for improving its capabilities in product design. The firm risks becoming "hollow."[19] These are not arguments against outsourcing; rather, they are arguments for ensuring that there is appropriate communication between the outsourcing specialist and the company. At Dell, for example, a great deal of attention is paid to making sure that the specialist responsible for providing technical support and onsite maintenance collects and communicates all relevant data regarding product failures and other problems to Dell, so that Dell can design better products.

KEY TERMS

TAKEAWAYS FOR STRATEGIC MANAGERS

1. A corporate strategy should enable a company, or one or more of its business units, to perform one or more of the value creation functions at a lower cost or in a way that allows for differentiation and a premium price.

2. The corporate-level strategy of horizontal integration is pursued to increase the profitability of a company's business model by (a) reducing costs, (b) increasing the value of the company's products through differentiation, (c) replicating

the business model, (d) managing rivalry within the industry to reduce the risk of price warfare, and (e) increasing bargaining power over suppliers and buyers.

3. There are two drawbacks associated with horizontal integration: (a) the numerous pitfalls associated with making mergers and acquisitions and (b) the fact that the strategy can bring a company into direct conflict with antitrust authorities.

4. The corporate-level strategy of vertical integration is pursued to increase the profitability of a company's "core" business model in its original industry. Vertical integration can enable a company to achieve a competitive advantage by helping build barriers to entry, facilitating investments in specialized assets, protecting product quality, and helping to improve scheduling between adjacent stages in the value chain.

5. The disadvantages of vertical integration include (a) increasing bureaucratic costs if a company-owned or in-house supplier becomes lazy or inefficient, (b) potential loss of focus on

those resources and capabilities that create the most value for the firm, and (c), reduced flexibility to adapt to a fast-changing environment. Entering into a long-term contract can enable a company to realize many of the benefits associated with vertical integration without having to bear the same level of bureaucratic costs. However, to avoid the risks associated with becoming too dependent upon its partner, it needs to seek a credible commitment from its partner or establish a mutual hostage-taking situation.

6. The strategic outsourcing of noncore value creation activities may allow a company to lower its costs, better differentiate its products, and make better use of scarce resources, while also enabling it to respond rapidly to changing market conditions. However, strategic outsourcing may have a detrimental effect if the company outsources important value creation activities or becomes too dependent upon the key suppliers of those activities.

DISCUSSION QUESTIONS

1. Under what conditions might horizontal integration be inconsistent with the goal of maximizing profitability?

2. What is the difference between a company's internal value chain and the industry value chain? What is the relationship between vertical integration and the industry value chain?

3. Why was it profitable for GM and Ford to integrate backward into component-parts manufacturing in the past, and why are both companies

now buying more of their parts from outside suppliers?

4. What value creation activities should a company outsource to independent suppliers? What are the risks involved in outsourcing these activities?

5. What steps would you recommend that a company take to build mutually beneficial, long-term, cooperative relationships with its suppliers?

CLOSING CASE

Outsourcing and Vertical Integration at Apple

At a dinner for Silicon Valley luminaries in February 2011, U.S. President Barack Obama asked Steve Jobs of Apple, "What would it take

to make iPhones in the United States?" Jobs replied, "Those jobs aren't coming back." Apple's management had concluded that overseas factories provided superior scale, flexibility, diligence, and access to industrial skills—"Made in the U.S.A." just did not make sense for Apple anymore.

As an example of the superior responsiveness of Chinese factories to Apple's needs, an executive described a recent event when Apple wanted to revamp its iPhone manufacturing just weeks before it was scheduled for delivery to stores. At the last minute, Apple had redesigned the screen, and new screens arrived at the Chinese factory at midnight. Fortunately, the 8,000 workers slept in dormitories at the factory—they were woken, given a cookie and a cup of tea, and were at work fitting glass screens into their beveled frames within 30 minutes. Soon the plant was producing 10,000 iPhones per day. The executive commented, "The speed and flexibility is breathtaking . . . There's no American plant that can match that."

"Foxconn City," a complex where the iPhone is assembled, has 230,000 employees, many of whom work 6 days a week and up to 12 hours a day. It is owned by Foxconn Technology, which has dozens of factories in Asia, Eastern Europe, Mexico, and Brazil. It is estimated that Foxconn assembles 40% of the world's consumer electronics. It boasts a customer list that includes Amazon, Dell, Hewlett-Packard, Motorola, Nintendo, Nokia, Samsung, and Sony, in addition to Apple. Foxconn can hire thousands of engineers overnight and house them in dorms—something no American firm could do. Nearly 8,700 industrial engineers were needed to oversee the 200,000 assembly-line workers required to manufacture iPhones. Apple's analysts estimated that it could take 9 months to find that many qualified engineers in the United States. It only took 15 days in China. Moreover, China's advantage was not only in assembly; it offered advantages across the entire supply chain. As noted by an Apple executive, "The entire supply chain is in China now. You need a thousand rubber gaskets? That's the factory next door. You need a million screws? That factory is a block away. You need that screw made a little bit different? It will take three hours." Of Apple's 64,000 employees, nearly one-third are outside of the United States. In response to criticisms about failing to support employment in its home country, Apple executives responded, "We sell iPhones in over a hundred countries. . . . Our only obligation is making the best product possible."

Although Apple epitomizes the opportunities for strategic outsourcing, it is also—paradoxically, perhaps—more vertically integrated than most computer or smartphone firms. Apple's decision to produce its own hardware and software—and tie them tightly together and sell them its own retail stores—was widely known and hotly debated. However, the vertical integration did not end there. Apple also spends billions of dollars buying production equipment that is used to outfit new and existing Asian factories that will be run by others (an example of quasi vertical integration), and then requires those factories to commit to producing for Apple exclusively. By providing the upfront investment, Apple removes most of the risk for its suppliers in investing in superior technology or scale. For decades, the computer and mobile phone industries have been characterized by commoditization and rapid cost reduction. Suppliers had to work hard to reduce costs to win competitive bids, and standardized production facilities trumped specialized facilities as they enabled suppliers to smooth out volatility in scale by working with multiple buyers. This meant that most suppliers to the computer and phone industry could produce cost-efficient hardware, but not "insanely great" hardware. Apple's strategy of paying upfront for both the technology and capacity enabled it to induce its suppliers to make specialized investments in technologies that were well beyond the industry standard, and to hold excess capacity that would enable rapid scaling. The net result is that Apple develops superior flexibility and technological sophistication that its competitors cannot match.

Seeming to acknowledge the advantages of Apple's strategy of controlling device design and production, Microsoft announced on June 18, 2012, that it too would design and produce its own tablet, the Surface. It also launched its own chain of dedicated Microsoft retail stores that looked remarkably similar to Apple stores. The success of this strategy

(continued)

is far from assured, however. Although Microsoft can imitate some of the individual integration strategies of Apple, it lacks both the tightly woven ecosystem that Apple has developed around those strategies, and its decades of experience in implementing them.

Sources: C. Duhigg and K. Bradsher, "How the U.S. Lost Out on iPhone Work," *New York Times*, January 21, 2012, p. 1; C. Guglielmo, "Apple's Secret Plan for Its Cash Stash," *Forbes*, May 7, 2012, pp. 116–120.

CASE DISCUSSION QUESTIONS

1. What are the advantages and disadvantages to Apple of outsourcing its production to factories in China?
2. What factors influence the choice of countries to which a firm might outsource its production?
3. Is there anything that might cause Apple to eventually shift production back to the United States?
4. Why is Apple more vertically integrated than many other computer makers?
5. What factors will help or impede Microsoft in matching the advantages Apple gains from its vertical integration strategies?

NOTES

[1]This is the essence of Chandler's argument. See A. D. Chandler, *Strategy and Structure* (Cambridge: MIT Press, 1962). The same argument is also made by J. Pfeffer and G. R. Salancik, *The External Control of Organizations* (New York: Harper & Row, 1978). See also K. R. Harrigan, *Strategic Flexibility* (Lexington: Lexington Books, 1985); K. R. Harrigan, "Vertical Integration and Corporate Strategy," *Academy of Management Journal* 28 (1985): 397–425; F. M. Scherer, *Industrial Market Structure and Economic Performance* (Chicago: Rand McNally, 1981).

[2]O. E. Williamson, *The Economic Institutions of Capitalism* (New York: Free Press, 1985). For another empirical work that uses this framework, see L. Poppo and T. Zenger, "Testing Alternative Theories of the Firm: Transaction Cost, Knowledge Based, and Measurement Explanations for Make or Buy Decisions in Information Services," *Strategic Management Journal* 19 (1998): 853–878.

[3]Williamson, *Economic Institutions of Capitalism*.

[4]J. M. deFigueiredo and B. S. Silverman, "Firm Survival and Industry Evolution in Vertically Related Populations," *Management Science* 58 (2012): 1632–1650.

[5]www.mcdonalds.com.

[6]Ibid.

[7]A. D. Chandler, *The Visible Hand* (Cambridge: Harvard University Press, 1977).

[8]Harrigan, *Strategic Flexibility*, pp. 67–87. See also A. Afuah, "Dynamic Boundaries of the Firm: Are Firms Better Off Being Vertically Integrated in the Face of a Technological Change?" *Academy of Management Journal* 44 (2001): 1121–1228

[9]K. M. Gilley, J. E. McGee, and A. A. Rasheed, "Perceived Environmental Dynamism and Managerial Risk Aversion as Antecedents of Manufacturing Outsourcing: The Moderating Effects of Firm Maturity," *Journal of Small Business Management* 42 (2004): 117–134; M. A. Schilling and H. K. Steensma, "The Use of Modular Organizational Forms: An Industry-Level Analysis," *Academy of Management Journal* 44 (2001): 1149–1169.

[10]X. Martin, W. Mitchell, and A. Swaminathan, "Recreating and

Extending Japanese Automobile Buyer-Supplier Links in North America," *Strategic Management Journal* 16 (1995): 589–619; C. W. L. Hill, "National Institutional Structures, Transaction Cost Economizing, and Competitive Advantage," *Organization Science* 6 (1995): 119–131.

[11]Williamson, *Economic Institutions of Capitalism*. See also J. H. Dyer, "Effective Inter-Firm Collaboration: How Firms Minimize Transaction Costs and Maximize Transaction Value," *Strategic Management Journal* 18 (1997): 535–556.

[12]Richardson, "Parallel Sourcing."

[13]W. H Davidow and M. S. Malone, *The Virtual Corporation* (New York: Harper & Row, 1992).

[14]J. Krane, "American Express Hires IBM for $4 Billion," *Columbian*, February 26, 2002, p. E2; www .ibm.com.

[15]Davidow and Malone, *The Virtual Corporation*.

[16]Ibid.; see also H. W Chesbrough and D. J. Teece, "When Is Virtual Virtuous? Organizing for Innovation," *Harvard Business Review*, January–February 1996, pp. 65 74;

J. B. Quinn, "Strategic Outsourcing: Leveraging Knowledge Capabilities," *Sloan Management Review*, Summer 1999, pp. 9–21.

[17]C. Duhigg and K. Bradsher, "How the U.S. Lost Out on iPhone Work," *New York Times*, January 21, 2012, p. 1.

[18]Schilling and Steensma, "The Use of Modular Organizational Forms."

[19]R. Venkatesan, "Strategic Sourcing: To Make or Not to Make," *Harvard Business Review*, November December 1992, pp. 98–107.

CHAPTER 10

CORPORATE-LEVEL STRATEGY: RELATED AND UNRELATED DIVERSIFICATION

sergign/Shutterstock.com

10.1 Differentiate between multibusiness models based on related and unrelated diversification

10.2 Explain the five primary ways in which diversification can increase company profitability

10.3 Discuss the conditions that lead managers to pursue related diversification versus unrelated diversification, and explain why some companies pursue both strategies

10.4 Describe the three methods companies use to enter new industries—internal new venturing, acquisitions, and joint ventures—and discuss the advantages and disadvantages associated with each method

OPENING CASE

LVMH: Getting Big While Staying Beautiful

In 1854, Louis Vuitton founded a trunk-making company in Paris. He had observed that most trunks could not be easily stacked because they had rounded tops; he thus began producing trunks with flat bottoms and tops out of trianon canvas, which was lightweight and airtight. The style became extremely popular, and soon competitors were imitating his design. To deter imitation, he began creating trunks with special patterns and a logo—creating the iconic look that distinguishes Louis Vuitton products today. After his death, his son, Georges Vuitton, took over the company and began to expand it worldwide. He exhibited the trunks at the Chicago World's Fair in 1893, and toured cities such as New York, Chicago, and Philadelphia, selling the trunks to retailers. Over the next 80 years, Louis Vuitton stores opened all over the world, including Bombay, London, Washington DC, Buenos Aires, Taipei, Tokyo, and Seoul. In 1987, Moët Hennessy and Louis Vuitton merged to create the LVMH group, one of the world's largest and best-known luxury goods companies.

Many brands that came to be owned by the LVMH group were even older than Louis Vuitton: Moët & Chandon, the champagne company, had been founded in 1743; Veuve Clicquot Ponsardin dated back to 1772; Hennessy (maker of fine cognac) was originally formed in 1765, and perfumery Guerlain dated back to 1829. The oldest company in the group, Château d'Yquem, began making wine in 1593. Each company

Mandritoiu/Shutterstock.com   CFimages/Alamy   iStockphoto.com/TkKurikawa   PETIT Philippe/Getty images   Bloomberg/Getty Images

brought a legacy of craftsmanship and a loyal following of customers. However, LVMH's biggest brand by far has continued to be the Louis Vuitton brand, which accounts for about one-third of its sales and almost half of its profit.

Much of LVMH's growth into the diversified, luxury goods group that it has become can be attributed to Bernard Arnault. Arnault's career in luxury goods began in 1984, when he bought Dior in the bankruptcy sale of an industrial group. A few years later, he bought Luis Vuitton, which at the time had 125 stores. He subsequently transformed the group into a luxury conglomerate with over 60 brands. One of his first moves was to take production and distribution back from license-holders to begin restoring the exclusivity of the brands. In the years that followed, he bought Celine, Givenchy, Fendi, Kenzo, Bulgari, Sephora, Tag Heuer, and more. In 2014, LVMH also opened a stunning new arts center in Paris, the Foundation Louis Vuitton. The center, designed by world-renowned architect Frank Gehry, generated a flurry of publicity for the group.

Perhaps ironically, luxury goods benefit from economies of scale: A large luxury group can help a new brand grow faster through its distribution reach and expertise in brand management. "Key money" to open a shop on a prestigious, high-traffic location such as London's Bond Street can cost as much as $16 million. On top of that, a vendor must pay to outfit the shop, and may pay annual rent of $1.5 million. A large luxury group can make such investments and wait for them to pay off; small brands usually cannot. Furthermore, large luxury groups have more bargaining power with fashion magazines, more access to important fashion shows, and more influence with "key opinion leaders." They can also better attract and retain managers because they offer a deep, broad career path. At LVMH, for example, managers can move from fashion to wine to jewelry, and can live in a range of the world's biggest cities, vastly increasing their experience and marketability.

According to Bain & Company, over the past 20 years the number of luxury-goods consumers has more than tripled to 330 million, and their spending on luxury goods has risen at double the rate of global GDP. Most new buyers are not superwealthy but rather are "merely prosperous," earning up to $188,000 annually. As luxury-goods makers have raced to capture this market, they have had to carefully balance growth on a global scale while preserving an artisan image and exclusivity. Expanding too fast or too far can tarnish a luxury brand by making it seem too accessible.

By 2014, LVMH was earning almost $31 billion in revenues and had a net profit margin of 18.4%. It operated over 400 stores under the Louis Vuitton name alone. LVMH had proven that a company could be big and global, yet have prestigious and exclusive brands. As noted by Arnault, "People said in 1989 that Louis Vuitton was already too big. Now it's ten times the size."

Sources: www.lvmh.com; Anonymous, "Beauty and the Beasts: The Business Case," *The Economist*, December 13, 2014, pp. 6–8; Anonymous, "Exclusively for Anybody," *The Economist*, December 13, 2014, pp. 3–5; Yahoo Finance.

▛ OVERVIEW

Diversification can create, and destroy, value. As shown in the Opening Case, diversification enabled Louis Vuitton to leverage its branding expertise, distribution reach, influence, and capital resources to help new brands grow more profitably than they would grow on their own. However, as shown in the Closing Case, overdiversification at Citibank led the company away from its key strengths in consumer retail banking and made it difficult for managers to provide adequate oversight within the organization. Diversification can be very alluring to managers, and it is easy to overestimate potential synergies. It is much harder to realize them.

In this chapter, we continue to discuss both the challenges and opportunities created by corporate-level strategies of related and unrelated diversification. A diversification strategy is based upon a company's decision to enter one or more new industries to take advantage of its existing distinctive competencies and business model. We examine the different kinds of multibusiness models upon which related and unrelated diversification are based. Then, we discuss three different ways companies can implement a diversification strategy: internal new ventures, acquisitions, and joint ventures. By the end of this chapter, you will understand the advantages and disadvantages associated with strategic managers' decisions to diversify and enter new markets and industries.

▛ INCREASING PROFITABILITY THROUGH DIVERSIFICATION

diversification

The process of entering new industries, distinct from a company's core or original industry, to make new kinds of products for customers in new markets.

diversified company

A company that makes and sells products in two or more different or distinct industries.

Diversification is the process of entering new industries, distinct from a company's core or original industry, to make new kinds of products that can be sold profitably to customers in these new industries. A multibusiness model based on diversification aims to find ways to use a company's existing strategies and distinctive competencies to make products that are highly valued by customers in the new industries it enters. A **diversified company** is one that makes and sells products in two or more different or distinct industries (industries *not* in adjacent stages of an industry value chain, as in vertical integration). As in the case of the corporate strategies discussed in Chapter 9, a diversification strategy should enable a company or its individual business units to perform one or more value-chain functions: (1) at a lower cost, (2) in a way that allows for differentiation and gives the company pricing options, or (3) in a way that helps the company manage industry rivalry better—*in order to increase profitability*.

Most companies consider diversification when they are generating *free cash flow;* that is, cash in excess of that required to fund new investments in the company's current business and meet existing debt commitments.[1] In other words, free cash flow is cash beyond that needed to make profitable new investments in the existing business. When a company's successful business model is generating free cash flow and profits, managers must decide whether to return that cash to shareholders in the form of higher dividend payouts or to invest it in diversification. In theory, any free cash flow belongs to the company's owners—its shareholders. So, for diversification to create value, a company's return on investing free cash flow to pursue diversification opportunities—that is, its future ROIC—*must* exceed the value shareholders would reap by returning the cash to them. When a firm does not pay out its free cash flow to its shareholders, the shareholders bear an opportunity cost equal to their next best use of those funds (i.e., another investment that pays a similar return at a similar risk, an investment that pays a higher return at a higher risk, or an investment that pays a lower return but at a lower risk). Thus, a diversification strategy must pass the "better off" test: The firm must be more valuable than it was before the diversification, and that value must not be fully capitalized by the cost of the diversification move (i.e., the cost of entry into the new industry must be taken into account when assessing the value created by the diversification). Thus managers might defer paying dividends now to invest in diversification, but they should do so only when this is expected to create even greater cash flow (and thus higher dividends) in the future.

There are five primary ways in which pursuing a multibusiness model based on diversification can increase company profitability. Diversification can increase profitability when strategic managers (1) transfer competencies between business units in different industries, (2) leverage competencies to create business units in new industries, (3) share resources between business units to realize synergies or economies of scope, (4) use product bundling, and (5) utilize *general* organizational competencies that increase the performance of *all* a company's business units.

Transferring Competencies Across Businesses

Transferring competencies involves taking a distinctive competency developed by a business unit in one industry and implanting it in a business unit operating in another industry. The second business unit is often one a company has acquired. Companies that base their diversification strategy on transferring competencies aim to use one or more of their existing distinctive competencies in a value-chain activity—for example, in manufacturing, marketing, materials management, or research and development (R&D)—to significantly strengthen the business model of the acquired business unit or company. For example, over time, Philip Morris developed distinctive competencies in product development, consumer marketing, and brand positioning that had made it a leader in the tobacco industry. Sensing a profitable opportunity, it acquired Miller Brewing, which at the time was a relatively small player in the brewing industry. Then, to create valuable new products in the brewing industry, Philip Morris transferred some of its best marketing experts to Miller, where they applied the skills acquired at Philip Morris to turn around Miller's lackluster brewing business (see Figure 10.1). The result was the creation of Miller Light, the first "light" beer, and a marketing campaign that helped to push Miller from number 6 to number 2 in market share in the brewing industry.

Companies that base their diversification strategy on transferring competencies tend to acquire new businesses *related* to their existing business activities because of commonalities between one or more of their value-chain functions. A **commonality** is a skill or attribute that, when shared or used by two or more business units, allows both businesses to operate more effectively and efficiently and create more value for customers.

For example, Miller Brewing was related to Philip Morris's tobacco business because it was possible to create important marketing commonalities; both beer and tobacco are mass-market consumer goods in which brand positioning, advertising, and

transferring competencies
The process of taking a distinctive competency developed by a business unit in one industry and implanting it in a business unit operating in another industry.

commonality
A skill or competency that, when shared by two or more business units, allows them to operate more effectively and create more value for customers.

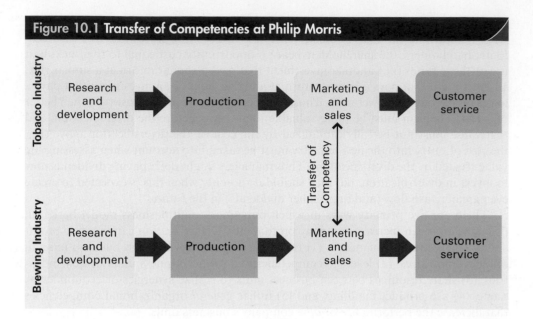

Figure 10.1 Transfer of Competencies at Philip Morris

product development skills are crucial to create successful new products. In general, such competency transfers increase profitability when they either (1) lower the cost structure of one or more of a diversified company's business units or (2) enable one or more of its business units to better differentiate their products, both of which give business-unit pricing options to lower a product's price to increase market share, or to charge a premium price.

To increase profitability, transferred competencies must involve value-chain activities that become an important source of a specific business unit's competitive advantage in the future. In other words, the distinctive competency being transferred must have real strategic value. However, all too often, companies assume that *any* commonality between their value chains is sufficient for creating value. When they attempt to transfer competencies, they find the anticipated benefits are not forthcoming because the different business units did not share some important attribute in common. For example, Coca-Cola acquired Minute Maid, the fruit juice maker, to take advantage of commonalities in global distribution and marketing, and this acquisition has proved to be highly successful. On the other hand, Coca-Cola once acquired the movie studio Columbia Pictures because it believed it could use its marketing prowess to produce blockbuster movies. This acquisition was a disaster that cost Coca-Cola billions in losses, and Columbia was eventually sold to Sony, which was then able to base many of its successful PlayStation games on the hit movies the studio produced.

leveraging competencies

The process of taking a distinctive competency developed by a business unit in one industry and using it to create a new business unit in a different industry.

Leveraging Competencies to Create a New Business

By **leveraging competencies a company** can develop a new business in a different industry. For example, Apple leveraged its competencies in personal computer (PC) hardware and software to enter the smartphone industry. Once again, the multibusiness model is based on the premise that the set of distinctive competencies that are the source of a company's competitive advantage in one industry might be applied to create a differentiation or cost-based competitive advantage for a new business unit or division in a different industry. For example, Canon used its distinctive competencies in precision mechanics, fine optics, and electronic imaging to produce laserjet printers, which, for Canon, was a new business in a new industry. Its competencies enabled it to produce high-quality (differentiated) laser printers that could be manufactured at a low cost, which created its competitive advantage, and made Canon a leader in the printer industry.

Many companies base their diversification strategy on leveraging their competencies to create new business units in different industries. Microsoft leveraged its long-time experience and relationships in the computer industry, skills in software development, and its expertise in managing industries characterized by network externalities to create new business units in industries such as videogames (with its Xbox videogame consoles and game), online portals and search engines (e.g., MSN and Bing), and tablet computers (the Surface).

Sharing Resources and Capabilities

A third way in which two or more business units that operate in different industries can increase a diversified company's profitability is when the shared resources and capabilities result in economies of scope, or synergies.[2] **Economies of scope** arise when one or more of a diversified company's business units are able to realize cost-saving or differentiation synergies because they can more effectively pool, share, and utilize expensive resources or capabilities such as skilled people, equipment, manufacturing facilities, distribution channels, advertising campaigns, and R&D laboratories. If business units in different industries can share a common resource or function, they can collectively lower their cost structure; the idea behind synergies is that 2 + 2 = 5, not 4, in terms of value created.[3] As shown in the Opening Case, LVMH can utilize its distribution channels and its influence with fashion editors to help newer brands reach a global market more quickly and cost effectively. Similarly, GE can leverage its consumer-products advertising, sales, and service activities across a wide range of products such as light bulbs, appliances, air conditioners, and furnaces, thereby reducing the average cost of these activities for each product line. There are two major sources of cost reductions.

There are two major sources of cost reductions. First, when companies can share resources or capabilities across business units, it lowers their cost structure compared to a company that operates in only one industry and bears the full costs of developing resources and capabilities. For example, P&G makes disposable diapers, toilet paper, and paper towels, which are all paper-based products that customers value for their ability to absorb fluids without disintegrating. Because these products need the same attribute—absorbency—P&G can share the R&D costs associated with developing and making even more advanced absorbent, paper-based products across the three distinct businesses (only two are shown in Figure 10.2). Similarly, because all of these products are sold to retailers, P&G can use the same sales force to sell its whole array of products (see Figure 10.2). In contrast, P&G competitors that make only one or two of these products cannot share these costs across industries, so their cost structures are higher. As a result, P&G has lower costs; it can use its marketing function to better differentiate its products, and it achieves a higher ROIC than companies that operate only in one or a few industries—which are unable to obtain economies of scope from the ability to share resources and obtain synergies across business units.

economies of scope
The synergies that arise when one or more of a diversified company's business units are able to lower costs or increase differentiation because they can more effectively pool, share, and utilize expensive resources or capabilities.

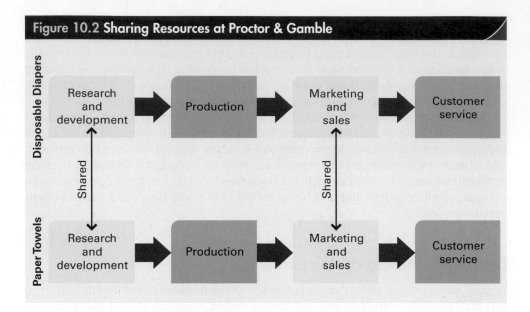

Figure 10.2 Sharing Resources at Proctor & Gamble

Similarly, Nike, which began strictly as a maker of running shoes, realized that its brand image, and its relationships with athletes and sports events, could be profitably leveraged into other types of athletic footwear, athletic apparel, and accessories such as sunglasses and headphones. Those products were more differentiated because of the Nike brand name and had better exposure because Nike was able to place them in suitable endorsement spots via its relationships with athletes and events, and Nike is able to amortize the cost of its brand-building activities across a wider range of products, thus achieving economies of scope.

To reiterate, diversification to obtain economies of scope is possible only when there are *significant* commonalities between one or more value-chain functions in a company's different business units or divisions that result in synergies which increase profitability. In addition, managers must be aware that the costs of coordination necessary to achieve synergies or economies of scope within a company may sometimes be *higher* than the value that can be created by such a strategy.[4] As noted in the Closing Case, although Citibank had anticipated major cost savings from consolidating operations across its acquisitions, and revenue-increasing opportunities from cross-selling, some synergies turned out to be small or difficult to reap. In retrospect, the coordination costs that Citi bore (in the form of massive losses due to inadequate oversight over its investment activities) probably vastly exceeded the synergies it gained. Consequently, diversification based on obtaining economies of scope should be pursued only when the sharing of competencies will result in *significant* synergies that will achieve a competitive advantage for one or more of a company's new or existing business units.

Using Product Bundling

In the search for new ways to differentiate products, more and more companies are entering into industries that provide customers with new products that are connected or related to their existing products. This allows a company to expand the range of products it produces in order to satisfy customers' needs for a complete package of related products. This is currently happening in telecommunications, in which customers are increasingly seeking package prices for wired phone service, wireless phone service, high-speed access to the Internet, television programming, online gaming, video on demand, or any combination of these services. To meet this need, large phone companies such as AT&T and Verizon have been acquiring other companies that provide one or more of these services, and cable companies such as Comcast have acquired or formed strategic alliances with companies that can offer their customers a package of these services. In 2010, for example, Comcast acquired GE's NBC division to gain control of its library of content programming. The goal, once again, is to bundle products to offer customers lower prices and/or a superior set of services.

Just as manufacturing companies strive to reduce the number of their component suppliers to reduce costs and increase quality, final customers want to obtain the convenience and reduced price of a bundle of related products—such as from Google or Microsoft's cloud-based commercial, business-oriented online applications. Another example of product bundling comes from the medical equipment industry, in which companies that, in the past, made one kind of product such as operating theater equipment, ultrasound devices, or magnetic imaging or X-ray equipment, have now merged with or been acquired by other companies to allow a larger, diversified company to provide hospitals with a complete range of medical equipment. This industry consolidation has also been driven by hospitals and health maintenance organizations (HMOs) that wish to obtain the convenience and lower prices that often follow from forming a long-term contract with a single supplier.

It is important to note that product bundling often does not require joint ownership. In many instances, bundling can be achieved through market contracts. For example, McDonald's does not need to manufacture toys in order to bundle them into Happy Meals—it can buy them through a supply contract. Disney does need to own airline services to offer a package deal on a vacation—an alliance contract will serve just as well. For product bundling to serve as a justification for diversification, there must be a strong need for coordination between the producers of the different products that cannot be overcome through market contracts.

Utilizing General Organizational Competencies

General organizational competencies transcend individual functions or business units and are found at the top or corporate level of a multibusiness company. Typically, **general organizational competencies** are the result of the skills of a company's top managers and functional experts. When these general competencies are present—and many times they are not—they help each business unit within a company perform at a higher level than it could if it operated as a separate or independent company. This increases the profitability of the entire corporation.[5] Three general organizational competencies help a company increase its performance and profitability: (1) entrepreneurial capabilities, (2) organizational design capabilities, and (3) strategic capabilities.

Entrepreneurial Capabilities   A company that generates significant excess cash flow can take advantage of it only if its managers are able to identify new opportunities and act on them to create a stream of new and improved products, in its current industry and in new industries. Companies such as Apple, 3M, Google, and Samsung

general organizational competencies

Competencies that result from the skills of a company's top managers and that help every business unit within a company perform at a higher level than it could if it operated as a separate or independent company.

are able to promote entrepreneurship because they have an organizational culture that stimulates managers to act entrepreneurially.[6] As a result, they create new, profitable business units more quickly than do other companies, and this allows them to take advantage of profitable opportunities for diversification. We discuss one of the strategies required to generate new, profitable businesses later in this chapter: internal new venturing. For now, it is important to note that, to promote entrepreneurship, a company must (1) encourage managers to take risks, (2) give managers the time and resources to pursue novel ideas, (3) not punish managers when a new idea fails, and (4) make sure that the company's free cash flow is not wasted in pursuing too many risky ventures that have a low probability of generating a profitable return on investment. Strategic managers face a significant challenge in achieving all four of these objectives. On the one hand, a company must encourage risk taking; on the other hand, it must limit the number of risky ventures in which it engages.

Companies that possess strong entrepreneurial capabilities achieve this balancing act. For example, 3M's goal of generating 40% of its revenues from products introduced within the past 4 years focuses managers' attention on the need to develop new products and enter new businesses. 3M's long-standing commitment to help its customers solve problems also ensures that ideas for new businesses are customer focused. The company's celebration of employees who have created successful new businesses reinforces the norm of entrepreneurship and risk taking. Similarly, there is a norm that failure should not be punished but instead viewed as a learning experience.

organizational design skills

The ability of a company's managers to create a structure, culture, and control systems that motivate and coordinate employees to perform at a high level.

Capabilities in Organizational Design   Organizational design skills are a result of managers' ability to create a structure, culture, and control systems that motivate and coordinate employees to perform at a high level. Organizational design is a major factor that influences a company's entrepreneurial capabilities; it is also an important determinant of a company's ability to create the functional competencies that give it a competitive advantage. The way strategic managers make organizational design decisions, such as how much autonomy to give to managers lower in the hierarchy, what kinds of norms and values should be developed to create an entrepreneurial culture, and even how to design its headquarters to encourage the free flow of ideas, is an important determinant of a diversified company's ability to profit from its multibusiness model. Effective organizational structure and controls create incentives that encourage business-unit (divisional) managers to maximize the efficiency and effectiveness of their units. Moreover, good organizational design helps prevent strategic managers from missing out on profitable new opportunities, as happens when employees become so concerned with protecting their company's competitive position in *existing* industries that they lose sight of new or improved ways to do business and gain profitable opportunities to enter new industries.

Chapters 11 and 12 of this book look at organizational design in depth. To profit from pursuing the corporate-level strategy of diversification, a company must be able to continuously manage and change its structure and culture to motivate and coordinate its employees to work at a high level and develop the resources and capabilities upon which its competitive advantage depends. The need to align a company's structure with its strategy is a complex, never-ending task, and only top managers with superior organizational design skills can do it.

Superior Strategic Management Capabilities   For diversification to increase profitability, a company's top managers must have superior capabilities in strategic management. They must possess the intangible, hard-to-define governance skills that are required to manage different business units in a way that enables these units to perform better than they would if they were independent companies.[7] These governance skills are a rare and valuable capability. However, certain CEOs and top managers seem to have them; they have developed the aptitude of managing multiple businesses simultaneously and encouraging the top managers of those business units to devise strategies that achieve superior performance. Examples of CEOs famous for their superior strategic management capabilities include Jeffrey Immelt at GE, Steve Jobs at Apple, and Larry Ellison at Oracle.

An especially important governance skill in a diversified company is the ability to diagnose the underlying source of the problems of a poorly performing business unit, and then to understand how to proceed to solve those problems. This might involve recommending new strategies to the existing top managers of the unit, or knowing when to replace them with a new management team that is better able to fix the problems. Top managers who have such governance skills tend to be very good at probing business-unit managers for information and helping them think through strategic problems, as the example of United Technologies Corporation (UTC) discussed in Strategy in Action 10.1 suggests.

10.1 STRATEGY IN ACTION

United Technologies Has an "ACE" in Its Pocket

United Technologies Corporation (UTC), based in Hartford, Connecticut, is a *conglomerate*, a company that owns a wide variety of other companies that operate separately in many different businesses and industries. UTC has businesses in two main groups, aerospace and building systems. Its aerospace group includes Sikorsky aircraft, Pratt & Whitney Engines, and UTC Aerospace systems, which was formed through the merger of Hamilton Sundstrand and Goodrich. Its building systems group includes Otis elevators and escalators; Carrier and Noresco heating and air-conditioning solutions; fire-detection and security businesses that include Chubb, Kidde, Edwards, Fenwal, Marioff, Supra, and Interlogix; and business that develop business automation systems (such as automatically controlled lighting and temperature) that include AutomatedLogic, Onity, Lenel, and UTEC.

Today, investors frown upon companies like UTC that own and operate companies in widely different industries. There is a growing perception that managers can better manage a company's business model when the company operates as an independent or stand-alone entity. How can UTC justify holding all these companies together in a conglomerate? Why would this lead to a greater increase in total profitability than if they operated as independent companies? In the last decade, the boards of directors and CEOs of many conglomerates such as Tyco and Textron have realized that by holding diverse companies together they were reducing, not increasing, the profitability of their companies. As a result, many conglomerates have been broken up, and their individual companies spun off to allow them to operate as separate, independent entities.

(continued)

UTC's CEO George David claims that he has created a unique, sophisticated, multibusiness model that adds value across UTC's diverse businesses. David joined Otis Elevator as an assistant to its CEO in 1975, but within a year, UTC acquired Otis. The 1970s was a decade when a "bigger is better" mindset ruled corporate America, and mergers and acquisitions of all kinds were seen as the best way to grow profits. UTC sent David to manage its South American operations and later gave him responsibility for its Japanese operations. Otis had formed an alliance with Matsushita to develop an elevator for the Japanese market, and the resulting "Elevonic 401," after being installed widely in Japanese buildings, proved to be a disaster. It broke down far more often than elevators made by other Japanese companies, and customers were concerned about the reliability and safety of this model.

Matsushita was extremely embarrassed about the elevator's failure and assigned one of its leading total quality management (TQM) experts, Yuzuru Ito, to head a team of Otis engineers to find out why it performed so poorly. Under Ito's direction, all employees—managers, designers, and production workers—who had produced the elevator analyzed why it was malfunctioning. This intensive study led to a total redesign of the elevator, and when the new, improved elevator was launched worldwide, it met with great success. Otis's share of the global elevator market dramatically increased, and David was named president of UTC in 1992. He was given the responsibility to cut costs across the entire corporation, including its important Pratt & Whitney division, and his success in reducing UTC's cost structure and increasing its ROIC led to his appointment as CEO in 1994.

Now responsible for all of UTC's diverse companies, David decided that the best way to increase UTC's profitability, which had been declining, was to find ways to improve efficiency and quality in *all* its constituent companies. He convinced Ito to move to Hartford and take responsibility for championing the kinds of improvements that had by now transformed the Otis division. Ito began to develop UTC's TQM system, also known as "Achieving Competitive Excellence," or ACE.

ACE is a set of tasks and procedures used by employees, from the shop floor to top management, to analyze all aspects of the way a product is made. The goal is to find ways to improve *quality and reliability*, to *lower the costs* of making a product, and, especially, to find ways to make the next generation of a particular product perform better—in other words, to encourage *technological innovation*. David makes every employee in every function at every level personally responsible for achieving the incremental, step-by-step gains that result in state-of-the-art, innovative, efficient products that allow a company to dominate its industry.

David calls these techniques "process disciplines," and he has used them to increase the performance of all UTC companies. Through these techniques, he has created the extra value for UTC that justifies it owning and operating such a diverse set of businesses. David's success can be seen in the performance that his company has achieved in the decade since he took control: he has quadrupled UTC's earnings per share, and its sales and profits have soared. UTC has been in the top three performers of the companies that make up the Dow Jones industrial average for most of the 2000s, and the company has consistently outperformed GE, another huge conglomerate, in its return to investors.

David and his managers believe that the gains that can be achieved from UTC's process disciplines are never-ending because its own R&D—in which it invests more than $2.5 billion a year—is constantly producing product innovations that can help all its businesses. Recognizing that its skills in creating process improvements are specific to manufacturing companies, UTC's strategy is to only acquire companies that make products that can benefit from the use of its ACE program—hence its Chubb acquisition. At the same time, David invests only in companies that have the potential to remain leading companies in their industries and can therefore charge above-average prices. His acquisitions strengthen the competencies of UTC's existing businesses. For example, he acquired Sundstrand, a leading aerospace and industrial systems company, and combined it with UTC's Hamilton Aerospace Division to create Hamilton Sundstrand, which is now a major supplier to Boeing and makes products that command premium prices. In October 2011, UTC acquired Goodrich, a major supplier of airline components, for over $22 billion in order to strengthen its aircraft division.

Source: http://utc.com.

Related to strategic management skills is the ability of the top managers of a diversified company to identify inefficient, poorly managed companies in other industries and then acquire and restructure them to improve their performance—and thus the profitability of the total corporation. This is known as a **turnaround strategy**.[8] There are several ways to improve the performance of an acquired company. First, the top managers of the acquired company are replaced with a more aggressive top-management team. Second, the new top-management team sells off expensive assets such as underperforming divisions, executive jets, and elaborate corporate headquarters; it also terminates staff to reduce the cost structure. Third, the new management team devises new strategies to improve the performance of the operations of the acquired business and improve its efficiency, quality, innovativeness, and customer responsiveness.

Fourth, to motivate the new top-management team and the other employees of the acquired company to work toward such goals, a companywide, pay-for-performance bonus system linked to profitability is introduced to reward employees at all levels for their hard work. Fifth, the acquiring company often establishes "stretch" goals for employees at all levels; these are challenging, hard-to-obtain goals that force employees at all levels to work to increase the company's efficiency and effectiveness. The members of the new top-management team clearly understand that if they fail to increase their division's performance and meet these stretch goals within some agreed-upon amount of time, they will be replaced. In sum, corporate managers of the acquiring company establish a system of rewards and sanctions that incentivize new top managers of the acquired unit to develop strategies to improve their unit's operating performance.

turnaround strategy
When managers of a diversified company identify inefficient, poorly managed companies in other industries and then acquire and restructure them to improve their performance—and thus the profitability of the total corporation.

◤ TWO TYPES OF DIVERSIFICATION

The last section discussed five principal ways in which companies use diversification to transfer and implant their business models and strategies into other industries and so increase their long-term profitability. The two corporate strategies of *related diversification* and *unrelated diversification* can be distinguished by how they attempt to realize the five profit-enhancing benefits of diversification.[9]

Related Diversification

Related diversification is a corporate-level strategy based on the goal of establishing a business unit (division) in a new industry that is *related* to a company's existing business units by some form of commonality or linkage between the value-chain functions of the existing and new business units. As you might expect, the goal of this strategy is to obtain benefits from transferring competencies, leveraging competencies, sharing resources, and bundling products, as just discussed.

The multibusiness model of related diversification is based on taking advantage of strong technological, manufacturing, marketing, and sales commonalities between new and existing business units that can be successfully "tweaked" or modified to increase the competitive advantage of one or more business units. Figure 10.3 illustrates the commonalities or linkages possible among the different functions of three different business units or divisions. The greater the number of linkages that can be formed among business units, the greater the potential to realize the profit-enhancing benefits of the five reasons to diversify discussed previously.

related diversification
A corporate-level strategy based on the goal of establishing a business unit in a new industry that is related to a company's existing business units by some form of commonality or linkage between their value-chain functions.

Figure 10.3 Commonalities Between the Value Chains of Three Business Units

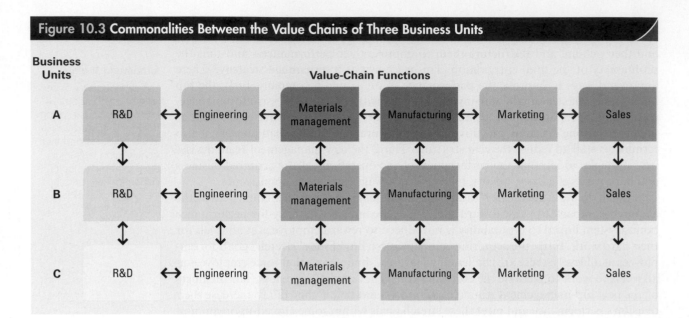

Another advantage of related diversification is that it can allow a company to use any general organizational competency it possesses to increase the overall performance of *all* its different industry divisions. For example, strategic managers may strive to create a structure and culture that encourages entrepreneurship across divisions, as Google, Apple, and 3M have done; beyond these general competences, these companies all have a set of distinctive competences that can be shared among their different business units and that they continuously strive to improve.

Unrelated Diversification

unrelated diversification
A corporate-level strategy based on a multibusiness model that uses general organizational competencies to increase the performance of all the company's business units.

internal capital market
A corporate-level strategy whereby the firm's headquarters assesses the performance of business units and allocates money across them. Cash generated by units that are profitable but have poor investment opportunities within their business is used to cross-subsidize businesses that need cash and have strong promise for long-run profitability.

Unrelated diversification is a corporate-level strategy whereby firms own unrelated businesses and attempt to increase their value through an internal capital market, the use of general organizational competencies, or both. Business organizations that operate in many diverse industries are often called *conglomerates*. An **internal capital market** refers to a situation whereby corporate headquarters assesses the performance of business units and allocates money across them. Cash generated by units that are profitable but have poor investment opportunities within their business is used to cross-subsidize businesses that need cash and have strong promise for long-run profitability. A large, diverse firm may have free cash generated from its internal businesses, or readier access to cheap cash on the external capital market than an individual business unit might have. For example, GE's large capital reserves and excellent credit rating enable it to provide funding to advanced-technology businesses within its corporate umbrella (e.g., solar power stations, subsea oil-production equipment, avionics, photonics) that would otherwise pay a high price (either in interest payments or equity shares) for funding due to their inherent uncertainty.

The benefits of an internal capital market are limited, however, by the efficiency of the external capital market (banks, stockholders, venture capitalists, angel investors, and so on). If the external capital market were perfectly efficient, managers could not create additional value by cross-subsidizing businesses with internal cash. An internal capital market is, in essence, an arbitrage strategy whereby managers make money by making better investment decisions within the firm than the external capital market would, often because they possess superior information. The amount of value that can be created through an internal capital market is thus directly proportional to the inefficiency of the external capital market. In the United States, where capital markets have become fairly efficient due to (1) reporting requirements mandated by the Securities and Exchange Commission (SEC), (2) large numbers of research analysts, (3) an extremely large and active investment community, (4) strong communication systems, and (5) strong contract law, it is not common to see firms create significant value through an internal capital market. As a result, few large conglomerates have survived, and many of those that do survive trade at a discount (that is, their stock is worth less than the stock of more specialized firms operating in the same industries). On the other hand, in a market with a less efficient capital market, conglomerates may create significant value. Tata Group, for example, is an extremely large, diverse, business-holding group in India. Founded during the 1800s, it took on many projects that its founders felt were crucial to India's development (for example, developing a rail transportation system, hotels, and power production). The lack of a well-developed investment community and poor contract law to protect investors and bankers meant that funds were often not available to entrepreneurs in India, or were available only at a very high cost. Tata Group was thus able to use cross-subsidization to fund projects much more cheaply than independent businesses could. Furthermore, the reputation of the company served as a strong guarantee that it would fulfill its promises (which was particularly important in the absence of strong contract law), and its long, deep relationships with the government gave it an advantage in securing licenses and permits.

Companies pursuing a strategy of unrelated diversification have *no* intention of transferring or leveraging competencies between business units or sharing resources other than cash and general organizational competencies. If the strategic managers of conglomerates have the special skills needed to manage many companies in diverse industries, the strategy can result in superior performance and profitability; often they do not have these skills, as is discussed later in the chapter. Companies such as UTC (discussed in Strategy in Action 10.1) have top managers who do possess these special skills.

▼ THE LIMITS AND DISADVANTAGES OF DIVERSIFICATION

Many companies, such as 3M, Samsung, UTC, and Cisco, have achieved the benefits of pursuing either or both of the two diversification strategies just discussed, and they have sustained their profitability over time. On the other hand, GM, Tyco, Textron, and Philips failed miserably and became unprofitable when they pursued diversification. There are three principal reasons why a business model based on diversification may lead to a loss of competitive advantage: (1) changes in the industry or inside a company that occur over time, (2) diversification pursued for the wrong reasons, and (3) excessive diversification that results in increasing bureaucratic costs.

Changes in the Industry or Company

Diversification is a complex strategy. To pursue it, top managers must have the ability to recognize profitable opportunities to enter new industries and implement the strategies necessary to make diversification profitable. Over time, a company's top-management team often changes; sometimes its most able executives join other companies and become CEOs, and sometimes successful CEOs retire or step down. When the managers who possess the hard-to-define skills leave, they often take their vision with them. A company's new leaders may lack the competency or commitment necessary to pursue diversification successfully over time; thus, the cost structure of the diversified company increases and eliminates any gains the strategy may have produced.

In addition, the environment often changes rapidly and unpredictably over time. When new technology blurs industry boundaries, it can destroy the source of a company's competitive advantage. For example, by 2011, it was clear that Apple's iPhone and iPad had become a direct competitor with Nintendo's and Sony's mobile gaming consoles. When such a major technological change occurs in a company's core business, the benefits it has previously achieved from transferring or leveraging distinctive competencies disappear. The company is then saddled with a collection of businesses that have all become poor performers in their respective industries because they are not based on the new technology—something that has happened to Sony. Thus, a major problem with diversification is that the future success of a business is hard to predict when this strategy is used. For a company to profit from it over time, managers must be as willing to divest business units as they are to acquire them. Research suggests managers do not behave in this way, however.

Diversification for the Wrong Reasons

As we have discussed, when managers decide to pursue diversification, they must have a clear vision of how their entry into new industries will allow them to create new products that provide more value for customers and increase their company's profitability. Over time, however, a diversification strategy may result in falling profitability for reasons noted earlier, but managers often refuse to recognize that their strategy is failing. Although they know they should divest unprofitable businesses, managers "make up" reasons to keep their collection of businesses together.

In the past, for example, one widely used (and false) justification for diversification was that the strategy would allow a company to obtain the benefits of risk pooling. The idea behind risk pooling is that a company can reduce the risk of its revenues and profits rising and falling sharply (something that sharply lowers its stock price) if it acquires and operates companies in several industries that have different business cycles. The business cycle is the tendency for the revenues and profits of companies in an industry to rise and fall over time because of "predictable" changes in customer demand. For example, even in a recession, people still need to eat—the profits earned by supermarket chains will be relatively stable; sales at Safeway, Kroger, and also at "dollar stores," actually rise as shoppers attempt to get more value for their dollars. At the same time, a recession can cause demand for cars and luxury goods to plunge. Many CEOs argue that diversifying into industries that have different business cycles would allow the sales and revenues of some of their divisions to rise, while sales and revenues in other divisions would fall. A more stable stream of revenue and profits is the net result over time. An example of risk pooling occurred when U.S. Steel diversified into the oil and gas industry in an attempt to offset the adverse effects of cyclical downturns in the steel industry.

This argument ignores two important facts. First, stockholders can eliminate the risk inherent in holding an individual stock by diversifying their own portfolios, and they can do so at a much lower cost than a company can. Thus, attempts to pool risks through diversification represent an unproductive use of resources; instead, profits should be returned to shareholders in the form of increased dividends. Second, research suggests that corporate diversification is not an effective way to pool risks because the business cycles of different industries are *inherently difficult to predict,* so it is likely that a diversified company will find that an economic downturn affects *all* its industries simultaneously. If this happens, the company's profitability plunges.[10]

When a company's core business is in trouble, another mistaken justification for diversification is that entry into new industries will rescue the core business and lead to long-term growth and profitability. One company that made this mistake is Kodak. In the 1980s, increased competition from low-cost, Japanese competitors such as Fuji, combined with the beginnings of the digital revolution, soon led its revenues and profits to plateau and then fall. Its managers should have done all they could to reduce its cost structure; instead, they took its huge free cash flow and spent tens of billions of dollars to enter new industries such as health care, biotechnology, and computer hardware in a desperate and mistaken attempt to find ways to increase profitability.

This was a disaster because every industry Kodak entered was populated by strong companies such as 3M, Canon, and Xerox. Also, Kodak's corporate managers lacked any general competencies to give their new business units a competitive advantage. Moreover, the more industries Kodak entered, the greater the range of threats the company encountered, and the more time managers had to spend dealing with these threats. As a result, they could spend much less time improving the performance of their core film business, which continued to decline.

In reality, Kodak's diversification was solely for growth, but *growth does not create value for stockholders*; growth is the by-product, not the objective, of a diversification strategy. However, in desperation, companies diversify for reasons of growth alone rather than to gain any well-thought-out, strategic advantage.[11] In fact, many studies suggest that too much diversification may reduce rather than improve company profitability.[12] That is, the diversification strategies many companies pursue may *reduce* value instead of creating it.[13]

The Bureaucratic Costs of Diversification

A major reason why diversification often fails to boost profitability is that, very often, the *bureaucratic costs* of diversification exceed the benefits created by the strategy (that is, the increased profit that results when a company makes and sells a wider range of differentiated products and/or lowers its cost structure). As we mention

bureaucratic costs

The costs associated with solving the transaction difficulties between business units and corporate headquarters as a company obtains the benefits from transferring, sharing, and leveraging competencies.

in the previous chapter, **bureaucratic costs** are the costs associated with solving the transaction difficulties that arise between a company's business units and between business units and corporate headquarters, as the company attempts to obtain the benefits from transferring, sharing, and leveraging competencies. They also include the costs associated with using general organizational competencies to solve managerial and functional inefficiencies. The level of bureaucratic costs in a diversified organization is a function of two factors: the number of business units in a company's portfolio, and the degree to which coordination is required between these different business units to realize the advantages of diversification.

Number of Businesses   The greater the number of business units in a company's portfolio, the more difficult it is for corporate managers to remain informed about the complexities of each business. Managers simply do not have the time to assess the business model of each unit. This problem occurred at GE in the 1970s, when its growth-hungry CEO Reg Jones acquired many new businesses. As he commented:

> I tried to review each plan [of each business unit] in great detail. This effort took untold hours and placed a tremendous burden on the corporate executive office. After a while I began to realize that no matter how hard we would work, we could not achieve the necessary in-depth understanding of the 40-odd business unit plans.[14]

The inability of top managers in extensively diversified companies to maintain control over their multibusiness models over time often leads them to base important resource-allocation decisions on a superficial analysis of each business unit's competitive position. For example, a promising business unit may be starved of investment funds, while other business units receive far more cash than they can profitably reinvest in their operations. Furthermore, because they are distant from the day-to-day operations of the business units, corporate managers may find that business-unit managers try to hide information on poor performance to save their own jobs. For example, business-unit managers might blame poor performance on difficult competitive conditions, even when it is the result of their inability to craft a successful business model. As such organizational problems increase, top managers must spend an enormous amount of time and effort to solve them. This increases bureaucratic costs and cancels out the profit-enhancing advantages of pursuing diversification, such as those obtained from sharing or leveraging competencies.

Coordination Among Businesses   The amount of coordination required to realize value from a diversification strategy based on transferring, sharing, or leveraging competencies is a major source of bureaucratic costs. The bureaucratic mechanisms needed to oversee and manage the coordination and handoffs between units, such as cross-business-unit teams and management committees, are a major source of these costs. A second source of bureaucratic costs arises because of the enormous amount of managerial time and effort required to accurately measure the performance and unique profit contribution of a business unit that is transferring or sharing resources with another. Consider a company that has two business units, one making household products (such as liquid soap and laundry detergent) and another making packaged food products. The products of both units are sold through supermarkets. To lower the cost structure, the parent company decides to pool the marketing and sales functions

Figure 10.4 Coordination Among Related Business Units

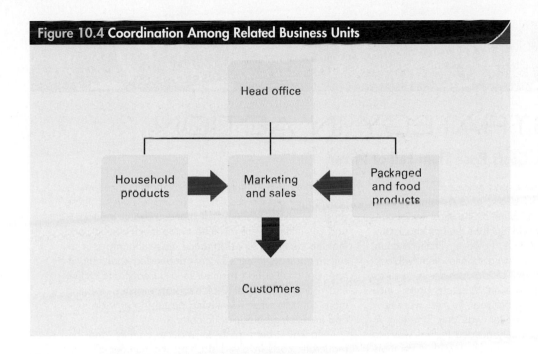

of each business unit, using an organizational structure similar to that illustrated in Figure 10.4. The company is organized into three divisions: a household products division, a food products division, and a marketing division.

Although such an arrangement may significantly lower operating costs, it can also give rise to substantial control problems, and hence bureaucratic costs. For example, if the performance of the household products business begins to slip, identifying who is to be held accountable—managers in the household products division or managers in the marketing division—may prove difficult. Indeed, each may blame the other for poor performance. Although such problems can be resolved if corporate management performs an in-depth audit of both divisions, the bureaucratic costs (managers' time and effort) involved in doing so may once again cancel out any value achieved from diversification. The need to reduce bureaucratic costs is evident from the experience of Pfizer, discussed in Strategy in Action 10.2.

In sum, although diversification can be a highly profitable strategy to pursue, it is also the most complex and difficult strategy to manage because it is based on a complex, multibusiness model. Even when a company has pursued this strategy successfully in the past, changing conditions both in the industry environment and within a company can quickly reduce the profit-creating advantages of this strategy. For example, such changes may result in one or more business units losing their competitive advantage, as happened to Sony. Or, changes may cause the bureaucratic costs associated with pursuing diversification to rise sharply and cancel out its advantages. Thus, the existence of bureaucratic costs places a limit on the amount of diversification that a company can profitably pursue. It makes sense for a company to diversify only when the profit-enhancing advantages of this strategy exceed the bureaucratic costs of managing the increasing number of business units required when a company expands and enters new industries.

10.2 STRATEGY IN ACTION

How Bureaucratic Costs Rose Then Fell at Pfizer

Pfizer is the largest global pharmaceuticals company, with sales of almost $50 billion in 2014. Its research scientists have innovated some of the most successful, profitable drugs in the world, such as the first cholesterol reducer, Lipitor. In the 2000s, however, Pfizer encountered major problems in its attempt to innovate new blockbuster drugs while its current blockbuster drugs, such as Lipitor, lost their patent protection. Whereas Lipitor once earned $13 billion in profits per year, its sales were now fast declining. By 2012, Lipitor was only bringing in $3.9 billion. Pfizer desperately needed to find ways to make its product development pipeline work. One manager, Martin Mackay, believed he knew how to do it.

When Pfizer's R&D chief retired, Mackay, his deputy, made it clear to CEO Jeffrey Kindler that he wanted the job. Kindler made it equally clear he thought the company could use some new talent and fresh ideas to solve its problems. Mackay realized he had to quickly devise a convincing plan to change the way Pfizer's scientists worked to develop new drugs, gain Kindler's support, and get the top job. He created a detailed plan for changing the way Pfizer's thousands of researchers made decisions, ensuring that the company's resources, talent, and funds would be put to their best use. After Kindler reviewed the plan, he was so impressed he promoted Mackay to the top R&D position. What was Mackay's plan?

As Pfizer had grown over time as a result of mergers with two large pharmaceutical companies, Warner Lambert and Pharmacia, Mackay noted how decision-making problems and conflict between the managers of Pfizer's different drug divisions had increased. As it grew, Pfizer's organizational structure had become taller and taller, and the size of its headquarters staff grew. With more managers and levels in the company's hierarchy there was a great need for committees to integrate across activities. However, in meetings, different groups of managers fought to promote the development of the drugs in which they had the most interest, and increas-

ingly came into conflict with one another in efforts to ensure they got the resources needed to develop these drugs. In short, Mackay felt that too many managers and committees were resulting in too much conflict, and that the company's performance was suffering as a result. In addition, Pfizer's success depended upon innovation, but conflict had resulted in a bureaucratic culture that reduced the quality of decision making, creating more difficulty when identifying promising new drugs—and increasing bureaucratic costs.

Mackay's bold plan to reduce conflict and bureaucratic costs involved slashing the number of management layers between top managers and scientists from fourteen to seven, which resulted in the layoff of thousands of Pfizer's managers. He also abolished the product development committees whose wrangling he believed was slowing down the process of transforming innovative ideas into blockbuster drugs. After streamlining the hierarchy, he focused on reducing the number of bureaucratic rules scientists had to follow, many of which were unnecessary and promoted conflict. He and his team eliminated every kind of written report that was slowing the innovation process. For example, scientists had been in the habit of submitting quarterly and monthly reports to top managers explaining each drug's progress; Mackay told them to choose one report or the other.

As you can imagine, Mackay's efforts caused enormous upheaval in the company, as managers fought to keep their positions and scientists fought to protect the drugs they had in development. However, a resolute Mackay pushed his agenda through with the support of the CEO, who defended his efforts to create a new R&D product development process that empowered Pfizer's scientists and promoted innovation and entrepreneurship. Pfizer's scientists reported that they felt "liberated" by the new work flow; the level of conflict decreased, and they felt hopeful that new drugs would be produced more quickly.

Source: www.pfizer.com.

CHOOSING A STRATEGY

Related Versus Unrelated Diversification

Because related diversification involves more sharing of competencies, one might think it can boost profitability in more ways than unrelated diversification, and is therefore the better diversification strategy. However, some companies can create as much or more value from pursuing unrelated diversification, so this strategy must also have some substantial benefits. An unrelated company does *not* need to achieve coordination between business units; it has to cope only with the bureaucratic costs that arise from the number of businesses in its portfolio. In contrast, a related company must achieve coordination *among* business units if it is to realize the gains that come from utilizing its distinctive competencies. Consequently, it has to cope with the bureaucratic costs that arise *both* from the number of business units in its portfolio *and* from coordination among business units. Although it is true that related diversified companies can create value and profit in more ways than unrelated companies, they also have to bear higher bureaucratic costs to do so. These higher costs may cancel out the greater benefits, making the strategy no more profitable than one of unrelated diversification.

How, then, does a company choose between these strategies? The choice depends upon a comparison of the benefits of each strategy against the bureaucratic costs of pursuing it. It pays for a company to pursue related diversification when (1) the company's competencies can be applied across a greater number of industries and (2) the company has superior strategic capabilities that allow it to keep bureaucratic costs under close control—perhaps by encouraging entrepreneurship or by developing a value creating organizational culture.

Using the same logic, it pays for a company to pursue unrelated diversification when (1) each business unit's functional competencies have few useful applications across industries, but the company's top managers are skilled at raising the profitability of poorly run businesses and (2) the company's managers use their superior strategic management competencies to improve the competitive advantage of their business units and keep bureaucratic costs under control. Well-managed companies such as UTC (discussed in Strategy in Action 10.1) have managers who can successfully pursue unrelated diversification and reap its rewards.

The Web of Corporate-Level Strategy

Finally, it is important to note that although some companies may choose to pursue a strategy of related or unrelated diversification, there is nothing that stops them from pursuing both strategies at the same time. The purpose of corporate-level strategy is to increase long-term profitability. A company can pursue multiple strategies as long as strategic managers have weighed the advantages and disadvantages of those strategies and arrived at a multibusiness model that justifies them. Figure 10.5 illustrates how Sony developed a web of corporate strategies to compete in many industries—a program that proved a mistake and reduced its differentiation advantage and increased its cost structure in the 2000s.

Sony's core business is in electronic products, and in the past, it was well known for innovative products that made it a leading, global brand. To protect the quality of its electronic products, Sony decided to manufacture a high percentage of the component

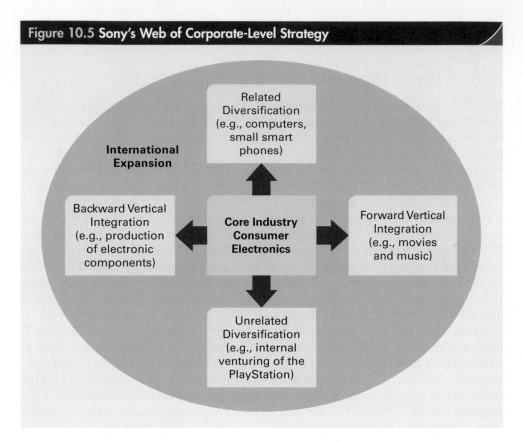

Figure 10.5 Sony's Web of Corporate-Level Strategy

Related Diversification (e.g., computers, small smart phones)

International Expansion

Backward Vertical Integration (e.g., production of electronic components)

Core Industry Consumer Electronics

Forward Vertical Integration (e.g., movies and music)

Unrelated Diversification (e.g., internal venturing of the PlayStation)

parts for its televisions, DVD players, and other units and pursued a strategy of backward vertical integration. Sony also engaged in forward vertical integration: for example, it acquired Columbia Pictures and MGM to enter the movie or "entertainment software" industry, and it opened a chain of Sony stores in shopping malls (to compete with Apple). Sony also shared and leveraged its distinctive competencies by developing its own business units to operate in the computer and smartphone industries, a strategy of related diversification. Finally, when it decided to enter the home videogame industry and develop its PlayStation to compete with Nintendo, it was pursuing a strategy of unrelated diversification. In the 2000s, this division contributed more to Sony's profits than its core electronics business—but the company has not been doing well.

As this discussion suggests, Sony's profitability has fallen dramatically because its multibusiness model led it to diversify into too many industries, in each of which the focus was upon innovating high-quality products. As a result, its cost structure increased so much it swallowed up all the profits its businesses were generating. Sony's strategy of individual-business-unit autonomy also resulted in each unit pursuing its own goals at the expense of the company's multibusiness model—which escalated bureaucratic costs and drained its profitability. In particular, because its different divisions did not share their knowledge and expertise, this incongruence allowed competitors such as Samsung to supersede Sony, especially with smartphones and flatscreen, LCD TV products.

▛ ENTERING NEW INDUSTRIES: INTERNAL NEW VENTURES

We have discussed the sources of value managers seek through corporate-level strategies of related and unrelated diversification (and the challenges and risks these strategies also impose). Now we turn to the three main methods managers employ to enter new industries: internal new ventures, acquisitions, and joint ventures. In this section, we consider the pros and cons of using internal new ventures. In the following sections, we look at acquisitions and joint ventures.

The Attractions of Internal New Venturing

Internal new venturing is typically used to implement corporate-level strategies when a company possesses one or more distinctive competencies in its core business model that can be leveraged or recombined to enter a new industry. **Internal new venturing** is the process of transferring resources to, and creating a new business unit or division in, a new industry. Internal venturing is used often by companies that have a business model based upon using their technology or design skills to innovate new kinds of products and enter related markets or industries. Thus, technology-based companies that pursue related diversification—for example, DuPont, which has created new markets with products such as cellophane, nylon, Freon, and Teflon—are most likely to use internal new venturing. 3M has a near-legendary knack for creating new or improved products from internally generated ideas, and then establishing new business units to create the business model that enables it to dominate a new market. Similarly, HP entered into the computer and printer industries by using internal new venturing.

A company may also use internal venturing to enter a newly emerging or embryonic industry—one in which no company has yet developed the competencies or business model to give it a dominant position in that industry. This was Monsanto's situation in 1979, when it contemplated entering the biotechnology field to produce herbicides and pest-resistant crop seeds. The biotechnology field was young at that time, and there were no incumbent companies focused on applying biotechnology to agricultural products. Accordingly, Monsanto internally ventured a new division to develop the required competencies necessary to enter and establish a strong competitive position in this newly emerging industry.

internal new venturing
The process of transferring resources to, and creating a new business unit or division in, a new industry to innovate new kinds of products.

Pitfalls of New Ventures

Despite the popularity of internal new venturing, there is a high risk of failure. Research suggests that somewhere between 33 and 60% of all new products that reach the marketplace do not generate an adequate economic return,[15] and that most of these products were the result of internal new ventures. Three reasons are often put forward to explain the relatively high failure rate of internal new ventures: (1) market entry on too small a scale, (2) poor commercialization of the new-venture product, and (3) poor corporate management of the new-venture division.[16]

Scale of Entry   Research suggests that large-scale entry into a new industry is often a critical precondition for the success of a new venture. In the short run, this means that a substantial capital investment must be made to support large-scale entry; thus, there is a risk of major losses if the new venture fails. But, in the long run—which can be as long as 5 to 12 years (depending on the industry)—such a large investment results in far greater returns than if a company chooses to enter on a small scale to limit its investment and reduce potential losses.[17] Large-scale entrants can more rapidly realize scale economies, build brand loyalty, and gain access to distribution channels in the new industry, all of which increase the probability of new-venture success. In contrast, small-scale entrants may find themselves handicapped by high costs due to lack of scale economies and lack of market presence, which limits the entrant's ability to build brand loyalty and gain access to distribution channels. These scale effects are particularly significant when a company is entering an established industry in which incumbent companies possess scale economies, brand loyalty, and access to distribution channels. In that case, the new entrant must make a major investment to succeed.

Figure 10.6 plots the relationship between scale of entry and profitability over time for successful small-scale and large-scale ventures. The figure shows that successful small-scale entry is associated with lower initial losses, but in the long term, large-scale entry generates greater returns. However, because of the high costs and risks associated with large-scale entry, many companies make the mistake of choosing a small-scale entry strategy, which often means they fail to build the market share necessary for long-term success.

Commercialization   Many internal new ventures are driven by the opportunity to use a new or advanced technology to make better products and outperform competitors in a market. To succeed commercially, the products under development must be tailored to meet the needs of customers. New ventures often fail because the company ignores these needs; its managers become so focused on the technological possibilities of the new product that customer requirements are forgotten.[18] Thus, a new venture may fail because it is marketing a product based on a technology for which there is no demand, or the company fails to correctly position or differentiate the product in the market to attract customers.

Figure 10.6 Scale of Entry and Profitability

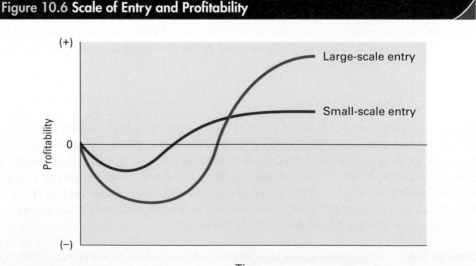

For example, consider the desktop PC marketed by NeXT, a company started by Apple founder Steve Jobs. The NeXT system failed to gain market share because the PC incorporated an array of expensive technologies that consumers simply did not want, such as optical disk drives and hi-fidelity sound. The optical disk drives, in particular, turned off customers because it was difficult to move work from PCs with floppy drives to NeXT machines with optical drives. In other words, NeXT failed because its founder was so dazzled by leading-edge technology that he ignored customer needs. However, Jobs redeemed himself and was named "CEO of the Decade" by *Fortune* magazine in 2010, after he successfully commercialized Apple's iPod, which dominates the MP3 player market. Also, the iPhone set the standard in the smartphone market, and the iPad quickly dominated the tablet computer market following its introduction in 2010.

Poor Implementation   Managing the new-venture process, and controlling the new-venture division, creates many difficult managerial and organizational problems.[19] For example, one common mistake companies make to try to increase their chances of introducing successful products is to establish too many internal new-venture divisions at the same time. Managers attempt to spread the risks of failure by having many divisions, but this places enormous demands upon a company's cash flow. Sometimes, companies are forced to reduce the funding each division receives to keep the entire company profitable, and this can result in the most promising ventures being starved of the cash they need in order to succeed.[20] Another common mistake is when corporate managers fail to do the extensive advanced planning necessary to ensure that the new venture's business model is sound and contains all the elements that will be needed later if it is to succeed. Sometimes corporate managers leave this process to the scientists and engineers championing the new technology. Focused on the new technology, managers may innovate new products that have little strategic or commercial value. Corporate managers and scientists must work together to clarify how and why a new venture will lead to a product that has a competitive advantage, and jointly establish strategic objectives and a timetable to manage the venture until the product reaches the market.

The failure to anticipate the time and costs involved in the new-venture process constitutes a further mistake. Many companies have unrealistic expectations regarding the time frame and expect profits to flow in quickly. Research suggests that some companies operate with a philosophy of killing new businesses if they do not turn a profit by the end of the third year, which is unrealistic given that it can take 5 years or more before a new venture generates substantial profits.

Guidelines for Successful Internal New Venturing

To avoid these pitfalls, a company should adopt a well-thought-out, structured approach to manage internal new venturing. New venturing is based on R&D. It begins with the *exploratory research* necessary to advance basic science and technology (the "R" in R&D) and *development research* to identify, develop, and perfect the commercial applications of a new technology (the "D" in R&D). Companies with strong track records of success at internal new venturing excel at both kinds of R&D; they help to advance basic science and discover important commercial applications for it.[21] To advance basic science, it is important for companies to have strong links with universities, where much of the scientific knowledge that underlies new technologies is discovered. It is also important to make sure that research funds are being controlled by scientists who understand the importance of both "R" and "D" research. If the "D" is lacking, a company will probably generate few successful commercial ventures no matter how well it does basic research. Companies can take a number of steps to ensure that good science ends up with good, commercially viable products.

First, many companies must place the funding for research into the hands of business-unit managers who have the skill or knowhow to narrow down and then select the optimal set of research projects—those that have the best chance of a significant commercial payoff. Second, to make effective use of its R&D competency, top managers must work with R&D scientists to continually develop and improve the business model and strategies that guide their efforts, and make sure that all its scientists and engineers understand what they have to do to make it succeed.[22]

Third, a company must foster close links between R&D and marketing to increase the probability that a new product will be a commercial success in the future. When marketing works to identify the most important customer requirements for a new product and then communicates these requirements to scientists, it ensures that research projects meet the needs of their intended customers. Fourth, a company should also foster close links between R&D and manufacturing to ensure that it has the ability to make a proposed new product in a cost-effective way. Many companies successfully integrate the activities of the different functions by creating cross-functional project teams to oversee the development of new products from their inception to market introduction. This approach can significantly reduce the time it takes to bring a new product to market. For example, while R&D is working on design, manufacturing is setting up facilities, and marketing is developing a campaign to show customers how much the new product will benefit them.

Finally, because large-scale entry often leads to greater long-term profits, a company can promote the success of internal new venturing by "thinking big." A company should construct efficient-scale manufacturing facilities and allocate marketing a large budget to develop a future product campaign that will build market presence and brand loyalty quickly and well in advance of that product's introduction. Also, corporate managers should not panic when customers are slow to adopt the new product; they need to accept the fact there will be initial losses and recognize that as long as market share is expanding, the product will eventually succeed.

ENTERING NEW INDUSTRIES: ACQUISITIONS

In Chapter 9, we explained that acquisitions are the main vehicle that companies use to implement a horizontal integration strategy. Acquisitions are also a principal way companies enter new industries to pursue vertical integration and diversification, so it is necessary to understand both the benefits and risks associated with using acquisitions to implement a corporate-level strategy.

The Attraction of Acquisitions

In general, acquisitions are used to pursue vertical integration or diversification when a company lacks the distinctive competencies necessary to compete in a new industry, and so uses its financial resources to purchase an established company that has those competencies. A company is particularly likely to use acquisitions when it needs to move rapidly to establish a presence in an industry, commonly an embryonic or growth industry. Entering a new industry through internal venturing is a relatively slow process; acquisition is a much quicker way for a company to establish a significant market presence. A company can purchase a leading company with a strong competitive position in months, rather than waiting years to build a market leadership position by engaging in internal venturing. Thus, when speed is particularly important, acquisition is the favored entry mode. Intel, for example, used acquisitions to build its communications chip business because it sensed that the market was developing very quickly, and that it would take too long to develop the required competencies.

In addition, acquisitions are often perceived as being less risky than internal new ventures because they involve less commercial uncertainty. Because of the risks of failure associated with internal new venturing, it is difficult to predict its future success and profitability. By contrast, when a company makes an acquisition it acquires a company with an already established reputation, and it knows the magnitude of the company's market share and profitability.

Finally, acquisitions are an attractive way to enter an industry that is protected by high barriers to entry. Recall from Chapter 2 that barriers to entry arise from factors such as product differentiation, which leads to brand loyalty, and high market share, which leads to economies of scale. When entry barriers are high, it may be very difficult for a company to enter an industry through internal new venturing because it will have to construct large-scale manufacturing facilities and invest in a massive advertising campaign to establish brand loyalty—difficult goals that require huge capital expenditures. In contrast, if a company acquires another company already established in the industry, possibly the market leader, it can circumvent most entry barriers because that company has already achieved economies of scale and obtained brand loyalty. In general, the higher the barriers to entry, the more likely it is that acquisitions will be the method used to enter the industry.

Acquisition Pitfalls

For these reasons, acquisitions have long been the most common method that companies use to pursue diversification. However, as we mentioned earlier, research suggests that many acquisitions fail to increase the profitability of the acquiring company and may result in losses. A study of 700 large acquisitions found that although 30% of these resulted in higher profits, 31% led to losses, and the remainder had little impact.[23] Research suggests that many acquisitions fail to realize their anticipated benefits.[24] One study of the postacquisition performance of acquired companies found that their profitability and market share often decline, suggesting that many acquisitions destroy rather than create value.[25]

Acquisitions may fail to raise the performance of the acquiring companies for four reasons: (1) companies frequently experience management problems when they attempt to integrate a different company's organizational structure and culture into their own; (2) companies often overestimate the potential economic benefits from an acquisition; (3) acquisitions tend to be so expensive that they do not increase future profitability; and (4) companies are often negligent in screening their acquisition targets and fail to recognize important problems with their business models.

Integrating the Acquired Company   Once an acquisition has been made, the acquiring company must integrate the acquired company and combine it with its own organizational structure and culture. Integration involves the adoption of common management and financial control systems, the joining together of operations from the acquired and the acquiring company, the establishment of bureaucratic mechanisms to share information and personnel, and the need to create a common culture.[26] Experience has shown that many problems can occur as companies attempt to integrate their activities. When the processes and cultures of two companies are very different, integration can be extremely challenging. For example, when Daimler Benz acquired Chrysler, the two companies discovered that the more formal and hierarchical culture at Daimler chafed Chrysler employees, who were used to a looser, more entrepreneurial culture. Furthermore, though Daimler had hoped to benefit from Chrysler's more rapid new-product development processes, they soon realized that to do so they would have to adopt a more modular approach to developing cars, for instance by re-using platforms across different car models. This contrasted sharply with Daimler's historic emphasis on holistic "ground up" development of car designs. In the end, few of the anticipated advantages of the acquisition materialized. After paying roughly $36 billion for Chrysler (through a stock swap), Daimler ended up having to *pay out* another $650 million to Cerberus Capital Management to shed the Chrysler group.[27]

Many acquired companies experience high management turnover because their employees do not like the acquiring company's way of operating—its structure and culture.[28] Research suggests that the loss of management talent and expertise, and the damage from constant tension between the businesses, can materially harm the performance of the acquired unit.[29] Moreover, companies often must take on an enormous amount of debt to fund an acquisition, and they are frequently unable to pay it once the management problems (and sometimes the weaknesses) of the acquired company's business model surface.

Overestimating Economic Benefits   Even when companies find it easy to integrate their activities, they often overestimate the combined businesses' future profitability. Managers often overestimate the competitive advantages that will derive from the acquisition and so pay more for the acquired company than it is worth. One reason is that top managers typically overestimate their own general competencies to create valuable new products from an acquisition (this is known as the "hubris hypothesis").[30] The very fact that they have risen to the top of a company gives some managers an exaggerated sense of their own capabilities and a self-importance that distorts their strategic decision making. Coca-Cola's acquisition of a number of mid-sized winemakers illustrates this. Reasoning that a beverage is a beverage, Coca-Cola's then-CEO decided he would be able to mobilize his company's talented marketing managers to develop the strategies needed to dominate the U.S. wine industry. After purchasing three wine companies and enduring 7 years of marginal profits because of failed marketing campaigns, he subsequently decided that wine and soft drinks are very different products; in particular, they have different kinds of appeal, pricing systems, and distribution networks. Coca-Cola eventually sold the wine operations to Joseph E. Seagram and took a substantial loss.[31]

The Expense of Acquisitions   Perhaps the most important reason for the failure of acquisitions is that acquiring a company with stock that is publicly traded tends to be very expensive—and the expense of the acquisition can more than wipe out the value of the stream of future profits that are expected from the acquisition. One reason is that the top managers of a company that is "targeted" for acquisition are likely to resist any takeover attempt unless the acquiring company agrees to pay a substantial premium above its current market value. These premiums are often 30 to 50% above the usual value of a company's stock. Similarly, the stockholders of the target company are unlikely to sell their stock unless they are paid major premiums over market value prior to a takeover bid. Collectively, this means that it is far easier to overpay for an acquisition target than to "get a bargain," and research shows that managers do regularly overpay for acquisitions.[32]

To pay such high premiums, the acquiring company must be certain it can use its acquisition to generate the stream of future profits that justifies the high price of the target company. This is frequently difficult to do given how fast the industry environment can change and other problems discussed earlier such as integrating the acquired company. This is a major reason why acquisitions are frequently unprofitable for the acquiring company.

The reason why the acquiring company must pay such a high premium is that the stock price of the acquisition target increases enormously during the acquisition process as investors speculate on the final price the acquiring company will pay to capture it. In the case of a contested bidding contest, where two or more companies simultaneously bid to acquire the target company, its stock price may surge. Also, when many acquisitions are occurring in one particular industry, investors speculate that the value of the remaining industry companies that have *not* been acquired has increased, and that a bid for these companies will be made at some future point. This also drives up their stock price and increases the cost of making acquisitions. This happened in the telecommunications sector when, to make sure they could meet the needs of customers who were demanding leading-edge equipment, many large companies went on acquisition "binges." Nortel and Alcatel-Lucent engaged in a race to purchase smaller, innovative companies that were developing new telecommunications equipment. The result was that the stock prices for these companies were bid up by investors, and they were purchased at a hugely inflated price. When the telecommunications boom turned to bust, the acquiring companies found that they had vastly overpaid for their acquisitions and had to take enormous accounting write-downs. Nortel was forced to declare bankruptcy and sold off all its assets, and the value of Alcatel-Lucent's stock plunged almost 90%.

Inadequate Pre-acquisition Screening   As the problems of these companies suggest, top managers often do a poor job of pre-acquisition screening—that is, evaluating how much a potential acquisition may increase future profitability. Researchers have discovered that one important reason for the failure of an acquisition is that managers make the decision to acquire other companies without thoroughly analyzing potential benefits and costs.[33] In many cases, after an acquisition has been completed, many acquiring companies discover that instead of buying a well-managed business with a strong business model, they have purchased a troubled organization. Obviously, the managers of the target company may manipulate company information or the balance sheet to make their financial condition look much better than it is. The acquiring company must be wary and complete extensive research. In 2009, IBM was in negotiations to purchase chip-maker Sun Microsystems. After spending 1 week examining its books, IBM reduced its offer price by 10% when its negotiators found its customer base was not as solid as they had expected. Sun Microsystems was eventually sold to

Oracle in 2010 for $7.4 billion. For the next 5 years, Sun Microsystems was a drain on Oracle's profit, but Ellison persevered in investing in Sun's technologies, and by 2015 it appeared his investment finally might be paying off.[34]

Guidelines for Successful Acquisition

To avoid these pitfalls and make successful acquisitions, companies need to follow an approach to targeting and evaluating potential acquisitions that is based on four main steps: (1) target identification and pre-acquisition screening, (2) bidding strategy, (3) integration, and (4) learning from experience.[35]

Identification and Screening   Thorough pre-acquisition screening increases a company's knowledge about a potential takeover target and lessens the risk of purchasing a problem company—one with a weak business model. It also leads to a more realistic assessment of the problems involved in executing a particular acquisition so that a company can plan how to integrate the new business and blend organizational structures and cultures. The screening process should begin with a detailed assessment of the strategic rationale for making the acquisition, an identification of the kind of company that would make an ideal acquisition candidate, and an extensive analysis of the strengths and weaknesses of the prospective company's business model compared to other possible acquisition targets.

Indeed, an acquiring company should select a set of top potential acquisition targets and evaluate each company using a set of criteria that focus on revealing (1) its financial position, (2) its distinctive competencies and competitive advantage, (3) changing industry boundaries, (4) its management capabilities, and (5) its corporate culture. Such an evaluation helps the acquiring company perform a detailed strength, weakness, opportunities, and threats (SWOT) analysis that identifies the best target, for example, by measuring the potential economies of scale and scope that can be achieved between the acquiring company and each target company. This analysis also helps reveal potential problems that might arise when it is necessary to integrate the corporate cultures of the acquiring and acquired companies. For example, managers at Microsoft and SAP, the world's leading provider of enterprise resource planning (ERP) software, met to discuss a possible acquisition by Microsoft. Both companies decided that despite the strong, strategic rationale for a merger—together they could dominate the software computing market, satisfying the need of large global companies—they would have challenges to overcome. The difficulties of creating an organizational structure that could successfully integrate their hundreds of thousands of employees throughout the world, and blend two very different cultures, were insurmountable.

Once a company has reduced the list of potential acquisition candidates to the most favored one or two, it needs to consult expert third parties such as investment bankers like Goldman Sachs and Merrill Lynch. These companies provide valuable insights about the attractiveness of a potential acquisition, assess current industry competitive conditions, and handle the many other issues surrounding an acquisition such as how to select the optimal bidding strategy for acquiring the target company's stock and keep the purchase price as low as possible.

Bidding Strategy   The objective of the bidding strategy is to reduce the price that a company must pay for the target company. The most effective way a company can acquire another is to make a friendly takeover bid, which means the two companies decide upon an amicable way to merge the two companies, satisfying the needs of each company's stockholders and top managers. A friendly takeover prevents speculators from bidding up stock prices. By contrast, in a hostile bidding environment, such as existed between Oracle and PeopleSoft, and between Microsoft and Yahoo!, the price of the target company often gets bid up by speculators who expect that the offer price will be raised by the acquirer, or by another company with a higher counteroffer.

Another essential element of a good bidding strategy is timing. For example, Hanson PLC, one of the most successful companies to pursue unrelated diversification, searched for sound companies suffering from short-term problems because of the business cycle or because performance was being seriously impacted by one underperforming division. Such companies are often undervalued by the stock market and can be acquired without paying a high stock premium. With good timing, a company can make a bargain purchase.

Integration Despite good screening and bidding, an acquisition will fail unless the acquiring company possesses the essential organizational-design skills needed to integrate the acquired company into its operations and quickly develop a viable multibusiness model. Integration should center upon the source of the potential strategic advantages of the acquisition; for instance, opportunities to share marketing, manufacturing, R&D, financial, or management resources. Integration should also involve steps to eliminate any duplication of facilities or functions. In addition, any unwanted business units of the acquired company should be divested.

Learning from Experience Research suggests that organizations that acquire many companies over time become expert in this process and can generate significant value from their experience of the acquisition process.[36] Their past experience enables them to develop a "playbook" they can follow to execute an acquisition efficiently and effectively. One successful company, Tyco International, never made hostile acquisitions; it audited the accounts of the target companies in detail, acquired companies to help it achieve a critical mass in an industry, moved quickly to realize cost savings after an acquisition, promoted managers one or two layers down to lead the newly acquired entity, and introduced profit-based, incentive-pay systems in the acquired unit.[37] Over time, however, Tyco tended to become too large and diversified, leading both investors and management to suspect it was not generating as much value as it could. In 2007, Tyco's health-care and electronics divisions were spun off. In 2012, Tyco was split again into three parts that would each have their own stock: Tyco Fire and Security, ADT (which provided residential and small-business security installation), and Flow Control (which sold water and fluid valves and controls).[38]

ENTERING NEW INDUSTRIES: JOINT VENTURES

Joint ventures, where two or more companies agree to pool their resources to create new business, are most commonly used to enter an embryonic or growth industry. Suppose a company is contemplating the creation of a new-venture division in an embryonic industry. Such a move involves substantial risks and costs because the company must make the huge investment necessary to develop the set of value-chain activities required to make and sell products in the new industry. On the other hand, an acquisition can be a dangerous proposition because there is rarely an established leading company in an emerging industry; even if there is, it will be extremely expensive to purchase.

In this situation, a joint venture frequently becomes the most appropriate method to enter a new industry because it allows a company to share the risks and costs associated with establishing a business unit in the new industry with another company. This is especially true when the companies share *complementary* skills or distinctive competencies, because this increases the probability of a joint venture's success. Consider the 50/50 equity joint venture formed between UTC and Dow Chemical to build plastic-based composite parts for the aerospace industry. UTC was already involved in the aerospace industry (it builds Sikorsky helicopters), and Dow Chemical had skills in the development and manufacture of plastic-based composites. The alliance called for UTC to contribute its advanced aerospace skills, and for Dow to contribute its skills in developing and manufacturing plastic-based composites. Through the joint venture, both companies became involved in new product markets. They were able to realize the benefits associated with related diversification without having to merge their activities into one company or bear the costs and risks of developing new products on their own. Thus, both companies enjoyed the profit-enhancing advantages of entering new markets without having to bear the increased bureaucratic costs.

Although joint ventures usually benefit both partner companies, under some conditions they may result in problems. First, although a joint venture allows companies to share the risks and costs of developing a new business, it also requires that they share in the profits if it succeeds. So, if one partner's skills are more important than the other partner's skills, the partner with more valuable skills will have to "give away" profits to the other party because of the 50/50 agreement. This can create conflict and sour the working relationship as time passes. Second, the joint-venture partners may have different business models or time horizons, and problems can arise if they start to come into conflict about how to run the joint venture; these kinds of problems can disintegrate a business and result in failure.

Third, while one advantage of joint ventures is that they allow frequent and close contact between companies, which facilitates learning and transfer of knowledge, this also creates a risk that a joint venture can lead to the unintentional leak of proprietary information across companies.[39] Even when collaboration agreements have extensive contractual clauses designed to protect the proprietary knowledge possessed by each partner or developed through the collaboration, it is still very difficult to prevent that knowledge from being expropriated. Secrecy clauses are very difficult to enforce when knowledge is dispersed over a large number of employees.[40] A company that enters into a joint venture thus runs the risk of giving away important, company-specific knowledge to its partner, which might then use it to compete with its other partner in the future. For example, having gained access to Dow's expertise in plastic-based composites, UTC might have dissolved the alliance and produced these materials on its own. As the previous chapter discussed, this risk can be minimized if Dow gets a *credible commitment* from UTC, which is what Dow did.

UTC had to make an expensive, asset-specific investment to make the products the joint venture was formed to create.

Restructuring

Many companies expand into new industries to increase profitability. Sometimes, however, companies need to exit industries to increase their profitability and split their existing businesses into separate, independent companies. **Restructuring** is the process of reorganizing and divesting business units and exiting industries to refocus upon a company's core business and rebuild its distinctive competencies.[41] Why are so many companies restructuring, and how do they do it?

restructuring
The process of reorganizing and divesting business units and exiting industries to refocus upon a company's core business and rebuild its distinctive competencies.

Why Restructure?

One main reason that diversified companies have restructured in recent years is that the stock market has valued their stock at a *diversification discount,* meaning that the stock of highly diversified companies is valued lower, relative to their earnings, than the stock of less-diversified companies.[42] Investors see highly diversified companies as less attractive investments for four reasons. First, as we discussed earlier, investors often feel these companies no longer have multibusiness models that justify their participation in many different industries. Second, the complexity of the financial statements of highly diversified enterprises disguises the performance of individual business units; thus, investors cannot determine if their multibusiness models are succeeding. The result is that investors perceive the company as being riskier than companies that operate in one industry, whose competitive advantage and financial statements are more easily understood. Given this situation, restructuring can be seen as an attempt to boost returns to shareholders by splitting up a multibusiness company into separate, independent parts.

The third reason for the diversification discount is that many investors have learned from experience that managers often have a tendency to pursue too much diversification or diversify for the wrong reasons: Their attempts to diversify *reduce* profitability.[43] For example, some CEOs pursue growth for its own sake; they are empire builders who expand the scope of their companies to the point where fast-increasing bureaucratic costs become greater than the additional value that their diversification strategy creates. Restructuring thus becomes a response to declining financial performance brought about by overdiversification.

A final factor leading to restructuring is that innovations in strategic management have diminished the advantages of vertical integration or diversification. For example, a few decades ago, there was little understanding of how long-term cooperative relationships or strategic alliances between a company and its suppliers could be a viable alternative to vertical integration. Most companies considered only two alternatives for managing the supply chain: vertical integration or competitive bidding. As we discuss in Chapter 9, in many situations long-term cooperative relationships can create the most value, especially because they avoid the need to incur bureaucratic costs or dispense with market discipline. As this strategic innovation has spread throughout global business, the relative advantages of vertical integration have declined.

KEY TERMS

TAKEAWAYS FOR STRATEGIC MANAGERS

1. Strategic managers often pursue diversification when their companies are generating free cash flow; that is, financial resources they do not need to maintain a competitive advantage in their company's core industry and so can be used to fund new, profitable business ventures.

2. A diversified company can create value by (a) transferring competencies among existing businesses, (b) leveraging competencies to create new businesses, (c) sharing resources to realize economies of scope, (d) using product bundling, (e) taking advantage of general organizational competencies that enhance the performance of all business units within a diversified company, and (f) operating an internal capital market. The bureaucratic costs of diversification rise as a function of the number of independent business units within a company and the extent to which managers must coordinate the transfer of resources between those business units.

3. Diversification motivated by a desire to pool risks or achieve greater growth often results in falling profitability.

4. The three methods companies use to enter new industries are internal new venturing, acquisition, and joint ventures.

5. Internal new venturing is used to enter a new industry when a company has a set of valuable competencies in its existing businesses that can be leveraged or recombined to enter a new business or industry.

6. Many internal ventures fail because of entry on too small a scale, poor commercialization, and poor corporate management of the internal new venturing process. Guarding against failure involves a carefully planned approach to project selection and management, integration of R&D and marketing to improve the chance new products will be commercially successful, and entry on a scale large enough to result in competitive advantage.

7. Acquisitions are often the best way to enter a new industry when a company lacks the competencies required to compete in the new industry, and it can purchase a company that does have those competencies at a reasonable price. Acquisitions are also the method chosen to enter new industries when there are high barriers to entry and a company is unwilling to accept the time frame, development costs, and risks associated with pursuing internal new venturing.

8. Acquisitions are unprofitable when strategic managers (a) underestimate the problems associated with integrating an acquired company, (b) overestimate the profit that can be created from an acquisition, (c) pay too much for the acquired company, and (d) perform inadequate pre-acquisition screening to ensure the acquired company will increase the profitability of the whole company. Guarding against acquisition failure requires careful pre-acquisition screening, a carefully selected bidding strategy, effective organizational design to successfully integrate

the operations of the acquired company into the whole company, and managers who develop a general managerial competency by learning from their experience of past acquisitions.

9. Joint ventures are used to enter a new industry when (a) the risks and costs associated with setting up a new business unit are more than a company is willing to assume on its own and (b) a company can increase the probability that its entry into a new industry will result in a successful new business by teaming up with another company with skills and assets that complement its own.

10. Restructuring is often required to correct the problems that result from (a) a business model that no longer creates competitive advantage, (b) the inability of investors to assess the competitive advantage of a highly diversified company from its financial statements, (c) excessive diversification because top managers desire to pursue empire building that results in growth without profitability, and (d) innovations in strategic management such as strategic alliances and outsourcing that reduce the advantages of vertical integration and diversification.

DISCUSSION QUESTIONS

1. When is a company likely to choose (a) related diversification and (b) unrelated diversification?

2. What factors make it most likely that (a) acquisitions or (b) internal new venturing will be the preferred method to enter a new industry?

3. Imagine that IBM has decided to diversify into the telecommunications business to provide on-line cloud-computing data services and broadband access for businesses and individuals. What method would you recommend that IBM pursue to enter this industry? Why?

4. Under which conditions are joint ventures a useful way to enter new industries?

5. Identify Honeywell's portfolio of businesses, which can be found by exploring its website (www.honeywell.com). In how many different industries is Honeywell involved? Would you describe Honeywell as a related or an unrelated diversification company? Has Honeywell's diversification strategy increased profitability over time?

CLOSING CASE

Citigroup: The Opportunities and Risks of Diversification

In 2015, Citigroup was a $70.1-billion, diversified financial-services firm known around the world. However, its history had not always been smooth. From the late 1990s through 2010, the company's diversification moves, and its role in the mortgage crisis, combined to bring the company to its knees, raising fears that the venerable bank—one of the oldest and largest in the United States—would not survive.

Citigroup traces its history all the way back to 1812, when it was formed by a group of merchants

in response to the abolishment of the First Bank of the United States (the First Bank's charter had been permitted to lapse due to Thomas Jefferson's arguments about the dangers of centralized control of the economy). The merchants, led by Alexander Hamilton, created the City Bank of New York in 1812, which they hoped would be large enough to replicate the scale advantages that had been offered by the First Bank. The bank played some key roles in the rise of the United States as a global power, including lending money

(*continued*)

to support the purchasing of armaments for the War of 1812, financing the Union war effort in the mid-1800s, and later pioneering foreign-exchange trading, which helped to bring the United States to the world stage in the early 1900s. By 1929, it was the largest commercial bank in the world.

The bank's capital resources and its trusted brand name enabled it to successfully diversify into a range of consumer banking services. The highly innovative company was, for example, the first to introduce savings accounts with compound interest, unsecured personal loans, checking accounts, and 24-hour ATMs, among other things. However, its business remained almost entirely within traditional, retail-banking services. That would soon change with the rise of a new concept: the "financial supermarket."

During the 1990s, there was much buzz in the financial industry about the value of having a wide range of financial services within the same bank. Why have your savings account in New Jersey, your stock broker in California, and your insurance agent in Maryland, when you could have them all under one roof? Merging such services would enable numerous "cross-selling" opportunities: Each company's customer bases could be more fully leveraged by promoting other financial products to them. Furthermore, cost savings might be realized by consolidating operations such as information technology, customer service and billing, and so forth. In 1998, Sanford "Sandy" Weill, who had already begun creating his own financial supermarket, which included Travelers insurance, Aetna, Primerica, Salomon Brothers, and Smith Barney Holdings, convinced Citicorp chairman and CEO John Reed that the two companies should merge. Travelers Group purchased all of Citicorp's shares for $70 billion, and issued 2.5 new Citigroup shares for each Citicorp Share. Existing shareholders of each company thus owned approximately half of the new firm. The merger created a $140-billion firm with assets of $700 billion. Renamed Citigroup, it was now the largest financial-services organization in the world.

Unfortunately, at almost exactly the same time, the Internet rendered the bricks-and-mortar financial supermarket obsolete: The best deals were to be found at the financial supermarket on the Web. To make matters worse, rather than cross-selling, the different divisions of Citi and Travelers began battling each other to protect their turf. Savings in consolidating back-office operations also turned out to be meager and costly to realize. Harmonizing each company's information technology systems, for example, was going to be so expensive that ultimately the legacy systems were left intact. Additionally, though the merged company shed more than 10,000 employees, it was harder to part with executives—indeed, the company kept so many pairs of executives with "co" titles (including co-CEOs Weill and Reed) that some people compared Citi to Noah's Ark. According to Meredith Whitney, a banking analyst who was an early critic of Citi's megabank model, Citi had become "a gobbledygook of companies that were never integrated… The businesses didn't communicate with each other. There were dozens of technology systems and dozens of financial ledgers."

To boost earnings Citi began investing in subprime loans, the risk of which was camouflaged by bundling the loans into mortgage-backed securities known as collateralized debt obligations (CDOs). Trouble began brewing before even Citi knew the scale of risk it had undertaken. Loose lending policies had resulted in a large number of poor-quality mortgages, the vast majority of which were adjustable-rate mortgages (i.e., the initial rate was very low, but would increase over time). This combined with a steep decline in housing prices that made it next to impossible for homebuyers to refinance their mortgages as their interest rates climbed—their homes were now worth less than what they owed. Delinquencies and foreclosures soared, meaning that banks holding those mortgages had assets whose value was rapidly declining. A lawsuit by Citi's shareholders in 2006 accused the company of using a "CDO-related quasi-Ponzi scheme" to falsely give the appearance that it had a healthy asset base and to conceal the true risks the company was facing, but even Citi's CEO at the time, Charles O. Prince III, did not know how much the company had invested in mortgage-related assets. Prince found out at a September 2007 meeting that the company had $43 billion in mortgage related assets, but was assured by Thomas Maheras (who oversaw trading at the bank) that everything was fine. Soon, the company was posting billions in losses, and its stock price fell to the lowest it had been in a decade (see the accompanying figures). To Lynn Turner, a former chief accountant with the Securities and Exchange Commission, Citi's crisis was no surprise. He pointed out that Citi was too large, did not have the right controls, and lacked sufficient accountability for individuals undertaking risks on the company's behalf, making such problems inevitable.

The amalgamation of businesses had created conflicts of interest, and Citi's managers lacked the ability to accurately gauge the risk of the exotic financial instruments that were proliferating. As the true scope of the problem was revealed, Citi found itself in very dire circumstances. The losses from writing down its mortgage assets threatened to destroy the entire company, bringing down even its profitable lines of business.

Citigroup's Revenues and Net Income (in $US millions), 2003–2014

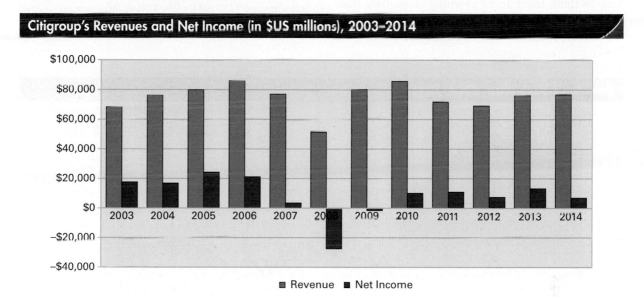

Revenue   Net Income

While the U.S. government kept the bank from failing with a $45-billion bailout (out of fear that Citi's failure would cause an even greater economic collapse—giving rise to the phrase "too big to fail"), Citigroup began reducing its workforce and selling off everything it could, dismantling its financial supermarket. Over the next 2 years, it slashed over 80,000 jobs and sold Smith Barney, Phibro (its commodities-trading unit), Diner's Club (a credit card), its Japanese brokerage operations, Primerica, and more. Furthermore, to raise capital it sold 5% of its equity to the Abu Dhabi Investment authority for $7.5 billion, and then raised another $12 billion by selling shares to a group of investors that included Prince Alwaleed Bin Talal of Saudi Arabia in 2008. It also restructured into two operating units: Citicorp for retail and institutional client business, and Citi Holdings for its brokerage and asset management.

This reorganization would help isolate Citi's banking operations from the riskier assets it wished to sell.

In 2010, Citigroup finally returned to profitability. It repaid its U.S. government loans, and its managers and the investment community breathed a sigh of relief, optimistic that the worst was over. In 2014, Citi posted $76.9 billion in revenues and $7.3 billion in net income. Today, roughly 50% of its revenues come from its consumer businesses (retail banking, credit cards, mortgages, and commercial banking for small-to-medium businesses); just over 40% comes from its Institutional Clients group (which provides investment and banking services for corporations, governments, institutions and ultra-high-net-worth individuals); and Citi Holdings accounts for just under 10% of revenues.

The saga of Citi seriously undermined the investment community's faith in the financial supermarket

(continued)

model, although in the wake of the mortgage crisis it was difficult to assess how much had been gained and lost through the diversification of the firm. One thing was clear, however: Having a very large, complex organization had made it more difficult to provide sufficient, and effective, oversight within the firm. This, in turn, allowed problems to grow very threatening before being detected. Citi's managers knew they would have to think much more carefully about their business choices in the future, and about how to manage the interdependencies between those businesses.

Sources: R. Wile, "Dramatic Highlights from Citi's 200-Year History," *Business Insider*, April 4, 2012, www. businessinsider.com/ presenting-a-history-of-citi-2012-4?op=1); "About Citi—Citibank, N.A.," www.citigroup.com; M. Martin, "Citicorp and Travelers Plan to Merge in Record $70 Billion Deal," *New York Times*, April 7, 1998, p. 1; A. Kessler, "The End of Citi's Financial Supermarket," *The Wall Street Journal*, January 16, 2009, p. A11; "Fall Guy," *The Economist*, November 5, 1998; E. Dash and J. Creswell, "Citigroup Saw No Red Flags Even as It Made Bolder Bets," *New York Times*, November 22, 2008, p. 14; P. Hurtado and D. Griffin, "Citigroup Settles Investors' CDO Suit for $590 Million," Bloomberg.com, August 29, 2012; D. Ellis, "Citi Plunges 26%–Lowest in 15 Years," CNNMoney .com, November 20, 2008; Citigroup 2014 10-K.

Citigroup's Stock Price, 2004–2015

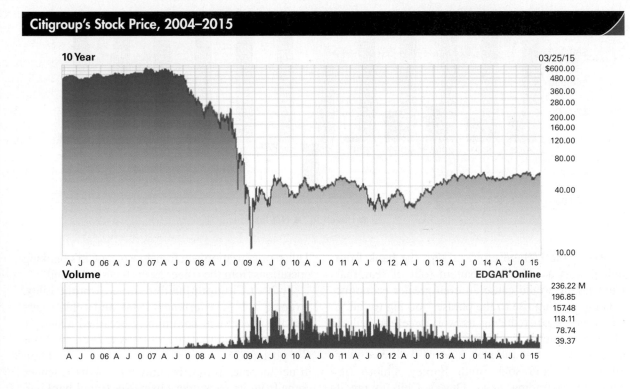

CASE DISCUSSION QUESTIONS

1. What advantages did Citigroup's managers think would result from creating a "financial supermarket"?

2. Why didn't the "financial supermarket" concept pay off the way Citi's managers had anticipated?

3. Why do you think it was so hard to integrate the different companies that were merged?

4. What are some challenges involved with managing a very large, diverse financial-services company?

NOTES

[1]This resource-based view of diversification can be traced to Edith Penrose's seminal book, *The Theory of the Growth of the Firm* (Oxford: Oxford University Press, 1959).

[2]D. J. Teece, "Economies of Scope and the Scope of the Enterprise," *Journal of Economic Behavior and Organization* 3 (1980): 223–247. For more recent empirical work on this topic, see C. H. St. John and J. S. Harrison, "Manufacturing Based Relatedness, Synergy and Coordination," *Strategic Management Journal* 20 (1999): 129–145.

[3]Teece, "Economies of Scope." For more recent empirical work on this topic, see St. John and Harrison, "Manufacturing Based Relatedness, Synergy and Coordination."

[4]For a detailed discussion, see C. W. L. Hill and R. E. Hoskisson, "Strategy and Structure in the Multiproduct Firm," *Academy of Management Review* 12 (1987): 331–341.

[5]See, for example, G. R. Jones and C. W. L. Hill, "A Transaction Cost Analysis of Strategy Structure Choice," *Strategic Management Journal* 2 (1988): 159–172; O. E. Williamson, *Markets and Hierarchies, Analysis and Antitrust Implications* (New York: Free Press, 1975), pp. 132–175.

[6]R. Buderi, *Engines of Tomorrow* (New York: Simon & Schuster, 2000).

[7]See, for example, Jones and Hill, "A Transaction Cost Analysis," and Williamson, *Markets and Hierarchies.*

[8]C. A. Trahms, H. A. Ndofor, and D. G. Sirmon, "Organizational Decline and Turnaound: A Review

and Agenda for Future Research," *Journal of Management*, 39 (2013): 1277–1307.

[9]The distinction goes back to R. P. Rumelt, *Strategy, Structure and Economic Performance* (Cambridge: Harvard Business School Press, 1974).

[10]For evidence, see C. W. L. Hill, "Conglomerate Performance over the Economic Cycle," *Journal of Industrial Economics* 32 (1983): 197–212; D. T. C. Mueller, "The Effects of Conglomerate Mergers," *Journal of Banking and Finance* 1 (1977): 315–347.

[11]For reviews of the evidence, see V. Ramanujam and P. Varadarajan, "Research on Corporate Diversification: A Synthesis," *Strategic Management Journal* 10 (1989): 523–551; G. Dess, J. F. Hennart, C. W. L. Hill, and A. Gupta, "Research Issues in Strategic Management," *Journal of Management* 21 (1995): 357–392; D. C. Hyland and J. D. Diltz, "Why Companies Diversify: An Empirical Examination," *Financial Management* 31 (Spring 2002): 51–81.

[12]M. E. Porter, "From Competitive Advantage to Corporate Strategy," *Harvard Business Review* (May–June 1987): 43–59.

[13]For reviews of the evidence, see Ramanujam and Varadarajan, "Research on Corporate Diversification"; Dess et al., "Research Issues in Strategic Management"; Hyland and Diltz, "Why Companies Diversify."

[14]C. R. Christensen et al., *Business Policy Text and Cases* (Homewood: Irwin, 1987), p. 778.

[15]See Booz, Allen, and Hamilton, *New Products Management for*

the 1980s (New York: Booz, Allen and Hamilton, 1982); A. L. Page, "PDMA's New Product Development Practices Survey: Performance and Best Practices" (presented at the PDMA 15th Annual International Conference, Boston, October 16, 1991); E. Mansfield, "How Economists See R&D," *Harvard Business Review* (November–December 1981): 98–106.

[16]See R. Biggadike, "The Risky Business of Diversification," *Harvard Business Review* (May–June 1979): 103–111; R. A. Burgelman, "A Process Model of Internal Corporate Venturing in the Diversified Major Firm," *Administrative Science Quarterly* 28 (1983): 223–244; Z. Block and I. C. MacMillan, *Corporate Venturing* (Boston: Harvard Business School Press, 1993).

[17]Biggadike, "The Risky Business of Diversification"; Block and Macmillan, *Corporate Venturing.*

[18]Buderi, *Engines of Tomorrow.*

[19]I. C. MacMillan and R. George, "Corporate Venturing: Challenges for Senior Managers," *Journal of Business Strategy* 5 (1985): 34–43.

[20]See R. A. Burgelman, M. M. Maidique, and S. C. Wheelwright, *Strategic Management of Technology and Innovation* (Chicago: Irwin, 1996), pp. 493–507. See also Buderi, *Engines of Tomorrow.*

[21]Buderi, *Engines of Tomorrow.*

[22]See Block and Macmillan, *Corporate Venturing*; Burgelman et al., *Strategic Management of Technology and Innovation,* and Buderi, *Engines of Tomorrow.*

[23]For evidence on acquisitions and performance, see R. E. Caves,

"Mergers, Takeovers, and Economic Efficiency," *International Journal of Industrial Organization* 7 (1989): 151–174; M. C. Jensen and R. S. Ruback, "The Market for Corporate Control: The Scientific Evidence," *Journal of Financial Economics* 11 (1983): 5–50; R. Roll, "Empirical Evidence on Takeover Activity and Shareholder Wealth," in J. C. Coffee, L. Lowenstein, and S. Rose (eds.), *Knights, Raiders and Targets* (Oxford: Oxford University Press, 1989), pp. 112–127; A. Schleifer and R. W. Vishny, "Takeovers in the 60s and 80s: Evidence and Implications," *Strategic Management Journal* 12 (Special Issue, Winter 1991): 51–60; T. H. Brush, "Predicted Changes in Operational Synergy and Post Acquisition Performance of Acquired Businesses," *Strategic Management Journal* 17 (1996): 1–24; T. Loughran and A. M. Vijh, "Do Long-Term Shareholders Benefit from Corporate Acquisitions?" *Journal of Finance* 5 (1997): 1765–1787.

[24]Ibid.

[25]D. J. Ravenscraft and F. M. Scherer, *Mergers, Sell-offs, and Economic Efficiency* (Washington, DC: Brookings Institution, 1987).

[26]F. Bauer and K. Matzler, "Antecedents of M&A Success: The Role of Strategic Complementarity, Cultural Fit, and Degree and Speed of Integration," *Strategic Management Journal* 35 (2014): 269–291.

[27]C. Isidore, "Daimler Pays to Dump Chrysler," *CNNMoney* (May 14, 2007).

[28]See J. P. Walsh, "Top Management Turnover Following Mergers and Acquisitions," *Strategic Management Journal* 9 (1988): 173–183.

[29]See A. A. Cannella and D. C. Hambrick, "Executive Departure and Acquisition Performance,"

Strategic Management Journal 14 (1993): 137–152.

[30]R. Roll, "The Hubris Hypothesis of Corporate Takeovers," *Journal of Business* 59 (1986): 197–216.

[31]"Coca-Cola: A Sobering Lesson from Its Journey into Wine," *Business Week* (June 3, 1985): 96–98.

[32]J. Harford, M. Humphery-Jenner, and R. Powell, "The Sources of Value Destruction in Acquisitions by Entrenched Managers," *Journal of Financial Economics* 106 (2012): 247–161; F. Fu, L. Lin, and M. C. Officer, "Acquisitions Driven by Stock Overvaluation: Are They Good Deals?" *Journal of Financial Economics* 109 (2013): 24–39.

[33]P. Haspeslagh and D. Jemison, *Managing Acquisitions* (New York: Free Press, 1991).

[34]J. Burt, "Oracle Continues to Grow Hardware Business 5 Years After Sun Deal," *eWeek* (February 16, 2015): 1.

[35]For views on this issue, see L. L. Fray, D. H. Gaylin, and J. W. Down, "Successful Acquisition Planning," *Journal of Business Strategy* 5 (1984): 46–55; C. W. L. Hill, "Profile of a Conglomerate Takeover: BTR and Thomas Tilling," *Journal of General Management* 10 (1984): 34–50; D. R. Willensky, "Making It Happen: How to Execute an Acquisition," *Business Horizons* (March–April 1985): 38–45; Haspeslagh and Jemison, *Managing Acquisitions*; and P. L. Anslinger and T. E. Copeland, "Growth Through Acquisition: A Fresh Look," *Harvard Business Review* (January–February 1996): 126–135.

[36]M. L. A. Hayward, "When Do Firms Learn from Their Acquisition Experience? Evidence from 1990–1995," *Strategic Management Journal* 23 (2002): 21–39; K. G. Ahuja, "Technological

Acquisitions and the Innovation Performance of Acquiring Firms: A Longitudinal Study," *Strategic Management Journal* 23 (2001): 197–220; H. G. Barkema and F. Vermeulen, "International Expansion Through Startup or Acquisition," *Academy of Management Journal* 41 (1998): 7–26.

[37]Hayward, "When Do Firms Learn from Their Acquisition Experience?"

[38]N. Zieminski, "Tyco Shareholders Approve Three-Way Break-Up," Reuters, September 17, 2012.

[39]A. C. Inkpen and S. C. Currall, "The Coevolution of Trust, Control, and Learning in Joint Ventures," *Organization Science* 15 (2004): 586–599; D. C. Mowery, J. E. Oxley, and B. S. Silverman, "Strategic Alliances and Interfirm Knowledge Transfer," *Strategic Management* 17 (1996): 77–91.

[40]M. A. Schilling, "Technology Shocks, Technological Collaboration, and Innovation Outcomes," *Organization Science* 26: 668–686.

[41]For a review of the evidence and some contrary empirical evidence, see D. E. Hatfield, J. P. Liebskind, and T. C. Opler, "The Effects of Corporate Restructuring on Aggregate Industry Specialization," *Strategic Management Journal* 17 (1996): 55–72.

[42]A. Lamont and C. Polk, "The Diversification Discount: Cash Flows Versus Returns," *Journal of Finance* 56 (October 2001): 1693–1721; R. Raju, H. Servaes, and L. Zingales, "The Cost of Diversity: The Diversification Discount and Inefficient Investment," *Journal of Finance* 55 (2000): 35–80.

[43]For example, see Schleifer and Vishny, "Takeovers in the '60s and '80s."

4

IMPLEMENTING STRATEGY

Igor Sokolov (breezel)/Shutterstock.com

CHAPTER 11

CORPORATE GOVERNANCE, SOCIAL RESPONSIBILITY, AND ETHICS

Igor Sokolov (breeze)/Shutterstock.com

OPENING CASE

Starbucks: Taking a Stand on Social Issues

When Howard Schultz founded Starbucks in 1987, he wanted to create a company that would genuinely care for the well-being of its employees. He had been very influenced by his memories of his father, noting that his father "struggled a great deal and never made more than $20,000 a year, and his work was never valued, emotionally or physically, by his employer … This was an injustice … I want our employees to know we value them." He also believed that happy employees are the key to competitiveness and growth. As he stated: "We can't achieve our strategic objectives without a work force of people who are immersed in the same commitment as management. Our only sustainable advantage is the quality of our work force. We're building a national retail company by creating pride in—and stake in—the outcome of our labor."

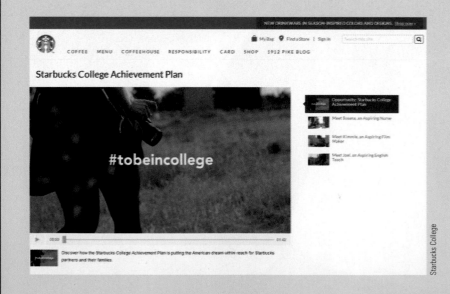

Starbucks College

Schulz set out to accomplish his goals by creating an empowering corporate culture, exceptional employee benefits, and employee stock ownership programs. While Starbucks enforces almost fanatical standards of coffee quality and customer service, the culture at Starbucks towards employees is laid back and supportive. Employees are empowered to make decisions without constant referral to management, and are encouraged to think of themselves as partners in the business. Starbucks wants employees to use their best judgment in making decisions and will stand behind them. This is reinforced through generous compensation and benefits packages.

In 2000, Schultz announced that he was resigning as CEO and left the firm to pursue other ventures (though he remained chairman of the board of directors). However, after Starbucks began to suffer from slumping net income and decreasing share price, Schultz returned to the helm in 2008. Rather than cutting costs and reducing the work force, Schulz announced his "Transformation Agenda"—a controversial plan to invest in Starbucks' employees, environment, and community. Schultz's plan included:

Competitive employee compensation plans that include equity-based compensation for nonexecutive partners. In 2013, $230 million was paid out in equity awards. In 2015, Starbucks gave all baristas and supervisors a pay raise and increased starting pay rates across the United States. In 2015, Starbucks's U.S. baristas earned between $7.59 and $10.92 an hour, plus $.33 to $1.91 an hour in tips, depending on location and experience.

Industry-leading health care benefits and 401K benefits for both part-time and full-time workers. Other companies that offer health benefits to part-time workers typically only do so for employees who work at least 30 hours a week. Starbucks broke with industry norms by creating benefits for employees who work at least 20 hours a week.

Tuition reimbursement for students. In June 2014, Starbucks unveiled a "College Achievement Plan" wherein employees who work more than 20 hours a week can work towards a bachelor's degree through an online program from Arizona State University.

An ethical sourcing plan. Starbucks' coffee must be purchased from suppliers that adhere to Starbucks' "C.A.F.E." standards. These standards include practices related to *product quality, economic accountability and transparency* (e.g., suppliers must provide evidence to demonstrate that the price Starbucks pays reaches the farmer), *social responsibility* (e.g., third-party verifiers provide audits to ensure that suppliers are using safe, fair, and humane working and living conditions, including minimum-wage requirements and the prohibition of child and forced labor), and *environmental leadership* (e.g., measures to manage waste, protect water quality, and reduce use of agrochemicals).

Whether investors and consumers were inspired by the Agenda, were encouraged by Schultz's return, or just floated up with the recovering economy is unclear, but Starbuck's stock price and balance sheet roared back to life. Revenues and net income began to climb again and, by September 2014, Starbucks' sales had reached $16.4 billion—160% of what sales had been when Schultz returned as CEO and an all-time high for the company. With a 12.6% net margin and 19.2% return on assets, Starbucks was one of the most profitable food retailers in the world.

In late 2014 and early 2015, Schultz decided to leverage the company's influence in the world by beginning to speak out on such issues as gay marriage (Schultz supports it), gun carrying laws (Starbucks requests that people not carry guns into their locations, even in states that permit it), and treatment of veterans (in March 2014, Schultz committed $30 million of his own money to posttraumatic stress disorder programs and other initiatives to help veterans, and vowed to hire 10,000 veterans and military spouses by 2018).

The company drew some ire in taking on issues that bear little relationship to its core activities. Critics admonished that such initiatives risked alienating some consumers and investors, and creating elevated expectations that the company might not always be able to meet. As Schultz noted, "I can tell you the organization is not thrilled when I walk into a room and say we're now going to take on veterans (issues)." But he adds, "The size and the scale of the company and the platform that we have allows us, I think, to project a voice into the debate, and hopefully that's for good ... We are leading [Starbucks] to try to redefine the role and responsibility of a public company."

Sources: C. Birkner, "Taking Care of Their Own," *Marketing News*, February, pp. 44–49; M. Rothman, "Into the Black," *Inc.*, January, 1993, p. 58; D. Ritter, "3 Reasons It's Hard to Hate Starbucks," *Wall Street Cheat Sheet*, July 6, 2014; www.usatoday.com, A. Gonzalez, "Starbucks as Citizen: Schultz Acts Boldly on Social, Political Issues," *Seattle Times*, March 15, 2015; www.seattletimes.com, www.starbucks.com (accessed April 28, 2015); Yahoo Finance, Hoovers.

▟ OVERVIEW

We open this chapter with a close look at the governance mechanisms that shareholders implement to ensure that managers act in the company's interest and pursue strategies that maximize shareholder value. We also discuss how managers need to pay attention to other stakeholders such as employees, suppliers, and customers. The Opening Case on Starbucks is a good illustration of how some companies incorporate a wide range of stakeholder needs into their strategy. Balancing the needs of different stakeholder groups is in the long-term interests of the company's owners, its shareholders. Good governance mechanisms recognize this truth. In addition, we will review the ethical implications of strategic decisions, and discuss how managers can make sure that their strategic decisions are founded upon strong ethical principles.

▟ STAKEHOLDERS AND CORPORATE PERFORMANCE

stakeholders

Individuals or groups with an interest, claim, or stake in the company—in what it does and in how well it performs.

internal stakeholders

Stockholders and employees, including executive officers, other managers, and board members.

external stakeholders

All other individuals and groups that have some claim on the company.

A company's **stakeholders** are individuals or groups with an interest, claim, or stake in the company, in what it does, and in how well it performs.[1] They include stockholders, creditors, employees, customers, the communities in which the company does business, and the general public. Stakeholders can be divided into two groups: internal stakeholders and external stakeholders (see Figure 11.1). **Internal stakeholders** are stockholders and employees, including executive officers, other managers, and board members. **External stakeholders** are all other individuals and groups that have some

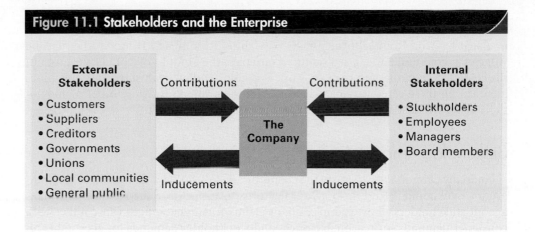

Figure 11.1 Stakeholders and the Enterprise

claim on the company. Typically, this group comprises customers, suppliers, creditors (including banks and bondholders), governments, unions, local communities, and the general public.

All stakeholders are in an exchange relationship with their company. Each stakeholder group listed in Figure 11.1 supplies the organization with important resources (or contributions), and in exchange each expects its interests to be satisfied (by inducements).[2] Stockholders provide the enterprise with risk capital and expect management to attempt to maximize the return on their investment. Creditors, particularly bondholders, also provide the company with capital in the form of debt, and they expect to be repaid on time, with interest. Employees provide labor and skills and in exchange expect commensurate income, job satisfaction, job security, and good working conditions. Customers provide a company with its revenues, and in exchange want high-quality, reliable products that represent value for money. Suppliers provide a company with inputs and in exchange seek revenues and dependable buyers. Governments provide a company with rules and regulations that govern business practice and maintain fair competition. In exchange they want companies to adhere to these rules. Unions help to provide a company with productive employees, and in exchange they want benefits for their members in proportion to their contributions to the company. Local communities provide companies with local infrastructure, and in exchange want companies that are responsible citizens. The general public provides companies with national infrastructure, and in exchange seeks some assurance that the quality of life will be improved as a result of the company's existence.

A company must take these claims into account when formulating its strategies, or stakeholders may withdraw their support. For example, stockholders may sell their shares, bondholders may demand higher interest payments on new bonds, employees may leave their jobs, and customers may buy elsewhere. Suppliers may seek more dependable buyers, and unions may engage in disruptive labor disputes. Government may take civil or criminal action against the company and its top officers, imposing fines and, in some cases, jail terms. Communities may oppose the company's attempts to locate its facilities in their area, and the general public may form pressure groups, demanding action against companies that impair the quality of life. Any of these reactions can have a damaging impact on an enterprise. A study by Witold Henisz, Sinziana Dorobantu and Lite Nartey on the impact of stakeholder opposition to gold mines, for example, found that the value of cooperative relationships with external stakeholders was worth twice as much as the market value of the gold itself.[3] As articulated by Yani Roditis, former COO of Gabriel Resources, "It used to be that the value of a gold mine was based on three variables: the amount of gold in the ground, the cost of extraction, and the world price of gold. Today, I can show you two mines identical on these three variables that differ in their valuation by an order of magnitude. Why? Because one has local support and the other doesn't."

Stakeholder Impact Analysis

A company cannot always satisfy the claims of all stakeholders. The goals of different groups may conflict, and, in practice, few organizations have the resources to manage all stakeholders.[4] For example, union claims for higher wages can conflict with consumer demands for reasonable prices and stockholder demands for acceptable returns. Often, the company must make choices, and t do so it must identify the most important stakeholders and give highest priority to pursuing strategies that satisfy their needs. Stakeholder impact analysis can provide such identification. Typically, stakeholder impact analysis follows these steps:

1. Identify stakeholders.
2. Identify stakeholders' interests and concerns.
3. As a result, identify the claims stakeholders are likely to make on the organization.
4. Identify the stakeholders who are most important from the organization's perspective.
5. Identify the resulting strategic challenges.[5]

Such an analysis enables a company to identify the stakeholders most critical to its survival and to make sure that the satisfaction of their needs is paramount. Most companies that have gone through this process quickly come to the conclusion that three stakeholder groups must be satisfied above all others if a company is to survive and prosper: customers, employees, and stockholders.

The Unique Role of Stockholders

A company's stockholders are usually put in a different class from other stakeholder groups, and for good reason. Stockholders are the legal owners and the providers of **risk capital**, a major source of the capital resources that allow a company to operate its business. The capital that stockholders provide to a company is seen as risk capital because there is no guarantee that stockholders will recoup their investments and/or earn a decent return.

Recent history demonstrates all too clearly the nature of risk capital. For example, many investors who bought shares in Washington Mutual, the large, Seattle-based bank and home loan lender, believed that they were making a low-risk investment. The company had been around for decades and paid a solid dividend, which it increased every year. It had a large branch network and billions in deposits. However, during the 2000s, Washington Mutual was also making increasingly risky mortgage loans, reportedly giving mortgages to people without properly verifying if they had the funds to pay back those loans on time. By 2008, many borrowers were beginning to default on their loans, and Washington Mutual had to take multibillion-dollar write-downs on

risk capital

Capital that cannot be recovered if a company fails and goes bankrupt.

the value of its loan portfolio, effectively destroying its once-strong balance sheet. The losses were so large that customers with deposits at the bank started to worry about its stability, and they withdrew nearly $16 billion in November 2008 from accounts at Washington Mutual. The stock price collapsed from around $40 at the start of 2008 to under $2 a share, and with the bank teetering on the brink of collapse, the federal government intervened, seized the bank's assets, and engineered a sale to JP Morgan. Washington Mutual's shareholders got absolutely nothing: They were wiped out.

Over the past decade, maximizing returns to stockholders has taken on significant importance as an increasing number of employees have become stockholders in the companies for which they work through employee stock ownership plans (ESOPs). At Wal-Mart, for example, all employees who have worked for more than 1 year are eligible for the company's ESOP. Under an ESOP, employees are given the opportunity to purchase stock in the company, sometimes at a discount or less than the market value of the stock. The company may also contribute a certain portion of the purchase price to the ESOP. By making employees stockholders, ESOPs tend to increase the already strong emphasis on maximizing returns to stockholders, for they now help to satisfy two key stakeholder groups: stockholders and employees.

Profitability, Profit Growth, and Stakeholder Claims

Because of the unique position assigned to stockholders, managers normally seek to pursue strategies that maximize the returns that stockholders receive from holding shares in the company. As we noted in Chapter 1, stockholders receive a return on their investment in a company's stock in two ways: from dividend payments and from capital appreciation in the market value of a share (that is, by increases in stock market prices). The best way for managers to generate the funds for future dividend payments and keep the stock price appreciating is to pursue strategies that maximize the company's long-term profitability (as measured by the return on invested capital, ROIC) and grow the profits of the company over time.[6]

As we saw in Chapter 3, ROIC is an excellent measure of the profitability of a company. It tells managers how efficiently they are using the capital resources of the company (including the risk capital provided by stockholders) to generate profits. A company that is generating a positive ROIC is covering all of its ongoing expenses and has money left over, which is then added to shareholders' equity, thereby increasing the value of a company and thus the value of a share of stock in the company. The value of each share will increase further if a company can grow its profits over time, because then the profit that is attributable to every share (that is, the company's earnings per share) will also grow. As we have seen in this book, to grow profits, companies must be doing one or more of the following: (a) increasing the margins earned on their products and services, (b) maintaining margins and share while participating in a market that is growing, (b) maintaining margins while taking market share from competitors, (c) or (d) developing new markets through innovation, geographic expansion, or diversification.

Although managers should strive for profit growth if they are trying to maximize shareholder value, the relationship between profitability and profit growth is a complex one because attaining future profit growth may require investments that reduce the current rate of profitability. The task of managers is to find the right balance between profitability and profit growth.[7] Too much emphasis on current profitability at the expense of future profitability and profit growth can make an enterprise less attractive to shareholders. Too much emphasis on profit growth can reduce the current profitability of the enterprise and have the same effect. In an uncertain world where the future is unknowable, finding the right balance between profitability and profit growth is as much art as it is science, but it is something that managers must try to do.

In addition to maximizing returns to stockholders, boosting a company's profitability and profit growth rate is also consistent with satisfying the claims of several other key stakeholder groups. When a company is profitable and its profits are continuing to grow, it can pay higher salaries to productive employees and can also afford benefits such as health insurance coverage, all of which help to satisfy employees. In addition, companies with a high level of profitability and profit growth have no problem meeting their debt commitments, which provides creditors, including bondholders, with a measure of security. Profitable organizations are also better able to undertake philanthropic investments, which can help to satisfy some of the claims that local communities and the general public place on a company. Pursuing strategies that maximize the long-term profitability and profit growth of the company is therefore generally consistent with satisfying the claims of various stakeholder groups.

Stakeholder management requires consideration of how the firm's practices affect the cooperation of stakeholders in the short term, the benefits of building trust and a knowledge-sharing culture with stakeholders in the long run, and the firm's profitability and growth that will enable it to serve stakeholder interests in the future.[8] The company that overpays its employees in the current period, for example, may have very happy employees for a short while, but such action will raise the company's cost structure and limit its ability to attain a competitive advantage in the marketplace, thereby depressing its long-term profitability and hurting its ability to award future pay increases. As far as employees are concerned, the way many companies deal with this situation is to make future pay raises contingent upon improvements in labor productivity. If labor productivity increases, labor costs as a percentage of revenues will fall, profitability will rise, and the company can afford to pay its employees more and offer greater benefits.

Of course, not all stakeholder groups want the company to maximize its long-run profitability and profit growth. Suppliers are more comfortable about selling goods and services to profitable companies because they can be assured that the company will have the funds to pay for those products. Similarly, customers may be more willing to purchase from profitable companies because they can be assured that those companies will be around in the long term to provide after-sales services and support. But neither suppliers nor customers want the company to maximize its profitability at their expense. Rather, they would like to capture some of these profits from the company in the form of higher prices for their goods and services (in the case of suppliers), or lower prices for the products they purchase from the company (in the case of customers). Roberto Garcia-Castro and Ruth Aguilera capture this dynamic nicely by breaking the traditional explanation of value creation and value capture (discussed in Chapter 3) down into more fine-grained categories that show how value is created and captured by multiple stakeholders, similar to Figure 11.2.[9] As shown, the total value that is created is the spread between the opportunity costs of the resources it employs and the willingness-to-pay of its customers. However, value is created and captured by different stakeholders. Suppliers create and capture value in the form of goods and services they sell to the firm; employees and management create value through their labor and capture value in the form of salaries and other benefits; government creates value in the form of providing the broad infrastructure in which the firm operates and

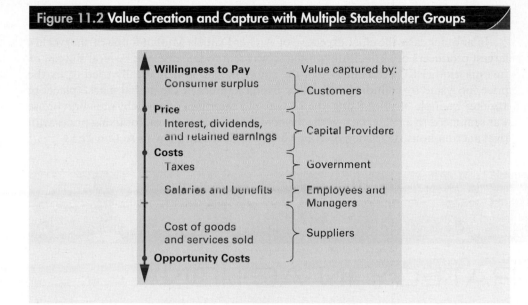

Figure 11.2 Value Creation and Capture with Multiple Stakeholder Groups

Source: Adapted from R. Garcia-Castro and R. Aguilera, "Increasing Value Creation and Appropriation in a World with Multiple Stakeholders," *Strategic Management Journal*, 36 (2015): 137–147.

captures value in the form of taxes; debt providers and stockholders create value by providing capital to the firm that it can use to finance its operations, and they capture value in the form of interest, dividends, and capital gains. Finally, customers capture value in the form of consumer surplus–the difference between the price they pay for goods and their true willingness-to-pay.

Despite the argument that maximizing long-term profitability and profit growth is the best way to satisfy the claims of several key stakeholder groups, it should be noted that a company must do so within the limits set by the law and in a manner consistent with societal expectations. The unfettered pursuit of profit can lead to behaviors that are outlawed by government regulations, opposed by important public constituencies, or simply unethical. Governments have enacted a wide range of regulations to govern business behavior, including antitrust laws, environmental laws, and laws pertaining to health and safety in the workplace. It is incumbent on managers to make sure that the company is in compliance with these laws when pursuing strategies.

Unfortunately, there is plenty of evidence that managers can be tempted to cross the line between legal and illegal in their pursuit of greater profitability and profit growth. For example, in mid-2003, the U.S. Air Force stripped Boeing of $1 billion in contracts to launch satellites when it was discovered that Boeing had obtained thousands of pages of proprietary information from rival Lockheed Martin. Boeing had used that information to prepare its winning bid for the satellite contract. This was followed by the revelation that Boeing's CFO, Mike Sears, had offered a government official, Darleen Druyun, a lucrative job at Boeing while Druyun was still involved in evaluating whether Boeing should be awarded a $17-billion contract to build tankers for the Air Force. Boeing won the contract against strong competition from Airbus and hired Druyun. It was clear that the job offer may have had an impact on the Air Force decision. Boeing fired Druyun and the CFO, and shortly thereafter, Boeing

CEO Phil Condit resigned in a tacit acknowledgment that he bore responsibility for the ethics violations that had occurred at Boeing during his tenure as leader.[10]

In another case, the chief executive of Archer Daniels Midland, one of the world's largest producers of agricultural products, was sent to jail after the Federal Bureau of Investigation (FBI) determined that the company had systematically tried to fix the price for lysine by colluding with other manufacturers in the global marketplace. In another example of price fixing, the 76-year-old chairman of Sotheby's auction house was sentenced to a jail term, and the former CEO to house arrest, for fixing prices with rival auction house Christie's over a 6-year period (see Strategy in Action 11.1).

11.1 STRATEGY IN ACTION

Price Fixing at Sotheby's and Christie's

Sotheby's and Christie's are the two largest fine-art auction houses in the world. In the mid-1990s, the two companies controlled 90% of the fine-art auction market, which at the time was worth approximately $4 billion annually. Traditionally, auction houses earn their profits by the commissions they charge on auction sales. In good times, these commissions can be as high as 10% on some items, but in the early 1990s, the auction business was in a slump, with the supply of art for auction shriveling. With Sotheby's and Christie's desperate for works of art, sellers played the two houses against each other, driving commissions down to 2%, or sometimes lower.

To try to control this situation, Sotheby's CEO, Dede Brooks, met with Christie CEO Christopher Davidge in a series of clandestine meetings held in parking lots that began in 1993. Brooks claimed that she was acting on behalf of her boss, Alfred Taubman, the chairman and controlling shareholder of Sotheby's. According to Brooks, Taubman had agreed with the chairman of Christie's, Anthony Tennant, to work together in the weak auction market and limit price competition. In their meetings, Brooks and Davidge agreed to a fixed and nonnegotiable commission structure. Based on a sliding scale, the commission structure would range from 10% on a $100,000 item to 2%

on a $5-million item. In effect, Brooks and Davidge were agreeing to eliminate price competition between them, thereby guaranteeing both auction houses higher profits. The price-fixing agreement started in 1993 and continued unabated for 6 years, until federal investigators uncovered the arrangement and brought charges against Sotheby's and Christie's.

With the deal out in the open, lawyers filed several class-action lawsuits on behalf of the sellers that had been defrauded. Ultimately, at least 100,000 sellers signed on to the class-action lawsuits, which the auction houses settled with a $512-million payment. The auction houses also pleaded guilty to price fixing and paid $45 million in fines to U.S. antitrust authorities. As for the key players, the chairman of Christie's, as a British subject, was able to avoid prosecution in the United States (price fixing is not an offense for which someone can be extradited). Davidge struck a deal with prosecutors, and in return for amnesty turned over incriminating documents to the authorities. Brooks also cooperated with federal prosecutors and avoided jail (in April 2002, she was sentenced to 3 years of probation, 6 months of home detention, 1,000 hours of community service, and a $350,000 fine). Taubman, ultimately isolated by all his former coconspirators, was sentenced to 1 year in jail and fined $7.5 million.

Sources: S. Tully, "A House Divided," *Fortune*, December 18, 2000, pp. 264–275; J. Chaffin, "Sotheby's Ex CEO Spared Jail Sentence," *Financial Times*, April 30, 2002, p. 10; T. Thorncroft, "A Courtroom Battle of the Vanities," *Financial Times*, November 3, 2001, p. 3.

Examples such as these beg the question of why managers would engage in such risky behavior. A body of academic work collectively known as agency theory provides an explanation for why managers might engage in behavior that is either illegal or, at the very least, not in the interest of the company's shareholders.

AGENCY THEORY

Agency theory looks at the problems that can arise in a business relationship when one person delegates decision-making authority to another. It offers a way of understanding why managers do not always act in the best interests of stakeholders and why they might sometimes behave unethically, and, perhaps, also illegally.[11] Although agency theory was originally formulated to capture the relationship between management and stockholders, the basic principles have also been extended to cover the relationship with other key stakeholders, such as employees, as well as relationships between different layers of management within a corporation.[12] Although the focus of attention in this section is on the relationship between senior management and stockholders, some of the same language can be applied to the relationship between other stakeholders and top managers, and between top management and lower levels of management.

Principal–Agent Relationships

The basic propositions of agency theory are relatively straightforward. First, an agency relationship is held to arise whenever one party delegates decision-making authority or control over resources to another. The principal is the person delegating authority, and the agent is the person to whom authority is delegated. The relationship between stockholders and senior managers is the classic example of an agency relationship. Stockholders, who are the principals, provide the company with risk capital but delegate control over that capital to senior managers, and particularly to the CEO, who, as their agent, is expected to use that capital in a manner consistent with the best interests of stockholders. As we have seen, this means using capital to maximize the company's long-term profitability and profit growth rate.

The agency relationship continues down the hierarchy within the company. For example, in a large, complex, multibusiness company, top managers cannot possibly make all the important decisions, therefore, they delegate some decision-making authority and control over capital resources to business-unit (divisional) managers. Thus, just as senior managers such as the CEO are the agents of stockholders, business-unit managers are the agents of the CEO (and in this context, the CEO is the principal). The CEO entrusts business-unit managers to use the resources over which they have control in the most effective manner in order to maximize the performance of their units. This helps the CEO ensure that he or she maximizes the performance of the entire company, thereby discharging agency obligation to stockholders. More generally, whenever managers delegate authority to managers below them in the hierarchy and give them the right to control resources, an agency relation is established.

The Agency Problem

information asymmetry

A situation where an agent has more information about the resources he or she is managing than the principal has.

Although agency relationships often work well, problems may arise if agents and principals have different goals, and if agents take actions that are not in the best interests of their principals. Sometimes this occurs because an **information asymmetry** exists between the principal and the agent: Agents almost always have more information about the resources they are managing than principals do. Unscrupulous agents can take advantage of such information asymmetry to mislead principals and maximize their own interests at the expense of principals.

In the case of stockholders, the information asymmetry arises because they delegate decision-making authority to the CEO, their agent, who, by virtue of his or her position inside the company, is likely to know far more than stockholders do about the company's operations. Indeed, there may be certain information about the company that the CEO is unwilling to share with stockholders because that information would also help competitors. In such a case, withholding information from stockholders may be in the best interest of all. More generally, the CEO, involved in the day-to-day operations of the company, is bound to have an information advantage over stockholders, just as the CEO's subordinates may have an information advantage over the CEO with regard to the resources under their control.

The information asymmetry between principals and agents is not necessarily a bad thing, but it can make it difficult for principals to measure an agent's performance and thus hold the agent accountable for how well he or she is using the entrusted resources. There is a certain amount of performance ambiguity inherent in the relationship between a principal and agent. Principals cannot know for sure if the agent is acting in his or her best interests. They cannot know for sure if the agent is using the resources to which he or she has been entrusted as effectively and efficiently as possible. This ambiguity is amplified by the fact that agents must engage in behavior that has outcomes for different time horizons. For example, investing in research and development may lower profits today but help to ensure the firm is profitable in the future. Principals who reward only immediate performance outcomes could induce myopic ("short-sighted") behavior on the part of the agent. To an extent, principals must trust the agent to do the right thing.

Of course, this trust is not blind: principals do put mechanisms in place with the purpose of monitoring agents, evaluating their performance, and, if necessary, taking corrective action. As we shall see shortly, the board of directors is one such mechanism, for, in part, the board exists to monitor and evaluate senior managers on behalf of stockholders. In Germany, the codetermination law (*Mitbestimmungsgesetz*) requires that firms with over 2,000 employees have boards of directors that represent the interests of employees—just under half of a firm's supervisory board members must represent workers. Other mechanisms serve a similar purpose. In the United States, publicly owned companies must regularly file detailed financial statements with the Securities and Exchange Commission (SEC) that are in accordance with generally agreed-upon accounting principles (GAAP). This requirement exists to give stockholders consistent, detailed information about how well management is using the capital with which it has been entrusted. Similarly, internal control systems within a company help the CEO ensure that subordinates are using the resources with which they have been entrusted to the best possible advantage.

Despite the existence of governance mechanisms and comprehensive measurement and control systems, a degree of information asymmetry will always remain between principals and agents, and there is always an element of trust involved in the relationship. Unfortunately, not all agents are worthy of this trust. A minority will deliberately mislead principals for personal gain, sometimes behaving unethically or breaking laws in the process, or engaging in behaviors that the principals would never condone.

The interests of principals and agents are not always the same; they diverge. For example, some authors argue that, like many other people, senior managers are motivated by desires for status, power, job security, and income.[13] By virtue of their position within the company, certain managers, such as the CEO, can use their authority and control over corporate funds to satisfy these desires at the cost of returns to stockholders. CEOs might use their position to invest corporate funds in various perks that enhance their status—executive jets, lavish offices, and expense-paid trips to exotic locales—rather than investing those funds in ways that increase stockholder returns. Economists have termed such behavior **on-the-job consumption**.[14]

Aside from engaging in on-the-job consumption, CEOs, along with other senior managers, might satisfy their desire for greater income by using their influence or control over the board of directors to persuade the compensation committee of the board to grant pay increases. Critics of U.S. industry claim that extraordinary pay has now become an endemic problem, and that senior managers are enriching themselves at the expense of stockholders and other employees. They point out that CEO pay has been increasing far more rapidly than the pay of average workers, primarily because of very liberal stock option grants that enable a CEO to earn huge pay bonuses in a rising stock market, even if the company underperforms the market and competitors.[15] In 1980, the average CEO in *Business Week's* survey of CEOs of the largest 500 American companies earned 42 times what the average blue-collar worker earned. By 1990, this figure had increased to 85 times. In 2013, the AFL-CIO's Executive PayWatch database reported that American CEOs made 331 times the pay of average workers.[16]

What rankles critics is the size of some CEO pay packages and their apparent lack of relationship to company performance.[17] In 2010, a study by Graef Crystal evaluated the relationship between CEO pay and performance and concluded that there virtually is none. For example, if CEOs were paid according to shareholder return, the CEO of CBS Corporation, Leslie Moonves, who earned an impressive $43.2 million in 2009, should have gotten a $28 million pay cut, according to Crystal.[18] Critics argue that CEO compensation is disproportionate to achievement, representing a clear example of the agency problem. However, in response to shareholder pressure, in recent years more companies have begun adopting compensation practices that more closely tie CEO pay to performance. For example, at Air Products & Chemicals, when the earnings per share fell short of its 9% growth target in 2012, CEO John McGlade paid the price in the form of a 65% cut in his annual bonus. His stock grants and stock options decreased as well, reducing his total direct compensation 19%, to 9.1 million.[19]

A further concern is that in trying to satisfy a desire for status, security, power, and income, a CEO might engage in empire building—buying many new businesses in an attempt to increase the size of the company through diversification.[20] Although such growth may depress the company's long-term profitability and thus stockholder returns, it increases the size of the empire under the CEO's control and, by extension, the CEO's status, power, security, and income (there is a strong relationship between company size and CEO pay). Instead of trying to maximize stockholder returns by seeking the right balance between profitability and profit growth, some senior managers may trade long-term profitability for greater company growth via new business

on-the-job consumption
A term used by economists to describe the behavior of senior management's use of company funds to acquire perks (lavish offices, jets, and the like) that will enhance their status, instead of investing the funds to increase stockholder returns.

purchases. For example, in the mid-1970s, Compagnie Générale des Eaux was primarily a water utility and waste-management company, operating "near-monopolies" in
local municipalities in France and generating strong, stable cash flows for its shareholders. However, a series of audacious, debt-funded acquisitions in the 1980s and
1990s, first by CEO Guy DeJouany and later by his successor, Jean-Marie Messier,
rapidly transformed the company into one of the world's largest media and telecom
empires, renamed "Vivendi." Then, in the 2000s, as the tech, media, and telecom bubble burst, the Vivendi empire came crashing down under the weight of its debt burden.
Jean-Marie Messier was investigated by both French and U.S. courts and accused of
misleading shareholders, misappropriating funds, and worsening the company's pre-
carious position. He was fined and forced to resign.[21]

Figure 11.3 graphs long-term profitability against the rate of growth in company
revenues. A company that does not grow is likely missing out on profitable opportunities.[22] A moderate revenue growth rate of G^* allows a company to maximize long-term
profitability, generating a return of π^*. Thus, a growth rate of $G1$ in Figure 11.3 is
not consistent with maximizing profitability ($\pi1 < \pi^*$). By the same token, however, attaining growth in excess of $G2$ requires moving into market segments that earn
lower profit margins or diversification into areas that the company knows little about.
Consequently, it can be achieved only by sacrificing profitability; that is, past G^*, the
investment required to finance further growth does not produce an adequate return,
and the company's profitability declines. Yet $G2$ may be the growth rate favored by
an empire-building CEO, for it will increase his or her power, status, and income. At
this growth rate, profitability is equal only to $\pi2$. Because $\pi^* > \pi2$, a company growing at this rate is clearly not maximizing its long-run profitability or the wealth of its
stockholders.

Figure 11.3 The Tradeoff Between Profitability and Revenue Growth Rates

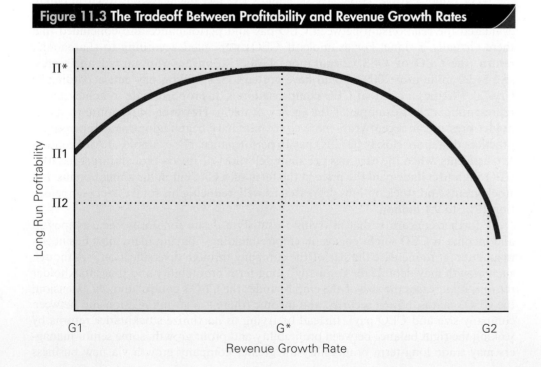

The magnitude of agency problems was emphasized in the early 2000s, when a series of scandals swept through the corporate world, many of which could be attributed to self-interest-seeking senior executives and a failure of corporate governance mechanisms to hold the largess of those executives in check. In 2003, an investigation revealed that the CEO of Hollinger, Conrad Black, had used "tunneling" to divert over $400 million in company funds to his family and friends (see the Strategy in Action 11.2 for more details on Hollinger and Black). Between 2001 and 2004, accounting scandals also unfolded at a number of major corporations, including Enron, WorldCom, Tyco, Computer Associates, HealthSouth, Adelphia Communications, Dynegy, Royal Dutch Shell, and Parmalat, a major Italian food company. At Enron, $27 billion in debt was hidden from shareholders, employees, and regulators in special partnerships that were removed from the balance sheet. At Parmalat, managers apparently "invented" $8 to $12 billion in assets to shore up the company's balance sheet—assets that never existed. In the case of Royal Dutch Shell, senior managers knowingly inflated the value of the company's oil reserves by one-fifth, which amounted to 4 billion barrels of oil that never existed, making the company appear much more valuable than it was. At the other companies, earnings were systematically overstated,

11.2 STRATEGY IN ACTION

Self-Dealing at Hollinger International Inc.

From 1999 to 2003, Conrad Black, CEO, and F. David Radler, chief operating officer (COO), of Hollinger International Inc. illegally diverted cash and assets to themselves, family members, and other corporate insiders. Hollinger International was a global publishing empire that owned newspapers around the world, such as the *Chicago Sun-Times*, the *Daily Telegraph* (in London), the *National Post* (in Toronto), and the *Jerusalem Post* (in Israel), among others. According to Stephen Cutler, the director of the SEC's Division of Enforcement, "Black and Radler abused their control of a public company and treated it as their personal piggy bank. Instead of carrying out their responsibilities to protect the interest of public shareholders, the defendants cheated and defrauded these shareholders through a series of deceptive schemes and misstatements." In a practice

known as "tunneling," Black and Radler engaged in a series of self-dealing transactions such as selling some of Hollinger's newspapers at below-market prices to companies privately held by Black and Radler themselves—sometimes for a price as low as one dollar. They also directly channeled money out of the firm under the guise of "noncompetition payments." The managers abused corporate perks, using a company jet to fly to the South Pacific for a vacation and spending corporate funds on a swanky, New York apartment on Park Avenue and a lavish, $62,000 birthday party for Black's wife. Black's ill-gotten gains are thought to total more than $400 million, and fallout from the scandal resulted in a loss of $2 billion in shareholder value. Although Black was sentenced to 6½ years in jail, he ultimately only served 42 months.

Sources: S. Taub, "SEC Charges Hollinger, Two Executives," *CFO*, November 16, 2004; www.cfo.com, U.S. Department of Justice, "Former Hollinger Chairman Conrad Black and Three Other Executives Indicted in U.S.–Canada Corporate Fraud Schemes," indictment released November 17, 2005; "Ex-Media Mogul Black Convicted of Fraud," Associated Press, July 13, 2007; A. Stern, "Ex-Media Mogul Conrad Black Sent Back to Prison," Reuters, June 24, 2011.

often by hundreds of millions of dollars, or even billions of dollars in the case of Tyco and WorldCom, which understated its expenses by $3 billion in 2001. In all of these cases, the prime motivation seems to have been an effort to present a more favorable view of corporate affairs to shareholders than was the case, thereby securing senior executives significantly higher pay packets.[23]

It is important to remember that the agency problem is not confined to the relationship between senior managers and stockholders. It can also bedevil the relationship between the CEO and subordinates, and between them and their subordinates. Subordinates might use control over information to distort the true performance of their unit in order to enhance their pay, increase their job security, or make sure their unit gets more than its fair share of company resources.

Confronted with agency problems, the challenge for principals is to (1) shape the behavior of agents so that they act in accordance with the goals set by principals, (2) reduce information asymmetry between agents and principals, and (3) develop mechanisms for removing agents who do not act in accordance with the goals of principals and mislead them. Principals deal with these challenges through a series of governance mechanisms.

◤ GOVERNANCE MECHANISMS

Principals put governance mechanisms in place to align incentives between principals and agents and to monitor and control agents. The purpose of governance mechanisms is to reduce the scope and frequency of the agency problem; that is, to help ensure that agents act in a manner that is consistent with the best interests of their principals. In this section, the primary focus is on governance mechanisms that exist to align the interests of senior managers (as agents) with their principals, stockholders. It should not be forgotten, however, that governance mechanisms also exist to align the interests of business-unit managers with those of their superiors, and likewise down the hierarchy within the organization.

Here we look at four main types of governance mechanisms for aligning stockholder and management interests: the board of directors, stock-based compensation, financial statements, and the takeover constraint. The section closes with a discussion of governance mechanisms within a company to align the interest of senior and lower-level managers.

The Board of Directors

The board of directors is the centerpiece of the corporate governance system. Board members are directly elected by stockholders, and under corporate law they represent the stockholders' interests in the company. Hence, the board can be held legally accountable for the company's actions. Its position at the apex of decision making within the company allows it to monitor corporate strategy decisions and ensure that they are consistent with stockholder interests. If the board believes that corporate strategies are not in the best interest of stockholders, it can take measures such as voting against management nominations to the board of directors or submitting its own nominees. In addition, the board has the legal authority to hire, fire, and compensate corporate employees, including, most importantly, the CEO.[24] The board is also responsible for making sure that the company's audited financial statements present a true picture of its financial situation. Thus, the board exists to reduce the information asymmetry between stockholders and managers, and to monitor and control management actions on behalf of stockholders.

The typical board of directors is composed of a mix of inside and outside directors. **Inside directors** are senior employees of the company, such as the CEO. They are required on the board because they have valuable information about the company's activities. Without such information, the board cannot adequately perform its monitoring function. But because insiders are full-time employees of the company, their interests tend to be aligned with those of management. Hence, outside directors are needed to bring objectivity to the monitoring and evaluation processes. **Outside directors** are not full-time employees of the company. Many of them are full-time, professional directors who hold positions on the boards of several companies. They need to maintain a reputation for competency and so are motivated to perform their role as objectively and effectively as possible.[25]

There is little doubt that many boards perform their assigned functions admirably. For example, when the board of Sotheby's discovered that the company had been engaged in price fixing with Christie's, board members moved quickly to oust both the CEO and the chairman of the company (see Strategy in Action 11.1). But not all boards perform as well as they should. The board of now-bankrupt energy company Enron approved the company's audited financial statements, which were later discovered to be grossly misleading.

Critics of the existing governance system charge that inside directors often dominate the outsiders on the board. Insiders can use their position within the management hierarchy to exercise control over the company-specific information that the board receives. Consequently, they can present information in a way that puts them in a favorable light. In addition, because insiders have intimate knowledge of the company's operations, and because superior knowledge and control over information are sources of power, they may be better positioned than outsiders to influence boardroom decision making. The board may become the captive of insiders and merely rubber-stamp management decisions instead of guarding stockholder interests.

Some observers contend that many boards are dominated by the company CEO, particularly when the CEO is also the chairman of the board.[26] To support this view, they point out that both inside and outside directors are often the CEO's nominees. The typical inside director is subordinate to the CEO in the company's hierarchy and therefore unlikely to criticize the boss. Nor can outside directors nominated by the CEO be expected to evaluate the CEO objectively. Sometimes CEOs sit on each other's boards as outside directors, forming "interlocking directorates" that may induce them to act in each other's interests. Thus, the loyalty of the board may be biased toward the CEO, not the stockholders. Moreover, a CEO who is also chairman of the board may be able to control the agenda of board discussions in such a manner as to deflect criticisms of his or her leadership. Notably, although shareholders ostensibly vote on board members, board members are not legally required to resign if they do not receive a majority of the vote. The Council of Institutional Investors (which represents pension funds, endowments, and other large investors) published a list of "zombie directors" in 2012—directors who were retained on boards despite being rejected by shareholders. The list includes a wide range of companies, from Boston Beer Company to Loral Space and Communications to Cablevision. In fact, Cablevision

inside directors

Senior employees of the company, such as the CEO.

outside directors

Directors who are not full-time employees of the company, needed to provide objectivity to the monitoring and evaluation of processes.

was listed as having three directors who lost their shareholder votes twice between 2010 and 2012, yet remained on the board.[27]

In the aftermath of the wave of scandals that hit the corporate world in the early 2000s, there are clear signs that many corporate boards are moving away from merely rubber-stamping top-management decisions and are beginning to play a much more active role in corporate governance. In part, they have been prompted by new legislation such as the 2002 Sarbanes-Oxley Act in the United States, which tightened rules regulating corporate reporting and corporate governance. A growing trend on the part of the courts to hold directors liable for corporate misstatements has also been important. Powerful institutional investors such as pension funds have also been more aggressive in exerting their power, often pushing for more outside representation on the board of directors and for a separation between the roles of chairman and CEO—with the chairman role going to an outsider. Partly as a result, 43% of firms on the Standard & Poor's 500 index split the chairman and CEO jobs as of November 2012—up from 25% 10 years earlier.[28] Separating the role of chairman and CEO limits the ability of corporate insiders, particularly the CEO, to exercise control over the board. Regardless, it must be recognized that boards of directors do not work as well as they should in theory, and other mechanisms are needed to align the interests of stockholders and managers.

Stock-Based Compensation

According to agency theory, one of the best ways to reduce the scope of the agency problem is for principals to establish incentives for agents to behave in the company's best interest through pay-for-performance systems. In the case of stockholders and top managers, stockholders can encourage top managers to pursue strategies that maximize a company's long-term profitability and profit growth, and thus the gains from holding its stock, by linking the pay of those managers to the performance of the stock price.

stock options
The right to purchase company stock at a predetermined price at some point in the future, usually within 10 years of the grant date.

Giving managers **stock options**— the right to purchase the company's shares at a predetermined (strike) price at some point in the future, usually within 10 years of the grant date—has been the most common pay-for-performance system. Typically, the strike price is the price at which the stock was trading when the option was originally granted. Ideally, stock options will motivate managers to adopt strategies that increase the share price of the company, for in doing so managers also increase the value of their own stock options. Granting managers stock if they attain predetermined performance targets is another stock-based, pay-for-performance system.

Several academic studies suggest that stock-based compensation schemes such as stock options and stock grants can align executive and stockholder interests. For instance, one study found that managers were more likely to consider the effects of their acquisition decisions on stockholder returns if they were significant shareholders.[29] According to another study, managers who were significant stockholders were less likely to pursue strategies that would maximize the size of the company rather than its profitability.[30] More generally, it is difficult to argue with the proposition that the chance to get rich from exercising stock options is the primary reason for the 14-hour days and 6-day workweeks that many employees of fast-growing companies experience.

However, the practice of granting stock options has become increasingly controversial. Many top managers earn huge bonuses from exercising stock options that were granted several years prior. Critics claim that these options are often too generous but do not deny that they motivate managers to improve company performance. A particular cause for concern is that stock options are often granted at such low strike prices that the CEO can hardly fail to make a significant amount of money by exercising them, even if the company underperforms in the stock market by a significant margin. A serious example of the agency problem emerged in 2005 and 2006, when the SEC investigated a number of companies that had granted stock options to senior executives and apparently "backdated" the stock to a time when the price was lower, enabling executives to earn more money than if those options had simply been dated on the day they were granted.[31] By late 2006, the SEC had investigated nearly 130 companies for possible fraud related to stock-option backdating. Major corporations such as Apple, Jabil Circuit, United Healthcare, and Home Depot were included in the list.[32]

Other critics of stock options, including the famous investor Warren Buffett, complain that huge stock-option grants increase the outstanding number of shares in a company and therefore dilute the equity of stockholders; accordingly, they should be shown in company accounts as an expense against profits. Under accounting regulations that were enforced until 2005, stock options, unlike wages and salaries, were not expensed. However, this has since changed, and as a result many companies are beginning to reduce their use of options. Microsoft, for example, which had long given generous stock-option grants to high-performing employees, replaced stock options with stock grants in 2005. Requiring senior management to hold large numbers of shares in the company also has its downside: Managers who hold a large portion of their personal wealth in the company they manage are likely to be underdiversified. This can lead to excessively risk-averse behavior, or overdiversification of the firm.

Financial Statements and Auditors

Publicly traded companies in the United States are required to file quarterly and annual reports with the SEC that are prepared according to GAAP. The purpose of this requirement is to give consistent, detailed, and accurate information about how efficiently and effectively the agents of stockholders—the managers—are running the company. To make sure that managers do not misrepresent financial information, the SEC also requires that the accounts be audited by an independent and accredited accounting firm. Similar regulations exist in most other developed nations. If the system works as intended, stockholders can have a lot of faith that the information contained in financial statements accurately reflects the state of affairs at a company. Among other things, such information can enable a stockholder to calculate the profitability (ROIC) of a company in which he or she invests and to compare its ROIC against that of competitors.

Unfortunately, this system has not always worked as intended in the United States. Despite the fact that the vast majority of companies do file accurate information in their financial statements, and although most auditors review that information accurately, there is substantial evidence that a minority of companies have abused the system, aided in part by the compliance of auditors. This was clearly an issue at bankrupt energy trader Enron, where the CFO and others misrepresented the true financial state of the company to investors by creating off-balance-sheet partnerships that hid the true state of Enron's indebtedness from public view. Enron's auditor, Arthur Andersen, was complicit with this deception and in direct violation of its fiduciary duty. Arthur Anderson had lucrative consulting contracts with Enron that it did not want to jeopardize by questioning the accuracy of the company's financial statements. The losers in this mutual deception were shareholders, who relied completely upon inaccurate information to make their investment decisions.

There have been numerous examples in recent years of managers' gaming of financial statements to present a distorted picture of their company's finances to investors (see the accusations made by HP about Autonomy in the Closing Case, for example). The typical motive has been to inflate the earnings or revenues of a company, thereby generating investor enthusiasm and propelling the stock price higher, which gives managers an opportunity to cash in stock-option grants for huge personal gain, obviously at the expense of stockholders, who have been misled by the reports.

The gaming of financial statements by companies such as Enron raises serious questions about the accuracy of the information contained in audited financial statements. In response, Congress passed the Sarbanes-Oxley Act in 2002, representing the most far-reaching overhaul of accounting rules and corporate governance procedures since the 1930s. Among other things, Sarbanes-Oxley established an oversight board for accounting firms, required CEOs and CFOs to endorse their company's financial statements, and barred companies from hiring the same accounting firm for both auditing and consulting services.

The Takeover Constraint

Given the imperfections in corporate governance mechanisms, it is clear that the agency problem persists at some companies. However, stockholders do have residual power—they can always sell their shares. If stockholders sell in large numbers, the price of the company's shares will decline. If the share price falls far enough, the company might be worth less on the stock market than the actual value of its assets. At this point, the company may become an attractive acquisition target and runs the risk of being purchased by another enterprise, against the wishes of the target company's management.

takeover constraint
The risk of being acquired by another company.

The risk of being acquired by another company is known as the **takeover constraint**—it limits the extent to which managers can pursue strategies and take actions that put their own interests above those of stockholders. If they ignore stockholder interests and the company is acquired, senior managers typically lose their independence, and likely their jobs as well. Therefore, the threat of takeover can constrain management action and limit the worst excesses of the agency problem.

During the 1980s and early 1990s, the threat of takeover was often enforced by corporate raiders: individuals or corporations that purchase large blocks of shares in companies that appear to be pursuing strategies inconsistent with maximizing stockholder wealth. Corporate raiders argue that if these underperforming companies pursued different strategies, they could create more wealth for stockholders. Raiders purchase stock in a company either to take over the business and run it more efficiently or to precipitate a change in top management, replacing the existing team with one more likely to maximize stockholder returns. Raiders are motivated not by altruism but by gain. If they succeed in their takeover bid, they can institute strategies that create value for stockholders, including themselves. Even if a takeover bid fails, raiders can still earn millions, for their stockholdings will typically be bought out by the defending company for a hefty premium. Called **greenmail**, this source of gain has stirred much controversy and debate about its benefits. Whereas some claim

greenmail
A source of gaining wealth whereby corporate raiders either push companies to change their corporate strategy to one that will benefit stockholders, or charge a premium for stock when the company wants to buy it back.

that the threat posed by raiders has had a salutary effect on enterprise performance by pushing corporate management to run companies better, others counter that there is little evidence of this.[33]

Although the incidence of hostile takeover bids has fallen off significantly since the early 1990s, this should not imply that the takeover constraint has ceased to operate. Unique circumstances existed in the early 2000s that made it more difficult to execute hostile takeovers. The boom years of the 1990s left many corporations with excessive debt (corporate America entered the new century with record levels of debt on its balance sheets), limiting the ability to finance acquisitions, particularly hostile acquisitions, which are often particularly expensive. In addition, the market valuation of many companies became misaligned with underlying fundamentals during the stock market bubble of the 1990s, and after a substantial fall in certain segments of the stock market, such as the technology sector, present valuations are still high relative to historic norms—making the hostile acquisition of even poorly run and unprofitable companies expensive. However, takeovers tend to occur in cycles, and it seems likely that once excesses are worked out of the stock market and off corporate balance sheets, the takeover constraint will reassert itself. It should be remembered that the takeover constraint is the governance mechanism of last resort and is often invoked only when other governance mechanisms have failed.

Governance Mechanisms Inside a Company

Thus far, this chapter has focused on the governance mechanisms designed to reduce the agency problem that potentially exists between stockholders and managers. Agency relationships also exist within a company, and the agency problem can arise between levels of management. In this section, we explore how the agency problem can be reduced within a company by using two complementary governance mechanisms to align the incentives and behavior of employees with those of upper-level management: strategic control systems and incentive systems.

Strategic Control Systems Strategic control systems are the primary governance mechanisms established within a company to reduce the scope of the agency problem between levels of management. These systems are the formal target-setting, measurement, and feedback systems that allow managers to evaluate whether a company is executing the strategies necessary to maximize its long-term profitability and, in particular, whether the company is achieving superior efficiency, quality, innovation, and customer responsiveness. They are discussed in more detail in Chapter 12.

The purpose of strategic control systems is to (1) establish standards and targets against which performance can be measured, (2) create systems for measuring and monitoring performance on a regular basis, (3) compare actual performance against the established targets, and (4) evaluate results and take corrective action if necessary. In governance terms, their purpose is to ensure that lower-level managers, as the agents of top managers, act in a way that is consistent with top managers' goals, which should be to maximize the wealth of stockholders, subject to legal and ethical constraints.

One increasingly influential model that guides managers through the process of creating the right kind of strategic control systems is the balanced scorecard model.[34] Managers have traditionally emphasized financial measures of performance such as ROIC to gauge and evaluate organizational performance. According to the balanced scorecard model financial information is extremely important, but it alone is not enough. If managers are to obtain a true picture of organizational performance, financial information must be supplemented with performance measures that indicate how well an organization has been achieving the four building blocks of competitive advantage: efficiency, quality, innovation, and responsiveness to customers. This is because financial results simply inform managers about the results of strategic decisions they have already taken; the other measures balance this picture of performance by informing managers about how reliably the organization has in place the building blocks to drive future performance.[35]

One version of the way the balanced scorecard operates is presented in Figure 11.4. Based on an organization's mission and goals, strategic managers develop a set of criteria for assessing performance according to multiple perspectives such as:

- *The financial perspective:* for example, ROIC, cash flow, and revenue growth
- *The customer perspective:* for example, satisfaction, product reliability, on-time delivery, and level of service

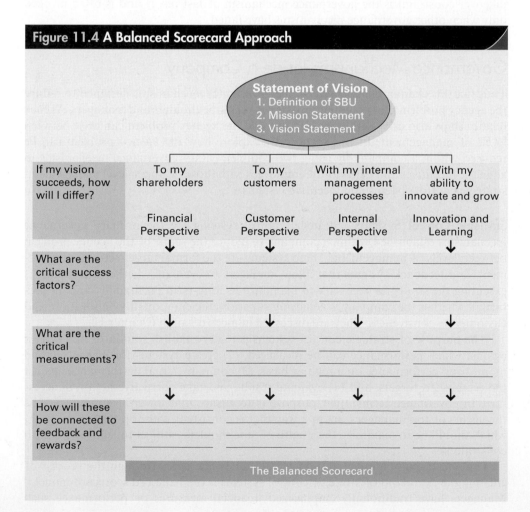

Figure 11.4 A Balanced Scorecard Approach

- *The internal perspective:* for example, efficiency, timeliness, and employee satisfaction
- *Innovation and learning:* for example, the number of new products introduced, the percentage of revenues generated from new products in a defined period, the time taken to develop the next generation of new products versus the competition, and the productivity of research and development (R&D)—how much R&D spending is required to produce a successful product

As Kaplan and Norton, the developers of this approach, suggest, "Think of the balanced scorecard as the dials and indicators in an airplane cockpit. For the complex task of navigating and flying an airplane, pilots need detailed information about many aspects of the flight. They need information on fuel, air speed, altitude, learning, destination, and other indicators that summarize the current and predicted environment. Reliance on one instrument can be fatal. Similarly, the complexity of managing an organization today requires that managers be able to view performance in several areas simultaneously."[36]

Based on an evaluation of the complete set of measures in the balanced scorecard, strategic managers are in a good position to reevaluate the company's mission and goals and take corrective action to rectify problems, limit the agency problem, or exploit new opportunities by changing the organization's strategy and structure—which is the purpose of strategic control.

Employee Incentives   Control systems alone may not be sufficient to align incentives between stockholders, senior management, and the organization as a whole. To help do this, positive incentive systems are often put into place to motivate employees to work toward goals that are central to maximizing long-term profitability. As already noted, ESOPs are one form of positive incentive, as are stock-option grants. In the 1990s, ESOPs and stock-ownership grants were pushed down deep within many organizations, meaning that employees at many levels of the firm were eligible for the plans. The logic behind such systems is straightforward: Recognizing that the stock price, and therefore their own wealth, is dependent upon the profitability of the company, employees will work toward maximizing profitability.

In addition to stock-based compensation systems, employee compensation can be tied to goals that are linked to the attainment of superior efficiency, quality, innovation, and customer responsiveness. For example, the bonus pay of a manufacturing employee might depend upon attaining quality and productivity targets, which, if reached, will lower the costs of the company, increase customer satisfaction, and boost profitability. Similarly, a salesperson's bonus pay might depend upon surpassing sales targets, and an R&D employee's bonus pay may be contingent upon the success of new products he or she had worked on developing.

ETHICS AND STRATEGY

The term **ethics** refers to accepted principles of right or wrong that govern the conduct of a person, the members of a profession, or the actions of an organization. **Business ethics** are the accepted principles of right or wrong governing the conduct of businesspeople. Ethical decisions are in accordance with those accepted principles, whereas unethical decisions violate accepted principles. This is not as straightforward

ethics
Accepted principles of right or wrong that govern the conduct of a person, the members of a profession, or the actions of an organization.

business ethics
Accepted principles of right or wrong governing the conduct of businesspeople.

ethical dilemmas

Situations where there is no agreement over exactly what the accepted principles of right and wrong are, or where none of the available alternatives seems ethically acceptable.

as it sounds. Managers may be confronted with **ethical dilemmas**, which are situations where there is no agreement over exactly what the accepted principles of right and wrong are, or where none of the available alternatives seems ethically acceptable.

In our society, many accepted principles of right and wrong are not only universally recognized but also codified into law. In the business arena, there are laws governing product liability (tort laws), contracts and breaches of contract (contract law), the protection of intellectual property (intellectual property law), competitive behavior (antitrust law), and the selling of securities (securities law). Not only is it unethical to break these laws, it is illegal.

In this book we argue that the preeminent goal of managers in a business should be to pursue strategies that maximize the long-term profitability and profit growth of the enterprise, thereby boosting returns to stockholders. Strategies, of course, must be consistent with the laws that govern business behavior: Managers must act legally while seeking to maximize the long-term profitability of the enterprise. Unfortunately, as we have already seen in this chapter, managers do break laws. Moreover, managers may take advantage of ambiguities and gray areas in the law, of which there are many in our common law system, to pursue actions that are at best legally suspect and, in any event, clearly unethical. It is important to realize, however, that behaving ethically surpasses staying within the bounds of the law. In the Opening Case, for example, we described how Starbucks goes well beyond legal requirements to ensure that its coffee is purchased from suppliers that use safe, fair, humane working and living conditions, including minimum-wage requirements and the prohibition of child and forced labor. On the other hand, research by Surroca, Tribó, and Zahra on 110 multinational firms found that often multinational firms deal with stakeholder pressures and legal concerns in their home country by simply transferring their socially irresponsible practices to their overseas subsidiaries. The researchers found that this was particularly likely when it was not overtly apparent that the subsidiary had a connection to the multinational, suggesting that managers knew the behavior was unethical and did not want to be associated with it, yet continued the practice anyway.[37]

In this section, we take a closer look at the ethical issues that managers may confront when developing strategy, and at the steps managers can take to ensure that strategic decisions are not only legal, but also ethical.

Ethical Issues in Strategy

The ethical issues that strategic managers confront cover many topics, but most are due to a potential conflict between the goals of the enterprise, or the goals of individual managers, and the fundamental rights of important stakeholders, including stockholders, customers, employees, suppliers, competitors, communities, and the general public. Stakeholders have basic rights that must be respected; it is unethical to violate those rights.

Stockholders have the right to timely and accurate information about their investments (in accounting statements), and it is unethical to violate that right. Customers have the right to be fully informed about the products and services they purchase, including the right to information about how those products might cause them harm, and it is unethical to restrict their access to such information. Employees have the right to safe working conditions, fair compensation for the work they perform, and just treatment by managers. Suppliers have the right to expect contracts to be respected, and the company should not take advantage of a power disparity between it and a supplier to opportunistically rewrite a contract. Competitors have the right to expect that the firm will abide by the rules of competition and not violate the basic principles of antitrust laws. Communities and the general public, including their political representatives in government, have the right to expect that a firm will not violate the basic expectations that society places on enterprises—for example, by dumping toxic pollutants into the environment, or overcharging for work performed on government contracts.

Those who take the stakeholder view of business ethics often argue that it is in the enlightened self-interest of managers to behave in an ethical manner that recognizes and respects the fundamental rights of stakeholders, because doing so will ensure the support of stakeholders and, ultimately, benefit the firm and its managers. Others go beyond this instrumental approach to ethics and argue that, in many cases, acting ethically is simply the right thing to do. They argue that businesses need to recognize their *noblesse oblige*, a French term that refers to honorable and benevolent behavior that is considered the responsibility of people of high (noble) birth, and give something back to the society that made their success possible. In a business setting, it is understood that benevolent behavior is the moral responsibility of successful enterprises.

Unethical behavior often arises in a corporate setting when managers decide to put the attainment of their own personal goals, or the goals of the enterprise, above the fundamental rights of one or more stakeholder groups (in other words, unethical behavior may arise from agency problems). The most common examples of such behavior involve self-dealing, information manipulation, anticompetitive behavior, opportunistic exploitation of other players in the value chain in which the firm is embedded (including suppliers, complement providers, and distributors), the maintenance of substandard working conditions, environmental degradation, and corruption.

Self-dealing occurs when managers find a way to feather their own nests with corporate monies, as we have already discussed in several examples in this chapter (such as Conrad Black at Hollinger). **Information manipulation** occurs when managers use their control over corporate data to distort or hide information in order to enhance their own financial situation or the competitive position of the firm, such as HP accused Autonomy of in the Closing Case. As we have seen, many accounting scandals have involved the deliberate manipulation of financial information. Information manipulation can also occur with nonfinancial data. An example of this is when managers at the tobacco companies suppressed internal research that linked smoking to health problems, violating the right of consumers to accurate information about the dangers of smoking. When this evidence came to light, lawyers filed class-action suits against the tobacco companies, claiming that they had intentionally caused harm to smokers; they had broken tort law by promoting a product that they knew was seriously harmful to consumers. In 1999, the tobacco companies settled a lawsuit brought by the states that sought to recover health-care costs associated with tobacco-related illnesses; the total payout to the states was $260 billion.

Anticompetitive behavior covers a range of actions aimed at harming actual or potential competitors, most often by using monopoly power, and thereby enhancing the long-run prospects of the firm. For example, in the 1990s, the Justice Department claimed that Microsoft used its monopoly in operating systems to force PC makers to bundle Microsoft's Web browser, Internet Explorer, with the Windows operating system, and to display the Internet Explorer logo prominently on the computer desktop. Microsoft reportedly told PC makers that it would not supply them with Windows

self-dealing
Managers using company funds for their own personal consumption

information manipulation
When managers use their control over corporate data to distort or hide information in order to enhance their own financial situation or the competitive position of the firm.

anticompetitive behavior
A range of actions aimed at harming actual or potential competitors, most often by using monopoly power, and thereby enhancing the long-run prospects of the firm.

unless they did this. Because the PC makers needed Windows to sell their machines, this was a powerful threat. The alleged aim of the action, which exemplifies "tie-in sales"—which are illegal under antitrust laws—was to drive a competing browser maker, Netscape, out of business. The courts ruled that Microsoft was indeed abusing its monopoly power in this case and, under a 2001 consent decree, the company was forced to cease this practice.

Legality aside, the actions Microsoft managers allegedly engaged in are unethical on at least three counts; first, by violating the rights of end-users by unfairly limiting their choice; second, by violating the rights of downstream participants in the industry value chain, in this case PC makers, by forcing them to incorporate a particular product in their design; and third, by violating the rights of competitors to free and fair competition.

opportunistic exploitation
Unethical behavior sometimes used by managers to unilaterally rewrite the terms of a contract with suppliers, buyers, or complement providers in a way that favors to the firm.

Opportunistic exploitation of other players in the value chain in which the firm is embedded is another example of unethical behavior. Exploitation of this kind typically occurs when the managers of a firm seek to unilaterally rewrite the terms of a contract with suppliers, buyers, or complement providers in a way that is more favorable to the firm, often using their power to force a revision to the contract. For example, in the late 1990s, Boeing entered into a $2-billion contract with Titanium Metals Corporation to purchase certain amounts of titanium annually for 10 years. In 2000, after Titanium Metals had already spent $100 million to expand its production capacity to fulfill the contract, Boeing demanded that the contract be renegotiated, asking for lower prices and an end to minimum-purchase agreements. As a major purchaser of titanium, managers at Boeing probably thought they had the power to push this contract revision through, and Titanium's investment meant that it would be unlikely that the company walk away from the deal. Titanium promptly sued Boeing for breach of contract. The dispute was settled out of court, and under a revised agreement Boeing agreed to pay monetary damages to Titanium Metals (reported to be in the $60-million range) and entered into an amended contract to purchase titanium.[38] This action was arguably unethical because it violated the supplier's right to have a purchaser do business in a fair and open way, regardless of any issues of legality.

substandard working conditions
Arise when managers underinvest in working conditions, or pay employees below-market rates, in order to reduce their production costs.

Substandard working conditions arise when managers underinvest in working conditions, or pay employees below-market rates, in order to reduce their production costs. The most extreme examples of such behavior occur when a firm establishes operations in countries that lack the workplace regulations found in developed nations such as the United States. For example, The Ohio Art Company ran into an ethical storm when newspaper reports alleged that it had moved production of its popular Etch A Sketch toy from Ohio to a supplier in Shenzhen Province where employees—mostly teenagers—work long hours for $0.24 per hour, below the legal minimum wage of $0.33 per hour. Moreover, production reportedly started at 7:30 a.m. and continued until 10 p.m., with breaks only for lunch and dinner. Furthermore, Saturdays and Sundays were treated as normal workdays, meaning that employees worked 12 hours per day, 7 days per week, or 84 hours per week—well above the standard 40-hour week authorities set in Shenzhen. Working conditions such as these clearly violate employees' rights in China, as specified by local regulations (which are poorly enforced). Is it ethical for the Ohio Art Company to use such a supplier? Many would say it is not.[39]

environmental degradation
Occurs when a company's actions directly or indirectly result in pollution or other forms of environmental harm.

Environmental degradation occurs when a company's actions directly or indirectly result in pollution or other forms of environmental harm. Environmental degradation can violate the right of local communities and the general public to clean air and water, land that is free from pollution by toxic chemicals, and properly managed forests.

Finally, **corruption** can arise in a business context when managers pay bribes to gain access to lucrative business contracts. For example, it was alleged that Halliburton was part of a consortium that paid nearly $180 million in bribes to win a lucrative contract to build a natural gas plant in Nigeria.[40] Similarly, between 2006 and 2009, Siemens was found guilty of paying hundreds of millions of dollars in bribes to secure sales contracts; the company was ultimately forced to pay hefty fines, and one Chinese executive who accepted $5.1 million in bribes was sentenced to death by Chinese courts.[41] Corruption is clearly unethical because it violates many rights, including the right of competitors to a level playing field when bidding for contracts, and, when government officials are involved, the right of citizens to expect that government officials will act in the best interest of the local community (or nation) and not in response to corrupt payments.

corruption
Can arise in a business context when managers pay bribes to gain access to lucrative business contracts.

The Roots of Unethical Behavior

Why do some managers behave unethically? What motivates managers to engage in actions that violate accepted principals of right and wrong, trample on the rights of one or more stakeholder groups, or simply break the law? Although there is no simple answer to this question, a few generalizations can be made.[42] First, it is important to recognize that business ethics are not divorced from **personal ethics**, which are the generally accepted principles of right and wrong governing the conduct of individuals. As individuals we are taught that it is wrong to lie and cheat, and that it is right to behave with integrity and honor and stand up for what we believe to be true. The personal ethical code that guides behavior comes from many sources, including parents, schools, religion, and the media. A personal ethical code will exert a profound influence on the way an individual behaves as a businessperson. An individual with a strong sense of personal ethics is less likely to behave in an unethical manner in a business setting; in particular, he or she is less likely to engage in self-dealing and more likely to behave with integrity.

personal ethics
Generally accepted principles of right and wrong governing the conduct of individuals.

Second, many studies of unethical behavior in a business setting have come to the conclusion that businesspeople sometimes do not realize that they are behaving unethically, primarily because they simply fail to ask the relevant question: Is this decision or action ethical? Instead, they apply straightforward business calculus to what they perceive to be a business decision, forgetting that the decision may also have an important ethical dimension.[43] The fault here is within the processes that do not incorporate ethical considerations into business decision making. This may have been the case at Nike and other textile companies when managers originally made subcontracting arrangements with contractors that operated factories as "sweatshops," with long hours, low pay, and poor working conditions. Those decisions were probably made on the basis of good economic logic. Subcontractors were probably chosen on the basis of business variables such as cost, delivery, and product quality, and key managers simply failed to ask: "How does this subcontractor treat its workforce?" If managers pondered this question at all, they probably reasoned that it was the subcontractor's concern, not the company's.

Unfortunately, the climate in some businesses does not encourage people to think through the ethical consequences of business decisions. This brings us to the third cause of unethical behavior in businesses: an organizational culture that de-emphasizes business ethics and considers all decisions to be purely economic ones. Individuals may believe their decisions within the workplace are not subject to the same ethical principles that govern their personal lives, or that their decisions within the firm do not really "belong" to them, but rather that they are merely acting as agents of the firm. A related fourth cause of unethical behavior may be pressure from top management to meet performance goals that are unrealistic and can only be attained by cutting corners or acting in an unethical manner. Thus the pressure to perform induces individuals to behave in ways they otherwise would not.

An organizational culture can "legitimize" behavior that society would judge as unethical, particularly when this is mixed with a focus upon unrealistic performance goals such as maximizing short-term economic performance regardless of the costs. In such circumstances, there is a greater-than-average probability that managers will violate their own personal ethics and engage in behavior that is unethical. By the same token, an organization's culture can do just the opposite and reinforce the need for ethical behavior. Recreational Equipment Inc. (REI), for example, has a strong culture around valuing environmental sustainability, respect for individuals, and trustworthiness. The firm backs up this belief system with such policies as producing an annual environmental stewardship report and providing health-care benefits for all workers (including part-time employees), a retirement plan that does not require individual contributions, and grants for employees to contribute to their communities or to buy gear to pursue personal outdoor challenges. The company has made *Fortune*'s "100 Best Companies to Work For" list every year since 1998.

This brings us to a fifth root cause of unethical behavior: *unethical leadership.* Leaders help to establish the culture of an organization, and they set the example that others follow. Other employees in a business often take their cues from business leaders, and if those leaders do not behave in an ethical manner, employees may not either. It is not what leaders say that matters, but what they do. A good example is Ken Lay, the former CEO of the failed energy company Enron. While constantly referring to Enron's code of ethics in public statements, Lay simultaneously engaged in behavior that was ethically suspect. Among other things, he failed to discipline subordinates who had inflated earnings by engaging in corrupt energy-trading schemes. Such behavior sent a very clear message to Enron's employees—unethical behavior would be tolerated if it could boost earnings.

Behaving Ethically

What is the best way for managers to ensure that ethical considerations are taken into account? In many cases, there is no easy answer to this question, for many of the most vexing ethical problems involve very real dilemmas and suggest no obvious right course of action. Nevertheless, managers can and should do at least seven things to ensure that basic ethical principles are adhered to and that ethical issues are routinely considered when making business decisions. They can (1) favor hiring and promoting people with a well-grounded sense of personal ethics, (2) build an organizational culture that places a high value on ethical behavior, (3) make sure that leaders within the business not only articulate the rhetoric of ethical behavior but also act in a manner that is consistent with that rhetoric, (4) put decision-making processes in place that require people to consider the ethical dimension of business decisions, (5) use ethics officers, (6) put strong governance processes in place, and (7) act with moral courage.

Hiring and Promotion   It seems obvious that businesses should strive to hire people who have a strong sense of personal ethics and would not engage in unethical or illegal behavior. Similarly, you would rightly expect a business to not promote people, and perhaps fire people, whose behavior does not match generally accepted ethical standards. But doing this is actually very difficult.

Is there anything that businesses can do to ensure they do not hire people who have poor personal ethics, particularly given that people have an incentive to hide this from public view (indeed, unethical people may well lie about their nature)? Businesses can give potential employees psychological tests to try to discern their ethical predisposition, and they can check with prior employees regarding someone's reputation, such as by asking for letters of reference and talking to people who have worked with the prospective employee. The latter approach is not uncommon and does influence the hiring process. Promoting people who have displayed poor ethics should not occur in a company where the organizational culture values ethical behavior and where leaders act accordingly.

Organization Culture and Leadership   To foster ethical behavior, businesses must build an organizational culture that places high value on ethical behavior. Three actions are particularly important. First, businesses must explicitly articulate values that place a strong emphasis on ethical behavior. Many companies now do this by drafting a **code of ethics**, a formal statement of the ethical priorities to which a business adheres—in fact, both the New York Stock Exchange and Nasdaq listing services require listed companies to have a code of ethics that identifies areas of ethical risk, provides guidance for recognizing and dealing with ethical issues, provides mechanisms for reporting unethical conduct, and notes procedures to ensure prompt action against violations.[44] Firms also sometimes incorporate ethical statements into documents that articulate the values or mission of the business. For example, the food and consumer products giant Unilever's code of ethics includes the following points: "We will not use any form of forced, compulsory or child labor" and "No employee may offer, give or receive any gift or payment which is, or may be construed as being, a bribe. Any demand for, or offer of, a bribe must be rejected immediately and reported to management."[45] Unilever's principles send a very clear message to managers and employees within the organization. Data from the National Business Ethics Survey, administered by the Ethics Resource Center, a U.S. nonprofit, has found that firms with strong, well-implemented ethics programs have significantly fewer cases of ethical misconduct.

Having articulated values in a code of ethics or some other document, it is important that leaders in the business give life and meaning to those words by repeatedly emphasizing their importance and then acting on them. This means using every relevant opportunity to stress the importance of business ethics and making sure that key business decisions not only make good economic sense but also are ethical. Many companies have gone a step further and hired independent firms to audit them and make sure that they are behaving in a manner consistent with their ethical codes. Nike, for example, has in recent years hired independent auditors to ensure that its subcontractors are adhering to Nike's code of conduct.

Finally, building an organization culture that places a high value on ethical behavior requires incentive and reward systems, including promotional systems that reward people who engage in ethical behavior and sanction those who do not.

Decision-Making Processes   In addition to establishing the right kind of ethical culture in an organization, businesspeople must be able to think through the ethical

code of ethics
Formal statement of the ethical priorities to which a business adheres.

implications of decisions in a systematic way. To do this, they need a moral compass, and beliefs about what determines individual rights and justice. Some experts on ethics have proposed a straightforward practical guide, or ethical algorithm, to determine whether a decision is ethical. A decision is acceptable on ethical grounds if a business-person can answer "yes" to each of these questions:

1. Does my decision fall within the accepted values or standards that typically apply in the organizational environment (as articulated in a code of ethics or some other corporate statement)?
2. Am I willing to see the decision communicated to all stakeholders affected by it—for example, by having it reported in newspapers or on television?
3. Would the people with whom I have a significant personal relationship, such as family members, friends, or even managers in other businesses, approve of the decision?

Ethics Officers   To make sure that a business behaves in an ethical manner, a number of firms now have ethics officers. These individuals are responsible for making sure that all employees are trained to be ethically aware, that ethical considerations enter the business decision-making process, and that employees adhere to the company's code of ethics. Ethics officers may also be responsible for auditing decisions to ensure that they are consistent with this code. In many businesses, ethics officers act as an internal ombudsperson with responsibility for handling confidential inquiries from employees, investigating complaints from employees or others, reporting findings, and making recommendations for change.

United Technologies, a large aerospace company with worldwide revenues of about $60 billion, has had a formal code of ethics since 1990. There are now some 450 "business practice officers" (the company's name for ethics officers) within United Technologies who are responsible for making sure that employees adhere to the code. United Technologies also established an ombudsperson program in 1986 that allows employees to inquire anonymously about ethics issues.[46]

Strong Corporate Governance   Strong corporate governance procedures are needed to ensure that managers adhere to ethical norms, in particular, that senior managers do not engage in self-dealing or information manipulation. Strong corporate governance procedures require an independent board of directors that is willing to hold top managers accountable for self-dealing and is capable of verifying the information managers provide. If companies like Tyco, WorldCom, and Enron had had strong boards of directors, it is unlikely that these companies would have experienced accounting scandals or that top managers would have been able to access the funds of these corporations as personal treasuries.

There are five cornerstones of strong governance. The first is a board of directors that is composed of a majority of outside directors who have no management responsibilities in the firm, who are willing and able to hold top managers accountable, and who do not have business ties with important insiders. Outside directors should be individuals of high integrity whose reputation is based on their ability to act independently. The second cornerstone is a board where the positions of CEO and chairman are held by separate individuals and the chairman is an outside director. When the CEO is also chairman of the board of directors, he or she can control the agenda, thereby furthering his or her own personal agenda (which may include self-dealing) or limiting criticism against current corporate policies. The third cornerstone is a compensation committee formed by the board that is composed entirely of outside directors. It is the compensation committee that sets the level of pay for top managers, including stock-option grants and additional benefits. The scope of self-dealing is reduced by making sure that the compensation committee is independent of managers. Fourth, the audit committee of the board, which reviews the financial statements of the firm, should also be composed of outsiders, thereby encouraging vigorous independent questioning of the firm's financial statements. Finally, the board should use outside auditors that are truly independent and do not have a conflict of interest. This was not the case in many recent accounting scandals, where outside auditors were also consultants to the corporation and therefore less likely to ask management hard questions for fear that doing so would jeopardize lucrative consulting contracts.

Moral Courage   It is important to recognize that sometimes managers and others need significant moral courage. It is moral courage that enables managers to walk away from a decision that is profitable but unethical, that gives employees the strength to say no to superiors who instruct them to behave unethically, and that gives employees the integrity to contact the media and "blow the whistle' on persistent unethical behavior in a company. Moral courage does not come easily; there are well-known cases where individuals have lost their jobs because they were whistleblowers on unethical corporate behaviors.

Companies can strengthen the moral courage of employees by making a commitment to refuse to seek retribution against employees who exercise moral courage, say no to superiors, or otherwise complain about unethical actions. For example, Unilever's code of ethics includes the following:

> Any breaches of the Code must be reported in accordance with the procedures specified by the Joint Secretaries. The Board of Unilever will not criticize management for any loss of business resulting from adherence to these principles and other mandatory policies and instructions. The Board of Unilever expects employees to bring to their attention, or to that of senior management, any breach or suspected breach of these principles. Provision has been made for employees to be able to report in confidence and no employee will suffer as a consequence of doing so.

This statement gives "permission" to employees to exercise moral courage. Companies can also set up an ethics hotline that allows employees to anonymously register a complaint with a corporate ethics officer.

Final Words   The steps discussed here can help to ensure that when managers make business decisions, they are fully cognizant of the ethical implications and do not violate basic ethical prescripts. At the same time, not all ethical dilemmas have a clean and obvious solution—that is why they are dilemmas. At the end of the day, there are things that a business should not do, and there are things that a business should do, but there are also situations that present managers with true predicament. In these cases a premium is placed upon the ability of managers to make sense out of complex, messy situations and to make balanced decisions that are as just as possible.

KEY TERMS

TAKEAWAYS FOR STRATEGIC MANAGERS

1. Stakeholders are individuals or groups that have an interest, claim, or stake in the company—in what it does and in how well it performs.

2. Stakeholders are in an exchange relationship with the company. They supply the organization with important resources (or contributions) and in exchange expect their interests to be satisfied (by inducements).

3. A company cannot always satisfy the claims of all stakeholders. The goals of different groups may conflict. The company must identify the most important stakeholders and give highest priority to pursuing strategies that satisfy their needs.

4. A company's stockholders are its legal owners and the providers of risk capital–a major source of capital resources that allow a company to operate its business. As such, they have a unique role among stakeholder groups.

5. Maximizing long-term profitability and profit growth is the route to maximizing returns to stockholders, and it is also consistent with satisfying the claims of several other key stakeholder groups.

6. When pursuing strategies that maximize profitability, a company has the obligation to do so within the limits set by the law and in a manner consistent with societal expectations.

7. An agency relationship is said to exist whenever one party delegates decision-making authority or control over resources to another party.

8. The essence of the agency problem is that the interests of principals and agents are not always the same, and some agents may take advantage of information asymmetries to maximize their own interests at the expense of principals.

9. Numerous governance mechanisms serve to limit the agency problem between stockholders and managers. These include the board of directors, stock-based compensation schemes, financial statements and auditors, and the threat of a takeover.

10. The term *ethics* refers to accepted principles of right or wrong that govern the conduct of a person, the members of a profession, or the actions of an organization. Business ethics are the accepted principles of right or wrong governing the conduct of businesspeople, and an ethical strategy is one that does not violate these accepted principles.

11. Unethical behavior is rooted in poor personal ethics; the inability to recognize that ethical issues are at stake; failure to incorporate ethical issues into strategic and operational decision making; a dysfunctional culture; and failure of leaders to act in an ethical manner.

12. To make sure that ethical issues are considered in business decisions, managers should (a) favor hiring and promoting people with a well-grounded sense of personal ethics, (b) build an organizational culture that places high value on ethical behavior, (c) ensure that leaders within

the business not only articulate the rhetoric of ethical behavior but also act in a manner that is consistent with that rhetoric, (d) put decision-making processes in place that require people to consider the ethical dimension of business decisions, (e) use ethics officers, (f) have strong corporate governance procedures, and (g) be morally courageous and encourage others to be the same.

DISCUSSION QUESTIONS

1. How prevalent has the agency problem been in corporate America during the last decade? During the late 1990s, there was a boom in initial public offerings of Internet companies (dot.com companies). The boom was supported by sky-high valuations, often assigned to Internet start-ups that had no revenues or earnings. The boom came to an abrupt end in 2001, when the Nasdaq stock market collapsed, losing almost 80% of its value. Who do you think benefited most from this boom: investors (stockholders) in those companies, managers, or investment bankers?

2. Why is maximizing ROIC consistent with maximizing returns to stockholders?

3. How might a company configure its strategy-making processes to reduce the probability that managers will pursue their own self-interest at the expense of stockholders?

4. In a public corporation, should the CEO of the company also be allowed to be the chairman of the board (as allowed for by the current law)? What problems might this present?

5. Under what conditions is it ethically defensible to outsource production to companies in the developing world that have much lower labor costs when such actions involve laying off long-term employees in the firm's home country?

6. Is it ethical for a firm faced with a labor shortage to employ illegal immigrants to meet its needs?

CLOSING CASE

HP's Disastrous Acquisition of Autonomy

In 2011, HP was churning on many fronts simultaneously. It had decided to abandon its tablet computer and was struggling with a decision about whether to exit its $40 billion-a-year personal computer (PC) business altogether. It also had a new CEO, Leo Apotheker (formerly the head of German software company SAP AG), who was intent on making a high-impact acquisition that would transform the firm from being primarily a hardware manufacturer into a fast-growing software firm. The firm also had a new chairman of the board, Ray Lane, who was also a software specialist as well as former president of Oracle.

Leo Apotheker had proposed buying two mid-sized software companies, but both deals fell through. The first was nixed by the board's finance committee, and the second fell apart during negotiations over price. In frustration, Apotheker told Lane, "I'm running out of software companies."

Then, in the summer of 2011, Apotheker proposed looking at Autonomy, a British company that makes software firms use to search for information

(continued)

in text files, video files, and other corporate documents. Lane was enthusiastic about the idea. When Apotheker brought the proposal to the board members in July 2011, half of them were already busy analyzing the decision to jettison the PC business, so only half of the board evaluated the acquisition proposal. The board approved a price for Autonomy that was about a 50% premium over its market value, which was already high at about 15 times its operating profit. HP announced the acquisition on August 18, 2011--the same day that it announced it would abandon its tablet computer and was considering exiting the PC industry. The price of the acquisition was $11.1 billion—12.6 times Autonomy's 2010 revenue. Notably, Oracle had already considered acquiring Autonomy and decided that, even if the numbers Autonomy was presenting were taken at face value, it was not worth buying even at a $6-billion price tag. HP's stock fell by 20% the next day.

In the days following the announcement, HP's stock continued to tumble, and backlash from shareholders and others in the investment community was scathing. Ray Lane asked HP's advisers if the company could back out of the deal and was told that, according to U.K. takeover rules, backing out was only possible if HP could show that Autonomy engaged in financial impropriety. HP began frantically examining the financials of Autonomy, hoping for a way to get out of the deal. In the midst of harsh disapproval from HP's largest stockholders and other senior executives within the firm, HP fired Leo Apotheker on September 22, 2012, less than a month after the acquisition's announcement, and only 11 months into his tenure as CEO.

By May 2012, it was clear that Autonomy was not going to hit its revenue targets, and Michael Lynch, Autonomy's founder (who had been asked to stay on and run the company) was fired. In late November 2012, HP wrote down $8.8 billion of the acquisition, essentially admitting that the company was worth 79% less than it had paid for it. Then the finger pointing began in earnest. HP attributed more than $5 billion of the write-down to a "willful

effort on behalf of certain former Autonomy employees to inflate the underlying financial metrics of the company in order to mislead investors and potential buyers. . . . These misrepresentations and lack of disclosure severely impacted management's ability to fairly value Autonomy at the time of the deal."

Michael Lynch denied the charges, insisting he knew of no wrongdoing at Autonomy, arguing that auditors from Deloitte had approved its financial statements, and pointing out that the firm followed British accounting guidelines, which differ in some ways from American rules. Lynch also accused HP of mismanaging the acquisition, saying "Can HP really state that no part of the $5-billion write-down was, or should be, attributed to HP's operational and financial mismanagement of Autonomy since acquisition? ... Why did HP senior management apparently wait six months to inform its shareholders of the possibility of a material event related to Autonomy?"

Many shareholders and analysts also pointed their fingers at HP, saying that the deal was shockingly overpriced. Sanford C. Bernstein & Company analyst Toni Sacconaghi wrote, "We see the decision to purchase Autonomy as value-destroying," and Richard Kugele, an analyst at Needham & Company, wrote, "HP may have eroded what remained of Wall Street's confidence in the company" with the "seemingly overly expensive acquisition of Autonomy for over $10B." Apotheker responded by saying, "We have a pretty rigorous process inside HP that we follow for all our acquisitions, which is a D.C.F.-based model.... Just take it from us. We did that analysis at great length, in great detail, and we feel that we paid a very fair price for Autonomy." However, when Ray Lane was questioned, he seemed unfamiliar with any cash flow analysis done for the acquisition. He noted instead that he believed the price was fair because Autonomy was unique and critical to HP's strategic vision.

According to an article in *Fortune*, Catherine A. Lesjak, the chief financial officer at HP, had spoken out against the deal before it transpired, arguing that it was not in the best interests of the shareholders and that HP could not afford it. Furthermore, outside auditors for Autonomy apparently informed HP (during a call in the days leading up to the announcement) that an executive at Autonomy had raised allegations of improper accounting at the firm, but a review had deemed the allegations baseless and they were never passed on to HP's board or CEO.

In the third quarter of 2012, HP lost $6.9 billion, largely because of the Autonomy mess. Its stock was trading at $13—almost 60% less than it had been worth when the Autonomy deal was announced. By April 4, 2013, Ray Lane stepped down as chairman of the board (although he continued on as a board member).

Did Autonomy intentionally inflate its financial metrics? Did Apotheker and Lane's eagerness

for a "transformative acquisition" cause them to be sloppy in their valuation of Autonomy? Or was the value of Autonomy lost due to the more mundane cause of integration failure? Financial forensic investigators are trying to answer these questions, but irrespective of the underlying causes, Sacconaghi notes that Autonomy "will arguably go down as the worst, most value-destroying deal in the history of corporate America."

Sources: J. Bandler, "HP Should Have Listened to Its CFO," *Fortune*, November 20, 2012; www.fortune.com, J. B. Stewart, "From HP, a Blunder That Seems to Beat All," *New York Times*, November 30, 2012; www.nytimes.com, M. G. De La Merced, "Autonomy's Ex-Chief Calls on HP to Defend Its Claims," *New York Times*, Dealbook, November 27, 2012, www.nytimes.com/pages/business/dealbook; B. Worthen and J. Scheck, "Inside HP's Missed Chance to Avoid a Disastrous Deal," *The Wall Street Journal*, January 21, 2013, pp. A1–A16.

CASE DISCUSSION QUESTIONS

1. Why do you think Apotheker was so eager to make an acquisition?
2. Why do most acquisitions result in paying a premium over the market price? Was the 50% premium for Autonomy reasonable?
3. Was it unethical for Apotheker to propose the acquisition at the 50% premium? Was it unethical for Autonomy to go along with the price at a 50% premium? Who suffers the consequences of an overpriced acquisition?
4. Is there anything HP and Autonomy could have done differently to avoid the public backlash and share price drop the company suffered?

NOTES

[1] E. Freeman, *Strategic Management: A Stakeholder Approach* (Boston: Pitman Press, 1984).

[2] C. W. L. Hill and T. M. Jones, "Stakeholder-Agency Theory," *Journal of Management Studies* 29 (1992): 131–154, and J. G. March and H. A. Simon, *Organizations* (New York: Wiley, 1958).

[3] W. Henisz, S. Dorobantu, and L. Nartey, L. "Spinning Gold: The Financial Returns to Stakeholder Engagement," *Strategic Management Journal*, 35 (2014):1727–1748.

[4] Hill and Jones, "Stakeholder-Agency Theory,; and C. Eesley and M. J. Lenox, "Firm Responses to Secondary Stakeholder Action," *Strategic Management Journal* 27 (2006): 13–24.

[5] I. C. Macmillan and P. E. Jones, *Strategy Formulation: Power and Politics* (St. Paul: West, 1986).

[6] T. Copeland, T. Koller, and J. Murrin, *Valuation: Measuring and Managing the Value of Companies* (New York: Wiley, 1996).

[7]R. S. Kaplan and D. P. Norton, *Strategy Maps* (Boston: Harvard Business School Press, 2004).

[8]J. S. Harrison, D. A. Bosse, and R. A. Phillips, "Managing for Stakeholders, Stakeholder Utility Functions, and Competitive Advantage," *Strategic Management Journal* 31 (2010): 58–74.

[9] R. Garcia-Castro, and R. Aguilera, "Increasing Value Creation and Appropriation in a World with Multiple Stakeholders," *Strategic Management Journal*, 36 (2015): 137–147.

[10]A. L. Velocci, D. A. Fulghum, and R. Wall, "Damage Control," *Aviation Week*, December 1, 2003, pp. 26–27.

[11]M. C. Jensen and W. H. Meckling, "Theory of the Firm: Managerial Behavior, Agency Costs and Ownership Structure," *Journal of Financial Economics* 3 (1976): 305–360, and E. F. Fama, "Agency Problems and the Theory of the Firm," *Journal of Political Economy* 88 (1980): 375–390.

[12]Hill and Jones, "Stakeholder-Agency Theory."

[13]For example, see R. Marris, *The Economic Theory of Managerial Capitalism* (London: Macmillan, 1964), and J. K. Galbraith, *The New Industrial State* (Boston: Houghton Mifflin, 1970).

[14]Fama, "Agency Problems and the Theory of the Firm."

[15]A. Rappaport, "New Thinking on How to Link Executive Pay with Performance," *Harvard Business Review,* March–April 1999, pp. 91–105.

[16]AFL-CIO's Executive Pay-Watch Database, www.aflcio.org/Corporate-Watch/CEO-Pay-and-You.

[17]For academic studies that look at the determinants of CEO pay, see M. C. Jensen and K. J. Murphy, "Performance Pay and Top Management Incentives," *Journal of Political Economy* 98 (1990): 225–264; Charles W. L. Hill and Phillip Phan, "CEO Tenure as a Determinant of CEO Pay," *Academy of Management Journal* 34 (1991): 707–717; H. L. Tosi and L. R. Gomez-Mejia, "CEO Compensation Monitoring and Firm Performance," *Academy of Management Journal* 37 (1994): 1002–1016; and J. F. Porac, J. B. Wade, and T. G. Pollock, "Industry Categories and the Politics of the Comparable Firm in CEO Compensation," *Administrative Science Quarterly* 44 (1999): 112–144.

[18]J. Silver-Greenberg and A. Leondis, "CBS Overpaid Moonves $28 Million, Says Study of CEO Pay," *Bloomberg News*, May 6, 2010.

[19]"'Pay for Performance' No Longer a Punchline," *The Wall Street Journal*, March 20, 2013.

[20]For research on this issue, see P. J. Lane, A. A. Cannella, and M. H. Lubatkin, "Agency Problems as Antecedents to Unrelated Mergers and Diversification: Amihud and Lev Reconsidered," *Strategic Management Journal* 19 (1998): 555–578.

[21]M. Saltmarsh and E. Pfanner, "French Court Convicts Executives in Vivendi Case," *New York Times*, January 21, 2011.

[22]E. T. Penrose, *The Theory of the Growth of the Firm* (London: Macmillan, 1958).

[23]G. Edmondson and L. Cohn, "How Parmalat Went Sour," *Business Week*, January 12, 2004, pp. 46–50; and "Another Enron? Royal Dutch Shell," *Economist,* March 13, 2004, p. 71.

[24]O. E. Williamson, *The Economic Institutions of Capitalism* (New York: Free Press, 1985).

[25]Fama, "Agency Problems and the Theory of the Firm."

[26]S. Finkelstein and R. D'Aveni, "CEO Duality as a Double Edged Sword," *Academy of Management Journal* 37 (1994): 1079–1108; B. Ram Baliga and R. C. Moyer, "CEO Duality and Firm Performance," *Strategic Management Journal* 17 (1996): 41–53; M. L. Mace, *Directors: Myth and Reality* (Cambridge: Harvard University Press, 1971); and S. C. Vance, *Corporate Leadership: Boards of Directors and Strategy* (New York: McGraw-Hill, 1983).

[27]J. B. Stewart, "When Shareholder Democracy Is a Sham," *New York Times*, April 12, 2013.

[28]"Goldman Union Deal Lets Blankfein Keep Dual Roles," Reuters, April 11, 2013.

[29]W. G. Lewellen, C. Eoderer, and A. Rosenfeld, "Merger Decisions and Executive Stock Ownership in Acquiring Firms," *Journal of Accounting and Economics* 7 (1985): 209–231.

[30]C. W. L. Hill and S. A. Snell, "External Control, Corporate Strategy, and Firm Performance," *Strategic Management Journal* 9 (1988): 577–590.

[31]The phenomenon of back dating stock options was uncovered by academic research, and then picked up by the SEC. See Erik Lie, "On the Timing of CEO Stock Option Awards," *Management Science* 51 (2005): 802–812.

[32]G. Colvin, "A Study in CEO Greed," *Fortune*, June 12, 2006, pp. 53–55.

[33]J. P. Walsh and R. D. Kosnik, "Corporate Raiders and Their Disciplinary Role in the Market for Corporate Control," *Academy of Management Journal* 36 (1993): 671–700.

12.1 STRATEGY IN ACTION

FEMA and Hurricane Katrina

A vivid example of the costs of making the wrong choice between centralization and decentralization occurred in 2005, when the Federal Emergency Management Agency (FEMA) responded to the devastating impact that Hurricane Katrina had on New Orleans. The hurricane flooded much of the city and resulted in a mandatory evacuation. However FEMA, the Federal agency responsible for disaster relief, was widely criticized for being very slow to respond to the plight of the hundreds of thousands of mostly poor people who had been made homeless. For several days, while thousands of homeless people huddled in the New Orleans Superdome, lacking food and adequate sanitary facilities, FEMA was nowhere to be seen.

A postmortem revealed that one reason for FEMA's slow response was that the once-autonomous agency had been placed under the direct supervision of the Department of Homeland Security after September 11,

2001. FEMA officials apparently felt that they had to discuss relief efforts with their superiors before proceeding. This cost the agency crucial time in the early hours of the disaster and significantly slowed its response, meaning that the relief effort was less effective than it might have been. In addition, FEMA was poorly managed. Its head, Mike Brown, a political appointee, had no experience in disaster relief. Moreover, the agency had been gutted by budget cuts.

In a report that was highly critical of FEMA, the U. S. Senate Committee charged with reviewing the response to Katrina cited a "failure of agility" and concluded that response plans at all levels of government lacked flexibility and adaptability, which often delayed response. In other words, decision making was too centralized, bureaucratic, and inflexible. Decentralization would have helped enormously in this case.

Sources: "A failure to innovate: Final report of the select bipartisan committee to investigate the preparation for and response to Hurricane Katrina". United States Government Printing Office, February 17th, 2006. *The Economist*, "When Government Fails – Katrina's aftermath", September 2005, page 25.

Tall Versus Flat Hierarchies

A second aspect of vertical differentiation refers to the number of levels in an organization hierarchy. **Tall hierarchies** have many layers of management, while **flat hierarchies** have very few layers (see Figure 12.2). Most firms start out small, often with only one or at most two layers in the hierarchy. As they grow, management finds that there is a limit to the amount of information they can process and the control they can exert over day-to-day operations. To avoid being stretched too thin and losing control, they tend to add another layer to the management hierarchy, hiring more managers and delegating some decision-making authority to them. In other words, as an organization gets larger it tends to become taller. In addition, growing organizations often undertake more activities, expanding their product line, diversifying into adjacent activities, vertically integrating, or expanding into new regional or national markets. This too creates problems of coordination and control, and once again the organization's response often is to add another management layer. Adding levels in the

tall hierarchies
An organizational structure with many layers of management.

flat hierarchies
An organizational structure with very few layers of management.

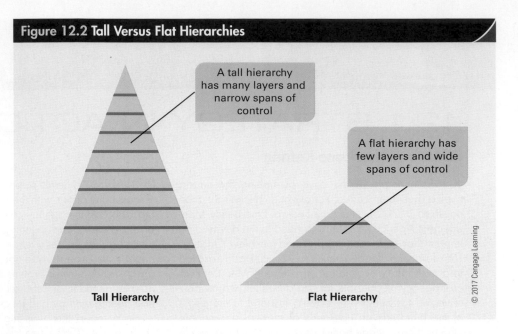

Figure 12.2 Tall Versus Flat Hierarchies

A tall hierarchy has many layers and narrow spans of control

A flat hierarchy has few layers and wide spans of control

Tall Hierarchy

Flat Hierarchy

© 2017 Cengage Learning

hierarchy is a problem that mounts when managers have too much work to do. The number of layers added is also partly determined by the span of control that managers can effectively handle.

span of control

The number of a manager's direct reports.

Span of Control   The term **span of control** refers to the number of direct reports that a manager has. At one time it was thought that the optimal span of control was six subordinates.[8] The argument was that, if a manager was responsible for more than six subordinates, he would soon lose track of what was going on and control loss would occur. Now we recognize that the relationship is not this simple. The number of direct reports a manger can handle depends upon (1) the nature of the work being supervised, (2) the extent to which the performance of subordinates is visible, and (3) the extent of decentralization within the organization. Generally, if the work being performed by subordinates is routine, if the performance of subordinates is visible and easy to measure, and if the subordinates are empowered to make many decision by themselves, and do not have to refer up the hierarchy for approval or consultation, managers can operate with a wide span of control. How wide is the subject of debate, but it does seem as if managers can effectively handle as many as 20 direct reports if the circumstances are right.

In sum, as organizations grow and undertake more activities, the management hierarchy tends to be come taller, but how tall depends upon the span of control that is feasible, and that in turn depends upon the nature of the work being performed, the visibility of subordinate performance, and the extent of decentralization within the organization. It is important to note that managers can influence the visibility of subunit performance and the extent of decentralization through organization design, thereby limiting the impact of organization size and diversity on the size of a management hierarchy. This is significant because we know that while adding layers to an organization can reduce the workload of higher-level managers and attenuate control loss, tall hierarchies have their own problems.

Problems in Tall Hierarchies   Several problems can occur in tall hierarchies that may result in lower organizational efficiency and effectiveness. First, there is a tendency for information to get *accidentally distorted* as it passes through layers in a hierarchy. The phenomenon is familiar to anyone who has played the game "telephone," in which players sit in a circle and each whispers a message to the person sitting next to them, who then whispers the message to the next person, and so on around the room. Often, by the time the message has been transmitted through all the players, it has become distorted and its meaning has changed (this can have very funny consequences, which of course is the point of the game). Human beings are not adept at transmitting information; they tend to embellish or omit data. In a management context, if critical information has to pass through many layers in a tall hierarchy before it reaches critical decision makers, it may well get distorted in the process, resulting in a message that differs from the one originally sent. As a result, decisions may be made based on inaccurate information and poor performance may result.

In addition to the accidental distortion of information as it travels through a management hierarchy, there is also the problem of *deliberate distortion* by mid-level managers trying to curry favor with their superiors or pursue a personal agenda. For example, the manager of a division might suppress negative information, while exaggerating positive information, in an attempt to "window dress" the performance of the unit under his control to higher-level managers and win their approval. By doing so he may gain access to more resources, earn performance bonuses, or avoid sanctions for poor performance. All things being equal, the more layers in a hierarchy, the more opportunities exist for people to deliberately distort information. To the extent that information is distorted, once again it implies that senior managers will be making important decisions on the basis of inaccurate information, which can result in poor performance. Economists refer to the loss of efficiency that arises from deliberate information distortions for personal gain within an organization as **influence costs**, and they argue that influence costs can be a major source of low efficiency.[9]

An interesting case of information distortion in a hierarchy concerned the quality of pre-war intelligence information on weapons of mass destruction in Iraq prior to the 2003 invasion by the United States and allied forces. The information on biological weapons that was used to help justify the invasion of Iraq was derived from a single Iraq defector, code named "Curveball," who was an alcoholic and, in the view of the one person who had interviewed him, a Pentagon analyst, "utterly useless as a source." However, higher-level personnel in the intelligence community took the information provided by Curveball, stripped out the reservations expressed by the Pentagon analyst, and passed it on as high-quality intelligence to U.S. Secretary of State, Colin Powell, who included the information in a speech he made to the United Nations to justify the war. Powell was apparently unaware of the highly questionable nature of the data. Had he been, he probably would not have included it in his speech. Apparently, gatekeepers who stood between Powell and the Pentagon analyst deliberately distorted the information, presumably to further their own agenda, or the agenda of other parties whose favor they were trying to curry.[10]

A third problem with tall hierarchies is that they are expensive. The salaries and benefits of multiple layers of mid-level managers can add up to significant overhead, which can increase the cost structure of the firm. Unless there is a commensurate benefit, a tall hierarchy can put a firm at a competitive disadvantage.

A final problem concerns the inherent inertia associated with a tall hierarchy. Organizations are inherently inert—that is, they are difficult to change. One cause of

influence costs
The loss of efficiency that arises from deliberate information distortions for personal gain within an organization.

inertia in an organization is that, in order to protect their turf, and perhaps their jobs, managers often argue for the maintenance of the status quo. In tall hierarchies there is more turf, more centers of power and influence, and more voices arguing against change. Thus, tall hierarchies tend to be slow to change.

Delayering–Reducing the Size of a Hierarchy   Many firms attempt to limit the size of the management hierarchy. **Delayering** to reduce the number of levels in a management hierarchy has become a standard component of many attempts to boost a firm's performance.[11] Delayering is based on the assumption that when times are good, many firms tend to expand their management hierarchies beyond the point at which it is efficient to do so. However, the bureaucratic inefficiencies associated with a tall hierarchy become evident when the competitive environment becomes tougher, at which time managers seek to delayer the organization. Delayering, and simultaneously widening spans of control, is also seen as a way of enforcing greater decentralization within an organization and reaping the associated efficiency gains.

The process of delayering was a standard feature of Jack Welch's tenure at General Electric, during which time he laid off 150,000 people and reduced the number of layers in the hierarchy from nine to five, while simultaneously growing General Electric's profits and revenues. Welch believed that GE had become too top heavy during the tenure of his successors. A key element of his strategy was to transform General Electric into a leaner, faster-moving organization, which required delayering. Welch himself had a wide span of control, with some 20 subordinates reporting directly to him, including the heads of GE's 15 top businesses. Similarly, Jeffery Immelt, the head of GE's medical-systems business under Welch, had 21 direct reports (Immelt eventually replaced Welch as CEO).[12]

Structural Forms

Most firms begin with no formal structure and are run by a single entrepreneur or a small team of individuals. As they grow, the demands of management become too great for one individual or a small team to handle. At this point, the organization is split into functions that represent different aspects of the firm's value chain (see Chapter 3).

Functional Structure   In a **functional structure**, the structure of the organization follows the obvious *division of labor* within the firm with different functions focusing on different tasks. There might be a production function, an R&D function, a marketing function, a sales function, and so on (see Figure 12.3). A top manager, such as the CEO, or a small top-management team oversees these functions. Most single businesses of any scale are organized along functional lines.

While a functional structure can work well for a firm that is active in a single line of business, problems develop once the firm expands into different businesses. Google began as a search company, but has expanded into operating systems (Android and Chrome), software applications (Google Apps, Gmail), digital media distribution (Google Play), and social products (Google Plus, Blogspot). As noted in the Opening Case, trying to manage these different businesses within the context of a functional structure creates problems of accountability, coordination, and control.[13]

With regard to control, it becomes difficult to identify the profitability of each distinct business when the activities of those businesses are scattered across various

---

delayering

The process of reducing the number of levels in a management hierarchy.

functional structure

The organizational structure is built upon the division of labor within the firm, with different functions focusing on different tasks.

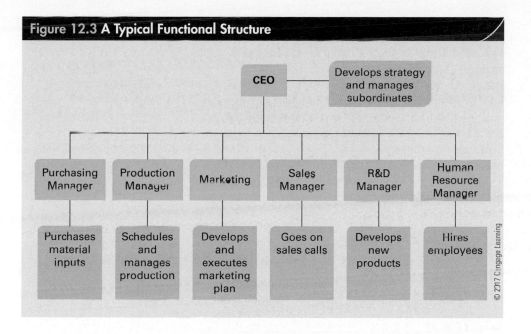

Figure 12.3 A Typical Functional Structure

© 2017 Cengage Learning

functions. It is hard to assess whether a business is performing well or poorly. More-over, because no one individual or management team is responsible for the perfor-mance of each business, there is a lack of accountability within the organization, and this too can result in poor control. As for coordination, when the different activities that constitute a business are embedded in different functions, such as production and marketing, that are simultaneously managing multiple businesses, it can be difficult to achieve the tight coordination between functions needed to effectively run a business. Moreover, it is difficult to run a functional department if it is supervising the value creation activities of several business areas.

Multidivisional Structure   The problems that we have just discussed were first recog-nized in the 1920s by one of the pioneers of American management thinking, Alfred Sloan, who at the time was CEO of General Motors, then the largest company in the world.[14] Under Sloan, GM had diversified into multiple businesses. In addition to making cars under several distinct brands, it made trucks, airplane engines, and re-frigerators. After struggling to run these different businesses within the framework of a functional structure, Sloan realized that a fundamentally different structure was re-quired. His solution, which has since become the classic way to organize a diversified, multibusiness enterprise, was to adopt a multidivisional structure (see Figure 12.4).

In a **multidivisional structure**, the firm is divided into different divisions, each of which is responsible for a distinct business area. The multidivisional structure has be-come the standard structural form for managing a diversified enterprise. Thus, as we saw in the Opening Case, in 2011 Google created seven core business divisions: Search, Advertising, YouTube, Mobile (Android), Chrome, Social (Google + and Blogger), and Commerce (Google Apps). In most multidivisional enterprises, each division is set up as a self-contained, largely autonomous entity with its own functions. Respon-sibility for functional decisions and business-level strategy is typically decentralized to the divisions, which are then held accountable for their performance. Headquarters is

multidivisional structure

An organizational structure in which a firm is divided into divisions, each of which is responsible for a distinct business area.

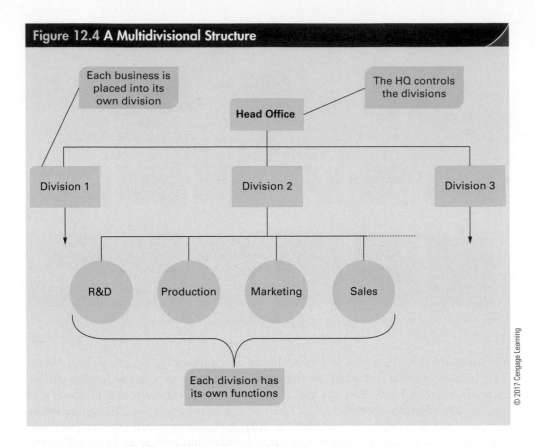

Figure 12.4 A Multidivisional Structure

Each business is placed into its own division

The HQ controls the divisions

Head Office

Division 1   Division 2   Division 3

R&D   Production   Marketing   Sales

Each division has its own functions

© 2017 Cengage Learning

responsible for the overall strategic development of the firm (corporate-level strategy), for the control of the various divisions, for allocating capital between divisions, for supervising and coaching the managers who run each division, and for transferring valuable knowledge between divisions.

The divisions are generally left alone to run day-to-day operations as long as they hit performance targets, which are typically negotiated on an annual basis between the head office and divisional management. Headquarters, however, will often help divisional managers think through their strategy. Thus, while Jeff Immelt does not develop strategy for the various businesses within GE's portfolio (that is decentralized to divisional managers), he does probe the thinking of divisional managers to see if they have thought through their strategy. In addition, he devotes much effort to getting managers to share best practices across divisions, and to the formulation and implementation of strategies that span multiple businesses.

One of the great virtues claimed for the multidivisional structure is that it creates an internal environment where divisional managers focus on efficiency.[15] Because each division is a self-contained entity, its performance is highly visible. The high level of responsibility and accountability implies that divisional managers have few alibis for poor performance. This motivates them to focus on improving efficiency. Base pay, bonuses, and promotional opportunities for divisional managers can be tied to how well the division does. Capital is also allocated by top management between the competing divisions depending upon how effectively top management thinks the division managers can invest that capital. The desire to get access to capital to grow their businesses, and to gain pay increases and bonuses, creates further incentives for divisional managers to focus on improving the competitive position of the businesses under their control.

On the other hand, too much pressure from the head office on divisional managers to improve performance can result in some of the worst practices of management. These can include cutting necessary investments in plant, equipment, and R&D to boost short-term performance, even though such action can damage the long-term competitive position of the enterprise.[16] To guard against this possibility, top managers need to develop a good understanding of each division, set performance goals that are attainable, and have personnel who can regularly audit the accounts and operations of divisions to ensure that each division is not being managed for short-term results or in a way that destroys its long-term competitiveness.

Matrix Structure High-technology firms based in rapidly changing environments sometimes adopt a **matrix structure**, in which they try to achieve tight coordination between functions, particularly R&D, production, and marketing.[17] Tight coordination is required so that R&D designs products that (a) can be manufactured efficiently, and (b) are designed with customer needs in mind—both of which increase the probability of successful product commercialization (see Chapter 4). Tight coordination between R&D, manufacturing, and marketing has also been shown to result in a quicker product development effort, which can enable a firm to gain an advantage over its rivals.[18] As illustrated in Figure 12.5, in such an organization an employee may belong to two subunits within the firm. For example, a manager might be a member of the manufacturing function and a product development team.

matrix structure

An organizational structure in which managers try to achieve tight coordination between functions, particularly R&D, production, and marketing.

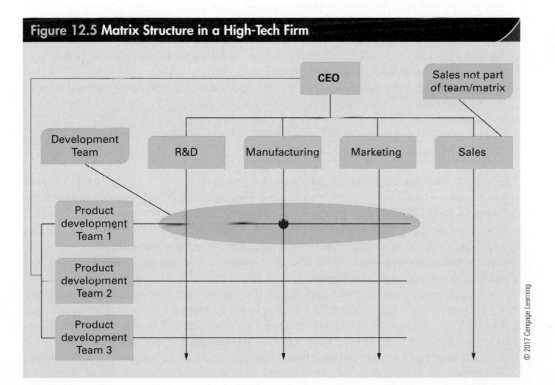

Figure 12.5 Matrix Structure in a High-Tech Firm

© 2017 Cengage Learning

A matrix structure looks nice on paper, but the reality can be very different. Unless this structure is managed very carefully it may not work well.[19] In practice, the matrix can be clumsy and bureaucratic. It can require so many meetings that it is difficult to get any work done. The dual-hierarchy structure can lead to conflict and perpetual power struggles between the different sides of the hierarchy. In one high-tech firm, for example, the manufacturing manager was reluctant to staff a product development team with his best people because he felt that would distract them from their functional work. The result was that the product development team did not work as well it might have.

To make matters worse, it can prove difficult to ascertain accountability in a matrix structure. When all critical decisions are the product of negotiation between different hierarchies, one side can always blame the other when things go wrong. As a manager in one high-tech matrix structure said to the author when reflecting on a failed product launch, "Had the engineering (R&D) group provided our development team with decent resources, we would have got that product out on time and it would have been successful." For his part, the head of the engineering group stated that "We did everything we could to help them succeed but the project was not well managed. They kept changing their requests for engineering skills, which was very disruptive." The result of such finger pointing can be that accountability is compromised and conflict escalated, and senior management can lose control over the organization.

Despite these problems, there is evidence that a matrix structure can work.[20] Making a matrix work requires clear lines of responsibility. Normally this means that one side of the matrix must be given the primary role, while the other is given a support role. In a high-tech firm, for example, the product development teams might be given the primary role, because getting good products to market as quickly as possible is a key to competitive success. Despite taking such steps, managing within a matrix structure is difficult. In light of these problems, managers sometimes try to build "flexible" matrix structures based more on enterprisewide management knowledge networks, and a shared culture and vision, than on a rigid, hierarchical arrangement. Within such companies, the informal structure plays a greater role than the formal structure. We discuss this issue when we consider informal integrating mechanisms in the next section.

Formal Integrating Mechanisms

There is often a need to coordinate the activities of different functions and divisions within an organization in order to achieve strategic objectives. For example, at the *business level* effective new product development requires tight integration between R&D, production, and marketing functions. Similarly, at the *corporate level*, implementing a related diversification strategy requires integration between divisions in order to realize economies of scope and to transfer or leverage rare, valuable resources such as knowledge across divisions.

The formal integrating mechanisms used to coordinate subunits vary in complexity from simple, direct contact and liaison roles, to teams, to a matrix structure (see Figure 12.6). In general, the greater the need for coordination between subunits (functions or divisions), the more complex the formal integrating mechanisms need to be.[21]

Direct contact between subunit managers is the simplest integrating mechanism: Managers of the various subunits simply contact each other whenever they have

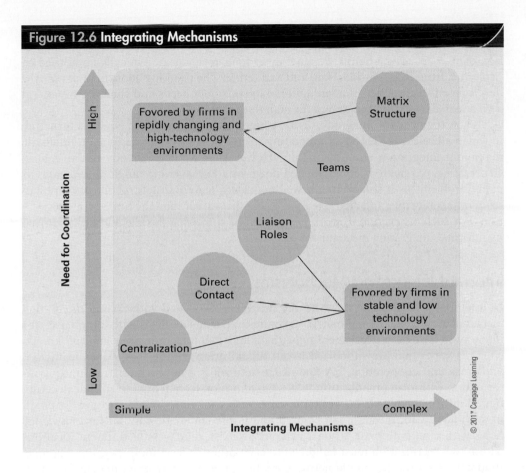

Figure 12.6 Integrating Mechanisms

a common concern. Direct contact may not be effective, however, if the managers have differing orientations that impede coordination, partly because they have different tasks. For example, production managers are typically concerned with issues such as capacity utilization, cost control, and quality control, whereas marketing managers are concerned with issues such as pricing, promotions, distribution, and market share. These differences can inhibit communication between managers. Managers from different functions often do not "speak the same language." Managers can also become entrenched in their own "functional silos," and this can lead to a lack of respect between subunits (for example, marketing managers "looking down on" production managers, and vice versa). This further inhibits the communication required to achieve cooperation and coordination. For these reasons, direct contact is rarely sufficient to achieve coordination between subunits when the need for integration is high.

Liaison roles are a bit more complex than direct contact. As the need for coordination between subunits increases, integration can be improved by giving one individual in each subunit responsibility for coordinating with other subunits on a regular basis. Through these roles, the employees involved establish a permanent relationship. This helps attenuate the impediments to coordination discussed above.

When the need for coordination is greater still, firms often use temporary or permanent teams composed of individuals from the subunits that need to achieve coordination. Teams are often used to coordinate product development efforts, but they can be useful when any aspect of operations or strategy requires the cooperation of two or more subunits. Product development teams are typically composed of personnel from R&D, production, and marketing. The resulting coordination aids the development of products that are tailored to consumer needs and can be produced at a reasonable cost (through design for manufacturing).

When the need for integration is very high, firms may institute a matrix structure in which all roles are viewed as integrating roles. The structure is designed to facilitate maximum integration among subunits. However, as we have already noted, matrix structures can quickly become bogged down in a bureaucratic tangle that creates as many problems as it solves. If not well managed, matrix structures can become bureaucratic, inflexible, and characterized by conflict rather than the hoped-for cooperation. For such a structure to work, it needs to be somewhat flexible and be supported by informal integrating mechanisms.[22]

Informal Integrating Mechanisms

In attempting to alleviate or avoid the problems associated with formal integrating mechanisms in general, and matrix structures in particular, firms with a high need for integration have been experimenting with an informal integrating mechanism: knowledge networks that are supported by an organization culture that values teamwork and cross-unit cooperation.[23] A **knowledge network** is a network for transmitting information within an organization that is based not on formal organizational structure but on informal contacts between managers within an enterprise.[24] The great strength of such a network is that it can be used as a nonbureaucratic conduit for knowledge flows within an enterprise.[25] For a network to exist, managers at different locations within the organization must be linked to each other, at least indirectly. For example, Figure 12.7 shows the simple network relationships between seven managers within a multinational firm. Managers A, B, and C all know each other personally, as do Managers D, E, and F. Although Manager B does not know Manager F personally, they are linked through common acquaintances (Managers C and D). Thus, Managers A through F are all part of the network; Manager G is not.

knowledge network

A network for transmitting information within an organization that is based not on formal organization structure but on informal contacts between managers within an enterprise and on distributed-information systems.

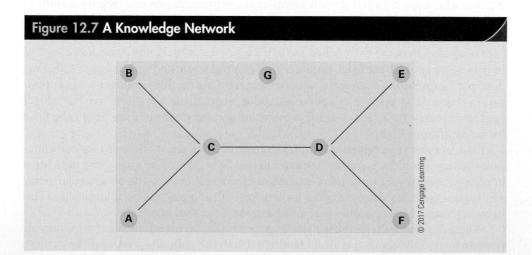

Figure 12.7 A Knowledge Network

© 2017 Cengage Learning

Imagine Manager B is a marketing manager in Spain and needs to know the solution to a technical problem to better serve an important European customer. Manager F, an R&D manager in the United States, has the solution to Manager B's problem. Manager B mentions her problem to all of her contacts, including Manager C, and asks if they know of anyone who might be able to provide a solution. Manager C asks Manager D, who tells Manager F, who then calls Manager B with the solution. In this way, coordination is achieved informally through the network, rather than by formal integrating mechanisms such as teams or a matrix structure.

For such a network to function effectively, it must embrace as many managers as possible. For example, if Manager G had a problem similar to manager B's, he would not be able to utilize the informal network to find a solution; he would have to resort to more formal mechanisms. Establishing firmwide knowledge networks is difficult. Although network enthusiasts speak of networks as the "glue" that binds complex organizations together, it is far from clear how successful firms have been at building companywide networks. The techniques that have been used to establish knowledge networks include information systems, management development policies, and conferences.

Firms are using their distributed computer and telecommunications information systems to provide the foundation for informal knowledge networks.[26] Email, video-conferencing, intranets, and Web-based search engines make it much easier for managers scattered over the globe to get to know each other, to identify contacts who might help to solve a particular problem, and to publicize and share best practices within the organization. Wal-Mart, for example, uses its intranet system to communicate ideas about merchandizing strategy between stores located in different countries.

Firms are also using their management development programs to build informal networks. Tactics include rotating managers through various subunits on a regular basis so they build their own informal network, and using management education programs to bring managers of subunits together in a single location so they can become acquainted. In addition, some science-based firms use internal conferences as a way to establish contacts between people in different units of the organization. At 3M, regular, multidisciplinary conferences bring together scientists from different business units and get them talking to each other. Apart from the benefits of direct interaction in the conference setting, the idea is that once the conference is over, the scientists may continue to share ideas, and this will increase knowledge flows within the organization. 3M has many stories of product ideas that were the result of such knowledge flows, including the ubiquitous Post-it Notes, whose inventor, Art Fry, first learned about the adhesive that he would use on the product from a colleague working in another division of 3M, Spencer Silver, who had spent several years shopping his adhesive around 3M.[27]

Knowledge networks alone may not be sufficient to achieve coordination if subunit managers persist in pursuing subgoals that are at variance with firmwide goals. For a knowledge network to function properly—and for a formal matrix structure to work as well—managers must share a strong commitment to the same goals. To appreciate the nature of the problem, consider again the case of Manager B and Manager F. As before, Manager F hears about Manager B's problem through the network. However, solving Manager B's problem would require Manager F to devote considerable time to the task. Insofar as this would divert Manager F away from his regular tasks—and the pursuit of subgoals that differ from those of Manager B—he may be unwilling to do it. Thus, Manager F may not call Manager B, and the informal network would fail to provide a solution to Manager B's problem.

To eliminate this flaw, an organization's managers must adhere to a common set of norms and values that override differing subunit orientations.[28] In other words, the firm must have a strong organizational culture that promotes teamwork and cooperation. When this is the case, a manager is willing and able to set aside the interests of his own subunit when doing so benefits the firm as a whole. If Manager B and Manager F are committed to the same organizational norms and value systems, and if these organizational norms and values place the interests of the firm as a whole above the interests of any individual subunit, Manager F should be willing to cooperate with Manager B on solving her subunit's problems.

ORGANIZATION CONTROLS AND INCENTIVES

One critical management task is to control an organization's activities. Controls are an integral part of an enterprise's organizational architecture. They are necessary to ensure that an organization is operating efficiently and effectively, and in a manner that is consistent with its intended strategy. Without adequate controls, *control loss* occurs and the organization's performance will suffer.

Control Systems

control

The process through which managers regulate the activities of individuals and units so that they are consistent with the goals and standards of the organization.

goal

A desired future state that an organization attempts to realize.

standard

A performance requirement that the organization is meant to attain on an ongoing basis.

subgoal

An objective, the achievement of which helps the organization attain or exceed it major goals.

Control can be viewed as the process through which managers *regulate* the activities of individuals and units so that they are consistent with the goals and standards of the organization.[29] A **goal** is a desired future state that an organization attempts to realize. A **standard** is a performance requirement that the organization is meant to attain on an ongoing basis. Managers can regulate the activities of individuals and units in several different ways to assure that they are consistent with a firm's goals and standards. Before considering these, we need to review the workings of a typical control system. As illustrated in Figure 12.8, this system has five main elements; establishing goals and standards, measuring performance, comparing performance against goals and standards, taking corrective action, and/or providing reinforcement.[30]

Most organizations operate with a hierarchy of goals. In the case of a business enterprise, the major goals at the top of the hierarchy are normally expressed in terms of profitability and profit growth. These major goals are typically translated into subgoals that can be applied to individuals and units within the organization. A **subgoal** is an *objective*, the achievement of which helps the organization attain or exceed it major goals. Goals and subgoals should be precise, measurable, address important issues, be challenging but realistic, and specify a time period.

To illustrate the concept of a goal hierarchy, suppose that the retailer Nordstrom has a goal of attaining a 15% return on invested capital (ROIC) in the coming year. This is the company's major profitability goal. One way of achieving it is to reduce the amount of capital needed to generate a dollars' worth of sales, and a good way of doing that is to reduce the amount of capital that Nordstrom has tied up in inventory. How does the company do that? By turning over inventory more rapidly. Thus, Nordstrom might operate with a subgoal of turning over inventory five times in the next year. If it hits that subgoal, which is precise, measurable, challenging, and has to be achieved

Figure 12.8 A Typical Control System

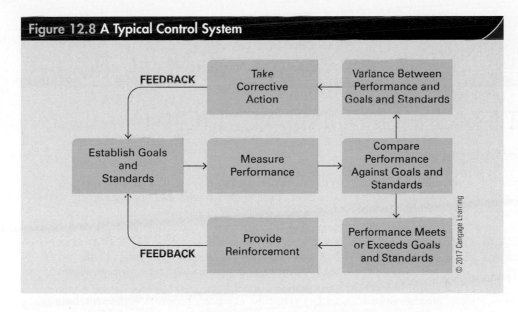

within a prespecified time period, the company's profitability, measured by ROIC, will increase. In fact, as explained in Strategy in Action 12.2, Nordstrom has done something very much along these lines.

Standards are similar to goals but tend to be objectives that the organization is expected to achieve as a part of its routine operations, rather than a challenging goal it is striving to attain. For example, an organization might operate with standards specifying that vendors should be paid within 30 days of submitting an invoice, that customer inquiries should be answered within 24 hours, that all employees should have a formal performance review and be given written feedback once a year, that safety checks should be performed on production equipment every six months, or that employees should fly coach when traveling on business trips.

A key element in the control process is generating the right goals, subgoals, and standards. Managers need to choose goals and standards carefully to avoid motivating the wrong behavior. There is a saying, "You get what you measure." If you chose the wrong goals and standards, you get the wrong behavior. Dysfunctional controls will generate dysfunctional behavior. A few years ago, a placement agency decided to start evaluating and rewarding its staff based on how many job seekers they sent to a job interviews. This productivity measure seemed to produce the desired results; over the next few months; more job seekers got interviews. However, after a while the numbers started to drop off quite alarmingly. When management looked into the issue, they found that several prospective employers would no longer interview people referred to them by the placement agency. The problem: In an effort to hit their numbers, staff members had been sending people to interview for jobs for which they were not qualified. This had damaged the reputation of the placement agency among prospective employers, and led to a fall-off in business for the agency—the opposite of what managers had been trying to achieve. Managers subsequently changed the measure to reflect the number of job seekers who were actually hired.

The next step in the control process is to compare actual performance against goals and standards. If performance is in line with goals or standards, that is good. However, the point made earlier still holds: Management needs to make sure that the reported

12.2 STRATEGY IN ACTION

Goal Setting and Controls at Nordstrom

A few years ago, Nordstrom, the venerable, high-end department store, was facing some challenges. Despite industry-leading sales per square foot, profits had fallen short of the company's goals for 3 years in a row and were down some 35%. The root of the problem was that poor inventory controls meant that Nordstrom either had too much merchandise that was in low demand, or too little of the merchandise that consumers wanted. To get rid of excess inventory, Nordstrom had to hold frequent sales, marking down produce and selling it at a lower profit margin. Moreover, the failure to stock popular items meant that Nordstrom was losing high-margin sales.

To correct this problem, Nordstrom revamped its inventory-control systems. The company invested heavily in information technology so that it could track its inventory on a real-time basis. It also built electronic links to provide suppliers with visibility of what was selling at Nordstrom and what the reorder pattern would be, so the suppliers could adjust their production schedules accordingly. The goal was to stock only what consumers demanded by having inventories delivered to stores on an as-needed basis. To measure the success of this program, Nordstrom focused on two metrics–inventory turnover and average inventory per square foot of selling space. When the company began to implement these systems it was turning over its inventory 3.73 times a year, and on average throughout the year had $60 of inventory for every square foot of selling space in a store. Three years later, as a result of better inventory controls, inventory was turning over 4.51 times a year, and the company held $52.46 of inventory for every square foot of selling space. Due to improved operating efficiency, net profits tripled over this time period.[31]

Endnote Crediting: J. Batsell, "Cost Cutting, Inventory Control Help Boost Nordstrom's Quarterly Profit", *Knight Ridder Tribune News*, Feburary 22, 2002, page 1. Nordstrom's 2004 10K statement.

performance is being achieved in a manner that is consistent with the values of the organization. If reported performance falls short of goals and standards, management needs to start digging to find out the reason for the variance. This typically requires collecting more information, much of which might be qualitative data gleaned from face-to-face meetings and detailed probing to get behind the numbers. The same is true if reported performance *exceeds* goals or standards. Management needs to find out the reason for such favorable variance, and doing so requires collecting more information.

Variances from goals (and standards) require that managers take corrective action. When actual performance easily exceeds the goal, corrective action might include raising the goal. When actual performance falls short of the goal, depending on what further investigation reveals, management might make changes in strategy, operations, or personnel. Radical adjustment is not always the appropriate response when an organization fails to hit a major goal. Investigation might reveal that the original goal was too aggressive, or that changes in market conditions outside the control of management accounted for the poor performance. In such cases, the response to a shortfall might be to adjust the goal downward.

If the goals and standards are meet, or exceeded, management needs to provide timely, positive reinforcement to those responsible. This can run from congratulations for a job well done, to awards, pay increases, bonuses, and enhanced career prospects for those responsible. Providing positive reinforcement is every bit as import an aspect of a control system as is taking corrective action. Behavioral scientists have long known that positive reinforcement increases the probability that those being acknowledged will continue to pursue the rewarded behavior in the future.[32] Without positive reinforcement, people become discourage, feel underappreciated, may not be willing to work as hard, and might look for other employment opportunities where they are better appreciated.

Methods of Control

There are several main ways of achieving control within an organization including personal controls, bureaucratic controls, output controls, incentive controls, market controls, and control through culture (which we consider in the next section on organizational culture).[33]

Personal Controls   As the term suggests, **personal control** is control by personal contact with and direct supervision of subordinates. Personal control consists of making sure, through personal inspection and direct supervision, that individuals and units behave in a way that is consistent with the goals of the organization. Personal control can be very subjective, with the manager assessing how well subordinates are performing by observing and interpreting their behavior. As an overarching philosophy for control within an organization, personal control tends to be found primarily in small firms where the activities of a few people might be regulated through direct oversight. By its very nature, personal control tends to be associated with the centralization of power and authority in a key manager, who is often the owner of the small business. Personal control may work best when this key manager is a charismatic individual who can command the personal allegiance of subordinates.

> **personal control**
> Control by personal contact with and direct supervision of subordinates.

Personal control has several serious limitations. For one thing, excessive supervision can be demotivating. Employees may resent being closely supervised and may perform better if given a greater degree of personal freedom. Moreover, the subjective nature of personal control can lead to a feeling that there is a lack of objectivity and procedural justice in the performance review process. Subordinates may feel that favoritism, personal likes and dislikes, and individual idiosyncrasies may be as important in performance reviews as actual performance. Personal control is also costly in that managers must devote considerable time and attention to the direct supervision of subordinates, which takes their attention away from other important issues. The real Achilles heel of personal control, however, is that it starts to break down as an overarching control philosophy when an organization grows in size and complexity. As this occurs, the key manager has no choice but to decentralize decision making to others within the hierarchy if the enterprise is to continue growing. Doing so effectively requires the adoption of different control philosophies.

Bureaucratic Control   **Bureaucratic control** is defined as control through a formal system of written rules and procedures.[34] As a strategy for control, bureaucratic control methods rely on prescribing what individuals and units can and cannot do; that is, on establishing bureaucratic standards. At the University of Washington, for example, there is a bureaucratic standard specifying that faculty members can perform no more

> **bureaucratic control**
> Control through a formal system of written rules and procedures.

than 1 day a week of outside work. Other standards articulate the steps to be taken when hiring faculty and promoting faculty, purchasing computer equipment for faculty, and so on.

Almost all organizations use bureaucratic controls. Familiar examples are budgetary controls and controls over capital spending. Budgets are essentially a set of rules for allocating an organization's financial resources. A subunit's budget specifies with some precision how much the unit may spend, and how that spending should be allocated across different areas. Senior managers in an organization use budgets to control the behavior of subunits. For example, an R&D budget might specify how much cash an R&D unit may spend on product development in the coming year. R&D managers know that if they spend too much on one project, they will have less to spend on other projects, so they modify their behavior to stay within the budget. Most budgets are set by negotiation between headquarters management and subunit management. Headquarters management can encourage the growth of certain subunits and restrict the growth of others by manipulating their budgets.

Although the term "bureaucratic" often has negative connotations, bureaucratic control methods can be very useful in organizations. They allow managers to decentralize decision making within the constraints specified by formal rules and procedures. However, too great a reliance on bureaucratic rules can lead to problems. Excessive formal rules and procedures can be stifling, limiting the ability of individuals and units to respond in a flexible way to specific circumstances. This can result in poor performance and sap the motivation of those who value individual freedom and initiative. As such, extensive bureaucratic control methods are not well suited to organizations facing dynamic, rapidly changing environments, or to organizations that employ skilled individuals who value autonomy. The costs of monitoring the performance of individuals and units to make sure that they comply with bureaucratic rules can also be significant and may outweigh the benefits of establishing extensive rules and standards.

Bureaucratic standards can also lead to unintended consequences if employees try to find ways around rules that they think are unreasonable. An interesting and controversial case in point concerns rules on forced school busing in the United States. In the 1970s, school districts around America started to bus children to schools outside of their immediate neighborhood in order to achieve a better racial mix. This well-intentioned bureaucratic rule was designed to speed racial integration in a society characterized by significant racial discrimination. Unfortunately, the rule had unintended consequences. Parents of all races objected to their children being bused to distant schools in order to comply with a bureaucratic rule. In many large cities where forced busing was practiced, white families with children responded by fleeing to the suburbs, where there were few minorities and busing was not practiced, or by sending their children to expensive, private schools within the city. The result: Far from advancing racial integration, busing had the opposite effect. A case in point was Seattle, where the percentage of white students in city schools dropped from 60 to 41% over the 20 years during which forced busing was enforced.[35] In the 1990s, most school districts ended forced busing.

Output Controls   Output controls can be used when managers can identify tasks that are complete in the sense of having a measurable output or meeting a criterion of overall achievement.[36] For example, the overall achievement of an automobile factory might be measured by the number of employee hours it takes to build a car (a measure of productivity) and the number of defects found per 100 cars produced by the factory (a measure of quality). Nordstrom measures the overall achievement of the unit responsible for inventory management by the number of inventory turns per year. FedEx measures the "output" of each of its local stations in its express delivery network by the percentage of packages delivered before 10:30 a.m. In a multibusiness company such as GE or 3M, senior management might measure the "output" of a product division in terms of that division's profitability, profit growth, and market share.

When complete tasks can be identified, **output controls** involve setting goals for units or individuals and monitoring performance against those goals. The performance of unit managers is then judged by their ability to achieve the goals.[37] If goals are met or exceeded, unit managers will be rewarded (an act of reinforcement). If goals are not met, senior management will normally intervene to find out why and take corrective action. Thus, as in a classic control system, control is achieved by comparing actual performance against targets, providing reinforcement, and intervening selectively to take corrective action.

output controls
Goals that are set for units or individuals and monitoring performance against those goals.

The goals assigned to units depend on the unit's role in the firm. Self-contained product divisions are typically given goals for profitability and profit growth. Functions are more likely to be given goals related to their particular activity. Thus, R&D will be given product development goals, production will be given productivity and quality goals, marketing will be given market-share goals, and so on.

The great virtue of output controls is that they facilitate decentralization and give individual managers within units much greater autonomy then either personal controls or bureaucratic controls. This autonomy enables managers within a unit to configure their own work environment in a way that best matches the particular contingencies they face, rather than having a work environment imposed upon them from above. Thus, output controls are useful when units have to respond rapidly to changes in the markets they serve. Output controls also involve less extensive monitoring than either bureaucratic or personal controls. Senior managers can achieve control by comparing actual performance against targets, and intervening selectively. As such, they reduce the workload on senior executives and allow them to mange a larger, more diverse organization with relative ease. Thus, many large, multiproduct, multinational enterprises rely heavily upon output controls to manage their various product divisions and foreign subsidiaries.

Output controls have limitations. Senior managers need to look behind the numbers to make sure that unit managers are not only achieving goals, but are doing so in a way that is consistent with the values of the organization. Managers also need to make sure that they choose the right criteria to measure output. Failure to select the right criteria might result in dysfunctional behavior. Moreover, output controls do not always work well when extensive interdependencies exist between units.[38]

The performance of a unit may be ambiguous if it is based upon cooperation with other units. For example, if the performance of a unit is declining, it may be because of poor management within that unit, or it may be because a unit with which it is cooperating is not doing its part. In general, interdependence between units within an organization can create performance ambiguities that make output controls more difficult to interpret. Resolving these ambiguities requires managers to collect more information, which places more demands on top management and raises the monitoring costs associated with output controls. It also increases the possibility that managers will become overloaded with information and, as a result, make poor decisions.

market controls

The regulation of the behavior of individuals and units within an enterprise by setting up an internal market for valuable resource such as capital.

Market Controls   **Market controls** involve regulating the behavior of individuals and units within an enterprise by setting up an *internal market* for valuable resource such as capital.[39] Market controls are usually found within diversified enterprises organized into product divisions, where the head office might act as an internal investment bank, allocating capital funds between the competing claims of the different product divisions based upon an assessment of their likely future performance. Within this internal market, all cash generated by the divisions is viewed as belonging to the head office. The divisions then have to compete for access to the capital resources controlled by the head office. Insofar as they need that capital to grow their divisions, the assumption is that this internal competition will drive divisional managers to find ways to improve the efficiency of their units. One of the first companies in the world to establish an internal capital market was Japanese electronics manufacturer Matsushita, which introduced such systems in the 1930s.[40]

In addition, in some enterprises divisions compete with each other for the right to develop and sell new products. Again, Japan's Matsushita has a long history of letting different divisions develop similar new products, and then assigning overall responsibility for producing and selling the product to the division that seems to be furthest along in the commercialization process. While some might view such duplication of product development effort as wasteful, Matsushita's legendary founder, Konosuke Matsushita, believed that the creation of an internal market for the right to commercialize technology drove divisional managers to maximize the efficiency of product development efforts within their unit. Similarly, within Samsung, the Korean electronics company, senior management will often set up two different teams within different units to develop new products such as new memory chips. The purpose of the internal competition between the two teams is to accelerate the product development process, with the winning team earning significant accolades and bonuses.[41]

The main problem with market controls is that fostering internal competition between divisions for capital and the right to develop new products can make it difficult to establish cooperation between divisions for mutual gain.[42] If two different divisions are racing against each other to develop very similar new products, and are competing against each other for limited capital resources, they may be unwilling to share technological knowhow with each other, perhaps to the determinant of the entire corporation. Companies like Samsung deal with this problem by using integrating mechanisms such as liaison role, and by assigning the responsibility for leveraging technological knowhow across divisions to key individuals.

Incentives Control   Incentives are the devices used to encourage and reward appropriate employee behavior. Many employees receive incentives in the form of annual bonus pay. Incentives are usually closely tied to the performance metrics used for output controls. For example, setting targets linked to profitability might be used to measure the performance of a subunit such as a product division. To create positive incentives for employees to work hard to exceed those targets, they may be given a share of any profits over above those targeted. If a subunit has set a goal of attaining a 15% ROIC and actually attains a 20% return, unit employees may be given a share in the profits generated in excess of the 15% target in the form of bonus pay.

The idea is that giving employees incentives to work productively reduces the need for other control mechanisms. Control through incentives is designed to facilitate *self-control*. Employees regulate their own behavior in a manner consistent with organizational goals in order to maximize their chance of earning incentive-based pay.

Although paying out bonus and the like costs the organization money, well-designed incentives pay for themselves. That is, the increase in performance due to incentives more than offsets the costs of financing them.

The type of incentive used may vary depending on the employees and their tasks. Incentives for employees working on the factory floor may be very different from the incentives for senior managers. The incentives must be matched to the type of work being performed. The employees on the factory floor of a manufacturing plant may be broken into teams of 20 to 30 individuals, and they may have their bonus pay tied to the ability of their team to hit or exceed targets for output and product quality. In contrast, the senior managers of the plant may be rewarded according to metrics linked to the output of the entire operation. The basic principle is to make sure the incentive scheme for an individual employee is linked to an output target that he or she has some control over and can influence. Individual employees on the factory floor may not be able to exercise much influence over the performance of the entire operation, but they can influence the performance of their team, so their incentive pay is tied to output at this level.

When incentives are tied to team performance, as is often the case, they have the added benefit of encouraging cooperation between team members and fostering a degree of peer control. Peer control occurs when employees pressure others within their team or work group to perform up to or in excess of the expectations of the organization.[43] Thus, if the incentive pay of a 20-person team is linked to team output, members can be expected to pressure those in the team who are perceived as slacking off and freeloading on the efforts of others, urging them to pick up the pace and make an equal contribution to team effort. When peer control is functioning well within an organization, it reduces the need for direct supervision of a team and can facilitate attempts to move toward a flatter management hierarchy.

peer control
The pressure that employees exert on others within their team or work group to perform up to or in excess of the expectations of the organization.

In sum, incentives can reinforce output controls, induce employees to practice self-control, increase peer control, and lower the need for other control mechanisms. Like all other control methods discussed here, controls through incentives have limitations. Since incentives are typically linked to the metrics used in output controls, the points made with regard to output controls also apply here. Specifically, managers need to make sure that incentives are not tied to output metrics that result in unintended consequences or dysfunctional behavior.

ORGANIZATIONAL CULTURE

Organizational culture refers to the values, norms, and assumptions that are shared among employees of an organization. By **values** we mean abstract ideas about what a group believes to be good, right, and desirable. Put differently, values are shared assumptions about how things ought to be. By **norms**, we mean social rules and guidelines that prescribe the appropriate behavior in particular situations.

Culture can exert a profound influence on the way people behave within an organization, on the decisions that are made, on the things that the organization pays attention to, and ultimately, on the firm's strategy and performance.

An organization's culture has several sources. There seems to be wide agreement that founders or important leaders can have a profound impact on organizational culture, often imprinting their own values upon it. In addition, the culture of an enterprise can be shaped by landmark events in its history. Culture is maintained and

values
The ideas or shared assumptions about what a group believes to be good, right, and desirable.

norms
Social rules and guidelines that prescribe the appropriate behavior in particular situations.

transmitted over time through formal and informal socialization mechanisms. These include hiring practices, procedures regarding rewards, pay, and promotions, and the informal rules of behavior that employees are expected to adopt if they want to fit in and succeed within the organization.[44]

Microsoft, for example, has a strong culture that was influenced by the company's founder and long-time CEO, Bill Gates. Gates always placed a high value on a technical brilliance, competitiveness, and a willingness to work long hours, something that he himself did. Gates hired and promoted people who shared these characteristics, and he led by example. He also had a tendency to dismiss the opinions of people who lacked technical brilliance. Talented engineers often "walked taller" within Microsoft, and they had a disproportionate impact on strategic decisions. The employees who gained Gates's confidence themselves hired and promoted individuals who were technically strong, competitive, and hardworking. The culture of the company was thus transmitted and enforced throughout the organization. As a result, Microsoft became a company where technical brilliance, competitiveness, and working long hours were highly valued attributes of behavior. New employees were socialized into these norms by coworkers who themselves had been similarly socialized.

History also shaped the culture at Microsoft. Most notably, it took three versions and 6 years before sales of Windows started to take off with the introduction of Windows 3.1 (Windows 1.0 and 2.0 did not do well). The lesson that Microsoft gained from this was that persistence can pay off. "We will get it right by version 3" is a phrase that is still used frequently at Microsoft. This culturally embedded value influences strategic decisions regarding investments such as Microsoft's long running commitment to its money-losing Bing search business. Reflecting the culture of Microsoft, many employees believe that if they stick with it, Bing will eventually turn profitable.

Culture as a Control Mechanism   Given that organizational culture shapes behavior within an organization, culture can be viewed as a control mechanism that mandates expected behaviors. At Microsoft, under the leadership of Gates, staff worked long hours not because bureaucratic rules told them to do so, and not because supervisors explicitly required them to do so, but because that was the cultural norm. In this sense, culture shaped behavior, thereby reducing the need for bureaucratic and personal controls. The company could trust people to work hard and behave in a competitive manner, because those norms were such a pervasive aspect of the culture.

Although cultural controls can mitigate the need for other controls, thereby reducing monitoring costs, they are not universally beneficial. Cultural controls can have dysfunctional aspects. The hard-driving, competitive aspect of Microsoft's culture was arguably a contributing factor in the antitrust violations that the company was found to have made in the 1990s (the U.S. Justice Department, which brought the antitrust case against Microsoft in the United States, used as evidence internal e-mails where one senior manager stated that Microsoft would "cut off a competitor's air supply"). Moreover, Microsoft's culture of working long hours clearly had a downside: Many good employees burned out and left the company. In the post-Gates era, the company has become attuned to this. As its work force has aged and started families, it has become more accommodating, stressing that the output produced is more important than the hours worked.

Implementing Strategy Through Culture   Given that culture can have such a profound impact upon the way in which people behave within organizations, it is important for managers to get culture right. The right culture can help a company execute its strategy; the wrong culture can hinder strategy execution.[45] In the 1980s, when IBM was performing very well, several management authors sang the praises of its culture, which among other things placed a high value on consensus-based decision making.[46] These authors argued that such a decision-making process was appropriate given the substantial financial investments that IBM routinely made in new technology. However, this process turned out to be a weakness in the fast-moving computer industry of the late 1980s and 1990s. Consensus-based decision making was slow, bureaucratic, and not particularly conducive to corporate risk taking. While this was fine in the 1970s, IBM needed rapid decision making and entrepreneurial risk taking in the 1990s, but its culture discouraged such behavior. IBM was outflanked by then-small enterprises such as Microsoft, almost went bankrupt, and had to go through a massive change to shift its organizational culture.

One academic study concluded that firms that exhibited high performance over a prolonged period tended to have strong but adaptive cultures. According to this study, in an adaptive culture most managers care deeply about and value customers, stockholders, and employees. They also strongly value people and processes that create useful change in a firm.[47] While this is interesting, it does reduce the issue to a very high level of abstraction; after all, what company would say that it doesn't care deeply about customers, stockholders, and employees? A somewhat different perspective is to argue that the culture of the firm must match the rest of its architecture, its strategy, and the demands of the competitive environment for superior performance to be attained. All these elements must be consistent with each other. Lincoln Electric provides a useful example (see Strategy in Action 12.3). Lincoln competes in a business that is very competitive, where cost minimization is a key source of competitive advantage. Lincoln's culture and incentive systems both encourage employees to strive for high levels of productivity, which translates into the low costs that are critical for its success. These aspects of Lincoln's organizational architecture are aligned with the low-cost strategy of the company.

ORGANIZATION PROCESSES

Processes, defined as the manner in which decisions are made and work is performed within an organization,[48] are found at many different levels within an organization. There are processes for formulating strategy, allocating resources, evaluating new-product ideas, handling customer inquiries and complaints for improving product quality, evaluating employee performance, and so on. Often, a firm's core competencies or valuable, knowledge-based resources are embedded in its processes. Efficient, effective processes can lower the costs of value creation and add additional value to a product. For example, the global success of many Japanese manufacturing enterprises in the 1980s was based in part on their early adoption of processes for improving product quality and operating efficiency, including total quality management and just-in-time inventory systems. Today, the competitive success of General Electric can in part be attributed to a number of processes that have been widely promoted within the company. These include the company's Six Sigma process for quality improvement, its process for "digitalization" of business (using corporate intranets and the Internet to automate activities and reduce operating costs), and its process for idea generation,

12.3 STRATEGY IN ACTION

Organizational Culture at Lincoln Electric

Lincoln Electric is one of the leading companies in the global market for arc welding equipment. Lincoln's success has been based on extremely high levels of employee productivity. The company attributes its productivity to a strong organizational culture and an incentive scheme based on piecework. Lincoln's organizational culture dates back to James Lincoln. Lincoln had a strong respect for the ability of the individual and believed that, correctly motivated, ordinary people could achieve extraordinary performance. He emphasized that Lincoln should be a meritocracy where people were rewarded for their individual effort. Strongly egalitarian, Lincoln removed barriers to communication between "workers" and "managers," practicing an open-door policy. He made sure that all who worked for the company were treated equally; for example, everyone ate in the same cafeteria, there were no reserved parking places for "managers," and so on. Lincoln also believed that gains in productivity should be shared with consumers in the form of lower prices, with employees in the form of higher pay, and with shareholders in the form of higher dividends.

The organizational culture that grew out of Lincoln's beliefs was reinforced by the company's incentive system. Production workers receive no base salary but are paid according to the number of pieces they produce. The piecework rates at the company enable an employee working at a normal pace to earn an income equivalent to the average wage for manufacturing workers in the area where a factory is based. Workers have responsibility for the quality of their output and must repair defects spotted by quality inspectors before the pieces are included in the piecework calculation. Production workers are awarded a semiannual bonus based on merit ratings. These ratings are based on objective criteria (such as an employee's level and quality of output) and subjective criteria (such as an employee's attitudes toward cooperation and his or her dependability). These systems give Lincoln's employees an incentive to work hard and generate innovations that boost productivity, for doing so influences their level of pay. Lincoln's factory workers have been able to earn a base pay that often exceeds the average manufacturing wage in the area by more than 50% and receive a bonus on top of this which, in good years, could double their base pay. Despite high employee compensation, its workers are so productive that Lincoln has a lower cost structure than its competitors.[49]

Endnote Crediting: J. O'Connell, "Lincoln Electric: Venturing Abroad," Harvard Business School Case No. 9-398-095, April 1998; and www.lincolnelectric.com.

referred to within the company as "workouts," where managers and employees gather for intensive sessions over several days to identify and commit to ideas for improving productivity.

An organization's processes can be summarized by means of a flow chart, which illustrates the various steps and decision points involved in performing work. A detailed consideration of the nature of processes and strategies for process improvement and reengineering is beyond the scope of this book. However, it is important to make two basic remarks about managing processes, particularly in the context of an international business.[50]

First, many processes cut across functions, or divisions, and require cooperation between individuals in different subunits. For example, product development processes require employees from R&D, manufacturing, and marketing to work in a cooperative manner to make sure new products are developed with market needs in mind and designed in such a way that they can be manufactured at a low cost. Because they cut across organizational boundaries, performing processes effectively often require the establishment of formal integrating mechanisms and incentives for cross-unit cooperation.

Second, it is particularly important for an enterprise to recognize that valuable new processes that might lead to a competitive advantage can be developed anywhere within the organization's network of operations.[51] Valuable and rare new processes may be developed within a team, function, product division, or foreign subsidiary. Those processes might then be valuable to other parts of the enterprise. The ability to create valuable processes matters, but it is also important to leverage those processes, and this requires both formal and informal integrating mechanisms such as knowledge networks.

IMPLEMENTING STRATEGY THROUGH ORGANIZATIONAL ARCHITECTURE

We are now in a position to make observations about the kind of organizational arrangements required to implement different strategies. Rather than construct an exhaustive list, we will focus on a limited number of business- and corporate-level strategies. We start by considering strategy and organization within the single-business firm. Then we look at strategy and organization within the diversified firm.

Strategy and Organization in the Single-Business Enterprise

As noted earlier, single-business enterprises are typically organized along functional lines (see Figure 12.3). However, the need for integration between functions will vary depending upon (1) the business-level strategy of the firm, and (2) the nature of the environment in which the firm competes (see Figure 12.9).

Strategy, Environment, and the Need for Integration   In general, the need for integration between functions is greater for firms that are competing through product

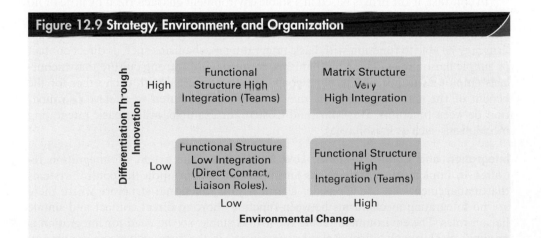

Figure 12.9 Strategy, Environment, and Organization

development and innovation.[52] This is typically the case when an organization's business-level strategy involves differentiation through the introduction of new and/ or improved product offerings. Apple, Google, Ford, Microsoft, Tesla, and Toyota, for example, all try to differentiate themselves through product development and innovation. As discussed earlier, in such organizations there is an ongoing need to coordinate the R&D, production, and marketing functions of the firm to ensure that (1) new products are developed in a timely manner, (2) that they can be efficiently produced and delivered, and (3) that they match consumer demands. We saw that a matrix structure is one way of achieving such coordination (see Figure 12.5). Another, more common, solution is to form temporary teams to oversee the development and introduction of a new product. Once the new product has been introduced, the team is disbanded and employees return to their functions or move to another team.

Firms that face an uncertain, highly turbulent, competitive environment,where rapid adaptation to changing market conditions is required, need coordination in order to survive.[53] Environmental change, such as that which occurs when an industry is disrupted by radical innovations, may require a change in product, process, business model, and strategy. In such cases, it is critical to make sure that the different functions of the firm all pull in the same direction, so that the firm's response to a changing environment is coherent and organizationwide. Temporary teams are often used to effect such coordination.

For example, in the mid-1990s, the World Wide Web emerged with stunning speed and in a way that almost no one anticipated. The rise of the Web produced a profound change in the environment facing computer software firms such as Microsoft, where managers quickly shifted their strategy so as to make their products Web enabled, and position their marketing and sales activities to compete in this new landscape. This shift required very tight coordination between different software engineering groups, such as those working on the software code for Windows, Office and MSN, so that all products not only were Web enabled but also worked seamlessly with each other. Microsoft achieved this by forming cross-functional teams.

In addition to using formal integrating mechanisms such as cross-functional teams, firms with a crucial need for coordination between subunits—for instance, those based in turbulent, high-tech environments—would do well to foster informal knowledge networks, for they too can facilitate coordination between subunits.

In contrast, if the firm is based in a stable environment characterized by little or no change, and if developing new products is not a central aspect of the firm's business strategy, the need for coordination between functions may be lower. In such cases, a firm may be able to function with basic integrating mechanisms such as direct contact or simple liaison roles. These mechanisms, coupled with a strong culture that encourages employees to pursue the same goals, and to cooperate with each other for the benefit of the entire organization, may be all that is required to achieve coordination between functions. Wal-Mart and Costco, for example, utilize basic integrating mechanisms such as liaison roles.

Integration and Control Systems: Low Integration   The extent of integration required to implement a strategy has an important impact upon the control systems that management can use. Consider a firm with a functional structure where there are no integrating mechanisms between functions beyond direct contact and simple liaison roles. The environment facing the firm is stable, so the need for integration is minimal. Within such a firm, *bureaucratic controls* in the form of budgets are used to allocate financial resources to each function and control spending by the functions. *Output controls* will then be used to assess how well a function is performing. Different functions will be assigned different output targets, depending on their specific tasks. The procurement function might be assigned an output target based on procurement costs as a percentage of sales; a manufacturing function might be given productivity and product quality targets such as output per employee and defects per thousand products; the logistics function might be given an inventory turnover target; the marketing and sales function might be given sales-growth and market-share goals; and the success of the service function might be measured by the time it takes to resolve a customer problem. To the extent that each function hits these targets, the overall performance of the firm will improve, and its profitability will increase.

Output controls might also be pushed further down within functions. A production process might be subdivided into discrete tasks, each of which has a measurable output. Employee teams might be formed and empowered to take ownership over each discrete task. Each team will be assigned an output target. To the extent that functions can be divided into teams, and output controls applied to those teams, this will facilitate (1) decentralization within the organization, (2) wider spans of control (since it is relatively easy to control a team by monitoring its outputs, as opposed to regulating behavior through bureaucratic rules), and (3) a flatter organization structure.

Within such a structure, the CEO will monitor the heads of the functions. They in turn will exercise control over units or teams within their function. There may also be some degree of *personal control,* with the CEO using personal supervision to influence the behavior of functional heads; they in turn do the same for their direct reports. *Incentives* will be tied to output targets. The incentive pay of the head of manufacturing might be linked to the attainment of predetermined productivity and quality targets for the manufacturing function; the incentive pay of the head of logistic might be linked to increases in inventory turnover; the pay of the head of marketing and sales to gains in market share, and so on. Incentives might also be pushed further down within the organization, with members of teams within functions being rewarded on the basis of the ability of their team to hit or exceed predetermined targets. A portion of the incentive pay for managers—and perhaps all employees—might be tied to the overall performance of the enterprise to encourage cooperation and knowledge sharing within the organization.

Finally, it is possible for such an enterprise to have strong *cultural controls.* Cultural controls may reduce the need for personal controls and bureaucratic rules. Individuals might be trusted to behave in the desired manner because they "buy into" the prevailing culture. Thus, cultural controls might allow the firm to operate with a flatter organization structure and wider spans of control, and generally increase the effectiveness of output controls and incentives, because employees may buy into the underlying philosophy upon which such controls are based.

Integration and Control Systems: High Integration   A functional structure where the strategy and/or environment requires a high degree of integration presents managers with a complex control problem. The problem is particularly severe if the firm adopts a matrix structure. As noted earlier, a firm based in a dynamic environment where competition centers on product development might adopt such a structure. Within such an enterprise, *bureaucratic controls* will again be used for financial budgets and as before *output controls* will be applied to the different functions. *Output controls* will also be applied to cross-functional product development teams. Thus a team might be assigned output targets covering development time, production costs of the new product, and the features the product should incorporate. For functional managers, *incentive controls* might be linked to output targets for their functions, whereas for the members of a product development team, incentives will be tied to the performance of the team.

The problem with such an arrangement is that the performance of the product development team is dependent upon the support the team gets from the various functions. The support needed includes people and information from production, marketing, and R&D. Consequently, significant performance ambiguity might complicate the process of using output controls to assess the performance of a product development team. **Performance ambiguity** arises when it is difficult to identify with precision the reason for the high (or low) performance of a subunit such as a function or team. In this context, the failure of a cross-functional product development team to hit predetermined output targets might be due to the poor performance of team members, but it could just as well be due to the failure of the functions to provide an appropriate level of support to the team. Senior management cannot determine which explanation is correct simply by observing output controls tied to team performance, because such outputs are not an unambiguous indicator of performance. Identifying the true cause of performance variations requires senior managers to collect information, much of it subjective, which increases the time and energy they must devote to the control process, diverts their attention from other important issues, and hence increases the costs of monitoring and controlling the organization. Other things being equal, this reduces the span of control that senior managers can handle, suggesting the need for a taller hierarchy which, as we saw earlier, gives rise to all kinds of additional problems.

The nature of the performance ambiguity problem in such an enterprise raises the question of whether there is a better solution to the control problem. In fact, there is. One step is to make sure that the incentives of all key personnel are aligned; that is, to use *incentive controls* in a discriminating way. The classic way of doing this is to tie incentives to a higher level of organization performance. Thus, in addition to being rewarded on the basis of the performance of their function, functional heads might also be rewarded on the basis of the overall performance of the firm. Insofar as the success of product development teams increases firm performance, this gives functional heads an incentive to make sure that the product development teams receive adequate support from the functions. In addition, strong *cultural controls* can be very helpful in establishing company wide norms and values that emphasize the importance of cooperation between functions and teams for their mutual benefit.

Strategy and Organization in the Multibusiness Enterprise

As discussed earlier, multibusiness enterprises typically organize themselves along divisional lines (see Figure 12.4). Within each division, there will be a functional organization. The extent of integration between functions *within divisions* may differ from division to division depending upon the business-level strategy and the nature of the environment. The need for integration *between divisions*, on the other hand, depends upon the specific corporate strategy the firm is pursuing. This will have an impact not only on the integrating mechanisms used, but also on the type of control and incentive systems employed.[54]

---

performance ambiguity
The difficulty of identifying with precision the reason for the high (or low) performance of a subunit such as a function or team.

If the firm is pursuing a strategy of related diversification and trying to realize economies of scope by sharing inputs across product divisions, or is trying to boost profitability by transferring or leveraging valuable competencies across divisions, it will have a need for integrating mechanisms to coordinate the activities of the different product divisions. Liaison roles, temporary teams, and permanent teams can all be used to ensure such coordination. On the other hand, if top management is focusing primarily on boosting profitability through superior internal governance, and if each division is managed on a stand-alone basis, with no attempt to leverage competencies or realize economies of scope, as is the case in firms pursuing a strategy of unrelated diversification, the firm may well operate well with minimal or no integrating mechanisms between divisions.

Controls in the Diversified Firm with Low Integration   In firms that focus primarily on boosting performance through superior internal governance where the strategy is one of unrelated diversification, the need for integration between divisions is low. Firms pursuing a strategy of unrelated diversification are not trying to share resources or leverage core competencies across divisions, so there is no need for complex integrating mechanisms, such as cross-divisional teams, to coordinate the activities of different divisions. In these enterprises, the head office typically controls the divisions in four main ways.[55]

First, they use *bureaucratic controls* to regulate the financial budgets and capital spending of the divisions. Typically each division will have to have its financial budgets approved for the coming year by the head office. In addition, capital expenditures in excess of a certain amount have to be approved by the head office; for example, any item of spending by a division in excess of $50,000 might have to be approved by the head office.

Second, the head office will use *output controls*, assigning each division output targets that are normally based on measurable financial criteria such as the profitability, profit growth, and cash flow produced by each division. Typically targets for the coming year are set by negotiation between divisional heads and senior managers at the head office. As long as the divisions hit their targets, they are left alone to run their own operations. If performance falls short of targets, however, top managers will normally audit a division to discover why this occurred, and take corrective action if necessary by instituting a change in strategy and/or personnel.

Third, *incentive controls* will be used, with the incentives for divisional managers being tied to the financial performance of their divisions. To earn pay bonuses, divisional managers have to hit or exceed the performance targets previously negotiated between the head office and the divisions. To make sure that divisional managers do not try to "talk down" their performance targets for the year, making it easy for them to hit their targets and earn bonuses, the head office will normally benchmark a product division against its competitors, take a close look at industry conditions, and use this information to establish performance targets that are challenging but attainable.

Fourth, the head office will use *market controls* to allocate capital resources between different divisions.[56] As noted earlier, in multidivisional enterprises the cash generated by product divisions is normally viewed as belonging to the head office, which functions as an internal capital market, reallocating cash flows between the competing claims of different divisions based on an assessment of likely future performance. The competition between divisions for access to capital, which they need to grow their businesses, is assumed to create further incentives for divisional managers to run their operations as efficiently and effectively as possible. In addition, the head office might use market controls to allocate the right to develop and commercialize new products between divisions.

Within divisions, the control systems used will be those found within single-business enterprises. It should also be noticed that head office managers might utilize some *personal controls* to influence the behavior of divisional heads. In particular, the CEO might exercise control over divisional heads by meeting with them on a regular basis and probing them to get rich feedback about the operations of the entity for which they are responsible.

Controls in the Diversified Firm with High Integration   The control problem is more complex in diversified firms pursuing a strategy of related diversification where they are trying to improve performance not only through superior internal governance, but also proactively attempting to leverage competencies across product divisions and realize economies of scope. Consider, for example, 3M, a highly diversified enterprise with multiple product divisions. The company devotes great effort trying to leverage core technology across divisions (for instance, by establishing internal knowledge networks). In addition, 3M tries to realize economies of scope, particularly in the areas of marketing and sales, where a marketing and sales division might sell the products of several 3M divisions. More generally, when a multidivisional enterprise tries to improve performance through the attainment of economies of scope, and via the leveraging of core competencies across divisions, the need for integration between divisions is high.

In such organizations, top managers use the standard repertoire of control mechanisms discussed in the last section (e.g. bureaucratic, output, incentive, and market controls). However, in addition, they have to deal with two control problems that are not found in multidivisional firms pursuing a strategy of unrelated diversification where there is no cooperation and integration between divisions. First, they have to find a control mechanism that induces divisions to cooperate with each other for mutual gain. Second, they need to find a way to deal with the performance ambiguities that arise when divisions are tightly coupled with each other, share resources, and the performance on one cannot be understood in isolation but depends upon how well it cooperates with others.

The solution to both problems is in essence the same as that adopted by single-business firms with high integration between functions. Specifically, the firm needs to adopt incentive controls for divisional managers that are linked to higher-level performance, in this case the performance of the entire enterprise. Insofar as improving the performance of the entire firm requires cooperation between divisions, such incentive controls should facilitate that cooperation. In addition, strong cultural controls can be helpful in creating values and norms that emphasize the importance of cooperation between divisions for mutual gain. At 3M there is a long-established cultural norm that, while products belong to the divisions, the technology underlying those products belongs to the entire company. Thus, the surgical tape business might utilize adhesive technology developed by the office supply business to improve its own products.

Despite such solutions to control problems, there is no question that top managers in firms where divisions are tightly integrated have to deal with greater performance ambiguities than top managers in less complex multidivisional organizations. Integration between various product divisions means that it is hard for top managers to judge the performance of each division just by monitoring objective output criteria. To accurately gauge performance and achieve adequate controls, they probably have to spend time auditing the affairs of operating divisions, and talking to divisional managers to get a comprehensive, qualitative picture of performance than can help them "dig behind" objective output numbers. Other things being equal, this might limit the span of control managers can effectively handle, and thus the scope of the enterprise.[57]

KEY TERMS

organizational
  architecture   386
organizational
  structure   386
controls   387
incentives   387
organizational
  processes   387
organizational
  culture   387
people   387

vertical
  differentiation   388
horizontal
  differentiation   388
integrating
  mechanisms   388
centralization   388
decentralization   388
autonomous subunit   389
tall hierarchies   391
flat hierarchies   391

span of control   392
influence costs   393
delayering   394
functional structure   394
multidivisional
  structure   395
matrix structure   397
knowledge network   400
control   402
goal   402
standard   402

subgoal   402
personal control   405
bureaucratic control   405
output controls   407
market controls   408
peer control   409
values   409
norms   409
performance
  ambiguity   416

TAKEAWAYS FOR STRATEGIC MANAGERS

1. Strategy is implemented through the organizational architecture of the enterprise.
2. It is useful to think of organizational architecture as a system that encompasses structure, controls, incentives, processes, culture, and human capital.
3. In general, a flat organizational structure where the performance of each subunit is visible, unambiguous, and can be measured by objective output controls, is preferable.
4. Implementing strategy may require cooperation between functions and product divisions. The need for cooperation requires integrating mechanisms. Extensive use of integrating mechanisms

may lead to performance ambiguity, and require more complex and varied control mechanisms.
5. At the business level, the need for integrating mechanisms to coordinate functional activities is greater for firms whose business-level strategy requires ongoing product development efforts and product innovation, and for firms based in rapidly changing market environments.
6. At the corporate level, the need for integrating mechanisms to coordinate the activities of different divisions is greater for companies pursuing a strategy of related diversification than for those pursuing a strategy of unrelated diversification.

DISCUSSION QUESTIONS

1. What is the relationship among organizational structure, control systems, incentives, and culture? Give some examples of when and under what conditions a mismatch among these components might arise.
2. What kind of structure best describes the way your (a) business school and (b) university operate? Why is the structure appropriate? Would another structure be better?
3. When would a company choose a matrix structure? What are the problems associated with managing this type of structure? How might these problems be mitigated?
4. What kind of structure, controls, incentives, and culture would you be likely to find in (a) a small manufacturing company based in a stable environment, (b) a high-tech company based in a rapidly changing market, and (c) a Big Four accounting firm?
5. When would a company decide to change from a functional to a multidivisional structure?
6. How would you design structure, controls, incentives, processes, and culture to encourage entrepreneurship in a large, established corporation? How might the desire to encourage entrepreneurship influence your hiring and management development strategy?

CLOSING CASE

Organization at Apple

Apple has a legendary ability to produce a steady stream of innovative new products and product improvements that are differentiated by design elegance and ease of use. Product innovation is in many ways the essence of what the company has always done, and what it strives to continue doing. Innovation at Apple began with the Apple II in 1979. The original Macintosh computer, the first personal computer (PC) to use a graphical user interface, a mouse, and onscreen icons, followed in 1984. After the late founder and former CEO Steve Jobs returned to the company in 1997, the list of notable innovations expanded to include the iPod and iTunes, the Mac Airbook, the iPhone, the Apple App store, and the iPad.

Unlike most companies of its size, Apple has a functional structure. The employees reporting directly to current CEO Tim Cook include the senior vice presidents of operations, Internet software and services, industrial design, software engineering, hardware engineering, and worldwide marketing, along with the CFO and company general council. This group meets every Monday morning to review the strategy of the company, its operations, and ongoing product development efforts.

The industrial design group takes the lead on new-product development efforts, dictating the look and feel of a new product, and the materials that must be used. The centrality of industrial design is unusual—in most companies engineers first develop products, with industrial design coming into the picture quite late in the process. The key role played by industrial design at Apple, however, is consistent with the company's mission of designing beautiful products that change the world. The industrial design group works closely with hardware and software engineering to develop features and functions for each new product, with operations to ensure that manufacturing can be rapidly scaled up following a product launch, and with worldwide marketing to plan the product launch strategy

Thus, product development at Apple is a cross-functional effort that requires intense coordination. This coordination is achieved through a centralized command and control structure, with the top-management group driving collaboration and the industrial design group setting key parameters. During his long tenure as CEO, Jobs was well known for clearly articulating who was responsible for what in the product development process, and for holding people accountable if they failed to meet his high standards. His management style could be unforgiving and harsh—there are numerous stories of people being fired on the spot for failing to meet his standards—but it did get the job done.

Even though Jobs passed away in 2011, the focus on accountability persists at Apple. Each task is given a "directly responsible individual," or DRI in "Apple-speak." Typically, the DRI's name will appear on an agenda for a meeting, so everyone knows who is responsible. Meetings at Apple have an action list, and next to each action item will be a DRI. By such clear control processes, Apple pushes accountability down deep within the ranks.

A key feature of the Apple culture is the secrecy surrounding much of what the company does. Information that reaches the outside world tightly controlled, and so is the flow of information within the company. Many employees are kept in the dark about new-product development efforts and frequently do not know what others are working on. Access to buildings where teams are developing new products or features is tightly controlled, with only team members allowed in. Cameras monitor sensitive workspaces to make sure that this is restriction is not violated. Disclosing what the company is doing to an outside source, or an unauthorized inside source, is grounds for termination—as all employees are told when they join the company. The goal is to keep new products under very tight wraps until launch day. Apple wants to control the message surrounding new products. It does not want to give the competition time to respond, or media critics time to bash products under development.

Sources: J. Tyrangiel, "Tim Cook's Freshman Year: The Apple CEO Speaks," *Bloomberg Businessweek*, December 6, 2012; A. Lashinsky, "The Secrets Apple Keeps," *CNNMoney*, January 10, 2012; and B. Stone, "Apple's Obsession with Secrecy Grows Stronger," New *York Times*, June 23, 2009.

CASE DISCUSSION QUESTIONS

1. Describe as best you can the organizational architecture at Apple, and specifically, its organizational structure, control systems, incentives, product development processes, and culture.

2. What do you think is different about the way Apple is organized compared to most high-tech firms?

3. What is Apple trying to achieve with its current organizational architecture? What are the strengths of this architecture? What are the potential weaknesses?

4. Are there changes that you think Apple should make in its organizational architecture? What are these changes? How might they benefit Apple?

NOTES

[1]D. Naidler, M. Gerstein, and R. Shaw, *Organization Architecture* (San Francisco: Jossey-Bass, 1992).

[2]G. Morgan, *Images of Organization* (Beverly Hills, CA: Sage Publications, 1986).

[3]The material in this section draws on J. Child, *Organizations* (London: Harper & Row, 1984).

Recent work addressing the issue includes J. R. Baum and S. Wally, "Strategic Decision Speed and Firm Performance," *Strategic Management Journal* 24 (2003): 1107–1120; D. I. Jung and B. J. Avolio, "Effects of Leadership Style and Followers Cultural Orientation on Performance in Groups and Individual Task Conditions," *Academy of Management Journal* 42 (1999): 208–218.

[4] This is a key tenet of the information-processing view of organizations. See J. Galbraith. *Designing Complex Organizations* (Reading, MA: Addison-Wesley, 1972).

[5] J. Kim and R. M. Burton, "The Effects of Uncertainty and Decentralization on Project Team Performance," *Computational & Mathematical Organization Theory* 8 (2002): 365–384.

[6] J. Birkinshaw, N. Hood, and S. Jonsson, "Building Firm Specific Advantages in Multinational Corporations: The Role of Subsidiary Initiatives," *Strategic Management Journal* 19 (1998): 221–241.

[7] K. M. Eisenhardt, "Making Fast Strategic Decisions in High Velocity Environments," *Academy of Management Journal* 32 (1989): 543–575.

[8] G. P. Hattrup and B. H. Kleiner, "How to Establish a Proper Span of Control for Managers", *Industrial Management* 35 (1993): 28–30

[9] The classic statement was made by P. Milgrom and J. Roberts, "Bargaining Costs, Influence Costs and the Organization of Economic Activity", in J. E. Alt and K. A. Shepsle (eds.), *Perspectives in Positive Political Economy*, (Cambridge: Cambridge University Press, 1990). Also see R. Inderst, H. M. Muller, and K. Warneryd, "Influence Costs and Hierarchy," *Economics of Governance* 6 (2005): 177–198.

[10] D. Priest and D. Linzer, "Panel Condemns Iraq Prewar Intelligence," *The Washington Post*, July 10, 2004, page A1; D. Jehl, "Senators Assail CIA Judgments of Iraq's Arms as Deeply Flawed," *New York Times*, July 10, 2004, page A1; M. Isikoff, "The Dots Never Existed," *Newsweek*, July 19, 2004, pp. 36–40.

[11] C. R. Littler, R. Wiesner and R. Dunford, "The Dynamics of Delayering," *Journal of Management Studies* 40 (2003): 225–240.

[12] J. A. Byrne, "Jack: A Close-up Look at How America's #1 Manager Runs GE," *Business Week*, June 8, 1998, pp 90-100. Also see *Harvard Business School Press*, "GE's Two Decade Transformation."

[13] A. D. Chandler, *Strategy and Structure: Chapters in the History of the Industrial Enterprise* (Cambridge, MA: MIT Press, 1962). Also see O.E. Williamson, *Markets and Hierarchies: Analysis and Anti-Trust Implications* (New York: Free Press, 1975).

[14] A. P. Sloan, *My Years at General Motors* (New York: Bantum Books, 1996). Originally published in 1963.

[15] C. W. L. Hill, M. A. Hitt, and R. E. Hoskisson. "Cooperative versus Competitive Structures in Related and Unrelated Firms," *Organization Science* 45 (1992): 501–521; O. E. Williamson, *Markets and Hierarchies: Analysis and Anti-Trust Implications* (New York: Free Press, 1975).

[16] C. W. L. Hill, M. A. Hitt, and R. E. Hoskisson, "Declining U.S. Competitiveness: Reflections on a Crisis," *Academy of Management Executives* 2 (1988): 51–60.

[17] P. R. Lawrence and J. Lorsch, *Organization and Environment* (Boston, MA: Harvard University Press, 1967).

[18] K. B. Clark and S. C. Wheelwright, *Managing New Product and Process Development* (New York: Free Press, 1993); M. A. Schilling and C. W. L. Hill, "Managing the New Product Development Process," *Academy of Management Executive* 12 (3) (August 1998): 67–68; S. L. Brown and K. M. Eisenhardt, "Product Development: Past Research, Present Findings, and Future Directions," *Academy of Management Review* 20 (1995): 343–378.

[19] L. R. Burns and D. R. Whorley, "Adoption and Abandonment of Matrix Management Programs: Effects of Organizational Characteristics and Interorganizational Networks," *Academy of Management Journal* (February 1993), pp. 106–138; C. A. Bartlett and S. Ghoshal, "Matrix Management: Not a Structure, a Frame of Mind," *Harvard Business Review* (July-August 1990), pp. 138–145.

[20] S. Thomas and L. S. D'Annunizo, "Challenges and Strategies of Matrix Organizations," *HR Human Resource Planning* 28 (2005): 39–49.

[21] See J. R. Galbraith, *Designing Complex Organizations* (Reading, MA: Addison-Wesley, 1977).

[22] M. Goold and A. Campbell, "Structured Networks: Towards the Well Designed Matrix," *Long Range Planning* (October 2003), pp. 427–460.

[23] Bartlett and Ghoshal, *Managing across Borders*; F. V. Guterl, "Goodbye, Old Matrix," *Business Month* (February 1989), pp. 32–38; I. Bjorkman, W. Barner-Rasussen, and L. Li, "Managing Knowledge Transfer in MNCs: The Impact

of Headquarters Control Mechanisms," *Journal of International Business* 35 (2004): 443–460.

[24] M. S. Granovetter, "The Strength of Weak Ties," *American Journal of Sociology* 78 (1973): 1360–1380.

[25] A. K. Gupta and V. J. Govindarajan, "Knowledge Flows within Multinational Corporations," *Strategic Management Journal* 21 (4) (2000): 473–496; V. J. Govindarajan and A. K. Gupta, *The Quest for Global Dominance* (San Francisco: Jossey-Bass, 2001); U. Andersson, M. Forsgren, and U. Holm, "The Strategic Impact of External Networks: Subsidiary Performance and Competence Development in the Multinational Corporation," *Strategic Management Journal* 23 (2002): 979–996.

[26] For examples, see W. H. Davidow and M. S. Malone, *The Virtual Corporation* (New York: Harper Collins, 1992).

[27] 3M. A Century of Innovation, the 3M Story. 3M, 2002. www.3m.com/about3m/century/index.jhtml.

[28] W. G. Ouchi, "Markets, Bureaucracies, and Clans," *Administrative Science Quarterly* 25 (1980): 129–144.

[29] J. Child, *Organization: A Guide to Problems and Practice* (Harper & Row: London, 1984).

[30] S. G. Green and M. A. Welsh. "Cybernetics and Dependence: Reframing the Control Concept," *Academy of Management Review* 13 (2) (1988): 287–301.

[31] J. Batsell, "Cost Cutting, Inventory Control Help Boost Nordstrom's Quarterly Profit," Knight Ridder Tribune News, Feburary 22, 2002, p. 1; Nordstrom 2004 10K statement.

[32] For a recent summary, see D. M. Wiegand and E. S. Geller. "Connecting Positive Psychology and Organization Behavior Management," *Journal of Organization Behavior Management* 24 (12) (2004/2005): 3–20.

[33] J. Child, "Strategies of Control and Organization Behavior," *Administrative Science Quarterly* 18 (1973): 1–17; K. Eisenhardt, "Control: Organizational and Economic Approaches," *Management Science* 31 (1985): 134–149; S. A. Snell, "Control Theory in Human Resource Management," *Academy of Management Review* 35 (1992): 292–328; W. G. Ouchi, "The Transmission of Control Through Organizational Hierarchy," *Administrative Science Quarterly* 21 (1978): 173–192.

[34] J. Child, *Organization: A Guide to Problems and Practice* (Harper & Row: London, 1984).

[35] R. Teichroeb, "End to Forced Busing Creates New Problems for Seattle's Schools," *Seattle Post Intelligencer*, June 3, 1999, online edition. www.seattlepi.com

[36] J. Child, *Organization: A Guide to Problems and Practice* (Harper & Row: London, 1984).

[37] Hill, Hitt, and Hoskisson, "Cooperative versus Competitive Structures in Related and Unrelated Diversified Firms."

[38] J. D. Thompson, *Organizations in Action* (New York: McGraw Hill, 1967).

[39] O. E. Wiliamson. *The Economic Institutions of Capitalism* (Free Press, New York, 1985).

[40] C. Bartlett. "Philips versus Matsushita: A New Century, a New Round," *Harvard Business School Press* Case No. 9–302–049, 2005.

[41] L. Kim. "The Dynamics of Samsung's Technological Learning in Semiconductors," *California Management Review* 39 (3) (1997): 86–101.

[42] Hill, Hitt, and Hoskisson, "Cooperative versus Competitive Structures in Related and Unrelated Diversified Firms."

[43] Peer control has long been argued to be a characteristic of many Japanese organizations. See M. Aoki, *Information, Incentives and Bargaining in the Japanese Economy* (Cambridge, UK: Cambridge University Press, 1988).

[44] E. H. Schein, *Organizational Culture and Leadership,* 2nd ed. (San Francisco: Jossey-Bass, 1992).

[45] J. P. Kotter and J. L. Heskett, *Corporate Culture and Performance* (New York: Free Press, 1992); M. L. Tushman and C. A. O'Reilly, *Winning through Innovation* (Boston, MA: Harvard Business School Press, 1997).

[46] The classic song of praise was produced by T. Peters and R. H. Waterman, *In Search of Excellence* (New York: Harper & Row, 1982). Ironically, IBM's decline began shortly after their book was published.

[47] Kotter and Heskett, *Corporate Culture and Performance*

[48] J. O'Connell, "Lincoln Electric: Venturing Abroad," Harvard Business School Press Case No. 9–398–095, April 1998, and www.lincolnelectric.com.

[49] M. Hammer and J. Champy, *Reengineering the Corporation* (New York: Harper Business, 1993).

[50] T. Kostova, "Transnational Transfer of Strategic Organizational Practices: A Contextual Perspective," *Academy of Management Review* 24 (2) (1999): 308–324.

[51] Andersson, Forsgren, and Holm, "The Strategic Impact of External Networks: Subsidiary Performance and Competence

Development in the Multinational Corporation."

[52] Ulf Anderson, Mats Forsgren, and Ulf Holm, "The strategic impact of external networks: Subsidiary performance and competence development in the multinational corporation," *Strategic Management Journal*, Vol 23(11), pp. 979–996.

[53] P. R Lawrence and J. Lorsch, *Organization and Environment.*

(Boston, MA: Harvard University Press, 1967).

[54] Hill, Hitt, & Hoskisson, "Cooperative versus Competitive Structures in Related and Unrelated Firms."

[55] Ibid.

[56] C. W. L. Hill, "The Role of Corporate Headquarters in the Multidivisional Firm," in R. Rumelt, D. J. Teece, and D. Schendel (eds),

Fundamental Issues in Strategy Research. (Cambridge, Mass: Harvard Business School Press, 1994), pp. 297–321.

[57] C. W. L. Hill and R. E. Hoskisson. "Strategy and Structure in the Multiproduct Firm," *Academy of Management Review* 12 (1988): 331–341.

CASE

STUDY

ANALYSIS

ANALYZING A CASE STUDY AND WRITING A CASE STUDY ANALYSIS

▌WHAT IS CASE STUDY ANALYSIS?

Case study analysis is an integral part of a course in strategic management. The purpose of a case study is to provide students with experience of the strategic management problems that actual organizations face. A case study presents an account of what happened to a business or industry over a number of years. It chronicles the events that managers had to deal with, such as changes in the competitive environment, and charts the managers' response, which usually involved changing the business- or corporate-level strategy. The cases in this book cover a wide range of issues and problems that managers have had to confront. Some cases are about finding the right business-level strategy to compete in changing conditions. Some are about companies that grew by acquisition, with little concern for the rationale behind their growth, and how growth by acquisition affected their future profitability. Each case is different because each organization is different. The underlying thread in all cases, however, is the use of strategic management techniques to solve business problems.

Cases prove valuable in a strategic management course for several reasons. First, cases provide you, the student, with experience of organizational problems that you probably have not had the opportunity to experience firsthand. In a relatively short period of time, you will have the chance to appreciate and analyze the problems faced by many different companies and to understand how managers tried to deal with them.

Second, cases illustrate the theory and content of strategic management. The meaning and implications of this information are made clearer when they are applied to case studies. The theory and concepts help reveal what is going on in the companies studied and allow you to evaluate the solutions that specific companies adopted to deal with their problems. Consequently, when you analyze cases, you will be like a detective who, with a set of conceptual tools, probes what happened and what or who was responsible and then marshals the evidence that provides the solution. Top managers enjoy the thrill of testing their problem-solving abilities in the real world. It is important to remember that no one knows what the right answer is. All that managers can do is to make the best guess. In fact, managers say repeatedly that they are happy if they are right only half the time in solving strategic problems. Strategic management is an uncertain game, and using cases to see how theory can be put into practice is one way of improving your skills of diagnostic investigation.

Third, case studies provide you with the opportunity to participate in class and to gain experience in presenting your ideas to others. Instructors may sometimes call on students as a group to identify what is going on in a case, and through classroom discussion the issues in and solutions to the case problem will reveal themselves. In such a situation, you will have to organize your views and conclusions so that you can present them to the class. Your classmates may have analyzed the issues differently from you, and they will want you to argue your points before they will accept your conclusions, so be prepared for debate. This mode of discussion is an example of the dialectical approach to decision making. This is how decisions are made in the actual business world.

Instructors also may assign an individual, but more commonly a group, to analyze the case before the whole class. The individual or group probably will be responsible for a 30 to 40 minute presentation of the case to the class. That presentation must cover the issues posed, the problems facing the company, and a series of recommendations for resolving the problems. The discussion then will be thrown open to the class, and you will have to defend your ideas. Through such discussions and presentations, you will experience how to convey your ideas effectively to others. Remember that a great deal of managers' time is spent in these kinds of situations: presenting their ideas and engaging in discussion with other managers who have their own views about what is going on. Thus, you will experience in the classroom the actual process of strategic management, and this will serve you well in your future career.

If you work in groups to analyze case studies, you also will learn about the group process involved in working as a team. When people work in groups, it is often difficult to schedule time and allocate responsibility for the case analysis. There are always group members who shirk their responsibilities and group members who are so sure of their own ideas that they try to dominate the group's analysis. Most of the strategic management takes place in groups, however, and it is best if you learn about these problems now.

ANALYZING A CASE STUDY

The purpose of the case study is to let you apply the concepts of strategic management when you analyze the issues facing a specific company. To analyze a case study, therefore, you must examine closely the issues confronting the company. Most often you will need to read the case several times— once to grasp the overall picture of what is happening to the company and then several times more to discover and grasp the specific problems.

Generally, detailed analysis of a case study should include eight areas:

1. The history, development, and growth of the company over time
2. The identification of the company's internal strengths and weaknesses
3. The nature of the external environment surrounding the company
4. A SWOT analysis
5. The kind of corporate-level strategy that the company is pursuing
6. The nature of the company's business-level strategy
7. The company's structure and control systems and how they match its strategy
8. Recommendations

To analyze a case, you need to apply the concepts taught in this course to each of these areas. To help you further, we next offer a summary of the steps you can take to analyze the case material for each of the eight points we just noted:

1. *Analyze the company's history, development, and growth.* A convenient way to investigate how a company's past strategy and structure affect it in the present is to

chart the critical incidents in its history—that is, the events that were the most unusual or the most essential for its development into the company it is today. Some of the events have to do with its founding, its initial products, how it makes new-product market decisions, and how it developed and chose functional competencies to pursue. Its entry into new businesses and shifts in its main lines of business are also important milestones to consider.

2. *Identify the company's internal strengths and weaknesses.* Once the historical profile is completed, you can begin the SWOT analysis. Use all the incidents you have charted to develop an account of the company's strengths and weaknesses as they have emerged historically. Examine each of the value creation functions of the company, and identify the functions in which the company is currently strong and currently weak. Some companies might be weak in marketing; some might be strong in research and development. Make lists of these strengths and weaknesses. The SWOT Checklist (Table 1) gives examples of what might go in these lists.

Table 1 A SWOT Checklist

Potential Internal Strengths	Potential Internal Weaknesses
Many product lines?	Obsolete, narrow product lines?
Broad market coverage?	Rising manufacturing costs?
Manufacturing competence?	Decline in R&D innovations?
Good marketing skills?	Poor marketing plan?
Good materials management systems?	Poor material management systems?
R&D skills and leadership?	Loss of customer good will?
Information system competencies?	Inadequate human resources?
Human resource competencies?	Inadequate information systems?
Brand name reputation?	Loss of brand name capital?
Portfolio management skills?	Growth without direction?
Cost of differentiation advantage?	Bad portfolio management?
New-venture management expertise?	Loss of corporate direction?
Appropriate management style?	Infighting among divisions?
Appropriate organizational structure?	Loss of corporate control?
Appropriate control systems?	Inappropriate organizational
Ability to manage strategic change?	structure and control systems?
Well-developed corporate strategy?	High conflict and politics?
Good financial management?	Poor financial management?
Others?	Others?

Potential Environmental Opportunities	Potential Environment Threats
Expand core business(es)?	Attacks on core business(es)?
Exploit new market segments?	Increases in domestic competition?
Widen product range?	Increase in foreign competition?
Extend cost or differentiation advantage?	Change in consumer tastes?
Diversify into new growth businesses?	Fall in barriers to entry?
Expand into foreign markets?	Rise in new or substitute products?
Apply R&D skills in new areas?	Increase in industry rivalry?
Enter new related businesses?	New forms of industry competition?
Vertically integrate forward?	Potential for takeover?
Vertically integrate backward?	Existence of corporate raiders?
Enlarge corporate portfolio?	Increase in regional competition?
Overcome barriers to entry?	Changes in demographic factors?
Reduce rivalry among competitors?	Changes in economic factors?
Make profitable new acquisitions?	Downturn in economy?
Apply brand name capital in new areas?	Rising labor costs?
Seek fast market growth?	Slower market growth?
Others?	Others?

© Cengage Learning 2013

3. *Analyze the external environment.* To identify environmental opportunities and threats, apply all the concepts on industry and macroenvironments to analyze the environment the company is confronting. Of particular importance at the industry level are the Competitive Forces Model, adapted from Porter's Five Forces Model and the stage of the life-cycle model. Which factors in the macroenvironment will appear salient depends on the specific company being analyzed. Use each factor in turn (for instance, demographic factors) to see whether it is relevant for the company in question.

    Having done this analysis, you will have generated both an analysis of the company's environment and a list of opportunities and threats. The SWOT Checklist table also lists some common environmental opportunities and threats that you may look for, but the list you generate will be specific to your company.

4. *Evaluate the SWOT analysis.* Having identified the company's external opportunities and threats as well as its internal strengths and weaknesses, consider what your findings mean. You need to balance strengths and weaknesses against opportunities and threats. Is the company in an overall strong competitive position? Can it continue to pursue its current business- or corporate-level strategy profitably?

What can the company do to turn weaknesses into strengths and threats into opportunities? Can it develop new functional, business, or corporate strategies to accomplish this change? *Never merely generate the SWOT analysis and then put it aside.* Because it provides a succinct summary of the company's condition, a good SWOT analysis is the key to all the analyses that follow.

5. *Analyze corporate-level strategy.* To analyze corporate-level strategy, you first need to define the company's mission and goals. Sometimes the mission and goals are stated explicitly in the case; at other times, you will have to infer them from available information. The information you need to collect to find out the company's corporate strategy includes such factors as its lines of business and the nature of its subsidiaries and acquisitions. It is important to analyze the relationship among the company's businesses. Do they trade or exchange resources? Are there gains to be achieved from synergy? Alternatively, is the company just running a portfolio of investments? This analysis should enable you to define the corporate strategy that the company is pursuing (for example, related or unrelated diversification, or a combination of both) and to conclude whether the company operates in just one core business. Then, using your SWOT analysis, debate the merits of this strategy. Is it appropriate given the environment the company is in? Could a change in corporate strategy provide the company with new opportunities or transform a weakness into a strength? For example, should the company diversify from its core business into new businesses?

Other issues should be considered as well. How and why has the company's strategy changed over time? What is the claimed rationale for any changes? Often, it is a good idea to analyze the company's businesses or products to assess its situation and identify which divisions contribute the most to or detract from its competitive advantage. It is also useful to explore how the company has built its portfolio over time. Did it acquire new businesses, or did it internally venture its own? All of these factors provide clues about the company and indicate ways of improving its future performance.

6. *Analyze business-level strategy.* Once you know the company's corporate-level strategy and have done the SWOT analysis, the next step is to identify the company's business-level strategy. If the company is a single-business company, its business-level strategy is identical to its corporate-level strategy. If the company is in many businesses, each business will have its own business-level strategy. You will need to identify the company's generic competitive strategy—differentiation, low-cost, or focus—and its investment strategy, given its relative competitive position and the stage of the life cycle. The company also may market different products using different business-level strategies. For example, it may offer a low-cost product range and a line of differentiated products. Be sure to give a full account of a company's business-level strategy to show how it competes.

Identifying the functional strategies that a company pursues to build competitive advantage through superior efficiency, quality, innovation, and customer responsiveness and to achieve its business-level strategy is very important. The SWOT analysis will have provided you with information on the company's functional competencies. You should investigate its production, marketing, or research and development strategy further to gain a picture of where the company is going. For example, pursuing a low-cost or a differentiation strategy successfully requires very different sets of competencies. Has the company developed the right ones? If it has, how can it exploit them further? Can it pursue both a low-cost and a differentiation strategy simultaneously?

The SWOT analysis is especially important at this point if the industry analysis, particularly Porter's model, has revealed threats to the company from the environment. Can the company deal with these threats? How should it change its business-level strategy to counter them? To evaluate the potential of a company's business-level strategy, you must first perform a thorough SWOT analysis that captures the essence of its problems.

Once you complete this analysis, you will have a full picture of the way the company is operating and be in a position to evaluate the potential of its strategy. Thus, you will be able to make recommendations concerning the pattern of its future actions. However, first you need to consider strategy implementation, or the way the company tries to achieve its strategy.

7. *Analyze structure and control systems.* The aim of this analysis is to identify what structure and control systems the company is using to implement its strategy and to evaluate whether that structure is the appropriate one for the company. Different corporate and business strategies require different structures. You need to determine the *degree of fit between the company's strategy and structure.* For example, does the company have the right level of vertical differentiation (e.g., does it have the appropriate number of levels in the hierarchy or decentralized control?) or horizontal differentiation (does it use a functional structure when it should be using a product structure?)? Similarly, is the company using the right integration or control systems to manage its operations? Are managers being appropriately rewarded? Are the right rewards in place for encouraging cooperation among divisions? These are all issues to consider.

In some cases, there will be little information on these issues, whereas in others there will be a lot. In analyzing each case, you should gear the analysis toward its most salient issues. For example, organizational conflict, power, and politics will be important issues for some companies. Try to analyze why problems in these areas are occurring. Do they occur because of bad strategy formulation or because of bad strategy implementation?

Organizational change is an issue in many cases because the companies are attempting to alter their strategies or structures to solve strategic problems. Thus, as part of the analysis, you might suggest an action plan that the company in question could use to achieve its goals. For example, you might list in a logical sequence the steps the company would need to follow to alter its business-level strategy from differentiation to focus.

8. *Make recommendations.* The quality of your recommendations is a direct result of the thoroughness with which you prepared the case analysis. Recommendations are directed at solving whatever strategic problem the company is facing and increasing its future profitability. Your recommendations should be in line with your analysis; that is, they should follow logically from the previous discussion. For example, your recommendation generally will center on the specific ways of changing functional, business, and corporate strategies and organizational structure and control to improve business performance. The set of recommendations will be specific to each case, and so it is difficult to discuss these recommendations here. Such recommendations might include an increase in spending on specific research and development projects, the divesting of certain businesses, a change from a strategy of unrelated to related diversification, an increase in the level of integration among divisions by using task forces and teams, or a move to a different kind of structure to implement a new business-level strategy. Make sure your recommendations are mutually consistent and written in the form of an action plan. The plan might contain a timetable that sequences the actions for changing the company's strategy

and a description of how changes at the corporate level will necessitate changes at the business level and subsequently at the functional level.

After following all these stages, you will have performed a thorough analysis of the case and will be in a position to join in class discussion or present your ideas to the class, depending on the format used by your professor. Remember that you must tailor your analysis to suit the specific issue discussed in your case. In some cases, you might completely omit one of the steps in the analysis because it is not relevant to the situation you are considering. You must be sensitive to the needs of the case and not apply the framework we have discussed in this section blindly. The framework is meant only as a guide, not as an outline.

WRITING A CASE STUDY ANALYSIS

Often, as part of your course requirements, you will need to present a written case analysis. This may be an individual or a group report. Whatever the situation, there are certain guidelines to follow in writing a case analysis that will improve the evaluation your work will receive from your instructor. Before we discuss these guidelines and before you use them, make sure that they do not conflict with any directions your instructor has given you.

The structure of your written report is critical. Generally, if you follow the steps for analysis discussed in the previous section, *you already will have a good structure for your written discussion*. All reports begin with an *introduction* to the case. In it, outline briefly what the company does, how it developed historically, what problems it is experiencing, and how you are going to approach the issues in the case write-up. Do this sequentially by writing, for example, "First, we discuss the environment of Company. . . . Third, we discuss Company X's business-level strategy. . . . Last, we provide recommendations for turning around Company X's business."

In the second part of the case write-up, the *strategic analysis* section, do the SWOT analysis, analyze and discuss the nature and problems of the company's business-level and corporate strategies, and then analyze its structure and control systems. Make sure you use plenty of headings and subheadings to structure your analysis. For example, have separate sections on any important conceptual tool you use. Thus, you might have a section on the Competitive Forces Model as part of your analysis of the environment. You might offer a separate section on portfolio techniques when analyzing a company's corporate strategy. Tailor the sections and subsections to the specific issues of importance in the case.

In the third part of the case write-up, present your *solutions and recommendations*. Be comprehensive, and make sure they are in line with the previous analysis so that the recommendations fit together and move logically from one to the next. The recommendations section is very revealing because your instructor will have a good idea of how much work you put into the case from the quality of your recommendations.

Following this framework will provide a good structure for most written reports, though it must be shaped to fit the individual case being considered. Some cases are about excellent companies experiencing no problems. In such instances, it is hard to write recommendations. Instead, you can focus on analyzing why the company is doing so well, using that analysis to structure the discussion. Following are some minor suggestions that can help make a good analysis even better:

1. Do not repeat in summary form large pieces of factual information from the case. The instructor has read the case and knows what is going on. Rather, use the

information in the case to illustrate your statements, defend your arguments, or make salient points. Beyond the brief introduction to the company, you must avoid being *descriptive*; instead, you must be *analytical*.

2. Make sure the sections and subsections of your discussion flow logically and smoothly from one to the next. That is, try to build on what has gone before so that the analysis of the case study moves toward a climax. This is particularly important for group analysis, because there is a tendency for people in a group to split up the work and say, "I'll do the beginning, you take the middle, and I'll do the end." The result is a choppy, stilted analysis; the parts do not flow from one to the next, and it is obvious to the instructor that no real group work has been done.

3. Avoid grammatical and spelling errors. They make your work look sloppy.

4. In some instances, cases dealing with well-known companies end in 1998 or 1999 because no later information was available when the case was written. If possible, do a search for more information on what has happened to the company in subsequent years.

  Many libraries now have comprehensive web-based electronic data search facilities that offer such sources as *ABI/Inform, The Wall Street Journal Index,* the *F&S Index,* and the *Nexis-Lexis* databases. These enable you to identify any article that has been written in the business press on the company of your choice within the past few years. A number of nonelectronic data sources are also useful. For example, *F&S Predicasts* publishes an annual list of articles relating to major companies that appeared in the national and international business press. *S&P Industry Surveys* is a great source for basic industry data, and *Value Line Ratings and Reports* can contain good summaries of a firm's financial position and future prospects. You will also want to collect full financial information on the company. Again, this can be accessed from Web-based electronic databases such as the *Edgar* database, which archives all forms that publicly quoted companies have to file with the Securities and Exchange Commission (SEC; e.g., 10-K filings can be accessed from the SEC's *Edgar* database). Most SEC forms for public companies can now be accessed from Internet-based financial sites, such as Yahoo's finance site (http://finance.yahoo.com/).

5. Sometimes instructors hand out questions for each case to help you in your analysis. Use these as a guide for writing the case analysis. They often illuminate the important issues that have to be covered in the discussion.

If you follow the guidelines in this section, you should be able to write a thorough and effective evaluation.

THE ROLE OF FINANCIAL ANALYSIS IN CASE STUDY ANALYSIS

An important aspect of analyzing a case study and writing a case study analysis is the role and use of financial information. A careful analysis of the company's financial condition immensely improves a case write-up. After all, financial data represent the concrete results of the company's strategy and structure. Although analyzing financial statements can be quite complex, a general idea of a company's financial position can be determined through the use of ratio analysis. Financial performance ratios can be calculated from the balance sheet and income statement. These ratios can be classified into five subgroups: profit ratios, liquidity ratios, activity ratios, leverage ratios, and shareholder-return ratios. These ratios should be compared with the industry average or the company's prior years of performance. It should be noted, however, that deviation from the average is not necessarily bad; it simply warrants further investigation. For example, young companies will have purchased assets at a different price and will likely have a different capital structure than older companies do. In addition to ratio analysis, a company's cash flow position is of critical importance and should be assessed. Cash flow shows how much actual cash a company possesses.

Profit Ratios

Profit ratios measure the efficiency with which the company uses its resources. The more efficient the company, the greater is its profitability. It is useful to compare a company's profitability against that of its major competitors in its industry to determine whether the company is operating more or less efficiently than its rivals. In addition, the change in a company's profit ratios over time tells whether its performance is improving or declining.

A number of different profit ratios can be used, and each of them measures a different aspect of a company's performance. Here, we look at the most commonly used profit ratios.

Return on Invested Capital (ROIC)   This ratio measures the profit earned on the capital invested in the company. It is defined as follows:

$$\text{Return on invested capital (ROIC)} = \frac{\text{Net profit}}{\text{Invested capital}}$$

Net profit is calculated by subtracting the total costs of operating the company away from its total revenues (total revenues − total costs). Total costs are the (1) costs of goods sold, (2) sales, general, and administrative expenses, (3) R&D expenses, and (4) other expenses. Net profit can be calculated before or after taxes, although many financial analysts prefer the before-tax figure. Invested capital is the amount that is invested in the operations of a company—that is, in property, plant, equipment, inventories, and other assets. Invested capital comes from two main sources: interest-bearing debt and shareholders' equity. Interest-bearing debt is money the company borrows from banks and from those who purchase its bonds. Shareholders' equity is the money raised from selling shares to the public, *plus* earnings that have been retained by the company in prior years and are available to fund current investments. ROIC measures the effectiveness with which a company is using the capital funds that it has available for investment. As such, it is recognized to be an excellent measure of the value a company is creating.1 Remember that a company's ROIC can be decomposed into its constituent parts.

Return on Total Assets (ROA)   This ratio measures the profit earned on the employment of assets. It is defined as follows:

$$\text{Return on total assests} = \frac{\text{Net profit}}{\text{Total assets}}$$

Return on Stockholders' Equity (ROE)   This ratio measures the percentage of profit earned on common stockholders' investment in the company. It is defined as follows:

$$\text{Return on stockholders equity} = \frac{\text{Net profit}}{\text{Stockholders equity}}$$

If a company has no debt, this will be the same as ROIC.

Liquidity Ratios

A company's liquidity is a measure of its ability to meet short-term obligations. An asset is deemed liquid if it can be readily converted into cash. Liquid assets are current assets such as cash, marketable securities, accounts receivable, and so on. Two liquidity ratios are commonly used.

Current Ratio   The current ratio measures the extent to which the claims of short-term creditors are covered by assets that can be quickly converted into cash. Most companies should have a ratio of at least 1, because failure to meet these commitments can lead to bankruptcy. The ratio is defined as follows:

$$\text{Current ratio} = \frac{\text{Current assets}}{\text{Current liabilities}}$$

Quick Ratio   The quick ratio measures a company's ability to pay off the claims of short-term creditors without relying on selling its inventories. This is a valuable measure since in practice the sale of inventories is often difficult. It is defined as follows:

$$\text{Quick ratio} = \frac{\text{Current assets} - \text{inventory}}{\text{Current liabilities}}$$

Activity Ratios

Activity ratios indicate how effectively a company is managing its assets. Two ratios are particularly useful.

Inventory Turnover   This measures the number of times inventory is turned over. It is useful in determining whether a firm is carrying excess stock in inventory. It is defined as follows:

$$\text{Inventory turnover} = \frac{\text{Cost of goods sold}}{\text{Inventory}}$$

Cost of goods sold is a better measure of turnover than sales because it is the cost of the inventory items. Inventory is taken at the balance sheet date. Some companies choose to compute an average inventory, beginning inventory, and ending inventory, but for simplicity, use the inventory at the balance sheet date.

Days Sales Outstanding (DSO) or Average Collection Period   This ratio is the average time a company has to wait to receive its cash after making a sale. It measures how effective the company's credit, billing, and collection procedures are. It is defined as follows:

$$DSO = \frac{Accounts\ receivable}{Total\ sales/360}$$

Accounts receivable is divided by average daily sales. The use of 360 is the standard number of days for most financial analysis.

Leverage Ratios

A company is said to be highly leveraged if it uses more debt than equity, including stock and retained earnings. The balance between debt and equity is called the *capital structure*. The optimal capital structure is determined by the individual company. Debt has a lower cost because creditors take less risk; they know they will get their interest and principal. However, debt can be risky to the firm because if enough profit is not made to cover the interest and principal payments, bankruptcy can result. Three leverage ratios are commonly used.

Debt-to-Assets Ratio   The debt-to-assets ratio is the most direct measure of the extent to which borrowed funds have been used to finance a company's investments. It is defined as follows:

$$Debt\text{-}to\text{-}assets\ ratio = \frac{Total\ debt}{Total\ assets}$$

Total debt is the sum of a company's current liabilities and its long-term debt, and total assets are the sum of fixed assets and current assets.

Debt-to-Equity Ratio   The debt-to-equity ratio indicates the balance between debt and equity in a company's capital structure. This is perhaps the most widely used measure of a company's leverage. It is defined as follows:

$$Debt\text{-}to\text{-}equity\ ratio = \frac{Total\ debt}{Total\ equity}$$

Times-Covered Ratio   The times-covered ratio measures the extent to which a company's gross profit covers its annual interest payments. If this ratio declines to less than 1, the company is unable to meet its interest costs and is technically insolvent. The ratio is defined as follows:

$$Times\text{-}covered\ ratio = \frac{Profit\ before\ interest\ and\ tax}{Total\ interest\ charges}$$

Shareholder-Return Ratios

Shareholder-return ratios measure the return that shareholders earn from holding stock in the company. Given the goal of maximizing stockholders' wealth, providing shareholders with an adequate rate of return is a primary objective of most companies. As with profit ratios, it can be helpful to compare a company's shareholder returns against those of similar companies as a yardstick for determining how well the company is satisfying the demands of this particularly important group of organizational constituents. Four ratios are commonly used.

Total Shareholder Returns   Total shareholder returns measure the returns earned by time $t + 1$ on an investment in a company's stock made at time t. (Time t is the time at which the initial investment is made.) Total shareholder returns include both dividend payments and appreciation in the value of the stock (adjusted for stock splits) and are defined as follows:

$$\text{Total shareholder returns} = \frac{\text{Stock price } (t + 1) - \text{stock price } (t) + \text{sum of annual dividends per share}}{\text{Stock price } (t)}$$

If a shareholder invests $2 at time t and at time $t + 1$ the share is worth $3, while the sum of annual dividends for the period t to $t + 1$ has amounted to $0.20, total shareholder returns are equal to $(3 - 2 + 0.2)/2 = 0.6$, which is a 60% return on an initial investment of $2 made at time t.

Price-Earnings Ratio   The price-earnings ratio measures the amount investors are willing to pay per dollar of profit. It is defined as follows:

$$\text{Price-earnings ratio} = \frac{\text{Market price per share}}{\text{Earnings per share}}$$

Market-to-Book Value   Market-to-book value measures a company's expected future growth prospects. It is defined as follows:

$$\text{Market-to-book value} = \frac{\text{Market price per share}}{\text{Earnings per share}}$$

Dividend Yield   The dividend yield measures the return to shareholders received in the form of dividends. It is defined as follows:

$$\text{Dividend} = \frac{\text{Dividend per share}}{\text{Market price per share}}$$

Market price per share can be calculated for the first of the year, in which case the dividend yield refers to the return on an investment made at the beginning of the year. Alternatively, the average share price over the year may be used. A company must decide how much of its profits to pay to stockholders and how much to reinvest in the company. Companies with strong growth prospects should have a lower dividend payout ratio than mature companies. The rationale is that shareholders can invest the money elsewhere if the company is not growing. The optimal ratio depends on the individual firm, but the key decider is whether the company can produce better returns than the investor can earn elsewhere.

Cash Flow

Cash flow position is cash received minus cash distributed. The net cash flow can be taken from a company's statement of cash flows. Cash flow is important for what it reveals about a company's financing needs. A strong positive cash flow enables a company to fund future investments without having to borrow money from bankers or investors. This is desirable because the company avoids paying out interest or dividends. A weak or negative cash flow means that a company has to turn to external sources to fund future investments. Generally, companies in strong-growth industries often find themselves in a poor cash flow position (because their investment needs are substantial), whereas successful companies based in mature industries generally find themselves in a strong cash flow position.

A company's internally generated cash flow is calculated by adding back its depreciation provision to profits after interest, taxes, and dividend payments. If this figure is insufficient to cover proposed new investments, the company has little choice but to borrow funds to make up the shortfall or to curtail investments. If this figure exceeds proposed new investments, the company can use the excess to build up its liquidity (that is, through investments in financial assets) or repay existing loans ahead of schedule.

◤ CONCLUSION

When evaluating a case, it is important to be *systematic*. Analyze the case in a logical fashion, beginning with the identification of operating and financial strengths and weaknesses and environmental opportunities and threats. Move on to assess the value of a company's current strategies only when you are fully conversant with the SWOT analysis of the company. Ask yourself whether the company's current strategies make sense given its SWOT analysis. If they do not, what changes need to be made? What are your recommendations? Above all, link any strategic recommendations you may make to the SWOT analysis. State explicitly how the strategies you identify take advantage of the company's strengths to exploit environmental opportunities, how they rectify the company's weaknesses, and how they counter environmental threats. Also, do not forget to outline what needs to be done to implement your recommendations.

Endnote

1. Tom Copeland, Tim Koller, and Jack Murrin, *Valuation: Measuring and Managing the Value of Companies* (New York: Wiley, 1996).

GLOSSARY

A

acquisition When a company uses its capital resources to purchase another company.

anticompetitive behavior A range of actions aimed at harming actual or potential competitors, most often by using monopoly power, and thereby enhancing the long-run prospects of the firm.

autonomous subunit A subunit that has all the resources and decision-making power required to run the operation on a day-to-day basis.

availability error A bias that arises from our predisposition to estimate the probability of an outcome based on how easy the outcome is to imagine.

B

broad differentiation strategy When a company differentiates its product in some way, such as by recognizing different segments or offering different products to each segment.

broad low-cost strategy When a company lowers costs so that it can lower prices and still make a profit.

bureaucratic control Control through a formal system of written rules and procedures.

bureaucratic costs The costs associated with solving the transaction difficulties between business units and corporate headquarters as a company obtains the benefits from transferring, sharing, and leveraging competencies.

business ethics Accepted principles of right or wrong governing the conduct of businesspeople.

business-level strategy The business's overall competitive theme, the way it positions itself in the marketplace to gain a competitive advantage, and the different positioning strategies that can be used in different industry settings.

business model The conception of how strategies should work together as a whole to enable the company to achieve competitive advantage.

business unit A self-contained division that provides a product or service for a particular market.

C

capital productivity The sales produced by a dollar of capital invested in the business.

centralization Structure in which the decision-making authority is concentrated at a high level in the management hierarchy.

chaining A strategy designed to obtain the advantages of cost leadership by establishing a network of linked merchandising outlets interconnected by information technology that functions as one large company.

code of ethics Formal statement of the ethical priorities to which a business adheres.

cognitive biases Systematic errors in decision making that arise from the way people process information.

commonality A skill or competency that, when shared by two or more business units, allows them to operate more effectively and create more value for customers.

competitive advantage The achieved advantage over rivals when a company's profitability is greater than the average profitability of firms in its industry.

control The process through which managers regulate the activities of individuals and units so that they are consistent with the goals and standards of the organization.

controls The metrics used to measure the performance of subunits and make judgments about how well managers are running them.

corruption Can arise in a business context when managers pay bribes to gain access to lucrative business contracts.

credible commitment A believable promise or pledge to support the development of a long-term relationship between companies.

cross-selling When a company takes advantage of or leverages its established relationship with customers by way of acquiring additional product lines or categories that it can sell to them. In this way, a company increases differentiation because it can provide a "total solution" and satisfy all of a customer's specific needs.

customer response time Time that it takes for a good to be delivered or a service to be performed.

D

decentralization Structure in which the decision-making authority is distributed to lower-level managers or other employees.

delayering The process of reducing the number of levels in a management hierarchy.

devil's advocacy A technique in which one member of a decision-making team identifies all the considerations that might make a proposal unacceptable.

dialectic inquiry The generation of a plan (a thesis) and a counterplan (an antithesis) that reflect plausible but conflicting courses of action.

distinctive competencies Firm-specific strengths that allow a company to differentiate its products and/or achieve substantially lower costs to achieve a competitive advantage.

diversification The process of entering new industries, distinct from a company's core or original industry, to make new kinds of products for customers in new markets.

diversified company A company that makes and sells products in two or more different or distinct industries.

divestment strategy When a company decides to exit an industry by selling off its business assets to another company.

dominant design Common set of features or design characteristics.

E

economies of scope The synergies that arise when one or more of a diversified company's business units are able to lower costs or increase differentiation because they can more effectively pool, share, and utilize expensive resources or capabilities.

employee productivity The output produced per employee.

environmental degradation Occurs when a company's actions directly or indirectly result in pollution or other forms of environmental harm.

escalating commitment A cognitive bias that occurs when decision makers, having already committed significant resources to a project, commit even more resources after receiving feedback that the project is failing.

ethical dilemmas Situations where there is no agreement over exactly what the accepted principles of right and wrong are, or where none of the available alternatives seems ethically acceptable.

ethics Accepted principles of right or wrong that govern the conduct of a person, the members of a profession, or the actions of an organization.

external stakeholders All other individuals and groups that have some claim on the company.

F

first mover A firm that pioneers a particular product category or feature by being first to offer it to market.

first-mover disadvantages Competitive disadvantages associated with being first to market.

flat hierarchies An organizational structure with very few layers of management.

focus differentiation strategy When a company targets a certain segment or niche, and customizes its offering to the needs of that particular segment through the addition of features and functions.

focus low-cost strategy When a company targets a certain segment or niche, and tries to be the low-cost player in that niche.

focus strategy When a company decides to serve a limited number of segments, or just one segment.

format wars Battles to control the source of differentiation, and thus the value that such differentiation can create for the customer.

fragmented industry An industry composed of a large number of small-and medium-sized companies.

functional managers Managers responsible for supervising a particular function; that is, a task, an activity, or an operation such as accounting, marketing, research and development (R&D), information technology, or logistics.

franchising A strategy in which the franchisor grants to its franchisees the right to use the franchisor's name, reputation, and business model in return for a franchise fee and often a percentage of the profits.

functional structure The organizational structure is built upon the division of labor within the firm with different functions focusing on different tasks.

G

general managers Managers who bear responsibility for the overall performance of the company or for one of its major, self-contained subunits or divisions.

general organizational competencies Competencies that result from the skills of a company's top managers and that help every business unit within a company perform at a higher level than it could if it operated as a separate or independent company.

generic business-level strategy A strategy that gives a company a specific form of competitive position and advantage vis-à-vis its rivals that results in above-average profitability.

global standardization strategy A business model based on pursuing a low-cost strategy on a global scale.

global strategic alliances Cooperative agreements between companies from different countries that are actual or potential competitors.

goal A desired future state that an organization attempts to realize.

greenmail source of gaining wealth whereby corporate raiders either push companies to change their corporate strategy to one that will benefit stockholders, or charge a premium for stock when the company wants to buy it back.

H

harvest strategy When a company reduces to a minimum the assets it employs in a business to reduce its cost structure and extract or "milk" maximum profits from its investment.

holdup When a company is taken advantage of by another company it does business with after it has made an investment in expensive specialized assets to better meet the needs of the other company.

horizontal differentiation The formal division of the organization into subunits.

horizontal integration The process of acquiring or merging with industry competitors to achieve the competitive advantages that arise from a large size and scope of operations.

hostage taking A means of exchanging valuable resources to guarantee that each partner to an agreement will keep its side of the bargain.

I

illusion of control A cognitive bias rooted in the tendency to overestimate one's ability to control events.

incentives The devices used to encourage desired employee behavior.

influence costs The loss of efficiency that arises from deliberate information distortions for personal gain within an organization.

information asymmetry A situation where an agent has more information about resources he or she is managing than the principal has.

information manipulation When managers use their control over corporate data to distort or hide information in order to enhance their own financial situation or the competitive position of the firm.

inside directors Senior employees of the company, such as the CEO.

integrating mechanisms Processes and procedures used for coordination subunits.

internal capital market A corporate-level strategy whereby the firm's headquarters assesses the performance of business units and allocates money across them. Cash generated by units that are profitable but have poor investment opportunities within their business is used to cross-subsidize businesses that need cash and have strong promise for long-run profitability.

internal new venturing The process of transferring resources to, and creating a new business unit or division in, a new industry to innovate new kinds of products.

internal stakeholders Stockholders and employees, including executive officers, other managers, and board members.

K

killer applications Applications or uses of a new technology or product that are so compelling that customers adopt them in droves, killing competing formats.

knowledge network A network for transmitting information within an organization that is based not on formal organizational structure, but on informal contacts between managers within an enterprise and on distributed information systems.

L

leadership strategy When a company develops strategies to become the dominant player in a declining industry.

leveraging competencies The process of taking a distinctive competency developed by a business unit in one industry and using it to create a new business unit in a different industry.

limit price strategy Charging a price that is lower than that required to maximize profits in the short run to signal new entrants that the incumbent has a low cost structure that the entrant likely cannot match.

localization strategy A strategy focused on increasing profitability by customizing a company's goods or services so that they provide a favorable match to tastes and preferences in different national markets

location economies The economic benefits that arise from performing a value creation activity in an optimal location.

M

market controls The regulation of the behavior of individuals and units within an enterprise by setting up an internal market for valuable resource such as capital.

market development When a company searches for new market segments for a company's existing products to increase sales.

market segmentation The way a company decides to group customers based on important differences in their needs to gain a competitive advantage.

mass market One in which large numbers of customers enter the market.

matrix structure An organizational structure in which managers try to achieve tight coordination between functions, particularly R&D, production, and marketing.

merger An agreement between two companies to pool their resources and operations and join together to better compete in a business or industry.

mission The purpose of the company, or a statement of what the company strives to do.

multidivisional company A company that competes in several different businesses and has created a separate, self-contained division to manage each.

multidivisional structure An organizational structure in which a firm is divided into divisions, each of which is responsible for a distinct business area.

multinational company A company that does business in two or more national markets.

N

network effects The network of complementary products as a primary determinant of the demand for an industry's product.

niche strategy When a company focuses on pockets of demand that are declining more slowly than the industry as a whole to maintain profitability.

non-price competition The use of product differentiation strategies to deter potential entrants and manage rivalry within an industry.

norms Social rules and guidelines that prescribe the appropriate behavior in particular situations.

O

on-the-job consumption A term used by economists to describe the behavior of senior management's use of company funds to acquire perks (such as lavish offices, jets, etc.) that will enhance their status, instead of investing it to increase stockholder returns.

organizational design skills The ability of a company's managers to create a structure, culture, and control systems that motivate and coordinate employees to perform at a high level.

opportunism Seeking one's own self-interest, often through the use of guile.

opportunistic exploitation Unethical behavior sometimes used by managers to unilaterally rewrite the terms of a contract with suppliers, buyers, or complement providers in a way that favors to the firm.

organizational architecture The totality of a firm's organizational arrangements, including its formal organizational structure, control systems, incentive systems, organizational culture, organizational processes, and human capital.

organizational culture The norms and value systems that are shared among the employees of an organization.

organizational processes The manner in which decisions are made and work is performed within the organization.

organizational structure The combination of the location of decision-making responsibilities, the formal division of the organization into subunits, and the establishment of integrating mechanisms to coordinate the activities of the subunits.

output controls Goals that are set for units or individuals to achieve and monitoring performance against those goals.

outside directors Directors who are not full-time employees of the company, needed to provide objectivity to the monitoring and evaluation of processes.

outside view Identification of past successful or failed strategic initiatives to determine whether those initiatives will work for project at hand.

P

parallel sourcing policy A policy in which a company enters into long-term contracts with at least two suppliers for the same component to prevent any incidents of opportunism.

peer control The pressure that employees exert on others within their team or work group to perform up to or in excess of the expectations of the organization.

people The employees of an organization, as well as the strategy used to recruit, compensate, motivate, and retain those individuals; also refers to employees' skills, values, and orientation.

performance ambiguity The difficulty of identifying with precision the reason for the high (or low) performance of a subunit such as a function or team.

personal ethics Generally accepted principles of right and wrong governing the conduct of individuals.

personal control Control by personal contact with and direct supervision of subordinates.

price leadership When one company assumes the responsibility for determining the pricing strategy that maximizes industry profitability.

price signaling The process by which companies increase or decrease product prices to convey their intentions to other companies and influence the price of an industry's products.

primary activities activities related to the design, creation, and delivery of the product, its marketing, and its support and after-sales service.

prior hypothesis bias A cognitive bias that occurs when decision makers who have strong prior beliefs tend to make decisions on the basis of these beliefs, even when presented with evidence that their beliefs are wrong.

process innovation Development of a new process for producing and delivering products to customers.

product development The creation of new or improved products to replace existing products.

product bundling Offering customers the opportunity to purchase a range of products at a single, combined price; this increases the value of a company's product line because customers often obtain a price discount when purchasing a set of products at one time, and customers become used to dealing with only one company and its representatives.

product innovation Development of products that are new to the world or have superior attributes to existing products.

product proliferation strategy The strategy of "filling the niches," or catering to the needs of customers in all market segments to deter entry by competitors.

profitability The return a company makes on the capital invested in the enterprise.

public domain Government- or association-set standards of knowledge or technology that any company can freely incorporate into its product.

Q

quasi integration The use of long-term relationships, or investment in some activities normally performed by suppliers or buyers, in place of full ownership of operations that are backward or forward in the supply chain.

R

razor and blade strategy Pricing the product low in order to stimulate demand, and pricing complements high.

reasoning by analogy Use of simple analogies to make sense out of complex problems.

related diversification A corporate-level strategy based on the goal of establishing a business unit in a new industry that is related to a company's existing business units by some form of commonality or linkage between their value-chain functions.

representativeness A bias rooted in the tendency to generalize from a small sample or even a single, vivid anecdote.

restructuring The process of reorganizing and divesting business units and exiting industries to refocus upon a company's core business and rebuild its distinctive competencies.

risk capital Equity capital invested with no guarantee that stockholders will recoup their cash or earn a decent return if a company fails and goes bankrupt.

S

scenario planning Formulating plans that are based upon "what-if" scenarios about the future.

segmentation strategy When a company decides to serve many segments, or even the entire market, producing different offerings for different segments.

self-dealing Managers using company funds for their own personal consumption, as done by Enron, for example, in previous years.

shareholder value Returns that shareholders earn from purchasing shares in a company.

span of control The number of direct reports that a manager has.

stakeholders Individuals or groups with an interest, claim, or stake in the company—in what it does and in how well it performs.

standard A performance requirement that the organization is meant to attain on an ongoing basis.

stock options The right to purchase company stock at a predetermined price at some point in the future, usually within 10 years of the grant date.

strategic alliances Long-term agreements between two or more companies to jointly develop new products or processes that benefit all companies that are a part of the agreement.

strategic commitments Investments that signal an incumbent's long-term commitment to a market, or a segment of that market.

strategic leadership Creating competitive advantage through effective management of the strategy-making process.

strategic outsourcing The decision to allow one or more of a company's value-chain activities to be performed by independent, specialist companies that focus all their skills and knowledge on just one kind of activity to increase performance.

strategy A set of related actions that managers take to increase their company's performance.

strategy formulation Selecting strategies based on analysis of an organization's external and internal environment.

strategy implementation Putting strategies into action.

standardization strategy When a company decides to ignore different segments, and produce a standardized product for the average consumer.

subgoal An objective, the achievement of which helps the organization to attain or exceed it major goals.

substandard working conditions Arise when managers underinvest in working conditions, or pay employees below-market rates, in order to reduce their production costs.

support activities Activities of the value chain that provide inputs that allow the primary activities to take place.

sustained competitive advantage A company's strategies enable it to maintain above-average profitability for a number of years.

SWOT analysis The comparison of strengths, weaknesses, opportunities, and threats.

T

takeover constraint The risk of being acquired by another company.

tall hierarchies An organizational structure with many layers of management.

tapered integration When a firm uses a mix of vertical integration and market transactions for a given input. For example, a firm might operate limited semiconductor manufacturing while also buying semiconductor chips on the market. Doing so helps to prevent supplier holdup (because the firm can credibly commit to not buying from external suppliers) and increases its ability to judge the quality and cost of purchased supplies.

technical standards A set of technical specifications that producers adhere to when making a product or component.

technological paradigm shift Shifts in new technologies that revolutionize the structure of the industry, dramatically alter the nature of competition, and require companies to adopt new strategies in order to survive.

technology upgrading Incumbent companies can deter entry by investing in costly technology upgrades that potential entrants have trouble matching.

transfer pricing The price that one division of a company charges another division for its products, which are the inputs the other division requires to manufacture its own products.

transferring competencies The process of taking a distinctive competency developed by a business unit in one industry and implanting it in a business unit operating in another industry.

transnational strategy A business model that simultaneously achieves low costs, differentiates the product offering across geographic markets, and fosters a flow of skills between different subsidiaries in the company's global network of operations.

turnaround strategy When managers of a diversified company identify inefficient, poorly managed companies in other industries and then acquire and restructure them to improve their performance—and thus the profitability of the total corporation.

U

unrelated diversification A corporate-level strategy based on a multibusiness model that uses general organizational competencies to increase the performance of all the company's business units.

V

value chain The concept that a company consists of a chain of activities that transforms inputs into outputs.

value innovation When innovations push out the efficiency frontier in an industry, allowing for greater value to be offered through superior differentiation at a lower cost than was previously thought possible.

values A statement of how employees should conduct themselves and their business to help achieve the company mission; ideas or shared assumptions about what a group believes to be good, right, and desirable.

vertical differentiation The location of decision-making responsibilities within a structure, referring to centralization or decentralization, and number of layers in a hierarchy, referring to whether to organizational structure is tall or flat.

vertical disintegration When a company decides to exit industries, either forward or backward in the industry value chain, to its core industry to increase profitability.

vertical integration When a company expands its operations either backward into an industry that produces inputs for the company's products (backward vertical integration) or forward into an industry that uses, distributes, or sells the company's products (forward vertical integration).

virtual corporation When companies pursued extensive strategic outsourcing to the extent that they only perform the central value creation functions that lead to competitive advantage.

vision The articulation of a company's desired achievements or future state.

INDEX

Logistics. *See* Materials management
Long-term contracting, 295–296
Long-term cooperative relationships, 295–297
Lorsch, J., 422, 424
Loughran, T., 346
Lovallo, D., 40–41
Lowenstein, L., 346
Lowes, 8, 175
LTV, 65
Lubatkin, M. H., 382
Luce, R. A., 74
Luft, H., 142
Lukach, R., 201
Lululemon, 2–7, 10
LVMH group, 308–309
Lyles, M. A., 277

M

Mackay, Martin, 326
MacMillan, I. C., 345, 381
Macroenvironment forces, 67–70
Madhok, A., 277
Mahoney, J. T., 107
Maidique, M. M., 345
Malone, M. S., 307, 423
Mambrick, D. C., 41
Management
    capabilities, 316–317
    of global strategic alliances, 272–273
Managers
    autonomous actions by, 23–24
    business-level, 12
    corporate-level, 11–12
    functional, 10, 12
    general, 10, 12
    levels of, 10–11
Mankin, E. D., 278
Mann, M., 74
Mansfeld, E., 108, 143, 237, 345
March, J. G., 381
Market controls, 408, 417
Market demand
    changing nature of, 178–181
    customer segment market share, 180
    market development and customer groups, 179
Market development strategy, 191
Market discipline, maintaining, 297
Market growth rate, 183–184

Market penetration strategy, 190
Market segmentation
    approaches to, 155–156
    definition of, 155
    and focus strategy, 156
    and mass customization, 157
    and segmentation strategy, 156
    and standardization strategy, 156
Marketing
    and efficiency, 120–121
    primary activities in value chain, 92
    reliability improvement methodologies, 129
    roles for achieving innovation, 135
    roles in achieving customer responsiveness, 139
    roles of value creation in achieving efficiency, 126
    strategies, 120–121
Markets
    expansion and product leverage, 247
    globalization of, 242–243
Marowits, R., 73
Marris, R., 382
Martin, A., 110
Martin, J. A., 107
Martin, X., 306
Mason, R. O., 40–41
Mass customization, 117–119, 157
Mass markets, 178
Materials management
    and efficiency, 121–122
    reliability improvement methodologies, 129
    roles for achieving innovation, 135
    roles in achieving customer responsiveness, 139
    roles of value creation in achieving efficiency, 126
    support activities in value chain, 92–93
Matlack, C., 241
Matrix structure, 397–398
Mattel, 191
Mature industries
    strategies to deter entry, 185–188
    strategies to manage rivalry, 188–194
Mature stage, industry analysis, 63
Matushita, 212
Matzler, K., 346
Mauborgne, R., 108, 164–165, 169, 201
Mauri, A. J., 39, 75
Mazer, R., 236